*Multinational Companies and
Global Human Resource Strategies*

Multinational Companies and Global Human Resource Strategies

Edited by
William N. Cooke

QUORUM BOOKS
Westport, Connecticut • London

Library of Congress Cataloging-in-Publication Data

Multinational companies and global human resource strategies / Edited by William N. Cooke.
    p. cm.
  Includes bibliographical references and index.
  ISBN 1–56720–583–6 (alk. paper)
    1. International business enterprises—Management. 2. Comparative industrial relations.
  3. Human capital. I. Cooke, William N.
  HD62.4.M837 2002
  331—dc21   2002017768

British Library Cataloguing in Publication Data is available.

Library of Congress Catalog Card Number: 2002017768
ISBN: 1–56720–583–6

First published in 2003

Quorum Books, 88 Post Road West, Westport, CT 06881
An imprint of Greenwood Publishing Group, Inc.
www.quorumbooks.com

Printed in the United States of America

∞

The paper used in this book complies with the
Permanent Paper Standard issued by the National
Information Standards Organization (Z39.48–1984).

10 9 8 7 6 5 4 3 2 1

To my wife, Julie
who warmly...in disbelief
at me, she does smile
and to my children
Benjamin, Jayna, Keegan and Connor
to whom, warmly...in disbelief
at them, I do smile
making family enriching beyond profession
yet making it too
all the more worthwhile

Contents

Tables

Figures and Exhibit

Acknowledgments and Tribute

Earlier versions of the chapters in this volume were first presented at the "Multinational Companies & Emerging Workplace Issues: Practice, Outcomes, and Policy" conference hosted by the Douglas A. Fraser Center for Workplace Issues, College of Urban, Labor and Metropolitan Affairs, Wayne State University (April 1-3, 2000). The papers presented were combined into several sessions, each chaired by a distinguished scholar who presented his or her assessment and comments of the papers and broader issues addressed. We wish to recognize and thank those session chairs for their valuable comments and insights. The chairs included:

- John Addison, Professor, University of South Carolina
- Heidi Gottfried, Professor, Wayne State University
- Tove Hammer, Professor, Cornell University
- Pradeep Kumar, Professor, Queens University
- Susan Schurman, Executive Director, George Meany Center and President, National Labor College

We also thank Ron Blackwell (Director of Corporate Affairs, AFL-CIO) for sharing his thoughtful perspective and insights regarding the union movement's challenges and strategic options in light of corporate globalization. We greatly appreciate, futhermore, the invitation by Greg Drudi (Regional Representative, United Auto Workers) who sponsored our visit to Auto Alliance in Flat Rock, Michigan and organized our discussion with both labor and management representatives of the history of Ford's joint venture with Mazda and its labor–management relationship. In addition, Jim Tucker provided invaluable editorial expertise and assistance in the preparation of this volume.

We also want to recognize our former friend and colleague Harvie Ramsay, who coauthored Chapters 3 and 13 in this volume. Only a few weeks following our conference, Harvie died most unexpectedly on April 24, 2000. For those of us who knew him personally, we will greatly miss a good friend, his quick but subtle humor, his warmth, and his graciousness. Harvie's death is also a substantial intellectual loss to our profession. Indeed, we will miss his penetrating analyses, the pure magic of his writing style and his unusual dedication to improving the lives of working men and women through his research and teaching.

The conference and preparation of this volume were supported by a generous gift from the Edward L. Cushman Endowment Fund in Labor-Management Relations, an endowment created by Edward Cushman's family, friends, and colleagues to honor his memory. As a showing of our gratitude, we pay tribute to Edward L. Cushman and his family.

Tribute to Edward L. Cushman: Edward Cushman held various appointments at Wayne State University, serving as the director of the Institute of Industrial Relations, as executive vice president and as the Clarence Hilberry University Professor. In 1954, Ed took a 12-year leave of absence from the university to become vice president of industrial relations at American Motors Company, during which time he negotiated with the United Auto Workers (UAW) the first profit-sharing agreement in the automobile industry. Ed helped draft the original Michigan Unemployment Compensation Act and served as the Michigan Director of the War Manpower Commission and U.S. Employment Service, as special assistant to the U.S. secretary of labor, on the staff of the U.S. delegation to the United Nations' Economic and Social Council and as chairman of the U.S. delegation to the Metal Trades Committee of the International Labor Organization (ILO). Ed was also a life member of the National Association for the Advancement of Colored People (NAACP) and a member of President Johnson's National Citizens Committee on Civil Rights and the National Business Council for the Equal Rights Amendment. Ed served on the board of the Detroit Urban League and was chairman of the Michigan Equal Worth Commission and the Detroit Commission on Community Relations.

Edward L. Cushman devoted his life's work—whether in a governmental, university, industrial, civic, or other capacity—to solving problems directly bearing on the well-being of people, be it by striving to enhance educational systems, reaching collective bargaining agreements, or seeking to improve government policies and services. He brought to all of these tasks superb intelligence, unusual patience, the highest integrity, an ability to always see the best in people, and unquenchable optimism.

Global Human Resource Strategies:
A Framework and Overview

William Cooke

Over the last two decades there has been an eightfold increase in the number of multinational companies (MNCs) worldwide. Today over 60,000 MNCs have ownership in over 800,000 foreign subsidiaries dispersed and integrated all around the globe. These foreign subsidiaries currently hold approximately U.S.$21 trillion in assets, generate roughly U.S.$16 trillion in annual sales, and employ over 45 million employees. If the rate of growth and expansion experienced just over the 1995–2000 period is maintained through 2010, there will be more than 90,000 MNCs holding roughly U.S.$41 trillion in assets across 1.8 million foreign subsidiaries (UNCTAD, 1995, 2001).

The ever-expanding transnational reach and influence of MNCs in an ever-increasingly competitive and uncertain global marketplace raise a complex set of global human resources issues for companies, workers, unions, public policy makers, and concerned citizen interest groups. Indeed, along with environmental concerns, transnational workplace issues have become central to a widening public debate about the effects of corporate globalization, which at the extreme has surfaced into highly visible social protests (a` la the mass demonstrations in Seattle, Melbourne, Seoul, Barcelona, Washington, D.C., Quebec City, Genoa, and elsewhere) over the perceived unfettered, reckless power of large multinationals. Stepping away from the glare of headlines and emotion-laden debates, the primary objective of this book is to systematically examine MNC global human resource management and labor relations (HRM/LR) strategies; the effects on, and response of, workers and unions to these strategies; and the influence of public policy on both the strategies pursued by companies and unions and workplace outcomes.

Our purpose is to provide a balanced and objective understanding of these workplace issues, that is beneficial to executives and managers as they develop and refine their global HRM/LR strategies, to union leaders as they respond to MNC investment decisions and HRM/LR initiatives affecting their members and as they might coordinate strategies across borders, and to public policy makers as they grapple with employment and workplace policies that best serve their national constituencies in a global marketplace. Toward this end, we examine:

1. National industrial relations systems and their effects on global business configuration strategies,
2. global HRM/LR strategies and the diffusion, adoption, and adaptation of practices across global operations,
3. transnational union strategies in response to MNC strategies, and
4. recently enacted transnational workplace legislation and its effects on workplace outcomes.

A thorough understanding of these issues demands not only in-depth analyses of each but also an understanding of how each is inextricably linked to the other. My objective in this introductory chapter is to lay out a highly simplified, but fairly comprehensive and coherent, framework, one that serves as a conceptual guide to more broadly understanding the complexity of these global workplace and labor–management issues and, in turn, a practical guide to companies, unions, and public policy makers as each develops its own strategies regarding global workplace and labor–management issues. Integrated into the framework are key observations and propositions made in the original, far richer analyses and case studies presented by the authors in the chapters that follow. In the final chapter, I synthesize a common theme of organizational power underlying the analyses in the various chapters and address the implications of the role of power in the development, implementation, and outcomes of strategies pursued by labor and management.

A FRAMEWORK

In this section, after briefly summarizing the logic of the framework used to guide the present analysis, I discuss each component and linkage more fully. As illustrated in Figure 1.1, MNC business and operational configuration strategies are shaped by the larger economic and sociopolitical environment. Within this environmental context are the industrial relations (IR) systems of home and alternative host countries. As these IR systems affect the benefits and costs associated with alternative operational configurations, they influence MNC decisions about where and how much to invest in alternative host locations and in their home countries. The IR systems of home countries also partially determine domestic HRM/LR strategies of parent companies. In addition to influencing operational configuration decisions, domestic HRM/LR strategies influence the HRM/LR strategies deployed in foreign subsidiaries.

Although influenced by MNC interests in diffusing preferred parent company HRM/LR practices abroad, the HRM/LR strategies of foreign subsidiary operations are shaped by the benefits and costs associated with

Figure 1.1
An Analytical Framework

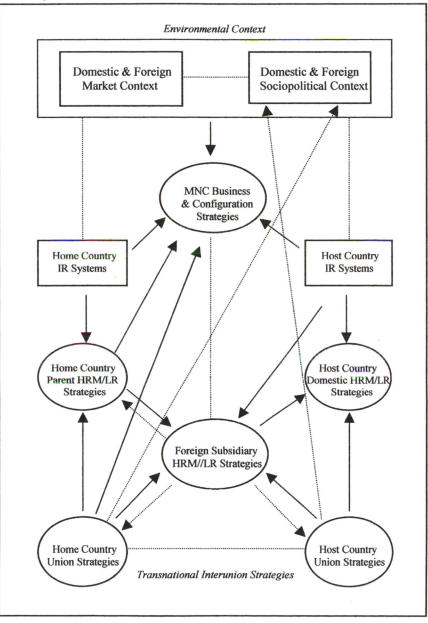

diffusing or creating HRM/LR advantages within host country IR systems. The HRM/LR strategies pursued in foreign subsidiaries, in turn, may ultimately influence both the domestic HRM/LR strategies pursued by parent companies in their home locations and by host country companies exposed to alternative HRM/LR strategies pursued by foreign subsidiaries in their countries. Whether acting independently or in concert across home and host countries, the strategies of unions in both home and host countries also influence domestic and foreign subsidiary HRM/LR strategies and MNC configuration strategies. Finally, both unions and MNCs attempt to influence the sociopolitical context in ways that help each achieve their respective goals.

Two admittedly oversimplified theoretical assumptions underlie the framework: namely, MNCs seek to act in ways *perceived* as optimizing profits, and unions seek to act in ways *perceived* as optimizing gains to workers. Such assumptions require that both employers and unions generally act rationally both economically and organizationally in their pursuit of optimizing gains. Optimization of gains is bounded, however, by the limits of the relative power that either party can exercise and the constraints placed on each by the environmental context within which the parties operate. The degree to which the parties act rationally, moreover, has limits. There are inherent limitations to having complete and accurate information and knowledge needed to make optimal decisions. Global market uncertainty, if not volatility, also limits a party's ability to predict and, hence, make longer-term rational decisions. Finally, given the complexity of organizations, comprising various stakeholders with varying priorities and influence within organizations, both companies and unions undoubtedly make some decisions inconsistent with rational optimizing behavior for their organizations. In other words, organizational mistakes are made. With these limitations to rational optimizing behavior in mind, competition in the global marketplace, nonetheless, rewards those parties that act in the most rational ways and penalizes those that act in the least rational ways in pursuing their objectives. In the longer run, therefore, those parties that act more rationally and can more quickly adjust to mistakes made prove to be the more successful in achieving their objectives.

MNC Business and Operational Configurations

In their persistent quest to optimize profitability, MNCs face a complex web of choices in configuring and reconfiguring their global operations. Given the highly dynamic nature and increasing speed of adjustment underlying the global marketplace, the reconfiguration of MNC global operations can occur regularly and quickly. As diagrammed in Figure 1.2, the primary configuration options include choices between investment in home operations, direct investment in foreign host operations, and trade. For MNCs seeking to penetrate foreign markets, the choice rests between either exporting to such markets or investing directly in such markets (i.e., market-seeking foreign direct investments [FDI]). For MNCs seeking to achieve lower operational costs, the choice rests between either importing from low-cost providers abroad or investing directly in low-cost locations (i.e., efficiency-seeking FDI). For MNCs seeking natural resources for further processing or production, the choice rests between either importing natural resources or directly investing in foreign locations to extract resources (i.e., resource-seeking FDI). Secondary configuration options include subcontracting, issuing licenses and franchises, creating joint ventures, and forming alliances. These options can entail either cross-national, domestic arrangements, or both. As diagrammed, each option may lead, furthermore, to importation and/or exportation to and from home and foreign host locations.

The fundamental strategic choices before MNCs are to decide on the optimal combinations of so-called external market transactions (exportation, importation, subcontracting, licensing, and franchising), so-called internal market transactions (investment in home operations and FDI), and hybrid arrangements that include both internal and external market transactions (joint ventures and alliances). As developed more fully by Jennifer Bair and Harvie Ramsay in Chapter 3, this web of configuration choices can be extended further by envisioning a commodity chain in which a final end customer product or service is linked to an array of MNCs and domestic companies serving as direct and indirect suppliers within and across industries. Viewed as such, one would link the configuration choices illustrated in Figure 1.2 for a given MNC with the configuration choices of all MNCs making up a commodity chain. Analyzed in this way, we obtain a yet richer understanding and appreciation for the nature of competition, dependencies, power relationships, and market vulnerabilities across MNCs. Providing a detailed example of the potential value of this kind of commodity chain analysis, Bair and Ramsay trace the mix of MNC configuration strategies developed differently by retailers, branded manufacturers, marketers, brokers, and textile manufacturers in the North American clothing industry.

Toward optimizing profitability, MNCs are driven to choose that combination of internal and external market transactions that offers the greatest market opportunities and the lowest costs. Of central interest to this volume are decisions by companies to invest abroad, an act that defines a company as a "multinational" company. By including FDI as part of their broader configuration strategies, companies have concluded that greater market opportunity and/or lower costs can be achieved through internal control of cross-border transactions than through alternative external transactions. In deciding to internalize some operations via FDI, MNCs perceive that they enjoy some inherent firm-specific competitive advantage over firms operating in other countries (Hymer, 1976; Buckley and Casson, 1976). Such firm-specific advantages may be derived, for example, from economies of scale, ready access to investment capital, and special expertise in marketing, research and development (R&D), logistics, or HRM.

Decisions about where and how much to invest across alternative locations (given potential competitive advantages) is, additionally, a matter of comparative location advantages (Dunning, 1993). Those foreign locations offering more advantage in terms of lower operational costs and greater ease in diffusing or creating competitive advantages attract greater FDI. Locations that offer greater market opportunity for MNCs to penetrate or to defend against competitors, likewise, attract greater FDI, as do locations that minimize the costs

Figure 1.2
MNC Business and Configuration Strategies

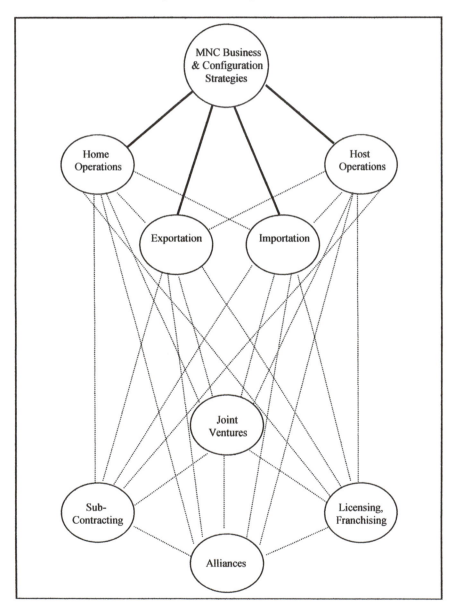

to MNCs of any divestment or downsizing (Hennart and Park, 1994; Buckley and Casson, 1998).

In deciding on optimal global configurations, MNCs are influenced by a wide range of economic and sociopolitical factors. As these factors decrease or increase either the market opportunities to exploit competitive advantages or the transaction costs associated with FDI vis-à-vis domestic investment, trade, and other options, MNCs choose to invest more or less abroad. Among economic market factors affecting these opportunities and transaction costs are relative differences in (1) market size, wealth, and growth, (2) proximity between parent headquarters, subsidiaries, customers, and suppliers, (3) availability and access to capital, R&D, and natural resources, (4) transportation, telecommunications, and utility infrastructures, (4) currency valuations and fluctuations, and (5) labor skills and compensation costs. Differences in sociopolitical factors across locations, likewise, affect transaction costs and opportunities to exploit firm-specific advantages, either directly or indirectly via effects on market factors. Sociopolitical factors of importance include differences in government taxation, incentives and disincentives to investment, tariffs, and related trade barriers. Indeed, there has been a marked liberalization in FDI policies over the last decade among developing nations, which have sought to gain access to needed finance, technology, and market channels, as well as to increase employment opportunities. Differences in cultures, languages, and political or social stability also influence MNC choices. Additionally, of special importance to the analyses developed in this volume are differences in IR systems between and across domestic and foreign locations. Finally, over the last decade there have been significant developments in bilateral and multilateral trade and FDI agreements between countries, which have altered the benefits and costs associated with configuration options.

In Chapter 2, Gabriele Köhler traces the increasingly important role of FDI in the world economy. In 1998, MNCs invested nearly U.S.$650 billion abroad, reflecting a twelvefold increase in unadjusted FDI flows over the last two decades. Over the same period, FDI as a proportion of total domestic capital formation has increased threefold to approximately 8 percent. These trends, however, do not indicate that there has been an increase in total global investment as a result of steadily rising FDI flows. Instead, there has been a shift in the origins of investment from domestic direct investment to FDI.

This shift in ownership composition, but not in the total amount of investment, of course, has implications for the amount of employment that MNCs generate via FDI. Köhler points out, for instance, that FDI has been associated with increased formal sector employment in a number of developing countries (especially in manufacturing), but this effect has been limited to a select, small set of countries. Taking into account rising productivity and rationalization of operations, she concludes that it is unlikely that the rising flow of FDI has had any appreciable effect on employment levels at the global level. The evidence is less clear-cut regarding the quality of employment opportunities arising from increased FDI. Here, Köhler finds the evidence to be mixed since

FDI can give rise to both a worsening of, or an improvement in, local employment conditions, depending on the environmental context.

IR Systems

Of special importance to the analyses developed in this volume are differences in IR systems between domestic and alternative foreign host countries. As I discuss in Chapter 4, in configuring their global operations, MNCs weigh the comparative advantages of their home country IR systems against alternative host country IR systems. The greater or lesser the comparative labor cost advantage of home IR systems vis-à-vis alternative host IR systems, ceteris paribus, the less or more MNCs invest abroad and the more or less they invest at home and export abroad. In addition to direct compensation costs for skills available, unit labor costs are determined in part by government workplace regulations and policies that (1) restrict employer freedom to set terms and conditions of employment and (2) impose significant transaction costs on making adjustments to terms and conditions of employment. An important further dimension of IR systems that influences MNC configuration strategies is the potential added cost associated with union representation and collective bargaining. On assessing potential net disadvantages or advantages of union representation and collective bargaining across home and alternative host locations, MNCs invest more in those locations where perceived net disadvantages are lower or net advantages are higher.

As reported in Chapter 4, several recent empirical analyses of the effects of selected IR system factors on FDI yield highly consistent evidence that various government workplace regulations and dimensions of collective bargaining contexts have had strong, independent effects on the distribution of FDI. In Chapter 5, Morris Kleiner and Hwikwon Ham take up this line of argument but make the case for viewing these kinds of IR factors more as a system of interdependent labor market institutions, rather than as a set of independent, additive factors. The authors, in turn, construct a composite scale of differences in IR systems, ranging from fairly unrestrictive to highly restrictive ones based largely on union and collective bargaining contexts. Constructed as such, the authors show how the U.S. IR system is sharply different from the IR systems found in the European Union and estimate the effects of these distinct differences in IR systems on FDI patterns. Consistent with the findings reported in Chapter 4, Kleiner and Ham find that distinct differences in IR systems have strongly influenced FDI decision making. Hence, one can reasonably conclude that MNCs generally give considerable weight to the perceived costs and benefits associated with different IR systems in deciding where and how much to invest abroad.

As diagrammed in Figure 1.1, home country IR systems, furthermore, influence parent domestic HRM/LR strategies. In particular, the kind of government workplace regulations and collective bargaining contexts described earlier, along with cultural norms, can be expected to shape domestic HRM/LR strategies deployed. Depending on these various kinds of characteristics underlying IR systems, employers are more or less able to develop HRM/LR ownership advantages at home. As I describe more fully in Chapter 4, MNCs enjoying HRM/LR ownership advantages at home have incentive to exploit such advantages abroad. MNCs lacking HRM/LR ownership advantages at home because of constraints placed on them by their home IR systems have reason, nonetheless, to attempt to create such advantage abroad under more flexible IR systems. The ease with which MNCs can either diffuse or create HRM/LR ownership advantages abroad, however, is dependent in part on the IR systems of host countries. As summarized in the following sections, a number of rich examples of such dependence are presented in this volume.

HRM/LR Strategies

At the center of most analyses in this volume is the issue of the transnational diffusion of HRM/LR strategies: diffusion within MNC operations and diffusion across MNCs and domestic companies in host countries. With regard to decisions about the kind of HRM/LR strategies pursued within MNC operations, MNCs make choices about whether to diffuse preferred domestic company policies and practices to their subsidiaries, to adopt policies and practices common to host countries, or to develop hybrid strategies incorporating both parent company and local HRM/LR practices. MNCs, moreover, may not only adopt host country HRM/LR practices in their foreign subsidiaries, but also, in turn, diffuse superior practices from selected foreign subsidiaries to other foreign subsidiaries and to their home operations.

In Part II, several authors describe how MNCs have sought to diffuse preferred HRM/LR practices and examine the conditions and salient factors that help explain the degree of success associated with MNC efforts at diffusion of preferred practices. In Part III, several authors also address MNC efforts to diffuse HRM/LR practices across national boundaries but from the perspective of union responses and transnational interunion strategies. Finally, in Part IV, Tony Royle and Brian Towers (Chapter 17) disentangle how McDonalds' Corporation has been able to successfully diffuse its antiunion American tradition across European countries in spite of fairly strong government policies and traditions of supporting extensive employee interest representation via works councils and unions.

In Chapter 6, Graeme Martin, Phil Beaumont, and Judy Pate develop a model of the strategic change process that captures the complex set of events, activities, discursive practices, emotions, and reactions underlying the process of diffusing parent HRM/LR strategies to foreign subsidiaries. Based on the case of American-owned AT&T in its efforts to diffuse a universal, corporate-wide style of leadership to its Scottish subsidiary NCR, the authors conclude that the successful diffusion of preferred HRM/LR practices from parents to subsidiaries depends heavily on two sets of factors. First, success is diminished to the extent that program champions are insensitive to the influence of diverse institutional differences between parent and subsidiaries. Second, the successful institutionalization of a change program is dependent on the extent to which managers and employees at all levels have the incentive and ability to read organizational messages of change positively and, in turn, implement those messages as effective HRM/LR practices.

Martin Kenney and Shoko Tanaka (Chapter 7) examine Japanese television assembly transplants in the United States. They find that the U.S. transplants have largely failed to re-create the "learning" bureaucracies characteristic of their sister plants in Japan. The authors attribute the inconsistency in HRM/LR strategies between the Japanese transplants and their domestic counterparts in Japan to differences found in deeply rooted labor–management relationships in the United States. In particular, the Fordist tradition of hierarchical job protection and seniority rights governing job assignments in both acquired and greenfield plants were or became highly ingrained for both the unionized workforces and local managers. For the most part there was little consideration of the adoption of more Japanese-style HRM/LR practices. Although some modest changes have been adopted in recent contract negotiations, it appears that all parties, even top Japanese management, have accepted the American Fordist traditions as simply part of doing business in the Japanese transplants.

Widely debated is the question of whether or not MNCs generally deploy superior (or so-called best practice) HRM/LR strategies and whether, as a consequence, domestic companies in host countries follow suit in order to remain competitive. To the extent that domestic companies adopt or imitate the HRM/LR strategies of MNCs, there is a growing convergence throughout the world of selected HRM/LR policies and practices mirroring those pursued by MNCs. However, as presented in the studies by Chris Brewster and Olga Tregaskis in Chapter 8 and by Sarosh Kuruvilla, Stephen Frenkel, and David Peetz in Chapter 9, there is only limited evidence that convergence toward MNC HRM/LR strategies is occurring.

Given the wide attention given to the emerging use of more flexible workplace practices and contingent employment relationships, Brewster and Tregaskis (Chapter 8) examine the use of various such practices across a large sample of MNCs and domestic firms in the United Kingdom, Germany, and Spain. More specifically, the authors examine the extent to which MNCs and domestic firms use part-time, temporary, and fixed-term contract employees and use shift work and annualized hours of work. Although differences are found, very little of that difference can be attributed to the status of the employer as a foreign MNC. Instead, differences in the extent of utilizing contingent workers and more flexible hours of work are largely a function of differences in country IR systems and industry concentration. Brewster and Tregaskis infer, therefore, that MNCs are far more likely to adopt local HRM/LR practices (at least of the kind studied) than to diffuse practices otherwise presumably preferred by MNCs. In light of the evidence, the authors conclude that the increasing global reach of MNCs does not portend convergence to any particular set of HRM/LR practices.

Kuruvilla, Frenkel, and Peetz (Chapter 9) also examine the degree to which MNCs are agents of horizontal diffusion of best practices in HRM/LR, but their focus is on diffusion to developing countries in which there may be greater receptivity by domestic companies to adopting best practices in HRM/LR, ostensibly mastered by MNCs in highly developed countries. The authors examine, in particular, the experience of key domestic and foreign companies operating in several industries in India and Malaysia. Kuruvilla et al. find that the degree to which there is diffusion of HRM/LR practices from foreign MNCs to domestic companies is clearly mixed and that such variation is associated more with differences in industry-level characteristics than in differences in national-level characteristics.

Union Strategies

As diagrammed in Figure 1.1, union strategies also influence both MNC configuration strategies and HRM/LR strategies, directly and indirectly. With respect to home country union strategies, unions first affect parent domestic HRM/LR strategies through the exercise of relative power via contract negotiations and administration. As such, unions partially determine whether or not domestic HRM/LR strategies yield competitive advantage. To the extent that unions enhance (diminish) company performance at home, MNCs have greater reason to invest more (less) at home than abroad, relying more (less) heavily than otherwise on trade than on FDI. In addition to indirectly influencing configuration strategies, unions may also directly influence business and configuration strategies. For example, unions can disrupt or threaten to disrupt domestic operations in response to an MNC's intentions to invest abroad at the expense of the domestic workforce.

With respect to host country union strategies, unions first need to organize a subsidiary's employees or at least bring them under centralized bargaining structures with extensions of union coverage to nonunion companies. Depending on the host country's IR system and the degree to which MNCs engage in union avoidance, the ability of unions to organize subsidiaries or bring them under contract varies. Although not captured explicitly in my framework but implicitly derived from my framing of strategic configuration choices, union organizing strategies need to encompass not only the home and foreign-owned operations of MNCs but also the network of suppliers that MNCs do not own or control directly. As highlighted by Jennifer Bair and Harvie Ramsay (Chapter 3), union power is derived by union success at critical points along broader commodity chain configurations, which include independent suppliers critically positioned in such chains.

On achieving representation, unions are in a position to modify foreign subsidiary HRM/LR strategies, the degree to which is a matter of union relative power. To the degree that unions enhance or diminish subsidiary performance, the more or less MNCs have reason to maintain their investment in foreign subsidiaries or otherwise attempt to marginalize unions. Given the ability of some MNCs to leverage or "whipsaw" unions across countries via explicit or implicit promises of investment and threats of divestment or movement of work, some unions may embark on more cooperative or, alternatively, concessionary strategies intended to protect the livelihood of their membership. Unions may also attempt to forge transnational strategies with unions representing an MNC's home sites and subsidiaries in other countries, the subject of several chapters herein. Lastly, as discussed earlier, unions attempt to influence public policy and sentiment more broadly in ways favorable to their membership and workers' rights to representation.

In Part III, several authors bring to life the transnational dimension of union strategies. Steve Babson (Chapter 10) examines Ford's dual sourcing of Escorts and Tracers in Ford's U.S. Wayne plant and its Mexican Hermosillo plant. He compares the union cultures of the local Confederation of Mexican Workers (CTM) union at Hermosillo and UAW locals in the United States, dispelling any misperception that local Mexican unions are docile, "kept" organizations. He then compares the "lean" production and team-based strategies deployed in the U.S. and Mexican sites. With the Hermosillo plant proving to be a model plant of quality and productivity (and marked by exceptionally low labor costs), Babson, furthermore, illustrates how Ford uses the Hermosillo operations as a benchmark operation in an effort to whipsaw the Wayne operations toward ever more lean production. Given the coercive comparison strategy of Ford (and other automakers) based on the implicit or explicit threat of movement of work from high-wage American and Canadian locations to low-wage Mexican locations, Babson addresses the need for North American union coordination. Arguing that the Ford Hermosillo experience shows that there is room for independent local union action and worker mobilization within the CTM in Mexico, a historic opportunity for cross-border collaboration between unions (especially between local unions producing the same product primarily for the same market) is waiting to be cultivated. But the first step in the realization of such an opportunity requires (1) direct and regular communication between unions and (2) a coordinated focus on opposition to the suppression of labor rights and exceptionally low wages of Mexican workers.

Christopher Huxley (Chapter 11) examines local union responses and workplace outcomes associated with GM's latest continental standardization of production and work organization in its truck assembly plants across Canada, Mexico, and the United States. In particular, he focuses on similarities and differences across four plants in regard to technology, employee involvement, health and safety, and outsourcing, finding that at each plant a distinct order has been negotiated. Like Babson, Huxley argues that given the similarities in workplace issues faced by local unions across North America and given that the long-term well-being of each local is inextricably linked to the same product and market, unions have good reason to communicate and exchange information among themselves. To date, however, they have not, which the author proposes may be explained by at least two fundamental challenges. First, local unions across borders may view each other as competitors for product and work.

Second, local unions must be able to identify with the struggles of the other before seeing the value of communication and cooperation with each other. These two factors, it would appear, have kept unions located in the highly industrialized countries of Canada and the United States from considering unions in Mexico as potential allies.

Against a backdrop of sharply falling union representation across foreign-owned subsidiaries in the United States, Tom Juravich and Kate Bronfenbrenner (Chapter 12) dissect the case of the U.S. Steelworkers' victory over Japanese-owned Bridgestone-Firestone's efforts to rid itself of union representation. The authors focus in particular on Bridgestone-Firestone's initial co-optation of the Rubber Workers through a "smoke-and-mirrors" program of Japanese-style employee involvement and the subsequent Steelworkers' transnational coalition strategy to thwart the company's displacement of workers. In addition to more traditional forms of national union resistance and leveraging of power, the Steelworkers engaged in an aggressive and ultimately effective transnational strategy of escalating confrontation. Of special note, the Steelworkers successfully enlisted support from unions in Japan, Europe, and Latin America, picketed both the Japanese embassy in Washington, D.C., and the company's European regional headquarters in Brussels, coordinated an "International Days of Outrage" campaign, and flooded the company with E-mail protests via a "cyberpicket." Juravich and Bronfenbrenner conclude that the global dimension of the Steelworkers' strategy (in conjunction with more traditional forms of resistance) provides a model for transnational union resistance to MNCs bent on undermining the rights and employment conditions of workers and destroying the unions that represent them.

Drawing on the recent experience and emerging union strategy of graphical worker unions in Europe, John Gennard and Harvie Ramsay (Chapter 13) describe and evaluate the elements and challenges to successfully deploying transnational union strategies. The authors first describe the changing graphical industry, characterized by radical technological change and alternative media options, expansion by merger and acquisition, growing concentration of corporate power, and HRM/LR strategies designed to achieve greater workforce flexibility and the reorganization of work. Gennard and Ramsay argue that the critical first step to the development of any successful transnational union strategy is the compilation and dissemination of relevant information, which require substantial coordination among unions across nations. Such information would necessarily focus on (1) the economic, political, and legal environments of pertinent countries, (2) the governance, financial circumstances, and HRM/LR strategies of key MNCs, and (3) the structures, priorities, policies, practices, and customs of cooperating unions. Once this kind of information is compiled, unions then need to collaborate among themselves, jointly analyzing and developing a cross-country strategy of coordinated common objectives. The authors conclude that given differences in environmental contexts, MNCs, and unions between countries, such a process of interunion, transnational cooperation and coordination is inherently problematic but, nonetheless, holds substantial, long-term promise.

The exceptional example of the coordinated strategy among graphical worker unions in Europe described and evaluated by Gennard and Ramsay is instructive. In a similar line of reasoning, Bair and Ramsay argue that an understanding of commodity chain configurations has a number of potential added advantages for unions. Among others, these advantages include enhancing a sense of mutual cause instead of conflict between labor at different points along a chain. Given the hollowing-out of trade union power along these chains and across many countries, furthermore, Köhler as well as Bair and Ramsay emphasize the opportunities for greater coordination of public campaigns between unions and civil society movements against MNCs engaged in or tolerating inequitable treatment and violations of basic human rights of workers across their subsidiaries and suppliers in developing countries.

Sociopolitical Context

As previously discussed, MNC configuration and FDI decisions are influenced by differences in national sociopolitical contexts more broadly and by national IR systems more narrowly. Given potential constraints arising out of the sociopolitical context, MNCs, of course, have incentive to press for changes in public policy favorable to their profit-optimizing objectives. Likewise, unions have incentive to influence public policy and sentiment more broadly in ways favorable to their membership and workers more generally. Both MNCs and unions, therefore, lobby and press for favorable provisions in domestic and transnational trade and investment policies. Whereas MNCs generally resist government infringement that increases their costs or reduces their freedom to conduct business, unions have sought to promulgate MNC codes of conduct and social clauses protecting workers from "social dumping" and the lack of minimal labor standards and worker rights (through conventions of the International Labour Organization (ILO), Organization for Economic Cooperation and Development (OECD) benchmark standards, and World Trade Organization (WTO) rule-making.

In addition, the recent enactment of two especially important multilateral agreements (containing policies governing the HRM/LR practices of MNCs across borders) has unfolded. The first is the directive establishing transnational works councils within the European Union, which is the only free trade area with a social dimension and a process for the establishment of cross-national minimum labor standards. The second is the labor side agreement of the North American Free Trade Agreement (NAFTA). In both cases, agreement among the signatory countries to these laws was preceded by fairly aggressive efforts, on the one hand, by organized labor that sought to achieve yet stronger legislation and, on the other hand, by MNCs that sought to avoid the passage of any such transnational legislation in the first place.

The issue of transnational legislation governing workplaces across borders and how MNCs and unions have attempted to use or skirt around these laws is examined in Part IV. First, it is worth examining how some MNCs may pursue HRM/LR strategies that allow them to exploit workforces in unregulated IR systems characterized by low skills, low wages, substandard work conditions, and expendable workforces. Such a case is reviewed by Clifford B. Donn (Chapter 14), who examines the increasing concentration in the maritime industry of so-called flag-of-convenience (FOC) ships and their crew-of-convenience workforces. Based on a strategy of minimizing government regulation and taxes, shipowners register ("flag") their vessels with Third World country registries. Under these FOC registries, maritime operators are virtually free of workplace and employment regulations. Typically staffed with Third World seafarers, work conditions on these vessels are often deplorable; marked by very low wages, long hours, a disregard for health and safety standards, and highly tenuous employment relations. Given the stateless nature of FOC operations, owners and operators are largely out of the reach of national regulations and ignore voluntary international conventions and standards set by the United Nations and its agencies. The largely union-free FOC vessels are, likewise, generally out of the reach of organized labor, although the International Transport Workers Federation (an international trade secretariat) has had some modest success in forcing FOC operators to negotiate with it over minimum pay and work standards.

Trevor Bain and Kim Hester (Chapter 15) next provide an overview of the 1994 European Works Council (EWC) directive, which applies to MNCs with at least 1000 employees in the European Union (EU) and with 150 or more employees in two or more member states. Affected MNCs were first given the option to voluntarily negotiate with employee representatives regarding the procedures and terms of an EWC in which employers would engage in information sharing and consultation with employees across locations in the EU. Failing to create such transnational forums for information sharing and consultation by September 1996, affected MNCs were given until September 1999 to establish EWCs that would comply with minimum requirements governing the composition, procedures, and authority of EWCs, as well as the kinds of information to be shared (including organizational, financial, employment, workplace, and operational changes anticipated). Based on a sample of 100 EWCs, Bain and Hester examine the recent history of EWCs and provide a comparison between voluntary and mandated EWCs. In their analysis, they assess the perceived costs and benefits of EWCs to companies, employees, and unions, and offer an explanation why neither the voluntary nor mandatory forms have yet to yield much benefit to the parties, except to provide MNCs with an avenue to share limited information or to justify their actions.

Thérèse Beaupain, Steve Jefferys, and Rachel Annand (Chapter 16) examine the initial stage of development of EWCs across three MNCs with locations in Belgium and the United Kingdom. The authors find that as of yet, EWCs have led to a very limited exchange of information and negligible consultation with employee representatives.   Beaupain et al. also find that substantial rivalry can arise between unions over influence and control of EWC activities, not only across countries but within countries.   Such rivalry has sometimes led to distrust between union leaders, which is exacerbated by language barriers, by a lack of understanding of each other's IR systems and organizational complexities, and by competition between locations over the allocation of investment and work.   One important result of interunion rivalry and distrust has been the failure of EWC delegates to communicate or consult effectively with union members at local levels about transnational issues.   In spite of these early-stage limitations of interunion cooperation and coordination, Beaupain et al. find a number of promising examples of interunion development and cooperation.   The authors conclude, nonetheless, that unions need to cooperate more fully to develop the transnational coordination and leverage needed to move the EWCs beyond providing just another channel for corporate communication.

Tony Royle and Brian Towers (Chapter 17) provide a close look at the diffusion of McDonalds' Corporation's HRM/LR strategy, which is marked by aggressive efforts at minimizing the effects of employee interest representation on its European operations.   Central to the company's strategy is a long tradition of avoiding union representation and avoiding the creation (or limiting the influence) of works councils mandated by national policies.   The authors trace the company's resistance in this regard across Austria, France, Germany, Spain, and Sweden.   They also identify a set of tactics pursued by McDonald's to minimize the influence of its required EWC, tactics designed to avoid any serious employee consultation or feedback and to keep trade unionists out of the process.   Among key factors allowing McDonald's to pursue its paternalistic HRM/LR strategy across Europe are its strong corporate culture, the nature of the labor force employed by fast-food restaurants, and the company's heavy reliance on franchise operations.

Finally, passage of NAFTA by the United States, Canada, and Mexico included a side agreement, the North American Agreement on Labor Cooperation (NAALC).   After describing the obligations and compliance procedures under NAALC, Mario F. Bognanno and Jiangfeng Lu (Chapter 18) examine the degree to which the objectives under the act have been fulfilled. The authors address, in particular, the hypothesized effect of the so called sunshine factor on compliance.   Through public scrutiny, exposure, and embarrassment associated with noncompliance, MNCs are expected to comply with the underlying intent and provisions of the act.   Toward testing the sunshine hypothesis, Bognanno and Lu review the published proceedings of complaints levied against employers through 1999 and survey trade unions and worker rights representatives involved in the submission of complaints.   Based on the evidence, the authors conclude that neither the direct compliance procedures nor the indirect sunshine factor has had any appreciable effect on MNC compliance with labor laws in the three cooperating countries.

CONCLUDING NOTE

As highlighted by the overview of analyses in this volume and the framework described, there is a host of strategic business, union, and public policy issues that need to be addressed to more fully understand the salient, transnational workplace and employment issues emerging from an ever-widening global market influence and context. In the chapters that follow, we flush out in much greater detail and with sharper analytical focus the various transnational workplace issues so briefly touched upon in this chapter. One underlying central theme running throughout this volume is that of power, which plays a dominant role in determining the development, implementation, and success of transnational strategies pursued by labor and management and, in turn, transnational workplace outcomes. In the final chapter, I draw on that theme of power to synthesize and integrate the various analyses herein. By integrating these analyses into a fairly coherent and comprehensive framework, it is our hope that the broader transnational workplace implications and challenges that lie ahead become clearer and that the contributions made in this volume help improve, in some small way, the workplace of tomorrow.

REFERENCES

Buckley, P. J. and Casson, M. C. (1976). *The Future of the Multinational Enterprise.* London: Macmillan.

Buckley, P. J. and Casson, M. C. (1998). "Models of the Multinational Enterprise," *Journal of International Business Studies* 29 (1), pp. 21–44.

Dunning, J. H. (1993). *Multinational Enterprises and the Global Economy.* New York: Addison-Wesley

Hennart, J. F. and Park, Y. R. (1994). "Location, Governance, and Strategic Determinants of Japanese Manufacturing Investment in the United States," *Strategic Management Journal* 15, pp. 419–36.

Hymer, S. (1976). *The International Operations of National Firms.* Cambridge, Mass: MIT Press

UNCTAD (1995, 2001). *World Investment Report.* New York and Geneva: United Nations.

Part I

Foreign Direct Investment Strategies and Industrial Relations Systems

2

Foreign Direct Investment and Its Employment Opportunities in Perspective: Meeting the Great Expectations of Developing Countries?

Gabriele Köhler

Developed and developing countries, alike, are increasingly turning toward foreign direct investment (FDI) as a means of increasing employment opportunities. In a global labor force of employable, working-age people estimated at 3 billion, some 140 million are unemployed, and another 175–200 million remain underemployed (ILO, 1998: 1). In developed economies, ensuring full employment is an acute concern, as industrial restructuring, changing capital-labor ratios, and enhanced productivity have decreased the demand for labor per unit of output and heightened frictional and structural unemployment. In developing countries, the relatively small size of the formal economies as well as the persistence of high levels of poverty make the creation of employment (notably in the formal sector) a pressing goal. Recent crises, furthermore, have exacerbated unemployment and underemployment, increasing the urgency to increase sustainable employment opportunities.

Achieving full employment is a primary objective in any society and constitutes the main economic and social development path toward overcoming poverty. The emphasis placed on the private sector in achieving this objective has increased significantly over the past decade, whereas the emphasis placed on governments as welfare states is being downplayed. Both developed and developing country governments, moreover, are increasingly ascribing to FDI an important role in generating employment, either directly in multinational company (MNC) affiliates or indirectly through links with MNCs, regardless of ownership and mode of entry. In the case of developing countries, there is also the expectation that employment in MNC affiliates will be of a *higher quality* than in firms owned by domestic investors. Additionally, there are expectations that FDI inflows will expedite integration into global production and trade chains or facilitate technology acquisition. For developing economies, furthermore, there is a hope that inward FDI will help close gaps between savings and investment.

The objective of this chapter is to examine the role of FDI and MNCs in creating employment, especially in developing countries. First, I provide an overview of trends in FDI, addressing the evolving role of FDI and MNCs, the direction, magnitude, and concentration of FDI flows, modes of entry, linkages to trade, and structural change. Second, against this profile of FDI trends, I examine the effects of FDI on generating employment opportunities in developing countries, exploring the extent to which FDI meets the great expectations that it raises among many economists and government policymakers in developing countries. Lastly, I reflect on the employment implications of the changing face and influence of MNC stakeholders on FDI decision making.

FDI: AN OVERVIEW

Long-Term Trends in FDI and the Changing Role of FDI and MNCs

In absolute terms, the long-term trend in FDI flows has increased substantially, despite intermittent slumps, since the mid-1970s, rising from U.S.$23 billion in 1975 to U.S.$1.3 trillion in 2000 (see Table 2.1). FDI growth rates have been accelerating, with FDI flows in 2000 roughly sixfold the level observed in the early 1990s. In relative terms, FDI, likewise, has increased. In particular, the share of FDI flows in gross fixed capital formation increased for all countries from an average three-year level of 3 percent at the outset of the 1980s, to 4 percent in the early 1990s, to 12 percent for the 1997–1999 period. For developing countries as a group, the respective averages also rose from 3 to 4 to 12 percent. Correspondingly, the share of inward FDI stock as a share of gross domestic product (GDP) almost tripled, from 5 percent in the early 1980s to 14 percent in the 1997–1999 period. For developing countries, the share rose from 6 percent to 22 percent (UNCTAD, 2001: 291–337; also see Table 2.2 on p.24).

The number of firms operating not just as single- or multiplant entities within one country but as multiplant entities in different economies has increased in parallel to the growth in FDI flows. It is estimated that there are currently some 60,000 MNCs worldwide, as compared to an estimated mere 7,300 at the end of the 1970s. These MNCs now control as many as 820,000 foreign affiliates (UNCTAD, 2001: 9). This rapid rise in the number of MNCs and FDI is attributable to several evolving patterns. First, more firms from the large developed economies that have been the "traditional" source countries of FDI (notably, the United States and the United Kingdom), have become ever more transnational. Second, more countries have become home to outward-investing firms. In particular, Japan has emerged as an international outward investor country since the mid-1980s, and several developing countries have also emerged as outward investors since the early 1990s. Third, different from the typical MNC of the 1960s or 1970s, small and medium-size enterprises in both developed and developing economies are increasingly investing outside their home countries. Moreover, it has become technically possible to decompose production into many discrete steps, allowing companies to exploit economies of scale across an ever wider range of dispersed production sites.

Due to regulatory liberalization, there also have been increasing opportunities for cross-boundary investment and greater accessibility (both physically and institutionally) of foreign economies. This liberalization is in itself, nonetheless, a response to the profit-maximizing interests and demands of foreign and domestic enterprises, as well as the economic and budgetary objectives of governments. Finally, political changes since the late 1980s and early 1990s have led to mass privatization programs. The number and scale of many such programs in transition and developing economies, in particular, have made it necessary for host economies to open to foreign investors.

In summary, the rise in FDI is both cause and result of what is often termed the "internationalization" or "transnationalization" of the global economy. The factors previously identified as accelerating the pace of FDI are mutually reinforcing. The rising absolute size and relative shares of FDI, furthermore, have changed the employment policy debate and, in turn, changed policy, in a process of circular causation.

Table 2.1
Total FDI Flows by Host Region (Millions of U.S. Dollars in Current Terms)

	1975	1980	1985	1990	1995	2000
World	23,223	54,625	57,265	205,183	331,068	1,270,764
Developed economies of which	14,446	42,100	37,837	170,182	208,462	1,005,178
- European Union	9,880	21,363	16,427	102,685	113,480	617,321
- United States	2,560	16,930	20,010	48,422	58,772	281,115
- Japan	230	80	642	1,753	39	8,187
Developing economies of which	8,756	10,106	11,475	34,433	113,338	240,167
- Latin America	3,997	7,378	7,225	9,276	51,279	86,172
- Asia	4,321	6,434	5,325	22,388	75,856	143,763
- Africa	397	319	2,871	2,355	4,694	8,198
Countries in Eastern Europe	na	11	15	568	12,730	25,419

Sources: UNCTAD, 1999c: 477–479; UNCTAD, 2001: 291–294.

Note: For all years, the European Union aggregate inflows refer to the union as at 1999, comprising Austria, Belgium, Denmark, Finland, France, Germany, Greece, Ireland, Italy, Netherlands, Luxembourg, Portugal, Spain, Sweden, and the United Kingdom.

Table 2.2
FDI in Selected Regions and Selected Indicators of the Role of FDI in Gross Fixed Capital Formation (GFCF) and Gross Domestic Product (GDP), Selected Periods

	FDI inflows (Millions of dollars)			Annual average								
				FDI inflows as a share of GFCF (Percentage)			FDI inward stock as a share of GDP (Percentage)			GFCF as a share of GDP (Percentage)		
	1980–82	1990–92	1997–99	1980–1982	1990–1992	1997–1999	1980–1982	1990–1992	1997–1999	1980–1982	1990–1992	1996–1998
World	60 548	180 414	748 504	2.7	3.7	11.6	5.3	8.5	14.2	21.7	21.9	21.1
Developed countries	41 095	132 859	528 120	2.5	3.6	11.2	5.0	8.1	12.4	21.2	20.9	20.0
Developing countries	19 438	45 052	199 244	3.2	4.1	12.1	6.2	11.2	21.5	23.6	26.2	24.9
Africa	1 198	3 064	7 946	1.6	4.5	9.4	7.2	14.1	18.9	22.9	20.0	19.9
Latin America and the Caribbean	7 842	14 413	88 212	3.7	5.6	20.3	5.9	11.4	20.8	24.1	18.0	19.3
Central Asia	..	55	2 931	..	1.2	25.3	..	0.2	24.1	..	9.5	22.9
Asia and the Pacific	10 357	27 461	101 076	3.4	3.7	9.5	15.0	15.5	24.6	24.6	31.9	28.4
Least developed countries:	440	1 433	3 944	3.5	6.1	6.7	2.4	5.5	9.1	10.5	14.4	14.8

Source: UNCTAD, FDI/MNC database.

Interestingly, though, the rise in cross-border investment flows mainly reflects a shift in the origins of investment, a shift from almost exclusively domestic investment to a relatively small, but rising, share of transboundary, transnational investment.   It is not indicative of an increase in total global investment, as is often implied.   That is, the share of *total* investment (measured as gross fixed capital formation) in GDP globally has not changed.   Instead, between 1980 and 1995, it remained at 21 to 22 percent for the world as a whole, 20 to 21 percent for all developed countries, and between 24 and 26 percent for developing countries.   Only the Central Asia and the Asian-Pacific regions display higher ratios of investment per GDP, while in Latin America the investment ratio has declined (Table 2.2).   In other words, the changing *ownership* composition of investment has not augmented the actual investment undertaken at the aggregate global level, which (as discussed later) has implications for the amount of employment that MNCs can be expected to generate.

Direction of Flows

Integral to the greater reliance on FDI has been the expectation that investment would flow to economies with relatively lower investment levels and capital-output ratios since the marginal return to investment would be higher in these locations.   Thus, it has been believed by many that differences among capital-rich and capital-poor countries would in due course even out.   This aggregate image, however, masks significant differences at the country and industry levels.   Contrary to the traditional neo-classical model, that is, most FDI flows circulate within the highly capitalized developed countries and to a small number of developing economies.

Indeed, over the past two decades, FDI flows have remained concentrated within the developed world, which has been receiving between 60 and 80 percent of all inflows.   Of total outflows, between 80 and 90 percent originate in developed economies, and with the exception of Japan, most FDI is directed to other developed countries.   In other words, the large MNCs domiciled in developed countries tend to invest in other developed countries, concentrating much of that within a small set of four to six countries.   The four largest recipients in given years (which have consistently included the United States and the United Kingdom) have been host to at least 60 percent of developed country inflows (Table 2.3).   Since 1990, moreover, six outward investor countries (the United States, the United Kingdom, Germany, France, the Netherlands, and Japan) have consistently accounted for roughly three-quarters of developed countries' (and, hence, total) FDI outflows (UNCTAD, 1999c: 483; UNCTAD, 1999a: 249).

The bulk of FDI flows, therefore, is concentrated not just among developed countries but within a certain set of countries among them.   For the early 1990s, they were the so-called triad countries comprising the United States, the European Union, and Japan (UNCTAD, 1991; Ohmae, 1985).   This

Table 2.3 Concentration of FDI Inflows in Developed Countries: The Four Largest Recipients, Selected Years (Billions of Dollars)

	1980		1990		1995		2000	
Country	Country	U.S.$ billion	Country	U.S.$ billion	Country	U.S.$ billion	Country	U.S.$ billion
	United States	17	United States	48	United States	59	United States	281
	United Kingdom	10	United Kingdom	32	France	24	Germany	176
	France	3	Spain	14	United Kingdom	20	United Kingdom	130
	Netherlands	2	France	13	Sweden	14	Belgium/Lux	87

Total developed country inflows in U.S.$ billion.

40	170	203	1,005

<u>Memorandum:</u> Share of four largest recipients in total developed country inflows in per cent

81	64	58	67

Sources: UNCTAD, 1999c: 476; UNCTAD, 2001: 291.

concentration is mirrored in capital stock data, whereby roughly 60 percent of all inward FDI stock is concentrated in these three locations (UNCTAD, 2001: 9).

In addition, the share of total FDI flowing to developing countries as a group fluctuates. Since 1980, it has varied between roughly 20 percent to more than one-third of total FDI flows (UNCTAD, 1999c: 477; UNCTAD, 2001: 291). This ratio suggests that FDI flowing into developing countries has indeed become a feature of the "globalizing" world economy, reflecting the shift in the organization of global production and the reach of MNCs. But this ratio can be misleading, nonetheless, as FDI flows are not evenly spread. The 10 largest recipient economies in the developing world have accounted for 70 to 80 percent of all developing country FDI, measured as averaged inflows for the three-year periods 1980–1982, 1990–1992, and 1996–1998. In 2000, six developing economies—Hong Kong, China, Brazil, Mexico, Argentina, and the Republic of Korea—accounted for 72 percent of all developing country inflows (UNCTAD, 2001: 291–95). With respect to total world FDI inflows, the 10 largest recipients among the developing economies accounted for just over 20 percent of all FDI inflows in the 1996–1998 period. (Figure 2.1; also see UNCTAD, 1999c: 18-19).[1]

Accordingly, FDI flows now present a somewhat different picture from the triad image of the early 1990s and might more aptly be captured as FDI clusters. There are four major FDI clusters. These clusters comprise the European Union, North America (with the United States as the lead FDI investor and host economy but also including Canada and Mexico), a group of developing economies in East Asia and Southeast Asia comprising China and the Asian newly industrializing economies (Hong Kong, the Republic of Korea, Singapore, and Malaysia), and the Mercosur group (including Brazil and Argentina). Together, these four clusters in the year 2000 accounted for 90 percent of all FDI flows (UNCTAD, 2001:291–95). Including Japan, they also represent the major source economies of FDI.

Although integration into the global economy is increasing for some developing economies, for most it is not. Whether the integration of economies through FDI leads to better performance depends on the measure of performance that one uses in making such judgments (e.g., growth rates of GDP, income distribution, value-added shares, or other economic indicators). A priori it can be argued that economies that are receiving negligible inflows of FDI and are not benefiting from other, steady inflows to capital accounts (such as from official development assistance or commercial loans) are likely to face problems on mustering the foreign exchange and foreign savings necessary to reach higher growth trajectories, unless, of course, domestic sources of development finance are not forthcoming.

Mode of Entry and the Impact of FDI

Increasingly, FDI flows, especially among developed countries, are in the form of mergers and acquisitions (M&As). A distinction between greenfield

Figure 2.1
Share of the Ten Largest FDI Recipients among Developing Economies
(Selected Periods)

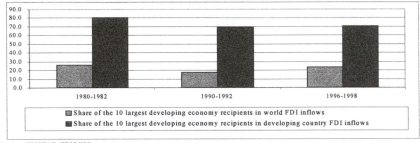

Source: UNCTAD, FDI/MNC.

Notes:
For 1980-1982: Saudia Arabia, Brazil, Mexico, Singapore, Hong Kong,
Malaysia, Argentina, Egypt, Bermuda, and Chile
For 1990-1992: China, Singapore, Malaysia, Mexico, Argentina,
Hong Kong, Thailand, Bermuda, Indonesia, and Brazil
For 1996-1998: China, Brazil, Hong Kong, Mexico, Singapore, Argentina, Malaysia, Chile, Thailand, and
Venezuela

investment that augments physical capital, on the one hand, and M&A flows associated with firm- or macrolevel restructuring, on the other hand, is warranted. These two forms of FDI occur for various reasons and in varied ways. Any employment and development assessment, in turn, is largely contextual (UNCTAD, 2000a).

M&As that (1) accommodate privatizations in economies where domestic entrepreneurs and capital are not readily available or (2) are made in developing countries catering to growing markets may initiate a process of restructuring that could result either in maintaining existing employment or, under beneficial circumstances, in expanding employment. Conversely, M&As that are undertaken by large MNCs seeking to control an industry globally and, hence, acquiring competitors as well as emerging firms in the same industries might well scale down or close acquired firms. These types of M&As can undermine "infant industries" and/or sever supplier linkages in the host developing countries. Each such scenario, consequently, leads to layoffs.

More fundamentally, when considering FDI as a source of investment, it is important to bear in mind that M&As do not (at least, initially) create new capacity. Therefore, any expectations based on FDI growth rates need to be tempered by the fact that, to some extent, they merely reflect flows of investment finance. They are not automatically indicative of incremental real investment, which would create additional employment.

FDI, Trade, and Structural Change

In terms of trade flows, MNCs are major economic players for a complex set of reasons. First, their large absolute size, measured in total assets or in market capitalization, is invariably intertwined with large sales volumes. For the 100 largest MNCs, total foreign sales were estimated at $4.3 trillion in 1999, with foreign sales accounting for half of these revenues (UNCTAD, 2001:94). Second, as MNCs invest abroad, they create a network of production plants. In many instances, the value chain is split up among the plants so that intermediate products are shipped among affiliates and frequently so across borders. Some estimates suggest that intrafirm trade of MNCs is equivalent to one-third of world exports and that two-thirds to three- quarters of world exports are handled by MNCs. The increasing transnationalization of productive activity has, in fact, augmented global trade flows in value terms. However, this is somewhat artificial, owing to multiple counting of the same final output as it is exported at various stages of processing.

Third, international trade and investment are interlinked in several ways. In some instances, MNCs invest in host countries or regions to avoid import tariffs and to sell output to large host markets. In other cases, MNCs invest in given locations for purposes of establishing export platforms, benefiting, for example, from preferential trade agreements or rules-of-origin arrangements in destination markets (notably, in the developed world). In these cases, FDI replaces earlier trade flows or is triggered by trade considerations. Given their rationale for investing abroad, many MNCs, therefore, tend to have higher export propensities than typical domestic firms.

There is also an interdependence among industries in which there is a higher degree of outward FDI, in part based on the industrial composition of MNCs and product groups experiencing high growth rates in international trade. In terms of its composition by sectors, at the global level, FDI flows are concentrated in manufacturing and services. Over time, the primary sector's weight has clearly diminished vis-à-vis the tertiary sector, in terms of growth rates of FDI-related capital stock and in terms of shares in the world FDI-based capital stock. Among developed economies, 36 percent of inward FDI stock in 1999 was in manufacturing, while services accounted for as much as 55 percent of inward FDI stock. In developing countries, the overall picture is practically inverse, whereby manufacturing FDI accounts for 55 percent and services roughly 37 percent of the inward FDI stock (1999) (UNCTAD, 2001: 66; 259–60).

In part, this profile mirrors the relative shares of the manufacturing and the tertiary sectors in the GDP of developed and developing countries respectively (e.g., see UNCTAD, 1999a: 332). It also reflects that, until recently, services were less open to foreign investment in developing countries. Table 2.4 provides a rough indication of the distribution of capital stock across industries at the global level. This profile is replicated in the industrial composition of the largest MNCs. They are centered on industries such as chemicals and pharmaceuticals, electronics, automobiles, and food and beverages (UNCTAD, 1999c: 78-80, 83). These are also the industries in which world trade has been the most expansionary, experiencing annual growth rates of world trade of 10 percent and more.

Table 2.4
Industrial Composition of FDI Inward Stock, 1988 and 1999

Sector/industry	Global investment stock			
	1988		1999	
	Billions of US$	percent of total	Billions of US$	percent of total
All industries	839	100	3633	100
Primary	**98**	**12**	**202**	**6**
Manufacturing	**347**	**41**	**1512**	**42**
of which				
Food, beverages and tobacco	30	4	102	3
Textiles, clothing leather	15	2	36	1
Chemical and chemical products	50	6	24	7
Basic metals		4	108	3
Machinery and equipment	37	4	92	4
Electric machinery		5	129	4
Unspecified manufacturing	25	3	392	11
Services	**355**	**42**	**1827**	**50**

Source: UNCTAD 2001: 259–60.

Note: Machinery and equipment denotes heavy machinery, while electric machinery comprises office, accounting and computing machinery, and radio, television, and communication apparatus.

Either as inward or outward investment, FDI may change the sectoral composition of capital stock and the profile of economic activities in both host and home economies. Thus, FDI is a contributing factor in economic restructuring. Economies can use FDI actively to induce structural change along certain desired paths or succumb to it passively by receiving FDI in patterns that cater to the MNCs' global positioning of production sites. In either case, FDI alters the sectoral composition of the economies concerned. This has direct implications for employment, since, broadly speaking, the primary sector and services tend to be associated with more workplaces per unit of capital. Within the manufacturing sector, capital stock is a somewhat misleading figure, in that capital–output and capital–labor ratios differ significantly by industry. Thus, the numbers of workplaces generated directly by a given size of capital investment vary significantly among industries, as well as, of course, among countries as a result of technologies deployed. The industrial composition of FDI also affects employment indirectly through its contractual, nonequity links, which again differ significantly across industries and product segments.

FDI AND ITS EMPLOYMENT OPPORTUNITIES: THE DEVELOPING COUNTRY VIEW

In all developing regions, unemployment was on the rise throughout the 1990s. In Central and Latin America, open unemployment reached 9.5 percent in 1999, as compared to 5.7 percent in 1990 (ILO Regional Office for Latin

America and the Caribbean, 1998: 6). In the Asian economies experiencing economic and financial crises, total job losses in 1997-1998 were estimated at 20 to 25 million (ILO, 1999b). As a result, formal sector workers are moving back into the informal sector, which is characterized by low productivity, extremely low income, and neither job nor social security. Such "casualization" of labor is also observed in the former planned economies, where the public sector and state-owned enterprises that once guaranteed full employment are undergoing privatization. In these economies, the restoration of the earlier formal sector employment levels is an obviously, politically and socially motivated objective. In addition, in many developing countries, high dependency ratios (the share of children under 15 in the total population) and rising labor force participation rates create an incessant need for additional jobs. Given the rising shares of FDI in total investment, hopes are set on capital inflows to provide the necessary employment growth.

The Role of FDI in Developing Economies

FDI has become a major preoccupation among those engaged in the development debate. This is partly because the role of FDI as a source of external finance has increased considerably over the past two decades. As one component of international financial flows to developing countries, net FDI flows accounted for only 5 percent of all financial flows in 1980, for 25 percent in 1990, and for as much as 66 percent of all financial flows in the late 1990s (Figure 2.2). As official development assistance has stagnated since the mid-1990s, moreover, private direct investment in developing countries currently far outstrips development cooperation flows in the form of grants and concessional loans, in effect, reversing the situation prevailing at the outset of the 1980s. For instance, in 1998, grants and concessional loans provided by international financial institutions and bilateral agencies amounted to roughly U.S.$38 billion, compared to U.S.$176 billion in FDI inflows to developing countries in that year (see Figure 2.1; UNCTAD, 2000b: 247, 254).

In response, development discourse has realigned itself as if to accommodate the changed realities. High expectations are fixed on the private enterprise sector as the place where investment and hence the source of economic growth and development, are centered. In the process, the assessment of MNCs as providers of an increasing share of "development finance", has changed. In large parts of the international community in the postwar period until the end of the 1980s, FDI and MNCs were seen to call for close monitoring. The concern over the noxious role of MNCs, expressed implicitly in the draft United Nations Code of Conduct on Transnational Corporations (1986), is one example of this position. Since the early 1990s, however, the perception regarding MNCs has metamorphosed.

MNCs are now welcomed by developing countries seeking to benefit from the access to finance, to marketing channels, to technology, and to employment accompanying FDI inflows. Competition among countries, including

Figure 2.2
FDI as a Share of International Financial Flows (1980, 1990, 1999)

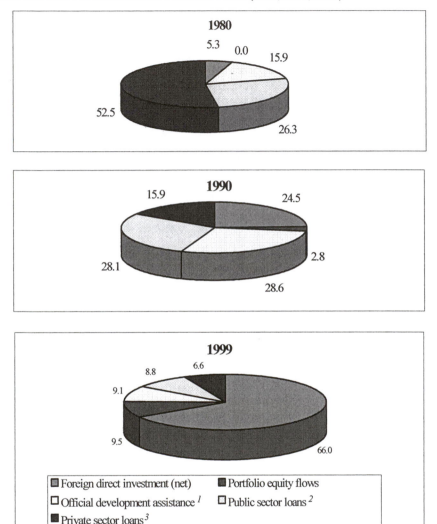

Source: World Bank, 2000.

Notes:
1.   Official development assistance (ODA) comprises grants excluding technical cooperation.
2.   Public sector loans refers to loans from official creditors such as the international financial
      institutions.
3.   Private sector loans are commercial bank loans and private, nonguaranteed loans.

among developing countries, to attract as much FDI as possible has replaced
their earlier, postcolonial wariness. This shift in perception mirrors a general

public to the private sector, and the role of the private commercial sector is cast prominently.

The Employment Concern and Trends in MNC-Based Employment

Estimates of total global employment in MNCs, including in both parent firms and affiliates, are in the range of 86 million people (1998 estimate, UNCTAD, 1999c: 265). Employment by all MNCs' affiliates in developing countries is estimated at between 17 to 26 million (UNCTAD, 1999c: 264). At least 4.5 million people are reportedly employed in enterprise processing zones (EPZs) in developing countries, and another 18–20 million in foreign invested firms in the special economic zones in China (UNCTAD, 1999c: 452–54; van Heerden, forthcoming). The largest 100 MNCs employ roughly 13 million of these people (estimated for 1998 and 1999; UNCTAD, 2001: 94). MNCs, nevertheless, account for only a minute share of total employment. Indeed, less than 1 percent of the global labor force of 3 billion people are directly employed by MNCs. In other words, their overall direct employment effect on a global scale is negligible. Why, then, does employment creation figure so prominently as a motive for countries (especially developing countries) to attract FDI? There are three fundamental reasons.

First, in some countries and industries, MNC-based employment makes up a large share of total formal sector employment (Table 2.5). Therefore, governments seeking to augment employment have come to see the establishment of MNC affiliates as a convenient avenue to ensuring a rise in domestic employment. Similarly, in distressed firms or areas, an incoming M&A investment may preserve workplaces that would otherwise be eliminated as companies reduce operations or close down altogether. Often, this expectation is fulfilled because in some industries MNCs establish contractual links with suppliers or distributors (backward and forward linkages), which, in turn, may lead to increases in employment. Depending on the industry involved, and the industrial and the MNC's global strategy, the extent of indirect employment runs from one to five additional workplaces in a host economy for each workplace created in an affiliate.

Examples of industries with high secondary employment effects include those that display backward linkages into natural-resource based activities (namely, in agriculture) or that have forward linkages (namely, production established to serve the host market). When host countries pursue effective employment policies and have strategies regarding "local content," some of the geographically highly dispersed industries (such as automobiles or electronics) can also result in employment linkages to supplier firms. Often these are serviced by supplier firms that relocate from the MNC's home country. To the extent that foreign-owned suppliers replace existing domestic firms, the gross employment effect may be large, but the net effect, nonetheless, may be negligible.

Second, MNCs and their individual plants are often large employers, especially MNCs domiciled in developed, Organization for Economic

Table 2.5
Share of MNCs in Employment, Selected Developing Economies and Industries

Economy	Year	Manufacturing sector	All industries
Brazil	1995	13.4	3.5
China	1997	..	4.1
Hong Kong, China	1994	16.0	12.8
Indonesia	1996	4.7	0.9
Malaysia	1994	43.7	..
Mexico	1993	17.9	3.3
Nepal	1998	1.9	..
Singapore	1996	52.1	..
Sri Lanka	1996	54.4	22.1
Taiwan Province of China	1995	21.1	11.1
Turkey	1990	3.2	..
Viet Nam	1995	14.9	5.3

Source: UNCTAD, 1999c: 265, Table IX.3.

Cooperation and Development (OECD) countries. Many of the largest MNCs employ 200,000 or more people, and among the 100 largest MNCs, 47 corporations employed 100,000 or more people in 1999 (including operations in home countries and abroad) (UNCTAD, 2001: 90 ff.). Listed in (Table 2.6) are the largest MNCs in terms of employment. As a result of mergers and acquisitions, total employment figures of the largest MNCs increased markedly in the late 1990s, with Wal-Mart becoming one of the world's largest employers.

Although assets, sales, and other measures of size are on a far smaller scale than for developed-country MNCs, a number of developing-country MNCs are also large employers. Six out of the 50 largest developing-country MNCs employed 40,000 or more workers in 1999 (UNCTAD, 2001: 105–6). MNCs are, consequently, highly visible as employers and, in a given location, might well be the largest employer. In addition, many MNC affiliates, especially in the food, textiles, and electronics industries, employ predominantly female workforces. Governments might, therefore, view MNC-based employment as a means of providing women, otherwise generally engaged in agriculture or home-based informal sector activities, with waged employment. Such FDI would, thus, augment formal sector employment, contributing favorably to overall household income and to GDP.

A third, less conspicuous reason that countries are motivated to attract FDI derives from some emerging patterns in MNC employment, observed at least tentatively during the 1990s. Large MNCs, in particular, tend to employ significant shares of their workforce in foreign affiliates. Among the group of 100 largest MNCs in 1997, 20 companies employed between 50 percent to over 90 percent in their foreign affiliates (calculations based on UNCTAD, 1999:

78–82 Table III.1: pp.). There is reason to expect that this trend may be on the rise. In 13 of these corporations, foreign employment increased by 20 to 40 percent over the 1993-1997 period, and in some instances, this occurred against a backdrop of a decrease in the firm's total employment. Similarly, developing-country MNCs tend to have a large share of overseas employment: 7 of 50 firms employed more than 50 percent of their workforce in foreign affiliates in 1997 (based on data from UNCTAD 1999c: 86–88;Table III.8). Likewise, for developing country MNCs, foreign employment as a share of total employment doubled or tripled between 1993 and 1997 in 12 of the 50 companies, albeit from a small base, which exaggerates the trend. There are also a number of MNCs where foreign employment has increased against a backdrop of decreasing total employment.

Table 2.6
MNCs Employing 200,000 or More Employees in 1999

	TNC	Employment Total	Foreign
1	Wal-Mart Stores	1 140 000	...
2	DaimlerChrysler AG	466 938	225 705
3	Siemens AG	443 000	251 000
4	General Motors	398 000	162 300
5	Ford Motor Company	364 550	191 486
6	Hitachi Ltd	323 827	...
7	McDonald's Corporation	314 000	260 000
8	General Electric	310 000	143 000
9	Royal Ahold NV	308 793	59 428
10	IBM	307 401	161 612
11	Volkswagen Group	306 275	147 959
12	Carrefour SA	297 290	...
13	Matsushita Electric Industrial Co	290 448	143 773
14	Vivendi SA	275 591	...
15	Unilever	246 033	222 614
16	Nestlé S.A.	230 929	224 554
17	Philips Electronics	226 874	...
18	Fiat Spa	221 319	98 589
19	Suez Lyonnaise des Eaux	220 000	150 000
20	Toyota Motor Corporation	214 631	13 500
21	SBC Communications	204 530	...
	Total employment in the 100 largest TNCs	13 279 327	6 050 283

Source: UNCTAD 2001: 90–94.

Note: Companies are ranked by total employment. The total for foreign employment is a minimum figure, as some firms do not provide data on foreign employment.

The only data available on the share of employment in foreign affiliates in developing countries are based on U.S. and Japanese MNCs. For MNCs domiciled in these two countries, employment has been increasing more in host countries than in their respective home countries. Also, roughly one-third of their overseas affiliate employment is in developing countries, and this trend has been on the rise (based on data from UNCTAD, 1999: 266, 450, 451). The available data, however, do not distinguish the form of investment. Some MNCs undertake greenfield investment predominantly outside the home country, pursuing asset-seeking or market-seeking growth strategies. Similarly, MNCs engaged in labor-intensive industries and pursuing efficiency-seeking strategies may be investing heavily in developing countries, where labor costs are relatively lower. The changing distribution of employment among parents and affiliates may also merely reflect M&A activity, whereby employees hitherto employed by domestic firms become employees in affiliates acquired by foreign MNCs. Under this latter scenario, host country employment would not necessarily increase despite investment inflows.

Because of the considerable share of MNC-based employment in some industries in some countries, because of the large employment numbers of some MNCs, and because of the high and possibly rising shares of foreign affiliate employment, MNCs are often wooed by prospective host economies for their expected contribution to employment at the national and local levels. Indeed, it is common for central or even local-level governments to invite MNCs to locate in their country, offering them a variety of incentives in exchange for creating local employment. The extent to which foreign-owned MNCs actually generate additional employment opportunities, however, is not readily apparent.

First, there may be a tendency for total employment numbers in the larger MNCs to decline. For example, several of the 100 largest MNCs have been downsizing their workforce over the past decade, with total employment dropping by anywhere from 1 to 40 percent in at least a quarter of the 100 largest MNCs (calculations based on UNCTAD, 1999c: 78–80). Similar to the pattern observed among the largest MNCs, roughly 20 percent of the developing-country MNCs appear to have downsized employment by between 10 and 50 percent during the 1990s. The reductions are almost certainly due, to some extent, to technological change that has increased productivity. Against this reduction in employment, however, a number of MNCs have increased their outsourcing, so that although employment within MNCs decreases, workplaces are not abolished but converted into indirect employment in supplier companies. In some instances, furthermore, MNCs have restructured, in which case employees might continue working but under new owners.

In many instances, declines in employee numbers may be related to M&A activity that results in layoffs. In developing countries, different scenarios and motivations might suggest an impact on employment, at the firm and country level, that is more varied than in developed countries. Empirical evidence on employment movements in developing countries, however, is patchy. As noted earlier, employment in MNCs' *foreign* affiliates has been on the rise, and possibly much of this increase is taking place in developing host countries. Cross-border M&As in developing countries, therefore, might not lead to employment reductions to the same extent as observed in developed countries. Nevertheless, any expected increase in employment opportunities derivable from FDI needs to be tempered by an analysis of the type of FDI made, namely, whether it is a greenfield or M&A investment.

Second, there is the general observation that from the enterprise perspective, production needs to be commercially viable and sustainable, predictable, and profitable. The logic of MNCs is no different, although the largest among them can easily accommodate losses in some affiliates in the short run without jeopardizing the performance of the MNC as a whole. As MNCs position their production sites in production chains across the global economy, the availability of labor, unit labor costs, and the mix of skills available in different locations shape their decisions. Hence, governments offering employment conditions favorable to the MNCs are more likely to win in the competition for employment-generating investment. Conversely, the capacity of MNCs to ascribe different roles to affiliates in their systems renders host countries vulnerable to a certain extent to the business decisions of MNCs. The employment impact, therefore, is once again subject to qualifications.

Quality of Employment as a Function of Type of FDI and Its Products

Debates on the effects of MNCs on employment are often highly emotional ones. MNCs are seen as either superior employers or as behemoths taking advantage of low-wage, suppressed workforces in developing countries, which allows MNCs to bargain down home-country employment standards and drive up profit rates. Observors with a positive assessment view MNCs as superior employers in terms of the quality of the actual shop floor and physical workplace, contractual arrangements, training programs, or compensation, including supplementary benefits such as sick or annual leave, provision of cafeterias, dormitories, and child care. This assessment is sometimes based on a comparison between MNC affiliates and domestic firms in the same industry. More generally, it is based on comparisons with workplaces in smaller enterprises or firms in the informal sector. In comparison with the work conditions in developed home countries, the image may be less flattering, but comparisons with home country conditions are often considered inappropriate given lower real wages and lower productivity prevailing in developing countries. Usually, positive assessments are based on comparisons to firms in the production of high-end, technology-intensive products that rely on consistent quality and reliability in their production.

Observers more critical of FDI and MNCs tend to focus their assessment on industries where there is strong global competition for investment and jobs and where wages and product prices have to be minimized accordingly. In these industries, products are essentially standardized, and mass-consumption goods produced on a large scale, with or without brand names. In these industries, MNCs may not provide favorable work conditions, possibly in collusion with host country governments willing to forgo employment quality in the interest of employment quantity. The prime examples are found in EPZs where, in some instances, industrial relations or employment conditions institutionalized in the host economy at large are waived in the zones in order to attract foreign investors (UNCTAD, 1999c: 271–72). Finally, in some industries, MNCs appear to deploy roughly the same technology across all affiliates, often obtaining levels of productivity approaching, if not commensurate with, those prevailing in comparable plants in their home countries. Given relatively lower wages existing in developing host countries, MNCs reduce their unit labor costs and, in turn, pay lower real unit wages.

In summary, the verdict is mixed and, again, is contextual. A decisive factor concerning the effects of MNCs on employment outcomes is the interplay between MNCs, the industry concerned, and the circumstances prevailing in host and home countries. This interplay is the subject of the following section.

FDI DECISION MAKING: THE CHANGING FACE AND INFLUENCE OF MNC STAKEHOLDERS

Traditionally, employers and their shareholders, employees and their representative institutions, and national governments have been the main stakeholders in employment policy. However, as global economic and sociopolitical environments are being transformed and as information technology increases transparency, the face and number of vocal stakeholders are, likewise, changing (at least for certain types of MNCs). First, MNCs are increasingly becoming differentiated between a company's management and its private and public shareholders. In addition, interests and positions among shareholders are becoming more divergent. On one hand, pressures on executives to meet earnings expectations of shareholders have led to decisions that adversely affect shareholder value in the longer term, for instance, by pushing for mergers or acquisitions that do not necessarily pay off (see UNCTAD, 2000a) and by reducing force or threatening layoffs as a means of appeasing stock markets to increase short-term shareholder value. On the other hand, institutional investors who have an interest in a company's financial performance but who are also under pressure to consider a company's social responsibility and performance are increasingly influencing MNCs' investment decisions or actions regarding employment conditions.

The second development influencing employment effects of FDI and human resourse management and labor relations (HRM/LR) policies is the changing nature of the trade union movement. Over the past decade, economic restructuring, internationalization, and economic crises have weakened trade unions. During the 1990s, union membership declined in many countries, including both developing and developed countries for a host of reasons (ILO, 1997). Consequently, the union movement's capacity to leverage employers and to influence governments toward labor-friendly policies has diminished. In response to globalization and to recapture their influence, international associations of trade unions are currently devising more transnational approaches to formulating negotiation and consultation strategies to achieve labor-related objectives. (For example, see the chapters in Part III of this volume.) Development of such transnational strategies of interunion cooperation, however, is an exceedingly difficult endeavor because the conflicts of interests within the trade union movement are becoming increasingly manifest. The labor movement in developed countries, where excess capacity in some industries and high productivity are displacing labor, eyes with wariness the movement of investment to developing countries and resulting "social dumping," especially in selected industries. Union counterparts and policymakers in developing countries seeking employment-enhancing FDI, in contrast, bristle at any proposed measures that might suggest "protectionist" motives.

Similarly, the influence of central governments has generally diminished in the course of structural adjustment programs designed to downsize governments, outsource traditional responsibilities, and otherwise reduce government revenues and expenditures. Decentralization of government activity, nonetheless, has allowed local governments to become more active in parallel to, or in place of, central governments. Local governments in developed and developing countries, alike, often attempt to increase employment by attracting new economic activity. These entities offer such incentives as tax advantages, industrial parks, technology centers, regional growth triangles, or the more classical EPZs. Such "locational tournaments" among local governments within countries intensify the already existent competition for FDI (Mytelka, 1998). Thus, in developing countries, central governments are less of a force than they were in much of the postwar period. However, at the international level, governments are increasingly making commitments to action to address unemployment and poverty. Adherence or at least reference to the normative frameworks of ILO conventions is more frequent than in earlier decades, partly as a result of greater transparency and open communication.

Lastly, other "stakeholders" have emerged to take a more active interest in labor issues. They include consumer groups, other nongovernment organizations (NGOs) concerned with environmental or human rights issues, and company shareholders. Consumer activism, for example, has served to reinforce trade union pressure, particularly in some consumer goods industries, as illustrated by the recent campaigns for better work conditions, higher remuneration, workplace safety, job security, or compliance with core International Labor Organization (ILO) labor standards. To a certain extent and in some specific areas, these emerging stakeholders are substituting for the weakened pro-labor efforts of unions. Some company shareholders and investor groups are also screening investment patterns against social criteria, including labor-related issues, with an eye on "ethical investment." This, too, is likely to influence MNC HRM/LR strategies and government employment policy, albeit indirectly and over time.

CONCLUSIONS: GREAT EXPECTATIONS BUT MIXED OUTCOMES

Clearly, the roles of FDI and of MNCs as global employers have increased over the past decade. The transnationalization of business and of investment implies that the share of MNC employment in total formal sector employment in developing countries is on the rise. In some countries, industries, or locations, MNC affiliates are indeed the largest employer. Whether or not FDI has increased employment in terms of numbers overall is an entirely different point. The share of FDI-linked employment in developing countries as a whole is negligible. Moreover, investment, as a share of GDP, has not increased over the past two decades. Therefore, it is unlikely that the existence of large international flows of capital, on the level of the global economy, would, per se, have generated net new employment in terms of numbers of workplaces, especially when the effects of productivity increases and operational rationalization are taken into consideration.

The observed transnationalization effect does mean that the quality and conditions of employment and how these are negotiated or derived have changed considerably over the past decade. Here, there is potential for change for the better, as the different emerging stakeholders and interest groups put pressure on MNCs to improve employment and workplace conditions and as there are a stronger global "watch" and understanding of employment issues as investment becomes more transnationalized. There is an equally strong risk for deterioration, though, as economies vie for FDI and are willing to sacrifice employment quality for quantity (Milberg, 1999: 105). Which outcome ultimately prevails depends, in the end, on the balance of power and influence of governments and civil society actors in developed and developing countries. In sum, the great expectations are met by, at best, mixed outcomes.

NOTE

1. In 1999 and 2000, cross-border mergers and acquisitions were particularly large, influencing total and developed country FDI inflow figures. Hence, the 1996–1998 period is a better reference period.

REFERENCES

ILO. (1997). *World Labour Report. Industrial Relations, Democracy and Social Stability 1997–1998*. Geneva: ILO.

ILO. (1998). *World Employment Report 1998–99. Employability in the Global Economy. How Training Matters*. Geneva: ILO.

ILO. (1999a). "Decent Work." Report of the Director-General. International Labour Conference, 87th session. International Labour Organisation: Geneva. www.ilo.org/public/english/10ilc.

ILO. (1999b). "The ILO's Response to the Financial Crisis in East and South-East Asia. Evolution of the Asian Financial crisis and Determination of Policy Needs and Response." GB. 247/4/2. Geneva: ILO.

ILO Regional Office for Latin America and the Caribbean (1998). "1998 Labour Review." www.lim.org.pe

Milberg, W. (1999). "Foreign Direct Investment and Development: Balancing Costs and Benefits." In *UNCTAD International Monetary and Financial Issues for the 1990s. Research Papers for the Group of Twenty-Four*, Vol. II. New York and Geneva: United Nations, pp. 99–116.

Mytelka, L. (1998). "Locational Tournaments for FDI: Inward Investment into Europe in a Global World". In Hood and S. Young, (eds.), *The Globalization of Multinational Enterprise Activity and Economic Development*. Basingstoke: Macmillan, pp. 278–302.

Ohmae, K. (1985). *Triad Power. The Coming Shape of Global Competition*. New York: Free Press.

UNCTAD. (1991). *World Investment Report 1991. The Triad in Foreign Direct Investment*. New York: United Nations.

UNCTAD. (1999a). *Handbook of International Trade and Development Statistics. 1996–1997*. New York and Geneva: United Nations.

UNCTAD. (1999b). *Trade and Development Report 1999*. New York and Geneva: United Nations.

UNCTAD. (1999c). *World Investment Report 1999. Foreign Direct Investment and the Challenge of Development*. New York and Geneva: United Nations.

UNCTAD. (2000a). *UNCTAD Handbook of Statistics 2000*. New York and Geneva: United Nations.

UNCTAD. (2000b). *World Investment Report 1999. Cross-border Mergers and Acquisitions and Development*. NewYork and Geneva: United Nations.

UNCTAD. (2001). *World Investment Report 2001. Linkages and Development*. New York and Geneva: United Nations.

van Heerden, A. (Forthcoming). *EPZs: The New Logic of Global Production*. Geneva: ILO.

World Bank. (2000). *World Development Indicators 2000*. Washington; D.C.: World Bank.

3

MNCs and Global Commodity Chains: Implications for Labor Strategies

Jennifer Bair and Harvie Ramsay

As briefly discussed by Cooke in Chapter 1, multinational company (MNC) production strategies can lead to diverse and complex global arrays of organizational arrangements linking domestic and foreign investment, trade, subcontracting, licensing, joint ventures, and alliances (see Figure 1.2). To more fully understand the emerging complexity, scope, and dynamics of MNC configuration choices, one needs to locate them within the broader intercompany networks of production and services in which MNCs operate. We suggest that a "commodity chain" approach provides an especially useful way to think about how goods and services are produced and delivered in today's world economy. Such an approach allows us (1) to trace the interorganizational networks that are increasingly central to global capitalism, (2) to identify and analyze how power is exercised through these networks by the leading agents that coordinate the different links in production and service chains, and (3) to think in a different way about strategic requirements for labor in confronting the power of global capital when embodied in often complex, cross-border chains.

We first discuss the scope of this commodity chain approach, comparing and contrasting it to related accounts of networks and value chains. Second, we provide an account based on current research of the apparel and textile industries supplying the North American clothing market. Included in this account is an assessment of the way in which the dynamics of the apparel chain shape labor issues in the industry. Third, we briefly consider the commodity chains that characterize several other sectors in an effort to identify salient factors that are likely to lead to more or less organizationally dispersed networks in different industries. Finally, we address the general implications for labor strategies in light of a commodity chain perspective.

THE TRADITIONAL VIEW OF THE MNC AND LABOR'S RESPONSE

The prevailing approach to analyzing the extent of the internationalization of capital and its impact on labor begins with the MNC. Although the distinctive aspects of MNCs gained no particular recognition until the early 1960s, once the idea took root, it gained extraordinary currency (Fieldhouse, 1986). In developmental theory, MNCs became the bearers of neoimperialism, the agents through which developing countries were exploited for the benefit of the richest nations at the core of the capitalist world system. Their independent power, moreover, was thought to make them formidable players even in the nation-states in which they were spawned and raised the specter of a future in which they would transcend their home countries and become truly transnational. At this stage they would be "monopoly capital" (Baran and Sweezy, 1966) with "global reach" (Barnet and Miller, 1974), spanning sectors as "transnational conglomerates" (Hymer, 1971) and exploiting the citizens of developed and less developed countries alike to fuel the engine of their continued growth.

Trade union accounts from the early 1970s, spearheaded by Levinson (see Ramsay, 1999 for a detailed review), picked up on this image and have arguably remained dominated by it ever since. The conventional wisdom has been that in order to provide an effective response to the power of the MNC, organized labor has to mirror the corporate behemoth of this image by becoming fully international or be continually outmaneuvered by the power of capital to regime shop, shift investment, and play off workers in each country against those elsewhere. This was buttressed by campaigns to get nation states to collaborate in intergovernmental forms of regulation, most notably through the Organization for Economic Cooperation and Development (OECD), International Labor Organization (ILO), United Nations (UN), and, more recently, regional trading blocs. The United Nations Conference on Trade and Development (UNCTAD) became a monitor of MNC activity, charted through annual recordings of foreign direct investment (FDI), which registered a combination of acquisitions and new investments by internationalizing enterprises.

International business analyses have also given the MNC all but exclusive attention in its courses and text.[1] Predictably, along with economic theory (Caves, 1982) it took a largely uncritical view of MNC growth, claiming positive net effects of FDI on both host and home countries. Human resource management and labor relations (HRM/LR) contributions instead sought to identify and suggest solutions for problems faced by MNCs as they expanded, whether they be cultural conflicts, political risks, "irrational" resistance from labor, or difficulties in finding organizational structures to cope with complexity, size, distance, and so on.

Thus, the terrain of analysis, for labor as for capital, has remained the international organization. The conventional profile of the MNC includes several characteristics. First, it is generally defined by ownership and characterized by a hierarchical, management-driven administration, having clear boundaries and a coherent identity. Second, it is typically measured and assessed by some combination of FDI, corporate sales, assets, profits, or sometimes number of employees.[2] Third, it is usually observed through the visible actions of the entity's management, as in making major acquisitions, opening or shutting down local operations, forging mergers, and the like. Even skeptics addressing globalization themes (Hirst and Thompson, 1999; Ruigrok and van Tulder, 1995; Boyer and Drache, 1996) take their departure from alternative measurements or assessments of these same indicators. The proportional spread of assets, composition of boards of directors, international ownership of shares, and evidence of merely "multidomestic" or "polycentric" internationalization are all mustered to demonstrate the limits of global capital.

This profile of MNCs presents a daunting challenge to labor, even in the modified picture offered by the skeptics. Sheer scale and financial muscle are backed by management sophistication drawn from cross-national experience, the capacity to disguise true accounting and performance, influence in political circles, and powers of whipsawing via threats of closure or downsizing should individual operations fail to be "competitive." The MNC of this image can seem to overwhelm labor's inherent limits in seeking coordinated internationalism (Thomson and Larsen, 1978; Olle and Schoeller, 1977). Such pessimism might be tempered by recognizing the limits to management coherence and knowledge (Ramsay and Haworth, 1990), but even in these moderated accounts, the MNC remains the core concept.

MARKETS, HIERARCHIES, NETWORKS, AND CHAINS

It is not a novel notion that traditional organizational theory and economic theory, both of which treat firms as monolithic and self-contained units of analysis, are inadequate for understanding much of what happens in contemporary capitalism. Transaction cost theory in economics (Williamson, 1975) seeks to explain why companies may choose to outsource some activities where the competencies of management are lower and services can be produced less expensively outside the organization. The growth of franchising, subcontracting, and other externalizing devices has also been seized upon by students of "flexibility," iconizing the practices of the Italian clothing firm Benetton, for example (Murray, 1985; Dicken, 1998; Segal-Horn, 1994; Piore and Sabel, 1984). Similar arguments have emerged from studies of the supplier networks for just-in-time manufacturing systems associated particularly with Toyota and other Japanese MNCs (Dore, 1983).[3]

These and other such innovations were initially understood as the externalization or "marketization" of some activities, by placing them outside the administrative structure of the organization and, consequently, allowing competition on price and quality. However, closer studies of Japanese supplier networks suggested that a greater priority was placed on interorganizational cooperation between suppliers and the core firm, with longterm, trust-based relationships often backed by technical, managerial, and financial support from the outsourcing firm (Dore, 1983). Market forces, therefore, did not operate unbound. Ambivalent relationships were also long established in supposedly more traditional settings, as in the case of the U.K. retailer Marks & Spencer, which has always outsourced the production of its line of clothes to a network of garment manufacturers, many of which are themselves MNCs. There were elements of cooperation rather than simple contractual or competitive relations in those arrangements, yet they did remove the management and detailed control of key processes from the hierarchy of the company outsourcing the production.

A series of other arrangements has provoked what has almost become a field of study in its own right (Child and Faulkener, 1998; Ebers, 1997). These arrangements include (1) the pooling of immense development costs (e.g., some forms of cooperation in the auto industry), (2) expanding internationally without the costs, preparation time, and other investments usually involved in such expansion (e.g., joint ventures in banking), and (3) realizing economies of scope and scale (e.g., through alliances in the airline industry). In response to the emergence of these arrangements, scholars have identified networks as representing a qualitative shift from both market and hierarchical relations, to a new structural form embodying different processes of economic activity (Thompson et al., 1991). For some, it even marks the end of "the enterprise" and the establishment of a new economy, based on fluidity, collaboration, and trust rather than power (Powell, 1990; Gerlach, 1992). This deconstruction of traditional organizational forms has the welcome effect of raising doubts about taken-for-granted ways of looking at MNCs and other companies. As it stands, however, it has some serious flaws, most notably, that it lacks a way to understand the dynamics and driving forces behind these new forms of organization. It also gives little attention to the labor processes that hierarchical analyses and more radical approaches provide.

An alternative way to disassemble the production process without losing all sense of organizational structure and constraint is found in the idea of the value chain, as developed by Porter (1985) to aid management strategy and accounting. This kind of analysis is viewed as a way to unpack elements of the production and distribution or delivery of a good or service so that the contributions of different activities to overall profitability can be identified. For Porter, there are five primary building blocks of corporate profitability: "inbound logistics," covering supply and storage; "operations," or the production process itself; "outbound logistics," or distribution; "marketing and sales"; and "services," which refers to after-sales support. Other functions, including HRM/LR, have only supporting roles. Porter's approach allows for a different view of the enterprise that can distinguish between profitable and unprofitable activities, with the implication that low value-added activities can be considered as candidates for hiring out. This quickly became a popular perspective as a rationale for outsourcing, subcontracting, downsizing, or reengineering, especially in Anglo-American corporate circles.

Value chain approaches remain trapped between orthodox managerial and more radical deconstructions, however, which is not surprising given that they are effectively still designed to serve management in large enterprises.

What is implied in the value chain concept, though, and becomes clearer still through critical examinations of specific networks, is that some key players dominate these chains (Kenney and Florida, 1992; Harrison, 1994). In short, the networks that are constructed following a value chain logic are hierarchically driven and primarily serve the interests of core or nodal organizations in the chain.

In order to escape the managerial straitjacket of value chain theory, we propose to extend the insights of a more sociological or political-economic account, namely, a commodity chains analysis. Since our interest is particularly in the nature, configurations, and effects of such chains in an internationalizing economy, we use Gereffi's label of "global commodity chains" (GCCs) (Gereffi and Korzeniewicz, 1994). A commodity chain has been defined as "a network of labor and production processes whose end result is a finished commodity" (Hopkins and Wallerstein, 1986: 159). We extend this definition to include distribution and sale of the commodity, especially as this allows us to address services as well as manufacturing industries.

GCCs, as we conceive them, comprise intra- and interfirm networks connecting all those involved in the complete chain of supply, production, and delivery of a good or service. These chains may well cross industry boundaries, as illustrated by our example of the apparel commodity chain, which includes the fiber, textile, apparel and retail industries. Chains are increasingly likely to cross national borders as well and to do so with a fair degree of fluidity and variation over time, at least for some products and services.

Gereffi (1994) identifies three dimensions of these GCCs: (1) an input-output structure, which describes the process of transforming materials into commodities, (2) a territoriality, or spatial dispersion of those activities, and (3) a governance structure, describing the power relations that are exercised along and through the chain. Only the first of these dimensions is addressed by value chain analysis, or most of the other theories discussed earlier. The territorial scope of these chains is now often potentially global, though, as the apparel case demonstrates, political and other contingencies may shape them into a largely regional pattern. Either way, the location of production in the chain has a specific geographical dimension not captured in value chain accounts. The GCC perspective highlights, moreover, the possibility that what may be thought of as the classic "core" activity, the actual production of commodities, is as likely to be externalized as peripheral elements.

Additionally, a GCC analysis links the configuration of chains to sociological and political factors, including institutional (state policy, political stability), cultural (work ethic, family and community structures that make labor available to capital in particular ways), and socioeconomic (wage levels, labor supply). Finally, the control of the chain remains largely in the hands of those occupying certain key "nodes" or links in the chain. In other words, the governance structure of a commodity chain embodies unequal relations of power and profitability. Each chain is dominated by a lead firm or set of firms that "drive" it, and these chain drivers are often MNCs.

The approach developed here seeks to extend the GCC approach, particularly emphasizing the ways that it can enhance our understanding of the political economy of production, capital, and labor. It combines the insights of market, value chain, and hierarchy and network analyses and adds the context of the wider political economy in which these chains operate. The resulting GCC framework does not remove MNCs from the analysis, nor does it confine itself to their boundaries, even defined broadly. The principal level of analysis is sectoral, keeping in mind that chains can cross several industries in the production and distribution of a particular good or service. Although the drivers of a chain (primarily MNCs) remain key coordinating agents, the configuration of the entire chain is of concern to worker organizations and others concerned with labor processes and their outcomes. Local and regional influences are incorporated as a level in the analysis, as are the less powerful enterprises that are incorporated into the chain at various links. Last and most importantly for our purposes, those whose very working lives are linked in and through these chains are also central actors. Hence, the dynamics of inequality and exploitation, which are generated, exacerbated, or mitigated by particular chains, are kept very much in the foreground of our analysis.

It will be evident that a chains perspective links the issues of concern to labor to those that motivate management (or governments) in a single approach. It elucidates how the employment relationship, as it is juridically and to a large extent experientially demarcated, is a poor guide to the real connections, dynamics, and interdependencies that determine labor's fate. As such, it allows us to identify and better understand the outcomes of global production arrangements for labor, including certain key dilemmas for labor organizations. It is problematic for workers along the length of a particular commodity chain if labor is organized only in the core firms, since MNCs can shift operations to links of the chain where labor is weaker and cheaper. It could be still more problematic if labor were strong only in the links *not* controlled by the drivers of the chain. The potential fluidity of chains is also an enormous problem for labor, as is the fact that labor organizations are divided across chains. The GCC approach highlights how labor interests may be divergent across different links and, hence, labor unity hard to forge. A GCC analysis, nonetheless, provides an excellent foundation for labor to identify information requirements and perhaps to even benchmark labor conditions.

CLOTHING CHAINS

In this section we present an overview of GCCs in the apparel industry, especially those that serve the U.S. market, which is the world's largest single-country market for apparel. This account is based on continuing research in Mexico, albeit compressed here to highlight the salient elements.[4] The apparel sector has been described as having the greatest global reach of any industry (Dickerson, 1995; Dicken, 1998) and traditionally has been regarded as a classic case of concentrated MNC power (Clairmonte and Cavanagh, 1981; Frobel,

Heinrichs, and Kreye, 1981). The two largest markets, the United States and the European Union (EU), both have import penetration levels measured at over 50 percent. Yet in each case, the majority of garments sold are marketed under brands owned by companies based inside these two corners of the global triad, which also includes Asia. The extensive development of East Asian subcontract suppliers for both markets has been analyzed at length (Bonacich et al., 1994; Gereffi, 1994, 1999). However, the shifting patterns of trade and apparel flows in recent years have shown just how fluid and sensitive to various circumstances the apparel supply chains may be, particularly in the context of pronounced regionalization within North America, Europe, and Asia.

Changing Chains

As has been well documented elsewhere (Bonacich et al., 1994; Appelbaum and Gereffi, 1994), there have been several shifts in the international production and sourcing of apparel. In the 1950s and early 1960s a large slice of assembly production moved from Europe and the United States to Japan; in the 1970s and 1980s it moved on to lower-cost locales in Asia, such as Hong Kong, Taiwan, and Korea. Later, in the 1980s, it was subcontracted on from these three countries to still lower-wage countries such as the Philippines, Vietnam, and, increasingly, China. Most recently there has been a major shift to Mexico and the Caribbean basin for production aimed at the U.S. market, while a similar shift to low-cost sites on the European periphery (such as Eastern Europe, Turkey, and North Africa) is under way for the EU. Each of these shifts has involved an interaction of local social and economic factors, various government policies, international competitive forces, and the changing composition and strategic mind-sets of the MNCs driving the chains. There is no reason to think that the shifting patterns have come to an end, especially with China's full entry into the world market still in its early stages.

These changing patterns demonstrate the fluidity of capital, especially with FDI and the internalization of production being the exception rather than the rule for how core MNCs expand and restructure their operations in this classically "footloose" industry. For example, the intra-Asian shift from the so-called Big Three (Hong Kong, Taiwan, and Korea) to yet cheaper locations has been largely coordinated by brokers and other companies. These intermediaries have set up triangle networks linking lead U.S. firms placing orders with East Asian companies to offshore manufacturers in lower-wage countries, such as China and Vietnam (Gereffi, 1994). Triangle networking arrangements indicate the organizational and geographic complexity of potentially remote linkages that can develop in cross-border chains.

MNC Drivers

Chains in apparel are far more complicated than might be understood from an initial description of the relocation of production to cheap labor sources.

As noted earlier, chains tend to have core MNCs from developed countries as drivers. Those MNCs are a heterogeneous group, however, differing in their outlook and priorities and in the types of chains that they construct and often competing with one another for control and market share (Gereffi, 1999; Bair and Gereffi, 2002). Drivers of the apparel commodity chain include:

1. *Retailers.* Originally clients of apparel manufacturers, retailers are increasingly competing with them, using subcontracting networks to produce their own private-label brands. Examples would include J. C. Penney, Wal-Mart, the Gap, and Marks & Spencer.

2. *Branded Manufacturers.* This set of lead firms includes companies such as Sara Lee (which owns brands such as Champion and Hanes), Levi's, and VF (which markets Wrangler and Lee jeans). Many have been compelled by intensifying competition to shift from a policy of domestic production, to establishing self-owned and operated offshore factories that supply intermediate inputs (cut fabric, thread, buttons), to using independent contract assemblers. This pattern of development has tended to lead to orders being placed in neighboring countries, with closer control over production than is exerted by commercial drivers (such as retailers) of subcontracting networks. There are increasing signs that branded manufacturers are abandoning this role and retreating from production altogether, which suggests that the cross-border sourcing networks of branded manufacturers and retailers will be more similar in the future.

3. *Marketers.* These chain drivers have never had their own factories and may not even have their own shops (though most have established some branded outlets as well as selling through major retail chains). Companies like Tommy Hilfiger, Liz Claiborne, Ralph Lauren, or Nautica began as brand design concepts and, following the classic example of Nike, have sourced their production globally from the outset. As such, they rely heavily on brokers and competent manufacturers, tending to protect their quality image by stringent vendor certification. These companies, nonetheless, have shown a strong willingness to relocate their sourcing for maximum advantage.

4. *Textile Manufacturers.* These companies, which produce the main input for apparel, are key players in the apparel commodity chain. They have found it necessary to seek ways of relocating production to cut costs and be closer to their increasingly offshore client base. However, textile production is more capital-intensive than apparel assembly. Consequently, the skills required are less widely available, favoring large-scale factory production and limiting the feasibility of adopting the kinds of far-flung, multitiered subcontracting chains that are typical of garment assembly. These manufacturers generally rely on a mix of FDI, joint ventures, and limited subcontracting to emerging local producers of quality fabrics (more often in East Asia than in Mexico, where quality problems with national producers remain significant).

5. *Sourcing Agents.* These agents are generally individual brokers or companies that manage cross-border production networks or help find local producers for lead firms looking to source offshore orders. These intermediaries played an important role in the development of sourcing networks between U.S. lead firms and Asian suppliers. With the development of full package production in Mexico as a new model existing alongside the *maquila* system (as discussed later), these coordinating agents are becoming increasingly important in North America, just as they did in the Asian Big Three.

The intricacy of the system containing these various players and their impact on each other as they vie to establish chains, seek possible alliances, lobby governments for favorable policies, and respond to changing environments make simple generalization about the configurations and dynamics of GCCs in the apparel industry perilous.

National and Trading Bloc Policies

National and trading bloc policies have exerted substantial influence on chain configurations over time. The outward processing trade (OPT) system in Europe and 807/9802 trade in North America[5] imposed customs regimes that strongly favored production in cheap adjacent labor sites using fabrics exported from the region's developed countries. This encouraged the growth of assembly production in Mexico, the Caribbean Basin, Eastern Europe, and North Africa during the 1980s and early 1990s. Subsequently, the North American Free Trade Agreement (NAFTA) and more recently the removal of OPT limitations by the EU for Eastern Europe have changed the rules of the game. Currently, there is a major shift toward far more of the production chain being located in low-cost locations within these regions, as the chain drivers noted earlier reorient their policies to take advantage of new institutional environments.

The Geography of Development

Countries where production is carried out are also strongly affected by the imperatives of emerging chains. Incoming MNCs are often drawn toward areas where there are prior clusters of apparel production. Local availability of fabrics and other key inputs may also be important, as well as a supply of skilled labor. Recent research on the Torreón-Goméz Palacio cluster in northern Mexico charts the startlingly rapid growth of denim jeans production in the area, with lead firms indicating their willingness to establish their own local operations or source in the area due in part to the availability of local inputs (Bair and Gereffi, 2001). Beyond the sheer size of the Torreón cluster (where during 2000 more than 4 million pairs of jeans were produced each week), its significance lies in the types of networks that connect U.S. and Mexican firms on the North American apparel commodity chain. While apparel production carried out in Mexico for the U.S. market has closely conformed to the classic *maquila* model of low value-added, assembly-only operations, new "full-package" production networks have emerged in Torreón to allow more steps in the production process (such as denim manufacture, cutting, laundering, and pressing) to take place in Mexico. Thus, the apparel commodity chain for blue jeans has lengthened in Mexico, with new links in the chain becoming rooted in areas like Torreón.

The Impact on Labor

The impact of the apparel chain on labor is even more problematic than that on local development per se. For workers in the textile and apparel industries in the United States or EU, the dominant consequence of proliferating cross-border networks has been job loss. In the United States, official figures suggest a fall from 1.3 million domestic apparel jobs in 1973 to 727,000 in January 1999 (NACLC, 2000). In the EU, 639,000 textile and apparel jobs were lost between 1988 and 1994 alone, representing 30 percent of all manufacturing job losses over this period. There were still 2.3 million jobs in these sectors in the EU in 1998, but declines have been running at over 2 percent per annum. Well-publicized closures in the last two years by Levi's in Belgium and Scotland, by VF across Europe, and by garment contractors in the United Kingdom hit by Marks & Spencer's new policy of relocating orders to cheaper offshore sites have underscored this process.

In Mexico, the flood of orders being placed by retailers, marketers, and branded manufacturers has certainly created jobs in some areas. Research in Torreón and other areas of Mexico, including interviews with U.S. companies, Mexican-owned "first tier" manufacturers, and smaller, more peripheral contractors, suggests that benefits in terms of wages, job security, and work conditions were more contingent (Bair and Gereffi, 2001). Employment was less precarious where established subcontractors had a reliable reputation with core MNCs, while more peripheral contractors bore the brunt of any fluctuations in demand. Wages were not found to be systematically higher even in companies filling full package orders for major U.S. clients, nor was it possible to conclude that companies producing for higher-end brands paid better. Faced by some upward pressure on wages in Torreón's tight labor market, some companies have moved sewing factories to rural areas surrounding the city where the recent privatization of communal farms (known as *ejidos*) has created a classic reserve army of labor, albeit one in need of training and acculturation to factory discipline. This suggests that even minor improvements in terms of employment provoke a certain response by local managers, who are quick to search for alternative, less expensive suppliers of labor. The greater technical complexity and capital intensity involved in textile production seem to create more security and higher wages, however, and in this sense, the development of full package networks in Mexico involving local fabric production can be seen as a positive development for Mexican workers.

Some of the ways in which workforce exploitation or particular inequalities emerge in chains exemplify the rootedness of these networks in local social structures. Lui and Chiu (1999) describe how family enterprise firms in

Hong Kong and Taiwan shape the way in which production is organized and, consequently, how the burdens and costs associated with it are distributed. The Mexican social and cultural context is different and, therefore, informality and/or homeworking networks operate in distinct ways, but with the same notably gendered consequences for women workers.[6]

For unions, the apparent tug-of-war for jobs creates classic and all too familiar divisions that are hard to bridge. This is especially true where the organizational strength of labor movements and cultures of organizations vary, making equal contributions to any shared resistance unfeasible even where common concerns over the longer run are recognized. The traditionally corporatist nature of trade unionism in Mexico, for instance, has made links between organized labor in the United States and Mexico particularly problematic historically. While difficulties exist in Europe, new unions in the East borne out of resistance to the old state regime offer a less fundamentally contentious basis for fraternal links. It is certainly clear in Mexico that the problems of organizing across subcontracting chains, especially among the most vulnerable and dispersed groups on the periphery, significantly hinder organizing efforts, including those made by independent unions. Furthermore, the country's aggressive neoliberal turn since the 1980s (which was accelerated under President Carlos Salinas [1988–1994] and continued under his successor, Ernesto Zedillo [1994–2000]) has seriously weakened the position of organized labor in Mexico, as suggested by the fact that average real wages remain below those prevailing prior to the 1994 devaluation (de la Garza, 1994; Dussel Peters, 1997).[7]

OTHER COMMODITY CHAINS

The apparel example is a singularly important and evocative one. It has also provoked particular responses from labor and other activist groups, as we will discuss in our final section. There is a danger, however, that we take it as representative of all firms in the sector, let alone of all sectors.[8] That danger also applies to analyses of autos and electronics as the other two sectors whose chains have been most extensively documented, especially by those sympathetic to labor issues. Even a comparison among these three demonstrates significant differences in the configuration, power distribution, and flexibility of chains. Such differences can be traced to differing implications for workers and unions. However, in this section we initiate a broader and more systematic analysis by considering a wider range of industries. Our initial proposition remains that all sectors can usefully be thought of in terms of commodity chains rather than as collections of firms dominated by MNCs. Our discussion of these examples constitutes a highly provisional attempt to build an analytical framework for understanding the varying configurations of GCCs and their implications for labor.

The factors that we consider likely to be important in shaping the configurations of GCCs fall into a few broad categories, under which a wide range of questions becomes apparent.

1. *Product/Process Contingencies.* How far is it possible to decompose and spatially/organizationally separate significant parts of the product and/or process? How transportable are the components or the entire product (since this affects the cost of transfer to market)? What economies of scale apply to the production process? What organizational economies or diseconomies of scope encourage or discourage internalization? To what extent is the product and/or process capital- or technology-intensive? To what extent is the product and/or process mature and widely understood or still in development?

2. *Labor.* How important are labor costs to competitiveness? How important are labor skills to productivity and/or quality? How widely available are these skills? What is the cost of training relative to other labor cost differentials? To what extent is control over, or motivation and commitment of, labor considered important?

3. *Market Contingencies.* To what extent is it necessary that production is visible in the market location? Is competition primarily based on price or quality distinctiveness? How long is the typical market response time?

4. *Organizational Capacity.* What is the available organizational capacity of contractors? What mind-set characterizes the sector in terms of dispersion and cross-border operations? What is the competence of management to organize and monitor outsourcing? To what extent does organizational structure facilitate or block externalizing activities? What institutional (legal or other regulatory) constraints to externalization exist?

We have space to illustrate the relevance of only a few of these factors with reference to sectors other than apparel. Electronics and automobiles have already been subjected to investigations similar to those that we have discussed for apparel (Carrillo, 1990, 1995; Dussel Peters, 1999). In the graphical sector (discussed in Chapter 13), the technological and other process constraints on geographical dispersion and perhaps externalization from a core MNC are few, especially with the digitalization of text and graphics. However, customer demand for one-stop local shops is high in many segments, and for some products (e.g., newspapers), delivery time is of the essence. In packaging or book printing, market restrictions are fewer. Still, management's global mind-set seems limited as yet, and internalization in MNCs growing by acquisition but regionally structured seems prevalent.

Brewing and distilling tend to require closely regulated processes with significant scale and some scope economies to maintain brand presence and distinctiveness. While bottling and warehousing are more labor-intensive and could be outsourced, they generally have not been (other than through tightly managed franchises). Food production offers a far wider range of processes and possibilities, and there is great scope for detailed examination of chains in this sector (where major MNCs like Nestlé, Philip Morris, or Unilever play dominant roles, but alongside many local niche suppliers).

Service industries are often neglected in the study of MNCs yet are increasingly globalizing in similar ways to manufacturing MNCs (Segal-Horn, 1994). In service industries generally, it has long been suggested that simultaneity of production and delivery severely limits flexibility in the configuration of service chains. However, the accuracy of this view has been questioned (Lovelock and Yip, 1996) on the grounds that some interactions can be remote (e.g., call center services), while others do not require any personal contact (e.g., Internet shopping, data management, financial management).

Hotels, especially when they seek to offer brand-distinct services, require close control of service delivery and content and, thus, tend to be largely internalized to fast-globalizing MNCs. Thompson et al. (1998) found hotels to be more centrally controlled and regulated than traditional manufacturers. Some peripheral activities (lobby shops and food sales, for instance) may be outsourced, nevertheless (Go and Pine, 1995; Nickson, 1999). Airlines, too, seek to establish distinctive brands and reputations for quality service (Hanlon, 1999). Cost margins are also critical, however, and there is evidence that work intensification and poor attention to progressive staff management lie just below the surface of rhetoric to the contrary (Boyd, 1999). Although some outsourcing of crewing occurs, greater economies of scale, capacity, and utilization are being sought through global alliances between airlines.

In software development, options are becoming complex and varied. Originally, bespoke software (i.e., produced specifically to one organization's needs) dominated, and in large companies was typically produced internally by a specialist management information systems department. In some companies (e.g., banks, particularly for legacy systems) this remains largely true, especially if information technology is believed to have become a core competence rather than a support service. However, a number of factors have made more dispersed chains feasible, especially due to developments in telecommunications technologies and digital information, which is instantly and almost costlessly transmittable across great distances.

First, software MNCs have emerged (most notably, Microsoft, but also Oracle, Lotus, Corel, SAP, and others) that develop generic software and then offer customization and support services. Most of these companies increasingly work through "partners" at the local level. Microsoft, for instance, develops programs and markets them but certifies external support and consultancy providers internationally. This gives rise to a supply chain that can become quite complex (though not cost-margin-driven, as in apparel). Second, database management companies, led by the multinational EDS with over 100,000 employees worldwide, offer to manage and increase the efficiency of information in client companies. On the face of it, this could be accomplished from anywhere but tends in practice to require on-site staff to learn from clients.

Third, the decomposition of systems analysis, programming, testing, debugging, and maintenance of software provides numerous possibilities for outsourcing. Some large software providers use help-line services that are actually outsourced to call centers. The global shift in the process is most visible in the use of cheap Indian programmers to carry out parts of the software development process. Initially, this involved the more routine coding and testing stages, but Indian subcontractors have sought to capture more value-added by moving toward what we might call "full-package" contracts. IBM's operations in the booming Guadalajara, Mexico, electronics cluster include not only the assembly of its laptop computers but also teams of young Mexican engineers involved in software customization for the Spanish-speaking market.

Over the last few years, the growth and globalization of these external chains of activities have become ever more visible. To illustrate, during a recent visit to a medium-size software company in the United Kingdom, itself largely implementing and supporting Microsoft systems as a local partner, we found the following: (1) some staff worked permanently on-site with clients, and others worked out of the company's own office; (2) some work was performed in India, both in a subsidiary that the U.K. multinational had established and in an independent company that served as its subcontractor; and (3) staff from both Indian companies were employees on a visiting basis in the U.K. office. Clearly, the levels of skill and the complexity and quality of work required differentiate this example from apparel production.

In comparison to the various chains that we have only briefly described, elaborately dispersed GCCs as described for the apparel sector are likely to remain the exception rather than becoming the rule across sectors. Having said this, detailed research in most sectors indicates potential areas of management innovation to create organizationally dispersed chains in at least some activities and sometimes (as with airlines) through complex alliances between MNCs rather than just by using small, local subcontractors. It is possible to work through a long list of sectors and subsectors using a GCC form of inquiry, analyzing the configuration strategies of MNCs and other organizations in the production and delivery of goods and services. The analysis of commodity chains that we have offered here is, of course, exploratory and provisional. We conclude by offering a simplified taxonomy to help draw out several implications.

Following our brief review of various industries in the previous section, Figure 3.1 displays more systematically and in visual form the key dimensions affecting the shape of commodity chains across sectors. Along the horizontal axis we position production and process constraints on the dispersion or integration of production, which would be determined to some extent by labor considerations. This is partly a geographical and internalization/externalization indicator in this rather simplified form, as we expect these two product/process contingencies to be distinct but related. As a function of market contingencies, the vertical axis is more specifically geographical. Again, international outsourcing will not prove feasible for sectors in which market demand requires a local presence, although some local decomposition may be possible depending on production constraints. As conceptualized, this produces a variant of the 2 x 2

Figure 3.1
Contingencies Shaping Commodity Chains

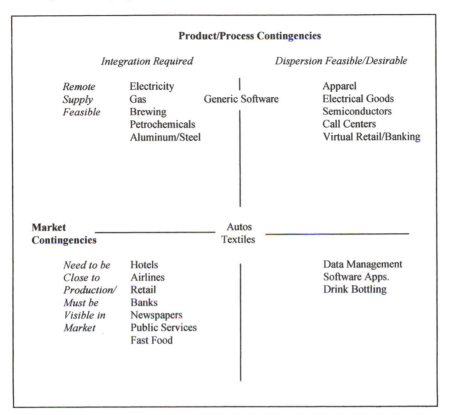

matrix. Organizational capability in each sector is not included, however, but acts to further enable or limit management responses to product/process and market contingencies as described.

Our main interests here are twofold. Our first interest is to help predict how far the classic, integrated MNC is likely to persist as labor's adversary and how far more dispersed chains (such as those in apparel) are likely to emerge. Our second interest is to consider the implications of the product/process and market contingencies for labor and their counterstrategies. In considering the first issue, it becomes evident that only organizations in the top right of the matrix are likely to display the kinds of radical dispersion seen in apparel. Having said this, dispersed chains driven by market location are likely in the bottom right corner. The classification is based, moreover, on core processes, and close examination of any sector may well show elements of production or delivery that could be more widely dispersed. Thus, retail outlets for petrol (or in the case of McDonald's restaurants) may offer a standard format yet can be dispersed organizationally by franchising. In brewing or distilling, the product can travel by tanker to locations but may be bottled and delivered by local operators in each market.

As highlighted by this type of matrix conceptualization, organized labor can benefit from carefully assessing both the present and likely future degree of geographical dispersion of commodity chains in selected industries. Companies in industries in the top right-hand corner, for example, generally have greater options in terms of globalizing their production activities. Hence, labor responses to capital in these sectors must acknowledge this greater degree of flexibility. Workers in industries found in the bottom left-hand quadrant of the matrix, on the other hand, may find different types or points of leverage vis-à-vis companies, since global dispersion and remote supply are more difficult for capital in these sectors to achieve. Next, we discuss the potential advantages to organized labor and its allies in developing strategies based on a careful exploration of chain configurations by sector and industry.

CONCLUSION: DEVELOPMENT OF LABOR STRATEGIES BASED ON GCC ANALYSES

We conclude by summarizing a number of advantages that can be derived by organized labor if it were to develop organizing and countervailing strategies to MNCs based on global commodity chain analyses. First, such analyses create the potential for a sense of mutual cause and understanding, rather than conflict, between labor in different parts of the chain, including across national frontiers. Second, such analyses allow for a greater understanding of likely management strategies and options, which in some circumstances can aid in the formulation of counterstrategies and assessments of strengths and weaknesses in any negotiation (as labor often underestimates its own power against the mysterious black box of management power and disinformation).

Third, such analyses can become a basis for valid comparison across companies and locations linked to given chains. The process of making such comparisons in itself, moreover, builds labor contacts through information exchange. Potentially, such comparisons also can be used quite effectively for labor benchmarking (emphasizing pay, working conditions, security, health and safety, stress, and so forth rather than unit costs and productivity-generating practices as in management benchmarking). This, in turn, can help guide union campaigns for upward leveling of workplace conditions. Fourth, such analyses provide a basis for linking firms, industries (usually a basis of identity and organization for labor), countries, and economic and sociopolitical environments, thus connecting employment relations to wider policy issues.

Finally, as previously noted, such analyses can form a basis for informed public campaigns against unconscionable and inequitable management practices. In the apparel industry, despite the seemingly daunting flexibility of the MNCs that drive chains, labor has already had some notable successes in mounting campaigns on a broad front. The National Labor Committee (NLC) in the United States has coordinated some of these; for instance, a 1995 exposé of child labor being used by a subcontractor in El Salvador to produce clothes for major U. S. retailer, the Gap (Sweatshop Watch, 1995). Although initially the company denied responsibility, the campaign ended with the Gap's promise to enforce an ambitious code of corporate conduct in all factories worldwide making clothing sold under its label. Despite its pledge to police its far-flung network of subcontractors more aggressively, continuing controversy about its global operations has kept the Gap in the media spotlight.[9]

In 1999, the NLC also blew the whistle on Liz Claiborne after the company claimed publicly to operate a code of conduct in all suppliers (National Labor Committee, 1998). Investigations showed that none of the workers in the El Salvador plants making Claiborne clothes had heard of the code, that monitoring visits were staged events, and that jackets retailing for U.S.$194 brought the young women sewing them a mere U.S.$0.84 each. The Internet is increasingly filled with campaign reports against companies like Nike or Guess, and there have been notable victories, though subsequent checks tend to show that only a minority of operators down the chain are strongly affected, and recent concerns have been raised about the effectiveness of monitoring (Greenhouse, 1997; O'Rourke, 1997). Where successes have occurred, however, they have occurred because activists have seized on the visibility of well-known brands marketed by corporations that feel vulnerable to negative press. It is far easier to embarrass companies that depend on public image than ones making products or providing services to other companies embedded in complex chains and less visible to the public.

The examples mentioned are just two of the numerous campaigns that have emerged as part of the antisweatshop movement (Greenhouse, 2000; Elliott and Freeman, 2001). These public campaigns and broader calls for raising labor standards via sanctions on MNCs responsible for substandard workplace conditions, however, raise a critical transnational dilemma for unions. Tensions are always implicit in efforts to build alliances between various stakeholders in a society, despite moments of transcendent solidarity such as the one that emerged between unionists and environmentalists (dubbed teamsters and turtles by the press) during protests against the World Trade Organization (WTO) in Seattle in December 1999. Forging alliances between groups *across* national borders is generally an even more contentious endeavor. As addressed by Köhler in Chapter 2, the governments of developing countries are increasingly seeking FDI as a means of job creation. These governments and some unions in developing countries often view demands to incorporate labor (and environmental) protections into trade and investment agreements as thinly veiled protectionism, largely on behalf of workers in the far richer, developed countries of the world.[10] Closer analysis of these tensions between labor in different countries and workers who may be connected across national borders by the same commodity chain will expose not only labor's weaknesses but also promising possibilities for new forms of collaboration and solidarity.

NOTES

1. Typical examples may be found for instance in Matsuura (1991) or Robock and Simmonds (1989).

2. As, for example, annual listings by the *Financial Times*, in *Fortune*, or *Eurobusiness* and the UNCTAD annual *World Investment Reports*.

3. A significant body of research in the 1990s contributed to our understanding of the lean production model and its critique (e.g., Boyer, 1998; Freyessenet, 1998). Bennett Harrison's (1994) seminal work emphasized that flexible production models can allow powerful firms to maintain control over their networks, even in the absence of ownership.

4. The discussion of apparel commodity chains is primarily based on research conducted by Bair and Gereffi. See, for example, Gereffi and Bair (1998); Bair and Gereffi (2001, 2002).

5. The 807 regime, which is also known as production-sharing, is so-called for the number of the clause in U.S. Trade Law; which describes this type of cross-border or offshore production. The relevant clause was later renumbered as 9802, and consequently this type of production is often referred to as 807/9802. In Mexico, it is known as the *maquila* system since the in-bond factories where these goods have traditionally been assembled are called *maquiladoras* in Spanish.

6. See Fernandez Kelly (1983) and Cravey (1999). A similar point can be made for just-in-time (JIT) systems in the United Kingdom (Newsome, 1999).

7. In July 2000, Mexicans elected to the presidency opposition candidate Vicente Fox from the center-right Partido Acción Nacional. In so doing, they ended the reign of the former ruling party, the Partido Revolucionario Institucional (PRI), which had managed to hold onto power in Mexico for over 70 years through a blend of corporatist patronage, corruption, and repression. While Fox's election has been hailed as proof that Mexico's decades-long transition to democracy has been consolidated, there is little evidence to date that Fox's political platform, particularly with regard to the issue of state–labor relations, differs markedly from that of his most recent PRI predecessors.

8. See, for example, Elson (1986) on the limitations of the "Babbage principle" as applied to all firms in the apparel and textiles sector.

9. The NGO Global Exchange has been focusing on the Gap as one of the main targets for its corporate accountability campaign. Recent attention has focused on the use of six Gap subcontractors in Saipan. See, for example, www.globalexchange.org/economy/corporations/saipan/WhyGap.html.

10. It should be noted that workers in developing countries do not always share their government's sentiments in this regard. For example, with the goal of creating a favorable investment climate for foreign capital, the Mexican government has made weakening the power of organized labor a priority. Some Mexican unions, however, have been working with their U.S. counterparts to resist these efforts and work for the establishment of genuine industrial democracy and effective representation in Mexico (Compa, 2001).

REFERENCES

Appelbaum, R. and Gereffi G. (1994). "Power and Profits in the Apparel Commodity Chain." In Bonacich, E., Cheng, L., Chinchilla, N., Hamilton, N., and Ong, P. (eds.), *Global Production: The Apparel Industry in the Pacific Rim.* Philadelphia: Temple University Press, pp. 42–62.

Bair, J. and Gereffi, G. (2001). "Local Clusters in Global Chains: The Causes and Consequences of Export Dynamism in Torreón's Blue Jeans Industry." *World Development* 29 (11), pp. 1885–1903.

Bair, J. and Gereffi, G. (2002). "NAFTA and the Apparel Commodity Chain: Corporate Strategies, Inter-firm Networks, and Local Development." In Gereffi, G., Spener, D., and Bair, J. (eds.), *Globalization and Regionalism: NAFTA and the New Geography of the North American Apparel Industry.* Philadelphia: Temple University Press, pp. 23–50

Bair, J. (eds.), *Globalization and Regionalism: NAFTA and the New Geography of the North American Apparel Industry.* Philadelphia: Temple University Press, pp. 23–50.

Baran, P. and Sweezy, P. (1966). *Monopoly Capital: An Essay on the American Economic and Social Order.* Harmondsworth: Penguin.

Barnet, R. and Miller, R. (1974). *Global Reach. The Power of the Multinational Corporations.* New York: Simon and Schuster.

Bonacich, E., Cheng, L., Chinchilla, N., Hamilton, N., and Ong, P. (eds.), (1994). *Global Production: The Apparel Industry in the Pacific Rim.* Philadelphia: Temple University Press.

Boyd, C. (1999). " Managing 'Our Most Important Asset': The Rhetoric and Reality of the Airline Industry", Ph.D. Thesis, University of Strathclyde, Glasgow.

Boyer, R. (ed.) (1998). *Between Imitation and Innovation: The Transfer and Hybridization of Productive Models in the International Automobile.* New York: Oxford University Press.

Boyer, R. and Drache, D. (eds.) (1996). *States against Markets: The of Globalization.* London: Routledge.

Carrillo, J. (ed.). (1990). *La Nueva era de la Industria Automotriz en México.* Tijuana: Colegio de la Frontera Norte.

Carrillo, J. (1995). "Flexible Production in the Auto Sector: Industrial Reorganization at Ford-Mexico." *World Development* 23 (1), pp. 87–101.

Caves, R. (1982). *Multinational Enterprise and Economic Analysis.* Cambridge: Cambridge University Press.

Child, J. and Faulkener, D. (1998). *Strategies of Cooperation: Managing Alliances, Networks and Joint Ventures.* Oxford: Oxford University Press.

Clairmonte, F. and Cavanagh, J. (1981). *The World in Their Web: The Dynamics of Textile Multinationals.* London: Zed.

Compa, L. (2001). "NAFTA's Labour Side Agreement and International Labour Solidarity." *Antipode: A Radical Journal of Geography* 33 (3), pp. 451–67.

Cravey, A. (1999). *Women and Work in Mexico's Maquiladoras.* Lanham, Md.: Rowman and Littlefield.

de la Garza, E. (1994). "The Restructuring of State-Labor Relations in Mexico." In Cook, M., Middlebrook, K. and Horcasitas, J. (eds.), *The Politics of Economic Restructuring.* LaJolla, CA: University of California Press, pp. 195–217.

Dicken, P. (1998). *Global Shift: Transforming the World Economy.* New York: Guilford Press.

Dickerson, K. G. (1995). *Textiles and Apparel in the Global Economy.* Englewood Cliffs, N.J.: Prentice-Hall.

Dore, R. (1983). "Goodwill and the Spirit of Market Capitalism." *British Journal of Sociology* 34, pp. 459–82.

Dussel Peters, E. (1997). *La Economía de la Polarización.* México, D.F. Editorial Jus.

Dussel Peters, E. (1999). *La subcontratacion como proceso do aprendizaje: el caso do la electronica en Jalisco (Mexico) en la decase de los noventa.* Santiago de Chile: Naciones Unidas.

Ebers, M. (ed.) (1997). *The Formation of Inter-Organizational Networks.* Oxford: Oxford University Press.

Elliott, K. A., and Freeman, R. B. (2001). "White Hats or Don Quixotes? Human Rights Vigilantes in the Global Economy." Working Paper 8102, National Bureau of Economic Research. Available on the Internet at www.nber.org/papers/w8102; downloaded May 2001.

Elson, D. (1986). "A New International Division of Labour in the Textile and Garment Industry: How Far Does the 'Babbage Principle' Explain it?" *International Journal of Sociology and Social Policy* 6 (2), pp. 45–54.

Fernandez Kelly, M. P. (1983). *For We Are Sold, I and My People: Women and Industry in Mexico's Frontier.* Albany: State University of New York Press.

Fieldhouse, D. K. (1986). "The Multinational: A Critique of a Concept." In Teichova, A.,Levy-Leboyer, M., and Nussbaum, H. (eds.), *Multinational Enterprise in Historical Perspective.* Cambridge: Cambridge University Press, pp. 9–29.

Freyssenet, M., (ed.). (1998). *One Best Way? Trajectories and Industrial Models of the World's Automobile Producers.* New York: Oxford University Press.

Hirst, P. and Thompson, G. (1999). *Globalization in Question.* Cambridge: Polity.

Frobel, F., Heinrichs, J., and Kreye, O. (1981). *The New International Division of Labour.* Cambridge: Cambridge University Press.

Gereffi, G. (1994). "The Organization of Buyer-Driven Global Commodity Chains: How U.S. Retailers Shape Overseas Production Networks." In Gereffi, G. and Korzeniewicz, M. (eds.), *Commodity Chains and Global Capitalism.* Westport, Conn.: Praeger, pp. 95–122.

Gereffi, G. (1999). "International Trade and Industrial Upgrading in the Apparel Commodity Chain." *Journal of International Economics* 48 (1), pp. 37–70.

Gereffi, G., and Bair, J. (1998). "US Companies Eye NAFTA's Prize." *Bobbin* 39 (7), pp. 26–35.

Gereffi, G., and M. Korzeniewicz (eds.). (1994). *Commodity Chains and Global Capitalism.* Westport, Conn.: Praeger.

Gerlach, M. (1992). *Alliance Capitalism.* Berkeley: University of California Press.

Go, F. and Pine, R. (1995). *Globalization Strategy in the Hotel Industry.* London: Routledge.

Greenhouse, S. (1997). "Sweatshop Raids Cast Doubt on Ability of Garment Makers to Police Factories." *New York Times*, July 18, p. A10.

Greenhouse, S. (2000). "Anti–Sweatshop Movement is Achieving Gains Overseas." *New York Times*, January 26, p. A10.

Hanlon, P. (1999). *Global Airlines.* Oxford: Butterworth Heinemann.

Harrison, B. (1994). *Lean & Mean: The Changing Landscape of Corporate Power in the Age of Flexibility.* New York: Guilford Press.

Hopkins, T. and Wallerstein, I. (1986). "Commodity Chains in the World Economy Prior to 1800." *Review* 10 (1), pp. 157–70.

Hymer, S. (1971). "The Multinational Corporation and the Law of Uneven Development." In Baghwati, J. (ed.), *Economics and the World Order.* New York: World Law Fund, pp. 113–40.

Kenney, M. and Florida, R. (1992). *Beyond Mass Production: The Japanese System and Its Transfer to the United States.* New York: Oxford University Press.

Lovelock, C. and Yip, G. (1996). "Developing Global Strageies for Service Businesses." *California Management Review* 38 (2), pp. 64–86.

Lui, T. and Chiu, M. (1999). "Global Restructuring and Non-Standard Work in Newly Industrialised Economies: The Organisation of Flexible Production in Hong Kong and Taiwan." In Felstead, A. and Jewson, N. (eds.), *Global Trends in Flexible Labour*. London: Macmillan, pp. 166–80.

Matsuura, N. (1991). *International Business: A New Era*. San Diego: Harcourt Brace Jovanovich.

Murray, R. (1985). "Benetton Britain. The New Economic Order." *Marxism Today* November, pp. 28–32.

National Labor Committee. (1998). "Liz Claiborne: Sweatshop Production in El Salvador." Available on the Internet at www.nlcnet.org/liz/claiborne.html; downloaded January 2000.

Newsome, K. (1999). "The Women Will Fill in the Gaps: New Production Concepts, Gender and Resistance." Paper presented at BUIRA, De Montfort University, Leicester.

Nickson, D. (1999). "A Study of the Internationalisation Strategies of Three Hotel Companies, with a Particular Focus on Human Resource Management". Ph.D. thesis, University of Strathclyde, Glasgow.

North American Commission for Labor Cooperation (NACLC). (2000). "Standard and Advanced Practices in the North American Garment Industry." Report published by the Secretariat of the Commission for Labor Cooperation, Washington, D.C.

Olle, W. and Schoeller, W. (1977). "World Market Competition and Restrictions upon International Trade Union Policies." *Capital & Class*, 2, pp. 56–75.

O'Rourke, D. (1997). "Smoke from a Hired Gun: A Critique of Nike's Labor and Environmental Auditing in Vietnam as Performed by Ernst & Young." Report published by the Transnational Resource and Action Center. Available on the Internet at www.corpwatch.org/trac/nike/ernst/; downloaded September 2001.

Piore, M. and Sabel, C. (1984). *The Second Industrial Divide: Possibilities for Prosperity*. New York: Basic Books.

Porter, M. (1985). *Competitive Advantage: Creating and Sustaining Superior Performance*. New York: Free Press.

Powell, W. (1990). "Neither Market nor Hierarchy: Network Forms of Organization." *Research in Organizational Behavior* 12, pp. 295–336.

Ramsay, H. (1999). "In Search of International Trade Union Theory." In Waddington, J. (ed.), *Globalization & Patterns of Labour Resistance*. London: Mansell.

Ramsay, H. and Haworth, N. (1990). "Managing the Multinationals: The Emerging Theory of the Multinational Enterprise and Its Implications for Labour Resistance." In Clegg, S. (ed.), *Organization Theory and Class Analysis: New Approaches and New Issues*. Berlin: de Gruyter, pp. 275–297.

Robock, S. and Simmonds, K. (1989). *International Business and Multinational Enterprises*. 4th ed. Homewood: Ill.

Ruigrok, W., and van Tulder, R. (1995). *The Logic of International Restructuring*. London: Routledge.

Segal-Horn, S. (1994). "Are Service Industries Going Global?" In Armistead, C. (ed.), *The Future of Service Management*. London: Kogan Page, pp. 137–155.

Sweatshop Watch. 1995). "Sweating for the Gap." *Sweatshop Watch Newsletter* 1 (1) p. 1.

Thompson, G., Frances, J., Levacic, R., and Mitchell, J. (eds.). (1991). *Markets, Hierarchies and Networks: The Coordination of Social Life*. London: Sage.

Thompson, P., Nickson, D., Wallace, T., and Jones, C. (1998). "Internationalisation and Integration: A Comparison of Manufacturing and Service Firms." *Competition and Change – A Journal of Global Political Economy* 3, pp. 387–415.

Thomson, D. and Larson, R. (1978). *Where Were You Brother? An Account of Trade Union Imperialism*. London: War on Want.

Williamson, O. (1975). *Markets and Hierarchies: Analysis and Antitrust Implications*. New York: Free Press.

4

The Influence of Industrial Relations System Factors on Foreign Direct Investment

William Cooke

To what extent do multinational companies (MNCs) weigh differences in industrial relations (IR) systems in deciding where and how much to invest or reinvest across alternative host countries? As argued in Chapter 1, profit-maximizing firms can be expected to invest more in those locations that provide the greatest market opportunities and the lowest operating costs, including costs associated with possible divestment at a later time. Both survey evidence and anecdotal evidence indicate that most MNCs (but not all) place considerable weight on labor costs in deciding where and how much to invest across alternative host locations. Obviously, those MNCs in industries in which the ratio of labor costs to total operational costs is relatively higher, place greater emphasis on labor cost considerations in making foreign direct investments (FDI) decisions than MNCs in industries in which labor–cost ratios are relatively lower. In contrast, MNCs that simply must locate in a country to successfully conduct business (e.g., supplier companies that must locate near their original equipment manufacturers or companies engaged in resource extraction) necessarily ignore or give limited consideration to labor costs in making decisions about where to invest.

In practice, labor cost assessments are made by MNCs against their own company-specific experiences abroad in deciding to expand or relocate work across existing foreign operations. In those instances wherein multinationals are considering investing in countries for which they have had no presence, companies typically deploy representatives to study a location. Engaging in due diligence inquiries common to merger and acquisition decisions, assessments and comparison of local markets and prevailing workplace practices are typically made.

My objective in this chapter is to examine the influence of differences in IR system factors on FDI decisions. As developed herein, net labor cost differences across countries are a function of differences in compensation, skills, government workplace regulations, and collective bargaining contexts. These factors not only directly affect net labor costs but, in part, indirectly affect labor costs as they influence the ability or ease with which MNCs can exploit existing human resource management and labor relations (HRM/LR) competitive advantages or create such advantages abroad. I first develop the logic behind exploiting or creating HRM/LR advantages abroad. Subsequently, I describe the kinds of salient IR system factors that influence both unit labor costs and the opportunity to exploit or create HRM/LR advantages abroad. As part of that discussion, a comparison of differences in IR system factors across highly developed and developing countries is made to highlight some distinct differences between and among both highly developed and developing countries in different regions of the world. Finally, I synthesize the empirical evidence about the influence of salient IR system factors on MNC FDI decisions of where and how much to invest abroad.

EXPLOITING OR CREATING HRM/LR ADVANTAGES ABROAD

Within the present framework, HRM/LR ownership advantages play an important role in inducing some companies to make foreign investments and exploit that advantage abroad (Cooke, 2001a). As proposed by Taylor, Beechler, and Napier (1996), MNCs face three basic choices: fully diffuse HRM/LR strategies abroad, fully adopt local HRM/LR practices, or integrate a mix of both parent and local HRM/LR practices. Although the authors do not explicitly link FDI decisions to these diffuse/adopt choices, their central propositions of why MNCs either diffuse parent or adopt local HRM/LR practices are especially relevant to the exploitation of ownership advantages.

MNCs, believing that their parent strategies offer resource-based assets that cannot be readily copied by competitors (Barney, 1991), have reason to diffuse such strategies to foreign locations. Believing that their HRM/LR strategies are superior to all others regardless of location, some Japanese MNCs have been insistent on replicating home strategies across foreign locations (Bird, Taylor, and Beechler, 1998). Firms not enjoying HRM/LR ownership advantages, on the other hand (either because they lack expertise in creating HRM/LR advantages or because they view HRM/LR strategies as relatively inconsequential to performance), have no incentive to diffuse home HRM/LR strategies abroad.

Firms that suffer HRM/LR ownership disadvantages as a result of constraints imposed on them by the IR system of their home countries, however, may have reason to diffuse some HRM/LR practices but not others to foreign locations. For example, companies located in countries that restrict employers' flexibility to lay off unneeded workers, hire temporary employees, or schedule hours of work may view their own restricted HRM/LR practices as disadvantageous relative to foreign competitors less restricted by foreign IR systems. These MNCs, therefore, face a disincentive to diffuse suboptimal

HRM/LR practices but may, nonetheless, invest more abroad than they would otherwise. Unable to create HRM/LR ownership advantages at home, that is, MNCs have incentive to invest in foreign locations offering less restrictive IR systems in which they can create or adopt more cost-effective HRM/LR practices.

It has been widely argued in the international HRM literature that MNC diffuse/adopt decisions are determined in part by the overall international orientation of control and centralization of decision making by MNCs. Based on the international orientation typology developed by Heenan and Perlmutter (1979), Schuler, Dowling, and DeCieri (1993) argue that MNCs in which top management attitudes and values are primarily "ethnocentric" in nature are generally inclined to diffuse preferred home-based HRM/LR practices to their foreign subsidiaries. At the opposite extreme are MNCs that have more "polycentric" orientations. For these MNCs, foreign subsidiaries are generally given considerable autonomy to manage their own operations, including the freedom to implement their own HRM/LR strategies. MNCs more "geocentric" in nature are inclined to formulate HRM/LR strategies that take into account the diverse interests and needs of both home and host country managers. As such, by integrating home and host practices, geocentric-minded MNCs will have developed strategies generally advantageous across all global operations.

In a similar line of reasoning, Hamill (1984) concludes that the most important factor determining the degree of centralization and parent control of labor relations policies is the degree of integration across foreign subsidiaries. Because more highly integrated configurations require greater overall coordination and are more vulnerable to single location disruption or poor performance, MNCs maintain more centralized control. In addition, the greater the capital investment and relative financial importance of subsidiaries, the greater the parent control over subsidiary labor relations policies.

Given differences in IR systems, however, the fungibility of HRM/LR strategies is bound to vary across host locations. Hence, the value of HRM/LR strategies may be reduced, if not lost, outside their given home-based, organizational context. (Taylor et al., 1996; Ferner and Quintanilla, 1998). In selecting locations, therefore, MNCs can be expected to weigh the transaction and opportunity costs associated with diffusing HRM/LR strategies abroad. Unless host country IR systems are sufficiently flexible and amenable to the diffusion of HRM/LR practices abroad, opportunity and transaction costs may be substantial.

On one hand, MNCs may attempt to mold foreign workplaces to fit their preferred strategies, incurring costs associated with intensive recruitment and selection activities and substantial reorientation and training of workers and managers. On the other hand, MNCs may not be able to cost-effectively diffuse their preferred HRM/LR practices abroad, causing them to adopt, instead, practices common to host country IR systems. As reported in a number of studies, many Japanese companies have adopted some practices more in common with host locations than those deployed in their home locations, while implementing other policies and practices core to their parent HRM/LR strategies (e.g., see Florida and Kenney, 1991; Doeringer, Evans-Klock, and Terkla, 1998; Purcell et al., 1999).

Except for a few studies, the literature has paid little attention to the transfer or adoption of union–management relations policies and practices. For those studies that have, the evidence indicates that MNCs (Japanese MNCs specifically) have generally pursued labor relations strategies similar to those common to host countries. As reported by Kenney and Tanaka in Chapter 7, Japanese transplants in the U.S. television assembly industry have largely adopted the U.S. Fordist tradition of hierarchical job progressions and seniority rules in their collective bargaining agreements. Florida and Kenney's (1991) study of Japanese automobile assemblers and parts transplants also shows that Japanese MNCs have vigorously avoided union representation in the United States. The exception is found in three cases in which joint ventures with U.S. automobile producers were created and in one case in which Ford Motor Company was a partial owner. In these cases, union representation was not seriously challenged. Furthermore, collective bargaining agreements were negotiated in which the Japanese HRM/LR and production systems were generally embraced but modified to varying degrees.

One component of the Japanese model that was not generally transferable to U.S. automotive plants was the use of individualized pay systems based on merit and seniority. U.S. workers in both the unionized and nonunion transplants and across both assemblers and part suppliers rejected or greatly resisted such individualized pay schemes, including the use of performance bonuses. Instead, U.S. workers and unions demanded more uniform wages based on job duties and classifications. According to Florida and Kenney, nonunion companies did not attempt to force Japanese-like pay schemes on their American workers for fear that such action would trigger union-organizing drives.

Purcell et al. (1999) found in their study of Japanese affiliates in Australia that among manufacturing subsidiaries over 80 percent became unionized, whereas among finance and tourism subsidiaries, only 1 out of 34 sites became unionized. As expressed by the authors and consistent with Florida and Kenney's (1991) findings, Japanese MNCs did not strongly contest unionization when it would have been especially costly to do so but otherwise aggressively avoided union representation. In an apparent attempt to marginalize unions, however, roughly three-quarters of the unionized firms established nonunion channels of joint consultation through the establishment of employee representation committees. Lastly, Purcell et al. also report that, unlike their home sites, only about one-third of the Japanese foreign affiliate sites surveyed (65 in total) paid bonuses to all of their employees.

In addition to the preceding studies, trends in union representation of foreign affiliates in the United States clearly indicate that foreign MNCs from nearly all major investor countries have adopted the union avoidance and deunionization culture prevalent within the American IR system (Cooke, 2001b).

More specifically, the union penetration rate of foreign-owned subsidiaries dropped substantially from above 29 percent in 1980 to below 15 percent by 1998. Between 1992 and 1997, not only did the penetration rate drop sharply (from 21.1 percent to 14.9 percent), but the number of employees covered by collective bargaining agreements plummeted 22 percent from a total of about 995,000 to about 775,000 employees. The sharp drop in coverage occurred, furthermore, during a period in which total employment in foreign-owned subsidiaries increased approximately 10 percent. Hence, foreign MNCs with operations in the United States have, of late, closed and reduced employment in their unionized sites, while expanding employment in their nonunionized sites and otherwise avoiding union representation in sites opened or acquired. It appears, therefore, that foreign MNCs have adapted their labor relations strategies to fit or take advantage of the IR system of their American host.

In summary, FDI decisions are partially determined by opportunities for MNCs to gain advantage via their HRM/LR strategies pursued abroad. Such advantage can be gained either by exploiting abroad HRM/LR strategies developed in home operations or by adopting host country HRM/LR practices considered superior to those practices common in their home operations. The limited evidence indicates that the collective bargaining contexts of host countries, in particular, have had the effect of either (1) limiting the opportunity for some MNCs to diffuse preferred HRM/LR strategies abroad or (2) providing opportunities to create HRM/LR advantages by avoiding union representation or circumventing collective bargaining altogether. The evidence suggests, therefore, that MNCs consider (or at least have reason to consider) the kinds of HRM/LR strategies that they can effectively pursue abroad in deciding in the first place where and how much to invest across alternative locations. As discussed next, the degree to which HRM/LR advantages might be achieved abroad is in large part determined by differences in the IR systems of alternative host countries.

IR SYSTEM FACTORS INFLUENCING FDI DECISIONS

Several recent analyses have identified a wide range of IR system factors that appear to have a substantial influence on the distribution of FDI across countries. The effects of IR system factors on FDI, it should be emphasized, are in addition to the influence of many other market and sociopolitical factors on FDI decisions. In summarizing the hypothesized or expected effects of various IR system factors on FDI decisions, therefore, it is important to keep in mind that such arguments are based on the presumption that "all else is the same." That is, all key variables relevant to interpreting the statistical association of IR variables with FDI must be accounted for. The evidence to date about the independent effects of IR system factors on FDI has focused primarily on differences in compensation costs for skill levels sought, government workplace regulations, and collective bargaining contexts. Missing from the empirical literature, consequently, is any evidence about the effects of differences in workplace cultures on FDI decisions not otherwise captured indirectly by the given IR system factors studied.

To provide the reader with a better appreciation of the variation in IR systems across countries, Table 4.1 identifies a set of IR system attributes across selected countries in most regions of the world. Given the simplicity of measurement necessary to create a comparative profile across a large number of countries, these variables, admittedly, provide only crude yardsticks for comparative purposes. Although they serve to illustrate significant differences in national IR systems, there remain more subtle, yet important, distinctions across systems. Readers, therefore, should interpret the distinctions highlighted in Table 4.1 with due caution. In particular, one should bear in mind that many countries are in various shorter-term and longer-term stages of transition out of centrally controlled communist, military, or (in the case of South Africa) apartheid states. The legacies of these transition economies have, consequently, colored existing institutions (especially unions), collective bargaining, and the application of labor laws. There are also differences in how some variables are measured in each country (e.g., union density and strike activity), in distinctions made between "formal" and "informal" labor markets among some less developed countries, and in public and private sector laws and collective bargaining (especially in transition economies).

The first variables reported provide a rough approximation of average differences in educational attainment and annual labor costs across countries. As shown, there are vast differences in education levels and in secondary education enrollment between the more highly developed countries of North America, Western Europe and the South Pacific, on the one hand, and, on the other hand, the less developed and transition economies of Eastern, Central and Southern Europe, Latin America, the Asia/Pacific, and Africa. These educational differences are highly correlated, moreover, with differences in average annual labor costs in manufacturing, although notable exceptions can be observed. For example, Italy, Spain, Brazil, Singapore, and South Africa are marked by relatively high average compensation costs in spite of relatively low educational attainment.

With respect to minimizing unit labor costs, MNCs can be expected to invest more in countries in which compensation costs are lower for given levels of skill and productivity sought. Efficiency-seeking MNCs that can readily staff operations with unskilled workforces, however, look to invest across low-skill, low-wage countries. As efficiency-seekers, MNCs invest more in countries with the lowest compensation costs, giving limited weight to differences in skills and productivity (Cooke and Noble, 1998). In contrast, market-seeking MNCs whose operations require a mix of various skill levels give substantial weight to differences in the skills and productivity of host country workforces.

Unit labor costs are also determined in part by government workplace regulations and policies restricting an employer's freedom or imposing significant transaction costs on employers when making adjustments in the terms and conditions of employment. Given the desire of MNCs to minimize

Table 4.1
Attributes of National Industrial Relations Systems

Country	Education Yrs	% Enrolled	Annual Labor Costs	Layoff Rest?	Works Coun?	Central Negot?	Union Density	Work Stoppages Days Lost	Work Stoppages % Invol	L-M Coop	Union Power (1-7 scale)
North America											
U.S.	12.4	90%	$28,907	No	No	No	14%	82	1%	5.0	4.1
Canada	12.2	91%	$28,424	No	No	No	30%	632	2%	4.8	4.6
Europe											
Western											
Austria	11.4	88%	$28,342	Yes	Yes	Yes	37%*	7	0%	6.1	5.5
Belgium	11.2	88%	$24,132	Yes	Yes	Yes	54%*	119	1%	4.4	5.2
Denmark	11.0	88%	$29,235	Yes	Yes	Yes	80%*	138	7%	6.0	5.0
Finland	10.9	93%	$26,615	Yes	Yes	Yes	79%*	157	9%	5.4	6.0
France	12.0	95%	na	Yes	Yes	Yes	10%*	79	1%	3.3	4.4
Germany	11.6	88%	$33,226	Yes	Yes	Yes	29%*	15	2%	5.3	5.3
Ireland	8.9	86%	$22,681	Yes	No	Yes	31%*	341	3%	5.2	4.8
Netherlands	11.0	91%	$34,326	Yes	Yes	Yes	28%*	23	4%	5.9	5.2
Norway	12.1	97%	$30,588a	Yes	Yes	Yes	60%*	17	1%	5.7	5.7
Sweden	11.4	99%	$26,601	Yes	Yes	Yes	80%*	79	1%	6.0	5.8
Switzerland	11.6	84%	na	Yes	No	No	25%*	1	1%	6.4	3.4
U.K.	11.7	92%	$23,843	No	No	No	30%	106	2%	5.1	3.5

Table 4.1 Continued

Country	Education Yrs	% Enrolled	Annual Labor Costs	Layoff Rest?	Works Coun?	Central Negot?	Union Density	Work Stoppages Days Lost	% Invol	L-M Coop	Union Power (1-7 scale)
Europe Southern											
Greece	7.0	87%	$12,753[a]	Yes	Yes	Yes	26%*	8886	10%	3.9	4.3
Italy	7.5	>75%	$34,859	Yes	Yes	Yes	35%*	462	41%	4.2	4.6
Portugal	6.4	78%	$ 7,577	Yes	Yes	Yes	26%*	75	12%	5.0	3.8
Spain	6.9	>75%	$19,329	Yes	Yes	Yes	15%*	542	36%	4.5	4.6
Central/Eastern											
Bulgaria	7.0	74%	$ 1,179	Yes	No	No	40%	na	na	4.3	4.3
Czech Rep.	9.2	87%	$ 1,876	No	No	No	30%	na	0%	5.1	4.2
Hungary	9.8	86%	$ 2,777	No	Yes	Yes	44%	3	9%	5.1	3.8
Poland	8.2	85%	$ 1,714	No	No	No	11%	75	6%	3.9	5.0
Russian Fed.	9.0	na	$ 1,528	No	No	Yes	54%	41	1%	4.1	3.0
Turkey	3.6	51%	$ 7,958	No	No	No	13%	2668	7%	3.6	4.0
Asia/Pacific More Developed											
Australia	12.0	89%	$26,087	No	No	No	25%	548	14%	4.3	4.9
Japan	10.8	99%	$31,687	Yes	No	No	22%	3	2%	6.1	4.2
N. Zealand	10.7	90%	$19,380[a]	No	No	No	20%	383	17%	5.6	3.6

Table 4.1 Continued

Country	Education Yrs	Education % Enrolled	Annual Labor Costs	Layoff Rest?	Works Coun?	Central Negot?	Union Density	Work Stoppages Days Lost	Work Stoppages % Invol	L-M Coop (1-7 scale)	Union Power (1-7 scale)
Asia/Pacific Less Developed											
China Mainland	5.0	>50%	$ 729	No	No	No	20%	na	na	5.0	5.0
Hong Kong	7.2	69%	$10,401[a]	No	No	No	22%	<1	1%	5.8	2.8
Taiwan	6.0	na	na	No	Yes	No	30%	na	na	5.6	3.7
India	2.4	<50%	$ 1,192	Yes	No	No	4%	na	21%	3.9	4.6
Indonesia	4.1	42%	$ 1,008	No	No	No	2%	na	13%	4.8	3.6
Korea, Rep.	9.3	97%	$10,743	No	No	No	12%	878	5%	3.9	4.6
Malaysia	5.6	<50%	$ 3,429	No	No	No	8%	10	2%	5.7	4.2
Philippines	7.6	59%	$ 2,450	No	No	No	11%	714	3%	4.3	4.7
Singapore	4.0	>50%	$16,070[a]	No	No	Yes	14%	0	0%	6.5	4.2
Thailand	3.9	<50%	$ 2,705	No	No	No	2%	43	2%	5.2	3.7
Latin America											
Argentina	9.2	>50%	$ 7,338	No	No	Yes	35%*	na	na	4.7	4.1
Brazil	4.0	20%	$14,134	No	No	Yes	16%*	2	23%	4.4	3.7
Chile	3.8	58%	$ 5,822	No	No	No	10%	na	33%	5.2	3.8
Colombia	7.5	46%	$ 2,507	Yes	No	No	5%	2	2%	4.0	4.1
Mexico	4.9	51%	$ 7,607	No	No	No	25%	1178	1%	5.4	4.2
Panama	6.7	<50%	$ 6,351	No	No	No	10%	43	2%	na	na
Venezuela	6.5	22%	$ 4,667	No	No	No	10%	na	na	4.2	4.6

Notes and Primary Sources:

<u>Notes</u>

* More than 50 percent of all wage and salary earners are covered by extensions of centralized collective bargaining agreements.

a Estimation based on trends between 1980-1984 and 1995-1999.

Education:

Yrs: average years of schooling, 1992 (*Human Development Report*, 1994, Table 1).

% Enrolled: the ratio of the number of children of official school age (as defined by the national education system) who are enrolled in secondary-level schooling or training to the population of the corresponding official school age, 1997) (*Social Indicators of Development*, 2001, Table 2.12).

Annual Labor Costs: the ratio of total compensation to the number of workers in the manufacturing sector. Compensation includes direct wages, salaries, and other remuneration paid directly by employers plus all contributions by employers to social security programs on behalf of their employees. Figures provided are based on dividing the total payroll by the number of employees engaged in manufacturing establishments over the 1990–1994 period (*Social Indicators of Development*, 2001, Table 2.5).

Works Coun?: "Yes" if country by law or custom requires the establishment of works councils and "No" otherwise (Cooke and Noble, 1998).

Layoff Rest?: "Yes" if government requires employers to notify government labor office and consult or negotiate with unions or works councils over pending layoffs and "No" otherwise (Cooke and Noble, 1998).

Notes and Primary Sources Continued:

Central Negot?: "Yes" if sectoral-wide or national collective bargaining agreements between federations of unions and employers play a *dominant* role in system and "No" if company level negotiations play a dominant role (*ILO*, 1997–1998, Table 3.1)

Union Density: percent of total workforce who are members of unions at or about 2000 (*OECD Labour Market Statistics*, 2001; *Country Reports on Human Rights Practices*, 2001).

Work Stoppages:

Days Lost: lost work days per 1000 employees due to strikes and lockouts (annual average over 1989–1993 period) (*ILO*, 1995, Table IV).

% Invol: percent of total union membership involved in work stoppages at or about 1995 (*ILO*, 1997–1998, Tables 1.1 and 4.2).

L-M Coop: average score from survey question "Labor/employer relations are generally cooperative." (1 = strongly disagree. 7 = strongly agree) (*Global Competitiveness Report*, 1999, Table 7.09).

Union Power: average score from survey question "The collective bargaining power of workers is high." (1 = strongly disagree. 7 = strongly agree) (*Global Competitiveness Report*, 1999, Table 7.10).

potential future divestment costs, regulations restricting employer freedom to lay off unneeded workers are perceived by companies as especially costly. Such restrictions include at a minimum that employers both notify government agencies and consult or negotiate pending layoffs with unions or works councils.

Some countries also require government authorization. Such restrictions, of course, limit (at least to some degree) an employer's discretion to adjust employment levels quickly, and they increase transaction costs in making such adjustments. As reported in Table 4.1, restrictions on employers' freedom to lay off workers are widespread across Europe but are not common elsewhere.

Another important form of government regulation or policy that may be viewed as costly to MNCs is one that requires the creation of works councils or representative employee committees. These councils, comprising elected workers, are given minimum rights ranging from access to business and operational information and consultation with management over workplace decisions to negotiation and approval rights of key workplace decisions. Such worker rights reduce an employer's discretion to implement preferred workplace policies and practices and, moreover, increase employer transaction costs when seeking adjustments in HRM/LR and operational practices. Employers, therefore, will view works councils as costly, an outcome consistent with the findings by Addison et al. (2000) that works councils reduce profitability. As with government restrictions regarding layoffs, government mandates and policies requiring employers to establish works councils are almost exclusively found in Europe.

The negative effects of these kinds of government constraints may, nonetheless, be offset to the degree that either government regulations improve workplace environments or MNCs find cost-effective alternatives to coping with such restrictions. For example, as a result of greater employment security, restrictions on laying off employees may improve employee loyalty and commitment and, consequently, performance (Emerson, 1988). Additionally, companies may find cost-effective alternatives to layoffs by retaining valued employees either through retraining redundant workers (Blank, 1994) or by reducing hours of work (Abraham and Houseman, 1995). With regard to works councils, these forms of employee voice can yield significant performance improvements as a result of improved labor–management relations and employee participation in workplace decisions (Rogers and Streeck, 1994; Freeman and Lazear, 1995). Works councils have been shown, furthermore, to provide an avenue for MNCs to transfer HRM/LR practices to foreign subsidiaries in the face of union objections (Martinez Lucio and Weston, 1994) or to marginalize unions more broadly (Rogers and Streeck, 1994: 103–4).

In addition to labor market and government workplace regulations, FDI decisions are influenced by the potential effects of union representation and collective bargaining on unit labor costs. Potential costs include higher current and future compensation costs, more restrictive workplace practices, greater divisions between labor and management, disruptions through strikes and lockouts, and greater transaction costs incurred through negotiations and contract administration than would otherwise be incurred in nonunion enterprises. Hence, unless MNCs view union representation and collective bargaining as adding value equal to, or greater than, potential costs (Freeman and Medoff, 1984; Cooke, 1994), MNCs seek to avoid union representation and collective bargaining. In calculating any net disadvantages, MNCs also consider the likelihood of being organized by unions and the transaction costs associated with avoiding or marginalizing unions.

Among the salient factors considered by MNCs in weighing the potential costs of union representation and collective bargaining are the extent of union coverage, the centralization of bargaining structures, the disruptive or cooperative nature of labor–management relationships, and the perceived power of unions. As reported in Table 4.1, the level of union membership density across countries is wide-ranging. Indeed, the most recent comparable estimates of the percent of wage and salary employees who are reported as being union members range from a low of 2 percent in Indonesia and Thailand to a high of 80 percent in Denmark and Sweden. Because of policies in which collective bargaining agreements can be extended to cover employees in nonunion companies via the practice of highly centralized negotiations, however, the extent of union contract coverage in some countries is typically much higher than membership density. That is, in a large majority of Western European countries and in some developing countries, negotiations are generally conducted on an industry- or occupation-wide basis or on a regional or national level between federations of employers and unions. Such centralized negotiations are frequently viewed as limiting a given company's flexibility to decide on compensation and workplace practices that best align with a company's business strategy and competitive circumstances (Hyman, 1994; Brown and Walsh, 1994). In nearly all developed countries with centralized negotiation structures, moreover, the extent of union contract coverage (irrespective of union membership) is quite high. Indeed, in Western European countries with centralized structures, union contract coverage exceeds the majority of workers in each country; and in all but Switzerland, union coverage reaches 75 percent or more. Making it difficult to avoid union representation or the effects of union power, this combination of centralized bargaining structures and pervasive union contract coverage can be expected to negatively influence FDI.

Providing some measure of the more confrontational or more cooperative nature of labor–management relationships, are several rough proxies in Table 4.1. First, using the latest comparable estimates available, two facets of work stoppages and lockout activity are provided: the annual average number of lost days of work per 1,000 employees over the 1989–1993 period and the percent of union membership involved in work stoppages at or about 1995. Across most countries, both the number of lost days and percent of members involved are relatively low. Nevertheless, lost days of work per 1,000 employees exceeded 500 days for Canada, Greece, Spain, Turkey, Mexico, Australia, South Korea, the Philippines, and South Africa. Second, I report on two perceptions of respondents to the worldwide survey conducted by the World

Economic Forum, which includes these perceptions in its global competitiveness index. The figures reported in Table 4.1 are based on scales of 1–7, wherein 1=strongly disagree and 7=strongly agree. In the first scale reported (L-M Coop), respondents were asked if they agreed or disagreed with the statement that "labor/employer relations are generally cooperative." Those countries receiving a relatively high score in which responses on average ranged from "agree" to "strongly agree" (6.0 or higher) are Austria, Denmark, Sweden, Switzerland, Japan, and Singapore. At the low end of the scale (averaging less than 4.0) are France, Greece, Poland, Turkey, India, South Korea, and South Africa.

In the second scale reported, respondents were asked if they agreed or disagreed with the statement that "the collective bargaining power of workers is high." Here we find a narrower range of average scores, with the highest union collective bargaining scores found for Finland (6.0), Norway (5.7), Sweden (5.8), Austria (5.5), Germany (5.3), and South Africa (5.3). The lowest union collective bargaining power scores are found for Hong Kong (2.8), mainland China (3.0), Poland (3.0), Switzerland (3.4), and the United Kingdom (3.5).

In summary, there is substantial variation in the IR systems across countries. Although there are some commonalities among countries within regions of the world, there remains, nonetheless, considerable variation across countries within regions. More subtle distinctions in labor market characteristics, government workplace regulations, and collective bargaining contexts between countries, furthermore, obviously exist. Hence, MNCs face a wide array of IR system factors to weigh across countries between and within regions of the world in making cost-benefit assessments about where and how much to invest across alternative host locations. In the following section, I review the empirical evidence about the influence of differences in IR system factors on FDI.

Empirical Evidence

On comparing several recent empirical analyses that I conducted or directed, considerable evidence is found that IR system factors shape FDI decisions. I have summarized the findings of these empirical inquiries in Table 4.2. Based on four different samples of data, in which FDI is measured either as accumulated assets or as ratios of assets expended across countries and made by both U.S.-based and foreign-based MNCs, the results are highly consistent across analyses. Not included in the table is a similar empirical inquiry by Bognanno, Keane, and Yang (2000), whose analysis of U.S. FDI abroad over the 1982–1992 period yields results highly consistent with those reported herein. Also consistent with these findings that IR systems influence FDI decisions is the analysis made by Kleiner and Ham in the following chapter.

Reported in Table 4.2 are positive and negative signs indicating the direction of relationships and the levels of statistical significance for each of the IR system variables regressed against the respective dependent variables identified. To give readers a sense of the magnitude of effects of the independent variables on FDI, yet avoid burdening readers with substantial detail (available in the respective reports), I discuss the size of effects based on my analysis of FDI ratios under Cooke (2001a). For ease of presentation, I have excluded the signs and significance levels of the control variables included in each regression model. Each regression estimate, nonetheless, included salient control variables for various measures of market size and wealth, proximity between home and host countries, taxation, FDI incentives, exchange rate trends, language differences, and, where possible, industry.

Across the four studies, the average number of years of education (treated as a rough proxy for differences in skills available and worker productivity) is found to be positively associated with FDI. The exception is found in regard to FDI in low-skill countries in which U.S. MNCs seek out the lowest-skilled workforces, arguably in the search for ever lower compensation costs when differences in skills are inconsequential to performance. Controlling for average education differences and compensation per unit of education, compensation costs are found to be negatively and highly significantly associated with FDI. When compensation costs per education are not controlled for, however, the association between FDI and compensation costs yielded mixed results (Cooke, 1997; Cooke and Noble, 1998). A plausible explanation for the various findings regarding compensation costs is that education differences do not fully capture skill and productivity differences. Since compensation is generally highly correlated with skill and productivity, differences in compensation costs can be expected to be capturing unobserved differences in skills and productivity.

With respect to government workplace regulations, restrictions on the layoff of workers (whether treated independently or in combination with works council requirements) are negatively associated with FDI in all four studies. On average, in comparing countries having government regulations restricting layoffs and requiring works councils to those countries that did not have both forms of regulation, the ratio of FDI was reduced by a factor of 25 points. In other words, a 1-to-1 ratio of FDI between otherwise similar IR systems would be reduced to a 25-to-1 ratio. With regard to the effects of works council policies on FDI, the results are mixed. In the two latter studies (Cooke, 2001a, 2001b), works council policies (in combination with government layoff restrictions) are found to be negatively related to FDI. In the two studies examining only U.S. FDI abroad (Cooke, 1997; Cooke and Noble, 1998), however, works councils are positively associated with FDI decisions. One plausible explanation for this finding is that U.S. MNCs have found works councils as useful avenues to offsetting union strength in countries in which centralized bargaining and contract coverage are widespread. In contrast, MNCs from other highly industrialized countries (the majority of which have works council policies) apparently view works councils as imposing greater restrictions on management discretion than offering avenues to marginalize unions.

Table 4.2
Summary of Results of Cross-Sectional Analyses of the Effects of IR System Variables on FDI

Variables	Cooke, 1997	Cooke and Noble, 1998	Cooke, 2001a	Cooke, 2001b
Dependent Variables and Sample	U.S. 1989 FDI assets by 2-digit industry across 19 OECD countries. N=126.	U.S. 1993 FDI assets by 2-digit industry across 33 developed and developing countries. N=244.	1994 ratio of FDI in country i to FDI in country j by 16 high-skill OECD countries. N=1021	1994 ratio of FDI in the U.S. to FDI in country j made by 15 high-skill OECD countries. N=151.
Yrs. Education	(+, $\leq$ .05 level)	(+, $\leq$ .01 level for high-skill countries.) (–, $\leq$ .01 level for low-skill countries.)	(+, $\leq$ .01 level)	(+, $\leq$ .05 level)
Compensation	(–, insignificant)	(+, $\leq$ .01 level)	(–, $\leq$ .01 level)	(–, $\leq$ .01 level)
Compensation per Year of Education	(Not included)	(Not included)	(+, $\leq$ .01 level)	(+, $\leq$ .01 level)
Layoff Restrictions	(–, $\leq$ .01 level)	(–, $\leq$ .05 level)	(As combination)	(As combination)

Table 4.2 Continued

Variables	Cooke, 1997	Cooke and Noble, 1998	Cooke, 2001a	Cooke, 2001b
Works Councils	(+, ≤ .01 level)	(+, ≤ .01 level)	(As combination)	(As combination)
Layoff Restrict. & Works Councils	(Not combined)	(Not combined)	(−, ≤ .05 level)	(−, ≤ .05 level)
% Union Membership	(−, ≤ .01 level)	(−, ≤ .01 level)	(−, ≤ .05 level)	(−, ≤ .05 level)
Centralized Bargaining	(−, ≤ .01 level)	(−, ≤ .05 level)	(As combination)	(As combination)
Cent. Barg. With ≥ 50 % Union Coverage	(Not combined)	(Not combined)	(−, ≤ .01 level)	(−, ≤ .01 level)
Lost Days Due to Work Stoppages	(Not included)	(Not included)	(−, ≤ .05 level)	(Not included)

Control Variables
Various controls for market size and wealth, proximity to hosts, taxation, FDI incentives, exchange rate trends, language differences, and, where possible, industry.

With respect to collective bargaining contexts, several variables are found to be associated with FDI. First, union density in a country as measured by the percent of all wage and salary employees belonging to union, is consistently negatively and statistically significantly related to FDI. Based on the ratio of FDI made in country i vis-à-vis country j, differences in union membership density rates have the effect of reducing the FDI ratio by a factor of .10 per each percentage point difference in union penetration. Based on the largest difference of penetration rates between countries, the maximum effect of union density rates reduces the FDI ratio by a factor of 7.3 to 1. Second, MNCs invest less than they would otherwise in countries characterized by negotiation structures centralized beyond company-wide levels. In the two studies reported in Table 4.2 that examine FDI made by MNCs from high-skill Organization for Economic Cooperation and Development (OECD) countries, centralized bargaining structures in combination with extensive union contract coverage are also found to be negatively and significantly associated with FDI decisions. On average, my estimates indicate that the effects are fairly substantial, decreasing the ratio of investment in a country characterized by both centralized bargaining and extensive union coverage by a factor of roughly 17 to 1.

Finally, statistically significant evidence is found that MNCs invest less in countries in which lost days due to work stoppages are greater. The estimated maximum difference between countries suggests that such forms of labor–management conflict have reduced the ratio of FDI by as much as a factor of 19, a rather sizable factor. One needs to be cautious, however, about the confidence placed in this latter result given inherent limitations in the measurement of union–management conflict and that such a measure was included in only one of the four studies summarized in Table 4.2.

CONCLUSION

In summary, there is highly consistent empirical evidence across published analyses that differences in IR systems have had major effects on MNC decisions of where and how much to invest abroad. It is inferred from the evidence available that in deciding on their FDI configurations, MNCs have chosen to invest more in host countries whose IR systems offer (1) greater net comparative unit labor cost advantages and (2) greater flexibility to either diffuse or create preferred HRM/LR practices. As such, host country IR systems marked by lower compensation cost for skills sought, by less imposing government workplace regulations, and by less extensive union representation and decentralized collective bargaining structures attract greater FDI.

Although the findings summarized about MNC FDI decision making are fairly straightforward, the implications for government policymaker and union leader strategic responses are not. Countries seeking to increase inward FDI or to prevent the erosion of inward FDI and domestic investment would apparently benefit from raising skill levels, reducing compensation, and offering greater flexibility to employers by minimizing government and collective bargaining constraints. Except for raising skill levels via increased training and education, however, policies aimed at reducing compensation or granting employers added workplace flexibility could prove costly in terms of other socially desirable outcomes for workers. As discussed at some length in Part IV of this volume, the feasibility of multilateral agreements governing workplace and collective bargaining practices across countries is complicated, furthermore, by the influences of differences in IR systems on FDI decisions. The implications for union responses are, likewise, complicated. As discussed by several authors in Part III of this volume, unions will need to refocus their strategic response to MNC FDI configuration and HRM/LR strategies pursued abroad. In particular, unions need to more effectively organize an MNC's operations and its competitors across countries, coordinate interunion actions across different unions in different countries, and block MNCs from deunionizing or otherwise marginalizing unions in their foreign subsidiaries.

REFERENCES

Abraham, K. and Houseman, S. (1995). "Earnings Inequality in Germany." In Freeman, R., and Katz, L. (eds.), *Differences and Changes in Wage Structures*. Chicago: University of Chicago Press, pp. 371–404.

Addison, J. T., Siebert, W. S., Wagner, J., and Wei, X. (2000). "Worker Participation and Firm Performance: Evidence from Germany and Britain." *British Journal of Industrial Relations* 38 (1), pp. 7–48.

Barney, J. B. (1991). "Firm Resources and the Theory of Competitive Advantage." *Journal of Management* 17 (1), pp. 99–120.

Bird, A., Taylor, S., and Beechler, S. (1998). "A Typology of International Human Resource Management in Japanese Multinational Corporations: Organizational Implications". *Human Resource Management* 37 (2), pp. 159–72.

Blank, R. (1994). "Does a Larger Social Safety Net Mean Less Economic Flexibility?" In Freeman, R. B. (ed.), *Working under Different Rules*. New York: Russell Sage Foundation, pp. 157–188.

Bognanno, M. F., Keane, M. P. and Yang, D. (2000). "The Influence of Wages and Industrial Relations Environments on the Production Location Decisions of U.S. Multinational Corporations." Working Paper, Industrial Relations Center, University of Minnesota.

Brown, W. and Walsh, J. (1994). "Corporate Pay Policies and the Internationalisation of Markets." In Niland, J., Lansbury, R., and Verevis, C. (eds.), *The Future of Industrial Relations*. London: Sage, pp. 377–88

Cooke, W. N. (1994). "Employee Participation Programs, Group-Based Incentives, and Company Performance: A Union-Nonunion Comparison." *Industrial and Labor Relations Review* 46 (3), pp. 594–609.

Cooke, W. N. (1997). "The Influence of Industrial Relations Factors on U.S. Foreign Direct Investment Abroad." *Industrial and Labor Relations Review* 50 (1), pp. 3–17.

Cooke, W. N. (2001a). "The Effects of Labor Costs and Workplace Constraints on Foreign Direct Investment among Highly Industrialized Countries." *International Journal of Human Resource Management*, 12 (5), pp. 697–716.

Cooke, W. N. (2001b). "Union Avoidance and Foreign Direct Investment in the U.S." *Employee Relations Journal* 23 (6), pp. 558–80.

Cooke, W. N. and Noble, D. S. (1998). "Industrial Relations Systems and U.S. Foreign Direct Investment Abroad." *British Journal of Industrial Relations* 36 (4), pp. 581–609. *Country Reports on Human Rights Practices*. (2001). U.S. Department of State www.state.gov.

Doeringer, P. B., Evans-Klock, C., and Terkla, D. G. (1998). "Hybrids or Hodgepodges? Workplace Practices of Japanese and Domestic Startups in the United States." *Industrial and Labor Relations Review* 51 (2), pp. 171–86.

Emerson, M. (1988). "Regulation or Deregulation of the Labour Market". *European Economic Review* 32, pp. 775-817.

Ferner, A. and Quintanilla, J. (1998). "Multinationals, National Business Systems and HRM: The Enduring Influence of National Identity or a Process of Anglo-Saxonization." *International Journal of Human Resource Management* 9 (4), pp. 710–31.

Florida, R. and Kenney, M. (1991). "Organization vs. Culture: Japanese Automotive Transplants in the U.S." *Industrial Relations Journal* 22, pp.181–96.

Freeman, R. and Medoff, J. (1984). *What Do Unions Do?* New York: Basic Books.

Freeman, R. and Lazear, E. (1995). "An Economic Analysis of Works Councils." In Rogers, J., and Streeck, W. (eds.), *Works Councils: Consultation, Representation, Cooperation.* Chicago: University of Chicago Press, pp. 27–50.

Global Competitiveness Report . (1999). Geneva: World Economic Forum.

Hamill, J. (1984). "Labour Relations Decision Making within Multinational Corporations." *Industrial Relations Journal* 15 (2), pp. 30–34.

Heenan, D. A. and Perlmutter, H. V. (1979). *Multinational Organization Development.* Reading, Mass.: AddisonWesley.

Human Development Report. (1994). United Nations Development Programme. New York: Oxford University Press.

Hyman, R. (1994). "Industrial Relations in Western Europe: An Era of Ambiguity?" *Industrial Relations* 33,pp. 1–24.

ILO. World Labour Report. (1995, 1997-1998). Geneva: ILO Publications.

Martinez Lucio, M. and Weston, S. (1994). "New Management Practices in a Multinational Corporation: Restructuring of Worker Representation and Rights?" *Industrial Relations Journal* 25, pp. 110–21.

OECD Labour Market Statistics. (2001). CD-ROM. Paris: OECD Paris Center.

Purcell, W., Nicholas, S., Merrett, D., and Whitwell, G. (1999). "The Transfer of Human Resource and Management Practice by Japanese Multinationals to Australia: Do Industry, Size and Experience Matter?" *The International Journal of Human Resource Management* 10 (1), pp. 72–88.

Rogers, J. and Streeck, W. (1994). "Workplace Representation Overseas: The Works Councils Story." In Freeman, R. (ed.), *Working under Different Rules* New York: Russell Sage Foundation, pp. 97–156.

Schuler, R. S., Dowling, P. J. and De Cieri, H. (1993). "An Integrative Framework of Strategic International Human Resource Management." *Journal of Management* 19 (2), pp. 419–59.

Social Indicators of Development. (2001). World Bank, www.ciesin.org/IC/wbank.

Taylor, S., Beechler, S., and Napier, N. (1996). "Toward an Integrative Model of Strategic International Human Resource Management." *Academy of Management Review* 21 (4), pp. 959–85.

5

The Effect of Different Industrial Relations Systems in the United States and the European Union on Foreign Direct Investment Flows

Morris Kleiner and Hwikwon Ham

In the preceding chapter, Cooke summarized the findings of research on the effects of various industrial relations (IR) system factors on foreign direct investment (FDI), showing that such factors have had important independent and additive effects on FDI. We next examine the influence of these kinds of factors on FDI but as a system rather than as a set of independent factors. Our fundamental proposition is that multinational company (MNC) investment decisions are based on fairly strong impressions of significant differences in IR systems in the whole and less so on differences in selected IR factors. By studying the effects of these kinds of variables in combination as a system, we can also capture the total net effect of these variables on FDI, including interaction effects among salient variables.

The emerging broader debate over appropriate policies governing labor markets in a global economic environment, furthermore, can be more fully informed by considering policy alternatives regarding the full system of IR policies and practices. Labor and human rights activists as well as politicians have become ever more concerned about the employment consequences and the appropriate role for government regulation of trade and the international movement of investment capital. The passion that these policy issues stir is witnessed in the protests staged at meetings of the World Trade Organization (WTO), the World Bank, and the International Monetary Fund. Often asked are questions about who benefits and who loses from international movements of capital and the determining factors of these movements across countries. An integral part of the controversy often focuses on the role of institutions in labor markets, in particular with regard to both the efficiency and equity effects of unions and government policies that enhance compensation and reduce employer flexibility in labor markets.

Given the increasingly competitive market for international trade and growth in the movement of international capital over the past decade, nations competing for international investments are increasingly concerned about developing and maintaining the appropriate economic climate for sustaining or creating employment opportunities (see Chapter 2). As reviewed in Chapter 4, MNCs have invested less in countries having national or industry-wide methods of wage determination, restrictions on the allocation of labor, works council policies, and higher levels of unionization and strike activity. Hence, policymakers have reason to reexamine and evaluate their IR systems.

Herein, we examine the role of the IR system and climate on both investing nations and countries receiving those investments. First, we synthesize the literature regarding the conceptualization of IR systems and make the case that differences in IR systems affect MNC FDI decision making. Second, we construct a composite scale of IR systems to illustrate the distinct and substantial difference between the U.S. and European Union (EU) IR systems. Third, we describe trends in FDI inflows between the United States and the EU and then analyze the effects of differences in IR systems on these FDI trends.

IR SYSTEMS AND MNC INVESTMENT DECISIONS

The general economic principle that motivates companies to invest abroad is the maximization of the present value of long-term profits. American companies, which operate in a less restrictive labor market, may be more closely guided by this principle than companies from EU countries, where a social contract between labor and management may modify solely private income-maximizing behavior (Kleiner and Ay, 1996). The economic returns to FDI, nonetheless, can be considered within the context of labor and other costs and returns. To the extent that companies in a country observe that relative labor costs and marginal products differ across countries, they have reason to invest or disinvest across those countries. To the degree that U.S. companies view the EU as a relatively high labor cost location due to its social contract, restrictions on management's ability to allocate labor or overall labor costs, U.S. FDI in the EU will be relatively low. To the degree that firms in the EU view the United States (with its relatively low direct and indirect social labor costs and largely union-free environment) as a good place to invest relative to other nations, then FDI in the United States will be relatively high. To the extent that labor productivity in EU countries does not offset higher labor costs, moreover, companies in the EU can be expected to invest even more in other countries, including the United States. In sum, market opportunities and relative factor costs and productivity in both the location of origin and destination are assumed to be important in the determination of FDI flows.

Whereas labor economists generally study the role of labor as a critical single factor of production in an economy (usually in the form of wages, the marginal product of labor, or unit labor costs), IR scholars usually study the role of labor in society as a system of compensation, productivity, workplace practices, and institutions. From the IR perspective, the labor economics approach is too narrow since it reflects only the view that supply and demand factors in the labor market are essential (Kaufman, 1988). The notion of an IR system has long been one of the basic theoretical concepts of the field, especially since the mid-1950s, following the publication of Dunlop's *Industrial Relations Systems* (1993). As conceptualized by Dunlop, IR systems comprise actors pursuing their respective objectives within a broader political and economic context, the outcome of which is a "web of rules" governing the workplace and labor market. The primary actors are workers and their hierarchies, managers and their hierarchies, and government policymakers and regulators. Embedded in an economic marketplace and political system, these actors pursue explicit and implicit rules and arrangements that govern industrial relations activity in the workplace and the respective roles of the actors within the broader system. An overarching theme within Dunlop's model, moreover, is that the actors and broader economic and political systems are interdependent, influencing each other and determining the outcomes of the system as a whole. In citing Slichter (1955), Dunlop suggests that "arrangements in the field of industrial relations may be regarded as a system in the sense that each of them more or less intimately affects each of the others so that they constitute a group of arrangements for dealing with certain matters and are collectively responsible for certain results." (Slichter, 1955: 168).

More recent analyses have drawn on the concept of IR systems in explaining various labor–management arrangements and labor market outcomes. For example, Cooke's (1990) conceptualization of cooperative vis-à-vis adversarial labor–management relations is dependent on both the relative and total power of companies and unions. Underlying his model are sources of power, which are largely a function of IR systems as framed by Dunlop. Freeman's (2000) comparative analysis of the role of labor market institutions on economic efficiency is similarly based on a holistic treatment of institutions, and on an integral set of laws and customs. In his analysis of the effects of different models of labor market institutions on economic efficiency, he assumes that there are inherent trade-offs between different types of labor market institutions, such as in wage and workforce allocation policies. In one model developed, he assumes, furthermore, that there are trade-offs between different types of labor market institutions and levels of economic efficiency. However, in other models of the labor market there can be multiple equilibrium, with many different systems of labor market institutions leading to optimal levels of economic efficiency. Within such models, the trade-off between economic efficiency and equity (e.g., reducing income inequality) is small; that is, large differences in equity lead to small changes in efficiency.

Drawing on these previous analyses of IR systems, we attempt to operationalize this concept for our purposes by creating a composite measure that reasonably distinguishes the U.S. IR system from other national IR systems. If differences in IR systems between countries are distinctive, one would hypothesize that business decision makers would behave as if they were important in making decisions to invest across countries. Consistent with the labor economist's perspective of the effects of any single variable such as wages on given outcomes, small differences may not matter much (Freeman and Katz, 1995). Large, systematic differences in IR systems, on the other hand, are likely to have substantial influence on FDI decisions. Therefore, we evaluate next whether or not there are such large differences in IR systems between the United States and EU countries.

MEASURING IR SYSTEM DIFFERENCES AND ASSESSING THEIR EFFECTS ON FDI FLOWS

Toward operationalizing differences in IR systems, we assume that there is an underlying latent structure for IR systems, ranging from more restrictive IR policies and practices to more lenient ones from management's perspective. Reported in Table 5.1 are five IR system variables that we use to construct a composite scale of differences in IR systems. Included are the average extent of union membership over the 1984–1992 period, union coverage rates for 1990, the average incidence of strike activity over the 1982–1991 period, centralization of bargaining, and estimates of worker representation. Since there can be substantial differences in union membership and collective bargaining coverage rates, we include both in Table 5.1. Our measure of bargaining centralization reflects the extent to which there is local or national wage bargaining based on measures developed by Calmfors and Drifill (1988), as well as by Traxler and Kittel (2000). Our estimates of worker representation are based on the interaction of the level of unionization and the existence of a detailed works council provision that covers a substantial proportion of the workforce (Kleiner and Ay, 1996).

Provided in the last column of Table 5.1 is a summated rating scale, which provides an aggregate measure of the IR system constraints on employers doing business in the countries included in the table. This summated rating scale is an additive one that measures the intensity of each factor included and aggregates these factors into one scale (Bartholomew, 1996). First, the variables in the table were subdivided into five discrete categories and given equal weights of 1. A score for each variable was then created, with a score of 5 depicting the greatest effect on reducing labor market flexibility and a score of 1 depicting the least effect. The extent of unionization variable was based on 20 percent intervals, wherein countries with penetration rates of 20 percent or lower, for example, were given a score of 1, and countries with penetration rates above 80 percent were given a score of 5. In creating this 1–5 score for union penetration, we used union contract coverage rates, except for Greece, Ireland, Portugal, and Spain, for which contract coverage rates are unavailable. For these four countries, we based the 1–5 union penetration score on the union density figures reported in Table 5.1. Similarly, the 1–5 point score depicting the degree of strike activity is based on five intervals of 100 days lost per year per 1,000 workers. Hence, for countries in which lost days averaged less than 100 over the

Table 5.1
EU/U.S. Industrial Relations Institutions

Country	Union Density[1]	Union Cover[2]	Strike Intens[3]	Cent Negot[4]	Workers' Rep[5]	Summated Rating
Belgium	55	90	45	3	2	11
Denmark	76	74	143	4	3	13
France	16	92	64	2	1	9
Germany	36	82	31	4	2	11
Greece	32	--	3630	4	1	12
Ireland[6]	62	--	318	5	5	18
Italy	44	83	492	2	4	16
Netherlands	30	71	20	4	1	10
Portugal	47	--	106	3	2	10
Spain	18	--	582	2	1	9
United Kingdom	46	47	272	2	4	12
EU Average[7]	35	63	328	3	2	11
United States	15	18	58	1	1	4

Sources:

[1,2] Golden, Wallerstein, and Lange Dataset (Golden, Wallerstein, and Wallerstein, 1998).

[3] ILO LABORSTA. Days lost by work stoppages per 1,000 workers averaged over the 1985-1995 period.

[4] Calmfors and Driffill (1998) (1 is the least and 5 is the most).

[5] Kleiner and Ay (1996) (1 is the least and 5 is the most).

[6] Bognanno, Keane, and Yang (1998).

[7] Weighted average of all 11 countries. Weight is generated using the total population in 1995.

1985–1995 period, the country was given a "lost days" score of 1; countries that averaged more than 400 lost days were given a score of 5. Although there has been some controversy regarding the validity of using the level of cross-country strike data, this information, nonetheless, is viewed as important by managers (Beggs and Chapman, 1987).

Our 1–5 point scores for "bargaining centralization" and "workers' representation" are based on scales that had been previously developed for other analyses. The "bargaining centralization" scale is based on both the degree to which there is government involvement in wage negotiations and whether wage negotiations are generally conducted at the national level or at the firm or establishment level (Calmfors and Driffill, 1998). The higher the score, the greater the degree of government involvement and the more centralized the level of wage negotiations. The "worker representation" scale is a multiple of the level of union penetration and the extent to which works councils have been established in a country (Kleiner and Ay, 1996). The higher the score, the greater the extent to which workers in a country have both union and works council representation.

On adding these four scores for union penetration, lost days, bargaining centralization, and workers' representation, a composite "summated rating" was created. As shown in Table 5.1, these summated ratings ranged from a low of 4 for the United States (making its IR system the most attractive to MNCs) to a high of 18 for Ireland (making its IR system the least attractive to MNCs). For Ireland, factors such as language and access to EU markets otherwise make it attractive for U.S. investment, which may serve to counterbalance the negative effects of potential labor market rigidities from management's perspective.

The data show a clear variation in the types of labor market institutions between the United States and EU countries. Relative to EU countries, the United States epitomizes the "free" labor market from a management perspective. Both union membership and union coverage are clearly among the lowest across countries. Although not the lowest, strike activity is relatively low in comparison to that in most EU countries. In addition, the United States has the lowest level of bargaining centralization and the lowest degree of employee representation. Using our summated rating scale scores, weighted by population in each of the EU countries, we calculate an overall average score for IR systems constraints in the EU. Although this average summary rating is clearly approximate, the EU average is almost three times the value estimated for the United States.

Not directly captured in our scaling but, nonetheless, important in comparing the U.S. to EU IR systems are several additional distinctions that generally reinforce the conclusion that there are substantial differences between the U.S. and EU systems. In comparison to the United States, many EU countries also place greater restrictions on employers' freedom to lay off or dismiss employees, to hire temporary employees, and to set hours of work. In contrast to the United States, furthermore, governments in the EU often play active roles concerning wage setting, grievance handling, and employment security more generally. The U.S. system, however, does appear to be much more litigious than EU IR systems, especially with regard to protecting workers from discrimination based, for example, on race, gender, age, and disability. Court enforcement of these U.S. laws can lead to large class-action damage suits, resulting in sizable make-whole awards, punitive damages, and substantial litigation costs for large firms in particular. In spite of these potentially higher U.S. workplace litigation costs, the costs associated with the constraints placed on employers by the EU social contract appear to be substantially greater overall (Freeman, 2000).

Given the distinct and substantial differences between the U.S. and EU IR systems, MNCs in the EU should find the United States a more attractive investment location than do MNCs in the United States regarding the EU. Furthermore, the greater degree to which IR systems in the EU lead to higher trade-offs of efficiency outcomes for equity outcomes, the more likely MNCs will view the United States rather than the EU as the more attractive investment location. This central hypothesis, of course, assumes that the observed differences in labor constraints is an important consideration in FDI decisions. The evidence fairly clearly suggests that it is.

First, we find support for such an assumption based on exploratory interviews with U.S. and German business executives in the chemical and automotive industries.[1] In general, U.S. executives reported that labor costs and restrictions on their freedom to allocate resources at the site or company-wide levels were major impediments to maximizing efficiency in Europe. Among German executives, many expressed envy of the American system marked, in particular, by low union penetration and coverage rates, opportunities to limit contract negotiations to the plant level, and freedom to hire and lay off workers as needed. Mercedes Benz executives also noted their ability to put added pressure on local German unions as a consequence of building new plants in regions of the United States where wages and union penetration are relatively low.

Second, the trends in FDI flows between the United States and EU show a distinct pattern consistent with the hypothesis that differences in labor constraints are associated with FDI decisions. Charted in Figure 5.1 are the annual percentages of total net FDI inflows between the United States and the EU over the 1985–1995 period. As illustrated, roughly 10 percent of the total investment flows to EU countries listed in Table 5.1 came from the United States. In contrast, about 35 percent of the total FDI flows to the United States came from the EU. Since the EU and United States are fairly comparable in terms of population and standards of living, it would appear that the United States has been viewed by MNCs in the EU as a more attractive FDI host than the EU has to U.S. MNCs.

Third, the evidence from estimating a multivariate model further supports our central hypothesis. Specifically, we specified a model using our measure of IR system constraint scaling described earlier to explain FDI flows. The dependent variable was measured as the proportion of annual total FDI made by countries over the 1985–1995 period. To increase the power of our estimates, however, we include annual FDI flows separately for 20 Organization for Economic Cooperation and Development (OECD)-member countries in our estimates. In order to estimate the average independent effects of IR system differences on these FDI flows, we controlled for a wide range of other variables identified in the literature as also likely to influence FDI decision making (see Chapter 4). These additional variables included measures of the cost of capital, wage differences, unemployment, education, language differences, and gross domestic product (GDP) per capita. Estimated as such, we found that differences in IR systems (as measured herein) have had a statistically significant effect on explaining the variation in FDI flows across countries. In particular,

Figure 5.1
US/ EU FDI Inflows

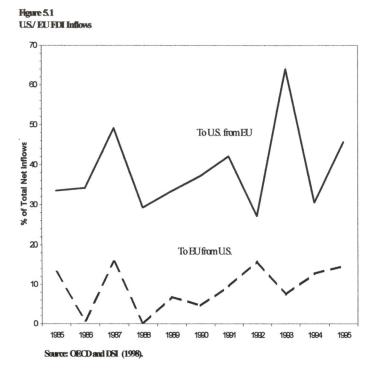

Source: OECD and DSI (1998).

we found that for every one-standard-deviation increase in our IR system constraint scale (i.e., the summated rating scale equivalent to the one reported in Table 5.1), the proportion of FDI flowing to countries was, on average, reduced by 1.5 percent, which is equal to a loss of approximately U.S. (1990) $1.8 billion. [2]

SUMMARY AND CONCLUSION

In this analysis, we first made a case for examining the effects of IR systems treated as a whole (rather than a set of strictly independent variables) on FDI decision making. At the heart of our case is the proposition that it is the broader IR system that matters to both potential investors and policymakers. On comparing the combination of several salient measures of labor market institutions (based on unionization rates, strike intensity, the centralization of collective bargaining, and degree of overall employee representation), we show distinct differences between the U.S. and EU IR systems. Indeed, based on our scaling of differences, European IR systems place substantially greater constraints in total on employers than does the American IR system.

Because the overall difference in IR system constraints on employer flexibility between the United States and EU are so substantial, there is reason to believe that these institutional differences as a whole influence where and how much profit-maximizing executives choose to invest abroad. Our exploratory interviews with both German and U.S. company executives clearly reinforce such an argument. In addition, a simple tracing of FDI flows from Europe to the United States and from the United States to Europe over the 1985–1995 period shows distinctly different FDI propensities, with MNCs from the United States expending much smaller shares of total FDI in the EU than MNCs from the EU expending in the United States. Finally, on estimating a model that controls for variables that might otherwise explain such sharply different FDI patterns, we infer from our estimates that differences in IR systems have had a significant and, arguably, sizable effect on FDI. Although different from previous analyses that have examined the independent, additive effects on FDI of various variables underlying IR systems (see Chapter 4), our results, which are based on a composite measure of IR systems, are fully consistent with the general implications of previous empirical studies. We conclude, therefore, that IR systems clearly matter to profit-maximizing executives in choosing where and how much to invest abroad.

Of course, differences in IR systems also clearly matter to union leaders and policymakers. In pursuing their interests to maximize gains for members, European union leaders have little or no interest in relaxing the constraints that they can impose on management (as can be derived from widespread representation, freedom to withdraw labor, and centralized bargaining structures). Given the threat that employers will increasingly move domestic investment abroad in the search for more flexible IR systems, nonetheless, we can expect that union leaders will increasingly forge transnational partnerships or alliances with other unions. Indeed, we are beginning to see a number of such strategic responses. For example, U.S. and EU commercial pilots have formed transnational alliances among unions in an effort to negotiate comparable salaries across regions of the world. Likewise, union leaders representing employees at DaimlerChrysler in Germany and the United States have met to establish common areas of interest for collective bargaining in their respective locations. In addition, several authors in this volume report on similar transnational union strategies being formed. If these kinds of efforts prove successful at diminishing the effects of different IR systems on workplace outcomes, the effect of IR systems on FDI in the future will likely narrow.

Given the stronger emphasis on achieving social equity vis-à-vis achieving economic efficiency in most European IR systems relative to the American IR system, EU countries have sacrificed greater FDI inflow and encouraged greater FDI outflow than the United States. EU policymakers interested in reversing these FDI flows in their desire to increase or otherwise maintain existing employment opportunities face two fundamental choices. Policymakers either must (1) trade off some equity outcomes for efficiency outcomes or (2) find ways to increase efficiency outcomes without diminishing equity outcomes. The first option may simply not be an acceptable alternative to policymakers. Providing workers with an IR environment in which they have greater say in the workplace and greater influence on wages and benefits (i.e., greater equity) may be worth the loss in efficiency and the unintended consequence of reduced investment. As pointed out earlier, moreover, achieving significant improvements in efficiency is likely to require substantial reductions in equity. The second option would require policymakers to restructure their IR systems in ways that maintain current equity outcomes but at the same time increase productivity and flexibility to achieve efficiency levels comparable to the U.S. IR system. Either option, we conclude, presents policymakers with an enormous challenge.

NOTES

1. We conducted two-hour structured interviews with senior executives at the headquarters of two multinational chemical manufacturing companies in both the United States and Germany. We also conducted two sets of interviews with executives of large German auto firms. This study was funded in part by the Austrian Ministry of Science and Transportation, but the views expressed are those of the authors only.

2. The detailed results of this estimation are available on request to the authors.

REFERENCES

Bartholomew, D. (1996). *The Statistical Approach to Social Measurement.* London: Academic Press.
Beggs, J. J. and Chapman, B. J. (1987). "Declining Strike Activity in Australia1983–85: An International Phenomenon?" *Economic Record* 63 (183), pp. 330–39.
Bognanno, M. F., Keane, M. P., and Yang, D. (1998). "The Influence of Wages and Industrial Relations Environments on the Production Location Decisions of US Multinational Corporations." Working paper, Industrial Relations Center, University of Minnesota.
Calmfors, L. and Driffill, J. (1988). "Bargaining Structure, Corporation and Macroeconomic Performance." *Economic Policy*, April, pp. 14–61.
Cooke, W. (1990). *Labor-Management Cooperation: New Partnerships or Going in Circles?* Kalamazoo, MI: Upjohn Institute for Employment Research.
Cooke, W. (1997). "The Influence of Industrial Relations Factors on U.S. Foreign Direct Investment Abroad." *Industrial and Labor Relations Review* 50 (1), pp. 3–17.
Cooke W. (2001). "The Effects of Labour Costs and Workplace Constraints on Foreign Direct Investment among Highly Industrialized Countries." *International Journal of Human Resource Management* 12 (5), pp. 697–716.
Cooke, W. and Noble, D. (1998). "Industrial Relations Systems and U.S. Foreign Direct Investment Abroad." *British Journal of Industrial Relations* 51 (2), pp.171–86.
Commons, J. R. (1934). *Institutional Economics.* New York: Macmillan.
Dunlop, J. T. (1958). *Industrial Relations Systems.* Boston: Harvard Business School Press.
Freeman, R. B. (2000). "Single Peaked vs. Diversified Capitalism: The Relation between Economic Institutions and Outcomes." NBER Working paper, w7556.

Freeman, R. B. and Katz, L. F. (1995). *Differences and Changes in Wage Structures.* Chicago: University of Chicago Press.

Golden, M., Wallerstein, P. and Wallerstein, M. (1998). *Union Centralization among Advanced Industrial Societies: An Empirical Study.* http://shelley.sscnet.ucla. edu/data.

Hufbauer, G. C. (1975). "The Multinational Corporation and Direct Investment." In Kenen, P. B. (ed.), *International Trade and Finance: Frontiers for Research.* Cambridge: Cambridge University Press, pp. 253–319.

ILO, Bureau of Statistics. LABORSTA.   http://www.ilo.org/public/English/support/lib/ dblist.htm.

Kaufman, B. (1988). "The Postwar View of Labor Markets and Wage Determination." In Kaufman, B. (ed.), *How Labor Markets Work.* Lexington, MA: D. C. Heath, pp. 145–204.

Kleiner, M. M. and Ay, C. R. (1996). "Unionization, Employee Representation, and Economic Performance: Comparisons among OECD Nations." *Advances in Industrial and Labor Relations* 7, pp. 97–121.

OECD. (1991). "Trends in Trade Union Membership." *Employment Outlook.* Paris: Organization for Economic Cooperation and Development, pp. 97–134.

OECD. (1994). "Collective Bargaining: Levels and Coverage." *Employment Outlook.* Paris: Organization for Economic Cooperation and Development, pp. 167–194.

OECD. (1997). "Economic Performance and the Structure of Collective Bargaining." *Employment Outlook.* Paris: Organization for Economic Cooperation and Development, pp. 63–92.

OECD and DSI. (1998). Data Service. *OECD Statistical Compendium*: CD-ROM.

Okun, A. M. (1975). *Equality and Efficiency, the Big Tradeoff.* Washington, D.C.: Brookings Institution.

Slichter, S. (1955). *Proceedings of the Eighth Annual Meeting of the American Academy of Arbitrators.* Boston: Bureau of National Affairs, pp. 167–86.

Traxler, F. and Bernard, K. (2000). "The Bargaining Systems and Performance: A Comparison of 18 OECD Countries." *Comparative Political Studies* 33 (9), pp. 1154–90.

Part II

Multinational Company Human Resource Management and Labor Relations Strategies

6

A Process Model of Strategic HRM/LR Change in MNCs: The Case of AT&T and NCR in the United Kingdom

Graeme Martin, Phillip Beaumont, and Judy Pate

The ways in which multinational companies (MNCs) configure and control their overseas operations has become a matter of some debate in recent years (Belanger, et al., 1999; Birkinshaw and Hood, 1997; Clegg, Ibarra-Colado, and Beuno-Rodriquez, 1999). As Taggart (1998) and others have pointed out, various models of MNC corporate strategy have been developed to answer the critical and sometimes antithetical problems of maintaining global cost advantages, local differentiation, and knowledge transfer and development among subsidiaries (Bartlett and Ghoshal, 1995). Common to most of these models, however, is the key role of the corporate center in shaping the strategic direction and strategic change programs in their subsidiaries, either directly as the source of innovations or indirectly by explicitly or tacitly structuring an agenda for acceptable human resource management and labor relations (HRM/LR) change strategies by subsidiaries.

Frequently, such change programs either have sought to modify the culture of subsidiaries through vision and values programs (Buller and McEvoy, 1999; Colville, Waterman, and Weick, 1999), with new or reformed HRM/LR policies being assigned a central role in normative control (Legge, 1995; Mabey and Salaman, 1995) or else have sought to transfer organizational HRM/LR best practices through internal benchmarking exercises (Kostova, 1999; Martin and Beaumont, 1998). These programs, however, have been criticized for their questionable "culture-free" operating assumptions (Cray and Mallory, 1998) and, in the case of culture change, their questionable ethical assumptions (Alvesson, 1993; McKinlay and Starkey, 1997). In addition, practitioners have been skeptical of their ability to deliver on the promises made for them (Harris and Ogbonna, 1998; Sparrow, 1998; Abrahamson and Fairchild, 1999).

Often, these criticisms arise because subsidiary line and human resource managers lack the incentive and/or ability to comply with headquarters' wishes

(Martin and Beaumont, 1999). Thus, for example, there is increasing evidence that certain types of overseas subsidiaries have been encouraged or allowed to become more autonomous (Birkinshaw and Hood, 1997) and in doing so, have become more resource-independent. Such units are usually under less pressure to comply with headquarters' directives than those subsidiaries that rely heavily on the center for finance and other key resources. At the same time, the influential business systems/institutionalist perspective (Guillen, 1998; Whitley, 1992) has shown how local subsidiaries may lack the ability to respond because of their embeddedness in developing host country product and labor market contexts, the influence of the host country state and financial markets, and other features of the host country national business system such as the historical relationships between capital and labor and the nature of the education and training.

While accepting the skepticism of the business systems perspective on the transfer of practices between different institutional contexts, clearly MNCs attempt to diffuse best practice, and some are relatively successful in doing so. Thus, an important theoretical and practical question for academics and human resource managers in MNCs is: What does it take to deliver a coherent and acceptable corporate-wide strategic HRM/LR change initiative, while simultaneously allowing for differential subsidiary development over time as a source of strategic change? In this chapter we answer that question by drawing on a previously developed process model of strategic HRM/LR change in MNCs (Martin and Beaumont, 2001) that identifies the factors and processes contributing to successful change. Second, we illustrate a number of the model's key features using a case study of a program of radical culture change launched by the headquarters of U.S.-owned AT&T by considering its response to, and the impact of, its program on one of its leading subsidiaries, NCR in the United Kingdom.   Third, we conclude with some lessons about the diffusion of universal programs of change throughout an MNC's international operations.

A MODEL OF STRATEGIC HRM/LR CHANGE

A number of highly useful frameworks for analyzing strategic change have been developed (e.g., Rajagopalan and Spreitzer, 1996; Pettigrew and Whipp, 1991; Pettigrew, 1997). These frameworks, however, have not been specifically designed with MNCs in mind, particularly with respect to problems posed by the crossborder diffusion of ideas among multiple layers of management. One valuable framework that has been designed specifically to analyze factors that contribute to success of the transnational transfer of organizational practices within MNCs is Kostova's (1999). Her framework, however, relies heavily on institutional theory and, while sympathetic to the notion of change, is redolent of theories that focus on "context" and "states" (Langley, 1999), which do not convey a sense of temporal dynamism or "changefulness" (Chia, 1999).

Accordingly, in a recent analysis (Martin and Beaumont, 2001) we synthesized diverse strands of literature on strategic change, institutional theory, and organizational discourse to provide a framework (see Figure 6.1) that acknowledges (1) the distinction between corporate level decision making and acceptance by subsidiary managers and employees and (2) significant stages for data collection and analysis of the process of diffusing and accepting the message of strategic change (Dawson, 1994). We also argue that the framework could be used to generate propositions about the likely organizational outcomes of HRM/LR changes, which can be tested for analytical generalization (Yin, 1994; Gummesson, 2000) using case study research.

Readers, nonetheless, should note two points. First, we do not make a distinction in the model between the corporate center and subsidiary units concerning the source of ideas for strategic HRM/LR change programs. As developed by Edwards (1998) and Ferner (2000), the developing relations in MNCs suggest that innovations in strategy may well arise in key subsidiaries that subsequently become corporate-wide policy. Second, in the interests of the trade-off in theory building between accuracy and simplification (Weick, 1999), our model is based on an idealized process theory of successful HRM/LR change that is unlikely to be achieved in reality. Our model's real contribution is to highlight the complex set of events, activities, discursive practices, emotions, reactions, and so on that help explain (1) what would be needed for successful HRM/LR change to occur and, in turn, (2) why most HRM/LR change initiatives are rarely ever fully successful or end in total failure. The key features of the model are as follows:

1. There is contextual embeddedness of HRM/LR change, of which receptive contexts for change are especially important (Pettigrew, Ferlie, and McKee, 1992; Ferner, 2000). Elaborating on Kostova's (1999) analysis of MNCs, four levels of context have been identified: the social, the outer organizational context, the inner organizational context, and the relational context. It is important to note that the process aspects of the model (the various stages, patterns of events, and communicative practices) are embedded in these changing contexts over time. This is particularly true of major labor relations changes, for example, decisions by MNCs to recognize unions for collective bargaining, which are inevitably bound up in different legislative practices and value systems concerning worker collectivism.

2. There is a conception stage, during which new HRM/LR strategies and discourse are developed. Note that the process model allows for two-way development of the strategic HRM/LR changes, in which the ideas are just as likely to come from subsidiary line and HRM/LR managers. It is recognized, however, that corporate support, adoption, and sponsorship of the change discourse and programs are a necessary, though not sufficient, condition of further implementation.

3. For the messages of change to progress to the transition stage, credible and novel culture changes and HRM/LR strategies (occurring in communicative practices) have to be read positively by subsidiary and other corporate-level managers.

**Figure 6.1 Integrating Institutional Theory and Strategic Discourse:
A Process Model of the Institutionalization of Strategic HRM/LR Change in MNCs**

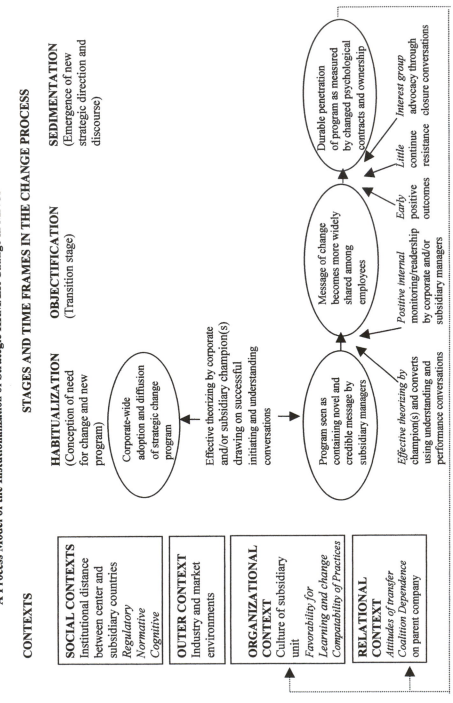

4. For the message of change to continue to progress toward the sedimentation stage, where a new strategic discourse has taken root, the communication of early positive outcomes, supported by evidence of such benefits, is necessary to overcome continued resistance or benign neglect of the change program.

5. There is an important feedback process in which the outcomes of strategic HRM/LR innovations (particularly with regard to employee psychological contracts, the capacity of employees to change, and employee favorability toward change) loop back into current and future contexts.

Key Propositions

We have argued that our process model can be used as the basis for more complex theory building and to generate hypotheses or practical propositions about the likely success of change strategies. These propositions are presented next.

The Conception Stage

Proposition 1. Without a convincing discourse of change, effectively theorized by corporate or midlevel management champions, corporate-wide adoption and diffusion of strategic HRM/LR change initiatives are unlikely to progress beyond the conception stage.

Proposition 2. Such discourse and stories generated by champions should draw on realistic initiating (and understanding conversations, including those that enhance the credibility and novelty of the assertions, declarations, and promises made at the outset, the rationale and evidence used to support these assertions, etc.), and the actions and benefits that will result from achieving the given changes.

Proposition 3. The messages of change as set out by the champions have to be read as containing a credible and novel message by lower-level (especially HRM/LR) managers to secure their acceptance to the change program.

The Transition Stage

Proposition 4. In the absence of a credible and novel message, other corporate and middle managers not yet involved in the change process are unlikely to have the incentive to read the story in a positive light and may look for reasons that the changes should be discontinued, resisted, or ignored.

Proposition 5. For the new discourse of change and its material realities to become more widely shared by employees at all levels in the organization, the champions of change, aided by their middle management converts, have to continue to draw on "new understanding" conversations and promises or directives that will engage or compel most employees to accept strategic change.

Proposition 6. For change to progress toward the sedimentation stage, there have to be evidence and publicity of early victories for managers and evidence and publicity of positive outcomes for the majority of employees.

Proposition 7. The champions of HRM/LR change have to continue to embed change in the organization by drawing on closure conversations intended to signify the success of these intermediate positive outcomes.

The Emergence of a New Strategic HRM/LR Discourse
Proposition 8. The extent to which strategic change is embedded in the organization can be measured by the degree of penetration and durability of changes in the attitudinal and behavioral dimensions of the outcomes of employee psychological contracts.

CASE STUDY EVIDENCE

To illustrate many of the features of our model and the propositions derived from it, we draw on case study data of a major attempt at culture change conducted by a U.S. MNC in one of its most successful subsidiaries in the United Kingdom.

Method

The case study is set during AT&T's brief ownership of the Ohio-based NCR Corporation during the early 1990s and involves the introduction of a major program of corporate culture change instituted by AT&T to integrate NCR into the wider AT&T empire. We have examined the research question from the perspective of the Scottish subsidiary of the then newly formed AT&T Global Products (the old NCR corporation). This subsidiary, based in Dundee, Scotland, was a good example of how a subsidiary, over time, could accumulate specific resources and capabilities, making it relatively resource-independent from NCR headquarters in Dayton, Ohio, and, subsequently, from AT&T's headquarters.

Our data have been collected over a period of four years of intermittent research in the U.K. plant and draw on earlier work by the present authors. To gain a measure of changes in the key dimensions of the culture change program, we have used secondary data from the corporate-wide employee surveys that were first conducted just prior to AT&T's acquisition of NCR. These surveys, which have undergone a series of adaptations to reflect the local language of the U.K. plant and the changing issues of the company as a whole, were conducted every six months with all of its 1,500 employees. It is important to note that between 1993 and 1997, results from the surveys were also used to reward managers, accounting for approximately 25 percent of their bonuses. While these data have been invaluable in providing a longitudinal set of reference points for our investigation, they are subject to at least three limitations: (1) changes in question content over the period 1993–1997, so that it was not always possible to compare "like with like" on certain key elements of the culture change program, (2) the way in which the data were made available to us in an already processed form, which meant that we were unable to produce tests of association between important explanatory variables, and (3) the broader shortcomings of surveys as a means of gaining insights into essentially subjective concepts (e.g., Despres, 1995) and of coping with questions of context.

To overcome some of the limitations associated with surveys and to provide an essentially interpretivist account of the effects of strategy storytelling, we also conducted a series of semistructured interviews during March-April 1998 with nine HRM/LR, senior and middle managers (formerly called "coaches") and 14 technical and shop-floor staff (formerly called "associates"). The senior and middle managers, technical staff, and shop-floor respondents were chosen on a theoretical sampling basis, drawn from all sections of the plant (Miles and Huberman, 1994). While an interview guide was used, the interviews were largely unstructured, with participants making largely uninterrupted responses. The interview transcriptions were then closely examined for dominant themes related to our research questions. In essence, our intention was to use these accounts to allow respondents to *theorize* about their own experiences of culture change (Silverman, 1997).

Attempts at Universal Change and the Failure of Program Champions to Understand Historical and Contextual Factors

To illustrate the key features of our model, it is necessary to embed the change program in the developing historical context (Pettigrew, 1995) of the relationship between the Scottish plant and its U.S. parent organizations.

The Context for Change: Changing Fortunes of the U.K. Subsidiary and Growing Resource Independence from NCR

Our case-study plant began life as a subsidiary of NCR, a midwestern-based U.S. MNC that underwent significantly changed fortunes during the period 1945–1979. During this period, when the U.K. plant was largely used as a second-source manufacturing facility to U.S. plants, employment rose dramatically to 6,300 employees in 1970 and fell to 820 employees in 1980 following a decline in traditional markets. At that time, there were strong rumors that the plant was scheduled for closure.

However, by the time of the launch of the cultural change program in the mid-1990s, the fortunes of the Scottish subsidiary had turned around dramatically, associated with what came to be tacitly known locally as the "Fortress Dundee" policy, in which local management sought and fought for "independence through local success." By 1985, it had acquired a significant design and development facility and had become NCR's headquarters for the newly created Self Service and Financial Systems Division. In short, it had turned the tables on its U.S. sister plants and had become something of a cash cow for the U.S. parent company. The Scottish subsidiary consistently outperformed sister NCR plants in the United States and Canada as measured by rate of return on assets, which grew from 54 percent in 1984 to a yearly average of over 100 percent from 1987 to 1992. Currently, it is the world's leading designer and producer of automatic teller machines; employs some 1,700 assembly workers, managers, and design and development engineers (including the largest private sector development community in Scotland); and has won the "Best Factory in Britain" award on two occasions.

This brief history of the changing fortunes of the Scottish subsidiary shows how it had become increasingly independent of NCR corporate headquarters for resources (Kostova, 1999) and how managers in the Scottish subsidiary have been less receptive to an externally initiated change program (Kostova, 1999; Pettigrew et al., 1992). Moreover, there was a history of opposition or reluctant compliance in the local subsidiary to previous headquarters' initiatives regarding HRM/LR practices. Much of this reluctance stemmed from headquarters' unsympathetic attitudes toward trade unions, which frequently posed problems for the local management of the highly unionized subsidiary. This uneasy relationship between corporate and local subsidiary management had played itself out in various ways over time. In particular, there were local subsidiary criticism and reluctance to adopt certain heavily American HRM/LR practices (e.g., the content and terminology of employee attitude questionnaires), and there was corporate-level coolness toward certain homegrown initiatives in the Scottish subsidiary intended to forge a closer working relationship with its union representatives.

AT&T's Takeover and Its Culture Change Program

Initiating a hostile takeover bid in 1990, AT&T acquired the NCR Corporation in 1991, eventually renaming it AT&T(GIS). Initially, the headquarters management of AT&T followed a financial control strategy, allowing the Scottish plant to function as a semiindependent unit, largely because its product range fell outside of top management's main interests. However, after an agreed period of two years of little or no intervention, AT&T's corporate management team sought to engineer a radical change throughout the corporation by attempting to pursue a globalization strategy integrating all businesses and units into a relatively homogeneous organization. This radical change was viewed as necessary by headquarters because of the large financial losses incurred by virtually every business unit in AT&T(GIS), apart, that is, from the Scottish subsidiary.

AT&T's president brought in a new U.S.-based president for AT&T(GIS), largely based on his high-profile track record in turning around an ailing electrical contracting company and another AT&T unit. Strongly influenced by academic-consultant "gurus" (Belasco and Stayer, 1993), the new president sought to reengineer AT&T(GIS) through a major attempt at cultural change. This reengineering process was marked by (1) the clearing out of many of the NCR management team, (2) the purging of AT&T(GIS) of its financial control focus, and (3) the introduction of a cultural change program that placed employees and customers at center stage. The program involved two central elements. The first was the "Common Bond," which included an ethical mission statement and set of working principles designed with the intention to empower employees and customers. The ethical and empowering facets of this program are worth emphasizing at this stage since it has been argued that the "mutuality model" of HRM/LR (based on treating people with respect) was more likely to lead employees to view the effort positively and to accept company actions that

Table 6. 1
Key Elements of the Cultural Change Program: "Opportunities, Vision, and Values"

---

1. "Common Bond" Values
    - respect for individuals
    - dedication to helping customers
    - highest standards of integrity
    - innovation
    - teamwork

2. Accompanying Education/Communication Sessions
    - opportunity and change: create an awareness of the forces of change and how each associate, by understanding the dynamics of change, could take advantage of the opportunities that arose
    - vision and direction forum: would ensure that all associates would understand, through interactive discussions, the major issues affecting the company

3. Supporting Actions
    - further attempts to flatten the organizational hierarchy
    - coach and associate labels assigned
    - casual dress policy introduced
    - introduction of diversity and harassment policies employee feedback sessions implemented based on repeated surveys
    - establishment of a 24-hour-a-day hot line to the U.S. president and Common Bond champion
    - introduction of a new company magazine

---

might have negative consequences for a minority of employees (Legge, 1998). Second, the program involved a further flattening of organizational structures and an attempt to reconstitute the more empowered workforce through, among other techniques, relabeling managers and supervisors as "coaches" and workers as "associates." Table 6.1 provides further details of the essentials of the cultural change program.

As a background to our subsequent empirical analysis, it is important to emphasize five key characteristics of the cultural change program:

1. The program was very much a personalized one that was driven by the new appointee as the U.S. president of AT&T(GIS) and the external academic consultant who worked closely with him. Although a small number of U.K. managers were incorporated into the design of the program, none of these were from the most important U.K. subsidiary on which this case is based.

2. The program was very much viewed by local management in the Scottish subsidiary as a U.S.-oriented program. This was because (1) it was driven by the two U.S. nationals from headquarters, (2) the language and content of the program were very American in nature, and (3) its track record of success was based on two U.S. organizations formerly managed by the new appointee.

3. This sense of U.S. parentage was markedly enhanced by an absence of prior consultation and discussion with local management in the Scottish subsidiary, apart from some HRM/LR staff. Quite simply, the views of the local chief executive officer (CEO) and many of his staff had not been sought with regard to the need for, and appropriateness of, such a change initiative in the Scottish cultural and operating context.

4. The president and lead consultant had set themselves very ambitious deadlines for launching the change program. The stipulated timetable was couched in months rather than years.

5. The president of AT&T(GIS), who championed the cultural change program, remained with the organization only for 18 months. Following his departure, his successor failed to continue to endorse the program.

The Reactions of Local Management and the Workforce to the Change Program

As we have suggested, the nature of the cultural change program and contextual factors (such as institutional distance and the organizational and relational context of the Scottish subsidiary) may have limited the incentive of local management to share the message of change and diffuse it throughout the plant. Our initial thoughts in this regard, however, run the risk of viewing local management as essentially a relatively homogeneous entity, in which all of local management either bought in or opposed the principles and content of the change program. Such an initial perspective would seem a somewhat oversimplified reflection of a more complex reality in that it does not take into account the all-important internal politics and divisions within local-level management (Purcell and Ahlstrand, 1994).

In fact, our interviews with managers in the Scottish subsidiary revealed, in keeping with this political perspective, some degree of variation in response to the principles and content of the cultural change program. For example, certain HRM/LR staff in the U.K. plant and U.K. head office were well disposed toward the program. In essence, it fitted in with their ideology of management. Thus, it was felt that the Common Bond would jointly raise the profile of human resources in the subsidiary's business development plans and also advance the career interests of those associated with the function. Fueled by some early enthusiasm from a minority of employees, moreover, some believed that the program was feeding through positively into the attitudes of significant groups of the workforce, with a consequent improvement in morale. In addition, younger managers in areas such as marketing and software development talked of the "electrical atmosphere" generated when the U.S. president walked into the room.[1]

In marked contrast, the manufacturing line managers whom we interviewed, in retrospect at least, were much less enthusiastic about the message of the program and its principal messenger. During our interviews with managers, four lines of criticism were voiced:

1. The official discourse of the culture change program, although designed to be "ethnoneutral," was seen to be overwhelmingly American in nature and inappropriate to the Scottish context and culture.[2] The voice used during the initiating conversations by program champions, particularly the company president, to deliver the message of the Common Bond generated a great deal of negative comment. The epic style of narrative used to create understanding of the program, furthermore, appeared to have undermined its aims. As a senior engineering manager commented: "I'm not saying I disagreed with the principles either; they were just common courtesy, common behavior. It was the way the message was delivered. The content was fine, there wasn't anything wrong with the message, it was the way it was delivered." Furthermore, the program was undermined by its U.S.-oriented, material symbolism, which was formalized through the use of differently colored cards to signify different levels of Common Bond violations.[3]

2. The perceived need for such a program was particularly resented, given that managers regarded themselves as already practicing commonsense principles such as "respect for individuals" and "dedication to helping customers." Messages concerning customers were seen as especially inappropriate, given the U.K. plant's outstanding financial performance and worldwide reputation for excellence in customer service.

3. Such a soft management approach was difficult to implement in practical, tangible terms and risked deprioritizing and undervaluing the pursuit of more rational financial and operational routes to improved performance. As the U.K. CEO put it: "It was like being asked to fly a plane on a wing and a prayer without having access to the aircraft's controls."

4. The program had cut across the further development of certain ongoing, homegrown HRM/LR initiatives in the Scottish subsidiary, such as a recently launched training and education initiative that was already proving popular with the local workforce and a "Vision and 10" values program introduced by the U.K. senior management team.

It comes as no surprise that the preceding arguments came from some of the more senior and long-serving managers in the Scottish subsidiary, since they had the most to lose from the threat to their identity from the change program (Schoenberger, 1997). Consequently, the weight of political forces and strength in the Scottish subsidiary were very much lined up against achieving a strong local management buy-in to the cultural change program. The majority of these managers regarded the story as neither particularly credible nor novel, despite (or because of) the theorizing by the program's champion, who insisted on senior managers in the U.K. plant speaking to the corporate voice and plan. Perhaps as significantly, these managers had not been involved in the design of the message, which was solely and literally a U.S. head office production, stage-managed in such a way as to provide a real sense of Hollywood-style epic theatre for the U.K. staff.

By and large, the response of shop-floor workers mirrored those of their managers, most workers claiming to have had little enthusiasm for, or interest in, the message of the Common Bond beyond the first few months of its existence. A small number of workers in assembly jobs, however, did see the program as providing them with a means of bringing about changes in the management of the company. Such sentiment was captured well by the following statement: "I really believed in it in the beginning. I thought there is no reason why this cannot work and if we can do this, pull it off as written down, we are going to make an improvement." In the majority of accounts, nonetheless, employees either were skeptical from the start or became disenchanted with the "halfhearted" local implementation of the program.

The reception of the message on the shop floor quickly came to reflect the views of their managers that the Common Bond was neither a credible nor a novel story, especially in the U.K. context. Assemblers, in particular (a dominant group in the factory), seemed to interpret the message as a crude attempt to impose an inappropriate set of American values on the factory. Indeed, any reception was likely to be lukewarm as a consequence of national stereotyping of Americans by Scottish workers. This line of argument from the workforce explaining the failure of the program figured prominently in most accounts but, as we shall argue later, may have hidden a more complex opposition to change.

Concerning the *materiality* (i.e., the formality and tangibility) of the message of the Common Bond, another assembler typified the views of those on the shop floor: "I don't think it affected the way people operated. If a manager is quite bolshie and shouts a lot, a bit of paper saying we all have a Common Bond isn't going to change the habits of a lifetime." A further factor in the program's lack of positive impact was the image of the champion held by the workforce, who saw him only on video.[4] He was seen by some as a rather comical figure and by others as a typical American evangelist, often in contrast to the U.K. CEO, who was generally held in high esteem by local employees.

Summarizing the case study data in line with the conception stage of our model, it is first clear that there was little local management buy-in to the story line of culture change. The interview data showed that the U.S. based program champion had a substantial negative effect on the credibility and novelty of the message of culture change. His claims to expertise and, thus, the right to impose top-down transformational change went largely unrecognized by the U.K. management team. Indeed, his role seems to have been counterproductive. According to the interviews with line managers and with the U.K.-based CEO of the plant, the local management team saw little that they could buy into that was new and that was going to improve the already highly successful plant. From the perspective of the U.K. managers, this lack of novelty appeared to be exacerbated by, and confused with, the eccentric voice and presentation style of the U.S. champions of change. Gradually, some of these key influencers became agnostics, either finding the message as insulting or, more significantly, attributing to it a negative commercial and organizational impact on the U.K. plant.

Viewed from a political perspective, it is clear that most managers in the U.K. plant had little incentive to change and had a strong measure of power or ability to block the changes being proposed, either through inaction or in the way that they transmitted the message down the line. Both facets of this political context can be sourced from the power that local managers already had, arising from their previously successful performance (Morgan, 1997) as well as their unwillingness to recognize the claims of expert power made by the U.S. champion of change. Therefore, we believe that the failure to create a strong local consensus was critical. The lack of impact of the program, in turn, can be explained largely by the U.S. president's manifest failure to collaborate with the U.K. managers and to build a powerful coalition in support of the change.

Effects on Workforce Attitudes

Concerning the *transition stage* of our model (which focuses on the wider acceptance of change among the workforce and the incentive and ability of local management to implement change), we expected to find that an ethically based story line would have a greater chance of acceptance by the U.K. workforce than a more utilitarian one. This expectation, however, was not borne out by some survey data regarding the Common Bond program (see Tables 6.2, 6.3). Indeed, the data show that there were significant negative changes in attitudes about key facets of the Common Bond and overall satisfaction with the company during the introduction of the Common Bond and the period immediately following its introduction (e.g., between 1993 and 1995 there were statistically significant declines in attitudes about how well the organization was doing in implementing respect for individuals, involvement, acting with integrity, and overall satisfaction with the company). The interview data suggest, furthermore, that so strong was the reaction of many of the U.K. management team and workforce to the evangelical, U.S.-style presentation that the American president's championing of the program virtually guaranteed its failure to achieve the desired effects on the U.K. plant.

Thus, we appear to have uncovered a case in which the usual story line of the positive impact of culture change champions can be turned on its head. In this case, that is, there is some strong evidence showing that the initial acceptance of a program of change can be negatively influenced by the presence and rhetoric of its champion and positively influenced by his or her departure (see later). Here, we speculate that the champion's role in raising initial expectations of empowerment among the workforce (which were subsequently either met with cynicism or, more critically, largely unfulfilled) may have been an important influence on the survey results in 1995 (Martin, Beaumont, and Staines, 1998), for, as some researchers have argued, the cynicism and lack of trust generated by unfulfilled expectations of change programs are often seen as one of the key problems of top-down change programs (Beer, Eisenstat, and Spector, 1990).

Table 6.2
Differences between Employee Ratings in 1993 and 1995 on Key Facets of the Common Bond

Questions	1993 Mean	1995 Mean	Two sample T-test of means (df. > 1000)
1. How good a job is the organization doing in acting in accordance with respect for individuals?	2.94	2.66	6.79**
2. How good a job is the organization doing in acting in accordance with the highest standards of integrity?	3.06	2.70	9.49**
3. How good a job is the organization doing in acting in accordance with dedication to helping customers?	3.29	3.68	-10.47**
4. How satisfied are you with your involvement in the decisions that affect your work?	2.85	2.61	5.35**
5. Sufficient effort is made to get the opinions and thinking of people who work here.	2.68	2.68	0.09
6. How satisfied are you with the recognition you receive from doing a good job?	2.48	2.53	-1.10
7. Considering everything, how would you rate your overall satisfaction with NCR?	3.47	2.89	13.84**
8. How would you rate NCR against other companies that you know?	4.09	3.66	13.48**
9. I am treated like an important member of this organization.	2.44	2.49	-1.01
10. My contributions are valued by this organization.	2.70	3.05	-8.18**

$* = p < 0.05$, $** = p < 0.01$.
Note: (Using 5-point Likert scales with 1=very poor/strongly disagree/very dissatisfied and 5 = very good/strongly agree/very satisfied).

Note here that we are not arguing that change had failed to occur as a consequence of the program; instead, the evidence for change is a little more uncertain and ambiguous (Pettigrew, 1985). The interview data point to a mixed and changing reception for the message ranging from active rejection by certain managers and workers, at least initially, to active acceptance by others (Harris and Ogbonna, 1998). Most accounts, however, suggest a range of employee responses in between these extremes of outright acceptance and rejection. Some of these accounts, moreover, implied that there were changes over time in employee perceptions of the program. Thus, for example, many workers claimed that they saw the new vision and values framework as nothing new or as something that did not affect them personally from the program's inception, a view that they continued to hold. Others, who had been initially more enthusiastic and sanguine because it provided them with a resource in their dealings with management, gradually became disaffected as the program fizzled out.

The survey data, however, point to an alternative, or at least slightly different, interpretation of events. First, the differences between responses to questions in 1993 and 1995, during the period in which the program champion was in position, show a generally negative change in employee perceptions about key ethical indicators of the Common Bond (such as "respect for individuals," "acting with the highest standards of integrity," and "involvement in the decisions that affect your work")[5] (see Table 6.2). Yet, during the period 1995–1997 (post–Common Bond period), perceptions became generally more positive regarding these same ethical indicators (see Table 6.3).

During the post–Common Bond period, furthermore, responses to questions related to the "involvement climate" showed a significant improvement, as did responses to questions about "recognition for doing a good job" and being "treated like an important member of the organization" (questions 4, 6, and 9). These positive indicators of ethical treatment, recognition, and involvement are all the more surprising given the adverse circumstances associated with the insecurity surrounding the future of the U.K. plant at the time that the last survey was conducted (perhaps borne out by the responses showing a decline in overall job satisfaction). Our alternative explanation for these latter changes in perceptions is that certain key facets of the change program, including the ethical messages of the Common Bond, may have become institutionalized or sedimented to such an extent that managers and workers had come to accept respect for individuals, acting with integrity, and involvement as embedded in the plant culture. It may be argued, therefore, that the retrospective interview accounts of the effects of the program were strongly influenced by rationalizations of an idealized version of the previously existing relationships between managers and workers, which were, in turn, unfavorably contrasted with the U.S.-oriented culture change program and its champion.

To summarize our story line, we have described a top-down, culturally insensitive approach to culture change, introduced into a context that was not conducive to radical transformation. Such an initiative could have been predicted to fail. Despite this, nonetheless, there is some evidence that positive changes occurred, particularly in the involvement climate and in how managers were seen to treat people with respect, particularly during the post–Common Bond period. How can this situation be explained, and what lessons can be drawn for managers?

Although much of the literature on organizational change emphasizes the manipulation of interpretivist facets of culture (such as values, rituals, heroes, and symbols), other researchers (e.g., Anthony, 1994) point to the importance of

Table 6.3
Differences between Employee Ratings in 1995 and 1997 on Key Facets of the Common Bond

Questions	1995 Mean	1997 Mean	Two sample T-test of means (df. > 1000)
1. How good a job is the organization doing in acting in accordance with respect for individuals?	2.66	2.97	-6.86**
2. How good a job is the organization doing in acting in accordance with the highest standards of integrity?	2.70	2.87	-3.95**
3. How good a job is the organization doing in acting in accordance with dedication to helping customers?	3.68	2.05	40.52**
4. How satisfied are you with your involvement in the decisions that affect your work?	2.61	3.06	-4.15**
5. Sufficient effort is made to get the opinions and thinking of people who work here.	2.68	3.31	-12.93**
6. How satisfied are you with the recognition you receive from doing a good job?	2.53	3.31	-15.67**
7. Considering everything, how would you rate your overall satisfaction with NCR?	2.89	2.41	10.53**
8. How would you rate NCR against other companies that you know?	3.66	3.83	-6.48**
9. I am treated like an important member of this organization.	2.49	2.85	-7.67**
10. My contributions are valued by this organization.	3.05	2.85	4.30**

* = p < 0.05, ** = p < 0.01.
Note: (Using 5-point Likert scales with 1=very poor/strongly disagree/very dissatisfied and 5=very good/strongly agree/very satisfied).

accompanying structural and systems changes in "winning hearts and minds" and in shaping behavior. Though it is little more than speculation at this stage, we suspect that the positive, longer-term changes that occurred, at least as revealed by the survey data, are associated with the introduction of employee attitude surveys and the linking of the results of these surveys to pay and to benchmarking among the various subsidiary plants in the AT&T(GIS), now

NCR Corporation. In short, to rework the old adage, "what is meaningful has become measurable," and "what is measurable has become meaningful," in this case at least.

We would not claim that our study is characteristic of all U.S. MNCs' attempts to globalize their operations. Yet, despite the criticisms often leveled at case studies due to their lack of statistical generalizability, qualitative researchers (especially ethnographers) have argued that the strength of case study research lies in analytical generalization and the contextualization of changes (Yin, 1994). Thus, we suggest that this case can offer some lessons for those MNCs that seek to diffuse top-down change across foreign subsidiaries.

LESSONS AND CONCLUSION

The first of several lessons that can be drawn, concerns some warning messages for those consultants and managers who believe in the power and application of transformational leadership regardless of circumstance. Our case has demonstrated the relative failure of one such champion of change who went by the "guru books" in managing by the key principles of transformational leadership (e.g., Bass, 1990) but, paradoxically, given the central message of employee empowerment underlying the program, did not sufficiently involve the local management team in the design of the message. At the same time, the data from the case seem to provide support for contingency approaches to leadership that take into account the nature of followership and their incentive and ability to support or resist radical change (Harris and Ogbonna, 1998).

A second and related lesson concerns international cultural differences, one of the principal contingencies that global transformation program champions are advised to take into account (Luthans, 1998). It is clear in this case that the messenger had a powerful, negative effect on the message of culture change, even that part of it that was regarded as unexceptional territory for managers and workers in the U.K. plant (i.e., respect for individuals and acting with integrity). Our case study, consequently, has important implications for transferring perceived best practices across national boundaries. That is, the choice of program champion and the terminology of the change program must be given particularly important consideration, for, as Cray and Mallory (1998) have hypothesized, leadership behavior that is not sensitive to context can produce negative results. Thus, not only the content of the message but what local managers and workers regard as success have to feature strongly in the design, implementation, and ongoing assessment of any cross-cultural program of change.

Finally, however, we would not wish to overplay the "national cultural card" (Adler and Boyacigiller, 1996). Although national cultural variables are always likely to influence organizational culture change (though often in an uncertain and indirect manner), we suggest that naive explanations of culture (Cray and Mallory, 1998), such as those given by some of the managers and workers in our case, were probably as much a rationalization as an underlying source of the problem.   Instead, we wish to stress the importance of understanding the embeddedness of subsidiaries in their institutional contexts and the nostrums of basic organizational politics (i.e., substantial change is likely to provoke substantial opposition).   Thus, managers and workers in the U.K. subsidiary of AT&T(GIS) would have been likely to react in a similar way to any outsider attempting to introduce a top-down program of change. The failure of this attempt to transfer U.S. best practices can probably be explained by the fact that little or no allowances were made for the variations in responses arising from (1) the institutional context of the plant's labor relations history, which in the Dundee area was characterized by a greater degree of opposition and conflict and skepticism regarding sophisticated HR initiatives than was likely to be found in many parts of the United States, (2) the local plant culture and history associated with the tacit "Fortress Dundee" policy of local management, and (3) the lack of incentive to change because of the plant's superior financial performance relative to those of sister plants in the United States.   The expectation by this agent of change that radical aims could be achieved in a short and definitive time frame, moreover, missed the point that most organizational change cannot be programmed in the sense of having definite aims, beginnings, and ends (Collins, 1998; Pettigrew, 1997).

In conclusion, we have sought to develop more fully a framework and underlying theory of strategic HRM/LR change in MNCs that incorporates contextual and processual elements in a multilevel analysis. This framework is intended to provide further clarity on the salient factors of success and failure in initiating and implementing change programs in complex MNC organizations. In addition to providing the basis for some new directions in research (particularly on issues such as international HMR/LR and international management generally), our framework can provide guidance to executives and managers in implementing programs of strategic change on a global scale. Finally, against our framework, the case study presented illustrates in practical terms some lessons for MNC executives and managers who seek to implement universal programs of so-called best practice.

NOTES

1. It has been pointed out that a significant number of managers in "younger" departments such as marketing, development, and information systems were much more enthusiastic about the program.

2. It was also criticized in other countries. For example, the various messages of "thank you" were translated, incorrectly, by U.S. headquarters into "dankashane" and "merci beaucoup."

3. The symbolism of differently colored cards represented a (rather patronizing) attempt to "Anglicize" the program by using the soccer metaphor. During soccer matches, players committing serious fouls are either warned or dismissed from the playing field through the symbolic gesture of showing them yellow or red cards, respectively.

4. In contrast, some managers who met the U.S. president were impressed by his "live" performance.

5. It is interesting to note that responses to question 10, "My contributions are valued by this organization" in Tables 6.2 and 6.3, show a trend in the opposite direction to those related to the key facets of the Common Bond and involvement. This apparent paradox might be explained by the fact that the attitude survey, in which people were asked to contribute, was introduced in 1993. Much was made of it during the period 1993–1995, and its importance in soliciting employee contributions was conveyed to the workforce in a number of meetings. Conversely, with the departure of the program champion, the attitude survey was played down by the plant management and treated in a less important way.

REFERENCES

Abrahamson, E. and Fairchild, G. B. (1999). "Knowledge Industries and Ideas Entrepreneurs." Paper presented at the Academy of Management Annual Conference, Chicago.

Adler, N. J. and Boyacigiller, N. (1996). "Global Management in the 21st Century." In Punnett, B. J. and Shenkar, O. (eds.) *Handbook for International Management Research.* Cambridge, MA: Blackwell, pp. 537–55.

Alvesson, M. (1993). *Cultural Perspectives on Organizations.* Cambridge: Cambridge University Press.

Anthony, P. D. (1994). *Managing Culture.* Milton Keynes: Open University Press.

Bartlett, C. A. and Ghoshal, S. (eds.). (1995). *Transnational Management: Text,Cases and Readings in Cross-Border Management. 2nd ed.* Chicago: Irwin.

Bass, B. (1990). "From Transactional to Transformational Leadership: Learning to Share the Vision." *Organizational Dynamics.* Winter, pp. 19–31.

Beer, M., Eisenstat, A., and Spector, B. (1990). "Why Change Programs Don't Produce Change." *Harvard Business Review* 67, November-December, pp. 158–66.

Belanger, J., Bergrren, C., Bjorkman, T., and Kohler, C. (eds.). (1999). *Being Local Worldwide: ABB and the Challenge of Global Management.* Ithaca,NY: Cornell University Press.

Belasco, J. A. and Stayer, R. C. (1993). *Flight of the Buffalo: Soaring to Excellence, Learning to Let Employees Lead.* New York: Warner Books.

Birkinshaw, J. M. and Hood, N. (1997). "An Empirical Study of Development Processes in Foreign-Owned Subsidiaries in Scotland." *Management International Review* 37 (4), pp. 339–64.

Buller, P. F. and McEvoy, G. M. (1999). "Creating and Sustaining Ethical Capability in the Multinational Corporation." In Schuler, R. S. and Jackson, S. E. (eds.), *Strategic Human Resource Management.* Oxford: Blackwell, pp. 396–412.

Chia, R. (1999). "A 'Rhizomic' Model of Organizational Change and Transformation: Perspectives from a Metaphysics of Change." *British Journal of Management* 10 (3), pp. 209–27.

Clegg, S. R., Ibarra-Colado, E. and Bueno-Rodriquez, L. (eds.). *Global Management: Universal Theories and Local Realities.* London: Sage.

Collins, D. (1998). *Organizational Change: Sociological Perspectives.* London: Routledge.

Colville, I. D., Waterman, R. H., and Weick, K. E. (1999). "Organizing and the Search for Excellence: Making Sense of the Times in Theory and Practice." *Organization* 6 (1), pp. 129–48.

Cray, D. and Mallory, G. R. (1998). *Making Sense of Managing Culture.* London:Thompson Business Press.

Dawson, P. (1994). *Organsational Change: A Processual Approach.* London: Paul Chapman.

Despres, C. J-N. (1995). "Culture, Surveys, Culture Surveys and Other Obfuscations: Questionnaire Approaches and the Culture Fallacy Approach." *Journal of Strategic Change* 2 (4), pp. 65–76.

Edwards, T. (1998). "Multinationals, Labour Management and the Processes of Reverse Diffusion: A Case Study *International Journal of Human Resource Management* 9 (4), pp. 696–709.

Ferner, A, (2000) "The Embeddedness of US Multinational Companies in the US Business System: Implications for HR/IR." Occasional Paper 61, Leicester Business School, De Montfort University.

Guillen, M. F. (1998). "International Management and the Circulation of Ideas." In Cooper, C. L. and Rousseau, D. M. (eds.), *Trends in Organizational Behaviour* 5. Chichester: Wiley, pp. 47–64.

Gummesson, E. (2000). *Qualitative Methods in Management Research. 2nd ed.* Thousand Oaks, CA: Sage.

Hamel, G. and Prahalad, C. K. (1994). *Competing for the Future.* Boston: Harvard Business School Press.

Harris, L. C. and Ogbonna, E. (1998). "Employee Responses to Cultural Change Efforts." Efforts." *Human Resource Management Journal* 8 (2), pp. 78–92.

Kostova, T. (1999). "Transnational Transfer of Strategic Organizational Practices: A Contextual Perspective." *Academy of Management Review* 24 (2), pp. 308–24.

Legge, K. (1995). *Human Resource Management: Rhetorics and Realities.* London: Macmillan.

Legge, K. (1998). "The Morality of HRM". In Mabey, C., Skinner, D., and Clark, T. (eds.), *HRM: The Inside Story.* London: Sage, pp. 14-32.

Luthans, K. (1998). "Using HRM to Compete in the 21st Century." *Management Quarterly* 38 (4), pp. 17–23.

Mabey, C. and Salaman, G. (1995). *Strategic Human Resource Management.* Oxford: Blackwell.

Martin G. and Beaumont P. B. (1998). "Diffusing Best Practice in Multinational Firms: Prospects, Practice and Contestation", *International Journal of Human Resource Management* 9 (4), pp. 671-695.

Martin, G. and Beaumont, P. B. (1999). "Coordination and Control of Human Resource Management in Multinational Firms: The Case of CASHCO. *International Journal of Human Resource Management* 10 (1), pp. 21-42.

Martin, G. and Beaumont, P. B. (2001). "Transforming Multinational Enterprises:Towards a Process Model of Strategic Human Resource Management Change", *International Journal of Human Resource Management* 12 (8), pp. 1234–50.

Martin, G., Beaumont, P. B. and Staines, H. (1998). "Changing Corporate Culture in a Scottish Local Authority: Paradoxes and Tensions". In Mabey, C., Skinner, D. and Clark, T. (eds.), *HRM: The Inside Story.* London: Sage.

McKinlay, A. and Starkey, K. (eds.). (1997). *Foucault, Management and Organization Theory: From Panopticon to Technologies of the Self.* London: Sage.

Miles, M. B. and Huberman, A. M. (1994). *Qualitative Data Analysis.* 2nd ed. Thousand Oaks, CA: Sage.

Morgan, G. (1997). *Images of Organization.* London: Sage.

Pettigrew, A. M. (1985). *The Awakening Giant: Continuity and Change in Imperial Chemical Industries.* Oxford: Blackwell.

Pettigrew, A. M. (1997). "What is Processual Analysis?" *Scandinavian Journal of Management* 13 (4), pp. 337–48.

Pettigrew, A. M., Ferlie, E., and Mckee, L. (1992). *Shaping Strategic Change.* London: Sage.

Pettigrew, A. M. and Whipp, R. (1991). *Managing Change for Competitive Success.* Oxford: Blackwell.

Purcell, J. and Ahlstrand, B. (1994). *Human Resource Management in the Multi-Divisional Company.* Oxford: Oxford University Press.

Rajagopolan, N. and Spreitzer, G. M. (1996). "Towards a Theory of Strategic Change: A Multi-Lens Perspective and Integrative Framework", *Academy of Management Review* 22 (1), pp. 48-79.

Schoenberger, E. (1997). *The Cultural Crises of the Firm.* Oxford: Oxford University Press.

Silverman, D. (ed.) (1997). *Analysing Qualitative Data.* London: Sage.

Sparrow, P. R. (1998). "New Psychological Forms, Processes, Jobs and Psychological Contracts". In Sparrow, P. and Marchington, M. (eds.), *Human Resource Management: The New Agenda.* London: Pitman, pp. 117-44.

Taggart, J. H. (1998). "Configuration and Control at Subsidiary Level: Foreign Manufacturing Affiliates in the UK", *British Journal of Management* 9 (4), pp. 327-340.

Weick, K. E. (1999). "Theory Construction as Disciplined Reflexivity. Tradeoffs in the 90s", *Academy of Management Review* 24 (4), pp. 797-807.

Whitley, R. (1992). *Business Systems in East Asia, Markets and Societies.* London:Sage.

Yin, R. K. (1994). *Case Study Research: Design and Method.* Thousand Oaks, CA: Sage.

7

Transferring the Learning Factory to America? The Japanese Television Assembly Transplants

Martin Kenney and Shoko Tanaka

The first great wave of Japanese foreign direct investment (FDI) in U.S. manufacturing was in television assembly in the 1970s and early 1980s. Faced by exceedingly intense global competition in recent years, only four Japanese-owned manufacturing plants in the United States are important survivors in the industry. Except for three fairly small enterprises,[1] seven other Japanese-owned television assemblers in the United States have closed their doors, having relocated operations to Mexico or left the industry altogether. In this chapter, we examine three of the four remaining major television assemblers in the United States and one that closed during the period of our study. In particular, we examine the extent to which Japanese parent companies have "transplanted" their production systems and embedded human resourse management and labor relations (HRM/LR) practices in their television assembly subsidiaries in the United States.

As framed in earlier chapters, multinational companies (MNCs) decide whether they will diffuse preferred HRM/LR strategies abroad and/or adopt practices more common to host country industrial relations (IR) systems. Evidence about the diffusion of Japanese practices is mixed. The general conclusion is that the most comprehensive transfer of Japanese HRM/LR methods has taken place within the automobile assembly and auto parts sectors (Kenney and Florida, 1993; Abo, 1994). While some studies have disputed this conclusion (Graham, 1995; Fucini and Fucini, 1990), there can be little doubt that a number of Japanese firms in the automobile and auto parts sectors have implemented core Japanese style HRM/LR practices in their subsidiaries. In contrast, most studies of Japanese-owned consumer electronics factories in the United States (Kenney and Florida, 1993; Sato, 1991; Abo, 1994) and the United Kingdom (Oliver and Wilkinson, 1988; Delbridge, 1998) found a more limited transfer of the Japanese production system. The study of television assembly in the United States, therefore, provides an important alternative perspective to the studies of Japanese-owned automotive operations, which to date have largely been the basis of our understanding of the diffusion of Japanese production systems in U.S. subsidiaries.

Herein, we first describe the production systems and associated HRM/LR practices in Japanese television factories, which we believe can be characterized as "learning" organizations (Adler, 1993). Second, we examine the extent to which the Japanese transplants in the United States have re-created these systems and address the factors that appear to have influenced differences between Japanese and U.S. practices. In particular, as three of the four transplants studied are unionized operations, we compare the more traditional Fordist practices to those preferred by Japanese companies. Finally, we assess the effects of American labor–management relations and customs on the diffusion of Japanese HRM/LR practices and learning environments.

THE PRODUCTION MANAGEMENT SYSTEM IN JAPANESE TELEVISION FACTORIES

To assess the extent to which Japanese MNCs have transplanted their production management systems to their U.S. subsidiaries, we first describe the salient HRM/LR practices common to television assembly factories in Japan. As in other large manufacturing companies, the basic form of the Japanese HRM/LR system in the television factories is characterized by a structure of job grades, substantial investments in training and skill development, complicated, individualized pay schemes, extensive upward mobility, the lack of job control or ownership, off-line small group activities, an emphasis on generating performance improvement suggestions, longterm employment, and enterprise union representation (Dore, 1973; Aoki, 1988; Koike, 1988). Such a system is markedly different from the workplace systems commonly found in traditional Fordist manufacturing in the United States. Hence, the diffusion of core Japanese practices to U.S. subsidiaries would generally require a significant transformation of the HRM/LR strategies pursued in more traditional American manufacturing, especially in unionized operations.

In the typical Japanese consumer electronics firm, regular, full-time workers are divided into five basic job grades, yet every individual's wage differs (Nakamura, Demes, and Nagano, 1994). Job grades correspond to the level of skill and experience needed to undertake a category of jobs. In addition, there are no categories such as skilled tradesperson or technician; these tasks are assigned to workers in higher job grades. Workers have no rights to specific jobs and can be reassigned at management's discretion. Seniority plays an important role, not because of years served per se but because workers with longer tenure have greater accumulated knowledge and training. Seniority, however, does not determine job assignment, even though it has a strong influence on pay (Kenney, 1999).

The compensation system for Japanese workers is extremely complicated. In all the consumer electronics firms there are five general categories of operators. In the past, there were also part-time and temporary workers in these factories, who were paid differently and did not have the rights of regular employees. However, by the late 1990s all of these workers had been laid off or retired. The top two categories of regular employees contain what in the U.S. unionized shops are the skilled trades and the lowest level of managerial supervisors. Wages are set according to a formula consisting of seniority (base), performance (merit), and ability components, though their percentage weighting differs by firm. There is also a bonus component that is approximately five months of salary paid in two installments. Salary increases are calculated once per year, and each individual receives a unique raise. For this reason, after a couple of years, it is likely that no two workers receive exactly the same wage.

Distinctions between managers and workers are not as clearly defined in Japan as they are in most Western nations. In most Japanese television factories, all supervisors and many upper-level managers have been promoted from among the workforce (albeit, top-level managers are often dispatched from corporate headquarters). For example, Kenney (1999) reports one case in which the factory manager, who was responsible for over 1,000 employees, began his career as an assembly line worker. Regular workers in Japan, therefore, are not limited in their opportunities for promotion into management positions by artificial glass ceilings (the exception being for women, who in theory face no barriers but in practice have little likelihood of reaching the upper levels of factory management). Higher-grade workers, furthermore, have job tasks encompassing a significant supervisory component (Kenney, 1999; Kenney et al., 1998; Nakamura et al., 1994). The responsibilities of these senior workers include drawing up work instructions (i.e., diagramming the physical motions and steps that workers must undertake to complete jobs), relieving workers, providing technical guidance and assistance to workers on the line, monitoring the status of lines, and even reassigning jobs to workers (Nakamura et al., 1994: 74).

One hallmark of Japanese management has been extensive training of workers (Liker, Fruin, and Adler, 1999; Kenney, 1999; Cole, 1989). Factory workers are hired locally after undergoing a battery of written, oral, and medical tests. Upon employment they normally receive an orientation session lasting between one and five days. Before being assigned to a work section, new employees are quickly rotated through a variety of simple jobs in different sections during the first one to three months of employment. Upon entry into their section, they receive on-the-job training (OJT) from senior workers and supervisors. The typical employee, however, does not remain assigned to a section permanently. About every two years employees are transferred to new sections as a means of promoting a better understanding of the entire production process and to otherwise challenge employees.

Investment in off-the-job or classroom training is also generally substantial. Regular workers receive classroom training from senior employees on a range of subjects, including quality control, inspection, operation of new machinery, machine maintenance, and special skills such as welding and soldering. These courses are not passive in nature as they include written homework assignments and examinations. As workers progress through job grades, there is a curriculum of classes provided to prepare them for examinations required for promotion to each higher-level grade. Not only do workers take factory-specific classes, but they also take company-wide classes. This broader training imparts to employees the skills to become managers and to improve overall factory operations. After completion of this training, operators can inspect their own equipment and perform routine equipment maintenance and cleaning functions. At higher grade levels, courses prepare employees for working with sophisticated electronics and programming, in addition to developing general management skills.

To fully exploit their investments in human capital, Japanese companies have every worker involved in off-line, "small group activities" (SGAs), such as quality control circles or safety improvement groups. SGAs have the dual purpose of improving operations and creating social solidarity (Cole, 1989). In addition, all factories have programs encouraging workers to individually suggest improvements in order to mobilize all individuals. The quality and number of suggestions received are considered very important and are a component of everyone's job performance evaluation, from the factory manager, to the novice operator. Indeed, the flow of suggestions is tracked closely, as illustrated in one interview, for instance, in which a factory manager reported having received precisely 13.2 suggestions per person in the previous six-month period. To help facilitate the flow of suggestions, supervisors are obligated to teach subordinates how to make useful suggestions.

Television factories in Japan, nevertheless, differ from the more commonly reported model of Japanese factory organization generalized from Toyota and the automobile industry (Cole, 1989; Adler and Cole, 1993). First, work is not organized into multifunctional teams. Instead, workers are grouped under a supervisor and, for the most part, work individually. In one plant, the manager stated candidly that "we do not really work on the team concept" (Kenney, 1999). At his factory, groups are considered administrative units and do not engage in collective problem solving, which is left to SGAs. Second, within groups there are long-term transfers from job to job but little short-term rotation between stations, even within groups. The most significant exception is found in picture adjustment, where eyestrain necessitates job rotation every two hours (this type of work, however, is being automated). Third, the physical process of assembling televisions is highly routinized, with detailed diagrams posted at every assembler's workstation. Workers do not have the responsibility or prerogative to stop the line, even if they notice a pattern of defects. Instead, their responsibility is solely to inform their supervisors, who make the determination as to whether or not the line should be halted.

In such a different work environment, the role of the union in Japan is much different than in the United States. In Japan, television factories are organized by enterprise unions representing only the firms' regular employees. Since lower-level management staff are members of unions, there is no strict separation between exempt and nonexempt employees. In general, bargaining takes place regarding any overall wage hikes and other benefits. The most important single goal of the unions has been to protect the long-term employment guarantee. Unions have little or no control over the movement of workers in the factories and other actions such as overtime distribution, though it should be stressed that unions have advisory roles, and good labor–management relations are an expressed goal of management. Although, from the perspective of critics, Japanese enterprise unions act as second personnel departments for management, their role is ambiguous. It is clear, nonetheless, that Japanese enterprise unions generally do not consider themselves in direct and constant conflict with management.

Despite the absence of work teams, Japanese television factories have some significant resemblance to Adler's (1993) "learning" bureaucracy, wherein the in-line work process is routinized and engineered in minute detail. Unplanned events and the introduction of new models create, for example, ample opportunities for more creative thinking and problem solving, and it is at these junctures that workers in higher labor grades are especially mobilized. In addition, the learning opportunities are manifested in the suggestion process and in the SGAs. Consequently, despite the routinized process (i.e., the bureaucracy), there is a constant emphasis on improvement, which requires learning.

JAPANESE TELEVISION ASSEMBLY IN THE UNITED STATES

Japanese success in exporting televisions to the United States in the 1960s and 1970s resulted in significant trade friction, as U.S. assemblers experienced a loss of market share (Porter, 1983). Fearing U.S. protectionism, Japanese television manufacturers opened or acquired assembly plants in the United States during the 1970s and 1980s (14 such plants in total). Initially, the plants were proverbial "screwdriver" factories, receiving both production equipment and critical components from Asia. By 1998, the U.S. market was controlled by two European firms, three Korean firms, and five Japanese firms, each of which also had factories in Mexico.

To examine the extent of diffusion of Japanese production and HRM/LR practices in the remaining Japanese transplants, we gained access to four of the five firms. Our assessment is based on a comprehensive review of secondary source material, plant tours, and personal interviews with selected executives, managers, and supervisors (which were taped and transcribed).[2] As a precondition for conducting our research, anonymity was granted to the respondents and firms. Hence, we refer to the respective factories as Factories W, X, Y, and Z. It should be noted that the present analysis is part of a larger research project examining the Japanese management system in television assembly factories in Japan, the United States and northern Mexico.[3]

Each factory studied had three to five conveyor belt assembly lines, each dedicated to a few different-sized televisions. Only one factory had a component insertion facility, whereas the other three factories imported their printed circuit boards from Mexico. The televisions arrived at a station and stopped, a single operator performed a set of routines in approximately one minute, and the sets then continued down the line. The group leader, the assistant, or in some cases an automated vehicle delivered the parts. Taken as a whole, the television assembly process was routinized, though not capital-intensive.

The plants in this study were located in three states: Georgia, Tennessee, and Arkansas. One plant was acquired in the 1970s, and the other three were greenfield factories built in the 1980s. Three factories were high throughput, mass production facilities. The other factory was also a mass production factory, but it specialized in large-screen and projection televisions and had shorter production runs. At the time of our investigation (1997), pay and benefits were competitive with those of other electronics plants in their respective regions. A newly hired operator's wage averaged about $10 per hour. The plants relied on state government employment bureaus for referral of potential operators, for which no company-administered written, oral, or medical examinations were required. Annual turnover has averaged less than 10 percent. No long-term employment guarantees were made to employees, and all plants have experienced both seasonal and long-term layoffs. Employment levels at two of the four plants had fallen from a decade earlier. The female–male ratios at the plants were approximately 60–40. Although we did not collect racial and ethnicity statistics, we observed that employees at two plants were predominantly white, whereas the other two plants employed substantial numbers of African Americans.

Unions and the Labor Environment

Of the 14 Japanese television assembly factories that have at one time operated in the United States, only 3 were ever unionized. Our sample includes those 3 unionized factories (Factories X, Y, and Z). The nonunionized plant (Factory W), which is now closed, never experienced a union-organizing campaign. When Sanyo purchased the Forrest City, Arkansas, factory, it was already organized by the International Union of Electronic, Electrical, Salaried, Machine, and Furniture Workers (IUE). The Toshiba and Sharp factories were organized in the early 1980s by the International Brotherhood of Electrical Workers (IBEW). All four factories were located in right-to-work states, which gave employees the right not to join the local unions but required the unions, nonetheless, to represent all hourly employees. The unionization rates were 60 percent at Factory Y and 78 percent at Factory Z. At Factory X the proportion of workers belonging to the union had dropped from a high of 90 percent in 1989 to only 44 percent by 1997. All contracts were three-year agreements covering only employees at the respective factories and within identified bargaining units. This contrasted sharply with sister plants in Japan where union contracts covered workers in all of a company's plants.

The history of labor confrontation at the unionized plants has been mixed. Factory X experienced a short strike in the early 1980s and a one-day strike in 1989. The only walkout at Factory Y was a brief one taken in the early 1980s immediately preceding unionization of the workforce. In contrast, Factory Z, which inherited a polarized situation (Beazley, 1988), has experienced substantial labor unrest. After a brief period of goodwill following the acquisition of the failing factory, the union struck in 1979 for eight weeks over wages and other issues (Harvard Business School, 1981). In 1985, the union struck again in response to management's demands for medical insurance cuts, seniority system changes, and the right to move workers from job to job. The strike was eventually settled, with management's achieving most of its demands. There was, however, a significant lingering level of animosity and distrust on both sides, as the strike was bitter and marked by violence. Management seriously considered closing the factory, but thanks to then-governor William Clinton, who visited Factory Z headquarters in Osaka, the plant remained open. In addition and importantly, Wal-Mart, the Arkansas-based retailer, began distributing Factory Z televisions (Byrne, 1986; Kotha and Dunbar, 1995).

Since the late 1980s, in contract negotiations across all plants, management has focused primarily on its demands for greater flexibility via reallocation of personnel and reductions in the number of job classifications. The primary emphasis of the unions, on the other hand, has been on protecting seniority and job rights. The bargaining environment has proved to be quite challenging for the local unions as a result of the relatively low union penetration rate in the industry and the persistent threat of plant closures and consolidation of operations in Mexico. Although the resulting union contracts can be characterized as fairly traditional ones by U.S. standards and highly rigid ones from the Japanese perspective, they have become increasingly flexible. Of particular note has been the creation of positions that have remained within the bargaining unit but have allowed union members to become team leaders, positions in which union members have assumed some duties previously retained solely by supervision. In effect, the sharp demarcations associated with U.S.-style job control unionism have become slightly blurred.

Work Organization, Job Classifications, and Seniority

Much like their counterparts in Japan, operators in the three unionized plants were divided into groups, which corresponded to a section of the assembly line and encompassed 25–30 operators. Supervisors in the United States, however, were considered members of management and very often had no hands-on assembly experience. In contrast to plants in Japan and the three unionized plants in the United States, a new American management team at Factory W had just begun to reorganize the entire factory into self-directed work teams. Absent from the design, however, were designated team leaders. All team members were to be cross-trained and involved in training. Teams were responsible, furthermore, for checking team members' time cards, assigning members to particular jobs, and participating in line rebalancing.

The three unionized television transplants differed little from other, more traditional U.S. factories, as they adopted fine-grained, complicated U.S. job classification structures and associated job control. An earlier 1986 reporter's interview with the personnel manager at Company Z highlights the sense of employee ownership of jobs and resistance to reassignment: "Here, it's Mary's chair. She's sat there for 15 years, and she'll be damned if she's going to move from that spot" (Byrne, 1986: 51). Only non-union Factory W had attempted to undergo any major revision of its job classification structure. At the time of our study, it was in the process of reducing 30 distinct job classifications down to 5 (production operator, warehouse operator, line support technician, maintenance technician, and quality assurance inspector). The new job titles and descriptions were deliberately left vague in an effort to include a wider number of different work activities within each. Within each job category there were three levels, whereas in the previous structure there were eight pay grades. In addition, the lead operator position, which had been a supervisory position, was eliminated. The motivation for these changes came from the new management team, which wanted to create a learning environment in which there could be rapid improvement in performance and cost reduction. The ideas for this reorganization, however, did not come from Japan but rather from other U.S. firms in the area.

Across all three unionized plants, seniority preference was tantamount and prevalent throughout each of the union contracts. All three had similar, but slightly different, plantwide job bidding and bumping rules based on seniority. These bidding systems awarded jobs to the most senior employees among all qualified applicants, not strictly to the most qualified applicants.

Factory X had seven labor grades and a total of 20 job classifications. Seniority and bumping privileges accrued in departments, of which there were four. With respect to job bidding and layoffs, however, accrued seniority privileges were applied on a plantwide basis. The company retained the right, nonetheless, to temporarily transfer workers between jobs for up to 30 days without regard to seniority or job-posting provisions. In addition, the top-level maintenance employees were not subject to the job bidding process and could be hired solely at management's discretion.

In Factory Y there were eight job grades each for operators and skilled tradespeople. Although employees could bid on jobs throughout the factory, bidding was usually based on identifiable departmental job ladders. In the case of layoffs, more senior workers had rights to bump junior employees at the departmental level. One provision in the contract allowing for some flexibility was management's right to temporarily reassign employees for up to 90 days without regard to the seniority or posting provisions in the agreement. But even in this case, the offer of reassignment was made first to the most senior employee in the affected classification. If that person refused, then management went down the seniority list until someone accepted or the least senior person was assigned.

At Company Z there were 11 labor grades and five pay groups. For bumping purposes all the jobs were divided into 15 job classification families in which there were seniority ladders. There was a total of 74 specific jobs across the factory covering only 400 bargaining unit employees. Workers accrued seniority in each of the 74 jobs and classification categories. Additionally, workers could not be reassigned except by seniority bumping or if jobs were eliminated.

Nonunion Factory W was in the process of implementing a more flexible job classification structure, though at the time of our study the restructuring had not yet been completed. In combination with a newly created self-directed work team system and cross-training, the evolving job classification and grading structure was viewed as providing management with sufficient flexibility to rotate workers through all tasks performed by teams.

In summary, the combination of job classifications and organization of work in the three unionized plants was far more rigid than that evolving in the nonunion plant. Governed by strict rules of seniority and a climate of job ownership and control, management in the unionized plants had little freedom to reassign or rotate employees through jobs. It is important to emphasize, however, that plant-level management appeared to endorse the U.S. system by accepting the notion that employees had rights to particular jobs. In Japan, on the other hand, management was free to move employees to any positions that management wished, albeit inexperienced, insufficiently skilled employees would not be assigned to positions requiring deep knowledge of a plant and its equipment. Management in Japan, therefore, was constrained by needed skill levels in the reassignment or rotation of employees, not by union resistance to such movement of employees.

Division of Labor and Management

The division between labor and management is often emphasized as an important difference between traditional Fordist and Japanese management. In the transplants there was a clear Fordist distinction between labor and management, but there were indicators that such division was being diminished. For example, at two unionized factories a category of bargaining unit members called "group leader" had been created. These group leaders were being used in lieu of the lowest category of production supervision, a change motivated by cost considerations. Although the appointment of group leaders was entirely at management's discretion, and seniority played no formal bearing on selection, the selection of group leaders was usually made among more senior workers who had significant experience and presumably a desire or willingness to move into the ranks of plant supervision. At the time of our study, the two companies were still phasing in the group leader positions, which included responsibilities for conducting morning meetings to discuss daily schedules and activities, delivering materials to the production lines, and training new operators. The group leader role, however, was more limited than the traditional supervisory role. In particular, as members of the bargaining unit, group leaders were restricted from issuing verbal instructions to other workers or taking any disciplinary actions.

Here, the unions were able to protect their principles of equality among members and strict separation between certain managerial tasks and bargaining unit work. Despite these restrictions, group leaders generally performed their new roles quite successfully. For example, at Factory Z a supervisor had to be reassigned to a new area, and the group leader assumed most of his responsibilities. According to the production manager, workers "haven't even missed the supervisor there. [Management] came in on Monday and [asked] will you take the job over. [They] then bid it and he has done a super job." Curiously, the managers expressed surprise at what bargaining unit employees were capable of or willing to do when offered opportunities to expand their responsibilities. It would appear, therefore, that management, like their union leader counterparts, had largely embraced and operated within the Fordist paradigm that divides managers and workers.

In addition, contracts specifically forbade managers and supervisors from engaging in bargaining unit work except under special circumstances, namely, during emergencies, for instruction and training, for purposes of checking on workmanship, quality, and equipment functioning, and during experimental and prototype runs. The unions' objective, we surmise, was to prevent any encroachment by supervision and management on bargaining unit work. As a result of this negotiated demarcation, bargaining unit work was largely restricted to more routine production work, leaving nonroutine work to managers and staff. For instance, maintenance work on both automated and test equipment was restricted to engineers. In Japan, such maintenance of equipment would be performed by highly trained high school graduates. In other words, the artificial job distinctions manifested in the U.S. agreements has meant that workers protect their rights to more routine jobs but forfeit many opportunities to engage in nonroutine jobs. Yet, from a Japanese management perspective, having workers engage in nonroutinized as well as more routinized jobs is key to increasing factory productivity, reducing costs, and otherwise enhancing competitive advantage.

In all four factories there also was a separation between technical duties and supervisory duties in the factory hierarchy. Whereas in Japan work instructions were drafted by the supervisor-class workers, all of these activities were assumed by industrial engineering sections in the United States. U.S. supervisors, furthermore, were not expected to be highly competent technically; they needed only to manage effectively. As one manager put it: "The group leader is probably more technical, like working on the line. The group leader is probably more skilled than the supervisors. Because they spend more time on the line. They know the jobs. But they are not there for the management skills standpoint, or motivational [standpoint], planning, or direct control." Hence, there was a separation not only between mental and manual labor but also between job skills and hierarchical control. Whereas in the transplants these separations were standard, they were not nearly as pronounced in the Japanese factories.

In addition to fairly sharp lines of demarcation based on tasks and responsibilities, it was uncommon for production workers in the unionized U.S. operations to cross the lines of demarcation through promotion. There were a number of instances of promotion from blue-collar to white-collar positions, but unlike in Japanese plants, these were the exception, not the rule, in the U.S. operations. For example, one assembly line worker in Factory Y had during his career at the factory advanced from a production relief operator to production quality assurance department manager. Another had begun at the lowest entry-level category (Assembler II) in 1988, but by 1997, she had been promoted to unit manager. As a unit manager she also had trained two other women, who, likewise, rose through the ranks to become unit managers. In our interview, she explained how she made the transition: "I would go to my supervisor and tell him that I wanted to learn everything that there was on the line. I learned all the positions. I wanted to know how to do things basically talking with them. I had a few Japanese bosses that were just fantastic and they taught me a whole lot of stuff. They helped me and here I am." She also expressed her frustration with lines of demarcation in her new role as a unit manager. For example, one frustration that she experienced as a manager was waiting for maintenance workers to repair machinery:

That was one of the hardest things for me, coming off the line into management. I was used to going up, seeing something wrong, and fixing or whatever to keep everything going. Now I have to walk around with my hands in my pocket, that was a hard habit to break. You know repairing boards or keeping the line flowing smoothly. You have certain people that can do certain things and it matters.

In summary, the lines between production workers and managers in the U.S. transplant operations were far more pronounced than in the Japanese operations. We encountered a number of exceptions, however, with respect to both production workers' taking on some traditional supervisory responsibilities and the promotion of production workers into management positions. Although the blue-collar/white-collar divide in the U.S. factories was permeable, there was almost no such divide in the Japanese factories. The traditional U.S. division between manual and mental labor was, in part, perpetuated and zealously guarded by unions, but the division is also attributable to how the Fordist tradition had become well ingrained in American management philosophy.

Training

Each transplant conducted between one and five days of orientation classroom training for new hires. This training included an introduction to factory rules, safety, general information about the factory and company, and sessions emphasizing the importance of quality control. These courses were purely informational, and there were neither homework assignments nor examinations. In general, initial orientation in the transplants very much resembled the Japanese orientation sessions. Since entry-level assembly jobs were extremely routinized in the U.S. factories and could be learned in a matter of days, additional training was minimal. Training, moreover, was almost exclusively delivered in the form of OJT provided by supervisors or group leaders. OJT by rotation through different jobs and tasks, however, could not be easily implemented in the unionized factories because of the rigid job classification structure negotiated by labor and management and enshrined in the union contracts. Opportunities for additional OJT occurred, nonetheless, as workers ascended through the seniority-based, job bidding process. Since the job bidding process was generally restricted to within departments, workers became increasingly specialized over time rather than increasingly generalized as in Japan.

With the exception of Factory W, the transplants engaged in far less off-the-job training than their counterparts in Japan. At Factory Y, all employees received only one one-hour class per year, each in handling chemicals and in ISO 9000 and ISO 14000 conformance/environmental awareness. Although other classes were provided, in no case did workers receive more than five hours of regularly scheduled training per year. In Factories X and Z, no classroom training was provided beyond legally required safety training. When there were important equipment or process changes, classroom training was offered only to selected individuals, usually supervisors, technicians, and/or skilled tradespeople.

Nonunion Factory W implemented the most thorough training program, which included substantial off the job training. Indeed, the factory's training investment per employee averaged $697 in 1997 (not including lost production time), a substantial increase over the mere $55 average invested a few years earlier. Operators received classroom and OJT training in statistical process control, teamwork, communications, safety, and continuous improvement techniques. As Factory W had just reorganized all production workers into teams and was introducing rotation among jobs, employees also received cross-training. Furthermore, the new team system had an intergroup training dimension, whereby team members were expected to train each other. This training effort was especially impressive in its thoroughness and was unmatched by the unionized factories.

In summary, the difference in training policies between the Japanese and U.S. factories could not be more striking. In Japan, management was clearly devoted to providing training, and all of the senior personnel served as instructors in various classes. In the United States, on the other hand, training investments were minimal, and few managers were involved in formal classroom training activities. In addition, with the exception of the newly reorganized nonunion plant, there was little effort to provide training beyond necessary OJT.

Machine Maintenance

Television assembly generally does not utilize sophisticated machinery, and, consequently, much of the machine maintenance is relatively simple. In the U.S. Fordist tradition, even the simplest maintenance has remained the province of skilled tradespeople, technicians, and engineers, whereas, in Japan, much of the responsibility for routine maintenance is performed by operators. The U.S. transplant record is somewhat mixed in this regard, and some managers expressed the desire to devolve routine maintenance to operators.

At the one nonunion plant, workers inspected the machinery before production began and cleaned their equipment, even though they had no formal maintenance obligations. In Factory Z, workers were responsible for keeping their work areas clean and neat, but inspection and routine maintenance were entirely within the purview of maintenance technicians. At Factory Y, operators were not involved in even the most routine maintenance; all maintenance was performed by a distinct maintenance group. Although operators were allowed to clean their machines, they were instructed that there was to be "no adjustment, no grease, or lubrication." The plant manager indicated, however, that he planned to have the maintenance group begin training operators to make minor adjustments on conveyors and other equipment at the start of their shifts. Similarly, operators in Factory X engaged in no equipment maintenance. As we were told, "They just use the machines and do not even clean them. Cleaning is done by a specialized group. Cleaning of the work place is also done by a specialized group."

The separation of even simple maintenance tasks from operator responsibilities is a legacy of U.S. functional specialization and the division of work between operators and more highly trained personnel. With the exception of management in the nonunion transplant, managers expected little contribution from their operators regarding machine maintenance. Therefore, unlike their Japanese counterparts, the U.S. transplants relied on more highly skilled technicians and engineers to perform necessary routine adjustment work, clearly, a costly underutilization of skill and capabilities.

Quality Improvement Involvement

Both the American transplants and the Japanese plants emphasized the importance of achieving high quality. Toward achieving ever-higher levels of quality, employers have focused on improving design and components, automating difficult or tedious tasks, increasing inspection, heightening worker awareness and responsibility for flagging problems, and involving workers in discovering and resolving quality problems. Although any factory must undertake some combination of these actions to achieve higher quality, it was the Japanese who generalized the use of quality control (QC) circles based on operator involvement (Cole, 1989). The Japanese transplants, however, repeatedly failed in their efforts to introduce or sustain worker involvement in QC circles and related small group activities; that is, workers monitored quality (a passive function) but for the most part were not engaged in quality improvement activities (an active function).

In the 1970s, when Japanese television assemblers began operations in the United States, they found a workplace environment radically different from their own in Japan. In Factory Z, which had been acquired, the new owners encountered what was, by all accounts, an example of the worst kind of quality consciousness in U.S. manufacturing. For instance, the quality assurance director described his initial impression of the acquired plant in the following way:

Compared with Japan, my first impression was that there was too much specialization. Sectionalism, I felt, was wrong among the departments, lines, and workers. It seemed to me that line workers thought quality control was the responsibility of the inspection or quality departments. I also felt that the concept of cooperation was totally lacking. Japanese workers would think of quality as the concern of the entire company. (Yonekura, 1985: 1)

Exacerbating circumstances, moreover, workers were generally opposed to inspecting the work of coworkers, an opposition common across unionized companies in the United States. As one Japanese manager complained, "They feel that it is wrong to say that a fellow worker has made an error, or even to correct the errors they see. But surely this is essential if the company is to turn out good products. If we make defective products, who will buy them? And where will these people work if nobody buys them?" (Harvard Business School, 1981: 10)

After purchasing the Arkansas plant, the company immediately reorganized production by installing new machinery, using higher-quality Japanese parts, and cleaning and upgrading the facility. To signal the importance of quality, furthermore, the Warwick plant quality control manager was made the plant manager (Kotha and Dunbar, 1995: 7). Although productivity and quality immediately improved, in some measure this might have been due to a "halo" effect as the result of the company's saving Factory Z from certain closure. The different perspectives of Japanese and American quality control managers, nonetheless, made efforts to transform the factory into a high performance operation most difficult. One Japanese QC manager stated, for instance, "Quality improvement can be achieved through cooperation among workers, lines, departments, and managers." In stark contrast, his American assistant argued, "The most important means [to achieve quality] is to introduce more advanced automation, digitalization, and consumer-oriented simple product design" (Yonekura, 1985: 4). As is apparent, one perspective of quality improvement emphasized cooperation among all employees, whereas the other emphasized the use of technical solutions.

The Japanese emphasis on the human element of quality improvement via the use of QCs never took hold in the transplants. In 1982, Factory Z introduced "Quality Improvement Groups" aimed at lowering defects (Yonekura,

1985), but a few years later no QC circles or SGAs were to be found (Abo, 1994). In our 1997 visit, we found QC circles in place, but these comprised strictly nonunion personnel. Similarly, in 1990, as reported by researchers at the University of Tokyo (Institute of Social Sciences, 1990), Factory Y had QC circles in place for the purpose of raising the sense of participation through communication between supervisors and employees. The Japanese manager interviewed stated that the purpose of the circles was to improve both product quality and productivity. The circles were voluntary, though there was a reported participation rate of 70 percent. However, several years later, we found that there was only limited voluntary participation in QC circles among operators, who usually met only one hour per month and after regular work hours. At Factory X, the QC circle program barely functioned. One Japanese manager attributed this to union discouragement of worker involvement, an allegation that we were unable to verify.

In the latter part of the 1980s, Factory W had also introduced QC circlelike activities, only to discontinue them two years later due to a lack of participation. However, as described earlier, management had recently introduced its new team-based structure. That new structure served as a basis for routine QC activity. In addition, Factory W instituted what was called "*kaizen* blitzes," which involved all levels of the factory organized into special teams for the purpose of resolving specific problems in targeted areas. The goal of the blitz was to bring rapid improvement in targeted areas, targets that could be suggested at any level within the organization.

In summary, with the exception of the recently renewed efforts at nonunion Factory W, the transplants diverged markedly from their counterparts in Japan with regard to worker involvement in QC circles and related SGAs. Beyond the simple flagging of quality problems included in their routines, workers contributed little to quality improvement. Hence, the Japanese achieved little success in diffusing QC circles and related employee involvement activities in their U.S. affiliates, an HRM/LR practice basic to the Japanese production systems.

Suggestions

Central to the Japanese production systems in television assembly were employee suggestion programs. In the U.S. transplants, however, there was a remarkable lack of success in implementing such suggestion programs. In Factory X, no suggestion programs had been implemented. Factory Z had a suggestion program, but neither the plant manager nor the other managers whom we interviewed had any idea of the number of suggestions that were being received. Tracking suggestions, we were told, was the responsibility of the quality control department.

At the time of our visit, Factory Y reported having introduced a new suggestion program to replace an earlier one that had fallen into disuse. A document provided by the company indicated that the objective of the new program, however, was "to build a more energized, productive manufacturing facility through activities geared toward eliminating job dissatisfaction caused by inconsistent or unfair treatment" and to aid the factory "in its objective of providing employees with a work environment that promotes the free exchange of communication with top management." In reality, this program appeared to be more of a mechanism to handle complaints than to solicit suggestions on performance improvements. In Factory Y, furthermore, upper-level management expressed much less interest in shop-floor suggestions than did two lower-level managers whom we interviewed. Unlike the upperlevel managers to whom they reported, these two managers (one was the former operator and union member mentioned earlier) were enthusiastic about worker contributions. Take for example, our discussion with the one supervisor:

Q. Is it hard to motivate feedback?
R. No. They are more than willing to give you an earful. If something doesn't work, they will let you know.

Q. It is one thing to let you know. The other would be to propose a solution.
R. They are good on that. They are really good on that. Like I said we encourage it. They tended to give me feedback in the past. And it has just kind of caught on as the years have gone by. They will, they will do it. Because I will ask, "what do you suggest?" [They] will come up with a countermeasure.

It was apparent from our interview that this supervisor was dedicated to improving performance and eliciting suggestions from operators to enhance performance. Her efforts to involve workers, nonetheless, appeared self-motivated and not part of an organized, plantwide effort.

In summary, what was striking about the transplants was the relative low priority that suggestion programs received. In Japan, all levels of management were extremely conscious of the number of suggestions received and actively sought to increase the number and quality of suggestions. At one Japanese factory, supervisors were trained explicitly in how to work with subordinates to increase the number and quality of suggestions. With the exception of the nonunion transplant, the U.S. transplants either attached only passing importance to generating employee suggestions or otherwise had not found ways to make suggestion programs an integral part of factory operations.

CONCLUSION

In our study of four of the five major Japanese-owned television assembly factories located in the United States, we have attempted to examine the extent to which standard Japanese production systems and embedded HRM/LR practices had been diffused to the United States. We found, on one hand, that much of the technical and physical configuration of Japanese television assembly operations had been diffused to the American operations. On the other hand, we found little evidence of diffusion of HRM/LR practices, except in the nonunion transplant. In essence, whereas the factories in Japan can be characterized as "learning" bureaucracies (Adler, 1993), the three unionized subsidiaries are best characterized as "static" bureaucracies. That is, in the unionized transplants there were few opportunities made for operators to learn much beyond fairly limited tasks and, in turn, little opportunity for operators to help improve factory-wide performance. These learning opportunities were especially limited by narrowly defined and complex classification schemes, by rigid seniority rules governing assignment and promotion, by sharp lines drawn between blue-collar and white-collar employees that restricted responsibilities and upward mobility, by relatively little investment in training, by restrictions on operator opportunities to maintain their own equipment, by the lack of QC circle or related small group activities, and by the low priority placed on employee suggestion programs.

Overall, we believe that the Fordist tradition of labor–management relationships in the United States had locked both American managers and their union leader counterparts into sustaining static bureaucracies that reinforced and perpetuated Braverman's (1974) dichotomy between managerial conception and worker execution. Such perpetuation is captured, in particular, by the hierarchical job-protection system long ingrained in U.S. union-management relations. That system made it virtually impossible to regularly reassign or rotate employees through different jobs and, hence, increase learning and employee understanding. Given that seniority governed nearly all job assignments, moreover, there was little incentive for management to invest in training beyond that necessary to satisfy the requirements of specific jobs.

Furthermore, in spite of examples wherein workers and supervisors demonstrated the capacity to move toward creating learning environments, the parties were unwilling or unable to capitalize on them. For example, we found a number of instances of promotion from hourly to supervisory ranks, but, curiously, managers viewed such mobility as the rare exception to the rule of hiring from outside. In other words, there was no effort to encourage such mobility, which is commonplace in the Japanese systems. Similarly, even when there were concrete examples of success (such as that of the promoted assembly worker and the group leaders who were able to manage production lines in ways that surprised management), upper-level management readily dismissed them as aberrations, not as examples for wider application. Apparently, these examples, which demonstrated that the workforce was capable of substantial change, were not salient enough to trigger a paradigm shift in managerial thinking.

In contrast to the unionized plants, the nonunion plant in our study eventually broke out of the Fordist tradition and began to create a learning environment more in line with that of sister plants in Japan. Consequently, the general nature of the HRM/LR practices embedded in Japanese production systems in television assembly was being replicated in this U.S. operation, and certain practices went beyond even the Japanese practices pursued in Japan. The plant, however, was closed shortly after our fieldwork. Suffering from a downturn in its fortunes globally, the company transferred production to Mexico.

In closing, the evidence from the unionized transplants confirms and deepens the findings of others regarding the general lack of diffusion of Japanese-style HRM/LR practices to television assembly operations in the United States and the United Kingdom. There were indications of some diffusion of practices in the unionized transplants, of which the development of the new group leader position was the most important. But only in the nonunion plant did we find substantial diffusion of Japanese-style HRM/LR practices. The stark contrast between the unionized transplants and the nonunion transplant strongly suggests that the U.S. union–management environment in which the parties were so rooted made diffusion of the HRM/LR practices impossible or too costly to justify (as illustrated by union willingness to strike over changes pursued by management). In particular, American management in the plants lacked the commitment to create the learning environments conducive to the diffusion of Japanese HRM/LR practices, albeit strongly reinforced by union insistence on maintaining hierarchical job-protection systems. In the end, all parties seem convinced that the socially constructed Fordist tradition was "natural" in these American facilities. We conclude that, unlike their counterparts in auto assembly, the Japanese television MNCs did not insist on the diffusion of their preferred HRM/LR practices, choosing instead to adopt workplace practices embedded in their American host environment.

NOTES

Martin Kenney gratefully acknowledges Frank Mayadas and Gail Pesyna of the Alfred P. Sloan Foundation for providing the support that made this research possible. The authors also thank Shuichi Hashimoto for his participation in the research.

1. There are three much smaller Japanese-owned factories still in operation: the Pioneer projection television plant in Chino, California, which employed approximately 100 people; the Orion television plant in Princeton, Indiana, which employed approximately 250 people; and the Matusushita television/videocassette recorder plant in Vancouver, Washington, which employed approximately 250 people.

2. We requested interviews with the factory manager, the quality control section manager, the production section manager, the production engineering manager, and a supervisor. All interviewees were chosen by management. Across the four plants, we conducted 22 in-depth interviews. At Factory W, we interviewed the plant manager, one vice president, two production managers, and two supervisors. At Plant X, we interviewed the executive vice president/general manager. At plant Y, we interviewed the president, three vice presidents, two directors, three middle-level managers, and one supervisor. At Plant Z, we interviewed two vice presidents and two directors.

3. Analyses of operations in Japan are reported in Kenney (1999). Analyses of operations in northern Mexico are reported in Kenney and Florida (1993) and Lowe and Kenney (1999).

REFERENCES

Abo, T. (1994). *Hybrid Factories*. New York: Oxford University Press.
Adler, P. (1993). "Time-and-Motion Regained." *Harvard Business Review* (January-February), pp. 97-109.
Adler, P., and Cole, R. (1993). "Designed for Learning: A Tale of Two Auto Plants." *Sloan Management Review* 34 (Spring), pp. 85-94.
Aoki, M. (1988). *Information, Incentives and Bargaining in the Japanese Economy*. Cambridge: Cambridge University Press.
Beazley, J. E. (1988). "In Spite of Mystique, Japanese Plants in U.S. Find Problems Abound." *Wall Street Journal* June 22, p. A1.
Braverman, H. (1974). *Labor and Monopoly Capital*. New York: Monthly Review Press.
Byrne, J. (1986). "At Sanyo's Arkansas Plant the Magic Isn't Working." *Business Week*, July 14, pp. 51-52.
Cole, R. (1989). *Strategies for Learning*. Berkeley: University of California Press.
Delbridge, R. (1998). *Life on the Line in Contemporary Manufacturing*. Oxford: Oxford University Press.
Dore, R. (1973). *British Factory —Japanese Factory*. Berkeley: University of California Press.
Fucini, S. and Fucini, J. (1990). *Working for the Japanese*. New York: Free Press.
Graham, L. (1995). *On the Line at Subaru-Isuzu*. Ithaca, NY: ILR/Cornell University Press.
Harvard Business School. (1981). "Sanyo Manufacturing Corporation—Forrest City, Arkansas." HBS Case No. 0-682-045.
Institute of Social Sciences. (1990). "Local Production of Japanese Automobile and Electronics Firms in the United States: The 'Application' and 'Adaptation' of Japanese Style Management." University of Tokyo, Report No. 23.
Kenney, M. (1999). "Transplantation?: Comparing Japanese Television Assembly Plants in Japan and the U.S." In Adler, P., Fruin, W. M., and Liker, J. (eds.), *Remade in America*. New York: Oxford University Press, pp. 256-93.
Kenney, M. and Florida, R. (1993). *Beyond Mass Production: The Japanese System and Its Transfer to the U.S.* Oxford: Oxford University Press.
Kenney, M., Goe, W. R., Contreras, O., Romero, J., and Bustos, M. (1998). "Learning Factories?: An Examination of Shopfloor Workers in the Japanese Electronics Maquiladoras." *Work and Occupations* 25 (3), pp. 269-304.
Koike, K. (1988). *Understanding Industrial Relations in Modern Japan*. New York: St. Martin's Press.
Kotha, S. and Dunbar, R. (1995). "Sanyo Manufacturing Corporation—1977-1990." Leonard N. Stern School of Business, New York University Case Study.
Liker, J., Fruin, W. M., and Adler, P. (eds.). (1999). *Remade in America*. New York: Oxford University Press.
Lowe, N. and Kenney, M. (1999). "Foreign Investment and the Global Geography of Production: Why the Mexican Consumer Electronics Industry Failed." *World Development* 27 (8), pp. 1427-43.
Nakamura, K., Demes, H., and Nagano, H. (1994). "Work Organization in Japan and Philipp-Franz-von-Siebold-Stiftung, Deutsches Institut fur Japanstudien.
Oliver, N. and Wilkinson, B. (1988). *The Japanization of British Industry*. Oxford: Basil Blackwell.
Porter, M. (1983). *Cases in Competitive Strategy*. New York: Free Press.

Sato, A. (1991). "Business as Usual: Management Practices of Japanese Consumer Electronics Companies in the United States." Program on U.S.-Japan Relations, Harvard University Occasional Paper 91-10.

Yonekura, S. (1985). "Sanyo Manufacturing Corp. (B)." Harvard Business School Case Study, revised September 1984.

8

Convergence or Divergence of Contingent Employment Practices? Evidence of the Role of MNCs in Europe

Chris Brewster and Olga Tregaskis

As discussed in several previous chapters, multinational companies (MNCs) decide whether they will adopt local human resource management and labor relations (HRM/LR) practices common to host countries or diffuse their preferred practices to host country subsidiaries. If their preference is diffusion, one can argue that MNCs serve as the engine of international convergence of HRM/LR practices. If, on the other hand, MNCs adopt host country practices, one can argue that the forces of local isomorphism are more powerful, in this respect at least, than the forces of convergence. This latter outcome would imply that there are significant limitations to the power of MNCs to organize work abroad in ways that they might prefer. We address this issue of diffusion/adaptation, using comparable samples from countries with distinctly different institutional and cultural settings. In so doing, we shed additional light on the debate about convergence/divergence and about the role of the MNC in determining employment practices worldwide.

First, we explore the issues of convergence and divergence and the role played by MNCs in diffusing innovative practices and, in turn, encouraging international convergence. As acknowledged in the general management literature, the convergence/divergence debate particularly focuses on HRM/LR issues since this is where the interface between business and national cultures is sharpest (Rozenzweig and Nohria, 1994). Second, we address the topic of contingent employment and workplace practices. These practices present one of the most contentious challenges to the established local institutional and legislative frameworks of some countries. As argued by some commentators, moreover, these contingent employment practices may serve as the new converging force in workplaces around the world (Piore and Sabel, 1984; Cappelli, 1999). To evaluate these issues regarding the convergence or divergence of contingent workplace practices, we subsequently examine contingent work practices across three fairly distinct national settings: Germany,

Spain, and the United Kingdom. Specifically, we estimate the effects of nationality, MNC status, and sector on the distribution of five contingent employment and workplace practices (part-time contracts, temporary contracts, fixed-term contracts, shift-working, and annualization of hours). Finally, we conclude by addressing the implications of the results of our empirical inquiry for theory and practice.

CONVERGENCE OR DIVERGENCE?

The convergence versus divergence debate has been an ongoing strand of the management literature for decades and has more recently been reflected in the associated HRM theorizing and empirical debate (Kerr, 1983; Muller, 2000; Mueller, 1994; Tregaskis, Heraty, and Morley, 2001). In brief, the convergence thesis argues that differences in management systems have arisen as a result of the geographical isolation of businesses and the consequent development of differing beliefs and value orientations of national cultures. These differences are being superseded, however, by the logic of technology and markets, which require the adoption of specific and, therefore, universally applicable management techniques (Kidger, 1991).

Early postwar thinking, for the most part, supported the convergence thesis. Galbraith (1967) contended that, given the evolution of modern industry, our "area of decision is, in fact, exceedingly small" and that much of what evolves across nations naturally converges since "the imperatives of organization, technology and planning operate similarly, and as we have seen, to a broadly similar result, on all societies" (336). Burnham (1941), Drucker (1950), and Harbison and Myers (1959) contended that there was a trend toward a worldwide rise of the professional manager who would successfully impose professional, as opposed to patrimonial or political, management systems on their respective societies. Closer to our field of interest, Kerr et al. (1960) believed not only that the convergence of industrial relations (IR) systems was inevitable but that the convergence would be toward U.S. practices. They argued that management systems represented attempts to manage technology as efficiently as possible. As the United States was the technological leader, it followed that U.S. management practices represented current best practice, which other nations would eventually seek to emulate as they sought to adopt U.S. technology. Thus, "patterns in other countries were viewed as derivative of, or deviations from, the U.S. model" (Locke, Piore, and Kochan, 1995: xvi).

A newer, alternative thesis argues that the effects of institutional arrangements in Europe (the dismantling of national boundaries to trade, and the movement of labor, the imposition of European Union (EU) wide standards of employment, etc.) may drive a form of convergence within the EU that is distinct from the U.S. model (Brewster, 1994; Due, Madsen, and Jensen, 1991). With the exception of the "institutional" arguments for convergence, what characterizes the various convergence perspectives is a mode of thought in which the practice of management is explained exclusively by reference to its contribution to technological and economic efficiency. It is a dependent variable that evolves in response to technological and economic change, rather than with reference to the sociopolitical context, so that "much of what happens to management and labor is the same regardless of auspices" (Kerr, 1983). This conceptualization has affected the paradigms through which such topics are researched and published (Brewster, 1999).

It has been argued by some in the industrial organization literature that firms tend to seek out and adopt the best solutions to organizing labor within their product markets, long-term survival being dependent on firms being able to implement them (Chandler, 1962, 1977; Chandler and Daems, 1980). More recent theories, such as transaction cost economics, also contend that at any one time there exists a best solution to organizing labor (Williamson, 1975, 1985). "Most transaction cost theorists argue that there is one best organizational form for firms that have similar or identical transaction costs" (Hollingsworth and Boyer, 1997: 34). These arguments promote the idea of convergent HRM/LR practices based on market and transaction cost commonalities, which transcend nationally bounded pressures for divergent organizational responses. The various convergence theorists recognize that in practice there are many variations in management approaches around the world. However, they argue that in the long term, these variations are ascribable to the industrial sector in which the firm is located, its strategy, its available resources, and its degree of exposure to international competition. These are factors that will be of diminishing salience over time, and, once taken account of, a clear trend toward the adoption of common management systems should be apparent.

Why might the managers of MNCs want to coordinate and integrate their HRM/LR practices across borders? There are five potential reasons (Dickmann, 1999). There is, first, the administrative heritage of a corporation. If a firm has a successful experience with specific practices, in the absence of strong countervailing arguments, it will wish to implement these approaches abroad (Bartlett and Ghoshal, 1989). Second, management may be persuaded of the ethical merit of the international standardization of certain practices. An example would be the establishment of a system that allows all long-term workers monetary security during their retirement (Schusser, 1992). Third, companies that rely on good relations or even want to sell their products to the host state may well want to install systems of training and career management that are perceived as internationally fair. Fourth, MNCs may pursue a global business strategy that encourages integration around a specific set of HRM/LR policies and practices (Schuler and Jackson, 1987). For example, a German firm may want to export its quality-centered strategy, encouraging extensive employee development and involvement in order to create products of high standards (Vitols et al., 1997). Fifth and most obviously, companies want to transfer their home policies if they see them as superior. The implementation of parent practices may be efficient in that it avoids duplication of efforts, it may be evaluated as better than alternative local solutions, and it may support global integration (Mayrhofer and Brewster, 1996). Each of these conditions would reinforce a convergence in HRM/LR practices among international organizations.

In direct contrast to those who look for convergence, proponents of the divergence thesis argue that personnel management systems, far from being economically or technologically derived, epitomize national institutional and cultural contexts. And they do not respond readily to the imperatives of technology or the market. According to this perspective, organizational choice is limited by institutional pressures, including those from the state, regulatory structures, interest groups, public opinion, and norms (Di Maggio and Powell, 1983; Oliver, 1991). Moreover, many of these pressures are so accepted, so taken for granted "as to be invisible to the actors they influence" (Oliver, 1991:148). One observable effect of differing institutional contexts is that "the same equipment is frequently operated quite differently in the same sectors in different countries, even when firms are competing in the same market" (Hollingsworth and Boyer, 1997: 20).

Divergence is also explained in that host country national business systems may offer MNCs competitive advantages that their own home country systems may not (Dunning, 1993, 1997; Porter, 1980). In such instances the parent may take a strategic decision not to transfer some of its practices. Guest and Hoque (1996) concluded that the lack of transfer of practices from German multinationals to U.K. subsidiaries was in part explained by the enhanced flexibility that the host context afforded. In other instances, the subsidiary may resist the imposition of parent practices, as detailed by Kenney and Tanaka in Chapter 7 of this volume. Endogenous organizational factors linked to structures, strategies, and control play a critical role in this respect. Depending on the strategic role of the subsidiary, the power of the parent in influencing subsidiary practice may be minimal (Birkinshaw and Morrison, 1995; Birkinshaw and Fry, 1998). Parent control over resources, the corporate culture, and authority structures act as vehicles for parent influence or lack of it. Normative or coercive isomorphic pressures promoted via host country legislation, professionalization, or collective bargaining also explain the limited transfer of practices (DiMaggio and Powell, 1983; Kenney and Tanaka, Chapter 7 of this volume). Divergence of HRM/LR practices across an MNC's foreign subsidiaries is, therefore, more likely, as well as convergence of practices at the level of the host country.

In a retrospective analysis of his work with Dunlop, Harbison, and Myers, Kerr concedes that they had been wrong to suggest that industrialism would "so overwhelmingly impose its own cultural patterns on pre-existing cultures; industrialism does conquer and it does impose, but less rapidly and less totally than we implied" (Kerr, 1983: 28). Divergence theorists, however, would not even subscribe to this thesis of partial and delayed convergence. They argue not only that national and, in some cases, regional institutional contexts are slow to change but that even when change does occur, this can be understood only in relation to the specific sociopolitical context in which it occurs (Maurice, Sellier, and Silvestre, 1986).

In summary and in broad terms, therefore, there are two distinct versions of the convergence thesis. On the one hand, there is the traditional version of the convergence thesis that contends that convergence of HRM/LR practices is driven by market and technological forces, making changes in the United States a harbinger of trends elsewhere. On the other hand, there is a new, institutionally based argument for convergence where there are international standards being set by supranational bodies (as in the EU). There is also a strong institutional and culturally based counterargument that the world is more likely to evince divergence than convergence (especially in matters of HRM/LR), because of the continuing differences between countries. Within the framework of this ongoing debate, we next examine the forces of convergence and divergence on shaping the specific context of contingent employment and workplace practices in Germany, Spain, and the United Kingdom.

CONTINGENT EMPLOYMENT AND WORKPLACE PRACTICES

It is argued that one of the key indicators of convergence is evidenced in the emergent model of organizational flexibility (Piore and Sabel, 1984). New, flexible production techniques emerged in the wake of advances in information technology, stimulating a shift in competitive strategy toward flexible specialization aimed at producing differentiated, high-value-added products. As a result, a new management model began to emerge. One element of this new model has been aimed at increasing individual flexibility and employee self-regulation of quality control. Furthermore, new, broader job designs have been created that allow employees in coordination with their supervisors to formulate their own job descriptions. On the premise that job security could be extended only to the core labor force, another feature of the new management model has been the increase in contingent or noncore employment, such as part-time, temporary, and contract work. In a comparative study of German, French, and U.K. industries, Lane (1989) found that each country responded differently to the same economic pressures for flexibility. She argued that whereas German industry embraced flexible specialization, British industry tended to adopt a combination of Fordist and contractual flexibility principles of management.

In terms of defining flexibility, a variety of wide-ranging options has been presented. Polivk and Nardone (1989) define contingent employment in broad terms as "any arrangement that differs from full-time, permanent, wage and salary employment" (10). An equally broad definition of "atypical" employment is that adopted by Delsen (1991), who describes it as deviating "from full-time open-ended work employment: part-time work, seasonal work" (123). Morishima and Feuille (2000) note that contingent employment can include a wide variety of workers. They conclude that "the common themes that unite the individuals in these diverse categories is that they receive few or no fringe benefits, they have little or no expectation of long-term employment with the firm on whose premises they work at any given time, and they occupy a secondary position to the regular, full-time (or core) employees in the firm's status hierarchy" (2). Although an accurate account of the United States and Japan, within the European context, such distinctions do not hold true. Apart from the fact that in many European countries local employment protection helps guard against any such discrimination, the EU has passed legislation guaranteeing the rights of part-time and temporary workers, which apply across the EU.

Different forms of contingent practices have different effects and implications. Herein, we examine five specific forms of employment and workplace practices, namely, part-time contracts, temporary contracts, fixed-term contracts, shift-working, and annualization of hours. Part-time, temporary, and fixed-term contracts have been selected as these are the most salient contingent employment practices in the available database used herein. Shift-working and annualization of hours were chosen for their contrast between the traditional and the new. Again, definitions across national boundaries can be complex. Part-time work, for example, applies to any work hours short of the normal working week for each country, which varies across the globe. Thus, in France and Belgium, part-time work is defined as four-fifths or less of the collectively agreed working time; in the Netherlands and the United States, as less than 35 hours; in the United Kingdom, as less than 30 hours, with lower thresholds in relation to social security contributions. Elsewhere, the norm is concentrated around 25–30 hours (see Bolle, 1997 or Brewster et al., 1996 for more complete listings). It is generally argued, on one hand, that judicious use of part-time employment allows employers to pay only for the most productive hours of an employee's time. On the other hand, such arrangements can be beneficial for those with family care responsibilities who find that longer working hours exclude them from participating full-time in the labor market. Approximately 85 percent of part-time workers in Europe, it can be noted, are female.

Temporary contracts are those that can be terminated with just the appropriate notice and are recognized by both parties as not intending to lead to permanent employment commitments. They can range from a few weeks' work to as many as three years, though typically they are at the lower end of such a distribution. Fixed-term contracts, in contrast, are those in which the parties agree will end on a certain date, often after 12 or 24 months. By law, these contracts are not treated as terminations of employment per se since they have simply been completed, not broken. Temporary and fixed-term contracts tend to overlap but often appear to substitute for each other depending on local legislation. Temporary contracts tend to be reached with lower-skilled workers, whereas fixed-term contracts tend to be reached with higher-skilled employees. Employers avoid expectations that either type of contract will lead to permanent employment and, consequently, avoid some of the legal obligations, as well as trade union reactions, that the termination of employment might otherwise prompt.

Shift-working is a familiar device in manufacturing and emergency services used as a means of extending production hours or customer coverage. It is now spreading into other industries that never used it before, such as in banking, in response to customer demand. Annualization of hours is an arrangement designed to cope with peaks and troughs in demand, by changing working hours over the year so that employees work longer hours during periods of peak demand than they do during the off-peak periods. Hours are arranged in advance, and wages are held level throughout the year. Justification for such annualization of hours is based on the argument that, provided the same number of hours are worked for the same income, employees are not penalized.

Overall, there are clear benefits for employers in deploying these various contingent practices, even when they do not pay lower wages. Employers, that is, pay just for the hours that are productive, have limited commitment, and enjoy increased flexibility. In some cases, moreover, these contingent employment practices are also advantageous for employees. Certain of these forms of contingent employment practices are further removed from the negative consequences identified by Morishima and Feuille (2000). For example, part-time employment can in many instances be of a permanent nature. Equally, fixed-term contracts in occupations that are in high demand and low in supply, such as software designers, can prove quite advantageous for individuals in terms of reward packages and opportunities for skill enhancement. De Grip, HoeVenberg, and Willems (1997) found that part-time employment in comparison to temporary employment was more likely associated with sales and service positions and younger and older workers. They also found (as have Tregaskis et al., 1998, and Brewster and Tregaskis, 2001), that the prevalence of part-time and temporary employment varies across countries, showing distinctive patterns.

The trend toward increasing use of contingent employment in Europe has complex antecedents. Competitive pressures have undoubtedly had a role to play in forcing managers to address the way that they utilize labor and introduce more innovative approaches to the organization of work. The European Commission has taken a "Janus" role in both promoting more flexible forms of organization and protecting worker rights associated with contingent work. Structural changes have also played a role. These include, for example, the shifts in employment from manufacturing to services, greater sexual and racial diversity within the labor market, rising levels of education, and changing attitudes toward work (Brewster et al., 1996). These structural changes have generated a demand for alternative working time and contractual arrangements. Such trends, which are common throughout Europe, would suggest that company responses may be similar across the continent, reflecting a shift toward the widespread use of contingent employment and workplace practices. As discussed later, there are institutional arguments, nonetheless, that might suggest otherwise.

The Cases of Germany, Spain, and the United Kingdom

We have selected Germany, Spain, and the United Kingdom for study here as cases that enable us to test the convergence influence of MNCs on different local environments. The three countries are significantly different in character both at a cultural level (Hofstede, 1980; Laurent, 1986; Trompenaars, 1993) and at an institutional level (Dickmann, 1999). To take an example that is relevant to the topic of flexibility in working patterns, social security and child-care provisions are widespread in Germany, less generous in the United Kingdom, and fairly limited in Spain (although here, reliance on family support is generally more prevalent). These variations in national systems influence variations in the use of certain forms of contingent employment, such as shorter working hours.

At the institutional level, Due et al. (1991) distinguish between countries such as the United Kingdom, on the one hand, in which the state plays a limited role in industrial relations, and countries such as Spain and Germany, on the other hand, in which the state functions as an actor with a central role in industrial relations. In the case of the latter, the state has a strong role in regulating the length of the working day and break periods. Consequently, the room for firm-level decision making is considerably less in the Spanish and German contexts relative to the U.K context. This difference in influence may diminish following the EU's recent legislation on working time, which provides for a basic minimum in hours worked, and breaks, and so on. However, as Covaleski and Dirsmith (1998: 562) point out, in Germany the strong regulatory environment, particularly in regard to employment, evokes a rule-oriented consensus that governs "social thought and action." In the United Kingdom, by contrast, the competitive environment allows greater organizational autonomy, promoting diversity in practice. We might conclude, therefore, that certain countries are more likely than others to encourage institutional consensus and conformity.

A review of the key characteristics of the business systems in Britain, Germany, and Spain by Dickmann (1999) suggests differences in three areas. First, he argues that the German business system is more long-term, compared to either the United Kingdom or Spain. This is made possible as a consequence of the stable political institutions (Goodhard, 1994), public-private ownership patterns, and investment supported through banking institutions as opposed to shareholders (Sally et al., 1992). In contrast, employment in Spain is dominated by the small and medium-size employer and by the tourism and service sectors, which are significant features of the economy (EIU, 1994; Aparacio-Valverde and Soler, 1996). Spain, moreover, has experienced some of the highest levels of unemployment in the EU, forcing the government to take action on job creation to reduce youth and long-term unemployment. Spain has also introduced significant reforms in employment legislation arising from the difficulties and costs that companies faced as a result of widespread retrenchment. In particular, these reforms promoted the use of contingent employment contracts for new labor market entrants, the long-term unemployed, and trainee positions. Together, the structure of the business sectors and the nature of the legislative approach to the employment relationship could be argued to promote more short-term investment strategies and more volatile market conditions.

Given these differences across countries, the pattern of contingent employment use across these three countries is likely to be quite different. In the case of Germany, we might expect less demand for contingent employment either by employees or by employers, at least in response to cost demands. In

Spain, the uncertainty of markets would encourage employers to use contingent employment relationships that offer them the greatest flexibility (e.g., temporary or fixed-term contracts). The United Kingdom potentially sits in the middle of these two extreme contexts, as business conditions would encourage employers to use a broad collection of contingent practices to meet both employee and employer demands regarding flexibility.

There is also an internal labor market case to be made. The well-known German *duales* vocational education and training systems, combined with the longer-term German investment perspective, encourage strong internal labor markets (Muller, 1997; Prais, Jarvis, and Wagner, 1991). In contrast, the low value placed on educational qualifications in the U.K. context in combination with the lower level of vocational training encourages poaching and reliance on external labor markets. In Spain, the uncertain economic conditions and heavy reliance on the tourist industry and family-run small businesses do not encourage the long-term investment and organic skills growth characteristic of internal labor markets. Consequently, as external labor markets are more commonly used by employers, it is more viable for them to adopt contingent employment options.

Finally, there is the influence of collective bargaining contexts. It is clear that, in general, European countries are more heavily unionized than the United States and most other countries. Trade union membership and influence vary considerably by country, of course, but are always significant (see Chapters 4 and 5 of this volume). Indeed, in many European countries the law requires union recognition for collective bargaining. In most European countries, many of the union functions in such areas as pay bargaining, for example, are exercised at industrial or national levels (outside the direct involvement of managers within individual organizations), as well as at the establishment level (Hyman and Ferner, 1994; Morley et al., 2000). Thus, in Europe, unlike in the United States, firms are likely to deal with well-founded trade union structures. There are still significant differences, nonetheless, in labor relations between Germany, Spain, and the United Kingdom. In Germany, the codetermination regulations promote greater employee influence in employment relations, enhancing the use of contracts that are more favorable in terms of job security and skill acquisition opportunities. For example, the influence of trade unions and collective bargaining arrangements has played a significant role in the restriction of weekend working in Germany. Unions are significantly less powerful in the United Kingdom (Lane, 1992) and weaker and more adversarial in Spain (Miguelez and Prieto, 1991; Filella and Soler, 1992). This calls into question the ability of employee representative groups to resist the introduction of contingent contracts with a managerialist agenda.

We have pointed to the fact that in the United Kingdom, Germany, and Spain, companies are constrained at a national level by culture, financial arrangements, and legislation and at the organizational level, companies are constrained by trade union involvement, consultative arrangements, and the viability of internal labor markets. Do these differences provide a barrier to MNCs' transferring personnel policies and practices across borders? Given the differences in the institutional, regulatory, and cultural arrangements across the three countries, some might expect divergent patterns of contingent employment use.   Given the imperatives of modern capitalism, others would expect convergence, or at least that MNCs would be distinctive (or "leading") in some way in their use of flexibility options. As the arguments for both convergence and divergence have merit, resolution of the debate ultimately requires empirical analyses.

EMPIRICAL INQUIRY

In this section, we draw on data collected in the 1995 Cranet-E survey to examine the extent of contingent employment and workplace practices across domestic companies and foreign-owned subsidiaries in Germany, Spain, and the United Kingdom. Although we cannot directly test for convergence/divergence, given the cross-sectional nature of our empirical inquiry herein, we can examine, nonetheless, the influence of nationality and MNC status on the distribution of contingent practices across firms in the sample. As such, we can shed some initial empirical light on the debate, first, on the extent to which MNCs have adopted local practices or have diffused contingent employment practices to their subsidiaries and, second, on whether the forces underlying convergence or divergence appear dominant.

Data

The Cranet-E survey data set that we examine is part of the larger, ongoing project of the Cranet network of universities and business schools that have collaborated on a cross-national survey of HRM/LR practices (Brewster et al., 2000). Our subsample of observations includes responses from just over 1,300 private sector companies in Germany, Spain, and the United Kingdom. As reported in Table 8.1, 518 are service sector companies, of which 310 are foreign- and home-owned MNCs and 208 are domestic companies.   The remaining responses are from 840 manufacturing companies, of which 639 are foreign- and home-owned MNCs and 201 are domestic companies.

Table 8.1
Distribution of Observations by Country, Sector, and MNC Status
(Totals in parentheses)

		Country			
		U.K.	Germany	Spain	Total
Service		(343)	(103)	(72)	(518)
	MNCs	223	42	45	(310)
	Domestic	120	61	27	(208)
Manufacturing		(470)	(227)	(143)	(840)
	MNCs	387	155	97	(639)
	Domestic	83	72	46	(201)
Totals		(813)	(330)	(215)	(1358)

Unlike most other studies, which have been constrained by having to grapple with these issues of comparability on the basis of sequential, country-by-country descriptions of HRM/LR practices without the benefit of access to strictly comparable measures (Locke et al., 1995), we are able to compare precisely defined HRM/LR practices across countries. Unlike most empirical comparisons of HRM/LR practices across countries, moreover, the given data allow us to compare company responses rather than employee responses as a means of understanding patterns of contingent employment in Europe.

Hypotheses

Within the limitations of the available secondary database, we state and test two hypotheses germane to the issues of adoption versus innovation and convergence versus divergence. As discussed earlier in this and preceding chapters, MNCs often have profit-maximizing and organizational incentives to diffuse preferred HRM/LR practices across their foreign subsidiaries unless the costs or benefits of doing so makes diffusion suboptimal. As developed herein, there is reason to believe that isomorphic constraints deeply embedded in the cultural, IR, and sociopolitical systems of Germany, Spain, and the United Kingdom make the use of innovative contingent employment and workplace practices that might be preferred by MNCs rather costly to diffuse. We anticipate, therefore, that while MNCs seek to diffuse innovative practices and, thus, their foreign subsidiaries exhibit a greater use of contingent practices than domestic firms, the cultural, IR, and sociopolitical systems of specific countries dominate. As such, MNCs tend to adopt the local practices prevalent in the host country. Hence, we hypothesize the following:

H1: The extent of contingent employment and workplace practices varies by country.

H2: The use of contingent employment and workplace practices by foreign-owned MNCs converges to the host country.

Statistical Analysis

To test these hypotheses, we first provide a multivariate analysis of variance (MANOVA) to estimate the effects of host country, MNC status, and sector on the distribution of contingent employment and workplace practices across our sample. The dependent variables consisted of the five contingent practices examined (i.e., the use of part-time, temporary, and fixed-term contracts, shift-working, and annualized hours). The extent to which these various practices are used was measured in terms of the average score on a scale of 0 to 5 (where 0 = not used, 1 = less than 1 percent of the workforce, 2 = 1-5 percent, 3 = 6-10 percent, 4 = 11-20 percent, and 5 = more than 20 percent). Host country is the country (German, Spain, or the United Kingdom) in which firms are located. MNC status is measured as one of three categories: foreign-owned MNC subsidiaries, domestic-owned MNCs, and domestic-only firms.

Sector distinguishes between companies operating in service and manufacturing industries. Additionally, we test for any added interaction effects associated with MNC status and host country, as well as for any interaction effects associated with sector and host country. Univariate tests of significance were made to establish the precise nature of the effect of the independent variables on each of the dependent variables.

The results from the multivariate estimates (Table 8.2) indicate that all three independent variables significantly influence the variance of contingent practices (measured in composite form) deployed by our sample of firms. Although statistically significant, the amount of variance accounted for by each of the variables differs considerably (see ETA values reported in Table 8.2). Country has the largest effect on variation, accounting for 25 percent of the variance. Sector also accounts for a substantial proportion (17 percent) of variance. MNC status, however, accounts for very little variance, a mere 1 percent. Our estimates also indicate that there is little added interaction effect among variables. The interaction between MNC status and country is insignificant, and although the interaction between country and sector is statistically significant, its effect is fairly negligible (accounting for only 2 percent of variance).

Table 8.2
MANOVA of the Determinants of Contingent Employment Practices

Effect	Wilks' Lambda	ETA Squared	DF	Sig.
Host Country	.57	.25	10	.000 *
MNC Status	.98	.01	10	.006 *
Sector	.83	.17	5	.000 *
MNC Status by Country	.97	.00	20	.562
Sector by Country	.97	.02	10	.000 *

* significant at the $\leq .05$ level.

Before drawing inferences from the multivariate results, we next examine in detail what these differences look like in practice. Reported in Table 8.3 are the mean scores of the five contingent employment and workplace practices by country, sector, MNC status, and the sector-by-country interaction. These mean scores are based on the scale of 0 to 5 indicating the percentage of the workforce engaged in each form of contingent employment, as outlined earlier. Reported in Table 8.4 are univariate tests of significance between these contingent practices and the set of variables used in our multivariate estimation. Using these data and statistics, we compare differences in the extent of usage where there are statistically significant patterns found at the univariate level.

In terms of country differences, it becomes clear from the univariate tests of significance that the three countries studied vary significantly in their use of part-time, temporary, and fixed-term employment but not in their use of shift-work or annualization of hours. As reported in Table 8.3, Spain has the lowest average score for the use of part-time contracts (mean score = .90), followed by the United Kingdom (mean score = 2.1), with Germany having the highest score (mean score = 2.6). This suggests that the use of part-time contracts varies on average from less than 1 percent of the workforce in Spain to just over 8 percent in Germany. The distributions of responses for part-time contracts across the United Kingdom and Germany are both normally distributed. However, the distribution for Spain is negatively skewed, with 96 percent of employers indicating that they use these contracts only to cover less than 10 percent of their workers.

With respect to temporary contracts, Germany is the lowest user (mean score = .93), and the United Kingdom is a medium user (mean score = 2.0), whereas Spain is by far the highest user (mean score = 2.8). The distribution of scores across the three countries is quite variable. For example, in the United Kingdom, the scores are normally distributed, with the majority of employers using temporary contracts to cover between 1 and 10 percent of their workers. In Germany, responses are negatively skewed, with 93 percent of employers using these contracts to cover 5 percent or less of their workers. In contrast, the distribution in Spain in positively skewed, with 83 percent of employers using temporary contracts to cover more than 20 percent of their workers.

Regarding fixed-term contracts, the pattern of use changes again, with the United Kingdom being the lowest user (mean score = 1.1), Germany the medium user (mean score = 1.8), and Spain, again, the highest user (mean score = 2.8). The distribution of organizational responses to the use of fixed-term contracts is also highly variable, with employers in Spain showing a very different pattern of use in comparison to both Germany and the United Kingdom. Specifically, 51 percent of employers in Spain indicated that they used fixed-term contracts to cover 10 percent or less of their workers, whereas 45 percent used them to cover more than 20 percent of their workers. In contrast, 84 percent of German employers and 97 percent of U.K. employers use fixed-term contracts to cover 10 percent or less of their workers.

Overall, the country variations show that the pattern of contingent practices used in Germany is marked primarily by the use of part-time contracts, a relatively moderate use of fixed-term contracts, and a minimal use of temporary contracts. The United Kingdom is characterized by a fairly even and relatively moderate utilization of all three practices. In Spain, temporary and fixed-term contracts are relatively widespread, whereas the use of part-time contracts is rare. As indicated earlier, there is no significant difference across the countries regarding the use of shift-working, which applies to approximately 8 percent of workers. Finally, we found no significant differences in the use of annualized hours, a practice that applies to less than 1 percent of workers across all three countries.

Differences between foreign-owned MNCs and domestic companies are found only in relation to the use of temporary contracts. Both domestic-only and home-owned MNCs are less likely to use temporary contracts (mean scores = 1.7 and 1.8, respectively) compared to foreign MNCs (mean score = 2.2). The difference in proportion of workers under temporary contracts is relatively small,

Table 8.3
Distribution of Contingent Practices by Country, Sector, and MNC Status

Country	Germany		Spain		U.K.	
Contingency practices:	Mean	SD	Mean	SD	Mean	SD
Part-time*	2.60	1.22	.90	1.09	2.10	1.37
Temporary*	.93	1.08	2.83	1.57	2.00	1.16
Fixed term*	1.80	.91	2.81	2.21	1.08	1.12
Shift work	2.67	2.04	2.62	2.17	2.72	1.97
Annual hours	.41	1.03	.67	1.48	.56	1.40

Sector	Manufacturing		Services			
Contingency practices:	Mean	SD	Mean	SD		
Part-time*	1.62	1.12	2.69	1.56		
Temporary	1.88	1.35	1.88	1.37		
Fixed-term	1.50	1.46	1.55	1.45		
Shift work*	3.20	1.94	1.87	1.87		
Annual hours	.56	1.38	.51	1.27		

Organization type	Home-MNC		Foreign MNC		Domestic-only	
Contingency practices:	Mean	SD	Mean	SD	Mean	SD
Part-time	2.10	1.39	1.63	1.18	2.30	1.52
Temporary*	1.78	1.25	2.16	1.31	1.73	1.49
Fixed-term	1.48	1.33	1.55	1.62	1.55	1.44
Shift work	2.82	1.95	2.96	1.99	2.28	2.07
Annual hours	.50	1.23	.65	1.53	.49	1.27

Country x Sector	Germany		Spain		U.K.	
Manufacturing:	Mean	SD	Mean	SD	Mean	SD
Part-time *	2.23	.97	.74	.94	1.61	1.05
Temporary *	1.05	1.12	2.71	1.49	2.02	1.19
Fixed-term	1.86	.82	2.74	2.21	.95	1.08
Shift work *	3.29	1.88	3.03	2.11	3.21	1.91
Annual hours	.34	.93	.68	1.53	.63	1.49

Country x Sector	Germany		Spain		U.K.	
Services:	Mean	SD	Mean	SD	Mean	SD
Part-time *	3.42	1.33	1.22	1.29	2.78	1.47
Temporary *	.65	.94	3.05	1.69	1.99	1.11
Fixed term	1.64	1.07	2.96	2.20	1.24	1.14
Shift work *	1.28	1.65	1.78	2.06	2.06	1.85
Annual hours	.57	1.21	.65	1.38	.47	1.26

*significant at the ≤ .05 level.

Table 8.4
MANOVA—Univariate Significance Tests

Effect		F	DF	Sig
MNC Status	Part-time	1.41	2	.245
	Temporary	4.23	2	.015 *
	Fixed-term	2.41	2	.090
	Shift-work	2.91	2	.055
	Annual hrs	0.97	2	.379
Sector	Part-time	122.87	1	.000 *
	Temporary	.006	1	.939
	Fixed-term	1.742	1	.187
	Shift-work	119.52	1	.000 *
	Annual hrs	.143	1	.705
Country	Part-time	119.40	2	.000 *
	Temporary	131.481	2	.000 *
	Fixed-term	136.54	2	.000 *
	Shift-work	2.48	2	.084
	Annual hrs	.797	2	.451
MNC Status	Part-time	.779	4	.539
by Country	Temporary	1.23	4	.292
	Fixed-term	1.67	4	.154
	Shift-work	.56	4	.689
	Annual hrs	.18	4	.949
Sector by	Part-time	5.49	2	.004 *
Country	Temporary	5.35	2	.005 *
	Fixed-term	2.73	2	.066
	Shift-work	5.24	2	.005 *
	Annual hrs	1.93	2	.145

* significant at the $\leq .05$ level.

nonetheless, with only about 6 percent of workers in foreign-owned MNCs and about 4 percent of workers in domestic companies covered under such contracts. However, foreign-owned MNCs are much more likely to have at least some workers covered by temporary contracts (71 percent) than home-owned MNCs (58 percent) and domestic-only companies (53 percent).

With respect to sectoral differences, the only statistically significant differences in variation are associated with the use of part-time employment contracts and shift-working. As expected, part-time employment is more widespread in service sector organizations (mean scores = 2.7 for services and 1.6 for manufacturing), with the reverse true for shift-work (mean scores = 3.2 for manufacturing and 1.9 for services). These mean scores show a range in the percentage of workers under part-time contracts from as low as about 3 percent to as high as about 10 percent. The distribution of responses among manufacturing companies shows that only 15 percent use part-time contracts for more than 5 percent of their workers, whereas this figure is 50 percent across service sector employers.

With regard to interaction terms, we first find no statistical evidence that there is variation in the usage of any of the five contingent practices across countries by MNC status. That is, any difference in the use of the five practices between foreign-owned MNCs and domestic firms is consistent across the countries. We find statistical evidence, however, that the usage of three contingent practices does vary across countries by sector. While the use of part-time contracts is greater in the services sector in both the United Kingdom and Germany, in Spain there is no significant difference in the use of these contracts between service and manufacturing organizations (they are low in both sectors). The use of temporary contracts significantly differs across the sectors in Germany but not in the United Kingdom and Spain. In Germany, the use of temporary contracts is greater in manufacturing (mean score = 1.1) compared to services (mean score = 0.6). Approximately 10 percent of the workforce in each of the three countries is employed on shift-work within manufacturing (mean scores = 3.2, 3.3 and 3.0, respectively). Within the service sector, however, the countries vary significantly, with the United Kingdom using shift-work the most (mean score = 2.1), followed by Spain (mean score = 1.8) and then Germany (mean score = 1.3). These mean scores reflect an approximate use of service sector shift-work varying between just over 1 percent of the workforce in Germany to about 5.5 percent of the workforce in the United Kingdom.

The standard deviations in scores (Table 8.3) across the five contingent employment practices suggest that the likelihood of using these practices varies considerably. In the case of part-time and temporary contracts, the distribution of responses is fairly similar, with about 74 percent of companies indicating that they use these contracts to cover 5 percent or less of their workers, and about 87 percent use them to cover 10 percent or less of their workers. Only 8 percent of employers use part-time contracts, and 6 percent use temporary contracts to cover more than 20 percent of their workers. In contrast, the distribution for the use of fixed-term contracts is narrower, with 82 percent of employers indicating that they use them to cover 5 percent or less of their workers, 89 percent use them to cover 10 percent or less of their workers, and only 8 percent use them to cover more than 20 percent of their workers. The use of shift-working conforms to a more bimodal distribution, with 56 percent of employers indicating that they use these contracts to cover 10 percent or less of their workers, and 33 percent use them to cover more than 20 percent of their workers.

The use of annualized hours, in comparison, is negatively and very heavily skewed, with 87 percent of employers indicating that they use them to cover 1 percent or less of workers and 90 percent of employers indicating that they use them to cover less than 10 percent of their workers. These distribution results suggest that annualized hours are the least likely to be used throughout Europe. Part-time and temporary contracts are more widespread, affecting larger proportions of workforces compared to fixed-term contracts. Finally, shift-working is not as widespread as, for example, part-time working.

However, in those organizations where shift-working is adopted, it is used extensively, affecting large proportions of workers.

In summary, the results from our statistical inquiry yield strong support for hypothesis 1 and partial support for hypothesis 2. First, we infer from our estimates that isomorphic constraints embedded in distinct cultural, IR, and sociopolitical systems have a dominant effect over any desires that MNCs might have to diffuse preferred contingent employment and workplace practices abroad. Indeed, country distinctions account for 25 percent of variance in the use of contingent employment and workplace practices across our sample, whereas MNC status accounts for a mere 1 percent of variance. Although we find some evidence that MNCs have deployed contingent employment practices to a greater extent than domestic companies, the evidence indicates that such innovation beyond the norm of the host country is quite limited. Not only does MNC status account for a nearly negligible amount of variance in practices, but it appears that such effect is found only in regard to the use of temporary contracts. Furthermore, we find no evidence of any interaction effects between MNC status and host country. Hence, we infer that the use of contingent employment and workplace practices of foreign-owned MNCs generally converge to the extent that such practices prevail in host countries.

DISCUSSION AND CONCLUSION

As framed by Cooke in Chapter 1, there is reason to believe and evidence to show that MNCs make decisions about whether to diffuse preferred HRM/LR practices to their subsidiaries abroad or to adopt practices common to host country locations. As addressed by Martin, Beaumont, and Pate in Chapter 6 and Kenney and Tanaka in Chapter 7, MNCs often face stiff resistance from host country managers, employees, and union representatives to the importation of selected practices. Among the wide range of alternative, innovative HRM/LR practices pursued by MNCs abroad, we have examined the diffusion of several contingent employment and workplace practices. Currently, the most widespread among these practices are part-time employment contracts, which cover about 18 percent of the European labor force (the vast majority held by women). Other contingent HRM/LR practices are less widely deployed, although most employers use them to some degree. Nevertheless, except for the relatively new experimentation with the annualization of hours, there has been a rising use of contingent employment practices throughout Europe and, in some cases, rather sharp rises (Brewster and Tregaskis, 2001).

We have sought to compare and explain any differences in the use of these contingent practices between MNCs and domestic companies, using Germany, Spain, and the United Kingdom as the basis for our analysis. Although the use of flexibility practices appears to be increasing in response to global competitive pressures and market uncertainty, our study shows that they are not deployed to the same extent across countries, nor appreciably more so by MNCs than by domestic firms. Either MNCs are not attempting to diffuse or impose contingent employment and workplace practices on their workforces in host countries (which we have argued, herein, is highly unlikely), or they have been constrained from doing so, in effect finding it too costly or of too limited benefit to justify pursuing in host locations in which workers are unreceptive. Based on our empirical inquiry, the evidence is consistent with, and strongly reinforces, the latter conclusion. It would appear, therefore, that the effects of institutions, legislation, trade unions, and related cultural differences substantially moderate the actions of MNCs.

Our finding that host country distinctions are the dominant influence on the deployment of contingent employment contracts, with no easier route for MNCs to introduce such practices in the (less regulated) United Kingdom than in (the more regulated, but more informal) Spain or in (the highly regulated, law-conscious) Germany, is at odds with some previous assessments. For example, Gooderham, Nordhaug, and Ringdal, (1998), contend that MNCs have tended to introduce contingent employment practices into at least some host countries, in particular, those where laws are more accommodating, such as in the United Kingdom. The difference between our findings and this earlier assessment may be that the earlier study is based on the practices of U.S. MNCs, which may have much in common with the United Kingdom in regard to favored HRM/LR practices. Hence, what the authors found might be the result of preexisting national similarities rather than the diffusion of innovative practices by U.S. MNCs.

The evidence here would suggest that the diffusion of contingent employment practices is heavily influenced by institutional factors that play a significant role in shaping organizational responses and, in turn, the adoption of contingent employment practices. That is, organizations operate not merely within economic environments but also within institutional ones. This affects not only the suitability or appropriateness of one particular form of HRM/LR practice over another but also the acceptance by the society, and hence by individuals within it, of alternative forms of workplace practices. Such a finding should give pause to those who assume that the reach and power of MNCs are unchecked, that their ability to impose their own patterns of work is unbounded, and that attempts to organize legislative, institutional, and trade union opposition to the imposition of contingent employment practices are fruitless. For some observers, these limits to the power of the MNCs may be viewed as encouraging. Since our evidence is not longitudinal, we cannot say that over time these statements about the power of the MNCs will prove lasting. What we can be sure of is that, at the time of our data collection (1995), they were manifestly false and that national institutional and cultural antecedents place significant constraints on MNCs from freely imposing those workplace practices that they prefer on foreign locations.

The importance of these institutional factors is worth careful consideration. Studies of HRM in the United States have tended to focus on the nonunion sector, of which there is a persistent assumption that innovative HRM practices are linked to nonunionism (see, e.g., Kochan, McKersie, and Capelli, 1984; Kochan, Katz, and McKersie, 1986). "In the U.S. a number of academics have argued that HRM [in concept and in practice] is anti-union and anti-collective bargaining" (Beaumont, 1991: 300).   In Europe, where such assumptions would be invalid (Brewster, 1995), the power of trade unions and the wider IR systems inevitably affect the ability of MNCs to introduce different employment and workplace patterns.

Not only does the same argument apply to the influence of legislation, but, as we have indicated, state involvement in HRM/LR in Europe is not restricted to the legislative role. Compared to the United States, the state in Europe has a higher involvement in underlying social security and social benefit provisions. Equally, it has a more directly interventionist role in the economy, providing far more HRM/LR services and acting as a more substantial employer in its own right, by virtue of a more extensive government-owned sector. Given these factors, it is perhaps not surprising that support for the argument for a converging common approach to flexible employment practices is not borne out by our data.

We do not want to build too much onto the foundation of these national differences in the adoption of certain workplace practices and the way that MNCs have had to accept and have adjusted to these differences. Nevertheless, the results of our limited inquiry should cause those whose vision is one in which MNCs have overwhelming power to consider the limitations of that power and the influence that this yields to national institutions. The evidence from our empirical inquiry would suggest that contingent employment practices are unlikely to operate as a force for convergence given their relatively limited use within the labor market and the strong institutional embeddedness of these practices in each country. It is going beyond the evidence here, but we might also suggest that in Europe at least, a more positive and cooperative approach to the introduction of contingent employment is possible (MacShane and Brewster, 2000). Such an approach would imply the melding of MNC interests with those of the local culture, institutions, and interests of local employees.

In spite of our findings' strongly supporting the argument for divergence of HRM/LR practices across national boundaries, on the one hand, and convergence of practices by MNCs to those prevailing within host countries, on the other hand, our study is clearly limited. In particular, we have examined only contingent employment and workplace practices, and these practices may, indeed, be ones that workers and their union representatives in Europe are especially opposed to, given the "contingency" nature of such employment arrangements. There may be much less resistance to HRM/LR practices that do not inherently threaten or limit the opportunities for stable, long-term employment. In addition, we have examined only the diffusion of these practices at the cross-section as of 1995 across three European countries. A much stronger test of the convergence thesis requires the analysis of longitudinal data, coupled with closer observation and accounting of employer and employee preferences. These limitations notwithstanding, the data and analysis presented herein clearly point to the need for greater "nuancing" of the arguments underlying the convergence/divergence debate and how subsequent empirical analyses are framed. In particular, there is a need to identify and assess the differing effects of institutions and cultures within various economic and

162   *Multinational Companies and Global Human Resource Strategies*

sociopolitical environments, as well as to make a coherent link (other than the overly simplistic "spearhead" argument) between the broader environmental factors and the role of MNCs on choices made about HRM/LR practices across host countries.

REFERENCES

Aparicio-Valverde, M. and Soler, C. (1996). *Working Time and Contract Flexibility*, Report prepared for the European Commission, Directorate-General V. Centre for European HRM, Cranfield University, pp. 56–76.

Bartlett, C. A. and Ghoshal, S. (1989). *Managing across Borders: The Transnational Solution.* Boston: Harvard Business School Press.

Beaumont, P. B. (1991). "The US Human Resource Management Literature: A Review." In Salaman, G. (ed.), *Human Resource Strategies*. Milton Keynes, U.K.:Open University Press, pp. 20–37.

Birkinshaw, J. M. and Morrison, A. J. (1995). "Configurations of Strategy and Structure in Subsidiaries of Multinational Corporations." *Journal of International Business Studies* 4, pp. 729–53.

Birkinshaw, J. M. and Fry, N. (1998). "Subsidiary Initiatives to Develop New Markets." *Sloan Management Review* 39 (3), pp. 51–62.

Bolle, P. (1997). "Part Time Work: Solution or Trap?" *International Labour Review* 136 (4), pp. 1–18.

Brewster, C. 1994). "European HRM: Reflection of, or Challenge to, the American Concept?" In Kirkbride, P. S. (ed.), *Human Resource Management in Europe*. London: Routledge, pp. 56–92.

Brewster, C. (1995). "IR and HRM: A Subversive European Model." *Industrielle Beziehungen*, 2 (4), pp. 395–413

Brewster, C. (1999). "Different Paradigms in Strategic HRM: Questions Raised by Comparative Research." In Wright, P., Dyer, L., Boudreau, J., and Milkovich, G. (eds.), *Research in Personnel and HRM*. Greenwich, CT.: JAI Press, pp. 213–38.

Brewster, C., Mayne, L., Tregaskis, O., Parsons, D., Atterbury, S., Hegewisch, A., Soler, C., Aparicio-Valverde, M., Picq, T., Weber, T., Kabst, R., Waglund, M., and Lindstrom, K. (1996). *Working Time and Contract Flexibility*. Report prepared for the European Commission, Directorate-General V. Centre for European HRM, Cranfield University.

Brewster, C. and Tregaskis, O. (2001). "Adaptive, Reactive and Inclusive Organisational Approaches to Workforce Flexibility in Europe." *Compartmento Organizational e Gestao* 7 (2), pp. 209–32.

Brewster, C., Tregaskis, O., Hegewisch, A. and Mayne, L. (2000). "Comparative Research in Human Resource Management: A Review and an Example." In Brewster, C., Mayrhofer, W., and Morley, M. (eds.), *New Challenges for European Human Resource Managemen*. London: Macmillan, pp. 324–48.

Burnham, J. (1941). *The Managerial Revolution*. New York: John Day.

Cappelli, P. (1999). *The New Deal at Work: Managing the Market-Driven Workforce*. Boston: Harvard Business School Press.

Chandler, A .D. (1962). *Strategy and Structure*. Cambridge: MIT Press.

Chandler, A. D. (1977). *The Visible Hand: The Managerial Revolution in American Business*. Cambridge: Harvard University Press.

Chandler, A. D. and Daems, H. (eds.). (1980). *Managerial Hierarchies: Comparative Perspectives on the Rise of the Modern Industrial Enterprise.* Cambridge: Harvard University Press.

Covaleski, M. A. and Dirsmith, M. W. (1988). "An Institutional Perspective on the Rise, Social Transformation, and Fall of a University Budget Category." *Administrative Science Quarterly* 33, pp. 562–87.

DeGrip, A., Hoevenberg, J., and Willems, E. (1997). "A typical Employment in the European Union." *International Labor Review* 136 (1), pp. 49–72.

Delsen, L. (1991). "Atypical Employment Relations and Government Policy in Europe." *Labor* 5 (3), pp. 123–49.

Dickmann, M. (1999). "Balancing Global, Parent and Local Influences: International Human Resource Management of German Multinational Companies." Ph.D. Thesis, University of London.

DiMaggio, P. J. and Powell, W. W. (1983). "The Iron Cage Revisited: Institutional Isomorphism and Collective Rationality in Organizational Fields." *American Sociological Review* 48, pp. 147–60.

Drucker, P. (1950). *The New Society: The Anatomy of the Industrial Order.* New York: Harper.

Due, J., Madsen, J. S., and Jensen, C. S. (1991). "The Social Dimension: Convergence or Diversification of IR in the Single European Market?" *Industrial Relations Journal* 22 (2), pp. 85–102.

Dunning, J. H. (1993). *Multinational Enterprise and the Global Economy.* New York: Addison Wesley.

EIU. (1994). *Country Report: Spain.* London: Economic Intelligence Unit.

Ferner, A. and Edwards, P. (1995). "Power and the Diffusion of Organizational Change within Multinational Enterprises." *European Journal of Industrial Relations* 1, pp. 229–57.

Filella, J. and Soler, C. (1992). "Spain." In Brewster, C., Hegewisch A., Holden, L., and Lockhart, T. (eds.), *The European Human Resource Management Guide.* London: Academic Press, pp. 439–82.

Galbraith, J. K. (1967). *The New Industrial State.* London: Hamish Hamilton.

Guest, D. and Hoque, K. (1996). "National Ownership and HR Practices in U.K. Greenfield Sites." *Human Resource Management Journal* 6 (4), pp. 50–74.

Gooderham, P.N., Nordhaug, O., and Ringdal, K. (1998). "When in Rome, Do They Do as the Romans? Subsidiaries of US Multinational Companies in Europe." *Management International Review* Special Issue, Feb.1998, pp. 47–64.

Harbison, F. and Myers, C. (1959). *Management in the Industrial World, an International Analysis.* New York: McGraw-Hill.

Hofstede, G. (1980). *Culture's Consequences: International Differences in Work-Related Values.* Beverly Hills, CA: Sage.

Hollingsworth, J. R. and Boyer, R. (1997). "Coordination of Economic Actors and Social Systems of Production." In Hollingsworth, J. R. and Boyer, R. (eds.), *Contemporary Capitalism.* Cambridge: Cambridge University Press, pp. 1–47.

Hyman, R. and Ferner, A. (eds.). (1994). *New Frontiers in European Industrial Relations.* Oxford: Blackwell.

Kerr, C. (1983). *The Future of Industrial Societies.* Cambridge: Harvard University Press.

Kerr, C., Dunlop, J. T., Harbison, F., and Meyers, C. (1960). *Industrialism and Industrial Man.* Cambridge: Harvard University Press.

Kidger, P. J. (1991). "The Emergence of International Human Resource Management." *International Human Resource Management* 2 (2), 149–63.

Kochan, T. A., McKersie, R. B., and Capelli, P. (1984). "Strategic Choice and Industrial Relations Theory." *Industrial Relations* 23, pp. 16–39.

Kochan, T., Katz H., and McKersie, R. (1986). *The Transformation of American Industrial Relations*. New York: Basic Books.

Lane, C. (1989). *Management and Labour in Europe*. Aldershot: Edward Elgar.

Lane, C. (1992). "European Business Systems: Britain and Germany Compared." In Whitley, R. (ed.), *European Business System*. London: Sage, pp. 64–97.

Laurent, A. (1986). "The Cross-Cultural Puzzle of International Human Resource Management." *Human Resource Management* 25 (1), pp. 91–102.

Locke, R., Piore M., and Kochan, T. (1995). "Introduction." In Locke, R., Kochan, T., and Piore, M. (eds.), *Employment Relations in a Changing World Economy*. Cambridge, MA: MIT Press.

Poole, M. (1986). *Industrial Relations - Origins and Patterns of National Diversity*. London: RKP.

Maurice, M., Sellier, F., and Silvestre, J. (1986). *The Social Foundations of Industrial Power*. Cambridge: MIT Press.

MacShane D. and Brewster C. (2000). *Making Flexibility Work*. London: Fabian Society.

Mayrhofer, W. and Brewster, C. (1996). "In Praise of Ethnocentricity: Expatriate Policies in European Multinationals." *International Executive* 38 (6), pp. 749–78.

Miguelez, F. and Priet, C. (1991). *Las Relaciones Laborales en Espana*. Madrid: Siglo Veintiuno.

Mueller, F. (1994). "Societal Effect, Organizational Effect and Globalisation." *Organization Studies* 15 (3), pp. 407–25.

Muller, M. (1997). "Institutional Resilience in a Changing World Economy? The Case of the Germany Banking and Chemical Industries." *British Journal of Industrial Relations* 35 (4), pp. 609–26.

Muller, M. (2000). "Employee Representation and Pay in Austria, Germany and Sweden." *International Studies of Management and Organization* 29 (4), pp. 67–83.

Morishima, M. and Feuille, P. (2000). "Effects of the Use of Contingent Workers on Regular Status Workers: A Japan-US Comparison." Paper presented at the IIRA conference, Tokyo, Japan.

Morley M., Brewster C., Gunnigle, P., and Mayrhofer, W. (2000). "Evaluating Change In Brewster, C., Mayrhofer, W., and Morley, M. (eds.), *New Challenges for European Human Resource Management*. Basingstoke: Macmillan, pp. 199–221.

Oliver, C. (1991). "Strategic Responses to Institutional Processes." *Academy of Mangement Review* 16 (1), pp. 145–79.

Piore, M. and Sabel, C. (1984). *The Second Industrial Divide*. New York: Basic Books.

Polivk, A. E. and Nardone, T. (1989). "The Definition of Contingent Work." *Monthly Labor Review* 112, pp. 9–16.

Porter, M. (1980). *Competitive Strategy*. New York: Free Press.

Prais, S. J., Jarvis, V., and Wagner, K. (1991). "Productivity and Vocational Skills in Services in Britain and Germany: Hotels." In Ryan, P. (ed.), *International Comparisons of Vocational Education and Training for Intermediate Skills*. London: Falmer Press, pp. 64–86.

Rosenzweig, P. M. and Nohria, N. (1994). "Influences on Human Resource Development Practices In Multinational Corporations," *Journal of International Business Studies*, second quarter, pp. 229–51.

Schuler, R. S. and Jackson, S. (1987). "Lining Competitive Strategy and Human Resource Management Practice." *Academy of Management Executive* 3, pp. 207–19.

Soler, C. and Aparacio-Valverde, M. (1996). "Flexibility in Spain." In *Cranet-E Working Time and Contract Flexibility in the E.U.*, report prepared for the European Commission, DGV, Cranfield School of Management.

Tregaskis, O., Brewster, C., Mayne, L., and Hegewisch, A. (1998). "Flexible Working in Europe: The Evidence and the Implications." *European Journal of Work and Organizational Psychology* 7 (1), pp. 61–78.

Tregaskis, O., Heraty, N., and Morley, M. (2001). "HRD in Multinationals: The Global/Local Mix." *Human Resource Management Journal* 11 (2), pp. 34–56.

Trompenaars, F. (1993). *Riding the Waves of Culture*. London: Economist Books.

von Hippel, C. Mangum, S. L., Greenberger, D. B., Heneman, R. L., and Skoglind, J. D. (1997). "Temporay Employment: Can Organizations and Employees Both Win?" *Academy of Management Executive* 11 (1), pp. 93–104.

Williamson, O. (1975). *Markets and Hierarchies: Analysis and Antitrust Implications*. New York: Free Press.

Williamson, O. (1985). *The Economic Institutions of Capitalism*. New York: Free Press.

9

MNCs as Diffusers of Best Practices in HRM/LR in Developing Countries

Sarosh Kuruvilla, Stephen Frenkel, and David Peetz

The purpose of this chapter is to explore the role of the multinational company (MNC) as a "diffuser" of best practices in human resource management and labor relations (HRM/LR) to domestic firms in developing countries. It is clear that in their search to find ways to compete globally and achieve rapid economic growth, many developing countries have increasingly sought foreign direct investment (FDI) (Chapter 2 in this volume). To be outside the global learning loop is a risk that local firms in developing countries can ill afford, especially in a period marked by fast-changing technology and markets. Hence, one potentially important benefit from FDI is the exposure gained by domestic firms in developing countries to alternative forms of management. Indeed, several authors have argued that MNCs play a critical role in the diffusion of best practices as such. At the center of the globalization process, MNCs can be viewed, therefore, as important transmitters of product, process, and organizational innovation to developing countries (Frenkel, 2000). The extent to which this transmission takes place is also relevant in the context of the global convergence debates in the literature. As reported by Brewster and Tregaskis in the preceding chapter, there is reason to doubt that there is emerging convergence of HRM/LR practices across borders, at least with respect to contingent employment practices across Europe.

There appear to be considerable optimism and some degree of consensus (especially in the business press), nonetheless, about the important role that MNCs play in the diffusion of organizational best practices in developing countries (Posthuma, 1994). The primary argument underlying this positive assessment of MNCs as important diffusers is that MNCs, with their superior knowledge, bring with them the latest in organizational (production and HRM/LR) innovations and that these innovations set a new standard in developing countries. For instance, Hoffman (1989: 89) argues that the nature of

MNC organizational innovations, given the resource constraints in finances and skills found in developing countries, are an important potential source of industrial practice and productivity upgrading. Hoffman suggests, furthermore, that diffusion of such practices in developing countries occurs fairly easily, given that organizational innovations are not scale-, product-, or function-specific. It has also been argued that there is little or no mystery behind how these practices work. Consequently, domestic firms can easily copy MNC practices to which they are exposed, and management consulting firms can readily advise domestic firms on how to implement them. The key assumption underlying this discourse (perhaps a "Western ethnocentric" one) is that because MNCs are from the advanced world, they will have developed best practices that firms in developing countries through replication could benefit from, having not otherwise developed such practices themselves.

It is important to note, however, that we found no systematic research focusing specifically on MNCs as diffusers of best practices in HRM/LR to developing countries, and there may be good reason for this. First, MNCs tend to specialize in high-end economic activities (e.g., Nike in marketing, design, and logistics). Thus, their HRM/LR practices are unlikely to be relevant to low-cost, low-end producers in developing countries. Second, MNCs, mainly based in advanced countries, face very different labor markets and IR systems from those in developing countries, and what is relevant in advanced countries may not be relevant in the developing country setting. Hence, it is possible that developing country firms may have developed local best practices in HRM/LR, which are more relevant to them and, in turn, superior to MNC practices pursued in that locale. Third, MNCs often decentralize HRM/LR, leaving it to local managers to decide best practices. Further, given low labor costs (as a percentage of total costs) in developing countries, HRM/LR practices may not be considered important to competitiveness. Although the answer to the question of whether MNCs are important diffusers or not is likely, therefore, to be locale-dependent, the identification of factors facilitating and inhibiting diffusion is, nonetheless, of general relevance.

The purpose of this chapter is to examine the extent to which the HRM/LR best practices of MNCs do in fact diffuse to domestic firms and to explore the processes, preconditions, and factors that increase or limit any such diffusion. Given the current lack of scientific evidence, our analysis is primarily inductive, exploratory, and preliminary in nature. It is conceived as a thought stimulator, a starting point for further discussion, research, and analysis. In the following section we first clarify the concepts of best practice in HRM/LR and diffusion, draw on the literature to generate some ideas and to conjecture about the diffusion of best practices in HRM/LR by MNCs, and describe the methodology and data on which this analysis is largely based. In the second section, we provide brief details of the industries studied and our findings about workplace practices in leading firms in each industry.[1] If diffusion has occurred, we expect to find it among leading firms. If diffusion has not occurred, we expect to find diverse HRM/LR practices among leading firms. In the third section, we discuss our findings in relation to our proposition of diffusion and factors associated with it. We conclude by arguing that there is a great degree of variation by country and industry in terms of the role of MNCs as diffusers and that the concept of "best practice" needs to be examined in terms of local effectiveness. Lastly, we advance a series of propositions about the salient factors influencing the diffusion of HRM/LR best practices.

LITERATURE AND METHODOLGY

Defining Best Practices and Diffusion

Given the absence of any existing literature that specifically addresses the question at hand, we first need to define both best practice in HRM/LR and diffusion. So-called best practice has been used in the literature to denote either a single HRM/LR practice or a "bundle" or system of different HRM/LR practices. In the case of diffusion of a single practice, domestic companies adopt one or two successful practices without adopting entire HRM/LR bundles deployed by MNCs. Pil and MacDuffie (1999) suggest, for example, that the extent of diffusion by multinationals varies considerably depending on the type of practice, whereby some practices are diffused more than others. On the other hand, there are examples of domestic companies adopting entire bundles of HRM/LR practices. Thus, if one examines diffusion based on bundles of practices instead of single practices, the test of diffusion is set rather high.

There is a tendency in the management literature, furthermore, to take a universalistic view of certain bundles of best practices. For example, there is the notion of best practices in automotive production derived from the "Toyota model," which is shorthand for a collection of managerial, technological, organizational, and institutional features associated with Japanese manufacturing (claimed to have set the standard for the worldwide automobile industry). Similarly, there is an emerging universalistic view of the applicability of a set of best practices in HRM/LR. One, for example, combines flexible compensation linked to productivity and skill acquisition, work organization with self-empowered teams, human resource development, flexible employment practices, strong organizational cultures, and collaborative labor–management relations, all of which are seen as applicable across many industries in different geographic contexts. This universalistic view tends to predominate in the international HRM/LR literature and is one of the underpinnings of the convergence argument (Lee and Kuruvilla, 2000). Indeed, writers such as Hoffman (1989) advocate the diffusion of organizational practices from developed to developing countries irrespective of the fact that the practices themselves are based on different cost structures and industrial relations (IR) systems. We do not, however, embrace such a universalistic view of what constitutes best practice or its central presumption that MNC HRM/LR practices will be diffused widely. We assume, instead, that there will be different sets of best practices in HRM/LR in different contexts because best practice can arise out of multiple sources, not just from MNCs.

With respect to diffusion, there are several different ways in which this concept has been used in the literature. On one hand, as developed by the authors in Chapters 6, 7, and 8, one can think in terms of *vertical* diffusion within given MNCs from and to both headquarters and subsidiaries. On the other hand, one can think in terms of *horizontal* diffusion, in which best practices are diffused across firms within the same industry or commodity chain (see Chapter 3) or diffused across industries to firms whose managers have been exposed to best practices in other industries. We focus, herein, specifically on the horizontal diffusion of HRM/LR practices within specific industries and within two developing countries.

Horizontal diffusion of HRM/LR practices, furthermore, can be more narrowly or broadly conceived, both in regard to both the application of HRM/LR practices and the range of industries across which such practices are diffused. With respect to the application of practices, diffusion may encompass more broadly both upper-level managers and lower-level production and service employees or more narrowly encompass either category of employee (or even some subset of either). Much of the international HRM literature focuses heavily on the study of managers, among which one might observe extensive diffusion of practices given the existence of a more global or regional labor market for that category of employees (Lee and Kuruvilla, 2000). With respect to the range of industries, horizontal diffusion may more broadly encompass diffusion across a number of industries within a commodity chain or across unrelated industries or more narrowly encompass diffusion within selected industries.

Figure 9.1 illustrates in a highly simplified way this range of possibilities of horizontal diffusion of best practices in HRM/LR. Along the vertical axis, diffusion can range from specific, individual practices to bundled sets of practices. Along the horizontal line, diffusion can range from one that is fairly narrow to one that is fairly broad with respect to the application of HRM/LR practices to categories of employees and to industries. Our focus is on quadrant 3, as we examine the horizontal diffusion of bundled HRM/LR practices but with a fairly narrow focus on the diffusion of practices to only lower-level production and service workers within selected industries. Our test for whether horizontal diffusion of best practices in HRM/LR has taken place in developing countries, therefore, is relatively high but a realistic one given our fairly narrow focus on diffusion of practices to only lower-level workers within single industries.

In addition to examining the extent of horizontal diffusion as previously defined, we explore what appear to be the primary processes of, and preconditions for, diffusion, as well as salient factors that facilitate or inhibit diffusion. As noted earlier, we have been unable to find published studies (at least written in English) regarding the diffusion of MNC HRM/LR practices between advanced and developing nations. Given that the available literature

Figure 9.1
Horizontal Diffusion of Best Practices in HRM/LR

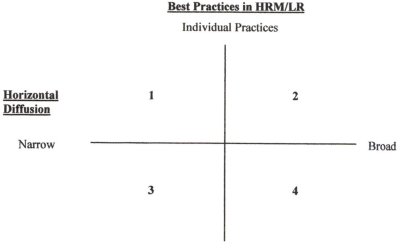

germane to our inquiry is limited and in the interests of conserving space, we provide a brief summary of the literature in Tables 9.1, 9.2. We distinguish between the process of diffusion, preconditions for diffusion, and factors facilitating and inhibiting diffusion. In Table 9.1, we include our expectations regarding important variables that affect horizontal diffusion. In Table 9.2, we highlight the various facilitators and inhibitors to such diffusion. Taken together, these tables provide background material used for suggesting several hypotheses explored in this chapter and testable in future research.

Methodology

The case studies examined herein are part of a larger research project designed to analyze national, industry-level, and workplace-level changes in HRM/LR resulting from the globalization process (see Frenkel and Royal, 1997; Kuruvilla, 1997). The results presented are preliminary to a more detailed analysis of workplace changes being conducted in the larger, ongoing project. The industries covered include white goods (i.e., domestic appliances), pharmaceuticals, banking, and electronics and information technology (IT) in India and banking and electronics in Malaysia. The focus of the present analysis is on a bundle of several HRM/LR practices: work organization, compensation, employment flexibility, training and skills development, and labor–management relations. In addition to examining these practices, we inquired about the perceived stimuli for any changes in HRM/LR practices and whether benchmarking was used, in particular, benchmarking against MNCs. We believe that it is reasonable to assume that most human resource (HR) managers know the best practices in their own industries, albeit we recognize that there may be a tendency by managers to present their own company practices as being the best in their industries. As such, we rely on perceptions of HR managers to define both what bundles of HRM/LR practices constitute best practices and, thus, whether these best practices have been diffused in their given industries.

Table 9.1
Previous Research and Authors' Conjectures Regarding Horizontal Diffusion

Research Focus	Previous Research	Authors' Conjectures
The process by which horizontal diffusion occurs between developed and developing economies through MNCs.	Mostly limited to developed economies and to selected industries (e.g., autos). Evidence suggests that increased competition in the auto industry led to the adoption of Japanese– style practices via benchmarking. Representative work includes Kenney and Florida (1993), Womack, Jones, and Roos (1990), Elger and Smith (1994), Kuruvilla (1995).	a. MNCs could affect the rules governing IR through pressure on national governments. b. MNCs introduce IR practices into their subsidiaries, and these spill over to contractors, suppliers, and possibly customers. c. If MNC practices are seen to be competitive, local firms will benchmark and adopt. d. Advice of global consulting firms that advocate best practices. e. Organizations of employers share information about best practices. f. Academic research.
Preconditions for horizontal diffusion to take place.	Length of time MNCs operate in developing nations is key (Bangert and Poor, 1993).	a. There must be a significant degree of FDI. b. The larger the number of MNCs in a given industry, the greater the potential for horizontal diffusion. c. Diffusion of MNC practices will be greater in virgin territory (economies that have been previously closed to foreign presence or under a completely different economic system; India before 1990 and China before 1978).
Inhibitors and facilitators	Diffusion (vertical) is not universal and influenced by a number of different conditions such as country of origin, product market factors, degree of production integration in an MNC, MNC structure (Edwards, Rees, and Collier, 1999). There are many barriers to transfer success such as legal, institutional, and being out of sync with local culture (Florkowski and Nath, 1993). Nature of product and labor markets, and selective diffusion, only of some practices. Representative works include Schuler, Dowling, and DeCieri (1993), DeCieri and Dowling (1999), Frenkel and Royal (1997), Taylor, Beechler, and Napier (1996), Carr (1994), Haddock and South (1994), Edwards, Ferner, and Sisson (1996), Beechler and Young (1994), Hannon, Huang, and Jaw (1995).	See Table 9.2

Table 9.2
Factors Facilitating and Inhibiting the Diffusion of Perceived Best Practices in HRM/LR in Particular Industries within Countries

Facilitators	Inhibitors
Product markets International. Rapidly changing. Strong integration across borders. Basis of competition -- quality/innovation but might include price.	Domestic. Stable. Weak. Price.
Local labor markets and IR institutions Tight. Weakly regulated (or regulated to encourage diffusion). Labor as critical resource – yes. Role of key actors*—positive. Industry-wide bargaining.	Loose. Strongly regulated (adverse affect on diffusion). No. Negative. Decentralized bargaining.
MNC characteristics Strategy: globalize and learning-oriented. ER strategy – global. Structure: facilitative (i.e., networked). Veteran status (age). Organizational culture strong. Dependent on headquarters. Presence of HQ-oriented expatriates. Founded by HQ.	Localize; nonlearning subsidiaries. Local. Hierarchical, information flows limited by localized strategy and undeveloped communications system. Newly established. Weak. Independent of HQ – powerful subsidiary or dependent on local firms. Absence of them. Founded by merger with local company.
Institutional (political/economic/cultural) environment Similar to headquarters' nation. MNC practices in sync with local culture.	Very different. Out of sync with local culture.

Note: * Refers to governments, employers, and unions.

Our analysis is based on interviews and documents collected in two or three leading firms in selected industries in India and Malaysia. We chose India and Malaysia because of their varying experience with "globalization," expecting to find some differences in the impact of MNCs as diffusers of best practices across these two nations. India is a more recent "globalizer," having liberalized its economy in 1991. In contrast, Malaysia has had a relatively open economy since the late 1970s. The industries studied include those that have been heavily affected by globalization, in terms of either increased product market competition or the recent entry of major MNCs. This is the case for the consumer goods sector in India and the electronics sector in Malaysia, as well as industries that are or have been relatively more sheltered, such as the banking industry in both countries.

Given the exploratory nature of our inquiry, we cast a wide net in an effort to capture any apparent variation in the diffusion of best practices in HRM/LR. Evidence that there is a tendency for HRM/LR practices deployed in lead firms in an industry to converge toward some general model would indicate that horizontal diffusion is taking place. Evidence that they also converge to the practices pursued by subsidiaries of MNCs would support the proposition that MNCs are important diffusers. Our findings, nonetheless, need to be treated with due caution, as we examine relatively few firms in each industry and as the industries studied are not necessarily representative of other industries. At this initial stage of our research agenda, moreover, our modeling remains incomplete. Hence, important dimensions of the diffusion of best practices in HRM/LR are not addressed. Given a growing attention and conjecture in the business press about MNCs as important diffusers, yet the complete absence of academic study on the subject, our study is intended to serve as a valuable starting point for more elaborate and analytically sophisticated analyses.

CASE STUDIES

India

Although MNCs have operated in India for many years (in some cases, for many decades), their equity investment had been limited to 40 percent. Consequently, many do not have majority control, and many have entered the country via the establishment of joint ventures. Only after economic liberalization in 1991 were MNCs allowed 100 percent ownership and since then inward FDI has soared from U.S.$83 million in 1991 to U.S.$8 billion in 1995. Nevertheless, by any measure of globalization, India cannot yet be regarded as a significant "globalizer." For instance, as a percentage of gross domestic product (GDP), exports and imports remain at under 12 percent and 14 percent, respectively. Furthermore, inward FDI as a percentage of gross fixed capital formation is less than 1.5 percent, and outward FDI is practically nonexistent (UNCTAD, 1998).

Much of the FDI in manufacturing is intended for India's large and growing domestic market, rather than for export. Although MNCs have entered all sectors, the consumer goods industries have attracted the most investment. In these industries, MNCs either compete directly with established Indian firms or ally themselves with established Indian firms or other established MNCs that have operated in India for a long time (e.g., Lever Brothers, Pfizer, and

Hoechst). We examine the diffusion of best practices in HRM/LR in four major industries.

White Goods Industry.

"White goods" refers to consumer durables such as refrigerators, washing machines, and air conditioners. Since liberalization, the industry has undergone considerable restructuring. Before liberalization, the market was dominated by Indian firms, including Godrej (accounting for a 45 percent market share), Allwyn, Videocom, and BPL. Following liberalization, U.S.-owned Whirlpool entered the market and subsequently purchased Indian-owned Kelvinator; Godrej merged with U.S.-owned GE; and Videocom has been considering some form of merger or acquisition with both Korean-owned Daewoo and Samsung. Within a few short years, therefore, the ownership and market share profile in this industry has changed substantially. The industry is now dominated by global firms through direct ownership or joint ventures, and most companies have recently established alliances with MNCs. Whirlpool has become the market leader with its 35 percent share, followed by Videocom, Godrej-GE, and BPL holding about 21 percent shares each. Industry sources suggest that there will be a major shake-up in this industry in the next two or three years.

We studied the two industry leaders, Godrej-GE and Whirlpool. Although Godrej-GE still owns several factories that have been in the Mumbai region for years, and Whirlpool has taken over the Kelvinator factory near Delhi, both companies have also pursued greenfield strategies since liberalization. Both have built new plants, investing in new technologies, hiring new workers, and creating new systems. In Table 9.2, we briefly summarize the changes in HRM/LR practices between the older and newer plants of these two companies. As shown, there is remarkable similarity between the new plants of both firms. Godrej-GE HR managers report that many of the work organization plans and the linking of compensation to skill acquisition were adopted from GE. Whirlpool has introduced its production and work organization practices (it follows a uniform pattern in the 28 countries where it has manufacturing units), and, as is clear, the HRM/LR practices at Godrej-GE and Whirlpool are remarkably alike. The HR manager at Videocom reported as well that their factories in southern India were implementing similar changes in HRM/LR practices.

The profile of practices shown in Table 9.3 indicates that there is clear convergence toward an international model in terms of what is contemporarily viewed by many as best practice in manufacturing. The movement toward this model occurred after liberalization in India and in a market dominated by multinationals. Although there are obstacles (Indian labor laws, in particular) to employer flexibility to adjust employment, the changes identified and the restructuring of the market strongly suggest that foreign-owned MNCs have had a significant effect on the diffusion of HRM/LR practices in this industry.

Table 9.3
Employment Relations in the White Goods Industry: India, 1997

	Godrej-GE (old)	Godrej-GE (new)	WOL (old)	WOL (new)
Work organization	Tayloristic.	Multiskilling and job rotation.	Tayloristic, with transitional efforts to multiskilling and job rotation.	Multiskilling and job rotation; self-directed work teams.
Compensation	Company welfarism; fixed.	Lead the market but without company welfarism; modest bonuses for skill acquisition.	Median; bonuses for skill acquisition.	High variable component, based on 360-degree appraisals.
Training emphasis	Low/not relevant.	High.	Attempted move from low to medium.	High.
Employment flexibility	Reduction by attrition.	Stable.	Substantial cuts via VRSs and transfers to other companies; looking to cut more.	Stable.
Labor–management relations.	Internal union; cooperative.	No union.	Internal union; conflictual.	No union.

The Pharmaceutical Industry.
India's economic liberalization policies, coupled with its entry into the World Trade Organization (WTO), have completely altered the economic environment of the pharmaceutical industry. Prior to liberalization, the pharmaceutical industry was tightly regulated to ensure that drugs were available to everyone at a reasonable price and protected against the vicissitudes of international competition. Additionally, Indian firms were granted patents to produce drugs if they could merely prove that the processes through which drugs were produced were different from those of the original creators of the drugs (usually MNCs). This spurred a number of firms to enter the market based on process innovations but also ensured a constant presence of MNCs in the country that wanted to "protect" their products. However, since India joined the WTO in 1995, international patent law applies to India. This means that Indian pharmaceutical firms' viability will depend heavily on their ability to develop their own drugs through investments in R&D. Poorly positioned to engage in

R&D relative to MNCs, there has been substantial consolidation and merger activity in the industry.

Many of the world's largest producers (e.g., Glaxo-Wellcome, Hoechst, Pfizer, Roussel, Novartis) have long been located in India in the form of joint ventures but, more recently, as wholly owned subsidiaries. As of 1997, the market share of foreign-owned firms was about 40 percent, with a large number of Indian firms that evolved under the protectionist regime accounting for the remaining 60 percent of the market. It is important to note that the rate of profit in the pharmaceutical industry has not been high. Profit before tax as a percentage of sales in the industry has varied between 1 percent in 1991 and 6.5 percent in 1994–1995. Maintaining profitability under a regime of continuing price controls has forced pharmaceutical firms to focus heavily on ways to cut costs and improve productivity, of which changes in organizational practices would appear to play a key role. Given this market imperative and the presence of several large successful MNCs, the Indian pharmaceutical industry can be cast as an ideal scenario in which MNCs would serve as important diffusers of best practices in HRM/LR.

We chose one MNC to study (Pfizer) based on the industry association's view that it was characterized by cutting-edge practices. A U.S.-owned MNC, Pfizer is one of the larger firms, with four modern factories and employing about 2,000 workers and medical sales representatives. We also chose two other leading Indian firms, I-Pharm and Lupin Laboratories, the second and third largest producers, respectively. According to industry association officials, Pfizer's best practices would gradually be imitated by the other firms in the market. Our preliminary inquiries clearly suggested that many of the MNCs such as Glaxo-Wellcome have modeled their new plants after Pfizer. Yet, as the practices identified in Table 9.4 suggests, there appears to be no sign of convergence of HRM/LR practices, despite heavy competition in a low-profit market.

While Pfizer's Kalanyi plant practices depict what one might expect from a leading MNC, Lupin's practices are based on an odd mix of paternalism and dynamic efficiency. Lupin does not have standardized compensation packages or salary scales and has the lowest labor turnover in the industry, at any level. Its work organization is quite Tayloristic, with relatively little multiskilling. On the other hand, employees are trained heavily in terms of the criteria that would enable Lupin to meet U.S. regulatory requirements on its products.

I-Pharm is one of the more successful Indian pharmaceutical producers, with 1,200 employees spread across seven plants. It is an Indian MNC, with operations in several countries. Its business strategy primarily focuses on producing pharmaceuticals derived from one or two complex molecules, for which there are few competitors. The HRM/LR practices in I-Pharm are not particularly noteworthy; none of the typical best practices such as multiskilling and team-based work organization had been adopted. Company officials, moreover, report that the company's Tayloristic work organization has proved quite sufficient given its business strategy.

This industry case is intriguing since there exist conditions likely to stimulate firms to adopt best practices in HRM/LR. These conditions include low profit rates, a highly competitive environment, and a change in patent regulation that creates new cost and development challenges for local firms. Our study of the major players and discussions with representatives of the industry association, however, suggest the following interpretation. Although Pfizer is praised as having the best practices among MNCs, the practices at Lupin are, to any informed observer of Indian industrial relations, much more innovative and, in regard to labor turnover, the most effective. This, in turn, raises the question: What constitutes best practice? Lupin provides the example of a case where the old, presumably antiquated style of paternalism works quite well. We conclude, therefore, that despite a significant presence of major MNCs, some having been present in India for a long time, there has been very little diffusion of MNC best practices in HRM/LR to domestic companies in the Indian pharmaceutical industry.

Table 9.4
Employment Relations in Pharmaceuticals: India, 1997

	Pfizer (Mumbai)	Pfizer (Kalanyi)	Lupin	I-pharm
Work organization	Tayloristic.	Extensive multiskilling; job rotation sporadic though.	Tayloristic.	Tayloristic.
Compensation	Median; fixed.	Mostly fixed; cash awards for skill acquisition.	Top 10 percent.	Top 10 percent.
Training emphasis	Low/mostly attitudinal.	High.	Low.	Medium.
Employment flexibility	Various VRSs over the last 15 years; most recent in 1995 covering 600 employees	Stable.	Stable; increase if anything.	Reduction via layoffs of current temporary workers.
Labor–management relations	Internal union with company wide federation; conflictual.	Limited unionism; conflictual.	No union; paternalist cooperation complete with workplace committees.	Internal/mix of conflict and acquiescence.

The Banking Industry.

Ever since the major banks were nationalized in 1969, the banking industry in India has been dominated by the public sector. The industry currently comprises some 27 public sector banks, 35 domestically owned private banks, and 29 foreign-owned banks. The public sector banks dominate the industry in terms of deposits, accounting for 92 percent of all deposits in 1996. In terms of profitability, however, they rank far below both the private sector domestic banks and foreign-owned banks. For instance, in terms of net profit per worker, the national banks reported estimates of Rs. 4614 crores, while the foreign-owned banks reported estimates of Rs. 456649 crores in 1995-1996 (1U.S.$ = 44 Indian rupees, October 2000). In the following year, most national banks suffered losses.

Given this scenario and consistent with broader economic reforms, the government has been implementing recommendations of the Narasimham Committee, which has been charged with designing ways to improve the performance of the financial sector generally. These reforms have included, for example, the restructuring of banks, bringing transparency to balance sheets, and establishing parity between public and private sector banks to enhance competition. These reforms have served to pressure the nationalized banks to become ever more efficient.

The banking sector is also characterized by strong unions and industry-wide bargaining. There are four major peak federations representing clerical employees and two major unions representing bank officers. HRM/LR practices are, by and large, regulated by the industry-wide collective bargaining agreements. There are major differences, nonetheless, in HRM/LR practices between nationalized and foreign-owned banks. In Table 9.5, we summarize the differences in selected practices between the public sector banks as a whole and three subsidiaries of foreign MNCs.

Although competition through increased foreign and domestic investment has not increased substantially, the banking industry is central to the government's liberalization plan. Consequently, there has been bureaucratic pressure placed on public sector banks to reform their work practices and ways of doing business that strengthen customer services and loan performance. This pressure is sometimes quite direct, as in the instance of the government's recent suggestion that employee pay should be tied to branch performance and its threat to close insolvent banks. Moreover, by opening some banking services heretofore closed to private investment, competition is expected to increase. These pressures are evident both in industry-level bargaining outcomes and at the level of the firm. A long tradition of job control and resistance to technological change is gradually giving way to deployment flexibility and multiskilling, led by the foreign-owned banks. Complementing these practices, there is an increased emphasis on training, even if actual implementation of programs has been very uneven across banks.

Government intervention in the diffusion of best practices in HRM/LR systems is noteworthy. The National Institute of Bank Management (NIBM), a government institute created to provide training, has been charged with the task of creating new training programs on work organization and customer service,

Table 9.5
Employment Relations in the Banking Industry: India, 1997

	Public Sector	**F-Bank**	**Grindlay's**	**Hong Kong Bank**
Work organization	Industry-level agreement on job rotation and multi-skilling; however, variation in implementa-tion at the local level.	Same industry agreement with successful implementation	Same industry agreement with successful implementation.	Same industry agreement with hard-fought-for implementation.
Compensation	Fixed; largely seniority-based.	Fixed plus great emoluments.	Fixed plus great emoluments; pushing for greater variable component.	Fixed plus great emoluments; pushing for a greater variable component.
Training emphasis	Low but increasing.	High.	High.	High.
Employment flexibility	Stable; reduction via attrition.	Stable but with substantial redeployment.	Stable.	Stable.
Labor–management relations	Union; conflictual.	Union; conflictual.	Union; conflictual but more recently cooperative.	Union; conflictual.

based specifically on studies of the foreign-owned banks. The NIBM is basing its training programs on the material offered at Grindlays Training College at Chennai, which is highly recognized for its training programs. There have been some notable successes in diffusing best practices to two public sector banks (Punjab National Bank and the Bank of Maharashtra) that have attempted to adopt the principles set out by the foreign-owned banks. Therefore, while the foreign banks serve as models for the public sector banks to emulate, the degree of diffusion of best practices in HRM/LR has been hindered significantly by the industry-wide collective bargaining agreement and antagonistic relationships between management and labor. On the other hand, these cases highlight the role of government and training institutions in the diffusion process.

The Electronics and IT Industry.
    The electronics and information technology industry in India is the fastest growing industry in the country, comprising several different segments, such as software, computer equipment and peripherals, computer maintenance, systems training, and scanners and related products. The industry has witnessed double-digit growth since 1991, and software exports have been growing at over

50 percent per year since 1991. The top 20 firms account for over 75 percent of the market share in the industry. In the nonsoftware sector, the industry is dominated by MNCs and Indian firms in partnership with MNCs. The largest firm is HCL-HP, followed by TATA-IBM and WIPRO (a domestic company). The other giants in the industry, such as INTEL, COMPAQ, and DIGITAL, have a growing presence. The industry's economic future appears favorable as domestic information technology spending has increased by a factor of eight since liberalization.

HRM/LR reforms, nonetheless, are imperative. An acute shortage of qualified people, especially in software professionals, has resulted in very high labor turnover rates. Indeed, in 1997 the average annual rate was 30 percent. These shortages and exceptionally high turnover rates have led to fast rising compensation levels and recruitment poaching. Further, rapidly changing technology requires high levels of training investment, but employees who have acquired the requisite training are immediately sought after by other companies. Thus, best practices in HRM/LR in this industry are those that yield high retention rates, which is the focus of our case studies in this industry.

We studied three firms (Table 9.6). The first was WIPRO, a diversified and highly successful Indian computer firm. There has been little change in the company's HRM/LR systems since liberalization. WIPRO enjoys one of the lowest turnover rates among the firms that we studied, with turnover of skilled labor at about 4 percent and turnover of software professionals at 6 percent annually. The second firm studied was TATA-IBM, a joint venture in which IBM has taken responsibility for management. All HRM/LR practices have been developed by IBM worldwide and thus, best practice systems from IBM are replicated here. The turnover rates at this company in 1997 were about 20 percent for software engineers and 10 percent for other personnel. The third company studied was Hewlett Packard (HP), which had recently severed its business relationship with HCL India. Because it has operated in India since 1969, it cannot be viewed as a new entrant (unlike TATA-IBM). HP's overall turnover rate is the best in the industry and, with respect to both software professionals and skilled workers, slightly better than WIPRO's at 4–5 percent on average. The low turnover rate appears to be attributable to the creation of a strong corporate culture that values the individual employee.

The information reported in Table 9.6 suggests that there has been very little diffusion of HRM/LR practices in the industry. These cases call into question any dominant role of MNCs as diffusers of HRM/LR practices. For example, in contrast to IBM's difficulty in introducing its systems, WIPRO's homegrown strategy (which was developed before liberalization) appears to be highly successful. Although HP has been successful in diffusing headquarters' model of HRM/LR practices to its Indian subsidiary, there is little evidence that it is being widely copied in this industry. In summary, despite similar industry-wide pressures that might force convergence to a high common standard of best practices in HRM/LR, we found very little such diffusion in the Indian electronics and IT industry.

Table 9.6
Employment Relations in the Electronics and Software Industries: India, 1997

	WIPRO	**TATA-IBM**	**HP**
Work organization	Fully autonomous teams with an open workplace culture.	Matrix organization that is team-based. Not very successful.	Autonomous teams with strong corporate culture.
Compensation	Pays market wages, but flexible linked to productivity.	75% of wage is flexible, based on company, division, and department profitability (IBM system).	Lead/lag compensation system tied to skills acquisition.
Training emphasis	Multiskilling, and training in teamwork.	Job-related training system with mentoring.	Multiskilling and training in culture.
Employment flexibility	No layoff guarantee, but also significant subcontracting via vendor development program.	Expanding market so flexibility not yet required.	Expanding market, flexibility not yet Required.
Labor–management relations	Nonunion.	Nonunion.	Nonunion.

Malaysia

Unlike India, the Malaysian economy has been relatively more exposed to globalization. Predicated on FDI, the government adopted an export-oriented industrialization strategy in the 1970s. This strategy proved remarkably successful. Exports and imports as a percentage of GDP in 1997 were 128 percent and 126 percent, respectively. As a percentage of gross fixed capital formation, inward FDI amounted to 12 percent, and outward FDI amounted to 8 percent. Not surprisingly, MNCs have a substantial presence in some industries, and, given a long history of FDI, Malaysia is a useful alternative location to India regarding MNC influence on the diffusion of best practices. In our effort to capture variation in the differences of best practices in HRM/LR, we chose one industry that is almost completely export-oriented (electronics) and a second that is almost exclusively focused on the domestic market (banking).

The Electronics Industry

The electronics industry is the largest industry in terms of exports and manufacturing employment in the country. The industry was established in the early 1970s, when Malaysia embarked on an export-oriented industrialization program. Malaysia is now home to almost all of the large semiconductor producers in the world, and production accounts for 37 percent of the country's export earnings. Our case studies were drawn from the state of Penang, which is the hub of electronics assembly, but we also rely on two case studies conducted in 1995 (see Kuruvilla, 1995). Trade unions were banned in this industry until 1988, but even after the ban on unionization was lifted, only enterprise based "in-house" unions have been permitted. Today, only 6 out of 50 factories in Penang have such in-house unions.

The electronics sector in Malaysia is diverse and has many segments, ranging from the design and manufacture of semiconductors, to the production of various electronics and computer-related items. Our cases are primarily drawn from the production of electronic components, largely because several studies exist on the narrower semiconductor sector (Kuruvilla, 1995). The central HRM/LR characteristic of the electronics industry is its tight labor market. The industry faces high turnover, which puts pressure on employers to create HRM/LR systems designed to retain employees and to develop adequate skills by investing in training. It has proved important, therefore, that companies be viewed by employees as attractive employers.

We studied four firms in the electronics industry. The first is a Japanese-owned subsidiary, Nippon Electronics, which produces cathode-ray tubes. The remaining three companies are subsidiaries of U.S.-based MNCs, the names of which are disguised to satisfy our agreement of confidentiality. The first of these subsidiaries produces key computer components (Micro), the second produces disk drives (Drive), and the third produces heads for drives (Elecomp). A summary profile of HRM/LR practices is provided in Table 9.7.

In sharp contrast to the other firms, Elecomp faces a considerably different economic circumstance than the others. It has been using an out-of-date technology and has suffered steady declines in sales, profitability and employment, which appears to have influenced its HRM/LR strategy and practices to a significant extent. Consequently, its HRM/LR practices are distinctly different from those of the three cases studied. Although there is some degree of variation in HRM/LR practices across the other three companies as a result of different business models pursued, there is, nonetheless, a high degree of similarity of practices. This high degree of similarity appears to be a product of the dynamics of the generally tight labor market, the dominance of MNC operations in the industry, and extensive benchmarking within the industry. Hence, in the electronics industry we observe an unusually high degree of diffusion and convergence in regard to best practices in HRM/LR.

Our investigation into the diffusion process revealed that there were both formal and informal networks in which human resource managers were able to track and compare HRM/LR innovations. On a formal network basis, all firms regularly benchmark their practices. Firms like Micro benchmark globally with other Micro plants in other nations and locally with all factories in the region. Micro also plays a leading role in the dissemination of HRM/LR innovations in the local area, to both its contractors and suppliers but also to the

Table 9.7
Employment Relations in the Electronics Industry: Malaysia, 1997

	Nippon Electronics	Micro	Drive	Elecomp
Work organization	Use of quality circles.	Highly automated. Quality circles.	Tayloristic (for operators). Some cross-training to enable mobility. Moving toward JIT.	Very Tayloristic. Quality circles aborted. Resistance to change. No JIT.
Training emphasis	High – avg. 40 hours/year. International.	High. Curriculum-based. International.	High – avg. 50 hours/year, but emphasis on technical and managerial employees. Provided in Malaysia. Not yet "refined." Some emphasis on people skills among supervisors.	Mainly for supervisors and managers. Mostly in-house.
Labor–management relations	High labor turnover (5%/month) before recession (though lower than competitors). Now under 1-2%.	High labor turnover (3-5%) before recession. But seen as attractive employer.	High labor turnover: 6% Jan. 98, falling to 3% Jan. 99. Wants to be an attractive employer in industry. Problems with performance appraisal.	High labor turnover: from 4-5% pre-recession to 2-2.5% now. Problems with performance appraisal, supervisors.
Compensation	Increment (individual based); contractual bonus (2 months); 1 variable bonus (profit-based). Aim to increase flexibility.	Starting wage RM490 + RM 160 allowances. Increment (individual and market); contractual bonus (6 weeks); 2 variable bonuses (profit, individual, work area: quality, rejects, attitudes); stock option plan.	Starting wage RM470. Increment (individual and market); contractual bonus (1 month); 4 variable bonuses (company profit; site performance - quality, timeliness, cost; ad hoc).	Starting wage RM450. Increment (individual); 2 variable bonuses (productivity, profit).
Employment levels/ changes	Falling slowly through attrition.	Major expansion in Malaysia.	Falling slowly through attrition.	Falling significantly.
Labor adjustment mechanisms	No retrenchments. Insourcing. Increase training time. No payment on variable bonus. Redeploy labor between companies.	Reduced increments due to slower market growth; still higher increase than industry. Reducing use of foreign workers as locals become available.	No retrenchments. Insourcing (work formerly done in Philippines). Reduced increments. Reduced bonus. Encourage use of leave.	800 layoffs (30%) through voluntary separation. Major cut in overtime. Reduce working days per week. Reduced bonus. Compulsory leave.

industry as a whole. There was general agreement among the HR managers whom we interviewed that Micro was the most attractive employer (and, in fact, Micro reported the lowest turnover rate in this high turnover industry). Micro also served as a model for other employers outside the electronics industry.

Perhaps more importantly, all of the companies are members of the Penang Skills Development Center (PSDC), a government organization that was formed for developing skills needed in the electronics sector. The organization relies on its member companies to donate equipment and provide training for operatives. In an area where labor is in short supply, such training has become essential. Thus, the PSDC provides the institutional base for human resource managers to learn from each other. As Kuruvilla (1995) explains, this arrangement is responsible for the remarkable situation wherein global competitors share knowledge about manufacturing processes and HRM/LR. Again, the high turnover rates in a tight labor market provide a strong incentive for companies to be seen as attractive employers, which in turn has induced a substantial degree of imitation of successful practices.

While these cases clearly support the notion that MNCs are important diffusers of HRM/LR practices, we underscore that this is an industry that almost exclusively comprises, and is dominated by, MNCs from all regions of the world. Consequently, our analysis of the diffusion of best practices observed here does not include diffusion to leading domestic firms, as in our previous analyses. Although the parent offices of MNCs vary in their influence on the development of HRM/LR practices in their subsidiaries, the remarkable similarity in practices found among foreign-owned operations is due to extensive benchmarking that has become formalized through the PSDC. Our case analysis of the electronics industry in Malaysia highlights, therefore, the key role of local institutions (such as the PSDC) in the diffusion of HRM/LR practices.

The Banking Industry

The commercial banking sector in Malaysia enjoyed steady growth during the 1990–1995 period, with major increases in the value of loans (260 percent), number of employees (46 percent), and profitability (300 percent). Until recently, Malaysia had 38 banks, including 14 foreign-owned banks. Arising from the financial crisis and the consequent losses reported by several banks, the government, through the national bank (Bank Negara), forced industry consolidation, reducing the number of banks to about 10. The banking sector remains incompletely open to the global marketplace given that there are several restrictions on the activities of foreign-owned banks, notably, in terms of the number of branches that they can open.

In general, HRM/LR practices in the banking industry are regulated by industry-wide collective bargaining agreements. There are 10 unions in the industry. Two are industry-wide unions: NUBE, representing about 30,000 clerical and bank employees, and ABOM, representing junior bank officers and managers. There are 8 in-house unions in the larger banks, which by and large represent bank officers. Through these in-house unions, represented employees are able to obtain higher benefits than negotiated in the industry-wide agreements. The employers in peninsular Malaysia are represented by the Malayan Commercial Banks Association (MCBA), which negotiates separate industry-wide agreements with NUBE and ABOM. Both employers and unions apparently view industry-wide bargaining as beneficial. Indeed, there has been little pressure from employers for decentralization in bargaining. For employers, industry-wide bargaining prevents unions from extracting above-normal wages from financially stronger banks or demanding wage increases that might cripple financially weaker banks. The benefits of solidarity among banks appear particularly high for employers during periods of downturn, such as during the financial crisis under way at the time of our inquiries. For the unions, industry-wide bargaining has ensured that employees doing like work receive like pay and core benefits, even though there may be differences at the margin from bank to bank. Although bank employees are prohibited from striking, they engage in other forms of protest, including picketing and slowdowns, which were reported to be effective.

As for much of the Malaysian labor market, the labor market for bank employees is very tight, even though the financial crisis had temporarily eased competition for labor, and the industry may incur employment redundancies as a result of anticipated further consolidation in the industry. The ABOM agreement covers retrenchments, whereas the NUBE agreement is silent on this issue. Although wage levels and bonuses are fixed via the industry agreement, banks attempt to provide more flexibility in compensation through a system of ex gratia payments. In addition, the recent NUBE agreement opened the way to introduce more flexible compensation systems tied to productivity, although no banks have as yet attempted to negotiate such provisions.

The government through its Bank Negara has exercised some centralized control regarding HRM/LR practices. Bank Negara requires, for instance, that all banks invest at least 2.5 percent of their annual wage and salary bill on training. In addition, the central bank has introduced a tax on the poaching of senior bank employees, requiring poachers to pay a six-month salary levy into a central fund. During the financial crisis, moreover, banks were discouraged from laying off employees. Foreign-own banks have been especially sensitive to any such guidelines as they do not want to be seen as acting contrary to the wishes of the government. In general, the financial crisis and the government-led reorganization of the industry have clearly reoriented the banking industry's view regarding the importance of productivity and spurred changes in bank systems to be more effective and efficient.

We studied four banks and again have disguised their identities. "Western Bank" is the Malaysian arm of a large London-headquartered banking group. Employing about 2,100 employees, it is the largest foreign-owned bank (based on market share) operating in Malaysia. "Local Bank," with roughly 2,500 employees, is owned by a government employee finance organization and claimed to be the sixth largest bank in Malaysia. "Conglomerate Bank" also claimed to be the sixth largest bank, employing approximately 2,500 employees.

"Bank East Asia" is a foreign-own bank based in East Asia and was ranked as the eighth or ninth largest bank at the time of our study. As shown in Table 9.8, there is some variation in HRM/LR practices, despite the industry-wide collective bargaining system.

Among the four banks studied, Western Bank had the more advanced HRM/LR innovations, practices that had been diffused from the bank's U.K. parent headquarters. Although many of its innovative practices had been copied or were being copied by other banks, other banks had not achieved Western Bank's level of sophistication. That was especially the case regarding employee

Table 9.8
Employment Relations in the Banking Industry: Malaysia, 1997

	Western Bank	**Local Bank**	**Conglomerate Bank**	**East Asia Bank**
Work organization	Leading edge in industry re empowerment, multiskilling.	Traditional – rudimentary changes.	Multiskilling employees past 2-3 years.	Traditional – rudimentary changes.
Training emphasis	Very high.	Moderately high.	High (increased in downturn).	Moderately high.
Labor – management relations	Cooperative.	Cooperative.	Accommodative.	Cooperative.
Compensation	Tenure-based increments plus contractual bonus, contingent bonus, possible shift to performance pay in future.	Tenure-based increments plus contractual bonus, contingent bonus.	Tenure-based increments plus contractual bonus. Contingent bonus for nonunion occupations.	Tenure-based increments plus contractual bonus, contingent bonus.
Employment levels/ flexibility	30% reduction before financial crisis.	May be forthcoming redeployments due to merger.	10-15% reduction across the group during financial crisis.	No staff cuts.
Labor adjustment mechanisms	VRS before financial crisis, no retrenchments during crisis, bonus still paid.	No retrenchments, pay rise for executives delayed.	No retrenchments in bank (but retrenchments elsewhere in group), cut in contingent bonus for non-union employees, executive privileges frozen.	Contingent bonus not paid, no retrenchments. Large cuts in overtime.

involvement, whereby Western Bank was viewed as the industry leader in employee empowerment and multiskilling. Although both kinds of practices were reportedly embraced in theory by other banks, only Conglomerate Bank had recently engaged in multiskilling, and none of the banks studied had implemented any formal programs of empowerment. In general, our cases show that Malaysian banks have been slow to introduce more innovative HRM/LR practices. Nevertheless, with Western Bank's bargaining agreement with NUBE, some degree of diffusion can be expected through the industry-wide collective bargaining agreement. Overall, in comparison to best practices in the worldwide banking industry, the HRM/LR practices of Malaysian banks remain underdeveloped.

Our study of banking firms in Malaysia suggests that despite local firms' recognizing the potential value of adopting best practices from lead MNC subsidiaries, the pace and nature of such diffusion can be significantly influenced by industry-wide bargaining agreements. We believe that this industry analysis highlights the important impact of labor market institutions on horizontal diffusion, notably, the role of unions and collective bargaining structures as potentially important agents in shaping the form and moderating the speed of diffusion. Given Malaysia's long exposure to globalization, this slow diffusion is all the more striking.

DISCUSSION AND CONCLUSION

Based on our preliminary study of HRM/LR practices among lead firms in four industries in India and two industries in Malaysia, we found considerable variation in practices, thus questioning the role of MNCs as important diffusers in these countries and perhaps in developing nations more generally. Our findings also question whether MNC HRM/LR practices can, indeed, be characterized as "best practices" in all of the industries studied. Variations in practices persist despite several market and regulatory pressures for reform toward achieving greater efficiency and possible convergence on the most effective HRM/LR models. These pressures include (1) tight labor markets for qualified workers and resultant high turnover (the electronics industries in India and Malaysia), (2) heightened competition and low profit margins (the pharmaceutical industry in India), (3) financial market crises (the banking industry in Malaysia) and (4) regulatory reforms targeting HRM/LR practices (the banking industry in both India and Malaysia).

What do these cases tell us about the importance of MNCs as diffusers? Our findings provide little support for some factors and some support for various other facilitators and inhibitors that were identified in Tables 9.1, 9.2. First, we find little support for the proposition that levels of diffusion will be higher in countries that have been exposed to globalization for a longer time. Diffusion appears no higher in Malaysia than in India, despite Malaysia's much longer exposure to dominant MNCs. This could, of course, be an artifact of our case selection. Second, our analysis points to several industry variables (e.g., the degree of domination of markets by MNCs, export-oriented production, and dependence on skilled labor) as a more likely source of variation. Third, the evidence supports the proposition that the extent to which MNCs dominate a particular industry affects the diffusion of HRM/LR practices in the industry. Support for such a proposition is nicely illustrated by our findings regarding the white goods industry in India and the electronics industry in Malaysia. In these industries, the major players are all MNCs, and diffusion is relatively strong, in contrast, for instance, with the Indian banking industry.

Fourth, a factor that does not appear to affect the diffusion of HRM/LR practices but influences the kinds of practices that are introduced by MNCs is the national IR system. For example, Indian labor law does not permit retrenchment, which limits management's ability to achieve numerical flexibility. Once a set of HRM/LR practices has been shown to work well within an IR system, however, diffusion is not inhibited by IR systems. Regarding the effects of differences in IR systems on diffusion is the question of whether or not MNCs affect diffusion by attempting to change national regulations to allow the introduction of HRM/LR practices favored by these companies. We found some evidence of such effects in the Malaysian electronics industry but not in India, despite calls by MNCs for liberalization of labor market regulations. It follows, therefore, that the greater the influence of MNCs on altering IR system regulations, the more likely MNC best practices in HRM/LR will be diffused.

To argue that IR system effects are limited is not to suggest that certain actors do not play significant roles as agents of diffusion. Our cases point to three especially important actors. The first is management. This is illustrated in the case of the Malaysian electronics industry, where formal and informal networks shaped ideas about HRM/LR best practices and influenced their implementation. Management, for example, played a strong role in the development of institutions that subsequently influenced the adoption of particular HRM/LR strategies associated with a more highly skilled workforce, as highlighted by the influence of the Penang Skills Development Center. This and other cases also highlight the role that governments can sometimes play in the diffusion process. Of special note is the important role played by the Indian government through its central bank, which helped diffuse specific HRM/LR practices throughout the Indian banking industry. Similarly, employers and unions together may promote diffusion by establishing institutions that assist in the process or, alternatively, limit diffusion via industry-wide bargaining agreements. Such is the case in the Indian and Malaysian banking industries, in which centralized bargaining had the effect of limiting diffusion despite intense pressures for reform and the presence of MNC banks that appear to have deployed superior HRM/LR practices. The Malaysian banking case suggests, however, that it is not always unions that block reform, as it was the unions that promoted decentralization of authority.

Fifth, our findings highlight the importance of labor market competition in encouraging convergence on best practices in HRM/LR. The intense competition for labor clearly creates incentives for firms to adopt best practices that help them attract and retain qualified workers. Labor market pressures were especially strong in the Malaysian electronics and Indian software industries, although diffusion appears to be much more widespread in Malaysian electronics. This difference suggests that there are joint or interaction effects underlying diffusion. That is, the Malaysian electronics industry is more homogeneous (focusing on semiconductors) and more tightly integrated into worldwide manufacturing networks controlled by innovative MNCs than the Indian software industry. In addition, Malaysian electronics manufacturers are primarily focused on export production, whereas the Indian industry produces for both export and domestic markets. In short, the combination of attributes such as tight labor markets, competitive export-oriented product markets, and industry dominance by MNCs is likely to have mutually reinforcing interaction effects that encourage more widespread and probably faster diffusion of best practices in HRM/LR.

Can the lack of convergence on best practice models be linked to the argument that HRM/LR may not be a source of competitive advantage in India and Malaysia or in developing countries more generally? Our results vary by industry. In several industries where there is considerable competitive pressure from both product and labor markets for improvements in HRM/LR, convergence is evident. Where these pressures are less intense (e.g., pharmaceuticals in India and banking in Malaysia), not only is there considerable variation, but some indigenous forms of HRM/LR practices appear to be as effective, if not more so, as so-called best practices developed by MNCs from advanced countries. Such a finding may suggest that in labor-intensive industries, including subsectors of high-tech industries, the development of best practice may require a careful blending of foreign-born practices with local customs. Preliminary evidence drawn from our studies of pharmaceutical company Lupin and electronics company WIPRO in India would support such a proposition.

The implications that we draw from the foregoing analysis of diffusion of MNC best practices in HRM/LR can be summarized by the following eight propositions.

1. Diffusion of MNC practices is not directly related to length of time that domestic companies in developing nations have been exposed to MNCs.

2. Diffusion of practices and the role of MNCs in that diffusion are more a function of industry-specific characteristics than national differences among developing countries.

3. The greater the market share and dominance of MNCs in an industry, the greater the diffusion of MNC best practices.

4. The tighter the labor market for qualified employees in an industry, the greater the diffusion of practices.

5. MNCs are more likely to be important diffusers of practices in industries that focus more on serving international than domestic markets.

6. The interaction and reinforcing effects of selected industry product and labor market factors increase diffusion.

7. The presence of formal and informal management networks, government support, and collective bargaining agreements influence the diffusion of new practices, either positively or negatively.

8. The greater the difference in the contexts within which practices were framed (developed countries, higher-skilled workforces) compared to where they might be diffused (developing countries, lower-skilled workforces), the less likely practices will be perceived as relevant, and, hence, the less MNC practices will be diffused.

We close with two conclusions. First, "best practices" in HRM/LR must be defined in both theoretically and empirically meaningful terms. Our research suggests that best practices are not equivalent to universalistic MNC practices. Rather, best practices need to be defined in a way that is industry-specific and also takes account of broad variations in local conditions. Second, we need to understand more thoroughly the processes of diffusion and, in turn, the factors influencing the speed of adoption by domestic companies. Other than to highlight the importance of specific institutions and actors in influencing diffusion, our cases reveal relatively little about the underlying processes and speed of diffusion. It will be important, therefore, to more richly understand the institutional contexts of decision making of both MNC diffusers and potential domestic company adopters, as well as the organizational characteristics that influence such decision making. The next stage of inquiry holds promise that much can be gained, not only theoretically but also in terms of guiding policy making on a critical subject that lies at the intersection of the global and the local.

NOTE

1. The original case studies in India and Malaysia can be found in Hiers and Kuruvilla (1999) and Peetz and Todd (1999). These studies form part of a wider canvass of national level studies of globalization and HRM/LR funded by the ILO.

REFERENCES

Adler, N. and Jelinek, M. (1986). "Is 'Organization Culture' Culture Bound?" *Human Resource Management* 25 (1), pp.73–90.

Bartlett, C. A. and Ghoshal, S. (1989). *Managing across Borders the Transnational Solution*. Boston: Harvard Business School Press.

Bangert, D. and Poor, J. (1993). "Foreign Involvement in the Hungarian Economy: Its Impact on Human Resource Management." *The International Journal of Human Resource Management* 4 (6), pp. 817–40.

Beechler, S. and Yang, J. Z. (1994). "The Transfer of Japanese-Style Management to American Subsidiaries: Contingencies, Constraints, and Competencies", *Journal of International Business Studies* 25 (3), pp. 467-487.

Caligiuri, P. and Stroh, L. (1995). "Multinational Corporation Management Strategies and International Human Resources Practices: Bringing IHRM to the Bottom Line." *The International Journal of Human Resource Management* 5 (5), pp. 494–504.

Carr, R. 1994). "The Development of a Global Human Resource Management Approach in ZENECA Pharmaceuticals." In Torrington, D. (ed.*), International Human Resource Management: Think Globally, Act Locally*. New York: Prentice-Hall, pp. 202–17.

De Cieri, H. and Dowling, P. J. (1999). "Strategic Human Resource Management in Multinational Enterprises: Theoretical and Empirical Developments." *Research in Personnel and Human Resources Management*, Supplement 4, pp. 305–27.

Dicken, P. (1992). *Global Shift: The Internationalisation of Economic Activity.* 2nd ed. London: Chapman.

Enderwick, P. (1985). *Multinational Business and Labour.* Beckenham: Croom Helm.

Edwards, T., Rees, C., and Collier, X. (1999). "The Structure, Politics, and Diffusion of Employment Practices in Multinationals." *European Journal of Industrial Relations* 5 (3), pp. 286–306.

Edwards, P., Ferner, A., and Sisson, K. (1996). "The Conditions for International Human Resources Management: Two Case Studies." *The International Journal of Human Resource Management* 7 (1), pp. 20–40.

Edwards, T. and Ferner, A. (2000). "Multinationals Reverse Diffusion and National Business Systems." Paper presented at the International Conference at Wayne State University, Detroit, April 1-3.

Elger, T. and Smith, C. (1994). *Global Japanization: The Transnational Transformation of the Labour Process.* London:Routledge

Ferner, A. (1997). "Country of Origin Effects and HRM in Multinational Companies." *Human Resource Management Journal* 7 (1), pp. 19–37.

Florkowski, G. and Nath, R. (1993). "MNC Responses to the Legal Environment of International Human Resource Management." *International Journal of Human Resource Management* 4 (3), pp. 305–24.

Frenkel, S. (2000). "Globalization and Employment Relations Systems: Trends and Strategies for the Future." Paper presented at the Conference of the ILO for Asian Employers Associations CEOs, April.

Frenkel, S. and Royal, C. (1997). "Globalization and Employment Relations." *Research in the Sociology of Work* 6, pp. 3–41.

Ghoshal, S. and Bartlett C. (1988). "Creation, Adoption, and Diffusion of Innovations by Subsidiaries of Multinational Corporations." *Journal of International Business Studies* 19 (3), pp. 265–388.

Haddock, C. and South, B. (1994). "How Shell's Organisation and HR Practices Help It to Be Both Global and Local." In Torrington, D. (ed.), *International Human Resource Management: Think Globally, Act Locally*. New York: Prentice-Hall, pp. 218–46.

Hannon, J. M., Huang, I. C., Jaw, B. S. (1995). "International Human Resource Strategy and Its Determinants: The Case of Subsidiaries in Taiwan." *Journal of International Business Studies* 26 (3), pp. 531–52.

Hiers, W. and Kuruvilla. S. (1999). *Globalization and Industrial Relations in India.* Bangkok:ILO.

Hoffman, K. (1989). "Technological Advancement and Organizational Innovation in the Engineering Industry." Industry and Energy Department Working Paper 4, the World Bank. March.

Kamoche, K. (1996). "The Integration-Differentiation Puzzle: A Resource-Capability Perspective in International Human Resource Management." *The International Journal of Human Resource Management* 7 (1), pp. 230–44.

Kedia, B. L. and Bhagat, R. S. (1988). "Cultural Constraints on the Transfer of Technologies across Nations: Implications for Research in International and Comparative Management." *Academy of Management Review* 13 (4), pp. 559–71.

Kogut, B. (1991). "Country Capabilities and the Permeability of Borders." *Strategic Management Journal* 12, pp.33–47.

Kenney, M. and Florida, R. (1993). *Beyond Mass Production: The Japanese System and Its Transfer to the U.S.* Oxford: Oxford University Press.

Koike, K. (1996). "Globalization, Competitiveness and Workers Skills." *Proceedings of the Regional Meeting of the Asian Industrial Relations Association*, Taipei, Taiwan, September.

Kostova, T. (1999). "Transnational Transfer of Strategic Organizational Practices: A Contextual Perspective." *Academy of Management Review* 24 (2), April, pp. 308–24.

Kuruvilla, S. (1997). *Globalization and Employment Relations: A Framework for Research.* Bangkok: ILO EASTMAT

Kuruvilla, S. (1995). "Industrialization Strategy and Industrial Relations Policy in Malaysia." In Frenkel, S. and Harrod, J. (eds.), *Industrialization and Labor Relations: Contemporary Research in Seven Countries.* Ithaca, NY: ILR Press, pp. 216–35.

Kuruvilla, S., Erickson, C., Anner, M., Amante, M., Ofreneo, R., and Ortiz, I. (1999). *Globalization and Industrial Relations in the Philippines.* Bangkok: ILO.

Lee, A. and Kuruvilla, S. (2000). "Review of the Literature on the Global vs. Local Question". Unpublished. Department of Collective Bargaining, Cornell University.

Oliver, N. and Wilkinson, B. (1988). *The Japanization of British Industry.* Oxford: Blackwell.

Pil, F. and MacDuffie, J. (1999). "What Makes Transplants Thrive? Managing the Transfer of Best Practice at Japanese Auto Plants in North America." *Journal of World Business* 34 (4), pp 372–91.

Peetz, D. and Todd, T. (1999). *Globalization and Employment Relations in Malaysia.* Bangkok: ILO. Unpublished.

Posthuma, A .C. (1994). "Japanese Production Techniques in Brazilian Automobile Components Firms: A Best Practice Model or Basis for Adaptation?" In Elger, T. and Smith, C. (eds.), *Global Japanization: The Transnational Transformation of the Labour Process.* London: Routledge, pp. 197–212.

Schuler, R. S., Dowling, P. J., and De Cieri, H. (1993). "An Integrative Framework of Strategic International Human Resource Management." *The International Journal of Human Resource Management* 6 (4), pp. 717–64.

Taylor, S., Beechler, S., and Napier, N. (1996). "Toward an Integrative Model of Strategic International Human Resource Management." *Academy of Management Review* 21 (4), pp. 959–76.

UNCTAD. (1998). *World Investment Report. 1998. Trends and Determinants.* New York and Geneva: United Nations.

Womack. J., Jones, J., and Roos, D. (1990). *The Machine That Changed the World.* New York: Rawson Associates.

Part III

Transnational Union Strategies

10

Dual Sourcing at Ford in the United States and Mexico: Implications for Labor Relations and Union Strategies

Steve Babson

North Mexico's growing production of auto parts and finished vehicles for export has gained it notoriety in recent years as "Detroit South" (Baker, Woodruff, and Weiner, 1992). In this emerging industrial region, the newest assembly plants of Ford, GM, and Daimler-Chrysler are said to have installed lean production practices comparable to, if not more advanced than, Detroit proper (Womack, Jones, and Roos, 1990: 87, 265–66; Harbour and Associates, 1999: 20-21). The growing output of this transplanted auto industry has also been matched by growing controversy, much of it centered on the intentions and consequences of corporate investment in Mexico. Debate has been especially polarized around labor issues (compensation, work rules, and collective bargaining) as they impact, and are impacted by, these trends.

This chapter presents preliminary results from a study comparing labor relations and work organization at the Ford assembly plants in Hermosillo, Sonora, and Wayne, Michigan, where the company has produced subcompact cars since the mid-1980s.[1] By centering on "paired" factories making the same product, comparative study can control for variables linked to company- and product-specific practices, isolating and clarifying variables linked to regional labor markets and national systems of workplace regulation. The process of collecting and comparing data from these two locations can also facilitate cross-border communication between researchers and unions in North America, establishing a basis for future collaboration in an industry moving rapidly towards regional integration.[2]

HERMOSILLO AND WAYNE

The Hermosillo and Wayne plants operate in the context of a rapidly changing North American auto industry. Of special interest to the concerns raised by this study is the dramatic growth in Mexican output of finished vehicles, from a total of 800,000 units in 1990, to 1,900,000 units in 2000. This rapid growth was accompanied by an equally dramatic shift toward production for export, particularly with the collapse of domestic sales in the middle years of the decade. In 1991, Mexican assembly plants exported 359,000 cars and light trucks, or 36 percent of total production; by 2000, exports had climbed to 1.4 million vehicles, representing 74 percent of total production. While domestic sales climbed to a record 854,000 vehicles in 2000 (half of them imports), this represented a growth of just 21 percent since the previous record year of 1992; in the same period, production for export had grown 260 percent. (Economist Intelligence Unit, 1999: 265, 292; Chappell, 2001).   This shift toward production for export entailed numerous qualitative changes, including a reduction in the number of models produced, a corresponding acceleration of production as model mix was simplified, an increase in automation, a shift toward certain lean production methods, and dramatic improvements in productivity and quality as these changes were implemented.

When Ford began to assemble Tracers in Mexico in 1986, six years after Escort production began at Wayne Assembly, Hermosillo was widely regarded as the harbinger and model for Mexico's incorporation into an integrated North American industry. By 1989, quality ratings for the plant's product had surpassed those for every other small car sold in the North American market except the Honda Civic, with which it was virtually tied (Shaiken, 1990: 26–28). By the mid-1990s, Hermosillo's rated productivity had also climbed dramatically, trailing the Wayne plant in workers-per-vehicle by just 5–8 percent (Harbour and Associates, 1995: 24). While this gap widened in the late 1990s, when the Harbour report began to measure productivity in hours-per-vehicle, the Hermosillo plant's performance was still a quantum leap ahead of the productivity levels in older Mexican assembly plants (Harbour and Associates, 1999: 46). The general data presented in Table 10.1 compare the two plants at the end of the 1990s, when the Wayne plant's rated productivity was roughly 25 percent higher than Hermosillo's, while the latter's labor costs were roughly 1/10th that of Wayne's.

Hermosillo's pathbreaking success in productivity, cost, and quality drew special attention to Ford's motives for building the plant, with debate focused on which of the inducements listed in Table 10.2 played the greater role in drawing Ford south (Womack et al., 1990: 265–66; Shaiken, 1990: 252–54; Baker et al., 1992; Carrillo, 1995b).   Discussion is ongoing over the relative weight of these factors in determining Ford's initial decision to invest U.S. $500 million in the Hermosillo plant and its subsequent decision to expand and upgrade the operation. Over time, the terms of the debate have also shifted as the sociopolitical context has changed, most notably, with the implementation of the North American Free Trade Agreement (NAFTA) in 1994 and the collapse of Mexico's domestic market in 1995.   While these transformations occurred outside the walls of the factory (and, therefore, outside the boundaries of this study), the remaining factors listed in Table 10.2 all focus on internal features of the Hermosillo plant's operation and performance. As part of a long-term research project on auto labor and lean production in North America, this

Table 10.1
Plant Characteristics and Performances

		Hermosillo	Wayne
General Data [1]			
Plant size		1.6 million sq. ft.	3.4 million sq. ft.
Date built		1986	Assembly, 1955; body/stamping, 1990
Product		Escort/Tracer, (99)	Escort/Tracer, (99)
		Focus hatchback	Focus sedan, wagon
Employment:	Total	2,288	3,393
	Hourly	2,058	3,136
	Salaried	230	257
	Ratio	1 salaried to 8.9 hourly	1 salaried to 12.2 hourly
Average age		30 years	41 years (1997)[2]
% women/minorities		0 / does not apply	13% / 34% [3]
Shift pattern		Two shifts	Two shifts
Working days available		240	235
Capacity line rate/hour		40.0	74.0
Annual capacity in units		150,400	278,240
1998 production		135,216	226,470
1998 utilization rate		90%	81%
1997 utilization rate		85%	100%
Productivity / Costs (Assy)			
A) Labor hrs per unit [4]		28.13	22.25
B) Hourly labor cost (U.S.)[5]		~$4.00	~$45.00
C) Labor cost per unit [6]		~$112	~$1,000

Notes:
1. Unless otherwise indicated, general data are drawn from plant interviews and from Harbour and Associates, (1999: 29, 34, 46, 88, 91). Harbour adjusts plant data in an attempt to commonize operations; because most assembly plants do not have stamping facilities, Harbour separates the two. Unless otherwise indicated, numbers reported here recombine assembly with stamping for 1998. For 1999, both plants reported a rise in the number of workers and hours per vehicle due to model launch. See *The Harbour Report 2000*, 48-49.
2. Michelle Kaminski, "Assembly Plant Template, Wayne ISA," International Research Conference, and "Working Lean: Labor in the North American Auto Industry," April 1997, Puebla, Mexico. The template is for body and stamping only.
3. Ibid., body & stamping only.
4. Does not include stamping. *Harbour and Associates, 1999*: 46, 64.
5. Compensation data for Hermosillo are drawn from "Summario de Compensación a Personal Técnico," VW de México, Departmento Administrativo de personal y nóminas, 1998. The exchange rate at that time fluctuated around 10 pesos to the U.S. dollar. Total daily compensation equaled $31.46, according to the Volkswagen estimate, including an average daily wage of $14.50, plus bonuses, food benefits, savings plan, vacation pay, etc. Calculation of the total cost of labor adds the cost to the company of the 14.7% payroll tax for health care and pension benefits applied to total daily compensation: 1.147 x $31.46 = $36.08; divided by daily hours (9) = $4.00. The $45 per hour figure for Wayne in 1998 is an industry estimate. The average hourly wage in the U.S. Big Three was $23.50 for skilled trades and $19.55 for production workers. See "Partsmaker Paranoia," *Ward's Auto World* (July 1999), 35.
6. A x B = C.

Table 10.2
Inducements for Ford to Invest in Mexican Auto Production

1. The promise of future growth in the Mexican market.

2. The opportunity to evade voluntary quotas on Japanese imports to the United States by locating production of the Mazda-based Tracer in Mexico and supplying it with parts and components imported from Japan.

3. The opening provided by government policies in Mexico that generally promoted greater foreign investment and, in particular, offered Ford significant subsidies to build the Hermosillo plant.

4. The lure of lower wages, said to be "dirt cheap" in the business press.

5. The prospect of exploiting a weak union culture on Mexico's northern frontier, offering little resistance to management initiatives.

6. The appeal of a "greenfield" environment that facilitated implementation of flexible, lean-production practices, including work teams.

7. The opportunity to use Hermosillo's performance measures as a benchmark for spurring (or, as union critics term it, "whipsawing") the Wayne, Michigan, workforce to improve quality while reducing labor costs.

chapter presents preliminary results comparing Hermosillo and Wayne against three human resource mangement and labor relations (HRM/LR) practices (items 5-7 in Table 10.2): union culture, "lean" work teams, and benchmarking/whipsawing.

Union Culture

If union culture is defined by the degree to which workers see collective action, independent organization, and adversarial bargaining as necessary and positive, then Hermosillo was not a place where Ford expected to find such an oppositional culture. In an internal assessment of 1984, the company concluded that its new plant would find "a workforce that is extremely docile, flexible, scarcely unionized, and with reduced capacity for negotiating collective bargaining agreements" (Carrillo, 1995b: 2). In fact, even as the plant demonstrated the success of the company's lean/flexible production system, Ford's expectations of a docile labor force soon confronted a budding union culture inside the Hermosillo plant.

The company's initial expectations of the Hermosillo workforce contrasted sharply with its assessment of the Ford assembly plant in Cuautitlán, a "brownfield" facility located near Mexico City. In this older plant, a union presence dating back to the 1960s had established work rules and classification structures aligned with Mexico's earlier production regime, centered on labor-intensive and low-volume production of varied models for domestic sale (Garcia and Hills, 1998). The Hermosillo plant, in contrast, was designed to produce a single platform at high volume targeted for export to the western United States and Canada. Ford, moreover, sought to recruit a labor force capable of managing the automated and robotic production equipment that the company planned to install. Accordingly, Ford recruited from an unusually large number of colleges and technical schools in the Hermosillo region to enlist a highly literate and technically competent workforce. While few of the initial recruits had any manufacturing experience, one-third reported some university training, and 90 percent reported 10 or more years of schooling—compared to just 55 percent at Cuautitlán (Shaiken, 1990: 23–25; Carrillo 1995a: 91).

Ford did not intend to insert these highly schooled workers into the detailed job classifications and seniority-based promotion system that characterized the Cuautitlán plant. Rather, Ford intended to deploy an HRM/LR strategy compatible with the lean/flexible production system deemed necessary for its new export strategy. Since operating nonunion would invite disruptive interunion competition to win bargaining rights, Ford sought an understanding with the Confederation of Mexican Workers (CTM), the same union representing workers at Cuautitlán and other Ford-Mexico plants (Middlebrook, 1995: 272–73). The CTM proved agreeable, and Mexico's decentralized structure of collective bargaining proved accommodating. Unlike in the United States, where local collective bargaining is constrained to varying degrees by a national pattern agreement applied across the Big Three, in Mexico there is no comparable pattern bargaining in any sector of the auto industry. Bargaining is emphatically local and company-specific, with wage rates as well as work rules varying across companies and regional labor markets. In this context, Ford enjoyed a unique opportunity to shape the initial collective bargaining agreement at Hermosillo. Before the plant was completed or the local union organized, the national CTM's leaders signed a letter of intent in 1985 committing the union to a sparse and "flexible" contract (Carrillo, 1995b: 1). There followed in 1986 a collective bargaining agreement of just 24 pages, with more of these devoted to wages and benefits than work rules and with no language regulating work teams, job rotation, or transfers within the plant.

Measured solely in terms of size, the contrast between the labor agreements at Hermosillo and Wayne could hardly be more sharply drawn. Even after seven rounds of renegotiation, Hermosillo's 1998-2000 agreement totaled only 30 pages. By comparison, the 1996–1999 United Automobile Workers (UAW)-Ford master agreement totaled 1,378 pages, with local contracts at Wayne pushing the total to 1,585 pages. *Quantitative* differences on this scale strongly suggest *qualitative* differences in workplace relations, a link suggested in a different context by Dennis Pawley, then vice president of Mazda's Michigan assembly plant, in his observation that "the big thick contracts you've got in your UAW [plants] across the country are there because management proved they couldn't be trusted with general language" (Fucini and Fucini, 1990: 47). On this score, it would appear that either Hermosillo's management has retained the trust of its union workers, or, as Ford anticipated in its initial assessment of northern Mexico, union culture remains weak and union workers docile, even when there is no trust between labor and management.

In practice, however, a collective bargaining agreement's comparative length is not always a reliable indicator of a union culture's comparative strength, particularly if the plants compared are situated within different national regimes of workplace regulation. This caveat applies with special force to the Hermosillo-Wayne comparison, since much of the UAW-Ford agreement addresses matters that, in Mexico, are covered by federal law. There is, for example, little language in the Hermosillo agreement specifying a grievance procedure, and there is none at all on health care, pensions, or profit sharing, matters that consume hundreds of pages in the UAW-Ford agreement. In fact, these issues are covered in Mexico by federal statute: grievance procedures (of a sort) under laws establishing Boards of Conciliation and Arbitration; health care and pensions under public programs administered by the Mexican Institute for Social Security (IMSS); and profit sharing under federal labor law.

A second consideration concerns the relative age of these two plants and their respective bargaining regimes. In 60 years of bargaining, the UAW-Ford agreement has grown into a dense thicket of closely worded contract language, yet it began as a relative seedling of just 24 pages when first negotiated in 1941. The scanty length of the initial agreement was hardly a measure of trust between the two parties, since there was little of this during the early years of union formation. The street battles and organizing campaigns of 1932–1941 were generating an emergent union culture at Ford, but the newborn UAW had only just found its legs in 1941, and was still struggling for survival. Its strength was measured by its capacity to win improvements in shop-floor conditions, and many of these were won in practice long before they were codified and protected in the collective bargaining agreement. To the degree that some of these workplace transformations were never codified (or once codified, were eroded in practice), the agreement's length as well as its content can be taken as only a crude first approximation of a union's current strength or potential for growth.

Compared with Wayne Local 900, founded in 1941, the Hermosillo local union is a relative newcomer. Though the slow rate of growth in contractual language in the Hermosillo agreement shows little evidence of acceleration, the growth of individual and collective protest is, nevertheless, discernible in the plant's short history, as indicated by the following sequence of highlighted events.

1986. In October, shortly after the plant opened, workers wore red-and-black armbands on the job to protest low wages (Carrillo, 1995a: 91).

1987. A two-month strike for a 70 percent wage increase ended with a 35 percent raise in the final settlement (Shaiken, 1990: 69).

1988. When the company fired the union's deputy secretary general for "inciting labor unrest," the local General Assembly voted overwhelmingly to censure the leaders who had acquiesced in the firing. Soon after, the fired leader began an

11-day hunger strike calling for his reinstatement, during which workers in the plant staged an illegal four-hour work stoppage on his behalf. Four days after this job action, local members voted by a 4–1 margin to elect an opposition slate promising greater militancy to improve working conditions. Three weeks later, Ford fired 35 workers, including newly elected officers and departmental stewards, charging them with sabotage of 160 vehicles during the work stoppage. The firings occurred immediately before a scheduled Christmas shutdown and were matched by the company's simultaneous announcement of a unilateral increase in wages and benefits, including a 23 percent raise, a similar jump in entry-level wages, an acceleration of the promotional process, and early payment of profit sharing. An interim leadership willing to accept this outcome was appointed (Shaiken, 1990: 50, 70–71; Associated Press, 1989; Witt, 1990).

1989. From the plant's opening in 1986 until July 1989, 679 workers quit Ford Hermosillo, representing 72 percent of an average plant population of 949. Low wages and narrowed opportunities for promotion accounted for much of the turnover, but work intensity evidently played a role as well, according to Shaiken's assessment: "Not surprisingly, those areas associated with the most repetitive and demanding jobs had the highest rates of voluntary quits. Final assembly was first, with a quit rate of 92%, followed by the body shop with 75% and the paint shop with 63%" (Shaiken, 1990: 81).

1990. Ford refused to comply with a federal labor board ruling ordering the company to reinstate all workers fired since 1987, prompting three workers to begin a new hunger strike. The local government council voted unanimously to censure Ford for defying the board ruling, and the archbishop accused the company of maintaining a blacklist to prevent fired workers from finding employment (Witt, 1990).

1993. An 18-day strike over wages ended with a raise of nearly 10 percent.

1995. Following Ford's announcement that there would be no profit sharing, workers reportedly scratched the paint on finished cars and set small fires. Ford eventually agreed to pay a bonus of approximately U.S.$200 (Angel Barroso, 1997).

1996. Under newly elected leadership, the local union conducted a shop-floor campaign to pressure the company to sell 500 rental units of worker housing to the tenants and count past rent toward the cost. The campaign was eventually successful.

1997. Local union members conducted a three-day unsanctioned strike (*paro*) over Ford's claim that it had made no profit in Mexico the previous year and, therefore, did not have to pay the legally mandated profit sharing to its hourly workers. After blocking the plant gates, 2,000 workers marched into the city and demanded government intervention to examine irregularities in Ford's accounts, including an unspecified line item under miscellaneous expenses, "Garantía y Politica" (Ford Motor, 1997), totaling more than the cost of Ford's Mexican payroll. The walkout spread to Ford's Cuautitlan and Chihuahua plants, prompting Ford to pay a "bonus" in lieu of the disputed profit sharing. The company lost a reported 1,000 units of production at Hermosillo during the walkout (Rivera Carrillo, 1997; Salinas Cano, 1997; Angel Barroso, 1997).

1998. Following an incident in which an injured worker was insulted and poorly treated by the IMSS, the local union led much of the first shift in a procession to the IMSS offices and conducted a blockade (*plantón*) of the building. After negotiations with state officials, the IMSS pledged improved services and designated a permanent delegate to attend to injured workers from the Ford plant (Juárez, 1999).

1999. Local union members again protested the amount that Ford would pay in profit sharing. Second-shift workers convened an open-air general assembly as they blocked the plant gates, and the next two shifts continued the protest. Stewards organized the demonstration as a "collective absence" rather than a strike, citing federal law that permits an employer to fire a worker only after three unjustified absences in a month. Continued agitation, marked by another brief sitdown in front of the gates, led to negotiations between the company and the union, with the company eventually agreeing to pay an average of $1,200 per worker, with no retributions for the collective absence. In addition to the issue of profit sharing, a second underlying grievance concerning supervisory abuse apparently animated much of this protest (Juárez, 1999). The "collective absence" was to some degree sparked by this issue, since it followed the day after the local union had successfully pressured the company to remove an offending supervisor from the plant, a German engineer who, while working on an in-plant project for a supplier firm, struck a union member without provocation, according to the union's protest letter (Escalente Lemus, 1999).

Based only on events through 1994, Carrillo's study of the Hermosillo plant concluded that "incidents such as the dismissal of union activists, stoppages and strikes showed clearly that the climate of consensus needed for the new work arrangements did not exist." The union made only limited gains in contesting managerial authority, but it did succeed, according to Carrillo, "in institutionalizing the role of union representatives within a system which had not, in fact, originally recognized their existence," allowing them to intervene "in such issues as the speed of the line, the relations between workers and technical staff and the division of labor" (Carrillo, 1995a: 93).

Events since 1994 confirm and amplify Carrillo's assessment, as the local has adopted a widening repertoire of collective actions: *paros* (sitdowns), *plantóns* ("collective absences"), and *tortugesas* (slowdowns). With the number of elected line stewards more than doubling from 25 in 1990, to 60 in 1999 (Shaiken, 1990: 47; Juárez, 1999), the Hermosillo local has also developed a representation system that is structurally different from that of Wayne Local 900 but comparably dense, the latter including more appointed and full-time representatives in union and joint labor-management positions, while the former includes more elected in-plant stewards who continue to work at their jobs. A growing union culture is equally evident in the extensive participation by local members in the annual May Day marches, with union leaders reporting a 90 percent turnout in recent years. Despite company objections, the union insisted that a photo of the local's spirited marchers be featured on the cover of the collective bargaining agreement. Furthermore, after years of housing its offices inside the factory, the local has purchased land near the plant to build a union hall.

For a factory said to have installed a Toyota-style production system, this is very un-Toyota-like behavior. It is of special interest when considering the plant's continuing capacity to perform at high levels of productivity and quality.[3] If nothing else, the record at Hermosillo suggests that a lean, team-based production system is not as "fragile" or as demanding of consensus as many observers (Womack, et al., 1990: 102–3) have claimed.

"Lean" Teams

Both the Hermosillo and Wayne plants are said to have installed team-based, lean manufacturing systems modeled after Japanese practice (Clark, 1990; Womack et al., 1990; Baker et al., 1992). However, as shown in Tables 10.3 and 10.4, there is considerable variation in job classifications and team organization not only between the two locations but also between different departments within the Wayne plant.

Much of this has to do with the timing of implementation and the changing expectations of the company and the union. In the late 1980s, Ford management had not implemented team-based production in any of its U.S. assembly plants, though in some engine plants and parts-making operations it had begun to install self-directed work teams, a reduced number of production-worker classifications, some job rotation, and some cross-training. While invoking Japanese practice, particularly Toyota's, the Ford variant was far less supervisor-centered than was the case in Japan, reflecting a hybrid derived from, among other things, U.S.-style collective bargaining and human relations theory. Hermosillo represented an opportunity for management to install this hybrid model with a relatively free hand, and the result was evident not only in the absence of job classifications but in the more radical absence of any distinction between production jobs and skilled trades (see Table 10.3). Workers received an unusually heavy dose of preparatory training before entering the plant. Follow-up training for selected workers included competencies normally reserved for the skilled trades at Wayne and elsewhere in the Big Three. Teams initially elected their hourly facilitators, played a role in selecting their supervisors, and also participated in decisions concerning rotation of jobs, training, and selection for maintenance work. Later, however, supervisors took responsibility for appointing team facilitators, and the number of employees rotated into maintenance work remained limited (Dearborn Assembly Plant and UAW Local 600, 1992).

Union leaders at Wayne Assembly were aware that Ford wanted to implement a team-based "Modern Operating Agreement" (MOA) in a U.S. plant and that the company was also considering construction of a new stamping plant. The local was prepared to bundle the two issues, agreeing in principle to

Table 10.3
Classifications

	Hermosillo	Wayne Assembly	Wayne Body / Stamping
Classifications, production workers	* One classification: "Ford Technician." [1] * Production workers rotate through a variety of jobs.	* 143 classifications within 5 wage groups, separated by $.50/hour, lowest group to highest. [2] Roughly half of the production workforce falls within three classifications: Assembler/Paint, Assembler/ Chassis, and Trim Stock to Car. * Production workers are assigned to tasks within a classification. * Senior workers in Utility and Relief classifications cover for absentees, personal leaves, and tag relief in each zone. [3] * Transfer requests to openings are awarded by (1) seniority in classifications of equal or lower pay, and (2) by merit and ability in classifications of higher pay, with seniority as a tie breaker. [4]	* One classification: "Body & Stamping Technician." [5] * Production workers rotate through a variety of jobs in their area. * Transfers to openings in five production areas are awarded to the most senior worker applying. Once a year, senior workers can bump into another area, displacing junior workers who move to the area the senior worker left. [6] * Three support areas (material handling, quality weld surveillance, and housekeeping-environmental) are reserved for senior workers who have reached the top Ability Rate Progression (see Table 10.4). [7]

Table 10.3, continued

	Hermosillo	Wayne Assembly	Wayne Body / Stamping
Classifications, production workers (con't)		* Management can "loan" workers to another classification, beginning with least senior. Workers retain wage rate or are paid a higher rate after 3 days if moved to a higher-paid classification. [9] * The union must agree to changes in classifications. [10]	
Classifications, skilled trades	* There are no separate skilled trades classifications. Maintenance work is performed by salaried personnel and outside vendors or by designated hourly workers who receive special training for routine servicing and programming of robots, machine maintenance, die repair, etc., depending on department and need. Members rotate back to production after 4 years. [8]	* 35 apprenticeable classifications, including blacksmith, carpenter, electrician, machine repair, millwright, plumber, pipefitter, repair, tinsmith, toolmaker, welder, and powerhouse/boiler repair. * Local contract reaffirms national contract's definition of "incidental work" which can be assigned outside of normal craft lines. [11]	* 13 apprenticeable classifications in three "umbrella" groups: electrical, mechanical, and tool and die. [12] * Within each umbrella, work is assigned according to the "core skills" of each trade. When the appropriate trades-person is not available, management can assign other skilled trades personnel. [13]

Notes:

1. Planta de Estampado y Ensamble de Hermosillo, *Contrato Colectivo de Trabajo*, Tabulador de Salarios, 27.

2. *Local Agreements, Letters of Understanding, and Rates between Local 900, UAW and the Ford Motor Company, Wayne Assembly Plant*, 1996, 94-99; hereafter, "*Wayne Assembly Local Agreement*."

3. *Wayne Assembly Local Agreement*, 14, 22, 26.

4. *Agreements between the UAW and the Ford Motor Company*, 1996, v.1, Article IV, Section 2; hereafter, "*UAW-Ford National Agreement*." National contract is reaffirmed in *Wayne Assembly Local Agreement*, 14-15. In practice, "merit and ability" are less determining than seniority.

5. *Local Agreements, Letters of Understanding, and Rates between Local 900, UAW and the Ford Motor Company, Wayne Body and Stamping*, 1990, 15; hereafter, "*Wayne Body and Stamping Local Agreement*."

6. *Wayne Body and Stamping Local Agreement*, 16-17, 36.

7. *Wayne Body and Stamping Local Agreement*, 17, 19, 77.

8. Interviews; Pat Burger, "Hermosillo Report," 1992, typescript, distributed to the Ford Dearborn Tool and Die Unit of UAW Local 600 by District Committee member Pat Burger. Burger was a union member of the joint study team that went to Hermosillo. See footnote 2, *Summary Report*.

9. *Wayne Assembly Local Agreement*, 33, citing the UAW-Ford *National Agreement*, Article VIII, Sec. 22(a). The length of time a worker can be "loaned" to another classification varies according to local and departmental practice. Local unions generally oppose extensive loaning, but management's contractual right to move production workers across classification has been upheld by the umpire, so long as wage rates are properly adjusted.

10. *Wayne Assembly Local Agreement*, 23.

11. *Wayne Assembly Local Agreement*, 100, citing the *National Agreement*, Skilled Trades Supplemental Agreement, Exhibit II, 327.

12. *Wayne Body and Stamping Local Agreement*, 56-73.

13. *Wayne Body and Stamping Local*.

Table 10.4 Work Groups

	Hermosillo	Wayne Assembly	Wayne Body / Stamping
Designation	* Team	* Continuous Improvement Work Group (CIWG)	* Team
Coverage	* 100% of plant, 60 groups of 30-40 workers	* 95% of plant, ~150 groups of 10-15 workers	* 100% of plant, 47 groups of 10-15 workers
Participation	* Mandatory	* Mandatory if during regular shift, voluntary if overtime	* Mandatory
Group is led by	* Product Specialist = supervisor Facilitators (F) = hourly workers	* "Scribe" = hourly worker (equivalent of a recording secretary)	* Team Leader (TL) = hourly worker
Selection	* Supervisor appoints facilitators	* Team members elect scribe	* Team members elect TL[2]
Meetings	* Weekly, 30 minutes, chaired by Product Specialist (Supervisor)	* Every two weeks, 30 minutes, chaired by Scribe. Supervisor rotates thru 3-5 CIWGs per zone	* Weekly, 30 minutes, chaired by Team Leader. Supervisor attends when invited by team
Training for production workers	* Extensive, 4 months, including gas welding, hydraulics, machine shop, etc.[1]	* Modest, with 28 hours training in CIWG; 12 in FPS overview; 8-16 in preventive maintenance	* Modest, including preventive maintenance, quality controls, team process
Overtime distribution by	* Supervisor	* Supervisor, with contractual obligation to equalize	* Elected hourly worker is paid TL premium to equalize overtime[3]

Table 10.4 Continued

	Hermosillo	Wayne Assembly	Wayne Body / Stamping
Scope of Task Rotation	* Rotate direct labor tasks, plus maintenance, repair, inspection, housekeeping. Team decides frequency	* Does not apply: No rotation across classifications	* Rotate direct labor tasks, minor maintenance, inspection, house-keeping, material handling.[7] Team decides frequency
Assignment of tasks	* By supervisor. Facilitator assists	* By classification. Supervisor assigns tasks inside classification	* By team. TL coordinates; supervisor decides if deadlock
Balancing job loads	* Supervisor, engineers, and team members	* Supervisors, engineers, and CIWG members, with hourly Quality Assurance Operator[5]	* Team members and engineers, plus supervisor if team disagrees on changes[8]
Pay for knowledge	* Total pay is determined by a ten-level progression. Evaluation by union-management committee[4]	* Does not apply	* Added to base pay as worker progresses through 5 Levels with $1/ hour spread, evaluated by team[9]
Workers can stop the line	* Yes	* Yes	* Yes
Group steward	* One delegate elected per group	* None. Elected scribe refers issues to union plant committee	* None. Elected TL refers issues to union plant committee
Contract defines team/group	* No, by policy	* Yes, by national contract on CIWGs, and local policy[6]	* Yes, by local contract

Notes:

1. "Summary Report: Dearborn Assembly Plant Visit of the Hermosillo Assembly Plant, June 2-5, 1992," typescript in author's possession, 2, 9-11. The report summarizes the findings of a joint labor-management delegation from the Dearborn Assembly Plant and UAW Local 600 that visited Hermosillo in anticipation of negotiating a new collective bargaining agreement.

2. *Local Agreements, Letters of Understanding, and Rates between Local 900, UAW and the Ford Motor Company, Wayne Body and Stamping*, 1990, 16; hereafter, "*Wayne Body and Stamping Local Agreement.*"

3. *Wayne Body and Stamping Local Agreement*, 25.

4. Planta de Estampado y Ensamble de Hermosillo, *Contrato Colectivo de Trabajo*, Capítulo III (A), 10-11.

5. *Local Agreements, Letters of Understanding, and Rates between Local 900, UAW and the Ford Motor Company, Wayne Assembly Plant*, 1996, 61. The Letter of Agreement concerning quality assurance operators (QAO) does not specify the QAO's role, only that the parties will seek approval from the national parties for the appropriate classification title and wage rate. The language was inserted at the union's request to protect the QAO position.

6. *Agreements between the UAW and the Ford Motor Company*, 1996, v.1, Appendix I, "Memorandum of Understanding—Continuous Improvement," 171-78.

7. *Wayne Body and Stamping Local Agreement*, 12-13.

8. *Wayne Body and Stamping Local Agreement*, 22.

9. *Wayne Body and Stamping Local Agreement*, 15.

an MOA if Ford agreed to build the stamping plant (generating 600 new jobs) at Wayne. At the same time, however, there was sharp debate within union ranks over team-based production systems. Older workers who had gained preferred jobs through seniority bidding did not welcome the prospect of job rotation; the skilled trades opposed the outsourcing or fragmenting of their work; and many workers regarded teams as a poor trade-off if they had to sacrifice hard-won work rules and seniority rights. In 1988, these issues attracted additional attention as an opposition caucus within the UAW, New Directions, ran a national slate of candidates opposed to the "Team Concept." While support for New Directions' defeated candidates was concentrated in GM locals, with comparatively few followers at Ford, Local 900 was wary of applying the controversial team concept across the entire incumbent workforce at Wayne Assembly. Further, there was no support in any sector of the local for abolishing the skilled trades or categorically jettisoning all work rules.

As a result, the union and the company agreed to split the Wayne operation in two: Wayne Assembly retained a more traditional agreement with job classifications and seniority rights in paint, chassis, and final assembly, while the new stamping and body-making plant (Integrated Stamping and Assembly, or ISA) implemented an MOA that consolidated production classifications but only modestly trimmed the trades classifications (see Table 10.3). The union also retained seniority bidding for transfers between work areas in the ISA plant, and team organization was codified in the local collective bargaining agreement, including the stipulation that team leaders be elected rather than appointed by supervision. By splitting the union's representational structure and installing separate bargaining committees in each of the two plants, the union also widened the opportunities for election and appointment of new leaders.

Finally, with Ford's resolve to implement the Ford Production System across all of its operations in the 1990s, teams (of a sort) came to Wayne Assembly as well. By the late 1990s, however, Ford was no longer wedded to the initial prescription for team-based production that had been deployed at Hermosillo and negotiated at Wayne ISA. While the same technical apparatus and related practices of lean production found their way into Ford plants (visual control "andon" boards, quality in station, standardized work, just-in-time inventory) the social imperative of employee involvement took a more muted form in the guise of "Continuous Improvement Work Groups" (CIWGs). As indicated in Table 10.4, these are essentially amplified quality circles with no job rotation or collective responsibility for a particular area or process. Unlike the older system of Employee Involvement (EI) at Ford in the 1980s, where volunteers met on company time to discuss work environment and quality issues, CIWGs now enlisted the entire work group in such meetings.

The question of why or to what degree Ford has abandoned self-directed work teams touches on issues that are central to any discussion of lean production in the auto industry. Although I cannot offer definitive answers based on this preliminary study, I can suggest several possibilities. First, a trend toward "lean without teams" was generally evident in U.S. and especially Canadian assembly plants during the 1990s, while other elements of the lean model gained widening acceptance (MacDuffie and Pils, 1997; Osterman, 2000).[4] The slowed pace of team implementation was partly the result of union opposition, ranging from the temporizing wariness of many UAW leaders and locals, to the overt hostility of the Canadian Auto Workers (Holmes and Kumar, 1998). In addition, the crisis conditions of the 1980s that had prompted so many amendments to Fordist mass production had moderated significantly by the mid-1990s. Dramatic downsizing had drawn attention to the inflexibility of classification systems and seniority-based transfers that continually "churned" the plant population. These concerns faded somewhat, however, in the 1990s as high sales and the rapid growth in market share for light trucks gave greater urgency to issues of capacity utilization, product development, and platform consolidation. Employee involvement was still deemed to be a critical ingredient in manufacturing success, but not at the expense of disrupting plant hierarchies anymore than necessary. These considerations seemed to apply with special force in brownfield settings producing trucks and sport-utility vehicles (SUVs) in the United States and Canada, where profit margins were high and the incidence of teams low.

Furthermore, while teams offered particular advantages in combining direct and indirect labor (reducing the need for off-line support personnel) and permitting flexible deployment (reducing the need for utility/relief workers), many managers were apparently persuaded that these outcomes could be achieved without the disruptive deployment of teams. Wayne Assembly is a case in point. The 143 production-worker classifications still listed in the plant's collective bargaining agreement may appear to be an obstacle to the flexible deployment of labor, but the system is more supple in practice than many critics would allow. Rather than prohibit the movement of people between job classifications, the contract stipulates only that wages be adjusted upward when workers are assigned to jobs rated at a higher levels of pay. Furthermore, roughly half of the Wayne Assembly workforce falls under just three classifications: Assembler/Chassis, Assembler/Paint, and Trim Stock to Car. Task assignments *within* these broad classifications are left to supervisory discretion, subject to constructive amendment by CIWG members and, when work intensity is disputed, the grievance procedure. Workers can be made responsible for inspection, line-side housekeeping, and "continuous improvement" without abandoning job classifications. In any case, the number of classifications that are actually utilized is smaller than the number listed in the contract; "cushion builder," for example, is still a listed classification in the trim department but has not been filled since Ford moved production of seats in the late 1980s to its Chesterfield, Michigan, plant.

Ironically, there is some evidence that Ford management would now *oppose* team-based production if it were modeled after the system negotiated in the Wayne ISA plant. Workers in ISA's body and stamping operation report high levels of support for a worker-centered approach that allows them to elect team leaders, to exclude supervisors from their meetings when they so choose, and to exercise a fair degree of control over task assignments, job rotation, and training (Kaminski, 1996, 1998). For management, such a worker-centered team is a mixed blessing, improving worker morale and commitment, on the one hand, but, on the other, generating a potentially contentious claim that the "self-directed" team is just that, a team centered too literally on worker initiative rather than management control. Concerns that the team concept could be "misinterpreted as a Democratic process" apparently motivated Ford management to redefine its expectations of teams in the early 1990s. The company's revised concept is more akin to the supervisor-centered groups found at Toyota, with an emphasis on the team "*not* as 'independent,'" as one management study put it, "but as '*inter*dependent' with other teams and line supervision" (emphasis in original; Ford Motor Co., 1994: 2.5, 4.2). This new perspective was consistent with Ford's decision at Hermosillo to eliminate team election of hourly facilitators. The lack of any contractual protection for team organization permitted management to make these changes unilaterally, while at Wayne ISA, team organization (including election of team leaders) was supported by the members and protected in the local agreement.

Placed side by side, this preliminary comparison of classification systems and team organization at Hermosillo, Wayne Assembly, and Wayne ISA reveals a remarkable range of outcomes in the implementation of "lean" production. The Hermosillo plant has moved from a more "worker-centered" to a more "supervisor-centered" team system, despite, or perhaps because of, a growing union culture and increasingly adversarial labor relations.[5] At Wayne ISA, the collective bargaining agreement has codified a decidedly worker-centered system, while at Wayne Assembly a more traditional classification structure has been amended to include plantwide quality circles that enlist the entire workforce in improvement activities.

Benchmarking/Whipsawing

For autoworkers in Canada, Mexico, and the United States, the emergence of an integrated North American industry raises the prospect of competition and collaboration between unions and workers in the three countries. Collaboration is comparatively underdeveloped, hindered by language barriers, cultural differences, and organizational dynamics that lag behind the transnational reach of corporations. Competition, on the other hand, is evident in the growing number of cases in which employers have used their widened mobility to discourage unionization and check advances in wages and working conditions (Bronfenbrenner, 1996, esp. pp. 11–12). With regional integration, automakers can source parts and finished vehicles in Mexico as well as in the United States or Canada, using the lowest-cost plant as the benchmark for spurring improvements elsewhere. Dual sourcing across the Mexican border is especially evident in the assembly sector for compact cars and light trucks: in 1999, Ford produced the Focus and the F-150 on both sides of the border;

Chrysler produced the Neon, Cirrus, Stratus, Plymouth Breeze, Sebring, and Dodge Ram in both the United States and Mexico; GM produced SUVs on the GMT800 platform in all three countries and the Cavalier and Sunbird in both the United States and Mexico. Disparities in pay, labor costs, and working conditions between these factories making the same product for the same market create downward pressure on high-cost locations threatened by divestment (Babson, 2000).

This whipsawing dynamic is usually presented as a one-way process pitting workers in brownfield sites in the United States and Canada against workers at greenfield sites in Mexico, with the latter gaining ground at the expense of the former. But consideration of the Wayne and Hermosillo plants also reveals a more complex and multilayered dynamic. Mexican autoworkers are subject to whipsawing as well, with greenfield sites in North and Central Mexico pitted against older sites closer to the Federal District and Mexico City. The key struggle in this regard was the 106-day strike in 1980 at GM's Federal District assembly plant. Affiliated with the Revolutionary Confederation of Workers and Peasants (CROC) since 1952, the GM-Federal District union had an unusually long tradition of democratic governance and militant bargaining, leading the first strike against a Big Three Mexican plant in 1965 and conducting five more walkouts over the next 15 years. By the late 1970s, the union had won language in the collective bargaining agreement protecting seniority rights, regulating work intensity, limiting the number of temporary workers, and establishing the union's legal claim to represent workers in any new GM-Mexico plant.

This last provision was the central issue in the 1980 strike, when GM refused to extend the contract to its new engine and assembly plants in Ramos Arizpe, located in the far northeast. With the defeat of the Federal District union, GM was able to open the northern plants with fewer encumbering work rules, under contracts negotiated with the regional CTM (Middlebrook, 1995: 225–87; Tuman, 1996). Thereafter, the lower wages and team-based production systems at the northern plants of GM and Ford were used to whipsaw pay and working conditions in the older factories near Mexico City, notably, the Ford Cuautitlán and GM Federal District plants. The most salient example occurred in 1987, when Ford refused to extend to Cuautitlán the wage increase that it had already granted at Hermosillo and Chihuahua, arguing that Cuautitlán's wages were already too high to be competitive. The company ended a 61-day strike over the issue by dismissing the entire Cuautitlán workforce and temporarily closing the plant (Middlebrook, 1995: 276–77; Garcia and Hills, 1998).

One should not conclude, however, that unions in the northern plants of Ford and GM are uniformly "kept" organizations, as we have seen in the growth of union culture and militancy at Hermosillo. In general, Mexico's local unions in assembly and engine making have retained some measure of representative governance from the 1970s, when a movement for democratic reform challenged the prevailing practice of appointing local leaders (usually from outside the workforce) and refusing to print, much less distribute, the negotiated agreement.

Middlebrook's detailed assessment of collective bargaining and labor relations in the Mexican auto industry demonstrates that even as Ford and GM moved north to shed work rules and implement lean production, the reforms of the 1970s still left their mark on local union practices at Ford-Hermosillo, the GM-Ramos Arizpe assembly plant, and the Ford-Chihuahua and GM-Ramos Arizpe engine plants:

There was regular turnover in elected union officials; rival slates of candidates often competed in union elections; and general assemblies were commonly held. Workers at each of the four plants received copies of the plant's collective contract for their inspection. Moreover, unions at all four Ford and General Motors plants exercised a degree of autonomy vis-à-vis their respective national union or state-level federation. In each case, the company provided full-time leave for several executive committee members (ranging from two in the General Motors plants to three at Ford Chihuahua and four at Ford Hermosillo). (Middlebrook, 1995: 273–74).[6]

Under these conditions, whipsawing might also be reversed, with unions in the North making their continued cooperation contingent on management's agreement to boost compensation and close the gap with the better-paying plants near Mexico City. Democratic union leaders in Hermosillo, for example, were able to assay more militant tactics in the space opened by the still greater militancy of the Cuautitlán workforce, which battled the company and the national CTM in a series of bitter confrontations in the late 1980s and early 1990s. Eager to avoid a "second front" in this prolonged conflict, Ford and the national CTM probably gave the Hermosillo local relatively more latitude than otherwise would have been the case (Juárez, 1999). Though the 1988 firings at Hermosillo were harsh enough, they paled in comparison with the mass dismissals and fatal violence visited on Cuautitlán's democratic movement (LaBotz, 1992: 148–59).

Whipsawing of a sort could also move in both directions between the Hermosillo and Wayne plants. The downward pressure on Wayne was evident enough in the late 1980s and early 1990s, when Hermosillo's potent combination of low labor costs, high productivity, and exemplary quality put considerable pressure on Wayne Local 900. Hermosillo's benchmark status was made explicit in 1988–1989, when Ford took local union leaders to both the Mazda plant in Hofu, Japan, and the Hermosillo plant to see firsthand how these model factories operated. But in a dynamic that, in effect, reversed the expected polarities of whipsawing, local union leaders borrowed selectively from Hermosillo's practice and turned several of these innovations into new work rules protecting members' workplace rights. Chief among these was the practice of using Quality Deployment Sheets (QDS) to standardize task assignments and sequence. The use of these visible charts posted at each workstation is a recognized feature of lean production and a contributing factor in Hermosillo's high quality ratings, since standardized procedures reduce variation in the assembly process, thereby reducing defects. Local 900's leaders favored the QDS for this reason, but they also reported a second factor that strengthened their support; by specifying the agreed-upon elements and task sequence of the job, the QDS also made it that much more difficult for second-shift supervisors to unilaterally add elements to the jobs of less-senior workers. By codifying in their agreement that workers, team leaders, and hourly "quality assurance operators" participate in developing a QDS for each workstation and that they also sign off on subsequent changes, this feature of flexible manufacturing was amended to include a degree of job control for workers.

CONCLUSION

This preliminary review of labor relations and work organization at Ford's Hermosillo and Wayne plants suggests several perspectives for developing union strategy in the assembly sector of the North American auto industry. First, Mexican autoworkers are potential allies. Unionists in the United States who oppose free trade have not always focused on this potential, in part because the relatively sudden appearance of "Detroit South" in the late 1980s initially cast Mexican workers as unknown competitors underbidding U.S. standards. Mexican autoworkers are, in fact, *put* in the role of competing for jobs in the North American auto industry, with the Mexican government clamping a lid on low wages to preserve this competitive advantage. Mexican workers generally do not welcome this policy, which has eroded real income for most of the last 20 years. A closer look at Hermosillo reveals individual and collective struggles that U.S. unionists can recognize as akin to their own; if nothing else, exposure to this history of collective action can dispel the stereotype of docile workers and uniformly "kept" unions in the assembly and engine sector of the industry.

Second, the CTM is not a monolith. Local and regional variations are evident in any case-by-case assessment, and the capacity for independent action and worker mobilization at Hermosillo suggests the potential for similar growth elsewhere. If cross-border collaboration with the national leadership of the CTM remains problematic, there may still be opportunities for local-to-local collaboration, particularly in cases where assembly plants are making roughly the same car, truck, or engine.

Third, local-to-local collaboration requires that U.S. unions reconsider strategies based on appeals to "Buy American." Regional integration of the North American auto industry has already made such a boycott of "foreign" products virtually impossible, given the extensive cross-border trade in finished vehicles and parts with Canada and Mexico. The problem with Hermosillo is not that Ford is investing in Mexican production but that Ford is investing in Mexican production without *also* enhancing Mexican consumption, a fact that becomes obvious when one looks at the plant's parking lot. The simple fact is that Hermosillo's workers cannot afford to buy the Escort or the Focus. The parking lot, consequently, is largely filled with the buses that Ford uses to transport workers to the plant. Mexican workers (like their U.S. and Canadian counterparts) need good-paying jobs, with real wages that are not only "good" compared to Mexico's falling standards but "good" compared to their rapidly rising productivity. This cannot happen overnight, but in a context where Mexican workers need substantial and steady improvements in purchasing power to become customers for their own product, a "Buy American" boycott is counterproductive as well as ineffective. To the degree that this kind of protectionist rhetoric has dominated the past discourse of U.S. unions, Mexico's business and government leaders have been able to portray the U.S. labor movement as a competitor rather than an ally. The admonition to "Buy *Union* and the increasingly popular call for "Fair Trade—Not Free Trade" are better rallying points for a common front opposing suppression of labor rights in Mexico and the United States.

Steps toward such an approach quickened in 1998, when American Federation of Labor and Congress of Industrial Organizations (AFL-CIO) President John Sweeney traveled to Mexico (the first visit by a national labor leader since John L. Lewis in 1938) and spoke with unionists from a wide range of organizations, including the CTM. "We want to work with our brothers and sisters in all parts of the Mexican labor movement and with freedom lovers throughout Mexican society," Sweeney said in his speech at the National Autonomous University of Mexico. The immediate need, Sweeney stressed, was to "find practical ways to work together by seeking and developing coordinated cross-border organizing and bargaining strategies" (LaBotz, 1998: 4). The recent participation of the UAW and the Canadian Auto Workers (CAW) in coalitions that have protested the suppression of labor rights at the Mexican supplier plants of Echlin/Dana and Han Young/Hyundai are also positive steps (Babson, 2000).

Fourth and last, communication is the obvious starting point for establishing such a transnational collaboration between unions. The lack of it is highlighted by two singular events of 1999, both concerning Ford workers. The first was the explosion in February at Ford's Dearborn power plant that killed six workers and temporarily closed the company's River Rouge production complex. The second was the "collective absence" and plant-gate sitdown that closed the Hermosillo plant in April. It is a measure of how integrated regional automaking has become that the Dearborn explosion, by halting operations at Rouge Steel, forced the closing of the Hermosillo plant some 2,000 miles away. Sadly, it is a telling measure of how little cross-border communication there is between unions in the United States and Mexico that no one at Wayne Local 900 knew that its counterparts in Hermosillo were on strike in April, while no one in the Hermosillo union knew why its plant was starved of steel in February. Indeed, the only information that Hermosillo's union members reported receiving was that there were "supplier problems" in Dearborn, as explained by management.

NOTES

1. This is the first study that places the two plants in a comparative context. There are no published studies of the Wayne Assembly plant, while the Hermosillo and Wayne Stamping plants have both been studied individually. On Hermosillo, see Shaiken (1990, 1995) and Carrillo (1995a, 1995b). On Wayne Body and Stamping, see Kaminski (1996, 1998).

2. Unless otherwise indicated, information on labor relations and work organization at the two plants is drawn from collective bargaining agreements, interviews with union leaders and members, plant visits, training manuals, and union newspapers.

3. According to Harbour and Associates (1999: 52), the Hermosillo plant ranked fifth out of 10 North American plants assembling subcompact cars, ahead of the Neon plant in Illinois, GM Lordstown, CAMI, Saturn, and Ramos Arizpe. The Wayne plant was third, ahead of NUMMI and trailing Toyota Cambridge and Honda East Liberty.

4. MacDuffie and Pils report on the International Motor Vehicle Program surveys of 1989 and 1993–1994, which indicate that the percentage of workers in teams in U.S. Big Three plants in North America actually declined from 10 percent to 6 percent (37). In the 1993-1994 survey (including plants not surveyed in 1989), 23 percent of workers in Big Three plants in the United States were in teams, and only 4 percent in Canada (17). Osterman's (2000) study of work organization has also found a dramatically slowed pace for team implementation in the private sector compared to other "high performance work practices."

5. For the distinction between worker-centered and supervisor-centered teams, see Babson (1998).

6. On pre-1970s conditions, see Middlebrook, (1995: pp. 226, 232–40). Both Middlebrook (pp. 239–47) and Tuman (1996: p. 324) argue that the more democratic the local union, the more likely it will seek to negotiate work rules. Tuman, however, focuses on the late 1980s and early 1990s and limits his analysis to only six assembly plants, none of them in the North. Consequently, his claim that democratic unions "were more likely to resist the use of team concepts and flexible production" (p. 324) misses the contrary case of Hermosillo. Middlebrook, in contrast, specifically recognizes (p. 283) that the northern plants of GM and Ford are relatively democratic at the same time that their collective bargaining agreements have relatively few work rules.

REFERENCES

Angel Barroso, M. (1997). "Otro paro en la Ford, piden pago de utilidades." Newspaper unknown, April 12. Clipping in author's possession.

Associated Press. (1989). "Vehicles Damaged, Ford Fires 35." *Automotive News* January 2, p.8.

Babson, S. (1998). "Ambiguous Mandate: Lean Production and Labor Relations in the United States." In Juárez, H. and Babson, S. (eds.), *Confronting Change: Auto Labor and Lean Production in North America / Enfrentando el cambio: Obreros de automóvil y producción esbelta en America del Norte.* Puebla, Mexico: Autonomous University of Puebla, pp. 23–51.

Babson, S. (2000). "Cross-Border Trade with Mexico and the Prospects for Worker Solidarity: The Case of Auto." *Critical Sociology* 26 (1/2), pp. 13–35.

Baker, S., Woodruff, D., and Weiner, E. (1992). "Detroit South: Mexico's Auto Boom, Who Wins, Who Loses." *Business Week* March 16.

Bronfenbrenner, K. (1996). *Final Report: The Effects of Plant Closing or Threat of Plant Closing on the Right of Workers to Organize.* Dallas: Labor Secretariat of the North American Commission for Labor Cooperation.

Carrillo, J. (1995a). "Flexible Production in the Auto Sector: Industrial Reorganization at Ford-Mexico." *World Development* 23 (1), pp. 87–101.

Carrillo, J. (1995b). "Hermosillo's Ford Plant: A Trajectory of Development of a Hybrid Model." Paper presented at the GERPISA Colloquium, "The New Industrial Models," Paris, June 15–17.

Chappell, L. (2001). "Mexico Splinters Mark for New-Car, Truck Sales." *Automotive News*, January 29, www.autonews.com. Clark, L. (1990). "Japanese Methods Flower at Ford." *Automotive News* March 19, pp. 1, 10.

Dearborn Assembly and UAW Local 600. (1992). "Summary Report: Dearborn Assembly Plant Visit of the Hermosillo Plant." June 2-5, typescript in author's possession.

Economist Intelligence Unit (EIU). (1999). *The Automotive Sectors of Latin America.* London: EIU.

Escalente Lemus, F. (1999). "Acta (Minutes) de Fernando Escalente Lemus, Secretario de Actas y Acuerdos, Comite Ejecutivo Local del sindicato Nacional de Trabajadores de Ford, 14 de Mayo." In author's possession.

Ford Motor Company. (1994). "B&AO Production System Study Group on Team Concept." Typescript in author's possession.

Ford Motor Company. (1997). "Estados de Resultados. Declaración de Ford Motor Co., 10 Abirl 1997, Renglón 46, Garantía y Politica." Document in author's possession.

Fucini, J. and Fucini, S. (1990). *Working for the Japanese: Inside Mazda's American Auto Plant.* New York: Free Press/Macmillan.

Garcia, R. and Hills, S. (1998). "Meeting 'Lean' Competitors: Ford de México's Industrial Relations Strategy." In Juárez, H. and Babson, S. (eds.), *Confronting Change: Auto Labor and Lean Production in North America / Enfrentando el cambio: Obreros de automóvil y producción esbelta en America del Norte.* Puebla, Mexico: Autonomous University of Puebla, pp. 143–54.

Harbour and Associates. (1995, 1999, 2000). *The Harbour Report: North America.* Troy, MI: Harbour and Associates, Inc.

Holmes, J. and Kumar, P. (1998). "Chrysler Canada's Windsor Assembly Plant: Lean Production Through Bargained Incremental Change." In Juárez, H. and Babson, S. (eds.), *Confronting Change: Auto Labor and Lean Production in North America / Enfrentando el cambio: Obreros de automóvil y producción esbelta en America del Norte.* Puebla, Mexico: Autonomous University of Puebla, pp. 257–78.

Juárez, H. (1999). Interview, Puebla, Mexico.

Juárez, H. and Babson, S. (eds.). (1998). *Confronting Change: Auto Labor and Lean Production in North America / Enfrentando el cambio: Obreros de automóvil y producción esbelta en America del Norte*. Puebla: Autonomous University of Puebla.

Kaminski, M. (1996). "Ford Wayne Stamping Plant/UAW Local 900." In Turner, B. (ed.), *Making Change Happen: Six Cases of Unions and Companies Transforming Their Workplaces*. Washington, DC: Work and Technology Institute, pp. 25–44.

Kaminski, M. (1998). "The Union Role in Team Concept." In Juárez, H. and Babson, S. (eds.), *Confronting Change: Auto Labor and Lean Production in North America / Enfrentando el cambio: Obreros de automóvil y producción esbelta en America del Norte*. Puebla, Mexico: Autonomous University of Puebla, pp. 157–72.

LaBotz, D. (1992). *Mask of Democracy: Labor Suppression in Mexico Today*. Boston: South End Press.

LaBotz, D. (1998). *Mexican Labor News*, February 2, www.ueinternational.org.

MacDuffie, J. P. and Pils, F. (1997). "Changes in Auto Industry Employment Practices: An International Overview." In Kochan, T., Landsbury, R., and MacDuffie, J. P. (eds.), *After Lean Production: Evolving Employment Practices in the World Auto Industry*. Ithaca, NY: ILR Press, pp. 9–42.

Middlebrook, K. (1995). *The Paradox of Revolution: Labor, the State, and Authoritarianism in Mexico*. Baltimore: Johns Hopkins University Press.

Osterman, P. (2000). "Work Reorganization in an Era of Restructuring: Trends in Diffusion and Effects on Employee Morale." *Industrial and Labor Relations Review* 53 (2), pp. 179–96.

Rivera Carrillo, M. (1997). "Demandan pago de utilidades." *El Independiente*, 12 April, p. 6A.

Salinas Cano, V. (1997). "Día de Marchas y Protestas en la Ciudad." *El Heraldo de Chihuahua*, 16 April, p. 3B.

Shaiken, H. (1995). "Lean Production in a Mexican Context." In Babson, S. (ed.), *Lean Work: Empowerment and Exploitation in the Global Auto Industry*. Detroit: Wayne State University, pp. 247–59.

Shaiken, H. (1990). *Mexico in the Global Economy: High Technology and Work Organization in Export Industries*. San Diego: University of California Press.

Tuman, J. (1996). "Unions and Restructuring in the Mexican Automobile Industry: A Comparative Assessment." *Industrial Relations Journal* 27 (4), pp. 317–30.

Witt, M. (1990). "Archbishop Condemns Ford for 'Persecuting' Mexican Unionists." *Labor Notes,* October, p. 8.

Womack, J., Jones, D., and Roos, D. (1990). *The Machine That Changed the World*. New York: Rawson and Associates.

11

Local Union Responses to Continental Standardization of Production and Work in GM's North American Truck Assembly Plants

Christopher Huxley

In 1997, General Motors (GM) launched the most expensive new motor vehicle manufacturing project in the history of the automotive industry, the GMT800 strategic initiative to assemble light trucks based on a common platform using standardized production and work in plants across the United States, Canada, and Mexico. As discussed in several preceding chapters, the ease and feasibility of diffusing preferred human resource management and labor relations (HRM/LR) strategies across borders have been seriously questioned in light of different industrial relations (IR) systems and workplace cultures. The GMT800 program offers an instructive opportunity to examine just how one multinational company (MNC) has attempted to transfer policies and practices across its continental operations and how unions have responded quite differently to GM's efforts at transnational standardization of work. My primary objective is to ascertain the extent of differences in local workplace organization as shaped by local unions in the context of unprecedented efforts to achieve continental rationalization and work standardization.

Although the GMT800 program has been in production only for a few years and the present research project is in its earliest stage, it is possible, nevertheless, to point to continuing differences such as in the conveyance technology used, the nature of work organization, union culture and representation, and collective bargaining in the context of different national social settlements that have proved to be most persistent in shaping workplace relations. Indeed, some distinct differences in union philosophies and perspectives regarding work organization and labor–management relations in the automotive industry are apparent across countries. Of note is the 1984–1985 breakaway of the Canadian Automobile Workers (CAW) from the United Automobile Workers (UAW). Continuing differences between the two auto unions are most evident in their stances toward joint union–management programs, with much greater institutional resistance to joint activities found in the CAW relative to the UAW (Huxley, Kettler, and Struthers, 1986; Kettler, Struthers, and Huxley, 1990). As addressed by Babson in the preceding chapter, local unions in the Mexican automotive industry have demonstrated increasing militancy over compensation and worker rights but, nonetheless, have more willingly embraced so-called high performance work practices than their UAW and CAW counterparts.

Toward understanding the local union responses and workplace outcomes associated with GM's GMT800 program, I first briefly discuss the program in the broader context of international reorganization of production. Subsequently, an overview of the GMT800 initiative is provided, covering the standardization of design, engineering, and work organization and the validation process. Third, I highlight similarities and differences in production systems, union responses, and work practices across four plants in Canada, the United States, and Mexico. Finally, I address several implications from the case analyses regarding transnational union strategies across the automotive industry in North America.

INTERNATIONAL REORGANIZATION OF PRODUCTION AND WORK

The value of international comparative workplace studies is enhanced when we understand the implementation of new managerial initiatives at the level of the workplace, on the one hand, and the outcomes and responses developed by workers and their organizations to these initiatives, on the other hand (Bélanger et al., 1994). The difficulties involved in the study of managerial strategies, working conditions, and union responses in workplaces across different industries have been widely noted, and these difficulties are only compounded at the international level of comparison (Berggren, 1992). One methodological approach that has been pursued with some success has involved the study of one particular MNC with operations in different countries (Bélanger et al., 1999). Findings based on such research suggest that while MNCs may be guided by well-developed managerial strategies, on-the-ground experiences in different countries or even in different locations in the same country usually prove to be marked by highly mediated processes (as shown in several preceding chapters).

Over the last two decades, GM's global reorganization of its operations in motor vehicle assembly has included heavy investment in technology, rationalization involving plant closures, the implementation of lean production (often referred to by GM as "synchronous manufacturing"), and an increased reliance on outsourcing (Katz, 1988). While the effects of these initiatives on the workplace have been the subjects of considerable debate, research has usually involved the study of the corporation's operations within one IR system. Although particular GM or GM joint-venture plants have been studied (e.g. Hamper, 1991; Milkman, 1997; Rinehart, Huxley, and Robertson, 1997), utilizing various methodologies, comparative studies of plants in different countries in the GM chain have been rare. A notable exception is a comparison and contrast of two GM plants in Europe by Shire (1994), who observed apparently different managerial strategies at each workplace.

Despite concerted managerial efforts to bring about greater standardization in the GMT800 program, as examined herein, actual work practices at the plant level take significantly different forms. This finding is consistent with reservations sometimes expressed with overarching typologies of managerial strategy towards the organization of work. Examples of such typologies range from those framed by liberal pluralist theories (e.g., lean production versus traditional production in Womack, Jones, and Roos, 1990), to those framed by radical theories (e.g., market despotic versus hegemonic factory regimes in Burawoy, 1985).

Work standardization has remained a constant in the industry since the original merging of scientific management principles with Fordist assembly line production. The reinvigoration of analyses of the capitalist labor process prompted in part by Braverman (1974) and continued in more recent debates on lean production (Rinehart et al., 1997) have maintained the focus on work standardization as a key element for understanding motor vehicle assembly. The major qualification to work standardization offered by proponents of lean production or high-performance workplaces has been to point to employee involvement programs and supposed positive outcomes resulting from *kaizen,* or continuous improvement initiatives at the workplace (Womack et al., 1990; Kenney and Florida, 1993; Appelbaum and Batt, 1994). These and other writers argue that, indeed, there is work standardization but that standards can be constantly improved, with positive outcomes for productivity, product quality, and the quality of work life. In the same vein, Adler (1995) concedes the continued application of scientific management principles but argues that lean production allows for experimentation with new variants of "democratic Taylorism."

There are two implications for HRM/LR research, one theoretical and one more concerned with empirical questions about how distinct, plantlevel managerial policies evolve at the workplace. The theoretical implication is to concur with those who question attempts to construct overly ambitious models of managerial strategy (Edwards, 1986; Williams et al., 1994). At the same time it would be inadvisable to abandon all attempts to construct ideal types for managerial strategy, since the challenge for research is precisely to ascertain the ways in which strategy is constantly redefined as a result of local circumstances, including union behavior. The empirical implication for the study of managerial policy is to suggest that MNC strategies may tolerate or even welcome some diversity of practices by local plant management in different locations in different countries. Indeed, MNCs may view such endeavors as providing valuable opportunities for learning and even experimentation. These observations suggest the fruitfulness of a study of workplace relations at different plants, across countries, and within a large MNC pursuing an ambitious transnational program such as the GMT800 initiative. The approach in this chapter emphasizes the "negotiation of order" in which the bases for conflict and consensus are constantly negotiated and renegotiated with consequences for the distinctive character of workplace relations at each workplace (Edwards, 1986; Clarke, 1997).

THE GMT800 PROGRAM FOR TRUCK ASSEMBLY

In 1993, GM began a complete redesign of its full-size pickup and cab/chassis trucks, including its full-size sport-utility vehicles (SUVs). Earlier versions of these vehicles had been built at seven assembly plants in the United States, Canada, and Mexico, supplied by five engine plants and numerous stamping facilities. Following broader motor vehicle industry trends, the company's new program, code-named GMT800 to distinguish it from GM's previous GMT400 program, used one vehicle platform for all of its North American truck assembly operations. According to one automotive analyst, the GMT800 initiative was so big that at an estimated cost of $6 billion, the program alone would have ranked 32nd if it were included on the *Fortune 500* list of U.S companies (Kobe, 1997:p. 41). In 1997, GM designated the Oshawa, Ontario, plant in Canada as the lead factory, followed by Pontiac East, Michigan, and Fort Wayne, Indiana. In 1998 the program was extended to include plants in Arlington, Texas; Flint, Michigan; Janesville, Wisconsin; and Silao, in the state of Guanajuato, Mexico.

At the core of the GMT800 program was the development of one vehicle chassis or platform, having as many common parts and processes as possible. Here, GM followed the automobile industry trend, led by Volkswagen, to create global vehicle platforms as a means of reducing costs and increasing profits ("Global Platforms," 1999: 15). While the development of one platform involved greater standardization, allowance was made for the manufacture of different vehicle models off the common platform. For example, the GMT800 frame for each model of truck or SUV (and up to 40 variations were planned), was designed to be modified by combining different frame elements to make up the particular frame for the model being produced. Thus, the program sought to accommodate the perceived marketing need for variation in product style. The Sierra pickup, for instance, was designed to be more upscale and stylized than the Silverado, which had more in common with the earlier version of the Chevrolet truck that was a product of the previous GMT400 program (Kobe, 1997: 41).

These new trucks were to be produced in different North American locations according to standardized engineering and work practice principles. The program was intended to allow for faster development of new truck models, with a sharp reduction in the time required to test or "validate" advances in design, engineering processes, and work practices, especially in the ramp-up phase prior to full production. The GMT800 program, moreover, involved developments in manufacturing design, technological processes, and the organization of work that reinforced key features of lean production, such as just-in-time production, work standardization, and initiatives to eliminate waste.

A number of features of the GMT800 program were consistent with evolving global strategies of the world's largest automakers. First, the program embraced the general industry move to design vehicles with fewer parts that could be assembled in less time. In particular, the GMT800 program aimed to produce a full-size pickup truck with 25 percent fewer parts, which could be assembled 10 percent faster than for previous models (Kerwin, 1999). Second, manufacture of the GMT800 frame involved many innovative technological processes. An example is "hydroforming," a process that used high internal water pressure to shape metal tubes within a die set. Advantages of the new technique included a stiffer frame for better vehicle handling and greater dimensional control, fewer welds, and a significant reduction in scrap.

Third and perhaps most importantly for developments in the global automobile industry, the use of parts requiring new manufacturing techniques was linked to the broader trend toward increased outsourcing. From the outset, the GMT800 program invited component suppliers to assume an increased role in product development, including taking on greater responsibility for design and engineering work (Murphy, 1998). Such outsourcing, furthermore, implied changes in the relationships with suppliers, especially a shift to emphasize "modular build" of components, involving different engineering disciplines in the production of more integrated component systems that had previously been produced as subcomponents by a number of suppliers and installed by assembly workers (Robertson, 1999).

The GMT800 Validation Process and Work Standardization

Since World War II, GM's North American operations department has compiled GM standard data for every possible facet of the motor vehicle assembly process and for years operated a validation process of truck manufacturing in Flint, Michigan. The GMT800 program's enhanced attention to design for manufacture and work standardization was accomplished, in part, by work carried out at the new truck Validation Center. Initially established for truck validation, this new facility was started up in 1996 next to GM's Pontiac, Michigan, truck headquarters to test-build prototypes and develop layout, tooling, and work procedures in body, chassis, and final assembly.

The new validation process, which was subsequently extended to include cars, was divided into two stages. First, there was a process of "slow build" that validated the task sequence, tooling, and "footprints" proposed by engineering staff. In this first stage, UAW skilled-trades workers validated the initial elements designed by engineering staff. A special category of skilled workers, named "vehicle builders," represented the largest trades classification. The second stage of the validation process was a "line-rate build," wherein vehicle builders worked with production workers to assemble vehicles at a rate of approximately 60 units per hour. In this second stage, visiting groups of production workers (assemblers and skilled trades) from designated plants were brought to Pontiac to work, learn, and evaluate the process, with their feedback incorporated into final validation. After a stay of several weeks, the production workers would return to their own assembly plants to help train their coworkers.

The role played by the Validation Center in the GMT800 program was based upon the principles of work standardization and product validation in an environment where four production issues became paramount. First, there was a speedup in the process from design to manufacture of new models. Second, there was an improvement in the capacity to test all manufacturing processes before they were installed in different assembly plants. Third, similar or even identical vehicle models could be assembled at more than one facility, with much quicker ramp-up to full production. Fourth, the program ensured a greater degree of knowledge and control over different assembly operations in the same vehicle program. Each of these developments increased the pressure for greater standardization of work procedures in all plants in the GMT800 system.

GM management personnel at the Validation Center reported that allowance was made for input at the GMT800 validation process by vehicle builders and by visiting production workers prior to the implementation of work routines at the plant level. However, what appeared to be absent from this process was any special reliance on plant-level continuous improvement activities, or *kaizening*, that analysts such as Kenney and Florida (1993:15) have argued is the "cornerstone" of lean production. Instead, there was an emphasis on work standardization developed by engineers, with some input by skilled trades, vehicle builders, and visiting production workers, but at the validation stage of job design. The one area for subsequent worker input and plant-level adjustment of work routines was in the development of more ergonomic work practices. This was required since the validation process did not claim to test for the consequences of carrying out repetitive tasks over longer periods of time.

In summary, the GMT800 program was designed to standardize truck production and, in turn, standardize some aspects of work organization. Work across assembly plants was linked directly to a validated sequence of tasks that workers at each plant would be expected to follow in performing their jobs. Not built into their standardized work tasks and processes, however, were methods for team working or employee involvement to achieve continuous improvements in performance. Decisions regarding these kinds of activities were left to the discretion of each assembly plant. The standardized work tasks and processes, moreover, allowed each assembly plant to adjust work routines in consideration of ergonomic issues that might arise. At the local level, therefore, management, employees, and the union leadership were faced with decisions about the form and extent of employee involvement (if any) and how work practices might be modified to achieve local ergonomic objectives.

Given that the GMT800 program also envisioned an increasing use of outsourced components in which suppliers would provide more integrated, preassembled component systems that would reduce assembly work in the plants, the issues of outsourcing and long-term employment security were given new prominence. Toward comparing local union responses to the GMT800 program, therefore, I examine, in particular, local responses to issues about employee involvement, health and safety, and outsourcing.

CASE STUDIES OF FOUR GMT800 ASSEMBLY PLANTS

Next, I examine similarities and differences in the implementation of work standardization in four North American GMT800 assembly plants operating with technology and work processes that were validated at the Pontiac Validation Center. These plants are located in Oshawa, Canada; Pontiac, Michigan; Fort Wayne, Indiana; and Silao, Mexico. The Canadian and Mexican plants are (to date) the only GMT800 plants located outside the United States. I also selected the first two U.S. plants that were designated by GM as GMT800 plants. The Pontiac East plant provides an example of a long-established and traditional assembly facility. A fairly recent greenfield plant, the Fort Wayne facility provides a useful case in contrast. Comparison of these two plants in the United States minimizes any misperception that might arise by generalizing from just one location as it offers a perspective on differences in plant cultures that can exist within the negotiated framework of the UAW-GM master agreement.

Emphasis is given to the identification of selected issues affecting the workplace at each facility. These include technology, employee involvement, health and safety, outsourcing and employment security, and other HRM/LR practices. For each plant I describe worker and union responses to these issues. My assessments are based on published sources and plant visits that included semistructured, open-ended interviews with managers, employees, and union officials conducted over the November 1999 to October 2000 period. For ease of comparison, a profile of the four plants studied is presented in Table 11.1.

Oshawa Truck Assembly, Canada

Following an abrupt change in company strategy precipitated by a strike at Pontiac East (involving both truck assembly and the Validation Center) in 1997, the Oshawa truck plant was designated as the lead facility for the GMT800 program. The Oshawa plant was selected for the assembly of two new-generation, large pickup truck models, the Chevrolet Silverado and the GMC Sierra. GM viewed these two products as strategically important for increasing, or at least preventing further decline in, its market share of the booming and highly profitable North American truck market. The only Canadian operation in the GMT800 program, the Oshawa truck plant is located alongside two other major motor vehicle assembly facilities in an established automotive community where the skilled trades have had a long presence. In 1999, the plant employed nearly 3,300 hourly workers who worked three shifts (Harbour and Associates, 2000).

In the late 1980s, GM had undertaken a major modernization of its Oshawa plants, at a cost of almost $10 billion (Canadian), at the time making the

Oshawa "Autoplex" the most modern vehicle complex in North America. As a result, the GMT800 program at Oshawa inherited distinct technological features that were retained, despite the GMT800 emphasis on increasing standardization of technology and production processes. The most important was the presence of a specific conveyance technology (automatic guided vehicles or AGVs), which continues to make Oshawa unique in the GMT800 program, although not to GM operations since similar technology is used at the company's Hamtramck plant in Detroit (Roberts, 1995; Clarke, 1997).

Table 11.1
Comparative Data for Four GMT800 Plants

Plant	Oshawa, Ontario, Canada	Pontiac East, MI U.S.A	Fort Wayne, IN U.S.A	Silao, GTO Mexico
Age of plant and start of GMT800	Brownfield 1965 rebuilt 1986 GMT400 1997 GMT800	Brownfield long-standing 1997 GMT800	Greenfield 1986 built 1987 2nd shift 1997 GMT800	Greenfield 1994 built 1998 GMT800
Plant size (sq. feet) 1999	3,100,000	2,940,745	3,361,300	2,197,372
Product	Full-size pickup (Silverado, Sierra)	Full-size pickup (Silverado, Sierra)	Full-size pickup (Silverado, Sierra)	Full-size SUV (Suburban/ Yukon XL, Avalanche)
Customers 1999	U.S., 92% Canada, 7% Other, 1%	U.S.	U.S.	Mainly U.S. Some Mexico
1999 (Dec.) Hourly production workers	3,235	3,312	2,591	2,721
# of Shifts	3	3	2	2
Production 1999	318,732	309,910	257,660	129,736
Average age of workforce (1999)	44 in 1997 with average of 18 years seniority	Mid-to-late 40s (estimate)	Mid-to-late 30s (estimate)	Mid-20s (estimate)
Plant specific features	Automatic guided vehicle system	Proximity to Validation Center	New material handling system	Less automation More subassemblies

Table 11.1 (continued)

	Oshawa	Pontiac East	Fort Wayne	Silao
Synchronous manufacturing	Yes	Yes	Yes	Yes
Teams	No	No	Yes	Yes
Rotation	No	No	Voluntary	Compulsory
Pay-for-knowledge	No	No	Yes	Yes
Profit sharing	No (not favored by CAW)	Yes (determined company wide)	Yes (determined company wide)	Yes (legally required for all large plants)
Union	Local 222 CAW	Local 594 UAW	Local 2209 UAW	Section 4 SITIMM-CTM
Bargaining	Industry-wide pattern bargain. GM-CAW master agreement & local 222 agreement	Industry-wide pattern bargain. GM-UAW master agreement & local 594 agreement	Industry-wide pattern bargain. GM-UAW master agreement & local 2209 agreement	Local agreement GM-SITIMM Silao plant
Work stoppages	1996: 3 week national GM strike. Impact of 1998 Flint strike	1997: 87-day strike over local issues. Impact of 1998 Flint strike	1997: 2-week strike over local issues. Impact of 1998 Flint strike	None. Impact of 1998 Flint strike
Contract and expiry	Three years (2002)	Four years (2003)	Four years (2003)	Two years (2002)
Cost-of-living allowance	Yes	Yes	Yes	Annual reopener on wages
Hours per vehicle*	1998: 31.2 1999: 22.5	1998: 40.6 1999: 29.0	1998: 33.0 1999: 25.5	1998: 38.1 1999: 50.5
Hours per vehicle**	1998: 24.9 1999: 22.5	1998: 31.3 1999: 29.0	1998: 27.0 1999: 25.5	1998: 38.1 1999: 36.8

Sources: Data for 1998 and 1999 based on Harbour Reports for 1999 and 2000, respectively.
Note: Two measures of hours per vehicle are used: *hours per vehicle (hpv) = actual hours/ actual production and **hpv = same as above adjusted for hours for new model launch.

Workers at the Oshawa truck plant are members of CAW Local 222, which, with nearly 13,500 members, is one of the largest private sector union locals in North America. In addition to the workers at the truck plant, the local union represents workers at the site's two car assembly plants and a number of independent motor vehicle component supplier companies. Local 222 has a long history of internal political life with two caucuses, the "Democrats" and the "Autoworkers," competing for local union leadership positions. Ideological differences once characterized the two caucuses, but in recent years the distinction has declined in importance, and only one caucus now functions. Neither caucus, moreover, was particularly identified with the national union leadership (Bourette, 1996). Internal differences have not usually affected the ability of the local to advance positions taken by the membership. For example, the negotiations with GM in 1996 led not only to a strike but also to the occupation of the Oshawa fabrication plant over the issue of outsourcing. In the 1999 round of contract negotiations, furthermore, the president of Local 222 chaired the CAW-GM master bargaining committee.

When it was first introduced at Oshawa, the Swedish-designed AGV technology was presented as having the potential to improve significantly the quality of work life in assembly. It was hoped that the new technology would allow groups of workers to work on more complex sets of tasks, without the pressures traditionally associated with the drag-chain assembly line. The promise of improved quality of work life, however, may not have been realized. A study of working conditions in nine assembly plants in Canada ranked GM plants, including the Oshawa truck plant, as the worst on fives indexes that included workload, workload change, physical risks, stress risks, and autonomy/control (CAW-Canada, 1996). Nevertheless, neither management nor the union has argued in favor of abandoning the technology, with both sides aware of the accruing benefits and costs.

GM management initially argued that the AGV technology was suited to ideas of natural work groups and self-directed teams associated with a sociotechnical systems approach to work organization. The Oshawa workers and their CAW local, however, resisted any formalized arrangements for teamwork. As such, the Oshawa facility can be characterized as a "traditional" plant with "completely informal mechanisms for employee involvement" (Kumar and Holmes, 1997:104). Although there are no formal teams or team leaders, "production leaders" fulfill some production coordination functions that are carried out in team-concept plants by team leaders.

Unlike the UAW, whereby in recent years negotiations on local issues have often continued after the ratification of the company-wide master agreement, the CAW practice has been to resolve all local plant issues prior to agreement on a company-wide settlement. Issues of importance for the truck plant in the 1999 contract bargaining were economic gains, including pensions, improvements in production standard contract language, and related items of job security and outsourcing. Outcomes on production standards included the negotiation of in-plant "production standard representatives" (including one designated for the Oshawa truck plant), a process for resolving problem jobs, and a focus on job design.

The tendency of the GMT800 program to place greater emphasis on outsourcing has been a longstanding issue at Oshawa. For the CAW, outsourcing emerged as a major issue in its 1996 round of bargaining with the Big Three automakers. Prior to the 1996 negotiations, the CAW claimed that GM Canada was outsourcing more than the Canadian subsidiaries of Ford or Chrysler ("1996 Auto Talks," 1996:143). The outcome of the 1996 negotiations, first negotiated with Chrysler but accepted by GM only after a strike, was described by the union as "precedent setting job security language against the threat of outsourcing" (CAW-Canada, 1999: 8). Appended to the collective agreement was a letter of understanding that defined the union's concept of "work ownership" as "protection against the outsourcing of work that had been performed on a historical basis in a quality and reasonable manner at reasonable cost." The 1999 round of bargaining extended the "work ownership" provisions to cover modular production, although the company insisted that it had no immediate plans to move to that level of restructuring.

The Oshawa truck plant has consistently been rated high on productivity measures compiled by the automobile industry analysts, Harbour and Associates. Table 11.1 provides comparative figures for the measure of hours per vehicle for 1998 and 1999 for all four GMT800 plants discussed in this chapter. Although such comparative measures need to be viewed with some caution, they, nonetheless, provide some indication of changes in comparative productivity over time. In the case of the Oshawa plant, a reluctance to embrace new forms of work organization has not been associated with more hours per vehicle than for the other three plants considered. Indeed, the Oshawa plant has consistently ranked as the most efficient in the GMT800 group. CAW leaders have been quick to point to these and other comparative data as evidence that their emphasis on long-established trade union principles, such as seniority rights, need not stand in the way of the development of a competitive workforce and a good working union–management relationship. However, the CAW, along with other observers, also points to additional factors that need to feature in any overall explanation for the relative competitive position of the Canadian plant. These include a cheaper Canadian dollar and lower benefit costs associated with a medical care system, which, according to the union, combine to contribute to a U.S$10 per hour advantage in Canada compared to the United States in 1996. ("1996 Auto Talks," 1996: 144).

Pontiac East Truck Assembly, United States

The Pontiac East truck assembly plant, which is the largest in the GMT800 chain, can be readily compared to the Oshawa facility in that it is also a "traditional" plant in an established automobile community with deep-rooted traditions in the skilled trades. With just over 3,500 hourly workers in 1999, working three shifts, the workforce is slightly greater than at Oshawa. As in

Oshawa, workers at the Pontiac East truck plant are members of a large union local that includes workers from more than one facility. UAW Local 594 includes workers from the Pontiac East truck assembly plant and from the Truck Product Center or Validation Center described earlier. According to Harbour and Associates, productivity measured by hours per vehicle at Pontiac East has ranked favorably compared to that at other GMT800 plants, especially when allowance is made for the more complex product mix in assembly (see Table 11.1).

A similar decision to that of the Oshawa plant to maintain more traditional workplace arrangements and to eschew new work organization practices appears to have been the result of an evolved consensus reached between the Pontiac East management and the local union. In 1999 a senior Pontiac East manager and an in-plant leader confirmed that both management and the union agreed that the facility was indeed a "traditional plant" without teams, team leaders, or pay-for-knowledge. However, as at Oshawa, although there are no teams, some hourly production workers are designated as "responders" who follow certain routines when "andon" cords are pulled to signal a problem on the assembly line.

One factor influencing the more traditional forms of work organization may have been the presence of an active union political culture in UAW Local 594 at Pontiac East. Again there are some similarities with Oshawa. In recent years, two caucuses at Pontiac East have run slates for union elections. For the last 15 years, a group called the Independent Slate has led the local, while the Union Democracy Slate, usually considered less friendly to management, has been in opposition. However, the May 1999 election for local union president was closely contested, with the incumbent from the Independent Slate narrowly winning by 52 percent to 48 percent over his opponent (McCracken, 2000).

Between April 22 and July 19, 1997, nearly 5,900 workers at the Pontiac East truck assembly plant and the Validation Center went on strike in a dispute with GM. The 87-day stoppage was the longest strike at GM since 1970. Staffing levels were at the center of the dispute. The issue had already surfaced at other GM facilities that had attempted to implement leaner methods of working. For example, between 1994 and 1997 strikes occurred at the Buick City complex in Flint, Michigan; at GM's AC Delco plant, also in Flint; at an assembly plant in Ste. Thérèse, Quebec; at two Dayton, Ohio, GM brake plants; and at an assembly plant in Oklahoma City. The problems arising during the preparations for the launch of the GMT800 program at Pontiac East had all the hallmarks of problems experienced elsewhere with lean production. As at other struck locations, the local agreement eventually ratified at Pontiac East went some way to addressing issues of production standards, health and safety, and hiring.

Another concern that had previously been expressed in the Pontiac East plant and that was reinforced with the introduction of the GMT800 program was outsourcing. In the period leading up to the 1999 negotiations, the Pontiac East Local 594 leadership identified outsourcing as a major issue in national bargaining between the UAW and GM. The local union president wrote in the union newspaper of the need to hold onto the jobs that the union represented, "as the company strives to shift more work to suppliers that pay less in wages and benefits and are often non-union" (Trandell, 1999: 1). These concerns were expressed at a time when modular production was receiving increased attention in auto union circles, especially centered on speculation over GM's "Yellowstone" project for small car assembly using modular techniques.

The eventual settlement between the UAW and GM on outsourcing extended job and income security protections for union employees that had been codified in previous national agreements (UAW, 1999; Savoie, 2000). First, job security provisions were strengthened by the requirement that new workers be hired as attrition replacements when staffing declined to unacceptable levels and the available pool of laid-off UAW members had been exhausted. Second, improvements were made to income security arrangements. Third, new contract language provided for increased union input into sourcing decisions at both the local and the national level, covering both permanent and temporary outsourcing, future product sourcing, and insourcing. Fourth and last, in response to growing union concerns over nonunion competition for work, the company agreed to send letters to each of its existing suppliers, as well as any new suppliers with whom it signed contracts during the four-year agreement, stating the company's commitment to "good corporate citizenship." The letters were to include a statement affirming the "positive and constructive relationship" that the company enjoyed with the UAW and GM's policy of neutrality toward new union organizing drives. The company also stated that it would not take retaliatory action against any supplier on the basis of "a decision by that supplier's employees to join a labor union" (UAW, 1999: 12).

Union input into sourcing decisions was supposed to be achieved through joint union–management committees that met at the company level as well as at some specific plants where union members were to be appointed to monitor sourcing issues. UAW locals such as at Pontiac East have participated in these joint processes, but on occasion they have also exercised their right to withdraw from these and other joint programs. Such was the case in 1998 at Pontiac East in a dispute with the company over several issues, including job assignments given to workers visiting the Validation Center from the GM plant in Silao (Trandell, 1998). The withdrawal from joint committees turned out to be temporary but was regarded by Local 594 as a bargaining weapon in defense of contract language in the Local Agreement.

Fort Wayne Truck Assembly, United States

The Fort Wayne truck assembly plant was built in 1986 and since 1987 has operated on a two-shift schedule. By 1999, the hourly production workforce just exceeded 2,600 (Harbour and Associates, 2000). GM points to the success of the plant in reducing the number of parts and the time required for truck assembly. The company claims that the plant has met its objectives for reducing the number of parts in its full-size pickups by 25 percent and for reducing the time required to assemble the trucks by 10 percent (General Motors, 1999: 19).

Although the factory was constructed on a new site, it was not entirely a greenfield facility insofar as much of the workforce included workers who had transferred from other GM plants across the country, often after having been laid off when plants were closed or downsized. Consequently, the average age of the workforce at the Fort Wayne truck plant, although younger than at Pontiac East, was not as young as might have been expected for a new plant. In spite of the transfers of laid-off UAW members to Fort Wayne, union traditions, nonetheless, are not as well established as at Pontiac East.

From the beginning, the plant adopted new forms of work organization such as teams, team coordinators, pay-for-knowledge, and, more recently, visual control "andon" boards. Some of these organizational forms were shaped in the course of local negotiations to address the concerns of Fort Wayne members of Local 2209. For example, task rotation within teams remained voluntary, with some high seniority workers declining to rotate. Team coordinators once rotated by seniority every six months, but more recent contract language provides for new team coordinator positions to be posted as permanent positions.

In other respects, such as job security and outsourcing, Fort Wayne's response to workplace issues arising out of the implementation of the GMT800 program bears more similarity to that at Pontiac East. Health and safety have been an especially important concern for the Fort Wayne local union. A long-standing feature of the national GM-UAW contract has been the right of workers to strike over health and safety issues. In March 1997, Fort Wayne UAW Local 2209 took strike action for two weeks for a new local agreement that addressed production standards, health and safety, and additional hiring. Many of the concerns proved to be the same as those that were subsequently taken up in the Pontiac East strike.

The major health and safety gains won by the Fort Wayne local union in the 1997 strike were remedies designed to relieve workers from being overburdened. These included the creation of additional permanent jobs, especially in those jobs designated as accident-prone. For some problem jobs, interim "administrative" controls were introduced in the form of contract language providing workers extra relief time every hour. Graham (1999) reports that these measures initially had a positive effect in ameliorating working conditions, although the model changeover to the GMT800 truck increased the intensity of work and the number of work-related injuries.

Health and safety issues continued to feature prominently in the subsequent round of negotiations, and by the year 2000, over one-third of the language in the Fort Wayne local contract covered health and safety issues. One example was the provision for a joint management–union canvass of the workforce to be conducted every two years asking questions about work-related pain or discomfort. Risk factors were to be identified based on feedback from the survey, which were then supposed to be resolved jointly.

Silao Truck Assembly, Mexico

As Shaiken (1987: vii) has observed, "a fundamental shift in the nature of comparative advantage" has been the realization that "highly advanced production processes can be successfully transferred to newly industrialized countries" such as Mexico. More than in the case of Fort Wayne, the Silao truck assembly plant is a textbook example of a greenfield facility. The plant was built in 1994 to replace the historic truck plant located in the Federal District area of Mexico City (Garcia and Lara, 1998). Considerations of dated, poorly designed buildings, a congested urban location, and the need to upgrade technology all featured in GM's decision to move operations from the Federal District plant to the new Silao location. More important may have been GM's decision to follow a general pattern of automotive multinational strategies in Mexico aimed at creating new, more highly flexible production systems (Middlebrook, 1991). I suggest this because workers at the Federal District plant, represented by the Revolutionary Confederation of Workers and Peasants (CROC), had a history of militancy, engaging in six strikes in just eight years between 1973 and 1980 (Middlebrook, 1995). Although given severance pay, workers were not given the option of transferring to Silao.

The Silao plant began by assembling large SUVs and in 1998 joined the GMT800 program when the plant started building two large SUVs, the Suburban and the Yukon XL. By the year 2000, the plant began producing another new, large SUV off the GMT800 platform—the Avalanche. The workforce rapidly increased from just over 2,000 hourly workers in 1998, to over 2,700 in 1999 (Harbour and Associates, 1999, 2000). All indications point to a further expansion of the GM complex at Silao. The facility serves as a distribution center for a range of GM products destined for shipment elsewhere in Latin America. As of late 2000, an engine plant was under construction next to the assembly operation. In addition, a new industrial park was being developed to accommodate the growing number of vehicle component supplier plants that supply the Silao truck facility. Future plans include construction of a direct road link between this industrial park and the truck plant that would bypass the existing highway system.

In comparison with other North American GM plants, the Silao facility quickly received favorable mention from Harbour and Associates (1998) for high product quality, good safety, low absenteeism, and, despite a lower level of automation, relatively high productivity. The level of technology deployed has remained lower at Silao than at each of the other three plants considered in this study. In the autumn of 2000, Silao plant managers reported that the number of robots was less than 100 compared to a 1998–1999 figure of more than five times that number for the Oshawa truck plant. The Harbour findings on productivity were further underscored in subsequent reports, which continued to report consistent improvement, although this may have been somewhat hidden by more model changeovers than for some of the other plants in the GMT800 program (see Table 11.1).

The trade union that GM recognized from the outset at Silao was the Confederation of Mexican Workers (CTM). As the official union arm of the then-governing Party of the Institutional Revolution (PRI), the CTM was accepted by GM as part of the process of gaining official encouragement for opening its truck assembly facility in an area of the country that was actively encouraging new export-oriented industry. As Tuman (1996) reports regarding other new export plants in Mexico, the CTM proved its loyalty to its government partner by helping to persuade local union leaders to accept many of the demands for new forms of work organization sought by the company.

Unlike in the United States and Canada, where negotiations for the Big Three cover both the company and the plant and where industry-wide pattern bargaining has become the norm, negotiations in the automobile industry in Mexico are restricted to each separate plant. There are no company-wide settlements, let alone any sort of industry-wide pattern. The result has been a decentralized process of plant-by-plant negotiations with little or no centralized coordination other than the involvement of national union officials in the actual bargaining. Stronger and more elaborate collective agreements, with higher wages, are the preserve of the well-established union locals. Hence, new local unions such as Section 4 of SITIMM (a federation of metal workers affiliated to the CTM representing production workers at the Silao plant) are left to struggle for contract language that addresses concerns specific to their individual workplaces.

Lower pay than elsewhere in the Mexican auto industry, continued inflation since the 1994–1995 peso devaluation, and strong export market demand for their product served to focus dissent in the Silao local around wages. In 1999, a new local plant leadership was elected that stressed the need to achieve economic gains in bargaining for a new contract in 2000. Union negotiations were more protracted than in previous rounds, and the final settlement, which exceeded the wage guidelines established by the government, was viewed by local union members (although not necessarily the CTM national leadership) with some satisfaction. Workplace issues other than wages, however, were not prominently addressed in the Silao negotiations. More recently, there has been some recognition by the new in-plant leadership of membership concerns over increasing work intensity. Questions are also being asked within the union about giving more recognition to seniority principles. Discussions of such topics are not generally encouraged given the dominant CTM/PRI ideology of support for fostering a "new work culture" in Mexican industry. Consequently, little has been negotiated regarding ergonomic or other health and safety provisions.

Some important features of collective bargaining agreements in Mexico are covered by the Mexican federal labor code. For example, provisions for profit sharing are required for all enterprises where the plant exceeds a certain size. By way of comparison, profit sharing in the United States has been agreed to in successive UAW–Big Three contracts since 1982. In Canada, the CAW has declined to negotiate profit sharing, preferring to emphasize annual percentage wage increases and other improvements, such as paid time off. Other concerns that feature large in the collective bargaining process in the United States and Canada, especially given the greater reliance on private health care in the United States, include benefits covering health care and retirement. By way of contrast, unionists in Mexico traditionally have placed more emphasis on securing improvements in these kinds of benefits as part of a broader social, political settlement.

For its short history, the Silao truck plant has experienced labor–management peace. This may partly be attributed to the presence of a young workforce in a region without automotive traditions and to the steady expansion of the plant in a favorable export market. From the outset, the plant has operated with new forms of work organization such as teams, team leaders, job rotation, and pay-for-knowledge (General Motors de México, 1998, 2000). The team-based system includes the "star system" in which different areas of responsibility are viewed figuratively as points on a star, which then become the special responsibility of one particular team member. The division of labor is based in part on several portfolios, which include production, quality control, health and safety, personnel, materials, maintenance, and finances.

Critics of the star system of team-based responsibilities argue that issues such as health and safety cannot always be adequately addressed at the level of the team. Rather, it is argued, plant and company-wide procedures can be developed more effectively through collective bargaining. In addition, regional, national, and international agencies set and enforce standards pertaining to health, safety, and ergonomics.

For the GMT800 program, the outsourcing of operations at Silao may both define the operation at that location and offer a learning opportunity for the parent company as it continues to experiment with new approaches to outsourcing and modular build. Well over half of the vehicle component parts, including the chassis and the engine, are imported from the United States and Canada. Although only in its early stages, the incorporation of workers employed by the suppliers into the assembly process has advanced further than at comparable motor vehicle assembly plants in the United States or Canada. For example, material handling is subcontracted out to Seglo, a German-owned company, which employs workers who work inside the assembly plant to supply the line on a just-in-time basis. These workers are members of another local of the same CTM affiliate but are paid less than workers employed by GM in the truck assembly plant.

The Silao Section 4 of SITIMM has begun to establish links with other auto union locals in Mexico, both in the GM chain and at other auto companies in Mexico and more recently with counterparts in the GMT800 program in the United States and Canada. The CTM affiliate has also applied to affiliate with the International Metalworkers Federation, which recently opened an office in Mexico (Juárez Núñez, 2001: 9). The union local regards these initiatives as important, especially since the union at all levels has much more limited resources than those of the UAW and CAW, especially in areas such as research and international affairs.

UNION RESPONSES AND TRANSNATIONAL WORKPLACE STRATEGIES

The foregoing observations suggest that while the GMT800 program is instructive both as an example of an employer strategy of continental integration of production and as a policy for achieving a greater degree of work standardization, the experience to date at the four workplaces has been quite varied. At each plant a distinct order has been negotiated with allowance for the accommodation of considerable differences in workplace regimes. With respect to arrangements to involve employees in continuous improvements programs, only workers at the Silao and Fort Wayne operations have engaged in formalized team-based and related activities. Although the Oshawa and Pontiac East plants have rejected formalized team-based activities, they, nonetheless, have allowed some workers to take on minor leadership roles in production. The rejection of formalized employee involvement programs at Oshawa and Pontiac East is primarily attributable to local union objections, but it is also true that local plant management has shown little interest in pursuing formalized programs (similar to the television assembly cases described by Kenney and Tanaka in Chapter 7).

Except for the Silao plant, unions at the other three plants have vigorously sought to restrict outsourcing of work and otherwise provide employment security. Although the issue of outsourcing has been a major concern of the UAW and CAW over the last decade of negotiations, the added emphasis on future outsourcing underlying the GMT800 program strengthened the resolve of both the UAW and CAW to negotiate tighter restrictions.

With respect to ergonomic and other health and safety issues, local unions in both U.S. plants and in Canada have given such issues high priority. Given the smaller number of GM assembly facilities in Canada, the CAW national headquarters may have played a more active role in the formulation of company-wide policies on ergonomic issues, especially in addressing problems resulting from work intensification. While language on health and safety is an important part of the UAW master agreement, much is left to joint committees, and specific policies are more likely to be developed at the plant level. The right to strike over health and safety issues has also given local unions in the United States an important means of leverage and one that workers at the two U.S. plants have exercised. Although GM management at Silao point to their data showing steady improvement in the plant's health and safety record, the absence of detailed union documentation on work-related injuries makes corroboration difficult. The fact that the union has not identified problems in this area may be attributable to the relatively short life of the plant and, the youth and lack of industrial experience of the workforce, or it may be that such issues have not yet surfaced as major bargaining concerns.

Despite all the emphasis on work standardization in the GMT800 program, GM may have adopted an approach in which different managerial strategies have been pursued at different facilities. Previous writers have drawn attention to GM's practice of pursuing a "dual strategy of management" where the corporation has simultaneously implemented different strategies at old and new factories (Shire, 1994). Thus, the greenfield factories of Fort Wayne and Silao became candidates for team concepts, while the modernized brownfield plants at Pontiac East and Oshawa maintained more traditional workplace practices. In the case of the GMT800 program, any such dual strategy may also have been influenced by union acceptance of, or resistance to, the introduction of new forms of workplace organization. Indeed, there is reason to believe that GM at least anticipated variation across plants. Most notably, GM did not build a team-based structure around the GMT800 initiative, leaving it open for each plant to negotiate any such terms as well as to decide on its own approaches to issues that would emerge concerning ergonomics and new work standards. In addition, note that GM (unlike AT&T in the case evaluated by Martin, Beaumont, and Pate in Chapter 6) involved skilled tradespeople and assembly workers in the design of the GMT800 program via the extensive validation process before diffusing it to various locations. Hence, given the corporation's willingness to allow local variation in some HRM/LR practices (especially concerning staffing, relief, and rotation) and the involvement of workers in establishing the new work standards, GM may have successfully diffused the core elements of its standardized production system and associated work standards. It appears, therefore, that GM recognized that variation at the local level was an inevitable result of the limitations of any attempt to impose standardization across an entire continent.

In an era of growing economic integration, the argument in favor of "transnational coordinative unionism" (Wells, 1998) or "transnational cooperation among unions" (Gordon and Turner, 2000) is increasingly advanced by labor-sympathetic researchers. The case for some expression of cross-border solidarity would appear to be especially compelling for workers and their unions in the GMT800 program. First, coordination can better prepare workers and their organizations against employer strategies to "whipsaw" one plant against another. Second, there is the more ambitious objective for solidarity in which workers in one plant might assist workers in another plant in resisting concessions or advancing common demands. A precondition for either form of coordination is the exchange and diffusion of comparative information (Ramsay, 2000).

The situation, at least in the period of strong market demand for GMT800 products that distinguished the period up to late 2000, may not have proved to be as dire as the regime of "hegemonic despotism" described by Burawoy (1985:148–52) in which concessions are constantly forced upon workers by "whipsawing." The threat, nonetheless, remains. During the period prior to the introduction of the GMT800 program, GM truck plants were closed, and, as has been noted, following the 1997 strike at Pontiac East, the designation of a lead plant was abruptly withdrawn from that facility and transferred to Oshawa.

By all accounts, communication between workers, unions, and union-sympathetic researchers across the North American automobile industry has been limited. This has also been the case for links between unions representing workers in the continental truck assembly operations of the GMT800 program. Information exchanges have occurred at the plant-to-plant level across each country, with reciprocal visits by unionists between each of the workplaces studied, as well as visits to other GMT800 plants ("Solidarity Across Borders," 2001). Comparative workplace research, even though it may at first be largely descriptive, can contribute to helping strengthen the future capacities of union locals and their national bodies to pursue initiatives based on a fuller understanding of transnational workplace developments (Chapter 13).

The most widely cited instance of cross-border solidarity associated with the GMT800 program occurred during the 1998 UAW Flint strikes when the CAW announced that union members at the Oshawa truck plant would not accept parts from an Ohio stamping facility made with dies from one of the struck Flint plants. The announcement was delivered to a UAW convention by CAW president Basil "Buzz" Hargrove as a gesture of solidarity and recognition for earlier support received from the UAW during the 1996 strike by the CAW against GM ("GM Workers," 1998). The refusal to accept struck work may even have had some influence on the outcome of the unprecedented stoppage that shut down most of GM's operations across North America (Babson, 1999).

For the most part, however, even where declarations in favor of solidarity between workers in different plants, especially across national borders, are forthcoming, they are unlikely to amount to much unless they are accompanied by ongoing efforts to build interunion coordination. In the final analysis, solidarity is more likely to be engendered by ongoing struggles at workplaces that produce concrete gains that can then be replicated or improved upon elsewhere. This follows a long-established postulate of labor movements that solidarity is more likely to be expressed by workers who have developed a capacity to pursue struggles at their own workplaces and who can then identify with other workers' struggles (as evidenced in the Bridgestone/Firestone case presented in the following chapter). According to this argument, gains at one workplace represent the best basis for extending solidarity and improving wages, working conditions, and worker livelihoods.

At first glance, economic issues might not appear to be the most obvious basis for transnational union coordination. Indeed, wage differences, most notably, the significant gap between autoworkers' pay in Mexico compared to pay in the United States and Canada, may have made it difficult to establish cross-border communication. Unions in the United States and Canada might have recognized a general need to support union struggles by their southern neighbors, if for no other reason than to reduce the likelihood that Mexican workers became lower-cost competitors. However, in the past U.S. and Canadian auto unions paid relatively little attention to the Mexican auto industry since it was viewed as largely a domestic industry producing for a national or Latin American market. Until recently, the Mexican automobile industry was also largely viewed as home to low-wage, nonunion, labor-intensive operations focused on producing auto parts and concentrated in border-industrialization zones.

Now, however, changes in the Mexican auto industry serve to alert unionists in the United States and Canada to the future importance of information exchange. Continental economic integration means that under a program such as the GMT800, similar or identical vehicles to those being produced in the United States or Canada are now being assembled in Mexico for export, primarily to the U.S. market. Although a large gap separates the wages of Canadian and Mexican autoworkers, both groups of workers find themselves in similar situations as the depreciated currencies of each country become part of an export promotion strategy that makes Canadian or Mexican plants more competitive in wage costs. Other similarities in workplace issues confront auto unionists in all three countries. The fortunes of workers at each GMT800 plant, in particular, become linked to the state of consumer markets in the United States. For the first few years of the program, the story was one of a booming U.S. domestic market. However, cyclical downturns remain a basic characteristic of the industry. Indeed, by early 2001 there were clear indications of a decline in U.S. consumer demand ("When America Sneezes," 2001). Cutbacks in hours worked have affected workers in GM plants across North America, including at some GMT 800 facilities.

The recent wage militancy of Mexican workers, furthermore, suggests that many of their plant-based local unions, whatever their national leadership, can no longer be so readily discredited as undemocratic, as company unions, or as uncritical instruments of government policy. The opening up of the Mexican labor movement may be an ongoing process marked by more initiatives to link struggles, both within the Mexican automobile industry and with counterparts in other countries.

Issues of health and safety and the common problems faced in each of the four GMT800 plants discussed in this chapter might be an obvious basis for information exchange between unionists in the different plants in the GMT800 program. However, differences in conveyance technology and the uneven introduction of mechanization in areas such as welding suggest that the nature of the concerns is likely to differ in each plant. National, state, or provincial health and safety standards also affect the way that workers at each plant pursue health and safety concerns. In addition, some health and safety concerns, especially of an ergonomic nature, are likely to vary according to the average age of a workforce. Newly hired young workers at the Silao facility may recoil at the demands expected of them in carrying out highly repetitive labor, as suggested by employee turnover figures reported during the first few years of operation. Those who stay on the job may tolerate conditions for a period but may eventually resist work intensification. Older workers in the U.S. or Canadian plants may be more likely to resist the demands placed upon them, especially if they encounter new expectations involving further reductions in the time between movements on the job or in the number of footsteps required to do certain tasks.

Union concerns over outsourcing and possible moves toward modular production have been registered throughout the North American automobile industry but most vocally in the United States and Canada. These concerns in U.S. automotive union circles have been exacerbated by a precipitous decline in union density in the U.S. motor vehicle component supplier industry, but that problem is by no means unique to U.S. operations. Whether outsourced operations are unionized or not has been a long-standing issue for the labor movements of each country. For instance, one of the major specialized suppliers of hydroformed frame parts for the GMT800 program has been Magna International, the Canadian based auto-parts multinational that has placed considerable emphasis on a strategy of remaining almost entirely nonunion.

Given the short period that it has been in operation, it is still too early to offer a final assessment of the different strategic initiatives undertaken in the GMT800 program, and the same applies to the workplace implications at each plant. Final consideration needs to take account of such features of the program as quicker and more flexible model change, work standardization, and multiple sourcing in the different countries. Eventually, as more vehicle models are built on the same platform, it is likely that the GMT800 program, or its successor, will be expanded to include more plants, possibly in additional countries.

This chapter has shown how, even in a best-case scenario for communication as in the GMT800 program, in which workers use similar manufacturing processes to assemble a similar product for the same market, there are reasons that workers and their unions have not taken significant steps toward international cooperation. These findings only serve to support the argument that information sharing among researchers and unionists based in comparable workplaces remains one of the most important contributions to both local struggles and transnational cooperation, as well as for understanding how MNCs operate.

NOTE

An earlier report on this research was presented to the second meeting of the International Research Network for Autowork in the Americas (IRNAA) at Wayne State University, Detroit, in November 1999. Special thanks are due to Morgan Gay for research assistance. Members of IRNAA from Canada, the United States and Mexico continue to be a source of encouragement and support for this ongoing project.

REFERENCES

Adler, P. S. (1995). "'Democratic Taylorism': The Toyota Production System at NUMMI." In Babson, S. (ed.), *Lean Work: Empowerment and Exploitation in the Global Auto Industry*. Detroit: Wayne State University Press, pp. 207–19.

Appelbaum, E. and Batt, R. (1994). *The New American Workplace*. Ithaca, NY: ILR-Cornell University Press.

Babson, S. (1999). "The 1998 Flint-GM Strike: Bellwether of Continental Integration and Lean Production." Paper presented to the 7th annual GERPISA international colloquium, Paris.

Bélanger, J., Edwards, P. K., and Haiven, L. (eds.). (1994). *Workplace Industrial Relations and the Global Challenge*. Ithaca, NY: IRL-Cornell University Press.

Bélanger, J., Berggren, C., Bjorkman, T. and Kohler, C. (eds.). (1999). *Being Local Worldwide: ABB and the Challenge of Global Management*. Ithaca, NY: ILR-Cornell University Press.

Berggren, C. (1992). *Alternatives to Lean Production: Work Organization in the Swedish Auto Industry*. Ithaca, NY: ILR Press.

Bourette, S. (1996). "Union's Feuding Factions Threaten GM Talks." *Globe and Mail* October 3, p. B6.

Braverman, H. (1974*). Labor and Monopoly Capital: The Degradation of Work in the Twentieth Century*. New York: Monthly Review Press.

Burawoy, M. (1985). *The Politics of Production: Factory Regimes under Capitalism and Socialism*. London: Verso.

CAW-Canada. (1996). *Working Conditions Study: Benchmarking Auto Assembly Plants*. North York, Ontario: CAW-Canada.

CAW-Canada. (1999). "CAW-Canada/General Motors Bargaining Report." October. North York, Ontario: CAW-Canada.

Clarke, L. (1997). "Changing Work Systems, Changing Social Relations? A Canadian General Motors Plant." *Relations Industrielles/Industrial Relations* 52 (4), pp.839-64.

Edwards, P. K. (1986). *Conflict at Work: A Materialist Analysis of Workplace Relations*. Oxford: Blackwell.

García G. A. and Lara R. A. (1998). "Cambio Tecnológico y Aprendizaje Laboral en G.M.: Los Casos del D.F. y Silao." In Juárez, H. and Babson, S. (eds.), *Confronting Change: Auto Labor and Lean Production in North America*. Puebla, Mexico: Benemérita Universidad Autónoma de Puebla, pp. 207–22.

Gardner, G. (1998). "GM Trucks Jump Back in the Saddle." *Ward's Auto World*, February, pp. 44–47.

General Motors. (1999). *GM Labor Negotiations Fact Book*. Detroit: General Motors.

General Motors de México [Planta Silao] con el Sindicato de Trabajadores de Industria Metal Mecanica, Automotriz Similares y Conexos de la Republica Méxicana (1998 and 2000). "Contrato Colectivo de Trabajo" [1998–2000 and 2000–2002].

"Global Platforms Take Over." (1999). *A1*, April p. 15.

"GM Workers to Reject Parts from U.S. Plant." (1998). *Globe and Mail* June 24, p. B11.

Gordon, M. E. and Turner, L. (2000). "Going Global." In Gordon, M. E. and Turner, L. (eds.), *Transnational Cooperation among Labor Unions*. Ithaca, NY: ILR-Cornell University Press, pp. 3–25.

Graham, L. (1999). "GMT800 Truck Assembly in Fort Wayne, Indiana." Paper presented to 2nd conference of the International Research Network on Autowork in the Americas, Detroit.

Graham, L. (2000). "Health and Safety Issues at Fort Wayne GM Truck Assembly." Paper presented to meeting hosted by IRNAA-SITIMM, May 22-24, Guanajuato, GTO.

Hamper, B. (1991). *Rivethead: Tales from the Assembly Line*. New York: Warner Books.

Harbour and Associates (1998, 1999, 2000). *The Harbour Report: North America*. Troy, MI: Harbour and Associates, Inc.

Huxley, C., Kettler, D., and Struthers, J. (1986). "Is Canada's Experience 'Especially Instructive'?" In Lipset, S. M. (ed.), *Unions in Transition: Entering the Second Century*. San Francisco: Institute for Contemporary Studies, pp. 113–32.

Juárez Núñez, H. (2001). "The VW Strike of 2000: Worker Resistance in a Setting of New Industrial Integration." *La Lettre du GERPISA* 149, February, pp. 3–9.

Katz, H. C. (1988). "Business and Labor Relations Strategies in the U.S. Automobile Industry: The Case of the General Motors Corporation." In Dankbaar, B., Jurgens, U., and Malsch, T. (eds.), *Die Zukunft der Arbeit in der Automobilindustrie*. Berlin: Sigma, pp. 249–61.

Kenney, M. and Florida, R. (1993). *Beyond Mass Production: The Japanese System and Its Transfer to the U.S.* New York: Oxford University Press.

Kerwin, K. with Muller, J. (1999). "Reviving GM: A Close-up Look at President Rick Wagoner and His Strategy." *Business Week* February 1, pp. 114-22.

Kettler, D., Struthers, J., and Huxley, C. (1990). "Unionization and Labour Regimes in Canada and the United States: Considerations for Comparative Research." *Labour/Le Travail* 25, Spring, pp. 161–87.

Kobe, G. (1997). "Inside GM's Massive New Truck Program." *AI*, December, pp. 40–47.

Kumar, P. and Holmes, J. (1997). "Canada: Continuity and Change." In Kochan, T., Lansbury, R., and MacDuffie, J. (eds.), *After Lean Production: Evolving Employment Practices in the World Auto Industry*. Ithaca, NY: ILR-Cornell University Press, pp. 85–108.

Kumar, P. and Holmes, J. (1998). "Recent Patterns of Production and Investment in the Canadian Auto Industry: Reflections on Management Strategy." In Juárez, H. and Babson, S. (eds.), *Confronting Change: Auto Labor and Lean Production in North America*. Puebla, Mexico: Benemérita Universidad Autónoma de Puebla, pp. 95–115.

McCracken, J. (2000). "UAW Election in Dispute." *Detroit Free Press*, August 24, p. 1A.

Middlebrook, K. J. (1991). "The Politics of Industrial Restructuring: Transnational Firms' Search for Flexible Production in the Mexican Automobile Industry. *Comparative Politics* 23 (3), pp. 275–97.

Middlebrook, K. J. (1995). *The Paradox of Revolution: Labor, the State, and Authoritarianism in Mexico*. Baltimore: Johns Hopkins University Press.

Milkman, R. (1997). *Farewell to the Factory: Auto Workers in the Late Twentieth Century*. Berkeley: University of California Press.

Murphy, T. (1998). "Welcome to the Table: Suppliers Part of Seamless Team Developing GMT800." *Ward's Auto World*, February, p. 46.

"1996 Auto Talks and Canada/U.S. Comparisons." (1996). *Collective Bargaining Review*, July-August, pp. 143–45.

Ramsay, H. (2000). "Know Thine Enemy: Understanding Multinational Corporations as a Requirement for Strategic International Laborism." In Gordon, M. E. and Turner, L. (eds.), *Transnational Cooperation among Labor Unions*. Ithaca, NY: ILR-Cornell University Press, pp. 26–43.

Rinehart, J., Huxley, C. and Robertson, D. (1997). *Just Another Car Factory? Lean Production and Its Discontents*. Ithaca, NY: ILR-Cornell University Press.

Roberts, B. (1995). "From Lean Production to Agile Manufacturing: A New Round of Quicker, Cheaper and Better." In Schenk, C. and Anderson, J. (eds.), *Re-Shaping Work: Union Responses to Technological Change*. Don Mills, Ontario: Technology Adjustment Programme, Ontario Federation of Labour, pp. 197–213.

Robertson, D. (1999). "Modular Production." Paper presented to CAW Auto Council, February, Port Elgin, Ontario.

Savoie, E. J. (2000). "The Auto Industry Labor Agreements: 1999–2003." *Enterprise* 13 (2), pp. 6–7, 13.

Shaiken, H., with Herzenberg, S. (1987). *Automation and Global Production: Automobile Engine Production in Mexico, the United States, and Canada*. San Diego: Center for U.S.-Mexican Studies, University of California.

Shire, K. (1994). "Bargaining Regimes and the Social Reorganization of Production: The Case of General Motors in Austria and Germany." In Bélanger, J., Edwards, P. K., and Haiven, L. (eds.), *Workplace Industrial Relations and the Global Challenge*. Ithaca: ILR-Cornell University Press, pp. 137–56.

Trandell, L. (1998). "Taking a Stand against General Motors!" *The Champ* 27 (9), p. 1.

Trandell, L. (1999). "We Must Preserve Jobs! Key Issue in '99 Negotiations." *The Champ* 28 (7), p. 1.

Tuman, J. P. (1996). "Unions and Restructuring in the Mexican Automotive Industry: A Comparative Assessment." *Industrial Relations Journal* 27 (4), pp. 317–30.

UAW. (1999). "UAW GM and Delphi Report: Contract Highlights." October. Detroit: UAW.

"Solidarity across Borders: UAW Local 95 Welcomes Mexican Auto Worker." (2001). *UAW Solidarity*, January-February, p. 23.

Wells, D. (1998). "Building Transnational Coordinative Unionism." In Juárez, H. and Babson, S. (eds.), *Confronting Change: Auto Labor and Lean Production in North America*. Puebla, Mexico: Benemérita Universidad Autónoma de Puebla, pp. 487–505.

"When America Sneezes." (2001). *Economist* January 6, pp. 66–7.

Williams, K., Haslam, C., Johal, S., and Williams, J. (1994). *Cars: Analysis, History, Cases*. Providence and Oxford: Berghahn Books.

Womack, J. P., Jones, D.T., and Roos, D. (1990). *The Machine That Changed the World*. New York: Rawson Associates.

12

Out of the Ashes: The Steelworkers' Global Campaign at Bridgestone/Firestone

Tom Juravich and Kate Bronfenbrenner

The demonstrations at the World Trade Organization (WTO) meeting in Seattle in the fall of 1999 brought together a diverse group of trade unionists, environmentalists, and anticorporate groups in a historic gathering. The size and the intensity of the action, coupled with the news and commentary in the weeks that followed, signaled a new and growing consciousness in the American public about economic globalization and its consequences. Indeed, the Seattle demonstrations marked a recognition that today's Nikes, Microsofts, and General Electrics represent new forms of global corporations fundamentally different from those of the past. The emergence of these megalithic structures has triggered renewed calls for global solidarity, for if the nature of capital has transmogrified in a new global order, then unions, environmental groups, and economic justice organizations can no longer be effective organizing on a national level. Labor and its allies must also build a global network.

The purpose of this chapter is to examine how unions and their allies can build global networks in the face of multinational company (MNC) efforts to deny workers their rights to representation and destroy the very unions that represent them. In particular, we examine the strike and the global contract campaign orchestrated by the United Steelworkers of America (USWA) against the Japanese-owned Bridgestone/Firestone company. The original strike, called by the United Rubberworkers (URW), had ended disastrously with an unconditional return to work, foreshadowing the deunionization of the entire tire industry. After merging with the Rubberworkers, the USWA mounted the largest and most comprehensive global campaign to date and, with its victory two years later, brought its new members at Bridgestone/Firestone out of the ashes of a certain and devastating defeat back into union jobs. We use this campaign to assess the key elements of a highly successful union strategy and from it to suggest what is becoming an emerging model of union global strategic campaigns in the face of human resource management and labor relations (HRM/LR) strategies pursued by MNCs to marginalize, if not to destroy, unions.

Our analysis is based largely on face-to-face interviews conducted with more than 50 participants in the Bridgestone/Firestone struggle. The interviewees ranged from top international staff and local officers to rank-and-file activists and community supporters. In addition to the interviews, we examined key union and company documents from the files of the USWA international office and the URW archives, as well as from the four local unions on strike against Bridgestone/Firestone. We also compiled and studied an extensive collection of media coverage of the strike and the subsequent global contract campaign.[1] We begin by tracing the evolution of labor relations at Bridgestone/Firestone, highlighting the HRM/LR and negotiation strategies pursued by the company that set the stage for confrontation with the URW. Second, we describe the birth of a new union global campaign that emerges following the merger of the URW and the USWA. Here, we focus on the essential elements of the USWA strategy; based on research, on constant escalation of external and internal resistance, and on the widespread involvement and mobilization of members, their families and communities, and, importantly, their allies from abroad. We close by summarizing the lessons learned from the USWA victory over Bridgestone/Firestone, suggesting an emerging model of union power in a global economy.

THE EVOLUTION OF LABOR RELATIONS AT BRIDGESTONE/FIRESTONE

Founded in 1900, the Firestone company grew in tandem with the bourgeoning auto industry. Bolstered by an increase in wartime production, by 1926 Firestone employed more than 20,000 workers (Firestone, 1926:136). In the postwar era, Firestone would remain among the top tire producers in the United States. During this same period Bridgestone began as a family business in Japan that in 1931 was transformed into the Bridgestone Tire Company by Shorijiro Ishibashi. By the mid-1950s, Bridgestone had become Japan's largest tire manufacturer.

While Bridgestone's profits and production continued to grow rapidly throughout the 1970s, by the end of the decade the U.S. tire industry was in trouble. Aging plants, coupled with the costly changeover to production of radial tires, left companies such as Firestone in serious financial difficulty. Firestone closed a number of its plants and laid off half its workforce. As part of this major reorganization effort, Firestone put its radial tire plant in La Vergne, Tennessee, on the block. The La Vergne plant was quickly purchased by the Bridgestone company, which saw it as an opportunity to move into the U.S. market. This left Firestone with only five plants in the United States: Decatur, Illinois; Oklahoma City, Oklahoma; Des Moines, Iowa; Noblesville, Indiana; and Akron, Ohio. Firestone continued to struggle and in 1988 was purchased by Bridgestone for U.S.$2.6 billion.

According to industry expert Mary Walton, "The news was greeted with considerable enthusiasm by most of Firestone's 53,500 employees; exactly half the 107,000 who had worked for the company as recently as 1979, before all but five North American plants were closed" (Walton, 1990: 197). Despite ambitious plans for the newly merged company, Bridgestone/Firestone struggled in its first years to absorb the debt from the Firestone purchase. The new Bridgestone management was also confronted with the need for extensive modernization of a number of the Firestone plants, which required them to allocate $1.5 billion for modernization within the first three years after the merger. Making matters worse, General Motors dropped the company as a supplier of automobile tires (Balfour, et al., 1999: 14). After losing more than U.S.$1 billion between 1989 and 1991, by 1992 Bridgestone/Firestone began to turn the corner, both in profits and in U.S. market share.

Central to Bridgestone's integration of the Firestone facilities and workers into its larger corporate structure and the return to profitability was the introduction of a new management philosophy, with an emphasis on employee involvement and new work systems. One of the Bridgestone/Firestone local union leaders described the changes:

Bridgestone came on board and in 1988 negotiations they introduced us to their new theme of cooperative management. We were introduced to Quality Circles, Employee Participation Teams, limited self supervision and other soothing, honey-coated programs. They talked of "life-time employment," never any layoffs, etc. and we bought into these ideas because, quite frankly, the majority of our workers thought aloud "it's worth a try" and "what have we got to lose?" And after all, they said we would no longer be referred to as employees, now we would be "ASSOCIATES." For the next couple of years we have a scramble of employees (oops!—ASSOCIATES) standing in line to become Team members and Team leaders. (Lessin, 1988: 9)

According to Lessin, the range of activities in these areas was dizzying:

Bridgestone/Firestone put employees through hours of training on "Total Quality Control" (TQC) with specific sections on TQC Problem Solving, brainstorming, the "PDCA cycle" (plan, do, check, act); Decision-making Prioritizing Checklist; Idea Growers and Idea Killers; Deming's 5W's and 1H: (who, what, where, when, why, how); Pareto Diagrams; Fishbone Diagrams; Problem Causation; Histograms; Flow charts; and Problem-solving exercises. (Lessin, 1998: 11)

Much of the activity centered on the Partnership for Involvement program. This program was discussed as part of bargaining in 1991 and was included in a Memorandum of Understanding in the final contract. The language is fairly typical of these kinds of efforts:

[The] Partnership for Involvement Mission Statement recognizes that our employees are our most important resource, our mission is to promote the safety, standard of living and quality of work life of all employees. Together we shall strive to insure continuous improvement in the quality of our products, better service to our customers and increased profitability of our company. ("Memorandum of Understanding," 1991: 1–2)

The agreement was seen as a model of cooperation for the entire industry and received the Federal Mediation and Conciliation Service Director's Award for Excellence in Industrial Relations ("Bridgestone/Firestone Fact Sheet," 1995). Bridgestone was back in the black, its market share was increasing, and it was building a stronger and more productive relationship with its workers and their union, the URW, through employee involvement and new work systems. The future appeared bright.

While these changes were taking place on the shop floor, Yoichiro Kaizaki moved into the top management position at Bridgestone/Firestone. Balfour, et al., describe the changes:

According to one industry analyst, Kaizaki, a 30-year Bridgestone veteran, was "sent as the agent of change." Armed with his reputation as the "ichiban" (number one) tough member of Bridgestone's hierarchy developed from his aggressive termination of losing operations and his relentless cost cutting ability, Kaizaki's presence would soon be felt by all. According to a 1992 interview, Kaizaki explained, through his translator, "of the four Ms, material, machine, method, and man, only this last one is different from our Japanese factories. We must focus on that." (Balfour, et al., 1999: 13)

During the same period that the company was touting cooperation on the shop floor, in the 1993 negotiations with the La Vergne local, the company, under Kaizaki's leadership, pushed for major concessions, threatening to close the plant if labor costs could not be lowered significantly. The local union struck for more than two weeks. Management's response to the strike proved that Bridgestone/Firestone's new Japanese management was no stranger to the kinds of aggressive antiunion tactics that had become so pervasive in the 1980s and 1990s in the United States. Former URW president, Ken Coss, remembers: "They put up guns on top of buildings, sandbags around. I mean, here's a place where they're supposed to have this cooperative joint-venture type of a location, and one of the first things is they [have] armed people roaming around in the plant. They had sandbags, they had gun emplacement on top of buildings" (Ken Coss interview, 1999:p. 9).

As the company prepared for the major negotiations in 1994, what it had begun in La Vergne continued. Much of the focus was on merging the master agreement and local supplemental agreements into one master contract. Decatur local president Roger Gates recalls, "They just went through our agreement and just ripped page after page out of it. They literally wiped out all the local language. And then of course from that they went on to work on the master language. So they just raped the agreement" (Roger Gates interview, 1999: 5–6).

Many might see this as the kind of hard bargaining that is a common occurrence in contract negotiations, especially with an industrial company struggling to get back on its feet. As in all negotiations, there would still be plenty of room for the company to move later in the bargaining process. The information that the Rubberworkers were receiving from their union contacts in other tire plants warned them that Bridgestone/Firestone's intentions went beyond traditional hard bargaining. The union quickly came to understand that Bridgestone/Firestone was using these demands to force a strike as part of an industry-wide effort to break pattern bargaining in the tire industry and severely weaken the URW's power and influence in the process. La Vergne local president Tommy Powell describes one of these reports:

We got word from Goodyear's corporate people. They contacted us, which they had always been great to work with, negotiate within the Rubberworkers' contracts in their chain. They called and said, "Look, Bridgestone's out beating the bushes. Want some of us to form a pact. They're willing to take you on at the International, to strike you, and they want us to help supply tires to them in addition to what they're going to supply to help keep their customers going while they destroy you all. We want you to know that we're not going to be a part of that." So they refused to be a part of it. (Powell interview, 1999: 14–15)

Despite Bridgestone/Firestone's failure to gain the full support of the tire industry giants, it pressed on with its campaign against the union in what in industry circles had already been secretly dubbed the "War of 94" (Bronfenbrenner and Juravich, 1998: 21).

TOWARD A MODEL OF UNION POWER IN A GLOBAL MARKET

The events at Bridgestone/Firestone provide an important opportunity to examine how unions function in the new global economy. Many have suggested that to gain power and restrain employers from moving production overseas or engaging in aggressive antiunion practices, unions and their members must prove that they are indispensable through a full commitment to new, more cooperative and productive work practices (e.g., see Cohen-Rosenfeld and Burton, 1987; Kochan and Osterman, 1994; Hecksher, 1996, 1998; Appelbaum et al., 2000). Heckscher provides the basic tenets of this approach:

First, institutions of worker representation cannot survive unless they are widely perceived as contributing to economic growth as well as economic justice. Second—and related—unions can succeed only if they essentially contribute to good management—not if they fundamentally undermine it. In fact, by making deals which are in the long-term interests of management as well as employees, they force management to act in its own interests. (Heckscher, 1998: 4)

As Lazes and Savage further explain, under this model of "new unionism,"

Unions must bargain for compensation tied to contributions that unions and workers make. These contributions may be in the form of improved business results, reduced total costs, reduced time to market, or the successful application of technology. Through strategic alliances, unions must fundamentally change the work systems of their workplaces, including work structure, decision-making and the use of technology. (Lazes and Savage, 1997: 185)

This model appears to advocate a form of enterprise unionism, with labor organizations more closely allied with company interests than those of their larger union (Juravich, 1998). It is based on the notion that the major avenue for power for workers and their unions in a global marketplace is primarily through the employer, not union power through the withholding of labor, building of solidarity, and other activities associated with a more traditional model of collective bargaining. What is strikingly absent from these discussions of "new unionism" is the development or growth of union power independent of the employer.

254   *Multinational Companies and Global Human Resource Strategies*

This mutual gains model is based on several assumptions about employer behavior. First and most important, it assumes that businesses act in rational ways to maximize their own self-interest. As a corollary, it also assumes that there is an alignment of human resource policy and practices with business strategies (Schuler and Jackson, 1987; Wright and McMahan, 1992). So not only does the firm as a whole act rationally, but the actions of its individual units are consistent across the firm.

The Rubberworkers were clearly operating under this model of "new unionism" at Bridgestone/Firestone. They assumed that through their active participation in the Partnership for Involvement program and the myriad of other new work schemes that were being introduced at the various Bridgestone/Firestone plants, they were securing their future with the company. Because many of the programs arose from the Japanese side of the firm, workers were especially convinced that this alignment with the larger corporation would assure them a strong future with Bridgestone/Firestone.

Yet, the Rubberworkers and their members found that these HRM/LR strategies and activities on the shop floor at Bridgestone/Firestone were entirely independent of the company's larger business practices. At the same time that the company was pursuing a cooperative strategy partnering with the workforce on the shop floor, it was developing a national tire industry strategy to completely undermine the union and the pattern agreement. Mike O'Connor, now president of the Akron Bridgestone/Firestone local, was one of the URW's most ardent supporters in the early days of the Employee Incentive Program. But it soon became apparent to O'Connor and others like him that the "emperor had no clothes":

I was actually one of the instructors in what they called TQC. We taught the Deming and Kaisan theories. I was the only hourly person—I was an officer of the union too—who was selected to go to the instructor school, and then I would teach a class once a week with a salaried guy. Quite frankly, in the beginning I thought this was kind of a neat concept. I really got kind of involved in it. I was all for it. But then, they never employed it. It was all smoke and mirrors. They'd put it together about halfway and then dropped it. I mean, this TQC was a big to-do, then after negotiations in '91 that was the end of that. They backed out and nothing came of it. They left an empty room. They didn't believe any concepts at all. (O'Connor interview, 1999: 2)

As Melman pointed out almost two decades ago, in modern global corporations the goal of maximizing profits is frequently not aligned with rational behavior in the marketplace (Melman, 1983). As we have witnessed in the wreckage of companies such as Eastern Airlines and Simplicity Patterns and whole industries such as footwear and consumer electronics, often profitable companies making quality products were destroyed because it was more profitable to break them up, sell them, or laden them with debt until they collapsed (Barlett and Steele, 1992). As capital has become more global, we should not assume that some invisible hand is guiding it to some higher purpose. Particularly during this era in which the interests of venture capital loom much larger than the long-term profits, productivity, product quality, or the focus on production of specific items, it is a leap of faith to assume that workers and their unions should place their future in human resources policies and practices. However enlightened, these practices are often inconsequential to the financial wizards of global capital.

Furthermore, it is important to explore the consequences of this enterprise-based unionism. First, as Parker and others have suggested, at the shop-floor level a cooperative approach often blurs lines between the company and union, particularly when key union officials are assigned as team leaders or facilitators reporting to management (Parker, 1985). While this new loyalty to the company may facilitate the success of these kinds of programs, it may also make more confrontational unionism less possible or effective. Similarly, a focus on company-based issues may also isolate one or more local unions from the larger national unions. Particularly when formal or informal pattern agreements are involved, this overemphasis on the enterprise may strain relationships and diminish the capacity of the larger national union organization (Juravich, 1998). Confronted with the failure of this type of cooperative model, the Rubberworkers and later the Steelworkers with which they merged were determined to employ a very different approach to gaining power in the global marketplace.

THE WAR OF 94: THE URW RESPONDS

In the wake of the bitter negotiations with the La Vergne local, contract negotiations for the five major locals of Bridgestone/Firestone began on March 21, 1994. The company came with a comprehensive proposal overflowing with concession demands. Their proposal began by radically altering the compensation system with a performance-based pay system linking wage increases to specified productivity targets. Balfour, et al., explain: "The company also wanted to eliminate paid union time; implement a considerably lower base wage rate; eliminate daily overtime payment and double-time payment for work on Sunday; impose a four crew/twelve hour fixed/seven day continuous operations schedule; implement major take-a-ways in health care coverage; and subject employees to a no-fault attendance program" (Balfour et al., 1999: 17).

That spring, the union and company met more than 40 times in bargaining sessions, but little progress was made. When the contract expired April 23, 1994, the union continued working without a contract, still hoping that, if it just kept bargaining, Bridgestone/Firestone would eventually move and it could reach a fair agreement. But no matter how many times the union attempted to work through the major issues, the company held firm to its original comprehensive proposal. Former URW president Ken Coss describes the process:

We couldn't get them to put forth any priorities. They had proposals, and they were such drastic proposals for the industry. It would have taken all of the uniform things that we had and just destroyed all of them. When we had the meeting, I said, "Chuck, if there's something in there that makes the difference whether you're going to survive or not we'll take a look at it location by location, you have to set priorities." He said, "We don't have any priorities. We want all of it." And I said, "But you know that that's not something that can happen. We want to avoid a strike." And he said, "Well, nobody likes the idea, but we think we're going to have to have one so the people will hurt badly enough that they're willing to give us what we want." (Coss interview, 1999: 7)

That June, the union reached the first tire industry agreement, settling with Goodyear for a package that included a 16 percent wage increase over three years. The union designated the Goodyear agreement as the pattern for the industry, but as it promised, Bridgestone/Firestone, along with three smaller companies, Pirelli, Yokohama, and Sumitomo, rejected the pattern.

After continuing negotiations through the summer, the union finally gave the company a five-day strike notice on July 7. No progress was made, and on July 12, 1994, more than 4,000 Bridgestone/Firestone workers from five URW locals in Ohio, Indiana, Iowa, Illinois, and Oklahoma went out on strike. A full complement of replacement workers was quickly brought in and management and salaried workers were reassigned to production jobs. Bridgestone/Firestone also imported tires from its Japanese plant to fill orders. On August 18, 1994, the company declared an impasse and implemented its final offer.

Unlike the Steelworkers and many other national unions that have established strike support structures and systems to assist local unions that go out on strike, the URW had little more to offer than $100 per week in strike benefits. Each of the locals had already made traditional strike preparations, organizing picket captains and cautioning its membership to build up their savings. But now it was up to the locals to establish whatever support systems they could to hold the striking workers and their families together, from discount groceries and family support groups to rallies and demonstrations outside the plants.

While the bargaining teams met sporadically over the fall, sometimes under the supervision of a federal mediator, no progress was made. On December 27, 1994, Bridgestone/Firestone's president Kaizaki announced that "he can crush" the now six-month-old strike, firing and permanently replacing more than 2,000 of the striking workers (Balfour et al., 1999: 36). In a devastating blow to the struggle, Local 7 in Akron broke ranks and returned to work, as did many of its counterparts at the other plants. Fearing the permanent loss of their jobs, by the end of the year more than one-fifth of the strikers had crossed the picket lines and returned to work.

The strike was quickly draining the financial reserves of the Rubberworkers, which was also coordinating strikes at Pirelli, Armstrong, Dunlop, and Yokohamo Tire. Fully 10 percent of their membership was on strike and, after paying out more than U.S.$12 million in strike funds, the Rubberworkers were near financial ruin. As a stopgap measure, a special convention approved a dues increase to keep the union solvent.

In addition to trying to get bargaining back on track, the Rubberworkers and their members attempted to bring pressure on the company through a boycott effort. Early targets were Sears, a major retailer of Firestone tires, and the MasterCare Centers, which are directly owned by

Bridgestone/Firestone. Yet clearly, the union was unable to mount a more comprehensive campaign necessary to bring Bridgestone/Firestone back to the table. As Doug Niehouse, former staffer from the Industrial Union Department of the AFL-CIO, suggests, "The reality was that the Rubberworkers just didn't have the resources or the people that were capable of doing the work" (Niehouse interview, 1999: 1).

The union was forced to borrow heavily from the American Federation of Labor and Congress of Industrial Organizations (AFL-CIO) and the United Automobile Workers (UAW) to keep the strike going, but its prospects for success, nonetheless, remained dim. By late spring 1995, it was becoming clear that labor's traditional model of bargaining in good faith and waiting for the courts and the National Labor Relations Board (NLRB) to deliver justice, which the URW and other industrial unions had relied on for decades, was no longer effective in the global economy. With members crossing the picket lines and returning to work, the Rubberworkers needed new ideas and different strategies, else the strike and most likely the entire union would be lost.

THE MERGER OF THE URW AND USWA: THE BIRTH OF A NEW CAMPAIGN

It is no accident that the URW looked to the USWA as a candidate for merger. Like the Rubberworkers, the Steelworkers had lost almost half of their membership during the 1970s and 1980s. The Steelworkers had also been one of the early industrial unions to jump on board with cooperative programs and new management initiatives, with their Labor Management Participation Teams (Camens, 1985). Just as the URW had experienced at Bridgestone/Firestone, the labor–management programs in steel did little to stop the hemorrhaging of jobs in the industry.

By the time of the Bridgestone/Firestone strike, the Steelworkers had stabilized their ranks and were building their comeback using a very different model. The approach began in 1986 with the strike at USX but became full-blown in a campaign in a small town in West Virginia. The aluminum plant in Ravenswood, West Virginia, had been spun off from Kaiser Aluminum and purchased through a leveraged buyout by a group of investors that included a former plant manager. As safety conditions worsened in the plant, where jobs were being speeded up and combined, the company essentially refused to bargain with the union, forcing a lockout on October 30, 1990. Three months later, with injunctions preventing little more than symbolic picketing and the plant running near capacity with a full complement of replacement workers, it looked like another long-drawn-out defeat for labor.

However, the Steelworkers, under the leadership of then vice president George Becker, turned the campaign around and developed a strategic campaign of unprecedented scope and intensity against Ravenswood Aluminum Corporation. This was not just a simple corporate campaign or a boycott but a multifaceted strategy based on extensive research that slowly unraveled a complex global ownership network of bankers, investors, and financiers. For the next 17 months, the Steelworkers, their members, and trade unionists across the globe mounted a spirited campaign that ultimately brought a decent contract for all 1,700 of their members.

On July 1, 1995 the Rubberworker/Steelworker merger was approved at a special convention in Pittsburgh. The more than 100,000 members of the URW, a significant number of them currently on strike, were now part of the USWA. Unlike many union mergers, where each of the former entities keeps its structure intact, the USWA knew that it would need to integrate the Rubberworkers more closely if it had any chance of winning at Bridgestone/Firestone. Jim English, assistant to the president of the USWA, describes what happened:

We've created an RPIC (Rubber and Plastics Industry Council) division. The RPIC division has responsibilities for coordinating bargaining, holding conferences, but the servicing all takes place within the context of the geographic districts of the union. I think that's significant in terms of Bridgestone/Firestone because what it meant was that the Bridgestone/Firestone locals were attending all of the same conferences that the Steelworkers' locals were during that period of time. They were very much brought into the life of the union. Had they remained as a separate entity, I don't think you would have had quite the same enthusiasm and commitment. (English interview, 1999: 21)

As part of the merger talks, the URW and the USWA had decided in late May to make an unconditional offer to return to work. Amid fear of decertification, the Decatur local had voted earlier in the month to return to work. More than one-quarter of its members had already closed the line and returned to work. After the return to work offer, however, only 153 of the remaining 2,400 workers were called back to work. In the wake of their huge victory at Ravenswood, the Steelworkers were not ready to admit defeat. But, to win, the USWA knew that it would have to take the campaign to the next level.

The Campaign Goes Global

The Steelworkers had learned four important lessons from Ravenswood and the campaigns that followed (Bronfenbrenner and Juravich, 1998). First was the importance of research in understanding how power flowed in a corporation and, in turn, for identifying as many vulnerabilities as possible. Second, in the words of George Becker, the emphasis must be on constant "escalation":

The last thing I wanted that company to think about before [they] went to bed at night, Monday, Tuesday, Wednesday, Thursday, Friday, Saturday, and Sunday, is all the problems and difficulties we caused them that day. And the first thing I wanted them to think of when they woke up is, oh, Christ, I've got to go out and face them sons of bitches again. We had to get them thinking about the Steelworkers continually, every day. If we let an hour go by that our name didn't cross their minds for some reason or another, then we were failing. (Juravich and Bronfenbrenner, 1999: 132)

Third, the union could not run a campaign of the scope and scale necessary to win by relying on existing staff and resources. A comprehensive global campaign like the one that they were beginning at Bridgestone/Firestone would take money, staff, and the involvement of thousands of their members, their families, and their allies. Fourth and finally, these campaigns could not be won by strategy and resources alone. They also depended on the determination, militancy, and solidarity of the strikers, their families, and their communities.

Following a model that the union had utilized in the Ravenswood campaign, Becker assembled a strategy team to coordinate the research and to use what they found in the research to develop both short-term tactics and a long-term strategy. The team included key leaders and staff from both the USWA and the former URW, as well as the Industrial Union Department (IUD) of the AFL-CIO. Jerry Fernandez, who had played a leading role in the Ravenswood international campaign, was appointed the overall USWA coordinator.

In June 1995, in perhaps the largest commitment of an American union in a strategic campaign, the USWA hired more than 50 boycott coordinators from each of the USWA districts. Rather than having boycott activities added to a long list of duties, their full-time job was to organize the boycott. For the first time since July 1994, the boycott would have dedicated staff support. This decentralized strategy of tapping already existing leadership in their communities also allowed the Steelworkers to involve a great number of their members.

In addition, as in the Ravenswood campaign, the union filed a massive list of health and safety, environmental, and NLRB charges. But unlike at Ravenswood, at Bridgestone/Firestone 1,000 union members had returned to work inside the struck plants (under conditions that some described as a "living hell"), and thousands of other USWA/URW members were working under extended contracts at Bridgestone/Firestone plants not part of the strike. Hence, in addition to the external campaign, the union launched a full-scale in-plant campaign, replete with solidarity days, mass grievances, phone and fax jamming of corporate offices, and escalating work-to-rule actions and slowdowns.

Based on their experience, however, Fernandez and the rest of the strategy team understood that the fight could not be won on American shores alone. Once the strategy team was established, they decided to move quickly in sending a delegation of strikers and their families to Japan to meet with labor, religious, and civil rights organizations. Fernandez remembers,

I wanted to put a human face to the strike. I wanted the Japanese to understand the suffering. I wanted the Japanese people and workers and unions to understand that they had essentially fired 2700 people. In these types of things you can't send officials of the union or paid professionals to do that kind of thing. You have to put a face to the struggle. (Fernandez interview, 1999: 5)

The decision having been made, the USWA and IUD realized that they had few connections to the Japanese labor movement. Rengo, the largest labor federation in Japan, did not want to get involved, but the USWA made an important link with a smaller, more militant labor organization, Zenrokyo.

Yet, just as plans for the trip to Japan began to come together, things seemed to unravel. On July 17, during a union protest involving 500 strikers and their supporters outside the Japanese embassy in Washington, a protester was photographed with a sign bearing the words, "Enola Gay, one more time." Featured in newspapers all over Japan, this display proved too offensive to bear for the Japanese unionists whom the Steelworkers were courting (Balfour et al., 1999: 47). Becker sent a personal apology, and the strategy teams made a commitment to stop the anti-Japanese sentiments that had been simmering below the surface since the strike began.

Despite the initial tensions with the Japanese unions, the visit of 12 strikers and family members in early September 1995 was an impressive success. Although refused a meeting with Kaizaki, they held a number of demonstrations with Japanese trade unionists and received tremendous media coverage. In the aftermath of the embassy debacle, Zenrokyo suggested that the workers' delegation visit Hiroshima and the Peace Park. As Balfour et al. explain, "The visit demonstrated, if in a small way, that the Steelworkers were not narrowly bent on pursuing their agenda to the exclusion of some of the greater issues of the campaign, namely tolerance and solidarity" (Balfour et al., 1999: 51). A second delegation of workers and their families returned in October 1995 to sustain the pressure.

Working with the ICEM (the Brussels-based International Federation of Chemical, Energy, Mine and General Workers' Unions), the Steelworkers returned to Europe in November 1995. In Brussels they picketed Bridgestone's European regional headquarters and went on from there to meet with Bridgestone union officials and workers in Madrid and Rome. Back at home the big news was that on January 31, 1996, the NLRB issued a formal complaint against Bridgestone/Firestone on eight counts, including illegally discharging strikers by falsely claiming that they were permanently replaced. A week later, a second complaint pushed the company's back-pay liability back to January 1995. The campaign was gaining momentum.

Almost immediately after the board decision, the USWA, ICEM, and the IUD pulled together a "World Conference for the Bridgestone Corporation" just outside Bridgestone/Firestone's lavish headquarters in Nashville, Tennessee. Held March 13 and 14, 1996, the conference brought together 65 union delegates from across the world. In the words of USWA's Becker, "We intend to develop a global union workers' action plan to counter this company's growing disregard for its workers' interests, and its exploitation of the economies of both Third World and industrially developed nations" (Balfour et al., 1999: 71). A number of international guests spoke, including representatives from Rengo, who, after the second trip to Japan, were now actively and publicly supporting the Steelworkers' effort. At the conclusion of the conference, delegates were joined by more than 1,000 union members as they marched to Bridgestone/Firestone's headquarters. After the rally, Steelworkers marched across the street and set up what would become Camp Justice.

Originally designed as a short-term media event, Camp Justice developed into a full-fledged campground, occupied and visited by thousands of trade unionists from around the world. Each day, rain or shine, there was a daily march on the plant by rank-and-file Bridgestone/Firestone workers and visiting trade union delegations. That spring, the boycott campaign picked up steam as well.   On May 14, 1996, at a news conference at AFL-CIO headquarters in Washington, D.C., USWA president Becker announced that the union was going to escalate its handbilling campaign to target hundreds of tire retailers nationwide, as well as to "black-flag"[2] Bridgestone/Firestone at the 1996 Indy 500, the Cleveland Grand Prix, and other auto races (Balfour et al., 1999: 79).

In the weeks that followed, USWA locals, under the leadership of the boycott coordinators, picketed and handbilled thousands of MasterCare and Sears tire retailers across the country. Several high-profile successes followed, whereby tire retailers posted announcements that they would no longer sell Firestone tires. The boycott campaign also targeted GM-Saturn and Ford, state and local governments, and pro-labor nongovernmental organizations (NGOs) to remove Bridgestone/Firestone tires from their vehicles. The effort paid off when, in July 1996, GM-Saturn announced that customers could have Bridgestone/Firestone tires replaced on new Saturn vehicles, free of charge. Several states and municipalities offered their support, including a strong resolution from the Alabama House of Representatives "in unequivocal support" of the USWA and a commitment from the Atlantic City Council not to purchase Bridgestone/Firestone tires.

The boycott effort, however, was most intense at the auto races, starting with the Indy 500 on May 26.   Action started weeks before the race with handbilling, rallies, balloons, marches, and a "black flag" motorcycle brigade. On the day of the race, more than 1,200 Steelworkers were at the race to handbill inside and outside the track and to pass out thousands of "Black Flag Firestone" flags.   In the weeks that followed, the USWA black-flagged Bridgestone/Firestone at auto races in Brooklyn, Michigan; Cleveland, Ohio; and Toronto, Canada.

Days of Outrage

As the two-year anniversary of the strike approached in early July, the USWA escalation strategy was beginning to take its toll on Bridgestone/Firestone on multiple fronts, locally and internationally. Determined to push even harder, the strategy team decided to plan for its "International Days of Outrage" to commemorate the anniversary of the strike. The hope was to have multiple events in Japan, the United States, Latin America, and Europe in the days surrounding the strike anniversary. In Japan, a delegation of workers from Des Moines and Decatur took part in a "Conference for the Solidarity of U.S. Bridgestone/Firestone USWA Workers" with leaders from the ICEM, Rengo and Tekko Roren affiliates. The assembled unions at the conference passed a unanimous resolution in support of the strikers, condemning Bridgestone for "breaking away from pattern bargaining, hiring union-busters, permanently replacing employees, and making unacceptable proposals in bargaining" and calling on the company to "settle a fair contract, and to comply with NLRB rulings by rehiring all strikers and compensating them with back pay" (Balfour et al., 1999: 96–97).

Another worker delegation traveled to Europe, where union leaders from Spain, France, and Italy drafted similarly forceful resolutions condemning Bridgestone/Firestone and pledging their solidarity with the striking workers. In Turkey, a U.S. striker, Pedro DeLeon, was brought into the plant by the Bridgestone union Lastik-Is. "Once inside, the workers stopped production, jumped up on tables, and held an impromptu rally on the shop floor" (Balfour, et al., 1999: 104).

This was followed by a series of solidarity work stoppages and rallies at Goodyear, Pirelli, Michelin, and Bridgestone plants in Brazil, Argentina, and Venezuela. Back in the United States the strike anniversary was commemorated through a series of rallies at Bridgestone/Firestone's Nashville headquarters. Around the globe, unions and labor supporters also joined in a "cyberpicket" against Bridgestone/Firestone whereby, through a link on the ICEM Web page, thousands of supporters could pass on their outrage directly to Bridgestone management, flooding the company with E-mail messages.

Settlement

All throughout the summer and fall, the international campaign, the boycott, and the local actions continued. Local union delegations traveled again to Japan and Latin America, and in late August 1996 a delegation of 20 Japanese trade unionists toured the United States in support of the strikers. On October 22, 1996, the USWA released "Running over the American Dream: A Case Study in Corporate Greed and Irresponsibility." Translated into four languages, the report was released worldwide, branding Bridgestone/Firestone as the world's "poster child for corporate irresponsibility." Just a few weeks later, the NLRB unfair labor practice hearing was due to open in Pittsburgh, along with the ever-ticking back-pay time clock, which by then had reached millions of dollars.

Finally, Bridgestone/Firestone had had enough. The scope and impact of the combined internal and external campaign had been staggering:

3.6 million handbills, nearly a million "Don't Buy Bridgestone/Firestone" stickers and bumper stickers, 250,000 campaign buttons, 115,000 small black flags, and 15,000 "Don't Buy" T-shirts were distributed; 63,000 yard signs were displayed. Thousands of separate campaign events involved over 60,000 USWA participants and volunteers; 1,100 separate USWA locals were actively involved. Camp Justice was occupied for 246 days; the campaign reached 86 countries, including 16 visited by replaced Bridgestone/Firestone workers; and 43 foreign workers visited the U.S. to lend their support. ("One Day Longer." 1997: 14)

The company came back to the bargaining table on October 28, 1996, ready to reach an agreement. On November 4, 1996, after 72 hours of uninterrupted bargaining, a tentative agreement was reached on all economic and noneconomic issues. With the exception of maintaining 12-hour shifts and the elimination of paid hours for union health and safety work, the settlement included major gains on almost every issue that had prompted the strike. Moreover, reinstatement was won for all union members, including all but four of those discharged for strike-related misconduct. Perhaps most significant of all, the new contract would expire simultaneously with other master agreements in the industry. Against the greatest odds possible, the union had truly snatched victory from certain defeat. In the words of University of Akron professor and tire industry expert David Meyer, the union's accomplishment was "drop-dead, jaw-to-the floor amazing" (Lessin, 1998: 68)

AN EMERGING MODEL OF UNION POWER IN A GLOBAL ECONOMY: SUMMARY AND CONCLUSION

While it may not be clear to the general public, over the past several decades American labor has made important strides out of its nationalist and, at times, jingoist past. "Buy American" campaigns and smashing Japanese cars have been replaced by an antisweatshop movement that has not only ignited college campuses but brought the plight of workers in developing countries into America's living rooms and into the consciousness of U.S. union leaders and members. The anticommunist International Labor Institutes of the AFL-CIO, which had isolated the federation from significant portions of the international labor community, have been abandoned, replaced by more workers' rights-oriented Solidarity Centers (Shailor, 1998).

At the same time, individual unions that throughout the 1980s were battered by plant closings, downsizing, whipsawing, and union busting have become increasingly sophisticated and aggressive in both organizing and contract campaigns. Central to many of these campaigns has been a global strategy linking workers and unions together across borders. The Communication Workers of America have built ongoing linkages and exchanges with British workers and unions in their efforts to organize the telecommunications industry (Borgers, 1999). Cross-border union coalitions were also an integral component of the Teamsters 1997 strike victory at United Parcel Service (UPS) (Russo and Banks, 1999), and the United Electrical Workers has established important connections to the independent Mexican union, Frente Autentico del Trabajo, for mutual support in organizing and contract struggles in both the United States and Mexico (UE, 2000). Faced by the same kinds of global pressures, the graphical worker unions in Europe have, likewise, embarked on cross-national coordination of union strategies (Chapter 13). But as discussed in the two preceding chapters, much more transnational communication and coordination among unions are called for to strengthen labor's hand in an increasingly integrated global economy.

With their victory at Bridgestone/Firestone, the Steelworkers demonstrated once again that labor can win, even in a highly competitive and uncertain global economy. In this and a string of victories that followed at Wheeling Pittsburgh Steel, Newport News, and Continental Tire in the United States, the Steelworkers proved that these victories were neither exceptional cases nor just lucky victories. These victories came not only against some of the nation's largest industrial employers but also against some of the world's most wealthy and powerful MNCs and financiers. Taken together, the Steelworkers' victories have provided an important model of unionism and trade union power in the global economy. The new model rejects the model coming from strategic management literature, suggesting that unions will gain power in the global marketplace only by making themselves invaluable and economical to their employers. Given the tremendous wage disparities that exist worldwide, it is difficult to see how American unions could ever gain any real security for themselves through bargaining away work rules and practices with their employers. While there has been a lot of talk about employers' taking the "high road" to economic success in developed economies, in reality, the "low road" strategies continue to dominate (Harrison, 1994).

Rejecting this "new unionism," the Steelworkers have built their power by directly confronting employers, using their members, their families, and community supporters as their allies and government regulation for enforcement of worker rights. But this is not a simple, old-fashioned model of confronting employers on the picket line and in the courts. This model of strategic contract campaigns is based on a thorough understanding of the structure and operation of global capital. Early in the twentieth century, the industrial giants seemed invincible from the viewpoint of trade unionists primarily experienced in dealing with local and regional employers. The CIO, nonetheless, found the leverage points of these new industrial giants and, in turn, became ever more successful in organizing them. Similarly, the victory at Bridgestone/Firestone and the ones that preceded and followed reveal that there are new opportunities for exercising leverage in MNCs, a theme emphasized in Chapter 3. Global companies such as Bridgestone/Firestone often have a very complex structure of management, control, and finances. Unlike privately held domestic firms, all these various players may in some way be vulnerable to union pressure. As the United Auto Workers have discovered with just-in-time production systems, these new corporate structures provide important new points of leverage.

Using this newfound understanding of global corporations, however, was not only about relying on the time-honored practices of the labor movement. The victory by the USWA called for bold new moves to reach across borders, down to their members, and deep inside their own organization, for the will and commitment to stay true to the union's purpose and values. As we have seen, it wasn't easy, and sometimes they faltered.

But in the Bridgestone/Firestone campaign, the Steelworkers left that past behind and created a different kind of new unionism that used the power of coalition. They made bold moves to move beyond the easy and traditional allies, forging relationships with environmental groups, international labor organizations, and even members of the financial community. The USWA's work with environmentalists as part of the Kaiser campaign and the alliances that they are building in the wake of the WTO protests have not only brought the Steelworkers closer to their allies but changed their allies in the process.

This model of strategic campaigns also understands that the work of labor relations is not just about money and simple economic self-interest. While successful strategic campaigns have to bring economic pressure to bear on a variety of players, campaigns are not won by economics alone. In both

Ravenswood and Bridgestone/Firestone, settlements were achieved because the Steelworkers and their worldwide allies made it clear that they would not go away, not ever, no matter how long it took. The commitment of the union, its members, their families, and their communities to win, whatever it would take, took on new meaning in the context of this new global strategic campaign.

As we begin this new millennium, it is not clear how this new global corporate order will evolve. Victories in campaigns such as Bridgestone/Firestone will need to become far more common for workers and their unions to have a just place in the world that is emerging. Victories like this one, however, cannot be reduced to a few winning battles in a losing war. They point to a new model of unionism, one not contingent on allegiance to corporate interests but allied with a broad coalition of workers, unions, environmentalists, and citizens worldwide. That is the real promise of what happened at Bridgestone/Firestone and more broadly in Seattle.

NOTES

1. This project was funded by the USWA, which provided unfettered access to individuals and documents related to the strike and campaign. The analysis presented, herein, is part of a multiyear research project with the USWA documenting contract victories in the 1980s and 1990s that began in 1993 with our research documenting the Steelworkers campaign at Ravenswood Aluminum (Juravich and Bronfenbrenner, 1999). It continued in 1998 with case studies of campaigns at USX, NIPSCO, WCI, Wheeling Pitt, Bayou Steel, and Allegheny Ludlum (Bronfenbrenner and Juravich, 1998). These studies provide important context for our analysis of the Bridgestone/Firestone campaign. As part of this project, a longer case study documenting the USWA campaign at Bridgestone/Firestone was compiled by Umass Labor Center students Jeff Balfour and Sue McNeil and Cornell industrial and labor relations students Jen Bloom and Ben Francis-Fallon. We also relied on Nancy Lessin's unpublished report about the Bridgestone/Firestone struggle.

2. In auto racing, a black flag signals disqualification from the race.

REFERENCES

Appelbaum, E., Bailey, T., Berg, P. and Kalleberg, A. L. (2000). *Manufacturing Advantage: Why High-Performance Work Systems Pay Off.* Ithaca,NY: Cornell University Press.

Balfour, J., Bloom, J., Francis-Fallon, B. and McNeil, S. (1999). "Documenting the Steelworkers' Victory at Bridgestone/Firestone." Unpublished manuscript.

Barlett, D. L. and Steele, J. B. (1992). *America: What Went Wrong.* Kansas City, MO: Andrews and McMeel.

Borgers, F. (1999). "Global Unionism—Beyond the Rhetoric: The CWA North Atlantic Alliance." *Labor Studies Journal* 24, (1), 107–22.

"Bridgestone/Firestone Fact Sheet." (1995). United Steelworkers of America internal document.

Bronfenbrenner, K. and Juravich, T. (1998). "The Evolution of Strategic and Co-ordinated Bargaining Campaigns in the 1990s: The Steelworkers' Experience." Paper presented at the Conference on the Revival of the American Labor Movement?: Arguments, Evidence, Prospects. Cornell University, October.

Camens, S. (1985). "Steel: An Industry at the Crossroad." In *Labor-Management Cooperation: Perspectives from the Labor Movement*. Washington, D.C.: U.S. Department of Labor, pp. 44–48. Carr, T. Interview, July 1, 1999.

Cohen-Rosenfeld, E. and Burton, C. (1987). *Mutual Gains: A Guide to Union-Management Cooperation*. New York: Praeger.

Coss, K.. Interview, June 16, 1999.

English, J. Interview, June 16, 1999.

Fernandez, G. Interview, June 6, 1999.

Firestone, H. S. (1926). *Men and Rubber: The Story of a Business*. New York: Double-day, Page.

Gates, R. Interview, June 18, 1999.

Harrison, B. (1994). *Lean and Mean: The Changing Landscape of Corporate Power in the Age of Flexibility*. New York: Basic Books.

Heckscher, C. (1996). *The New Unionism*. Ithaca, NY: Cornell University/ICR Press.

Heckscher, C. (1998). "Taking Transformation Seriously." Paper presented at the *Conference on the Revival of the American Labor Movement?: Arguments, Evidence, Prospects*. Cornell University, October.

Juravich, T. (1998). "Employee Involvement, Work Reorganization, and the New Labor Movement: Towards a Radical Integration." *New Labor Forum* Spring, pp. 84–91.

Juravich, T. and Bronfenbrenner, K. (1999). *Ravenswood: The Steelworkers' Victory and the Revival of American Labor*. Ithaca, NY: Cornell University Press.

Kochan, T. and Osterman, P. (1994). *The Mutual Gains Enterprise: Forging a Winning Partnership among Labor, Management, and Government*. Boston: Harvard Business School Press.

Lazes, P. and Savage, J. (1997). "New Unionism and the Workplace of the Future." In Nissen, B. (ed.), *Unions and Workplace Reorganization*. Detroit: Wayne State University Press, pp. 181–207.

Lessin, N. (1998). "The URW/USWA Campaign against Bridgestone/Firestone: A Tale of Two Bridgestones?" Unpublished manuscript, Labor Center, University of Massachusetts, Amherst.

Melman, S. (1983). *Profits without Production*. New York: Alfred A. Knopf.

"Memorandum of Understanding." (1991). United Rubber Workers-Bridgestone/Firestone.

Niehouse, D. Interview, July 28, 1999.

O'Connor, M. Interview, June 18, 1999.

"One Day Longer: The Road to Victory at Bridgestone/Firestone." (1997). United Steelworkers of America internal doucument.

Parker, M. (1985). *Inside the Circle*. Boston: South End Press.

Powell, T. Interview, July 4, 1999.

Russo, J. and Banks, A. (1999). "How the Teamsters Took the UPS Strike Overseas." *Working USA*, 2 (5), pp. 74–87.

Schuler, R. and Jackson, S. (1987). "Linking Competitive Strategies and Human Resource Management." *Academy of Management Executive* (3), pp. 207–19.

Shailor, B. (1998). "A New Internationalism: Advancing Workers Rights in the Global Economy." In Mort, J. (ed.), *Not Your Father's Union Movement*. London: Verso, pp. 145–55.

UE. "Strategic Organizing Alliance." http://www.igc.apc.org/unitedelect/#About Alliance "Bridgestone Bets It Can Defeat Rubber Workers Strike." (1994). *Wall Street Journal,* December 27.

Walton, M. (1990). *Deming Management at Work.* New York: G. P. Putnam's Sons.

Wright, P. M. and McMahan, G. C. (1992). "Theoretical Perspective for Strategic Human Resource Management." *Journal of Management* 18, (2), pp. 295–320.

13

Strategic International Laborism: MNCs and Labor in the Graphical Sector

John Gennard and Harvie Ramsay

Comprising printing and publishing, the graphical sector has been ranked as the fourth largest industry in the world (Birkenshaw, Minio, and Smyth, 1999). Advances in digital technology are changing the nature of print-related operations and transforming the graphical sector from craft-based, to modern, manufacturing-based production. The graphical industry is evolving, furthermore, as part of a larger communications industry. Magazine and newspaper publishers, in particular, are diversifying into radio and television and experimenting with on-line information services, some of which are Internet-based.

Printing, nonetheless, retains a distinct industrial identity. It covers a number of market segments (books, magazines, newspapers, brochures, catalogs, security printing, corporate publications, packaging and labels), each generating different market, technological, and organizational requirements. The printing industry continues to grow but at a slower rate than the new media industry based on electronic communications technologies. It is predicted that by 2005, printing will account for only 34 percent of the communications industry compared with 57 percent today. It will, nonetheless, continue to grow in terms of sales and employment (Gennard et al., 1998). Publishing firms typically outsource their printing to major graphical companies, though some employ significant numbers of graphical employees themselves. Newspaper publishers, in contrast, do their own printing as part of integrated operations that allow for greater speed of production and adjustments across editions. Where local editions are produced, however, work is outsourced to local graphical firms.

Based primarily on a wide range of interviews with union and business officials,[1] we focus on labor's strategic response to the effects of global restructuring in the graphical sector. We first trace the recent and ongoing restructuring of the graphical sector. Marked by increasing industry concentration, a series of mergers, and acquisitions, the emergence of large multinational companies (MNCs), international expansion, and the cross-border transfer of production, we highlight the effects of global restructuring on labor. Second, we examine the emerging development of transnational union strategies being pursued across graphical trade unions as a countervailing force to the growing power of graphical MNCs. In particular, we examine graphical union efforts at coordinating transnational collective bargaining objectives via the collection and analysis of information shared among unions through a variety of transnational forums. Third, we conclude by assessing obstacles faced by unions in successfully achieving interunion, cross-border cooperation and coordination.

INTERNATIONAL RESTRUCTURING OF THE GRAPHICAL SECTOR

The generic dimensions of international restructuring in the graphical sector that pose challenges to graphical unions may be summarized as follows:

1. the concentration of economic and managerial power in fewer, larger organizations,

2. the effects of growth by merger and acquisition, destroying smaller firms with ensuing job losses,

3. the globalization of companies, making decisions more remote and less easy to influence by labor, whether directly or indirectly through sympathetic nation-state efforts,

4. the concentration of production into a few locations, chosen for economies of scale and minimization of other costs, allowing locations to be leveraged against each other in the competition to survive,

5. the shift of production to low unit labor cost locations, creating pressures for "social dumping" and/or major job losses in the countries where unions are strongest,

6. the segmentation of the value chain and the use of outsourcing networks (effectively dividing labor, cutting wages, downgrading workplace conditions, and making core employers harder to pin down) and, thus, weakening union organization, and

7. restructuring, usually linked to technological and market shifts, which reconfigure industry boundaries and labor's organizational identities.

Based on this catalog of restructuring and its effects on labor, we next consider the prominent changes in corporate structure in the graphical sector.

Mergers, Acquisitions, and Increasing Concentration

In both North America and Europe, the graphical industries have historically been characterized by a large number of firms employing few workers and serving local niche markets (Intergraf, 1998). Recently, however, there have been an emergence of some relatively large graphical companies and, in turn, increasing industry concentration. These firms increasingly account for a disproportionately large share of sales and employment (Howkins, 1996; Howitt, 2000). It appears, nonetheless, that the smallest firms have escaped the attention of the largest, that is in their quest to expand into additional product segments and localities, the largest firms have found it easier and more cost-effective to acquire medium-size operations.

Fueled by technological advance and global competitive pressures, more and more firms have sought (1) to increase sales by penetrating wider and more diverse markets and (2) to reduce costs by finding advantage through economies of scale and scope (e.g., via spreading out overhead costs and reallocating resources to new technology investments). Central to these growth strategies have been mergers and acquisitions (M&A), which have allowed many firms to expand and diverge fairly quickly (Compass Report, 1998). In the United States, for instance, the number of mergers and acquisitions involving printing firms with at least U.S.$5 million in sales rose from 34 in 1992, to 80 in 1996, to 101 in 1997, and to 188 in 1998 (PIA, 1999). As a result of these rising recent trends in M&As, the current pattern of sales concentration varies markedly by subsector. In the United States, firms with over 100 employees account for 88 percent of the magazine and periodical market, 86 percent of the book printing market, 50 percent of the label and wrapper market, and 36 percent of the commercial printing market (PIA, 1998).

The growing concentration of larger firms in the graphical industry can be highlighted by a number of examples. In 1998, St. Ives (a U.K.-based MNC) purchased Hunters Armly, doubling its share of the expanding direct response and direct mailing printing market. U.S.-based Mail Well, which describes itself as "a leading consolidator in the highly fragmented envelope, high impact printing, speciality printing and glue-applied consumer product label industries," has grown at extraordinary speed over the last few years through takeover and acquisition activity. Since 1996, it has acquired 32 printing plants and now operates 75 such plants in North America, employing over 9,000 people. De La Rue, a U.K.-based MNC, has mainly expanded its security printing operations by investing in greenfield sites, often on a joint basis with the government or central bank of the host country. In 2000, for example, it opened a new facility in Washington, D.C., to produce American Express Travellers Cheques. Today, De La Rue produces approximately 60 percent of the world's printed banknotes. Worldwide, it employs over 11,000 people, of whom some 7,300 are located in Europe, 3,000 in the Americas, and 1,000 in the rest of the world.

Quebecor World, the world's largest graphical MNC, is the product of a recent series of acquisitions made by former, Canadian-owned Quebecor and its merger with U.S.-owned World Color. Quebecor's acquisition and expansion strategy is perhaps best summarized by its strategy statement in its 1997 *Annual Report*:

Our aim is to make the company stronger through acquisitions, not just bigger. We strive for diversity, emphasising investment in markets that show rising demand. Moreover, we constantly seek to widen the scope of the products and services we offer, strengthen our established networks and move into high potential enterprises that challenge the limits of print and digital media. (Quebecor Annual Report, p. 20)

In addition to acquiring a number of European-owned graphical companies in Germany, Sweden, and Finland in recent years, in 1999 it merged with World Color, formerly the second largest printer in the United States (employing some 16,000 employees across 58 facilities). Today, Quebecor World operates 173 production sites in 14 countries across four continents and employs roughly 42,000 people.

Other major graphical MNCs include R. R. Donnelly, Bertelsmann, and News Corporation. U.S.-based R. R. Donnelly, until recently the largest printing firm in the world, has long had a strong European presence. It employs some 29,000 employees in over 100 manufacturing facilities, sales offices and service centers in the United States, the United Kingdom, Germany, France, the Netherlands, the Republic of Ireland, Spain, and Luxembourg. Bertelsmann is a global media operation based in Germany, employing 57,000 people worldwide; approximately 8,000 of its 13,000 graphical employees work in Germany. The ever-increasing global spread of Australian-owned News Corporation has made it one of the most highly internationalized companies in the world (ranked 12th in 1999 by UNCTAD, 2001: 90).

Although there is increasing concentration of sales and employment in large MNCs competing in the graphical industry, these companies, nevertheless, do not figure prominently among the ranks of the world's largest MNCs. Indeed, no graphical firms were included in the *Financial Times* 1998 rankings of the top 500 global companies ("1998 Rankings," 1999). Two Japanese companies, with graphical interests, had fallen out of the top 500 due to the reduction of asset values as a result of currency devaluations between 1997 and 1998. Only seven publishing and two newspaper groups made it onto the list, with the highest rank going to Time Warner (ranked 54th in 1998, up from 198th in 1996), which has recently been acquired by America Online. A number of graphical companies figure rather higher in European and U.S. listings but remain far from being at the forefront.

Patterns of Internationalization

As graphical firms have gotten larger, they have tended to move beyond national boundaries. McArthur (1990) identified four salient patterns of this increasing internationalization in the graphical sector: international marketing and acquisition, the tailoring of products for local markets, the transfer of production to lower labor cost sites, and the development of international production strategies. A prime aim of companies has been to expand their markets for graphical products through international marketing and through acquiring operations in new target markets. For example, U.K. printers at present are primarily seeking to market their products and services to other European markets (Howitt, 2000). International marketing and acquisition are also apparent in publishing, as with Bertelsmann's takeover of Random House and Pearson's acquisition of Simon & Schuster, both in 1998. In both cases, the companies gained access to the lucrative U.S. market by acquiring distribution and other networks. At the same time, both companies gained new products compatible with their existing offerings, which they could, in turn, sell more effectively in their traditional base markets.

A distinct, if related, strategy has been for companies to tailor products to local markets, either through translation (as with the *Wall Street Journal, Financial Times,* and *The Economist*) or through locally adjusted coverage around core news and information resources. The latter approach, however, is more of a multidomestic than a global strategy as it uses local assets to at least some degree, rather than entirely centralizing production. This is, nonetheless, more the case with most cross-border attempts to expand in printing, where the expansion of operations is primarily achieved by increased scale through acquisition of increased numbers of outlets in more locations and local markets.

The pattern of transfer of production by MNCs from higher-cost to lower-cost sites is also important to restructuring of the graphical sector. For the most part, economies of scale seem limited to the production of newspapers and to lithographic printing. In general, medium-size plants with sufficient investment finance can match the unit costs of much larger operations. Despite reduced changeover times in the press stage and between prepress and press stages, the savings on all but very long runs are small and easily offset by greater convenience and accessibility to customers. Moreover, especially in commercial printing faced by pressure to reduce stocks and to print to need, printing runs are getting shorter and supply time ever more essential. While there are some large printing plants in key locations, the industry remains highly distributed (as witnessed by the 170 locations of Quebecor World).

However, technological changes in the industry do hold out the prospect of a significant shift of production from higher to lower cost labor locations (Gennard et al., 1998). The digitalization of inputs allows easy and instant transfer of work between locations. It is possible, that is, for skilled prepress work to be performed close to the customer but for press and postpress tasks (cutting, collating, binding, packing, etc.) to be carried out at remote locations. Time sensitivity, furthermore, is a critical factor. Some printed products (e.g., newspapers and local stationery supplies) rely on rapid delivery to market, while others (e.g., packaging and books) have potentially far longer lead times, with a range of time-sensitivity operations in between these extremes.

There is evidence of transfer of time-insensitive work to lower-cost areas. Some U.S. companies, for instance, have transferred their packaging operations to Mexico, whereas the printing of books has long been undertaken by printers in Asia. Similarly, the transfer of work from Scandinavia to cheaper labor locations in the Baltic States and Poland is of growing concern to Nordic graphical unions, especially as distances are relatively short. Given that R. R. Donnelly has established a prepress operation in Barbados to distribute work electronically for printing in Canada and the United States, the possibility is that even for time-sensitive products, prepress work might be lost in the future.

In general, however, the extent of work transfer has remained limited to date. Over four-fifths of printing work is still carried out in Europe and North America. For the time being, limited skills availability, rapid technological change, and corporate strategies emphasizing integration of all stages of the printing process seem likely to keep it that way. There are still benchmarking exercises, risks to jobs, and remote decision making, but not in the way experienced in apparel, automobiles, or electronics or even to the extent currently emerging in software production. Similarly, the restructuring of local supply chains through outsourcing is still at an early stage.

The greatest internationalization challenge to graphical unions is the development by graphical multinationals of international production strategies. For publishers, print is no longer the exclusive mode of publication. Compact discs (CDs) and other digital formats, videotapes and audiotapes, and the Internet all provide parallel alternative modes of publication. As the distribution of news and other materials diversifies, many graphical companies see their futures tied to the new media sector, as well as to the paper-based communications world, and are combining, acquiring, or redirecting their expansion accordingly. Some media MNCs, such as News Corporation and Bertelsmann, are particularly energetic in repositioning themselves, with the former diversifying aggressively into broadcasting media. For graphical firms, the risk is fairly obvious, but the digital capture of text and graphics allows them also to consider diversifying the output formats that they offer to customers. Indeed, most companies, including some small ones, are already going down this new path. The result has been that the frontiers of the graphical sector are becoming blurred with those of the new media, in which many companies are owned by traditional graphical companies.

THE UNION RESPONSE

The conclusion drawn by graphical trade unions from the trends and patterns just outlined is that they cannot continue to live in "splendid isolation" from each other. Nor can they effectively represent the interests of their members by confining their industrial and political lobbying activities within nation-state borders. The employers with which graphical unions deal in one world region are increasingly the same as those that their counterparts face in other regions. Their members are increasingly, throughout the world, becoming employed by the same companies. Like capital, they need to organize internationally. To counterbalance the power of graphical and media MNCs, graphical trade unions must cooperate across national boundaries, creating effective and well-resourced international structures and networks whose priorities reflect the everyday needs of graphical trade unionists.

The driving force in this regard has been the Graphical, Paper, and Media Union (GPMU),[2] which has a working membership of 127,000 employed in the United Kingdom and the Irish Republic. Their strategy and approach have found strongest backing from the graphical unions of the Nordic countries [3] and the Graphic Communications International Union (GCIU) in North America. In developing an international trade union response, these unions start from the premise that the maintenance of a strong graphical trade union presence in Europe is a necessary precondition for the establishment of a strong international graphical workers' organization.

There are a number of reasons for this. First, in terms of sales, workforce, capital investment, and total output, Western Europe accounts for some 60 percent of the global graphical industry. Second, the total membership of the graphical unions affiliated to Union Network International (UNI) Graphical [4] is 750,000, of whom 80 percent live and work in Europe. Third, the total income of UNI-Graphical is 24 million Belgian francs, of which 85 percent is contributed by its European affiliates. Finally, the European Union is the only free-trade area that includes a social dimension. The Social Chapter of the Treaty of Rome (1957) provides, inter alia, a mechanism for employer and trade union bodies at the European Union (EU) and EU-sector levels to be consulted on social regulation proposals and to negotiate framework agreements on such issues if they both voluntarily agree to do so. Through this system, graphical trade unions are bound into the EU lawmaking process, gaining opportunities to create a more favorable legal/political environment in which to counterbalance the activities of graphical MNCs.

In devising policies to protect and advance the interests of their members in light of the growth of MNCs, the GPMU, the Nordic graphical unions, and the GCIU also assume that the harmonization of pay and other employment conditions across companies within and between nation-state boundaries are best achieved by bilateral and multilateral industrial and political initiatives, coordinated by either UNI-Graphical at the world level or UNI Europa Graphical (UEG) at the European level. Seeking to offset the activities of MNCs to downgrade labor standards, these organizations have sought to establish common minimum levels via the classical trade union methods distinguished nearly a century ago by Webb (1902), namely, regulation and collective bargaining.

Regulation

The social dimension of the EU, designated to ensure that companies operating within its boundaries maintain minimum employment standards, has grown in importance in recent years. The Working Time Directive, for example, provides minimum standards regarding working hours, holidays, and rest periods. The European Works Council Directive provides employees in Pan-

European companies with legal rights to information and consultation on issues such as investment plans, restructuring intentions, and company accounts. Additionally, the Part-Time Worker Directive guarantees part-time employees the right to conditions of employment pro rata to those of full-time employees.

In Europe, the graphical unions through the UEG are using the "social dialogue" process to create a more favorable legal/political environment in which to counterbalance the activities of graphical MNCs. UEG, as the EU industry federation for the graphical industry, is developing greater contact with other industry federations, such as the European Metalworkers Federation, to learn of their strategies regarding European-level collective bargaining and to develop a corresponding appropriate legal framework (see "Metal Unions," 1999). Previously, the graphical industry federation had operated in isolation from other industry federations, but since the mid-1990s it has raised its profile within the European Trade Union Congress (ETUC) and committed that body to a policy of establishing legally based transnational rights for workers and trade unions with regard to union membership, collective bargaining, and industrial action.[5] The UEG's influence within the EU has also increased, as evidenced by its membership on the ETUC's bargaining team, which concluded a framework agreement on fixed-term employment contracts and is currently attempting to negotiate a framework agreement on the employment of temporary (agency) workers.

Graphical unions are, furthermore, counteracting the activities of graphical MNCs by playing a leading role in seeking changes to the European Works Council (EWC) Directive, whose operation is currently under review by the commission (EGF, 1999c).[6] Graphical unions welcomed the directive as recognizing the legitimacy of workers' transnational representation by its imposition on multinational employers of an obligation to negotiate with worker representatives over the establishment of permanent information and consultation structures. Indeed, graphical unions have regarded EWCs as institutions in which there is potential for the terms and conditions of employment in a company to be determined on a European-wide level by collective bargaining. (See Chapters 15, 16, and 17 in this volume for further discussion and assessment of EWCs.)

However, the UEG believes that the spirit and intention of the EWC Directive have been too easily circumvented by employers taking advantage of loopholes and ambiguities. The UEG successfully moved a motion to the 1999 ETUC Congress outlining its desired changes to the directive. These include the right of participation of full-time trade union officials in the affairs of EWCs; rights to skills training for EWC members to prepare better for their role; improved resources to enable EWC representatives to communicate and consult with the workforces that they represent, to be consulted at the agenda-planning stage, and to meet and discuss issues prior to full EWC meetings; and the right for EWCs to call timely "extraordinary" meetings in certain circumstances (e.g., in the case of company's restructuring and sudden job losses). On December 3,

1999, the ETUC detailed its position during meetings on the directive's review, at which all of these issues were incorporated.

In seeking to counterbalance the behavior of graphical MNCs by being an effective political force at the EU level, again with the GPMU and the Nordic graphical unions as the driving forces, the UEG established an effective and direct graphical worker voice to the EU political institutions (the commission, the Council of Ministers, and the European Parliament). The latest such initiative took place in December 1999 with the creation of a *"graphical group"* within the European Parliament. This group consists of one member of the European Parliament elected from each of the member states, to maintain a close association with the graphical union(s) in their country. The group provides access for the UEG and its affiliate unions to a parliamentary group, which assists them in representation, lobbying, and the initiation of contacts within the European Parliament (including its committees, the commission, and, if necessary, the social affairs commissioner).

In its statement on the promotion of European Social Dialogue, adopted on May 20, 1998, the commission proposed a new framework, the creation of sectoral dialogue committees within which social dialogue can develop and deepen. These committees, which provide the focus for sectoral dialogue (consultation, joint actions, and declarations), can be set up by the commission only on a joint request made by the sectoral-level social partners. In the graphical industry, these include the UEG on the employees' side and Integraf on the employers' side. However, the latter, mainly due to the opposition by German graphical employers, is reluctant to engage in sectoral social dialogue, arguing that it presents a further level of regulation when improvements in the industry's competitiveness require deregulation of labor markets. It is unlikely, therefore, that a sectoral dialogue committee for the graphical industry will be established in the near future. This weakens the possibility of graphical trade unions regulating the activities of graphical MNCs operating in the EU via common standards established across the graphical industries of member states by sector-level framework agreements.

Coordination of Collective Bargaining Objectives

To engage effectively in collective bargaining with graphical MNCs, trade unions need to collect, analyze and distribute among themselves information on the economic and sociopolitical environments across countries and on the corporate governance of multinationals, particularly their locus of decision making. Financial information on production, sales, investments, profitability, and so on of individual companies is also necessary if graphical unions are to assess effectively whether a company is justified in undertaking the action that it proposes, for example, to close a plant or reject a claim for improvements in pay and working conditions. Information on pay and conditions of employment within and between graphical MNCs enables unions to *"benchmark"* one group of employees relative to others. Knowledge and understanding of the employment relations, work organization practices, available technology, and other factors influencing performance (which are beyond the control of workers yet may be used as leverage through comparison between plants in different countries) are necessary if workers in one country are not to be leveraged against their fellow workers in different geographical areas.

Unions must also exchange information about each other's behavior, policies, priorities, customs, and practices. Graphical unions have different cultures and have evolved historically in different ways. Cross-national differences exist in density of membership, in decision-making machinery, in the role of officials, in industrial and political policies, and in bargaining arrangements with employers (Gennard et al., 2000). In some countries (e.g., France) there is trade union competition for membership of graphical workers, while elsewhere (e.g., the United Kingdom, Canada, the United States, and the Nordic countries) there is one dominant trade union. Without mutual knowledge and understanding, the construction of effective industrial structures and networks at an international level is more difficult, if not impossible, to achieve.

As part of their strategy toward developing countervailing power to the growing influence of MNCs, graphical unions individually and collectively have developed databases on the behavior and activities of such companies. This information is then exchanged across national borders at the appropriate levels in the respective graphical union decision-making structures. The GPMU has produced a database that contains a profile of all the U.S. and Canadian graphical and paper companies with establishments in the United Kingdom and the Republic of Ireland (in terms of their location, products, sales, number of employees, other European locations, etc.). The Nordic unions' overarching body, the Nordic Graphical Union,[7] maintains a database on legislation, economic circumstances, and the scope of collective agreements in the graphical and media sectors inside the five Nordic countries. For instance, the GCIU has a comprehensive database on Quebecor World, which covers information on sales, turnover, profitability, corporate governance, corporate strategy, employment, enterprise location, and union membership on a worldwide basis.

Since 1995, as part of its European strategy for the coordination of collective bargaining policies, the UEG has maintained a database developed from an annual, systematic survey of changes in collective bargaining institutions, the anniversary dates of agreements, the number of workers covered, and changes in wages and other employment conditions (working hours, holidays, overtime, shift working, etc.) in national agreements for each affiliate union. This provides a source of comparative information for UEG affiliates to draw upon when negotiating agreements with employers (EGF, 1996a, 1998a, and 1999a). It is also soon to provide, on an annual basis, the same information for each establishment of the major graphical MNCs.

In producing and maintaining such data bases, however, a major difficulty for graphical unions has been getting branches/locals and affiliates to provide up-to-date and, hence, relevant information. The relevance of information required depends upon the purpose for which it is sought.

Information is likely to be of higher quality, moreover, when it comes through formal channels in which trade unions and/or members participate jointly with employers (as unions are better able to obtain from employers the information that they need in the form that they require). The forum through which the graphical unions receive and analyze information is, thus, important, and they have obtained information through several broad forums: European works councils, world company councils, bilateral links between individual graphical unions, and multinational links via their international and European-wide organizations.

European Works Councils.

Graphical unions in Europe are supportive of EWCs, seeing them as providing a platform that allows workers employed by the same firm in different countries to come together, share experiences, and exchange information on working conditions. Currently, within the EU, 40 companies in the graphical and packaging sector have established EWCs. An additional 35 companies fall within the size criteria qualifying them for EWCs but have not yet established them (EGF, 1998a; "EWCs in the Paper and Printing Sector", 1998). All 40 agreements distribute employee representative seats on a country-by-country basis in preference to division or business area. The EWC members' terms of office vary between one and four years, with the majority fixed at three to four years. The UEG is keen to ensure that trade union officials have the right to serve as members of an EWC or to ensure that EWCs may call upon full-time officials to provide expert consultation. Twenty of the EWC agreements give trade union officials the right to attend meetings, mostly in an expert or advisory capacity and without prior discussion with the company. In the United Kingdom and the Irish Republic, trade unions have played the major role in the selection of EWC members. Early in 1998, the UEG established a European Works Council Network, which meets at least once a year to exchange information about companies, to develop training programs for current and future EWC members, and to develop a coordinated strategy for EWCs in the graphical sector.

World Company Councils.

The graphical unions are committed, but with little success to date, to extending EWCs into worldwide company councils where appropriate. Because there is no legislative support for the establishment and development of such institutions, multinational employers will have to be persuaded to accept the extension of EWCs. There is little reason to believe that they will do so of their own volition. However, under the auspices of the former International Graphical Federation, there have been some ad hoc meetings on a worldwide scale of representatives of employees of graphical MNCs. In 1999, a meeting was held in Belgium of trade union representatives from all countries within which Quebecor World has plants. Representatives attended from France, the United Kingdom, Germany, Finland, Spain, Canada, the United States, Mexico, and Chile. The meeting exchanged information on employment conditions, the company's employment practices, the strategic use of the impending EWC for Quebecor World for coordination of action with respect to its European operations, and the role of UNI-Graphical in coordinating activities on a global scale.

In March 2000, UNI-Graphical organized a meeting in Santiago, Chile for union representatives of Quebecor World employees in North, Central, and South America. The purpose of the meeting was to coordinate union activities across the company in the Americas. Representatives at the meeting shared experiences of relationships with Quebecor World and agreed to exchange collective agreements and information on working conditions prevailing in their respective countries. Additional meetings are planned for the purpose of constructing a common agenda for the Americas that can be used as a basis for approaching corporate level management. It is an aspiration that these European and Americas approaches will eventually be brought together in a worldwide company council for Quebecor World.

Bilateral Linkages.

Western Europe. The GPMU and the four Nordic graphical unions have developed a network of key officials at the national and plant levels. This was achieved by systematic exchange visits between the officers of the respective unions responsible for servicing the membership employed by graphical MNCs having plants in the respective countries. There have also been officer visits to exchange information on the industrial and political policies of the respective unions. There are, in addition, regularly structured visits designed to help national and plant representatives from the respective unions to understand how each union operates, why certain features and practices in each union are valued,and how their respective national and industry-level IR systems operate.

Relations between the GPMU and the Nordic graphical unions, on the one hand, and the three Italian graphical unions on the other, have developed considerably over the past two years (especially in terms of national officer exchange visits designed to better understand how each other's union functions and its industrial and political priorities and to exchange information on employment conditions). Bilateral links between the GPMU and the French graphical union FILPAC-CGT were limited until 1998. Since then, however, regular, structured exchange-of-information meetings have taken place, at one of which an agreement was reached on a joint approach to the establishment of an EWC at Quebecor World. The information exchanged mainly relates to the contents of collective agreements to which the two unions are signatories and the employment practices of the company's affiliates with which they deal.

In the early 1990s, relationships between the GPMU and IG Medien (Germany)[8] were close, resulting in the development of bilateral links based on joint training courses. The European Commission financed courses for chapel officials and covered the costs of six monthly meetings of the senior officers of the two unions and an officer exchange program. Arising out of these meetings was a joint statement on "Co-operation and Commitment to Further Joint

Action," which pledged the two unions to help and support each other in national pay and other employment conditions bargaining.

Since 1995, however, relationships have been strained between the union organizations, the result of several factors. First, the graphical industry members of the IG Medien felt a loss of identity and began to resign membership in significant numbers. Second, the presence of printers on the decision-making bodies of the union declined, such that by 1999 only one member of the Executive Committee and only one full-time officer had a graphical worker background. In addition, IG Medien's influence with the German graphical employers declined as it began to experience severe financial problems. These financial problems resulted from IG Medien's failure to recruit new members in the former East Germany, as graphical employers there declined to join the graphical employers' association and, thereby, avoided coming within the jurisdiction of the national agreement.

Central and Eastern Europe. The replacement of a communist planning economy model by a market-based economy model in Central and Eastern Europe in the late 1980s to the early 1990s posed a threat to the graphical unions of Western Europe. In Central and Eastern Europe, the pay and conditions of graphical workers are relatively poor, and, as a low-cost region, it is attractive to foreign direct investment (FDI). The emergent graphical unions in the former communist countries are characterized by weak national levels of organization, lacking physical, capital, and staff resources and experiencing declining membership.[9] In Hungary, the major MNC is Polestar, which is U.K.-owned and, employs 350 people, only 15 percent of whom are members of the Hungarian Graphical Workers Union.

West European graphical unions recognized that help and assistance to fellow graphical unions and workers in Central and Eastern Europe were essential if, indeed, effective unions of graphical workers were to emerge in the medium-term to long-term future in this part of Europe. The GPMU, with assistance from the European Commission, has developed close links with the graphical unions of the Czech Republic, Slovakia, and Hungary. The Nordic unions have developed and maintained similar links with such organizations in Estonia, Latvia, Lithuania, and Bosnia. The main feature of these links has been the provision of basic industrial relations skills training courses (interviewing, grievance and discipline handling, bargaining and communication, etc.). These courses have been designed to provide national officials and workplace representatives the opportunity to acquire and develop the skills, knowledge, and expertise needed to represent effectively members employed in a market economy.

North America. Given the growth in the number of U.S. and Canadian companies that have entered the graphical and packaging sector in the United Kingdom, the GPMU has developed strong links with the GCIU.[10] A network of key officials of both unions has been developed at the national/international and plant levels. This is the result of systematic exchange visits of senior officials, especially those with specific responsibilities for MNCs that have plants on both sides of the Atlantic. Further, senior officials from the two unions have attended meetings of each other's top policy-making bodies, as well as meetings of union representatives below the national/international level. In 1996, the parties signed a Memorandum of Agreement that committed them to coordinating their research and educational resources as a means of building up data banks on MNCs with which the two unions deal.

The development of a network of key officials at the plant level is furthest developed between the Canadian and U.K. employees of Quebecor World, which has over 60 plants in the United States and Canada, as well as establishments in Sweden, Finland, the United Kingdom, and Germany. In 1996, representatives of GCIU locals in both Canada and the United States with members employed by Quebecor World exchanged information and experiences and discussed common bargaining objectives and strategies. This conference was also attended by plant representatives of the GPMU and French officials of FILPAC-GCT responsible for bargaining with Quebecor World in their respective countries. Two years later, the GCIU in Canada hosted a GPMU delegation representing workers employed at the company's Corby establishment in the United Kingdom. The delegation included rank-and-file activists as well as GPMU officials, who toured Quebecor World plants in Toronto and met with their counterparts to exchange information and experiences and discuss common concerns.

South Africa. Following the end of apartheid, South Africa became attractive to graphical MNCs and the GPMU. The GPMU soon developed links with the black graphical workers union (the Paper, Printing, Wood, and Allied Workers Union), which in 1999 merged with the Chemical Workers Union to form the Chemical, Energy, Paper, Printing, Wood, and Allied Workers Union (CEPPWAWU).[11] Like other trade unions in South Africa, this graphical workers union has experienced a high turnover of experienced officials who have taken positions either in government or in private, not-for-profit organizations such as joint industrial councils.

Hence, an immediate priority for the black South African graphical workers union is to find skilled officials and leaders. The GPMU, from its own resources and those of the European Commission, has provided industrial relations training courses to assist in the development and growth of black South African union organization. In July 1997, the GPMU conducted two, two-week-long industrial relations skill training programs for 60 national and regional officials of the then Paper, Printing, Wood, and Allied Workers Union. The programs centered on developing skills and competencies on a variety of topics, including interpersonal communication, leadership, administration, finance, and in the preparation and negotiation of collective bargaining agreements.

This training was followed up by providing the union's national education officer with an intensive two-week course in the United Kingdom, during which he observed the facilities and training opportunities that Western trade unions provide for their activists. The third stage of assistance was completed in November 1999, when the GPMU provided a Training-for-

Trainers program designed to help 36 CEPPWAWU officials acquire and develop the skills necessary to train their own regional, local, and national officials. This program has provided the union with a pool of trainers who now have the skills, knowledge, and confidence to plan, budget, and execute training courses, which will create a new cadre of competent trade union officials for the union. In this way, the GPMU has helped the union develop its leadership and management capacity, which is essential, if in the long term, it is to protect effectively its members employed, inter alia, by graphical MNCs.

Multinational Collective Bargaining Policies.

Since the early 1990s, graphical MNCs, regardless of the country in which they are located, have pursued at the negotiating table similar demands, in particular, demands for greater labor market flexibility and changes in working patterns. Furthermore, where such companies have had interests in several countries, they have on occasion backed up their demands by switching work between plants in different countries. Facing such a considerable disadvantage, the graphical unions' coordinated collective bargaining policy began to emerge in the mid-1990s, one designed to counter the power of MNCs' exerting downward pressures on wages and working conditions. The driving force behind the strategy was the GPMU, whose coordination policy is based on a number of premises and principles (EGF, 1994, 1996b, and 1999b). First, the UEG serves as the key organization for providing and analyzing information and coordinating the European collective bargaining strategy of its affiliates. Second, national bargaining in the graphical industry within member states is to continue relatively undisturbed. Harmonization of wages and other employment conditions are to be achieved by affiliates' pursuing coordinated common claims across countries in the annual negotiations with the national graphical employers' federation and MNCs operating within their national boundaries.

Third, the convergence of such demands is to be met with due regard to the different levels, forms, stages of development, and bargaining priorities of each national graphical union. Fourth, given that 60 percent of graphical workers in the EU are covered by just five national collective agreements (in France, Germany, the United Kingdom, Spain, and Italy), the chances of achieving harmonization between collective agreements, other than on wages, are seen as genuinely realistic. A fifth principle underpinning the European graphical unions' coordinated approach to Pan-European level bargaining is that it is not sensible in the short to medium term to harmonize wages because of wide disparities between countries in wage levels, productivity, and economic performance. Fundamental to the coordinated approach, bargaining objectives in the initial phase are expected to be cautious and restricted. In the medium to long term, however, unions will adopt a more ambitious bargaining agenda to include provisions governing hours, holidays, harassment, equality, health and safety, and part-time and temporary workers.

A further principle of the collective bargaining strategy is that the UEG will establish, review, and recommend on a regular basis the common bargaining objectives for each successive bargaining round in the light of an annual conference of affiliated union negotiators. Finally, the coordinated policy calls for increased participation in the ETUC as a means of influencing that body's strategy for coordinating bargaining policies in Europe at the interprofessional and sectoral level. An underlying policy of the ETUC is based on the premise that trade unions within the Euro-zone should adopt similar negotiating objectives to guard against cross-border "wage dumping."

At its annual general meeting in 1999, the UEG began the process of cooperation and coordination in Pan-European-wide collective bargaining by instructing its collective bargaining committee to draw up a standard clause for inclusion in collective agreements with employers covering:

1. the joint commitment of unions and employers to sector-level dialogue at the European Union level,

2. the introduction of a 35-hour week and 30 days' paid leave for all European graphical workers,

3. equality, training, and health and safety provisions,

4. the harmonization of the start and finish dates of collective agreements, and

5. the convening of an annual conference of union negotiators to review the national collective bargaining strategies of affiliate unions and then agree to coordination at the European level for the next bargaining round.

The initial conference of the graphical union negotiators to establish national bargaining strategies and to coordinate activities at a European level took place in November 1999. A six-point, coordinated collective bargaining strategy for the year 2000 round of bargaining was adopted, which directed unions to:

1. improve the quality of information by completing the UEG Collective Bargaining Survey, designed to improve existing data on national agreements,

2. pressure national graphical employer organizations to persuade Intergraf to agree to establish a graphical industry Sector Dialogue Committee,

3. seek a wage improvement of inflation plus productivity,

4. claim a working year of 1,750 hours (approximately 38 hour per week),

5. seek common minimum standards regarding vocational training (including lifelong learning), the right to reskill, equality, and health and safety, and

6. take common actions of solidarity among affiliate organizations in pursuit of these claims.

CONCLUSION

Although the graphical unions have taken, and continue to take, positive steps toward building cross-border cooperation to protect and advance the interests of their members who work in MNCs, much remains to be accomplished. There are many barriers to be overcome if effective and well-resourced international structures and networks are to be established. Among these barriers are policy differences between unions, lack of resources, management opposition, outdated structures (in which some branches/locals harbor long-standing jealousies, making them resistant to merger and coordinated action), and differences in language and laws across countries.

The greatest obstacle to achieving effective cross-border coordination is the continued erosion of union membership and penetration and, hence, relative power among graphical sector unions. Except for the Nordic countries, where union density of graphical workers remains over 90 percent, trade union membership has continued to decline in the United Kingdom, the Irish Republic, Germany, France, Central and Eastern Europe, North America, and Australia. Given that total industry employment continues to rise, the figures are telling. In 1983, the GCIU membership stood at 200,000; today it is half that. In 1991, the GPMU had a total membership of 282,000, but today the figure is 203,000. In the United Kingdom, only one-third of the people employed in printing, publishing, and papermaking are organized. In the U.K. printing industry itself, union density is much higher, with 100 percent membership in many production departments but as low as 10 percent in some newspapers. In North America, graphical union density is about 20 percent, and deunionization continues. The decline in membership and penetration has occurred despite some of the unions' promoting aggressive organizing and introducing improved internal management cultures. In both Europe (excluding the Nordic countries) and North America, the failure to attract young people into membership remains a worrisome trend.

The relative success to date of cross-border union collaboration in the graphical sector is attributable, in large part, to its markets and MNCs remaining relatively "traditional." As described earlier, MNCs in printing and, to a large extent, publishing have thus far expanded in a classic and relatively visible way. In particular, the limited extent of subcontracting and other desegregations of the value chains in the industry allows the opponents, while dauntingly powerful and often distant in terms of ultimate decision making, to remain relatively easily identified. Likewise, differences in labor relations practices and commonality of interests between unions are relatively easily identified. The multidomestic nature of the marketplace in most cases, furthermore, means that the extent to which national unions are likely to see themselves in competition for jobs is limited. The scope of most bargaining and labor-related decisions, moreover, remains national, allowing a focus on comparison of best employer practice and information exchange to be particularly helpful. The emergence of new technologies in product and process and the restructuring that is just beginning as a result may, nevertheless, pose far more serious problems later. Unions, therefore, will need to prepare themselves now if they are to maintain, let alone improve, their effectiveness on the global stage.

NOTES

  1. The data for the chapter were collected from 26 semistructured interviews with graphical union officials (at all levels), with three representatives of trade union central (peak) bodies, and with six officers of graphical multinational companies and officials of national organizations of graphical employers. Data were also obtained from the official and public records of these organizations. This report is part of a wider research project being undertaken by the Centre for European Employment Research (CEER) at the Department of Human Resource Management of the Strathclyde Business School on behalf of the Nordic Graphic Unions, the Graphical Paper and Media Union, the Graphic Communications International Union, IG Medien, FILPAC-CGT, and UNI-Europa Graphical Section.

  2. The Graphical Paper and Media Union is the largest graphical union in the world with a working membership of 127,000 and total membership of 203,229. Its members include printers, planners, platemakers, keyboard and applemac operators, bookbinders, designers, artists, photographers, estimators, sales staff, press and guillotine operators, warehouse staff, and dispatch and delivery drivers.

  3. These are the Norwegian Graphical Union (10,700 members), the Swedish Graphical Union (32,000 members), the Finnish Media Workers (20,356 members), and, in Denmark, the HK-Industrial (26,000 members). In 1999, the Danish Union of Graphical Workers dissolved itself. Its membership split between three unions. The prepress and printer membership joined HK, its photographer members joined the Journalist Union, and the papermaking members joined the General Workers Union. For an explanation of this unusual event, see Gennard et al., 1998.

  4. The Union Network International (UNI) came into being on January 1, 2000, and was created by a merger of four International Trade Union Secretariats: FIET, the Post and Telecommunications International, the Media and Entertainment International, and the International Graphical Federation (IGF). UNI is the largest International Trade Union Secretariat, with a total membership of some 16 million divided into four regions: Europe, Asia, the Americas, and Africa. Inside each region and also at the world level, UNI is partitioned into 14 autonomous sectoral structures, of which the graphical sector is one. The graphical sector represents 6 percent of UNI's total membership. The Dutch and German graphical unions initiated the move to take the IGF into UNI on the grounds that technological developments, particularly the growth of new media, were changing graphical employees from manufacturing to service workers. The GPMU, GCIU, the Nordic Unions, and graphical unions of Hungary, the Czech Republic, and Slovakia were skeptical of such a merger but became supportive once it was clear that the identity and autonomy of graphical workers would be protected in the merger (GPMU, 1999). In 1985, the European Graphical Federation (EGF) became a regional organization of the IGF. The EGF is now UNI Europa Graphical Section (UEG).

  5. Currently, under the Social Chapter of the Treaty of Rome (1957) health and safety, working conditions, information and consultation, and equal treatment and integration of persons excluded from the labor market can be harmonized between member states on the basis of qualified majority voting. Social security, protection of workers when their employment contract is terminated, representation and collective defense of the interests of workers and employers, employment conditions for third-

country nationals, and financial contributions for promotion of employment and job creation can be harmonized only on the basis of all agreeing. However, the right to association, the right to strike, and the right to impose lockouts are excluded from the mechanism of the Social Chapter.

6. However, to date the commission has made little progress on this matter.

7. The Nordic Graphical Union (NGU) was formed in 1985 and grouped together all the graphical unions from the Nordic countries. Although the NGU is not a federal body, and each member union retains its autonomy and does not have its own resources or full-time employees (the acting president's union is responsible for all administrative work), decisions taken by the NGU are expected to be binding on its members

8. The IG Medien was formed in 1985. It then had a membership of 250,000, but today the figure is 150,000. It organizes in printing and publishing, paper and plastics, broadcasting, television and filmmaking, journalism, literature, art, performing arts, and music production. The number of graphical workers in membership is 85,000. IG Medien is currently in negotiations with four other unions (public services, transport and traffic union, German white-collar workers union, postal workers union, and commerce, banking, and insurance union) to create the Unified Service Sector Union, which would have a membership of some 3.2 million across more than 1,000 occupations.

9. In the Czech Republic, the Typographical Circle was formed in 1862, went underground in the period 1938–1989, and officially came back into existence in 1990. It has 4,000 members today compared with 13,000 in 1990. The Slovakia Graphical Trade Union now has a membership of 600 compared with 1,500 in 1993. In both these unions, most of the financial resources are held at the workplace level. The Hungarian Graphical Workers Union was formed in 1852 and went underground between 1938 and 1989. It came back officially in 1989. Today it has a membership of 5,000 compared with 11,000 in 1990.

10. The Graphic, Communications International Union was formed in 1983 by a merger of the International Printing and Graphic Communications Union and the Graphic Arts International Union. It is the largest printing and publishing union in North America with a working membership of 100,000. The International Typographical Union merged in the United States with the Communication Workers Union and in Canada with the Communications, Energy, and Paperworkers of Canada. It had a small working membership at the time.

11. The Chemical, Energy, Paper, Printing, Wood and Allied Workers Union has 100,000 members, of whom 12,000 are employed in the graphical industry. About 16 percent of these are in skilled occupations where the dominant union remains the white South African Typographical Union (SATU).

REFERENCES

Birkenshaw, J. W., Minio, R., and Smyth, S. (1999). *Five Year Technology Forecast of Printing and Publishing*. Leatherhead, U.K.: PIRA International.

Canadian Printing Industries Association. (1995). *Profile of the Commercial Printing Industry in Canada*. Toronto: CIPA/Entre Sy.

Compass Report. (1998). *Corporate Development Activities and Strategies of the Printing Industry*. Radnor, PA.: Compass Capital Partners.

Engelbach, W., Fahnrich, K. P. and Van Hoof, A. (1999). *Sustaining Development and Competitiveness for the European Printing Industry.* Brussels: European Commission, Employment and Social Affairs DG.

European Graphical Federation. (EGF). (1994). *Policy Statement in European Collective Bargaining.* Brussels: EGF.

European Graphical Federation. (EGF). (1996a). *Collective Bargaining Survey.* Brussels: EGF.

European Graphical Federation. (EGF). (1996b). *Proposals for a Common Approach to Collective Bargaining in Europe.* Brussels: EGF.

European Graphical Federation. (EGF). (1998a). *Collective Bargaining: What's in It for Our Workers?* Brussels: EGF.

European Graphical Federation. (EGF). (1998b). *European Works Councils and the EGF—The Progress So Far.* Brussels: EGF.

European Graphical Federation. (EGF). (1999a). *Collective Bargaining: What's new in 1999?* Brussels: EGF.

European Graphical Federation. (EGF). (1999b). *Declaration by the EGF Annual Meeting concerning the Co-ordination of Collective Bargaining at the European Level.* Brussels: EGF.

European Graphical Federation. (EGF). (1999c). *Opening up New Horizons for EWCs.* Brussels: EGF.

European Graphical Federation. (EGF). (1999d). *Report of Collective Bargaining Conference*, November. Brussels: EGF.

European Graphical Federation. (EGF). (1999e). *Report of 5th Annual General Meeting.* Brussels: EGF.

"EWCs in the Paper and Printing Sector." (1998). *European Industrial Relations Review.* no. 291, April, pp. 29–32.

Gennard, J., Bain, P., Baldry, C. J., Ramsay, H., and Snape, E. (1998). *Globalisation of the Graphical Industry and the Future of the Graphical Trade Unions.* Glasgow: Centre for European Employment Research, University of Strathclyde.

Gennard, J., Ramsay, H., Baldry, C., and Newsome, K. (2000). *Strengthening the Social Dialogue and Cross Border Trade Union Networks in the Graphical Sector.* Glasgow: Centre for European Employment Research, University of Strathclyde.

Gennard, J. and Newsome, K. (2001). "European Co-ordination of Collective Bargaining: The Case of UNI-Europa Graphical Sector." *Employee Relations* 23 (6), pp. 576–94.

Graphical, Paper, and Media Union (GPMU). (1999). *European and International Activities, 1997–1999.* Special Report to the 1999 Biennial Delegate Conference.

Howitt, S. (ed.). *Printing: 2000 Market Report.* Chartered Institute of Marketing, Keynote Report.

Howkins, M. (1996). *UK Printing Industry and Its Market, 1996.* Leatherhead U.K.: PIRA International.

Intergraf. (1997). *The Evolution of the European Graphical Industry, 1996–97.* Brussels: Intergragh

McArthur, R. (1990). "The Internationalisation of Print: Trends, Socioeconomic Impact and Policy." Sectoral Activities Programme Working paper. Geneva: International Labour Office.

"Metal Unions to Co-ordinate Bargaining Strategy." (1999). *European Industrial Relations Review*. no. 300, January, pp. 20–21.

"1998 Rankings." (1999). *Financial Times*, January 30, p. 4.

Printing Industries of America. (PIA). (1993). *The Printing Firm of the Future.* Alexandria, VA: Office of the Chief Executive.

Printing Industries of America. (PIA). (1998). "A Look at Market Segments." *Economic Trends Advisory*, December, p. 2.

Printing Industries of America. (PIA). (1999). "The Changing Economic Structure of the Printing Industry." *Economic Trends Advisory*, April, p. 1.

Quebecor Annual Report. (1997 and 1998).

UNCTD. (1997). *World Investment Report 2001. Promoting Linkages.* New York and Geneva: United Nations.

Webb, S. W. (1902). *Industrial Democracy*. London: Longmans.

Part IV

Transnational Workplace Regulation

14

Sailing Beyond the Reach of Workplace Regulations: Worker Exploitation by MNCs on the High Seas

Clifford B. Donn

In June 1998, a Canadian court ruled that the oceangoing vessel *Atlantis Two* should be auctioned off to pay wages owed to its crew. The vessel had been at anchor in Vancouver since November 1997, apparently abandoned by its owners after a Canadian port inspector had the vessel detained because of excessive corrosion. The vessel was registered in Cyprus but was operated by a British company "in connection with" a U.S. firm. The 25 crew members from India had been stranded on the ship the entire time that it was anchored in the Vancouver port and were owed hundreds of thousands of dollars in back wages (Bate, 1998). This is but one incident of the kinds of practices that have become commonplace in the international maritime industry. As a result of an increasing concentration of so-called flag-of-convenience (FOC) ships and crew-of-convenience workforces, the multinational companies (MNCs) that own these shipping vessels sail beyond the reach of workplace regulations, often exploiting their crews with impunity (Donn, 1988a, 1994).

In this chapter, I first describe the emergence of FOC fleets and the changing face of the international maritime industry. Second, the several limited avenues by which international standards, regulation, and oversight of maritime employment conditions have been pursued are discussed. Third, I construct a profile of the often deplorable working conditions and consequences of employment on FOC vessels. Finally, I reflect on the need for stepped-up oversight and meaningful enforcement mechanisms to ensure compliance with minimum standards.

EMERGENCE OF FOC FLEETS

Until after World War II, most shipping vessels were registered in the nations in which both their owners and seafarer crews lived. Accordingly, the employment relationships on most vessels were governed principally by the laws and customs of the home country, with some exceptions (Panama, in particular). After the war, the Liberian vessel registry (promulgated in the United States) was created largely for the benefit of American ship owners who sought an inexpensive host location to register their excess wartime tonnage. There was also some concern among American vessel owners that Panama, which had opened its registry largely in response to cruise ship owners wanting to serve alcoholic beverages during Prohibition in the United States, was attempting to exploit its monopoly position with U.S. shipowners. The operation of the Liberian registry to this day remains almost completely independent of the Liberian government. This is evidenced by the growth in registration under the flag during the Liberian civil war, a war that led to the complete breakdown of civil authority in Liberia. Further evidence is provided by the fact that the Liberian government found it necessary in the late 1990s to sue in a U.S. court to change the registry operator from one American firm to another (Freudmann and Baldwin, 1998; McElroy, 1995).

Over time, a growing number of developing nations took advantage of the ease and income associated with making their vessel registries open and convenient to foreign owners. Indeed, little is required either of a host nation in establishing a registry or of foreign owners to "flag" their vessels under foreign registries. Owners merely register as "paper" corporations, pay modest taxes, and enjoy lax regulations. By the 1980s, many nations were competing for the registration of vessels owned by foreigners. By December 1997, five of the six largest vessel registries in the world (in terms of gross tonnage) were FOC registries in Panama, Liberia, Bahamas, Cyprus, and Malta (ITF, 1999c: 39).

Unlike the registries in the traditional maritime nations (e.g., Britain, the United States, and Norway), the FOC registries impose only minimal safety regulations and virtually no regulation of the employment relationship and working conditions. Those regulations that they have imposed have often been weakened or eliminated once vessel owners have threatened to relocate to other registries. Gradually, vessel owners came to realize that registration in FOC countries enabled them to employ crews from any country and (as discussed later) allowed them to impose much harsher conditions on those crews than any of the traditional maritime nations would permit. Accordingly, the employment of such crew-of-convenience workers became universal among FOC vessels and became increasingly more common among vessels registered in traditional maritime nations.

These crew-of-convenience workforces share neither the nationality of the flag of the vessel nor that of the vessel owner. While some less-developed, poorer countries have found making their registries available to foreign owners a source of substantial income, others have learned that placing workers on foreign vessels can also be a substantial source of income. These countries, moreover, have actively marketed their workforces not primarily on the basis of their having requisite skills but primarily on their being low-wage, compliant workers. Vessel owners, in turn, have often promised wages two or more times as high as workers can earn onshore (plus room and board) and, hence, have had little difficulty recruiting seafarers (Magnier, 1995). As of 1999, the top seafarer labor suppliers were the Philippines (which supplies three times as many as any other country), Indonesia, Turkey, China, Russia, India, Japan, Greece, Ukraine, and Italy (ITF, 1999c: 28). Some countries, Japan and Greece in particular, largely supply seafarers to shipowners in their own countries or at least to ships carrying the given country's flag. In contrast, other countries supply crews to vessels having no relationship to the supplier countries.

The impact of this transformation of the maritime industry on traditional maritime countries has been substantial and the impact on the U.S. oceangoing fleet has been dramatic, as job opportunities have declined precipitously, dropping from around 48,000 in the 1960s, to below 10,000 in the late 1990s (Goldberg, 1971: 262; Donn, 1988b). There is little that unlicensed seafarers can do to counter job losses, but licensed officers can sometimes find work aboard FOC vessels, which often choose some of their officers from among the well-trained seafarers of the traditional maritime countries (Gillis, 1996). Having despaired of competing with FOC, crew-of-convenience operations, some of the traditional maritime nations began to adopt policies in the 1980s based on the premise that "if you can't beat them, join them." This gave rise to the establishment of "second registries" in traditional maritime states. These second registries, available generally only for international shipping, typically impose levels of taxation and regulation similar to FOC registries and generally allow the use of crews-of-convenience. Norway created the prototype second registry with the creation of the Norwegian International Ship Registry in 1987. Other traditional maritime nations such as the Netherlands and the United Kingdom have relaxed or removed restrictions on crew nationality (ITF, 1999c: 27).

The stateless nature of the industry makes the maritime multinational enterprise uniquely different from that in manufacturing or services. First, the movement or transfer of "production" abroad by ocean shipping MNCs is a virtual paper transaction, as FOC vessels are easily and quickly flagged and reflagged. Foreign direct investment (FDI) of this kind, is a simple matter of registration, sometimes with a law office or company not even located in the flag state. As described earlier, other than to impose minimal standards and taxes, flag state "host" countries rarely have anything to do with foreign-owned FOC fleets, and there is no physical presence of the MNC in the host country.

Second, whereas most foreign-owned subsidiaries largely employ host country nationals and executives and managers from the home headquarters, employees of FOC fleets are often nationals from a third country or, quite commonly, nationals of several third countries. Lastly, foreign-owned subsidiaries operate under the jurisdiction and laws of the country in which they are physically located. FOC vessels, in contrast, operate on the open sea except as they temporarily enter foreign ports. Many vessels literally never enter the physical jurisdiction of the nations where they are registered. Only at various times and for various purposes are FOC vessels subject to the jurisdiction of international law, the laws of port states, or the laws of flag states. As described later, there is a wide disparity between the laws and regulations governing the workplaces of foreign-owned subsidiaries within nations and those of FOC vessels outside national jurisdictions.

In summary, many considerations that are important in determining where to locate foreign manufacturing or service sites (see Chapter 4 in this volume) have no influence on the choices made by multinational shipping companies regarding registry of their vessels. Indeed, the only relevant economic factors are differences in taxation and the convenience afforded shipping companies across regulatory regimes (that of flag states and those of the countries whose cargoes companies wish to transport).

An example of a maritime MNC may provide a sense of the international dynamics of the industry. Take, for instance, the U.S.-based Crowley Maritime Corporation, which owns a vessel called the *Sea Wave*. In 1996 that vessel was registered in Greece. The paper corporation that serves as the formal owner, however, is based (at least technically) in Liberia. The company that operates the vessel is Swiss. Although some crew members come from Greece because the Greek registry requires that they do, most of the crew of 21 come from countries other than the United States, Switzerland, or Liberia. In similar fashion, Crowley owns and operates another 28 vessels, which are registered in the Bahamas, the Cayman Islands, Chile, China, Cyprus, Denmark, Germany, Greece, Liberia, Norway, and Panama, as well as in the United States (Gillis, 1996). Nothing about this arrangement is unusual in the maritime industry, whereas it would be rare to find a foreign-owned manufacturing or service subsidiary this "international" anywhere in the world.

INTERNATIONAL STANDARDS, REGULATION, AND OVERSIGHT OF MARITIME EMPLOYMENT

The United Nations (UN) and two of its agencies have played the lead roles in setting standards against which the international maritime industry is expected to comply. Among UN conventions is the UN Law of the Sea convention, which has established a set of responsibilities for flag states, including safety rules. As such conventions are voluntary in nature, however, they "contain no mechanism to really enforce implementation by those governments party to the conventions" (Bruce, 1997). Similarly, under the auspices of the UN, the International Labor Organization (ILO) has long been involved in setting minimum pay and working conditions aboard ships. ILO minimum standards, however, are typically very low. For instance, effective January 1, 1998, the minimum monthly pay for an able seaman (the key occupational grade for nonofficers) was raised from $385 to $435, and the maximum workday set to 14 hours (Zarocostas, 1996). There is no effective mechanism, however, to enforce these minimum standards.

Another UN agency, the International Maritime Organization (IMO), establishes voluntary minimum standards for training, certification, leave time, and watchkeeping. In an attempt to improve training standards and to reduce the number of accidents attributable to human error (the primary cause of maritime accidents), the IMO recently adopted a more stringent set of standards called the "Standards of Training, Certification and Watchkeeping" (STCW). Effective in early 1998, these standards require countries that supply maritime labor to be accredited by the IMO. A number of major suppliers of maritime labor, including the Philippines, however, had considerable difficulty meeting the STCW standards (Bangberg, 1997). Concerned with the lack of compliance, officials from the European Community, Australia, Britain, and Canada have proposed to the IMO that various sanctions (including expulsion from the IMO) be taken against flag states that fail to enforce international standards (Porter, 1996c, 1997). To date, there have been no such sanctions established, as the many countries that have operated flags-of-convenience or feel they might choose to do so in the future have resisted. Thus, the only consequence in most cases for states that fail to enforce these standards is negative publicity. Ironically, that publicity can have positive effects for flag states seeking ship operators in search of low-cost/low-regulation flags for their vessels.

During the 1980s, many nations came to recognize that neither UN standards nor national regulations were proving effective, leaving many unsafe vessels and many vessels characterized by abysmal employment conditions operating on the high seas. In an attempt to rectify such conditions, members of the international community took steps to enhance the role of port state control. Specifically, in 1982, a group of 14 Western European nations (now 19, including Canada) signed a Memorandum on Port State Control. This memorandum gave national authorities in the ports that vessels entered greater authority to inspect and detain vessels for failure to meet minimal safety, environmental, and working conditions standards. Through this agreement, an active program of inspections of the vessels visiting ports was instituted.

The results have been both enlightening and disheartening. By the early 1990s, the 16 countries coordinating the port state control system were detaining growing numbers of vessels, reaching over 1,800 in a given year (Porter, 1995a, 1996a; *Blue Book*, Chap. 1). Safety violations and unsanitary crew quarters were the most commonly cited violations. FOC vessels were typically detained the most often, including ships registered in Panama, Malta, Cyprus, Honduras, St. Vincent, and Grenadines (Porter, 1995b, 1996b). Widespread violations of standards were made evident from a three-month "inspection blitz" undertaken in European ports in late 1997. These inspections focused on crew living and working conditions. Some 25 percent of all the vessels inspected "failed at least one of the internationally agreed minimum standards." Of these, approximately 35 percent of deficiencies were so serious that ships were detained or their masters required to correct them before leaving port (ITF, 1999c: 25). The difficulty encountered in tracing the actual owners of many of these vessels has been particularly frustrating to port state control authorities.

In addition to the efforts by the UN, its agencies, and port authorities to ensure that minimum standards are observed by FOC fleets, the International

Transport Workers Federation (ITF) has provided some oversight and sought to pressure FOC operators into observing minimum workplace conditions. The ITF, an international trade secretariat bringing together transportation unions from around the world, has long been concerned about the proliferation of FOC fleets. The ITF has expressed several concerns about FOC fleets, including the loss of employment opportunities in the economically developed maritime nations, the exploitation of Third World seafarers, the use of Third World seafarers as leverage to reduce wages and diminish working conditions on the fleets of developed countries, and poor health and safety conditions on ships.

The ITF's long campaign against FOC fleets has had the ultimate goal of forcing vessel owners to flag their ships in the nations in which they live. Since most vessel owners are nationals of developed countries, and since the national flag fleets of such countries are overwhelming unionized, this would effectively unionize the large majority of the international fleet vessels. While the ITF has had little success in achieving that goal, it has had some modest success in forcing FOC operators who have no collective bargaining agreements with legitimate national unions to bargain with the ITF, to meet certain minimum conditions, and to contribute to a fund maintained by the ITF itself for the benefit of seafarers (Northrup and Rowan, 1983; Donn and Phelan, 1991). The ITF also attempts to enforce international health and safety standards.

With regard to health and safety and other working conditions, the ITF has carried out a campaign to alert seafarers, governments, and the public to what it sees as the myriad of deficiencies associated with FOC fleets. For example, in 1999, the ITF claimed that the Panamanian fleet was number one in the world: number one "for maritime casualties," number one "for port state control detentions," number one "for deficiencies in certification, safety, navigation, pollution and operations," number one "for cheating seafarers," number one "for ships abandoned, low salaries, substandard accommodation and victimization and unfair dismissal of seafarers," number one "for poor seafarer living conditions," and number one "for neglecting their obligations to seafarers" (ITF, 1999b).

Given the disparity between what Third World seafarers can earn aboard even the low-wage FOC vessels and what they can earn onshore, crews-of-convenience often tolerate quite extraordinary conditions. As one can readily imagine, without protection against management reprisal, FOC seafarers are generally reluctant to complain about substandard work conditions or mistreatment to authorities or to the ITF, let alone attempt to join or form unions. Consequently, lacking international standards that are effectively enforced and lacking extensive union coverage of FOC vessels, the effects of the ITF on improving the work conditions suffered by crews-of-convenience remain quite limited.

CONSEQUENCES OF AN UNREGULATED INDUSTRY

Neither systematic data on working conditions nor detailed case study analyses are available for constructing a detailed profile of working conditions and workplace practices on FOC vessels. In order to provide the reader with a sense of the unsafe and frequently deplorable workplace conditions and practices on FOC vessels, I necessarily rely heavily on various press reports and stories. Most of these accounts arise out of reporter investigations of accidents, missing vessels, and abandonment of ships and crews at port. In conjunction with information obtained from other sources, I attempt to construct a profile that highlights the too-often-serious disregard for seafarers on FOC fleets.

Many more people are killed in ship mishaps than in airplane crashes in a typical year (Porter, 1996c). During any given year, over 1,000 people die at sea, although the typical loss (which involves the sinking or disappearance of a cargo ship with a crew of approximately 20 mostly Third World seafarers) gets little press notice in the United States. Whereas ferry sinkings attract substantial public attention because of the large loss of life, and tanker accidents attract significant public attention because of their implications for serious environmental damage, the large majority of vessel losses involve older, smaller general cargo or bulk cargo ships. In 1996 (the last year for which complete figures are available) 120 vessels were lost, more than 2 per week (ITF, 1999a).

The ITF claims that ship casualties are disproportionately found among FOC vessels. Panamanian-flag vessels suffered the most losses in 1996 (and for all of the four previous years). Since the Panamanian flag is the largest in the world, this is not surprising, but the ITF claims Panamanian ship losses exceed its fraction of the world fleet, as do losses by the fleets of Cyprus, Malta, St. Vincent, and Honduras (ITF, 1999a).

Poorly maintained vessels are involved in a disproportionate share of maritime casualties for several reasons. "Ships that don't spend money and time to ensure decent living and safety conditions don't attract quality crews. As a result, those ships, already maintained poorly, usually are operated poorly as well. Eighty percent of ship accidents are due to human error. And when those accidents happen, they endanger lives" (Porter, 1995b). In addition, the use of mixed, multilingual crews has given rise to increasing instances of cultural misunderstandings, as well as outright failures of communication. That is, seafarers from different cultures, especially relatively new seafarers without a thorough understanding of maritime discipline, react in different and unexpected ways to authority. Indeed, at times misunderstandings among crew members and between officers and their crews "have even resulted in near-mutinies or threats to the safety of the vessel" (Magnier, 1995). Although in the words of one vessel captain, "it isn't so difficult to communicate. We'll use hand gestures in difficult circumstances" (Gillis, 1996), one can readily imagine that in a crisis (e.g., arising from a fire on board or a major storm) miscommunication could prove dangerous, if not fatal.

Another consequence of insufficient regulation that all too frequently strikes crews on FOC vessels is abandonment. In a typical such scenario, the crew of an older vessel that belongs to a small (often one-ship) company finds that the ship is arrested in some foreign port, perhaps because of failure to pay its crew the agreed- upon wages (or sometimes any wages at all), because of lack of food or water or inadequate safety equipment, or because of an unpaid debt unrelated to the seafarers on board. The owner, who may have few assets or none within easy reach of the authorities of the port state or who may not be easily identified, will simply abandon the vessel, leaving the crew aboard ship with little or no food, no money, and no way home. In other instances, the owner can be identified but refuses to comply with the demands of the port authorities and/or the crew. It is not unusual for crews to be stranded on such vessels in a foreign port for months.

For example, the Filipino crew of a Japanese-owned, but Panamanian-registered, vessel protested the failure of the owner to pay them at the ITF approved rate. The vessel had initially been inspected in a Japanese port by an ITF inspector who found it substandard. The crew demanded not only that the vessel be brought up to standard but also that they receive back pay and be permitted membership in the ITF. For four months the crew refused to sail the ship, with the owner cutting off all pay in June and cutting off food supplies in August, leaving the crew dependent on charity and the ITF. The owner sued in a Japanese court in September to force the crew to leave the ship, but the court refused and instead insisted on a negotiated settlement. Eventually, the owner agreed to a 50 percent pay increase to bring the seafarers up to ITF pay levels. However, the seafarers were not enrolled in the ITF, the pay increase was not made retroactive, and the wage increase applied only until the seafarers' contracts expired a few months later in January, when they would certainly be replaced by another crew (Kutota, 1995a, 1995b).

Perhaps the most extreme approach to escaping debts or obligations by vessel operators is to report that a ship has been lost, only to have it reappear, repainted with a new name and identity. The original crew has likely been abandoned, if not thrown overboard. Although hard to comprehend and although documentation of cases in which crew members have been thrown overboard has not been forthcoming, there have been cases in which stowaways have been ordered overboard to face almost certain death.[1] Crew members who dare report such tragedies find themselves without assistance or support and certainly without jobs (Malcolmson, 1997).

Finally, hundreds of cases of abuse of the rights of seafarers have been documented, ranging from the irritating to the life-threatening (Chapman, 1992). Most of these abuses take place on FOC vessels. For instance, a seafarer was told that he would be required to leave his vessel in an upcoming port, despite having seven months remaining on the contract that he had signed. The shipowner was Greek, the registry was Cyprus, and the port was Indian. The seafarer shared none of these nationalities, but none of the authorities in any of three countries were interested in compelling the vessel captain to honor the seafarer's contract (Chapman, 1992: 41). Many other cases simply depict cruelty. For example, an ITF port inspector in Seattle reported the case of a Panamanian registered vessel that docked in November 1998. Among other abuses, the inspector discovered crew members had been hit by the captain with his helmet and that the captain had locked up the fresh water supply (Rahner,

1999). Although many cases of abuse have raised questions of appropriate state jurisdiction, more have been marked by the lack of interest by any authorities that might potentially assert jurisdiction. In summation, the stateless maritime corporation faces no state to regulate its behavior of employees or the conditions of work. The result is too often abuse of seafarers, which, if not ubiquitous, is undeniably widespread.

SUMMARY AND CONCLUSION

The growth in both the registry of FOC fleets and crew-of-convenience workforces from Third World countries has allowed multinational shipping companies to escape the reach of regulation and oversight of shipping and workplace conditions otherwise imposed by traditional maritime nations or negotiated by national unions. The various international workplace standards set by the ILO and IMO are not backed by the necessary oversight and enforcement required to ensure that the employment and working conditions of FOC vessels meet minimum international standards. The only successful effort at oversight and enforcement of minimum standards has been the occasional concerted and coordinated inspection sweeps by 19 Western European countries (including Canada), which have imposed their port authority rights to investigate and retain vessels.

Furthermore, the inability of unions to organize crew-of-convenience workers and, in turn, negotiate improved employment and working conditions denies these seafarers the alternative course of collective action. Faced by the near certain loss of employment were they to complain publicly about living and working conditions on board, crew-of-convenience seafarers tolerate substandard conditions to keep their low-paying jobs, but jobs that pay them significantly more than they can obtain otherwise onshore in their home countries. Although the ITF has attempted to pressure FOC fleets into meeting some minimum standards, its successes (albeit many) remain relatively limited. In the absence of enforceable international regulations or extensive union representation across FOC fleets, the relative power exercised by the ITF and its member organizations is simply inadequate for the enormity of the task.

Largely out of the reach of enforceable international regulation and union coverage, FOC vessel owners and operators have been relatively free to set the terms and conditions of employment for crew-of-convenience labor forces. Although a thorough and systematic accounting of these conditions is not available, the evidence available allows us to piece together a limited profile. As previously discussed, that profile highlights what would appear to observers from advanced economies as highly substandard workplaces and working conditions, too often marked by exceptionally unhealthy and unsafe environments, extraordinarily long hours and low wages, unchecked management reprisal, and abandonment of crews.

Although the global dilemma faced in the international maritime industry in many ways parallels that faced by global production more generally, it is exacerbated by circumstances unique to the maritime industry. That is, the wide gulf between wealthier, advanced nations and poorer, less-developed countries has created equally wide disparities in employment and working conditions. MNCs seeking to exploit this disparity have ample opportunity to do so whether they are engaged in onshore production or offshore shipping. Given the lack of either national or international standards, oversight, and enforceable regulation in the maritime industry, however, the opportunity to exploit Third World seafarers is greater than for shoreside workers. Out of the eye of the general public and consumers of products shipped to ports worldwide, moreover, there is little social consciousness of the employment and working conditions on the high seas. It will likely take such visibility and consciousness, however, to muster the social pressure apparently necessary for the international community to monitor the stateless nature of FOC fleets and to fully enforce minimum, internationally accepted standards.

NOTE

1.These extreme actions appear motivated by policies that hold the vessel operating company responsible for the cost of repatriating stowaways who arrive in port on their vessels. The courts of any nation that might otherwise be willing to punish offending companies, however, lack jurisdiction.

REFERENCES

Bangberg, P. T. (1997). "Training Seafarers Leaves Asians at Sea." *Journal of Commerce*, December 5.
Bate, A. (1998). "Bulk Ship Stranded in Vancouver Since '97, to Be Sold to Pay Crew." *Journal of Commerce,* June 8.
Blue Book. (1999). Paris Memorandum on Port State Control.
Bruce, D. (1997). "Mediocrity Rules Safety at Sea." *Journal of Commerce*, December 4.
Chapman, P. K. (1992). *Trouble on Board: The Plight of International Seafarers.* Ithaca, NY: ILR Press.
Donn, C. B. (1994). "National Regulation of International Industry: Industrial Relations in the Maritime Industry." *International Journal of Employment Studies* 2 (2), pp. 211–27.
Donn, C. B. (1988a). "Flag of Convenience Registry and Industrial Relations: The Internationalization of National Flag Fleets." *Proceedings*, 25th Annual Meeting, Canadian Industrial Relations Association, pp. 139–50.
Donn, C. B. (1988b). "Foreign Competition, Technological Change, and the Decline in U.S. Maritime Employment." *Transportation Journal* 27 (4), pp. 31–41.
Donn, C. B. and Phelan, G. (1991). "Australian Maritime Unions and Flag of Convenience Vessels." *Journal of Industrial Relations* 33 (3), pp. 329–39.
Freudmann, A. and Baldwin, T. (1998). "Liberia Taps DC Lawyers to Handle Registry." *Journal of Commerce*, December 21.
Gillis, C. (1996). "A Tale of Two Ships." *American Shipper*, July, pp. 60–68.

Goldberg, J. P. (1971). "Modernization in the Maritime Industry: Labor Management Adjustments to Technological Change." In Levinson, H., et al *Collective Bargaining and Technological Change in American Transportation* Evanston, Il: Transportation Center at Northwestern University, pp. 245–419.

International Transport Workers Federation (ITF). Press Release, (1999a). "Cordigliera: What Price an Indian Seafarer's Life?" *ITF Home Page* (www.itf.org.uk/SECTIONS/MAR/Cordig.htm), March 3.

International Transport Workers Federation (ITF). (1999b). "Proud to Be an FOC?" *ITF Home Page* (www.itf.org.uk/SECTIONS/MAR/Cordig.htm), March 3.

International Transport Workers Federation (ITF). (1999c). *Seafarers Bulletin*, no.13.

Kutota, C. (1995a). "Striking Crew Detains Ship in Tokyo." *Journal of Commerce*, September 24.

Kutota, C. (1995b). "Japanese Shipowner, Filipino Crew End 4-Month Standoff over Wages." *Journal of Commerce*, November 30.

Magnier, M. (1995). "Captains Work Overtime to Prevent Culture Clashe." *Journal of Commerce*, August 7.

Malcolmson, S. L. (1997). "The Unquiet Ship." *The New Yorker*, January 20, 72–81.

McElroy, C. (1995). "Liberian Shipping Fleet Grows in Spite of War." *Journal of Commerce*, March 3.

Northrup, H. R. and Rowan, R. L. (1983). *The International Transport Workers' Federation and Flag of Convenience Shipping*. Philadelphia: Industrial Research Unit, Wharton School.

Porter, J. (1995a). "Ship Detentions Set Record in Europe, Canada." *Journal of Commerce*, July 26, 1A, 8A.

Porter, J. (1995b). "Chain Reaction: Wretched Conditions Compromise Safety." *Journal of Commerce*, August 8, 1A, 5B.

Porter, J. (1996a). "Bad-Ship Lists Found Useful But Where Are Shipowners?" *Journal of Commerce*, June 28.

Porter, J. (1996b). "Vessel Detentions Increased in '95." *Journal of Commerce*, July 11.

Porter, J. (1996c). "Many More Killed at Sea than in Air Crashes" *Journal of Commerce*, August 6.

Porter, J. (1997). "IMO Urged to Get Errant States Out." *Journal of Commerce*, May 29, 1B, 8B.

Rahner, M. (1999). "Crews Find an Advocate in Labor Representative." *seattletimes.com*, November 26.

Zarocostas, J. (1996). "ILO Conventions Benefit Seafarers." *Journal of Commerce*, October 23.

15

Carrot or Stick? How MNCs Have Reacted to the European Works Council Directive

Trevor Bain and Kim Hester

The culmination of a 20 year effort to require multinational companies (MNCs) to disclose information and consult with their employees on a European-wide basis, the European Works Council Directive (94/95/EC) (ETUI, 1994) was issued by the Council of Ministers of the European Union on September 22, 1994. With the initial exclusion of the United Kingdom and Northern Ireland, the directive was made binding on all other European Union (EU) countries and several remaining countries of the European Economic Area. Under the directive, MNCs and their employees were given the option of either voluntarily establishing structures and processes for information exchange and dialogue before September 1996 under Article 13 or negotiating structures and processes by September 1999 as mandated under Article 6.

The literature has only recently begun to examine the structure, processes, and success of these European transnational works councils and then only in regard to the earliest voluntary agreements. The objective of this chapter is to assess the choices made by MNCs between those that took the "carrot" by voluntarily establishing European Works Councils (EWCs) and those that took the "stick" by negotiating mandatory EWCs. In making this comparison, we first provide a review of the EU Directive, including an analysis of issues arising out of the directive. Second, we compare the structures of a sample of 50 voluntary (Article 13) agreements and 50 mandated (Article 6) agreements. Here, we draw a profile of the two forms of EWCs based on country of ownership and governing national law, on structure and processes, and on the substantive issues addressed by the councils. Third, we frame the potential benefits and costs associated with EWCs as perceived by companies and employee representatives and, how these benefits and costs are likely to differ under Articles 13 and 6 and, in turn, address why the parties would choose to establish voluntary or mandatory EWCs. Based on our comparison of EWCs and the extant literature, we conclude by assessing the implications of these decisions on the longer-term prospects of the underlying purpose of the directive being realized.

THE EWC DIRECTIVE

For a long time it looked as though an EWC Directive stood little or no chance of ever being passed. Employer groups such as the Union of Industries of the European Community, as well as individual MNCs, particularly those based in the United Kingdom and United States, vigorously resisted passage of any such directive. Initial efforts at creating the existing EWC Directive date back some 20 years. The Treaty of Rome (1957), which sets out the powers of the EU, confined the social policy jurisdiction of the EU to social protection related to work and employment. (See Addison and Seibert, 1991, 1994 on the evolution of EU social policy.) Even within these restrictions, social policy has always had a narrow interpretation, primarily related to freedom of movement, an integrated European labor market, and equal pay for women and men (Streeck, 1997a). The treaty, as it pertains to employment and workplace legislation, moreover, requires the unanimous vote of the Council of Ministers.

In October 1980, the so-called Vredeling Directive was presented to the Council of Ministers. The draft directive was based on the assumption that important decisions of multinational groups of companies were generally made in the head offices of the groups and often resulted in serious negative consequences for employees. Workplace rights and mechanisms for influencing head-office decisions by employees and their representatives were limited, however, to a large extent by national legislation in MNCs' home countries. Existing codes of conduct applicable to MNCs already issued by the Organization for Economic Cooperation and Development (OECD) and International Labor Organization (ILO), furthermore, were regarded as inadequate since they were based on *voluntary* guidelines. To overcome these effects and limitations, the Vredeling draft directive required MNCs to share information at least every six months with their subsidiaries, in particular with regard to policies relating to plant closures, transfers of work, plant reductions and related expenses or changes to plant organization, and compensation. The draft directive was vigorously resisted by employers, especially a clause that would enable workers to deal directly with their parent company, regardless of its geographic location, in the event that a subsidiary did not fulfill its obligations to provide information.

The draft was never actually rejected but was ultimately watered down by 217 proposed amendments stemming, in large part, from mounted resistance from U.K. employers. Although the Vredeling Directive faced vigorous opposition by some, it can be viewed, nevertheless, as a clear signal that the EU was determined to promote European-wide employee consultation across MNCs within its borders. Finally, in late 1991, EU ministers met in Maastricht to address social policy, including the Vredeling Directive, an effort again strongly resisted by the United Kingdom. To overcome U.K. opposition, the ministers of the 12 member states agreed that directives could be approved and take effect with only 11 votes in favor of passage (commonly called the "U.K. social opt-out"). Under the Maastricht settlement called the *Protocol on Social Policy*, EU social policy would thereafter be dealt with, not in the Treaty of Rome itself but in an attachment that need not be signed by the United Kingdom.

The EWC Directive that eventually emerged from the Maastricht meetings applies to MNCs with at least 1,000 employees and operations with at least 150 employees in two or more EU or European Economic Area (EEA) member states, with the exclusion of the United Kingdom. A later directive (97/74/EU), however, imposed the same requirements on the United Kingdom beginning in December 1999. In spite of its name, the EWC Directive does not necessarily require that a works council-type body be established, only that some structure and process be established for the purposes of informing and consulting employees across borders. The ministers, furthermore, envisioned a process that would take several years before all affected MNCs would be compelled to comply. Estimates of the number of MNCS covered by the directive range from 860 to 1,844 (Hall, et al., 1995; Lecher and Platzer, 1998).

Unlike most other directives, the EWC Directive was designed to encourage voluntary compliance, allowing the social partners considerable flexibility in negotiating agreements covering procedures for information sharing and consultation (Bellace, 1997). As envisioned by the Council of Ministers, nonetheless, EWC representatives were expected to represent employees in information sharing and consultation processes with management when decisions affecting employees were taken in a EU member state other than that in which they were employed. Information to be shared included changes in company structure; economic and financial situation; probable development of the business, including production and sales; the situation and probable trend of employment and investments; substantial changes regarding organizations and introduction of new working methods or production processes; transfers of production, mergers, cutbacks, or closures of undertakings; and collective redundancies.

Under Article 6, the EU Directive outlined the procedures for the initial establishment of "special negotiating bodies" consisting of employee representatives whose primary goals were to negotiate with central management regarding the establishment of mandated EWCs. These special negotiating bodies were established within the following general framework. Individual member states would determine the actual methods used for the election and appointment of the members of the body; each member state in which the community-scale undertaking has one or more establishments would be represented by at least one member, with supplementary members in proportion to the number of employees working in the establishments; the special negotiating body would have a minimum of 17 members; and certain expenses relating to the negotiations would be borne by central management. However, the special negotiating bodies could by two-thirds majority votes choose not to open negotiations or to end them and, thus, choose not to create EWCs.

The directive also contained instructions on the content of the negotiations between central management and the special negotiating bodies. Both parties were expected to negotiate in a spirit of cooperation, with the expressed goal of agreement on the detailed arrangements for implementation of the directive. Specifically, the two parties would jointly determine six major components within agreements reached: (1) which establishments in the EU would be covered by the negotiated agreement, (2) the composition of the EWC in number of members, allocation of seats, and terms of office, (3) the functions and procedures for the information-sharing and consultation process, (4) the venue, frequency, and duration of scheduled meetings, (5) the financial and material resources to be allocated to the councils, and (6) the duration of the agreement and the procedure for negotiation and subsequent renegotiations.

The EU Directive also addressed a number of other important issues. The official determination of the thresholds for the size of company workforces would be based on the average number of employees, including part-time employees, employed in the EU during the previous two-year period. In addition, a confidentiality clause would be included in the agreements to address the issue of company proprietary information. An important inclusion was also the assurance of protection for representatives serving either on the special negotiating body or in the EWC over rights, wages, and assignment of duties during the performance of their official duties under the directive. Finally, in the event of noncompliance, member states were required to provide the necessary administrative or judicial procedures for enforcement.

To encourage MNCs to establish EWCs early, the directive offered a "carrot." Article 13 in the directive allowed for the establishment of voluntary agreements, which could be negotiated within a two-year period (September 22, 1994, to September 22, 1996). Under Article 13, companies that established voluntary agreements by September 1996 providing for transnational information and consultation with their employees were not required to establish new agreements with employees if, indeed, similar mechanisms were already in place that addressed the same core issues. For example, an MNC that already had a group-level works council could approach that body with the goal of concluding an Article 13 agreement. Alternatively, any interested group of at least 100 workers from two countries or their representatives could initiate the creation of a special negotiating body with the purpose of creating EWCs. Whichever kind of approach was taken, Article 13 agreements, nonetheless, had to cover the entire workforce and provide for transnational information exchange and consultation. The directive, however, did not specify which employee representatives MNCs should negotiate with, which opened up the possibility of MNCs initiating human resource consultation strategies separate and distinctly different from EWCs.

The "stick" arises from Article 6 and the supplementary Annex, requiring that after September 22, 1996, Article 6 mandatory agreements had to be negotiated. The directive set out a series of requirements in the Annex that would apply automatically after three years and would have to be included in agreements. These agreements were to be initiated by management or 100 employees from at least two member states who could initiate a special negotiating body. Article 6, however, offers only general guidance as to the content of mandatory agreements. It states that the agreement has to name the undertaking to be covered, the composition of the EWC, the number of members, the allocation of seats, and the terms of office. Procedures for participation, information exchange, and consultation, on the other hand, were left to the parties to determine.

Only if the central office of an MNC did not commence negotiations within six months of September 1996 or had not received a request to negotiate a mandatory agreement would the "Subsidiary Requirements" in the Annex to the directive go into effect. The requirements in the Annex placed on MNC subsidiaries are the only requirements delineated in the directive. Lacking any detail, however, most obligations were left quite open-ended. Indeed, the information to be shared and which issues were to be consulted on with the MNC employees were confined to a single paragraph. If negotiations did not begin or were not concluded in three years, the subsidiary requirements would take effect as of September 22, 1999, and the outline of an agreement would be imposed on the MNC.

EWCs have the right to meet with central management once a year. It is to be informed and consulted with on the basis of a report drawn up by the central management regarding the progress and prospects of any business of community-scale undertaking (or community-scale groups of undertakings). Meetings should relate, in particular, to the structure, economic, and financial situation of the company; the probable development of the business and of production and sales; the situation and probable trend of employment, investments, and substantial changes concerning the organization; the introduction of new working methods or production processes; transfers of production, mergers, cutbacks, or closures of undertakings, and establishments or important parts thereof; and collective redundancies. Local management should also be informed on such matters.

COMPARISON OF VOLUNTARY AND MANDATORY EWCS

Sample

We next compare the voluntary (Article 13) and mandatory (Article 6) EWCs (Bain and Hester, 2000). The data used are drawn from the inventory of EWCs compiled by the European Trade Union Institution (ETUI) in cooperation with seven research institutes in the EU.[1] Of the 587 agreements included in the ETUI database, 534 were concluded before September 1996, and 53 were concluded between September 1996 and December 1998. Additional agreements have been concluded since that date; however, the largest number was concluded before September 1996. For purposes of our comparison, we selected the first 50 voluntary agreements and the first 50 mandatory agreements listed in the ETUI database, which are listed in alphabetical order. Because some information is missing from the agreements, our comparisons are not always based on 100 agreements. Although we did not take a strictly random sample of agreements (and, hence, cannot claim that our sample is fully representative of the total number of agreements), based on the distribution of home countries in our sample and that of the full database (ETUI, 2000), it appears that our sample is fairly representative. Specifically, the 17 countries represented in our sample of EWC agreements (Table 15.1) account for 89 percent of the countries represented in the 587 EWC agreements included in the full ETUI database. Although we have no reason to believe that the first 50 voluntary agreements are not representative of all voluntary agreements, it is important to note that the mandatory EWC agreements that we are able to examine at this point are the earliest ones negotiated (between October 1996 and December 1998), well before the September 1999 deadline.[2]

Structure of EWCs

Country of Ownership.

Across our sample of 100 EWC agreements, 86 were negotiated with MNCs based in nine countries, and the remaining were negotiated with MNCs based in six other countries. As reported in Table 15.1, we find that MNCs from several countries were more likely to have negotiated either voluntary or mandatory agreements. Among those showing preferences for establishing the earlier voluntary over the later mandatory agreements were France (6 voluntary and 3 mandatory), Germany (10 voluntary and 4 mandatory), and the United States (6 voluntary and 3 mandatory). Among those showing preferences for negotiating mandatory over voluntary agreements are Belgium (5 mandatory and 2 voluntary), Finland (3 mandatory and 1 voluntary), Italy (4 mandatory and 1 voluntary), and the Netherlands (7 mandatory and no voluntary agreements).

Country of Governing Law.

As required by the EWC Directive, the parties to agreements were to stipulate a country whose laws would govern in the event of noncompliance. In two cases in our sample, however, the parties simply designated the host countries of subsidiaries as having the governing laws. As reported in Table 15.1, some preference has been shown for designating the laws of countries other than the one of ownership. In particular, whereas there were only 3 Irish-owned MNCs with EWCs in our sample, 8 EWCs designated Ireland as the governing state. Similarly, 11 EWCs designated the Netherlands as the governing state, although only 7 MNCs were Dutch-owned. Of those EWCs designating Ireland and the Netherlands as the governing states, the large majority of EWCs were negotiated as mandatory agreements. In sharp contrast, whereas there were 20 U.K.-owned MNCs in our sample, only 11 EWCs designated the United Kingdom as the governing member state. Not surprisingly (given geography), only 3 EWCs designated the United States as the governing nation, even though 9 MNCs are U.S.-owned enterprises. Of those 11 EWCs designating the United Kingdom as the governing state, the large marjority (9 of 11) were negotiated as voluntary agreements. It appears, therefore, that some EWCs found benefit in designating countries as governing member states that differ from the country of ownership.

In addition, some distinction was found in our sample regarding whether or not EWCs were more or less likely to select as their governing law countries those countries mandating works councils (either through national law or centralized labor-management agreements). Of those EWCs that concluded voluntary Article 13 agreements, 73 percent selected countries with mandated works councils as their governing law country. In comparison, of those EWCs that concluded mandatory Article 6 agreements, 82 percent selected countries with mandated works councils as their governing law country.

EWC Structure and Design.

Based on a review of provisions describing the structure and design of EWCs, we find no substantial differences between voluntary and mandatory EWCs. With respect to size, EWCs are fairly wide-ranging, with the smallest having 7 members and the largest having 54 in our sample of 100. Most included between 10 and 25 members, the average being 22.4 for voluntary agreements and 19.4 members for manadatory agreements. Members generally serve for 3–4 years, although in several cases members were scheduled to serve only for 1–2 years and in one case for 5 years. The average years of service is 3.4 years for voluntary agreements and 3.8 years for mandatory agreements. In nearly every agreement, the official designated meeting venue was the corporate headquarters of the MNC's home country. Only one or two annual meetings were scheduled across all EWCs. A slightly larger proportion (36 percent) of voluntary agreements than mandatory agreements (28 percent) scheduled two regular annual meetings. In addition, however, most agreements included a

Table 15.1
Country of Ownership and Governing Law by Article 13
and Article 6 Agreements

Country	Country of Ownership		Designated Governing Country	
	Article 13	Article 6	Article 13	Article 6
Austria	2	2	1	2
Belgium	2	5	4	5
Canada	1	1	0	0
Denmark	0	1	0	1
Finland	1	3	1	3
France	6	3	7	4
Germany	10	4	11	4
Ireland	1	2	2	6
Italy	0	4	0	4
Luxembourg	1	0	2	0
Netherlands	0	7	1	10
Norway	0	1	0	1
Spain	0	1	0	1
Sweden	6	5	5	6
Switzerland	2	0	1	0
U.K.	12	8	9	2
U.S.	6	3	2	1
Total	50	50	48	50

provision for holding nonscheduled meetings that could be called if "unusual circumstances" so warranted (but very few describe what these circumstances would entail).

The lengths of EWC agreements are wide-ranging, the shortest set for three months and the longest for 10 years, but the majority ranging between 2 and 4 years in duration. Among voluntary agreements, there was a greater tendency to conclude short agreements of six months (28 percent), whereas among mandatory agreements, 46 percent reached 4-year agreements. The average length of agreements is 3.0 years for voluntary and 3.3 years for the mandatory agreements. Included in virtually every agreement was a clause specifying that either side could terminate the EWC by giving notice, usually after an initial six-month period commencing with the official ratification of the agreement by the two parties. There were few requirements placed on eligibility for election or appointment to the EWCs. Only in about one-fourth of both the voluntary and mandatory agreements did the parties stipulate length of tenure with companies, ranging from a minimum of six months to a maximum of 3 years.

In three of the voluntary agreements, employee representatives were required to be union representatives. No such union status requirement was found in the mandatory agreements. Union influence or involvement in the EWCs, nonetheless, is apparent in a significant proportion of agreements when such influence is gauged more broadly. Including agreements in which union representatives were involved in the negotiation of agreements or were signatories to agreements or were listed as available experts, we found that unions had influence in 37 percent of voluntary agreements and 22 percent of mandatory agreements.

Finally, in most agreements, some provision was included specifying the language adopted for deliberations. In roughly 60 percent of both voluntary and mandatory EWCs, the parties selected English. In three of the voluntary agreements, the parties further agreed that only candidates proficient in English were eligible to serve on the given EWCs. In a larger proportion of mandatory EWC agreements (40 percent) than voluntary agreements (24 percent), however, central management agreed to provide the necessary language training for EWC members needing and requesting such training. Of those EWCs not providing language training, necessary translation services were to be provided to assist members in fulfilling their official duties and responsibilities.

Substantive Issues.

The EWC Directive actually says very little about the substantive issues on which the companies are to share information and consult with employee representatives. The general statement in the EWC Directive states that:

The European Works Council, must, in order to fulfill the objective of this Directive, be kept informed and consulted on the activities of the undertakings or group of undertakings so that it may assess the possible impact on employees' interests in at least two different Member States; whereas, to that end, the undertaking or controlling undertaking must be required to communicate to the employees' appointed representatives general information concerning the interests of employees and information relating more specifically to those aspects of the activities of the undertaking or group of undertakings which affect employees' interests. (ETUI, 1994: 3)

In addition, a brief statement is provided in the directive's Annex under Item 2, which lists the issues that central management should report to EWCs. "The meeting shall relate in particular to the structure, economic and financial situation, the probable development of the business and of production and sales, the situation and probable trend of employment, investments, and substantial changes concerning organization, introduction of new working methods or production processes, transfers of production, mergers, cut-backs or closures of undertakings, establishments or important parts thereof, and collective redundancies" (ETUI, 1994: 11). This Annex was available to MNCs whether they chose to establish voluntary or mandatory EWCs. However, in neither case were MNCs required to include the list of topics from the Annex in negotiating agreements.

From a strategy perspective, each of the 16 items could have an impact on workforces. However, half, or 8 of the items can be labeled primarily as "employee interests," or those issues that would directly impact employees and about which they could be expected to have a special interest in receiving information and consulting. These issues are the employment situation and probable trend of employment; substantial changes in the production process; transfers of production; mergers; cutbacks; closures of undertakings, establishments, or important parts thereof; and collective redundancies. The other 8 items can be labeled "employer interests," but since these issues indirectly have effects on employees, we argue that management would want to share information and discuss these issues with its employee representatives to gain support for business strategies. These issues include the structural, economic, and financial situation, the probable development of the business, production and sales, the probable trend in investments, and substantial changes concerning organizations.

On comparing voluntary Article 13 agreements to mandatory Article 6 agreements regarding these substantive issues, we find some distinct differences in coverage (Table 15.2). First, with regard to the eight "employee interests" topics, nearly twice the proportion of mandatory agreements (41 percent) than voluntary agreements (21 percent) listed all eight topics. Whereas the large majority of both voluntary and mandatory agreements listed at least one of the eight topics, 35 percent of voluntary agreements but only 25 percent of the mandatory agreements failed to list any topics.

Of the eight different topics, the most widely cited in voluntary agreements were the employment situation and probable trend in employment (52 percent), substantial changes concerning the introduction of new working methods (44 percent), and substantial changes in production (42 percent). Among mandatory agreements, the most widely cited topics were closures (65 percent), cutbacks (61 percent), the employment situation (61 percent), and substantial changes concerning new working methods (61 percent).

Second, with regard to the eight "employer interest" topics, only 18 percent of voluntary agreements and 42 percent of mandatory agreements listed all eight topics. Nearly all agreements, however, listed at least one of the eight topics (89 percent of voluntary agreements and 83 percent of mandatory agreements), and few failed to list any (17 percent of voluntary and 16 percent of mandatory agreements). Of the eight different topics, the most widely cited among voluntary agreements were the financial situation (73 percent), economic situation (69 percent), investment plans (50 percent), and substantial changes concerning organizations (50 percent). Among mandatory agreements, the most widely cited topics were similar to those listed in voluntary agreements, including the financial situation (76 percent), economic situation (69 percent), investments (67 percent), and the structural situation (67 percent).

Finally, in addition to coverage of the 16 items listed in the Annex, a large number of other employeerelated issues were included in both voluntary and mandatory agreements. In decreasing order, these issues included health and safety, environment, training, diversity, and equal employment. A small number of agreements also covered union rights, working hours, working conditions, human resource development, strategic human resource mangement and labor relations (HRM/LR) policies, and compensation. Since several of these latter issues are often negotiated in collective bargaining contracts, their absence from most agreements suggests that employers generally wished to avoid reaching agreements that closely resembled collective bargaining contracts (Beaupain and Jefferys, 2000).

Summary

Our comparison of voluntary and the earliest mandatory EWC agreements shows that both forms are more alike than they are different (at least on paper). There are some modest differences, nonetheless, which we summarize next. First, MNCs from some home countries appear to have greater or lesser proclivities for having chosen to voluntarily establish agreements under Article 13. MNCs from France, Germany, and the United States were substantially more likely to have established voluntary agreements, and MNCs from Belgium, Finland, Italy, and the Netherlands were substantially more likely to have negotiated agreements under the directive's mandatory Article 6 provision. In choosing countries whose national laws would govern in the event of noncompliance, most chose the MNC's home country. However, those MNCs that negotiated mandatory agreements showed some disproportionate preference for selecting Ireland and the Netherlands. MNCs that negotiated mandatory agreements were also somewhat more likely to choose governing states that had nationally mandated works councils than MNCs that established voluntary agreements.

As previously discussed, there are no apparent differences between voluntary and mandatory EWCs regarding size, venue, and frequency of meetings. There was, however, a greater tendency for voluntary EWCs to conclude relatively short (six-month) agreements and for mandatory EWCs to negotiate lengthier, four-year agreements. Although the majority of both

Table 15.2
Employee and Employer-Related Subjects Specifically Included in Voluntary and and Mandatory EWC Agreements

	Art. 6 Agreements		Art. 13 Agreements	
	#	%	#	%
Employee Interest Items				
Employment Situation and Probable Trend of Employment	30	61	25	52
Substantial Changes concerning Introduction of New Working Methods	30	61	21	44
Substantial Changes in the Production Process	26	53	20	42
Transfers of Production	26	53	17	35
Mergers	29	59	18	38
Cutbacks	30	61	15	31
Closures of Undertakings	32	65	17	35
Collective Redundancies	29	59	16	33
Employer Interest Items				
Structural Situation	33	67	18	38
Economic Situation	34	69	33	69
Financial Situation	37	76	35	73
Development of the Business	28	57	20	42
Development of Production	28	57	20	42
Development of Sales	27	55	17	35
Investment	33	67	24	50
Substantial Changes concerning Organization	31	63	24	50

Source: ETUI, 1999 CD-ROM.

voluntary and mandatory agreements selected English as their preferred language, mandatory EWCs were much more likely to provide language training than were voluntary EWCs. Mandatory EWC agreements were more likely to explicitly list more topics of direct interest to employees (for which companies would share relevant information and engage in consultation with employee representatives) than were voluntary EWCs. At the same time, mandatory agreements were no more likely to list topics more directly relevant to management than were voluntary agreements. Lastly, voluntary EWC agreements were more likely to involve trade union representatives than mandatory EWCs

POTENTIAL PERCEIVED COSTS AND BENEFITS: FINDING ADVANTAGE UNDER ARTICLES 13 AND 6

Concerned that capital mobility had negative consequences for workers, the EU Council of Ministers issued the EWC Directive to provide a transnational mechanism for employees to become better informed about global competitive pressures and business strategies. In turn, through dialogue and consultation with company executives, employee representatives would have opportunity to suggest alternatives that might ameliorate anticipated negative consequences arising out of MNC strategic business and workplace decisions. For the EWC mechanism to provide such benefit to workers, however, management as well as trade union representatives in many cases, would, likewise, need to benefit; otherwise, any promise of benefit to workers would prove illusive. Therefore, in assessing why some MNCs chose to create voluntary Article 13 EWCs and others chose to create mandatory Article 6 EWCs, it follows that we need to examine the potential benefits and costs to employers and unions associated with establishing voluntary and mandatory EWCs. Simply stated, the parties would be expected to choose that form of EWC (voluntary or mandatory) that was perceived as providing the greater advantage or the least disadvantage.

Alternatively, as provided in the directive, the parties could choose by a two-thirds majority not to create EWCs or subsequently to terminate EWCs, presumably because neither employee representatives nor management perceived or found any net benefit arising out of EWCs. In addition, it appears that many MNCs falling under the directive have yet to establish mandatory EWCs. As such, some MNCs have apparently chosen to test the enforcement procedures provided in the directive, which were left to member states to establish and enforce. Although there have been a few court cases, these have not received widespread publicity, and no clear direction has developed out of them. Neither the existing literature nor the available data, therefore, allow us to examine those cases in which MNCs have not yet complied with the September 1999 deadline under Article 6 or in which the parties have chosen not to establish EWCs.

Next, we first identify the potential perceived costs and benefits to employer and employee representatives, drawing on the literature to provide some guidance on the kinds and salience of perceived costs and benefits reported, at least based on the earlier voluntary EWC agreements. Subsequently, we highlight the basic distinctions between Articles 13 and 6 to speculate about how the parties would choose between establishing voluntary and negotiating mandatory EWCs.

Potential Perceived Costs and Benefits

We start with the presumption that most (but not all) MNCs would rather avoid establishing EWCs than creating them. In short, if MNCs saw net benefit from such transnational councils, they would have already established them on their own prior to the directive. As reviewed by Rehfeldt (1998), some did, especially among French companies. But, as Rehfeldt concludes, most such transnational European councils were generally informal and fairly limited in sharing information and consulting with employee representatives. Faced by a directive requiring EWCs, on the other hand, affected MNCs can be expected to have weighed the potential costs against the potential benefits of EWCs and, in turn, decided how best to proceed.

Perhaps the most obvious management costs associated with EWCs are the added direct costs and administrative burden of creating new structures, convening meetings, compiling information, and establishing the communication apparatus necessary to provide feedback to employees at the subsidiary level. Second, there are the potential costs incurred from openly sharing confidential information and from consultation that could unnecessarily hinder or delay corporate-wide, transnational decision making. Given that the directive is silent with regard to disclosure of confidential business information and does not restrict companies from having final decision-making power, these kinds of potential costs are likely to prove minimal. In addition, there are the potential perceived costs that the establishment of EWCs would serve as a first critical step toward transnational collective bargaining, enhancing the relative power of trade unions in negotiating the terms and conditions of employment and deployment of workforces across locations. Here, there is no specific right granted to unions that they will be included in the formation or membership of EWCs. Hence, except where unions can exercise sufficient relative power to be included, employers may minimize any such perceived costs by excluding unions from, or marginalizing unions in, EWC deliberations (Royle, 1999). By way of example, General Motors apparently attempted to exclude union representatives from its voluntary EWC, but its unions, exercising their relative power, prevailed (*Economist*, 1995).

Against these real and perceived potential costs are, nonetheless, a variety of potential benefits. Among the benefits that might be derived from EWCs are ones that would lead to continuous improvements in performance. For instance, EWCs could provide important channels for communication with employees, creating a spirit of cooperation that might increase employee acceptance of (or reduce resistance to) corporate decisions and otherwise facilitate the development of European-wide company cultures and HRM/LR strategies (Bain, 2000). Second, information sharing and consultation with employee representatives may improve employee commitment and company decision making, leading to improvements in company-wide performance (Freeman and Rogers, 1993; Addison and Belfield, 2000). Third, over the longer run, EWCs may provide forums that supersede more stringent existing national regulations in regard to employee rights to information, consultation, and codetermination at the subsidiary level. As Streeck (1997a, 1997b) has suggested, that is, there ultimately may be competition between national institutions for employee representation and the EWC Directive. Countries having long provided for relatively stronger statutory rights for employee representation at the company level (e.g., Germany and France) may face the issue of which set of provisions (the older national or newer transnational) takes precedence. Indeed, Streeck emphasizes that under the EWC Directive, member countries are required to adopt the directive into their national laws. Once embodied in national law, it may be possible, if not probable, that the business community will press governments for having the less stringent EWC provisions take precedence. To date, we are not aware of any such governmental decisions or employer campaigns to achieve that end.

For trade union and nonunion employee representatives, the central promised benefit of the Directive derives from having access to company-wide information regarding business and workplace issues and strategies. Although not clearly provided by the directive, such sharing of information and ensuing dialogue over pertinent issues would possibly generate opportunities for employee representatives to consult with, and recommend alternative strategies to, corporate management. For trade union representatives, there is the added potential benefit that national unions could use EWC arrangements as avenues for strengthening cross-national interunion cooperation and coordination. Moreover, as noted, union representatives could use the formation of EWCs as a springboard to engage in transnational collective bargaining across MNC locations.

The potential costs incurred by employee representatives that must be weighed against potential benefits are threefold. First, there are the costs associated with developing interunion coordination and planning. These include underwriting the costs of communication and premeetings of union representatives across borders and among representatives speaking different languages and accustomed to different union structures and policies. The second potential cost entails the possibility that agreements reached at EWCs between trade union representatives and management could override or interfere with negotiations at local levels. Although such agreements might best serve the combined workforces across all locations, some unions at the local level could incur unwanted sacrifice in the name of the whole. Third, as previously noted, the EWC Directive might ultimately erode the protections of existing works councils and other forms of employee input mandated by national laws, ones superior to that envisioned in the EWC Directive. Hence, unions located in countries with existing superior institutions of employee input may ultimately contribute to losing such opportunities if they fully endorse and mobilize around EWCs. To maximize benefits under such a scenario, unions would need to perceive that EWCs would not become substitutes for existing national provisions but, instead, serve as added or extended avenues for obtaining valued information and further opportunities to engage in consultation. In contrast, for unions located in countries offering very limited rights to information and consultation (e.g., the United Kingdom and Spain), unions have greater reason to endorse and mobilize around EWCs.

Finding Advantage: Carrot or Stick?

With the preceding potential costs and benefits in mind, both management and trade union representatives could be expected to have pursued either the carrot or stick option depending on which option allowed each party to maximize net benefits or minimize net costs. Decisions regarding which option would provide greater advantage or lesser disadvantage would first depend on whether the primary objective was to use EWCs proactively as mechanisms to improve corporate-wide cooperation and performance or whether the primary objective was to minimally comply with the directive. Second, each party would need to have decided which option would more likely maximize gain or minimize loss in light of its primary objective.

Several distinctions between Article 13 and Article 6 are likely to have influenced the choice of options. First, Article 13 allowed the parties substantially greater latitude in the design of EWCs and the topics for which companies would be required to provide information, dialogue, and possible consultation. Second, parties establishing EWCs or the equivalent under Article 13 were not required to create the special negotiating bodies of elected representatives charged with negotiating the terms of an EWC under Article 6. Hence, more formalized negotiations could be avoided upon voluntarily establishing EWCs. Third, under Article 13, voluntary agreements could be reached without complying with the enabling member state legislation, provided an EWC-type of agreement was established prior to passage of such legislation (legislation due no later than September 1996). The opportunity to avoid pending legislation can be expected to have provided a carrot to some companies to opt for the voluntary establishment of EWCs, especially given the early uncertainty about the nature of member state requirements and procedures for enforcement. Fourth, under Article 13 but not under Article 6, MNCs that had already created forums for company-wide employee representation could choose to have these existing forums serve in place of newly created EWCs, which would, thus, allow companies to forgo the costs of creating EWCs. Finally, under Article 13 only, non-EU-based MNCs could play key roles in the EWCs. Consequently, MNCs based outside the EU Directive could exercise greater control under Article 13 than under Article 6. This provision may help explain why both U.K.-based and U.S.-based companies in our sample of 100 companies were much more likely to have established voluntary than mandatory EWCs.

The preceding distinctions suggest that MNCs would generally find greater advantage under Article 13 than under Article 6, for both employers and employee representatives. Indeed, only under limited circumstances would the parties appear to have reason to negotiate EWCs under Article 6. In large part, the advantage to voluntarily establishing EWCs was derived from the greater freedom and flexibility in designing EWCs granted under Article 13. That is, Article 13 (but not Article 6) allowed MNCs to pursue their primary objectives, whether their objective was to use EWCs proactively to improve corporate-wide cooperation and performance via dialogue and consultation with employee representatives or their objective was to create superficial councils. The same advantage applies, moreover, to employee representatives.

First, in all cases in which management would seek to be proactive in creating company-wide processes for meaningful dialogue and consultation, Article 13 provided greater advantage as the parties would have greater freedom to construct EWCs most suitable to their wider organizations. This proposition holds regardless of whether or not companies were unionized, whether unions involved were relatively strong or relatively weak, and whether employee representatives sought to create meaningful or superficial EWCs. The rationale here is fairly straightforward. Among nonunion companies, there would be no apparent reason for employee representatives to resist or reject the formation of EWCs since, although there might only be minimal benefit, there would be no apparent costs incurred by employees.

Among unionized companies, union representatives opposed to creating an EWC would gain greater advantage under the highly flexible provisions of Article 13 than under the somewhat more explicit, mandated provisions of Article 6. The only other options available to union representatives opposed to EWCs would be to attempt to muster a two-thirds vote against the formation of an EWC via Article 6 or to test the directive via refusal to comply. But obtaining a two-thirds majority opposed to establishing an EWC would be highly improbable if, indeed, company representatives appointed to EWCs truly sought to create meaningful structures and processes, at least for ones that would be administered jointly by labor and management. In those cases in which unions are relatively weak, the likelihood of generating a two-thirds majority vote would, indeed, be implausible.

Second, in those cases in which MNCs sought to minimize net costs by establishing superficial EWCs, the freedom and flexibility under Article 13, likewise, provided greater advantage for management than the more explicit provisions mandating information sharing and dialogue under Article 6. Since Article 13 provided no means by which employee representatives could negotiate with management over much of the structure and process of EWCs, in non-union companies and in companies with relatively weak union representation employees would have little or no leverage to block management from establishing superficial EWCs.

Only where strong unions existed could employee representatives be expected to mount sufficient leverage to redirect management's efforts aimed at establishing superficial EWCs, minimally compliant with the directive. It is under this kind of scenario, in which unions sought to create meaningful EWCs but companies sought to create only superficial ones, that the parties are likely to have waited until after September 1996 to negotiate EWCs under the provisions of Article 6. Where strong unions existed but shared the view of management that EWCs would be more costly than beneficial, we might also find that the parties would choose to respond to the stick over the carrot. Parties, that is, could choose to "negotiate" over the creation of EWCs under Article 6 with the expressed purpose of obtaining two-thirds votes from special negotiating bodies, not to establish EWCs. Short of taking this route through Article 6, the parties could merely create superficial EWCs under Article 13, that would minimize the costs to each and remain outside the purview of the enabling EWC legislation enacted by member states.

Finally, among those MNCs that waited to negotiate mandated EWCs under Article 6, some may have simply waited until compelled to establish EWCs, for several reasons. Some MNCs and their employee representatives may not have been either sufficiently opposed or sufficiently in favor of creating EWCs to warrant any effort to establish EWCs until so compelled under Article 6. Viewing EWCs as only moderately costly or moderately beneficial *and* not perceiving that mandated councils would be sufficiently more costly than voluntarily established councils, the parties had neither the motivation to create voluntary EWCs nor the motivation to avoid creating EWCs under Article 6. Some companies may have also simply sought to avoid incurring the costs of establishing EWCs for as long as possible by waiting out the compliance period (i.e., up to five years from enactment of the directive). Some advantage, however, could be obtained by commencing negotiations within the first six months under Article 6 since the parties could avoid complying with the "Subsidiary Requirements" embodied in the Annex. Others may have waited out the compliance period hoping that the directive might be further watered down by subsequent opposition mounted before the Council of Ministers. Lastly, some MNCs may have postponed establishing EWCs until after September 1996 to see if any or which member states in promulgating enabling legislation gave existing national regulations or the EWC Directive precedence over the other, then choosing the member state that provided the greatest advantage as the governing law country.

Assessment of Choices

Currently, there is very little information about mandatory, Article 6 agreements, and the existing literature has examined only voluntary, Article 13 agreements. Consequently, although we have laid out a framework for comparison and analysis of choices made between Article 13 and Article 6 agreements, our ability to examine either the motives underlying or the factors influencing these choices is presently quite limited. We can, nonetheless, summarize a few key points about the choices made and, in turn, highlight issues that need to be addressed more fully.

First, it's worth noting that of those EWCs established by the end of 1998, the overwhelming choice had been to establish voluntary EWCs. Hence, as predicted by our analysis of potential costs and benefits, greater advantage was generally perceived by MNCs and employee representatives in taking the carrot under Article 13 than responding to the stick under Article 6. Second, the evidence indicates that many, if not the large majority of the voluntary agreements are of a fairly superficial nature. Indeed, all case studies to date have found that voluntary EWCs have provided little more than limited information sharing. For instance, Knudson and Brunn (1998) found in their study of EWCs established in four Nordic countries that the parties established EWCs of only a minimalist nature. That is, no more influence or resources were provided to employee representatives beyond those narrowly specified in Article 13 of the directive. As discussed at some length by Royle and Towers in Chapter 17, the EWC formed by McDonald's was one "captured" by the company primarily for management purposes. Indeed, most members of the EWC are salaried managers, trade union representatives have been excluded from membership and denied input, meetings and the sharing of information are fully controlled by management, and there is no process for consultation or feedback to employees.

Wills (2000) concludes from her study of one of the first U.K.-owned MNCs to establish an EWC (in 1995) that the company viewed its EWC only as a forum for information exchange. Despite the company's difficulties encountered as the result of business decline and job losses, no substantive consultation with employee representatives occurred, nor were employee representatives able to develop any cross-border coordination among themselves. In their extensive study of eight companies across four countries, Lecher, Nagel, and Platzer (1999) echoed these findings. They found that management's primary objective was to use EWCs to raise the acceptance of corporate decisions on the part of employees and their representatives and, in turn, minimize losses during corporate restructuring. The authors also report that EWCs had to struggle to obtain recognition as institutions to which information was to be disclosed. Lastly, a somewhat more positive view of EWCs was reported by managers in Nakano's (1999) survey of Japanese managers. The majority of managers perceived that EWCs were useful mechanisms for disseminating company information among employees, for exchanging opinions with employee representatives, and for promoting a spirit of corporate-wide cooperation. At the same time, however, managers generally reported that EWCs seriously affected neither corporate decision making nor company competitiveness.

Third, it appears that at least with respect to voluntary EWC agreements, trade unions and their representatives have played minimal roles. Trade unionists, consequently, either (1) have been unable to leverage the relative power to insist that voluntary EWCs be used for consultation, if not the basis of transnational collective bargaining or (2) have, like their management counterparts, embraced the minimalist perspective. Based on the literature, the minimal role of unions appears to be attributable more to the lack of relative power in the face of employer resistance than any general perspective that EWCs were more costly than beneficial.

For instance, earlier efforts by European trade unions to establish so-called world group councils for the purpose of negotiating with MNCs on a transnational basis have generally ended in failure. Included among the earliest attempts were the world group councils convened in 1966 at Ford, General Motors, Chrysler, Volkswagen, and Daimler-Benz, which were followed by the formation of as many as 50 more such councils. In his assessment of these group councils, Rehfeldt (1998) concludes, however, that most of these group councils were short-lived and fairly weak, in large part because MNCs refused to recognize and negotiate with them, and the unions involved failed to coordinate multinational collective bargaining strategies among themselves. As discussed at some length in Part III of this volume, the challenge before unions across countries is substantial, but unions will necessarily have to move well beyond the limited transnational, interunion cooperation and coordination that exists today if they hope to muster the leverage required to confront MNCs.

With regard to EWCs specifically, Beaupain et al. (Chapter 16) highlight the challenges for unions in creating optimal benefit from EWCs. In particular, in their study of three unionized MNCs with locations in Belgium and the United Kingdom, the authors found substantial and sometimes crippling rivalry between unions over influence and control of EWCs. Often faced by suspicion and distrust of each other (exacerbated by language barriers and limited understanding of each other's organizational differences and national industrial relations [IR] systems), union delegates from different countries, moreover, have failed to communicate or consult effectively with union members about transnational issues addressed in EWCs. The authors also found that except to endorse the establishment of EWCs, national union leaders have done little to prepare or support EWC delegates in fulfilling their transnational roles and responsibilities.

It appears, therefore, that a primary motivation among MNCs choosing to establish voluntary EWCs has been to minimize costs by creating fairly superficial councils, rather than to negotiate meaningful ones intended by the directive. Given the barriers to transnational cooperation and coordination of strategies among unions, furthermore, employers have been relatively uninhibited in pursuing minimalist objectives. Lacking sufficient resources and well-defined Pan-European strategies to confront MNCs, that is, the opportunity for unions to transform voluntary EWC agreements into meaningful processes of information sharing and consultation is apparently quite limited.

The existing case study literature, is consistent with the generally minimalist nature of the 50 Article 13 agreements that we examined. In particular, with respect to the eight topics of employee interests identified in the directive's Annex, more than one-third of our sample of voluntary agreements failed to list any of the eight topics, and except for addressing the company's "employment situation and probable trend of employment," less than a majority of the agreements listed any of the remaining seven topics. About one-fourth of our sample of voluntary agreements, nonetheless, listed all eight items, suggesting that at least a small proportion of MNCs may have intended to establish meaningful forums in which substantial information of direct interest to employees is shared. Given that about one-third of the voluntary agreements also provided some measure for trade union representation input into the activities of EWCs, there also may be valuable dialogue, if not consultation, ongoing in a small proportion of Article 13 EWCs.

As discussed earlier, there would appear to be limited circumstances in which MNCs would opt to establish mandatory EWCs over voluntarily established ones. One explanation would be that strong unions seeking to establish meaningful EWC structures and processes in the face of employer opposition would forestall the formation of EWCs until after September 1996 to take advantage of the mandated provisions embodied in the Annex of the directive. Support for such an explanation, however, is fairly modest, as we found that only in about one-fifth of Article 6 EWCs was there any provision in the agreements that provided unions with input or influence. Hence, it appears that those MNCs choosing to respond to the stick of Article 6 were either motivated by potential benefits derived from waiting out the compliance period or not sufficiently motivated to create EWCs short of being compelled to by Article 6.

If the primary motivation were the avoidance of administrative costs, one would expect companies to not comply with the directive until close to September 1999. Since the 50 Article 6 agreements that we examined were all reached by December 1998, long before the September 1999 deadline, it follows that an explanation based on avoidance of costs is limited. Based on our examination of nearly all of the Article 6 agreements reached by December 1998, it would appear that a large proportion are the product of initial indifference between establishing voluntary EWCs under Article 13 or mandatory ones under Article 6. Hence, most parties, we surmise, merely waited until compelled by law to establish EWCs. Such an interpretation is based, in particular, on the observation that 41 percent of the mandatory agreements list all eight topics of employee interests listed in the Directive's Annex. In addition, in nearly half of the cases, the parties agreed to relatively lengthy four-year agreements.

CONCLUSION

We have argued that underlying decisions by MNCs regarding the structure and processes of EWCs and, in turn, the choices made between establishing voluntary EWCs under Article 13 and negotiating EWCs under Article 6 of the Directive are a function of perceived potential costs and benefits. The evidence clearly indicates that MNCs falling within the reach of the EWC Directive found greater advantage under the carrot offered in Article 13 than under the stick held in Article 6. As discussed, there is a wide range of factors influencing such perceived costs and benefits under Articles 13 and 6, ones that favored establishing EWCs under Article 13. Among these varied factors, we conclude that the large majority of MNCs have viewed the forum of information exchange, dialogue, and consultation itself as more costly than beneficial and have, consequently, sought to minimize costs by minimizing the degree to which they share information and engage in dialogue (let alone, consultation) with employee representatives. As such, the promise or objective of the EU Council of Ministers has largely gone unfulfilled, in particular, we believe, with respect to the voluntary agreements established. In summary, rather than having the intended incentive effect of creating meaningful forums, the carrot offered under Article 13 ironically has had the effect of minimizing the value of EWCs to employees who were the supposed beneficiaries.

In no small way, the lack of meaningful dialogue and consultation being offered by EWCs is the result of limited employee leverage in the face of employer resistance. As constructed, that is, the directive presumes either that MNCs will see that substantial benefit from employee input can be derived by these transnational forums (and, thus, be motivated to develop meaningful EWCs) or that employees will muster sufficient leverage to force resistant employers to fully share information and engage in dialogue and consultation. The evidence to date, however, strongly suggests that only in a small proportion of cases have either MNCs viewed EWCs as beneficial or employees been able to exercise such leverage. Given the substantial barriers and limited ability of trade union organizations to mount effective transnational strategies, the prospect that the directive will over time achieve its intended objective appears rather dismal.

In closing, lest the reader get the wrong impression, our assessment of EWCs is clearly preliminary. Whether one is a "Euro-Skeptic" or a "Euro-Optimist" with regard to the directive depends on one's view of the benefits and costs to employers and unions of the directive over the longer run (Lecher and Rüb, 1999). Our intended contribution has been to help highlight the critical issues and offer an initial perspective of MNC decision making regarding the directive based on a cost-benefit framework. A much more extensive study of EWCs, especially those negotiated under Article 6, is warranted before one comes to any conclusive assessment of EWCs or prescribes amendments to the directive. Central to such a study and assessment would be an analysis of EWCs created just prior to the September 1999 deadline and cases in which the parties have chosen to terminate or not establish EWCs by exercising the two-thirds majority vote option. Finally, information is sorely lacking on the extent to which affected MNCs failed to meet the September 1999 deadline, how the directive has or has not been enforced, and how member states have integrated the directive into national laws and policies governing employee representation rights.

NOTES

1. The ETUI database was originally issued in hard-copy format in 1997 but later released as a 1999 CD-ROM containing 470 full-text agreements. These agreements were supplemented by a 1998 database containing company profile information along with additional sources.

2. The baseline research here was conducted by the European Foundation for the Improvement of Living and Working Conditions (Marginson, et al., 1998). They examined 386 voluntary agreements, which had been signed under Article 13. The report provides both an item-by-item review and some broader analysis. The authors conclude that a significant number of Article 13 agreements depart from the guidelines of the Annex. These voluntary agreements were often concluded with substantial union involvement, which carried over to the foundations of EWCs. Although the Annex also provides for employee-only EWCs without union or employer representation, most of the voluntary agreements established joint management-employee councils. One-quarter of the voluntary agreements, moreover, set up single-tier EWCs at division levels rather than at groupwide structure levels.

REFERENCES

Addison, J. T. and Belfield, C. R. (2000). "The New European Works Councils: Determinants and Impacts." Working paper, University of South Carolina.

Addison, J. T. and Seibert, W. S. (1991). "The Social Charter of the European Community: Evolution and Controversies." *Industrial and Labor Relations Review* 44 (4), pp. 597–625.

Addison, J. T. and Seibert, W. S. (1994). "Recent Developments in Social Policy in the New European Union." *Industrial and Labor Relations Review* 48(1), pp. 5–27.

Bain, T. (2000). "If Works Councils Came to North America from Europe, Would They Matter?" *Tijdschrift voor Economie en Management* 65 (1), pp. 5–22.

Bain, T. and Hester, K. (2000). "Similarities and Differences in a Sample of European Works Council Agreements." *Proceedings of the 52nd Annual Meeting, Industrial Relations Research Association*, Madison, WI.

Beaupain, T. and Jefferys, S. (2000). "European Works Councils: A New Institution but with What Content? The Early Belgium Experience." *Proceedings of the 52nd Annual Meeting, Industrial Relations Research Association*, Madison, WI.

Bellace, J. R. (1997). "The European Works Council Directive: Transnational Information and Consultation in the European Union." *Comparative Labor Law Journal* 18 (3), pp. 325–61.

Economist. (1995). December 2, Untitled. 337, p. 73.

European Trade Union Institute (ETUI). (1994). Council Directive 94/95EC of September 22.

European Trade Union Institute (ETUI). (2000). *Information Letter.*

Freeman, R. B. and Rogers, J. (1993). "Who Speaks for Us? Employee Representation in a Nonunion Labor Market." In Kaufman, B. and Kleiner, M. (eds.), *Employee Representation: Alternatives and Future Directions.* Madison, WI: Industrial Relations Research Association, pp. 13–79.

Hall, M., Carley, M., Gold, M. Marginson, P., and Keith Sisson. K (1995). *European Works Councils: Planning for the Directive.* London: IRS.

Knudsen, H. and Brunn, N. (1998). "European Works Councils in the Nordic Countries: An Opportunity and a Challenge for Trade Unionism." *European Journal of Industrial Relations* 4 (2), pp. 131–56.

Lecher, W., Nagel, B., and Platzer, H. (1999). *The Establishment of European Works Councils.* Aldershott: Ashgate

Lecher, W. and Platzer, H. (1998). *European Union—European Industrial Relations?* London: Routledge.

Lecher, W. and Rüb, S. (1999). "The Constitution of European Works Councils: From Information Forum to Social Actor." *European Journal of Industrial Relations* 5 (1), pp. 7–25.

Marginson, P., Gilman, M., Jacobi, O., and Krieger, H. (1998). *Negotiating European Works Councils: An Analysis of Agreements under Article 13.* Dublin, Ireland: European Foundation for the Improvement of Living and Working Conditions.

Nakano, S. (1999). "Management Views of European Works Councils: A Preliminary Survey of Japanese Multinationals" *European Journal of Industrial Relations* 5 (3), pp. 307–26.

Rehfeldt, U. (1998). "European Works Councils—An Assessment of French Initiatives." In Lecher, W. and Platzer, H. (eds.), *European Union—European Industrial Relations?* London: Routledge, pp. 217–22.

Royle, T. (1999). "Where's the Beef? McDonald's and It's European Works Council." *European Journal of Industrial Relations* 5 (3), pp. 327–47.

Streeck, W. (1997a). "Industrial Citizenship under Regime Competition: The Case of the European Works Councils." *Journal of European Public Policy* 4 (4), pp. 643–64.

Streeck, W. (1997b). "Neither European nor Works Councils: A Reply to Paul Knutsen." *Economic and Industrial Policy* 18, pp. 325–37.

Wills, Jane. (2000). "Great Expectations: Three Years in the Life of a European Works Council." *European Journal of Industrial Relations* 6 (1), pp. 83–105.

16

Early Days: Belgian and U.K. Experiences of European Works Councils

Thérèse Beaupain, Steve Jefferys, and Rachel Annand

The 1994 European Works Council (EWC) Directive fueled hopes that it was an important first legislative step toward the development of a European industrial relations (IR) system (Marginson and Sisson, 1994; Schulten, 1996). As described and assessed by Bain and Hester in the preceding chapter, to date the prospects that the EWC directive will have laid the foundation for such a European-wide IR system are not promising. Given employer apathy and general resistance to forming meaningful EWCs that not only exchange information but allow for consultation, it becomes imperative that labor greatly expand its capacity to take greater advantage of the legislative opportunity laid down in the directive. Herein, we seek to more fully understand the early and practical challenges faced by organized labor in utilizing EWCs to promote a transnational labor agenda regarding the European operations of multinational companies (MNCs).

Toward delineating and assessing these challenges, we report on the initial phase of our in-depth study of EWCs of three MNCs with subsidiaries in Belgium and the United Kingdom and whose EWCs are governed by Belgian law. Such a comparison allows us to compare responses to this "new tier" of IR institutions from contrasting IR systems: the Belgian, wherein trade unions are strongly institutionalized within labor market regulatory processes, and the British, wherein just the opposite is the case. The cases studied include one MNC from the engineering sector and two MNCs from the insurance sector, allowing us to examine and compare responses from both traditionally strongly unionized and traditionally weakly unionized firms. Our findings and analysis are based on one- to two-hour interviews conducted between the autumn of 1998 and the spring of 1999 with six senior human resource managers, 15 employee representatives, and two national union representatives in the target multinationals.[1]

We first describe the Belgian and U.K. IR systems to provide the broader and very different contexts in which the three EWCs are placed. Second, we describe the evolution and practice of the three EWCs, focusing on the processes, the interaction among EWC representatives, the extent and form of information exchange and consultation, the development of a broader community of interest among trade union representatives, and management objectives. Lastly, we draw on our exploratory analysis to summarize several critical challenges faced by trade union organizations across countries in forging cooperative and coordinated efforts in light of the EWC promise.

THE BELGIAN AND U.K. CONTEXTS

Whereas there were some similarities between the Belgian and U.K. IR systems in the era of Britain's social contract and multiemployer bargaining in the 1970s, by the 1990s the two systems differed quite sharply. Thus, if Belgium is still a "*concertation* economy" (Beaupain, 1994), Britain is now virtually its antithesis. The strong working relationship that exists between Belgian trade unions and employers has played a key role in elaborating a bipartite negotiating process that takes place at three levels: at the intersectoral, the sectoral, and, largely based on the guidelines that the former establish, at the enterprise level. This system remains intact in spite of a trend toward growing intervention by the state. In Britain, by contrast, while growing state intervention has also been a feature of the 1980s and 1990s, intersectoral bargaining has been totally absent, and multiemployer sectoral bargaining is but a shadow of its former self. Even where enterprise- and establishment-level collective bargaining continues to take place in Britain, such bargaining is generally less likely to reflect a strong union presence than to reflect an employer calculation that the system provides net advantages over nonrecognition.

U.K. union density declined continuously from the 1970s, falling from over 50 percent to 30 percent by 2000, although its precipitous drop has been halted by the return of a Labor government in 1997. In Belgium, by contrast, one of the major reasons for the continuing importance of concertation is the presence of strong union organizations. Recent reports indicate that union density as a share of the employed labor force is relatively high, estimated at about 52 percent in 1995 (ILO, 1997) and that total membership (including employed, unemployed, and retired workers) rose nearly 12 percent between 1990 and 1995 (Vilrokx and Van Leemput, 1998: 320–21). Belgian unions are legitimated, furthermore, both by their sectoral and intersectoral institutional roles (including their important consultative functions and their role in the administration of social security—the Ghent system) and by their strong presence at the enterprise level, particularly in all large firms.

There is not just greater breadth of trade union presence in Belgium than in the United Kingdom; there is also greater depth. Even before the EWC Directive was issued, Belgian employees enjoyed several distinct channels of representation: through workplace trade union delegates, through health and safety committees, and through enterprise works councils (in which nearly 98 percent of employees vote for union representatives) (Vilrokx and Van Leemput, 1998: 323). Britain, by contrast, effectively has but a single channel of representation.[2] In two-thirds of those workplaces where employers recognize trade unions (44 percent of all workplaces, according to the 1998 Labour Force Survey), primarily in large private manufacturing firms and in the public sector, employees elect workplace trade union representatives (218,000 in 1998). The opt-out by Britain's Conservative government from the Maastricht Social Chapter also meant that, unlike Belgian-owned MNCs, qualifying British-owned MNCs were not legally obliged to implement the EWC Directive by 1996. In Britain, therefore, not only did the addition of a EWC represent something conceptually novel, but it was also initially far from being the rule. In Belgium, on the other hand, the EWC Directive was brought within the enabling national law in February 1996 through an interindustry collective agreement concluded under the framework of the National Labour Council between employer associations and unions. This agreement expressed a wish that "national representative organisations of employees" (i.e., unions) rather than mere "employee representatives," play a key role both in any special negotiating bodies and in the EWC itself. The three Belgian representative unions, moreover, will be the only ones to play a role and to nominate delegates on the Belgian side. Under the Subsidiary Requirements of the Annex, it also established that an EWC should be an *employee-only* body, in opposition to the existing consultative structures, which are normally *joint* committees under Belgian law.[3]

Another significant difference between Belgian and British employee representation is that while both are pluralist, multiunion systems, workers in Belgium choose between union confederations differentiated along religious and political lines, whereas in Britain, union choice is most likely to be differentiated by occupation.   Hence, the largest Belgian union confederation (the Confederation of Christian Unions, CSC)[4] has links with the two (Flemish and French-speaking) Catholic Christian Democratic Parties. The next largest confederation (the Belgian General Federation of Labor, FGTB) is socialist-oriented with links to the two socialist parties. The much smaller General Federation of Belgian Liberal Trade Unions (CGSLB) has its historical origin in the Liberal Party (Miroir, 1982). While blue-collar CSC and FGTB members are organized by industry, white-collar members are organized into interindustry unions: in the Union for Technicians, White Collar Employees and Middle Management (SETCA), for the FGTB and for the CSC, in the National Center for White Collar Employees (CNE). As a consequence of this system of representation, large firms employing both blue-collar and white-collar workers located in just one of the linguistically defined regions of the country, are likely to have to deal with five unions and occasionally with a corporate-level staff union. In Britain, by contrast, although about four out of five trade unionists are affiliated with the effectively powerless peak union confederation (the Trades Union Congress, TUC), the key choice is among a declining number of still highly independent unions (which are essentially rooted in occupational divisions and rivalries rather than in ideology).

THE EVOLUTION AND PRACTICE OF THREE EWCs

Management in all three of our case study MNCs favored concluding agreements before the September 22, 1996, deadline in order to fall under Article 13, which allowed the voluntary establishment of EWCs. Three fundamental reasons were offered. First, there was an intention to demonstrate their openness to dialogue with their employees. A senior British human resource manager at company B explained why he had recommended that it go ahead with an EWC even before the British opt-in:

I was very much of the view, you know, that to be King Canute-like and so sort of endeavour to ignore what appears to me to be really quite inevitable, and so on, that that would not be in our interests and we really ought to—in terms of our own pragmatism—we ought to welcome this and we ought to seize the opportunity afforded and to try and shape a European Works Councils which suited what we were endeavouring to be as an organization. We very much sought to do it in a kind of partnership way. We had our own sort of little working party and "think tank" and whatever, but really, you know, we were very much interested in having a dialogue with the trade unions, as indeed we did.

Second, the human resource managers involved felt that the September 1996 deadline would help "us focus the mind". One described it as "gingering up the decision-making process." One can interpret such responses as reflecting how human resource professionals viewed using European social policy to enhance their status and power within their firms. Third, managers expressed a wish to take advantage of the possibility of designing their own agreements.

Company A is a non-European-owned, engineering sector MNC. In Belgium, it is located in the Walloon French-speaking industrial region, a traditional bastion of the more combative factions of the working class. In the United Kingdom, it has plants in various regions generally identified with low levels of labor–management conflict. After long and difficult negotiations, its EWC agreement was reached after the 1996 deadline. After initially excluding British delegates, it agreed to allow them in as of 1998 after the new Labor government decided to end the United Kingdom's social policy opt-out. Company B, which is British-owned, and company C, which is Swiss-owned, are both in the insurance sector. Their Belgian operations are mainly located in Brussels, and their U.K. operations are located in London and in various medium-size urban locations elsewhere. Both MNCs concluded EWC agreements in the month preceding the 1996 deadline for establishing voluntary agreements. At the time of our interviews, company B was completing a merger with another British insurance MNC, and the fate of their respective EWCs was still in debate. In all three cases, therefore, the EWCs are still very young institutions, and, thus, the research reported herein effectively covers at most their first two years of activity. The principal characteristics of the three MNCS and their EWCs are reported in Table 16.1.

In all three MNCs, management responded to the new institution by investing considerable resources in the formal structure. They ensured the presence of top, European-level management at meetings, prepared highly professional presentations, covered the costs of travel, expensive lodging, and food and drink, and provided the meeting place, along with extensive and costly interpreting facilities for at least the plenary meetings. The cost to management of covering meetings is obviously high, raising the issue of whether there is a discrepancy between the material value apparently attached to the EWCs and the substantive value derived from the meetings. Given that the MNCs concerned had decided to establish their EWCs under Belgian law, it comes as no surprise that the Belgian national unions played important or major roles in the negotiating process. In company B, SETCA took the initiative in organizing a first international meeting in Belgium for both sides, including British management, but left the subsequent talks in London to a British delegate mandated by the European Regional Organization of the International Federation of Commercial, Clerical, Professionals and Technical Employees (Euro-FIET), the European industry federation. In companies A and C, the national Belgian unions led the negotiations with management while staying in close touch with their respective European industry federations. In line with the European Trade Union Confederation (ETUC) position, both federations had guidelines stipulating that the national unions of the country where the headquarters are situated (or where the agreement would be signed) should lead the negotiations. In companies B and C, this gave the Belgian unions more responsibility than their numerical proportion would have entitled them to in determining the distribution of seats between different countries. The unions also allocated the seats on the EWCs between the Belgian delegates, in theory in such a way as to loosely reflect the strength of representation in each company. In practice, however, this process did not always go smoothly, revealing interunion rivalries. In company C, for example, the majority FGTB denied the minority CSC one seat because in another company the majority CSC had done likewise to the FGTB.

The allocation of seats on EWCs appears to be a major concern and sometimes contentious issue for trade union delegates during periods of corporate restructuring associated with mergers or acquisitions, which threatens the existing balance of seats. For instance, in company A the distribution of the United Kingdom's six seats was just having to be redrawn at the time of our interviews because of the parent company's purchase of another very large subsidiary in Northern Ireland. The reconfiguration would clearly have the effect of reducing the number of seats held by the British Amalgamated Engineering and Electrical Union (AEEU) delegation. One of the delegates worried that this might not be done amicably: "They [interunion relations] are not too bad here honestly. But I mean you can go to some areas where they just don't talk to each other, and I don't think you experience that in Belgium, even with the diversity of the trade unions out there. I don't think you would ever experience something like that. They just don't talk. But it does happen in British industry unfortunately." Once the reallocation of seats was agreed to, the

Table 16.1
Profile of EWCs across Companies A, B, and C

A	Country of headquarters and core business	U.S.; engineering
	Evolution	Approx. 18,000 employees in Europe in 1999 (about 45% in U.K. and 21% in Belgium). Has experienced both redundancies and expansion.
	Date of agreement creating EWC	December 11, 1996
	Composition	Workers representatives only; 11 members in 1996 (6 from Belgium); 25 members in 1999, (6 new ones from U.K.).
	Select committee	2 workers reps. from Belgium; 1 from France
	Plenary meetings held up to June 1999	3 ordinary meetings
B	Country of headquarters and core business	U.K.; insurance
	Evolution	Approx. 17,000 employees in Europe in 1999 (about 50% in U.K.; 400 in Belgium). Merger decision in 1998 with another British insurance company.
	Date of agreement creating EWC	September 9, 1996
	Composition	Worker representatives only; 14 members (4 from U.K., 1 from Belgium + 2 experts).
	Select committee	President is U.K. worker rep.; 2 other members: 1 member from Belgium representing other European countries; 1 member of staff.
	Plenary meetings held up to June 1999	2 ordinary meetings in 1997 and 1998.
C	Country of headquarters and core business	Switzerland; insurance
	Evolution	Approx. 23,000 employees in Europe in 1997 (5% in Belgium and 9% in U.K.). Acquired in 1997 by another large Swiss financial services group.
	Date of agreement creating EWC	September 12, 1996
	Composition	Bilateral. Worker representatives: 19 in 1997 (2 from Belgium); 22 in 1999 (3 from the U.K.).
	Secretariat	1 secretary (Belgian); 1 adjunct secretary (Italian) chosen among the worker representatives.
	Plenary meetings held up to June 1999	3 ordinary meetings; 1 extraordinary meeting in 1997

delegates who took up the seats were generally first among existing senior plant-level, lay union officers.

Different procedures were used in allocating seats on the EWCs of company B and company C's U.K. locations. In company B, the only union present was an in-house, certified independent "staff" union, which was not a TUC affiliate. As the Euro-FIET was a major partner in setting up the EWC, the in-house union was originally given just an expert position in the EWC, but subsequent to the 1998 merger with a company in which the Manufacturing, Science, Finance Union (MSF), a TUC affiliate was strongly represented, no meetings of the EWC took place at all while the dispute about U.K. representation continued. Company C used different methods in allocating seats across its three principal U.K. subsidiaries, varying from a nomination process and genuine election to a simple appointment by the human resource department. In each subsidiary, a nontrade unionist was selected, although in one subsidiary in which the MSF union was present, a trade unionist was the second selection. The MSF full-time official subsequently offered and provided information on the EWC to the nonunion representatives on the grounds that in helping them become better representatives, the union was more likely either to recruit them or to have a positive impression on other nonmembers than if he ignored them.

We asked the nonunion representatives in company C why they had stood for election or appointment. One woman replied that they were among the few staff in their company who had had business contacts outside the subsidiary and within Europe: "Obviously the senior managers visit Switzerland and that sort of thing, but they have started to have more opportunities, certainly within the last year, of people getting involved in projects in other countries and I really enjoyed that, and thought it would be a nice thing to do. And the fact that I had been here quite a long while." One other delegate from company C nominated himself because he thought that it would look good on his curriculum vitae. The human resourse director explained how the company avoided holding an election. "What we decided to do was advertise the opportunity on the e-mail. We spiced it up to make it sound interesting and a trip to Brussels and that sort of thing." He then chose the delegate from among those who responded.

Experiencing the EWC

The meetings with management are, of course, the formal purpose of the EWC. There was a general consensus among union interviewees that meetings were simply too short to be as effective as desired, lasting half a day, except in company B, where it convened for a full day. Some delegates complained of senior managers' dictating the duration and pace of the meeting by their flight schedules. Most agreed that the preparatory meeting for employee representatives was a key element, though again too brief, permitting, in the best of these meetings, only limited genuine exchange of information between delegates from different countries. Preparatory meetings also lasted for just half a day, usually the afternoon or evening of the day before the meeting with management. The one social occasion tends to be the evening meal between the preparatory employee-side meeting and the meeting with management. In company A, a formal follow-up meeting of employee representatives takes place and is highly valued.

The first positive result of the existence of EWCs, therefore, appears to be that they bring together and foster contact between employees from different national establishments of the same MNC, an outcome that, nonetheless, needs to be qualified.[5] We found considerable suspicion among the Belgian delegates about the independence of the three nonunion British delegates on the EWC of company C. When "it came out in conversation" with the German delegates that the British delegates were not union representatives, their surprise was evident. "You know it was 'Ah..,'" reported one of British nonunion delegates. Similar suspicion concerning the independence of British trade union delegates was also held by Belgian EWC delegates in company A. In the latter, unlike in companies B and C, over the first two years the evening meals of delegates had excluded management. However, when they arrived, the British AEEU delegates refused to attend the meal without their personnel manager and subsequently complained informally about their fellow delegates' being "too left-wing." The Belgian CSC-metal president of the EWC also told us of his concern about the fact that the AEEU delegates from company A received their faxes from him through their personnel departments' fax machines. In company B, on the contrary, the relationships between the Belgian delegate and his British colleagues were reportedly very good.

Besides attending the formal meetings, the day-to-day functioning of the EWCs involves very little additional work for most delegates. Union delegates use the same facilities as provided for other facets of their representative and union work. In the case of the British nonunion representatives, delegates are allowed a limited amount of time to meet to prepare a feedback report for their colleagues. More dedicated time is involved, however, for the employee-side EWC secretary (or president[6]), who is also responsible for the smaller employee-side EWC select committee. The committee also plans the annual meeting (and any extraordinary meetings) with its national human resource manager, reports on them, and exchanges information and maintains loose contacts during the time between annual meetings. In all three MNCs, the secretaries usually contact (by phone or fax) their select committee colleagues before convening meetings to share views and to write to the other delegates asking for issues and ideas to be included in the agenda. Often the secretaries include suggestions that they consider important, but only after having raised them with the manager responsible for the EWC. The secretaries reported having received little response at this stage, either from locations in other countries or from other unions, suggesting a lack of engagement by a number of delegates and probably reflecting inexperience for the new ones, such as for many of the British representatives. Although the agenda is formally set up jointly, in reality the greater majority of time is spent on the presentation of management views. Consequently, there is little time left fully open to responses by the delegates. Their views and the opportunity for a genuine exchange of opinion or consultation have been squeezed into a few questions.

Information Rather than Consultation

Much of the substance of the regular EWC meetings consists of a presentation of the company's operations, often reported in terms of annual returns, market share in different sectors and countries, and employment trends. The evolution or restructuring of companies has not been included in the agendas. Furthermore, in no case in the nine meetings that had occurred before our interviews was information provided in advance. One delegate commented that delegates felt drowned by the volume of information exchanged and were often incapable of fully comprehending and evaluating its implications within the time constraints imposed. Others expressed the need to have some expertise in corporate accounting to take advantage of the meetings as scripted.

Since an important rationale behind the EWC directive was to persuade MNCs to adjust their information and consultation procedures to the Europeanization of the firm, we inquired whether the EWCs really added any information beyond what was already generally available at the subsidiary level (wherein a strong trade union presence or preexisting legal obligations or negotiating traditions were in place). Responses from the union delegate interviewees were wide-ranging. While some delegates believed that the EWCs had not added anything substantial, many others believed that they had widened their understanding, particularly in giving them a better knowledge about their company's operations in countries other than their own. An AEEU delegate from company A suggested that the information that they were given was "half and half" (half useful and half not) but that the absence of information in advance and the format of meetings with "your one session there, your questions at the end of it" made it somewhat frustrating. Another AEEU delegate from a different subsidiary of company A summarized the general view: "Some I already knew, but a lot of it was financial. A lot of it was international movements of different things and what the aspects for the future probably were, you know. So, yes, it was interesting and quite useful, but there wasn't anything I would say that was of paramount importance there, really, I wouldn't have thought." As a nonunion representative from company C added: "Nothing was totally new to me. Some things like the group results we would get presented to us here anyway. One of the projects particularly, I had read about that in the European Group magazine. You know, things like that."

In addition to requiring MNCs to share pertinent transnational information, the EWC Directive encouraged consultation with employee representatives over issues that could directly affect employment. Included among the potentially most sensitive issues of this kind are merger and acquisition activity, which occurred in our three case studies. Company A was expanding through a series of acquisitions, company B was completing a merger at the time of our interviews, and company C had just completed a merger. Given the disruption and possible displacement of employees associated with mergers and acquisitions, clearly the issues raised by these transformations are ideally suited for consultation rather than just "information after the fact" being provided. Yet, in all three cases, the companies provided no opportunity for consultation, over either the decisions or the effects of the decisions on employees.

Company B merely informed its EWC secretary of the merger 12 hours prior to the public announcement. Information about the merger was shared only at the next regular meeting of the EWC, and no serious consultation with employee representatives about the effects of the merger took place. Company C gave no prior notice of its merger, and following a request by EWC members an "extraordinary" meeting was held. The absence of proper consultation led both EWCs to protest vigorously. At company C, a formal reprimand was issued by the Euro-FIET expert, who warned the Swiss managers that if they did not take the EWC seriously, he would take whatever steps necessary to ensure that they did, not excluding legal action. "This really threw the Swiss management. 'What are you going on about there?' They had a bit of a panic. Anyway, we'll see" (SETCA delegate, Company C). At the time of our interviews, this skeptical SETCA observer was not entirely convinced that company C would comply with the demand for consultation. Indeed, according to managers involved, secrecy was imposed by stock market rules.

Resource Mobilization Rather than Negotiation

Information and consultation may be viewed as part of a continuum of employee participation in decision making in which the next step could be negotiation. We, therefore, inquired whether there were any signs of the EWCs' facilitating moves in this direction. It appeared that the information provided the EWC and still more importantly the possibility of directly exchanging information with colleagues from other countries had the indirect result of allowing the unions in company A to cross-check information given by management at the national level. In certain cases, EWC delegates believed that they had more information than local managers. We also found that the very existence of the EWC and the opportunity that it provided for having access to top management led to the formulation of a demand by EWC members in company C for an assurance that there would be no Belgian reductions in force during a fixed period following the merger, a demand subsequently realized.

Although the EWCs in these two cases served as vehicles for local bargaining objectives, there was never anything arising out of the EWC meetings remotely approaching group-level, transnational negotiations. Within the relatively short time frame that EWCs have existed, however, two *preconditions* for such negotiations are beginning to emerge. The first, appearing among only a few union activists, is a deeper recognition and sense of common interests. Largely the consequence of the informal comparisons of national working conditions and rights of workers' representatives, this recognized commonality may encourage a gradual escalation of national demands toward greater parity (at least on broad principles in human resource management). The second precondition is the emergence of some friendships and, perhaps, a small degree of trust between a handful of delegates from different countries.

At the most basic level, the main result of the EWC process to date has been to bring employee representatives from different countries into brief contact with each other, which has had the effect of highlighting the need for members of the EWC select committees to keep in touch more frequently. The trust that can emerge from such contact is, of course, a necessary condition for the development of any common position across countries. Indeed, members of the EWCs affected by merger activity managed at one point or another to adopt a common position and, in one of them, to write a common resolution. Reaching that common resolution, however, was far from an easy task, and where common interests would appear to be clear under the given circumstances, they marked a significant advance over national particularities.

Perhaps sensing these possibilities, practically all our Belgian union interviewees believed that the EWCs would lead to collective bargaining over the next 5 to 10 years or later:

I think it must happen given time, the issues, the discussions, the decisions that we're going perhaps to make. Because now we can't take decisions in an EWC. But I think that perhaps in ten years, and I really hope it happens, that will be the case. But in my view it must happen, it must develop and it's going to develop. That's my personal view now. And I think that in five years we will be clearly further forward than we are now. Because, really, we're only at the infancy of these committees now. (SETCA delegate, Company C)

Talking about Europe-wide collective agreements, I'd say that five, ten years for a perspective is a bit short. It would be great to have such an agreement, even if it was just on the reduction of working time. But anyway, I wish with all my heart that it could happen. (CSC-metal delegate, Company A)

Despite an honest recognition of the present limits of the role of EWCs, these Belgian union representatives appear to sense a slow development of a broader European community of interests. Among the British representatives, however, there was no similar vision. Perhaps the difference between the Belgian and British delegates is that the Belgian delegates whom we interviewed generally had greater international exposure and experience. The difference could also be due to the newness of the EWC experience in conjunction with the greater weakness of a trade union presence in the Unied Kingdom that made the prospect of an effective collective presence among U.K. representatives much more remote. Additionally, EWC representatives in company A were learning that their U.K.-based trade union structure handicaps coordinated activity at the wider EWC level.

Currently, EWCs operate largely and unsatisfactorily as avenues for information exchange, used more or less effectively in the same way as are national union information resources to help legitimate negotiable demands. Perhaps over time, a better way of understanding the role of EWCs as a new tier of European trade union coordination is to view them as an additional resource, rather than as a system that operates alone as an information, consultation, or negotiating body. To date, the EWCs have contributed only modestly to a broader spectrum of employee representation, but the Belgian union delegates may, nonetheless, be right when they suggest that the EWC is likely to evolve very slowly toward a greater role in transnational union cooperation and coordination.

EWCs: A Forum for Management?

As described by Bain and Hester in the preceding chapter, MNCs strongly resisted the sheer existence of the EWC Directive, which in its present form imposes very few obligations as far as information and consultation are concerned. But having to face the reality of the directive, many MNCs are learning how to take advantage of it. In particular, some saw their early compliance as a way to improve their image, and some have also learned that EWC meetings can serve as platforms from which MNCs can legitimate their views and enhance corporate identity with their employees. Asked about the potential advantages to them of EWCs, our management interviewees described three advantages consistent with a recent British survey (Wills, 1998): (1) getting across management's vision to employee representatives, (2) exchanging information with employee representatives, and (3) building new relationships with unions. In company B, one British manager also found the EWC advantageous in helping make the company appear more "European" as part of the process of market expansion.

Potential disadvantages were also identified by management, although with varying accents and importance. Among these disadvantages were increased bureaucracy, unnecessary duplication in employee relations, direct financial expenses and indirect costs of lost time, the tendency to compare employment conditions between different countries, the likelihood of European collective bargaining (opposed by all but one Belgian manager interviewed), delays in decision making, and heightened employee expectations. Management in company A insisted that it was their responsibility to ensure that these potential costs were avoided or minimized. One way that management has circumvented unwanted decisions or developments has been to impose certain restrictions, for instance, by refusing to make any comparison of employment conditions or, following the subsidiarity requirements of the Annex to the directive,[7] by rejecting any questions pertaining to what takes place in one country only, even when (as occurred in company C) a takeover could be considered an important element of group strategy. In addition, employers avoid expending resources for other than the required annual meetings of EWCs, for while the day-to-day functioning of an EWC is not expensive per se, annual meetings are; yet MNCs often spend much more on these annual meetings than is required. At the same time, nevertheless, they regularly use the cost of meetings as an excuse to deny additional meetings between employee representatives. Perhaps not surprisingly, companies appear ready to spend substantially on improving their image but only minimally on helping create stronger employee representation.

CONCLUSIONS

While we must emphasize that our research is still in progress, we can summarize three main themes running through our initial interviews. First, contrary to the level of employer complaints about being obliged to establish EWCs and to the contrasting enthusiastic support for them given by many European industry federations, we found that the new EWC institution is very "thin" indeed. This is true with respect to the restricted *information* flow of EWCs, their negligible *consultative* effects, and the minimal *numbers* of individual actors seriously engaged in them. Second, in contrast with the strong, national-level British trade union enthusiasm for European social policy since 1987, we found that while there were more similarities than differences in attitudes, the British representatives were even more tentative and doubtful than were the Belgian representatives as to whether the EWCs provided "added value." There was, nonetheless, a positive feeling among the British that at least they were meeting delegates from other parts of the United Kingdom. Third, despite the hopes that the EWCs would strengthen solidarity and understanding, we detected a rather strong sense of rivalry and suspicion both between the unions *within* Britain and Belgium and *between* the unions internationally in regard to the EWCs. From the subtext of our interviews, moreover, EWC participation was sometimes viewed as a means to the end of maintaining or increasing the union's local legitimacy and status rather than as an effective European-wide forum in and of itself.

We can also draw some further general conclusions about the dynamics of union representation in the EWC process. Having been imposed upon MNCs, if EWCs supplement existing union and employee representative structures, they also crosscut them, often creating a "democratic deficit" that is the source of a number of potential difficulties (Lecher, Nagel, and Platzer, 1999). That is, EWCs are not merely councils molded by those who participate directly in them; they are also shaped by the related actions of those who inhabit other institutional structures. The paradox of a subordinate, but simultaneously "superior," institution, in turn, causes some special problems.

First, *intra-EWC delegate relations* present, perhaps, the greatest challenge. We can distinguish two facets of this challenge. *National* divisiveness arises in which interunion rivalry under union pluralism impedes the process of establishing cohesion and reduces the effectiveness of the EWC as a communication forum. This divisiveness can entail disdain by one union for the activities of another union, including its participation or its leadership in the EWC, which can lead to a lack of either valorization or even curiosity toward EWCs. Furthermore, for the union holding a dominant position in an EWC, interunion rivalry can lead to the retention of valuable information vis-à-vis the other union(s). Indeed, we saw examples in our case studies wherein the Belgian EWC secretaries functioned without much contact with their own "minority" unions. Negative *transnational* divisiveness also arises partly as a result of language barriers but nearly as much from distrust stemming from a lack of understanding of each other's IR systems and respective organizations. Such divisiveness can be exacerbated, moreover, by competition between different sites for production.   Both national and/or transnational divisiveness can be further compounded in cases in which mergers or acquisitions lead to a reshaping of EWCs.   Our observations suggest that these changes in company configurations present major obstacles to the coherent functioning of the EWCs.

A   second   problem faced by EWCs   arises out of ineffective *enterprise-level union articulation*.   In general we found, according to our interviewees, very little interest in the EWCs, yet demonstrating their relevance is critical if EWCs are to achieve any legitimacy and, in turn, be effective.   In part, this is a function of EWC member selection and communication with constituents.   Neither in the Belgian subsidiaries nor in the U.K. subsidiaries of company A were there direct elections of members to the EWC, and in company C, the selection process was not an independent one.   In all three cases studied, EWC delegates, moreover, have done little to communicate European issues to the employees whom they represent or consult with their constituents about the issues brought before the EWCs.

Flawed *national-level union articulation* is a third problem encountered by EWCs.   In all three cases, senior national union officials were the main actors on the employee side in setting up the EWCs, but they usually acted without the full participation of all the key actors in the MNC.   While continuing in all cases to wish the EWCs well, some unions, furthermore, failed to follow up with the necessary support for success, in part because of limited resources but in part because of concerns about the role of EWCs.   Continuing training and support for EWC delegates were variable, and the national unions were not prepared to fund travel by EWC delegates between countries to strengthen links and coordination among delegates between EWC meetings.   Some Belgian national officials, moreover, expressed a fear, not without reason, that the EWC delegates might "get out of control" and that "enterprise unionism" might inadvertently enter through the back door.   Lastly, one union official strongly opposed the prospect of negotiating collective agreements at the level of the multinationals, believing that it would interfere with the Belgian structure of sectoral collective bargaining.

Putting the preceding special problems of union dynamics underlying the EWC process into the broader context of our inquiry, we offer several final comparative observations.   The responses from human resource managers to the EWCs appear to be conditioned by the particular company union context and, linked to this, by their national origin.   Thus, while Belgian managers tended to be positive about the costs and benefits of EWCs, this view was shared only by the British managers of companies A and B (where the trade union presence was strong) and not by those of company C, where the trade union presence was weak or nonexistent.

Among the employee representatives, similar national and contextual differences emerge.   In particular, we found that the EWCs are the active concern of a paper-thin layer of lay union activists.   In Belgium, these activities include mainly the secretaries and some especially interested delegates.   These delegates tend to be the most European-minded, often speaking more than one language themselves. They also appear to hold views that are fairly remote from their constituents' views about EWCs and even sometimes from those of other lay activists who are not EWC delegates. In the United Kingdom, the interest appeared strongest in company B, where international management is most supportive and where interunion cooperation is exceptional. Not surprisingly, interest was lowest in company C, where there is no union. From the early meetings of the EWCs, the parties had not yet established any clearly important purpose for the new institution, and the possibility of the contacts set in motion leading to improvements in resource mobilization was not explicitly recognized by two delegates.

At this early stage in the evolution of EWCs in both countries, therefore, the role of EWCs appears most clearly to be in helping management improve corporate communications and image. Somewhat less clearly, the EWCs may also have a slightly subversive effect on this end by helping create an international employee counterculture network, especially where trade unions are stronger. Furthermore, there is certainly a very long way to go before EWCs become significant vehicles of a European union consciousness. As many delegates insisted, nonetheless, the EWCs are still very young. Given the issues, the time, adequate support, a continuing dedication on the part of the most active delegates, and the opportunity to make good the "democratic deficit" separating them from their constituencies, it is possible that EWCs will eventually become valued institutions, evolving from simply an annual, formal meeting, to playing some form of coordinating role between different national groups of workers who increasingly trust each other and have converging interests. For this to be realized, however, we suggest that EWCs will need further political support from both their national unions and from the European industry federations. At a time when the ETUC has proposed a number of revisions of the directive (Buschak, 1999), our findings suggest that providing this support is at least as important as legislative changes.

EWCs, therefore, may be considered as providing a platform for a start toward creating some union response to the internationalization of capital and a step toward a European labor movement. Turner (1996) rightly argues that what is still more important than the growth of employee representation institutions is that they encourage a thickening web of cross-national union contacts. Our analysis of three Belgian law-based EWCs tends to confirm his argument that "unless the new structures can open space for cross-national collective action or mass protest, the European labour movement is likely to remain a rather formal construct" (Turner, 1996: 326). Based on the early experiences of our case studies, we cannot conclude that such space has been opened. What perhaps makes a case for cautious optimism about the EWC institutional innovation is our finding that it has encouraged a small-scale process of active and conscious national and cross-national networking. Although such networking exists on a very small scale presently, it has certainly not closed off the possibility of transnational union cooperation and coordination and has probably increased its likelihood.

NOTES

1. The first phase of comparative study was in part funded by the Belgian Federal Services for Scientific, Technical and Cultural Affairs, contract no. SE/11/038, the Belgian National Fund for Scientific Research, the French Community of Belgium and the British Council. Of the 23 semistructured interviews in this first phase of our research, as many as possible (11) were conducted jointly by mixed Belgian-British teams speaking either French or English according to the language of origin of the interviewee, which we believe greatly facilitated genuinely comparative insights into the IR processes in the two countries

2. Health and Safety Committees in Britain are more rarely viewed as vehicles of employee representation than in Belgium.

3. Supplementing this bipartite agreement, the government passed a law covering confidentiality, the employment protection of the employee representatives, and the coverage of public enterprises.

4. We use the French acronyms instead of Flemish ones.

5. For all the British delegates, there was another basic effect of the EWC meetings. Because they had no opportunities to meet together with the United Kingdom, the hosting of the meetings abroad brought them together and gave them an opportunity to compare conditions across different companies and plants.

6. The nomenclature varies. In the two insurance companies, the leading employee representative was called the EWC secretary, whereas in the metalworking companies, he or she was called the EWC president, based on the model of the German *Betriebsrat*, even if he or she did not actually preside during the EWC meeting with management. Although this distinction does not entail any practical difference, it can lead to different expectations. Herein, we use the term secretary throughout.

7. The competence of the EWC is limited to information and consultation on issues that concern the whole of the Community-scale undertaking or group or at least two group establishments situated in two different Member States. (See Article 1, paragraph b of the Annex).

REFERENCES

Beaupain, Th. (1994). "Belgium." In Trebilock, A., et al., *Towards Social Dialogue: Tripartite Cooperation in National Economic and Social Policy-Making.* Geneva: ILO, pp. 121–63.

Buschak, W. (1999). "Five Years After: A Look Forward to the Revision of the EWC Directive." *Transfer* 3 (5), pp. 384–92.

International Labor Organization. (ILO). (1997). *World Labour Report 1997–98: Industrial Relations, Democracy and Social Stability.* Geneva: ILO.

Lecher, W., Nagel, B., and Platzer, H. (1999). *The Establishment of European Works Councils. From Information Committee to Social Actor.* Aldershot: Ashgate.

Marginson, P. and Sisson, K. (1994). "The Structure of Transnational Capital in Europe: The Emerging Euro-company and Its Implications for Industrial Relations." In Hyman, R. and Ferner, A. (eds.), *New Frontiers in European Industrial Relations.* Oxford: Basic Blackwell, pp. 15–51.

Miroir, A. 1982). "Le syndicalisme libe'ral. Contribution a' l'e'tude des familles politiques." Revue belge d'histoire contemporaine 10 (1), pp. 59–81.

Schulten, T. (1996). "European Works Councils: Prospects for a New System of European Industrial Relations." *European Journal of Industrial Relations* 3 (2), pp. 303–24.

Turner, L. (1996). "The Europeanization of Labour: Structure before Action." *European Journal of Industrial Relations* 3 (2), pp. 325–44

Vilrokx, J. and Van Leemput, J. (1998). "Belgium: The Great Transformation." In A. Ferner and Hyman, R. (eds.), *Changing Industrial Relations in Europe.* Oxford: Blackwell, pp. 315–47.

Wills, J. (1998). "Making the Best of It? Managerial Attitudes Towards, and Experiences of, European Works Councils in UK-Owned Multi-National Firms." Working paper No. 3, Department of Geography, Southampton University, pp. 1–34.

17

Regulating Employee Interest Representation: The Case of McDonald's in the European Union

Tony Royle and Brian Towers

Given the limitations of national and transnational trade union organization (Chapters 10–13), it has long been argued that the organizational structures and global mobility of multinational companies (MNCs) allow them to pursue their interests with little regard for the employment standards and employee rights of national industrial relations (IR) systems (Levinson, 1972). It has also been argued that various voluntary forms of cross-border regulation embodied in *public codes* of conduct, such as Organization for Economic Cooperation and Development (OECD) guidelines and International Labor Organization (ILO) conventions, have had minimal effects on MNC behavior. As these codes specifically exclude interference with national workplace laws and lack enforcement mechanisms, MNCs can choose to ignore such codes with impunity. Likewise, the substantial growth and increasing popularity of *private codes* of conduct appear to have much more to do with protecting corporate reputations than with protecting the rights of workers and adhering to national workplace regulations (Hepple, 1999; Maitland, 1999).

In contrast to voluntary codes aimed at cross-border self-regulation, there are regional forms of regulation found in the treaty provisions of the European Union (EU). These treaty provisions are binding on member states and enforceable through supranational institutions, including legally binding directives on important human resource management and labor relations (HRM/LR) issues such as discrimination, health and safety, working time, and parental leave; institutions deriving from directives extending information and consultation rights to workers and their representatives (i.e., European Works Councils); and the legally based, EU-wide framework agreement processes of the Social Dialogue.

The EU regional model of regulation, nonetheless, is marked by several notable limitations. First, the development of maximum competition within the single market is not conditional upon the parallel development of employment rights. Second, EU directives are not intended to impose detailed, supranational regulation on national systems. Third, the directives arising from the Social Dialogue seek compromises over conflicts of interests rather than advancing *social* rights per se (Keller and Sörries, 1999). Fourth, the legal scope of EU directives precludes the regulation of rights to freedom of association, and access to collective bargaining, the right to strike, and minimum pay and benefits.

The European Works Council (EWC) Directive (described in detail in Chapter 15) is a good example of the limitations of EU legislation in the promotion and regulation of employment rights. This directive was intended to provide employees with some voice in the decision-making process of MNCs operating in more than one European country, but the directive that finally emerged in 1994 offers businesses a menu of alternative rules and structures from which they can choose. In other words, the specific framework of each EWC is the result of a complex bargaining process reflecting the relative bargaining power of employee representatives, unions, and employers. It is not just European-wide legislation, however, that is threatened by the activities of MNCs. National systems have also come into conflict with the HMR/LR policies pursued by MNCs. U.S. MNCs, in particular, are well known for their efforts at undermining legislatively underpinned systems of employee interest representation, including those that require works councils and employee representation on supervisory boards (De Vos, 1981; Martinez and Weston, 1994; Shire, 1994; Wever, 1995).

In this chapter, we trace the HRM/LR policies and practices of McDonald's Corporation in selected countries of the EU. Our purpose is to examine how and to what extent well-organized, well-resourced, and determined MNCs can evade the objectives and outcomes intended by legislated systems of employee interest representation at both the national and supranational levels. Our findings are based on more than six years of investigation using a variety of methods, including direct observation, analyses of documentation, questionnaire surveys, and one-on-one interviews. The results presented here are primarily based on approximately 200 semistructured interviews, lasting about two hours each. These interviews were conducted with various McDonald's senior managers, restaurant managers, franchise operators, employees, works councillors, trade union representatives (including local trade unions, union federations, and international union organizations), and representatives from national and international employer associations.

After providing a brief summary of McDonald's Corporation's operations in the EU, we examine and analyze national-level mechanisms of worker representation across McDonald's restaurants. In particular, we describe the extent to which McDonald's restaurants have embraced or evaded national IR systems of worker representation as embodied in various works council and union representation arrangements. Such behavior is examined across five EU countries (Germany, Austria, France, Spain, and Sweden). Second, we evaluate the company's involvement in EWCs and the impact that this supranational regulation of workplaces has had on transnational employee representation.

Lastly, we summarize our key findings and offer several general conclusions about the prospects that national and supranational IR regulation can have on MNCs bent on evading or marginalizing such regulation.

THE MCDONALD'S CORPORATION IN THE EU

At the beginning of 2000, the McDonald's Corporation employed well over 1.5 million people in over 25,000 restaurants worldwide. It is the best-known fast-food service brand in the world and the largest food service system in terms of sales (valued at over U.S.$40 billion in 1998). McDonald's plans to open between 2,500 and 3,200 new restaurants every year, the equivalent of one new restaurant every three hours. If this rate of expansion can be achieved, the corporation will have more than doubled in size to well over 50,000 restaurants by 2010. At the end of 1999, McDonald's employed over 200,000 people across roughly 4,000 restaurants in the 17 countries of the European Economic Area (EEA). McDonald's first invested in Europe in 1971, when it opened restaurants in Holland and Germany. Restaurants were subsequently opened in Sweden in 1973, the United Kingdom in 1974, Austria and Ireland in 1977, Belgium in 1978, France in 1979, Denmark in 1981, Spain in 1982, Norway in 1983, Finland in 1984, and Italy in 1985.

Some 65 percent of McDonald's European restaurants are operated as franchises. As discussed elsewhere (Royle, 2000), although franchises are legally distinct entities, in economic terms and for all practical purposes they are tightly controlled by the corporation, essentially acting as its de facto subsidiaries. This control is achieved by a combination of stringent processes for selection, training, socialization, and financial incentives and controls. Despite these tight controls, McDonald's frequently iterates its claim that franchisees are independent operators and, therefore, that the corporation cannot be held responsible for their actions. Nevertheless, we suggest that if MNCs are determined to avoid union involvement and statutory mechanisms of worker representation, then this legal "separation" can prove extremely useful both at national and supranational levels.

National-Level Mechanisms of Worker Representation

The company's standard approach to worker participation (what we term "McParticipation") is based on communication and limited employee involvement (Marchington, 1995). It is not a system that provides worker rights to consultation, information, or codetermination. Instead, it largely comprises newsletters, suggestion schemes, team briefings, and RAP (Real Approach to Problems) sessions. The latter are meetings called by management, in which, in concept at least, employees are allowed to express their views and grievances, but in practice, worker complaints are rarely acted upon, and many workers are not even invited to such sessions (especially if they are union members). In short, "McParticipation" of this kind is at best a management-dominated, paternalistic consultation regime. Most countries of mainland Europe, however, have statutory mechanisms that provide workers with rights to information and consultation over management decisions that affect them and sometimes rights to codetermine decisions with management. Next, we describe and evaluate how McDonald's has dealt with such mechanisms in practice across a number of EU countries.

Germany

The German model of codetermination provides for employee representation on supervisory boards in larger firms. The 1952/1972 Works Constitution Act and the 1976 Co-determination Act govern these institutions for private businesses outside the coal and steel industries. The former legislation deals with supervisory boards of limited liability companies with over 500 employees and works councils at plant, company, and group levels. The 1976 act is concerned with employee representatives on the supervisory boards of companies with over 2,000 employees (Müller-Jentsch, 1995). With over 50,000 employees in over 1,000 restaurants, one might expect that McDonald's Germany would have employee representatives sitting on a supervisory board, but this is not the case, and the main reason is that McDonald's Germany has retained American registration, making it a wholly owned subsidiary of the American McDonald's Corporation registered in Oak Brook, Illinois. This arrangement is permitted under the German-American Trade Agreement of 1954, under which the usual obligation for a supervisory board according to either the 1952 or 1976 acts cannot be imposed.

However, the issue of the German works council is not quite so straightforward. The Works Constitution Act provides for a works council in all businesses with five or more employees aged 18 and older. The works council cannot call a strike, but it can sue management for any alleged breach of rights. The council must meet with management every four weeks, and the law grants the councils a broad range of rights to information, consultation, and codetermination. In addition, in any business or unit with 300 employees, a works council member can be released from his or her normal duties to work full-time on works council business. The number of these full-time works councillors increases in proportion with the size of organizations. This act also provides for a "central" works council at the company level (*Gesamtbetriebsrat*—GBR) where there are two or more works councils in the same business. Similarly, where there is a group of companies with works councils, a group-level or concern-level works council (*Konzernbetriebsrat*—KBR) can be established, but only if this is requested by the works councils of subsidiaries employing at least 75 percent of the group's workforce. The works councillors represented on the GBR or KBR are also quite likely to be the same representatives on the supervisory board where one exists (Müller-Jentsch, 1995; Jacobi, Keller, and Muller-Jentsch, 1998).

Given that 65 percent or more of McDonald's restaurants are franchise operations, only about 350 of McDonald's German restaurants (employing about 18,000 workers) are company-owned. McDonald's also operates some of these restaurants through a number of holding companies, called *Anver* companies. The typical McDonald's restaurant employs between 45 and 100 employees, and, thus, there could be a works council in every McDonald's restaurant in Germany. One might also expect that there would be a company-level works council (GBR) or possibly a concern-level works council (KBR). In fact, in 1999 there were only between 40 and 50 works councils across 1,000 restaurants, no KBR, and until five years ago, no GBR either.

How can the limited number of works councils be explained? Union officials and McDonald's workers allege that over the years, the corporation has used some rather extreme measures to block the establishment of works councils in their restaurants. There have been many instances of unfair dismissals and so-called flying squads of managers sent to restaurants to persuade employees that there was no need for works councils. One infamous management exponent of this practice was known among works councillors as "Commando Mueller." McDonald's has also transferred restaurants into different ownership, which has had the effect of delaying or stopping altogether the election of works councils. The corporation has also been adept at "arranging" the nomination of management candidates to serve on works councils in order to capture them for a management-sponsored agenda.[1] Franchises are frequently at the center of this kind of activity, wherein the corporation has often sold off "unruly" restaurants to franchise owners, not only to dissuade workers from becoming involved in works councils but also to interfere with the establishment of a GBR. Once a works council is transferred in this way, it cannot be included in any attempt to create a GBR within the corporation. In similar fashion, franchises have sometimes been taken back under corporate ownership to avoid the establishment of a GBR among a group of franchise restaurants operated by one franchisee.

When managers suspect that workers are planning to elect a works council, McDonald's Germany has a standard procedure for its managers to follow. Documentation distributed to McDonald's restaurant managers (*Practical Help in Dealing with Works Councils*)[2] states that employee attempts to establish works councils are a serious problem and a failure of management. It states, moreover, that the reactions of managers to any such initiative must be carefully handled and the head office in Munich immediately informed, which, in turn, must make all major decisions. Specifically, the document states:

A works council representative from another restaurant visits your store how do you behave? Information about the visit must be sent immediately to headquarters personnel operations, any further measures will not be taken by operations but only by headquarters. You must never talk with union representatives without first having authority from head office (and) never give employees the impression that you are against the trade unions or the works council. The incentive to lead someone to do something is much greater than you think. (p. 8)

Indeed, in one case recently reported in an article in the German *Stern* magazine ("Abgebraten bis die Kasse Stimmt," 1999), a restaurant manager was allegedly demoted to assistant manager for allowing his workers to elect a works council in his restaurant in 1997. It is worth noting, furthermore, that no works councils have been established in the old East German states. Union officials state that McDonald's workers in the new federal states are not familiar with the works council legislation and that because of the continuing high unemployment in the East, they are much more afraid of upsetting management and losing their jobs.

In addition to efforts to suppress the establishment of works councils, there remains the problem with the election of a company-level works council (GBR) at McDonald's. In 1998, two separate GBRs with two different chairmen were both claiming to be the legitimate body to represent McDonald's German workers. Union officials argue that after years of trying to block or nullify the union-supported GBR, McDonald's Germany had decided to establish its own GBR (despite a court ruling that suggested that the corporation had acted illegally and that the GBR election would have to be held again). After what could be described as more "underhanded" tactics, the corporation managed to have its preferred candidates elected. As we discuss in the next section, the outcome of the reelection also had implications for the McDonald's European Works Council. Indeed these kinds of avoidance activities appear to be increasing rather than subsiding.

As we have already suggested, the corporation has used a variety of tactics in its efforts to avoid or rid itself of works councils, but its most effective weapon appears to be the "buyout" (Royle, 1998). Unions have no effective response to this tactic. In 1995 alone, union officials and the press reported that McDonald's spent close to U.S.$375,000 to buy out 46 works councillors and their supporters (Langenhuisen, 1995). More recently, according to union officials (and reported in "Abgebraten," 1999), a works council chairman in Wiesbaden was allegedly offered roughly U.S.$105,000 to leave McDonald's. He refused, and, according to the same sources, management has since tried to block his works council activities by various means. The *Stern* article also states that the chairman of McDonald's Germany (Raupeter) wrote a letter in September 1999 to the chairman of the employer association (BdS), Thomas Heyll, regarding this stubborn works council. Heyll is well known for his "rough stuff" when it comes to dealing with trade unions. In the letter, Raupeter (in James Bond-like tones) grants the license to dismiss: "With regard to this matter you are authorised to carry out every necessary measure within individual employment contract and works council law" ("Abgebraten," 1999: 128). We surmise that the conflict over effective worker representation at McDonald's Germany is likely to continue.

Austria

Works councils in the private sector in Austria are regulated by the Works Constitution Act, a law similar to that in Germany. Works councils can be established in any business with at least five permanent employees, and the number of works council members increases with the size of the business. Austrian works councils also enjoy similar but not quite as many rights as their German counterparts (Traxler, 1998). In addition, there are provisions for company-level works councils (*Zentralbetriebsrat*—ZBR) and group-level works councils.

There are approximately 4,000 people working in 80 restaurants at McDonald's in Austria. On paper at least, there could be a works council in each one of these restaurants. But there are none, for which there is a fairly straightforward reason: the majority of employees are foreign workers. Similar to McDonald's Germany's workforce, the McDonald's Austrian workforce is made up of a large proportion of foreign workers (the remainder includes students over 18 years old and second-income earners such as housewives). Union officials estimate that roughly 60 to 70 percent of McDonald's employees in Austria are foreign workers. In addition to the fact that foreign workers are less likely to be aware of their rights regarding representation in works councils, they are less likely to question managerial authority.

The distinguishing factor with regard to the employment of foreign workers, however, is the requirement that candidates for works council offices be Austrian citizens or citizens of EU member states. For the last 27 years, Austria has been the only European country to restrict employee representation on the basis of citizenship. There has been little, if any, attempt, moreover, to give foreign workers equal rights. With the exception of some union pressure groups *("Sesam öffne dich!")* and smaller unions like HGPD, even the larger unions and the main union confederation (*Österreichischer Gewerkschaftsbund*) have done little in practice to support their cause.[3] Anyone who wishes to be elected to the works council, furthermore, must have worked at the company for at least six months. In short, large proportions of the McDonald's workforce do not enjoy EU citizenship, and, as elsewhere, many others do not stay long enough with the corporation. Under these circumstances, it is hardly surprising that no works councils have been established at McDonald's in Austria.

The lack of Austrian works councils throughout McDonald's restaurants has the effect of also denying workers any employee representation on supervisory boards. Although employee representatives are normally appointed by trade unions, only works council members may be nominated and then only those entitled to vote in works council elections. These legal requirements automatically exclude union officials normally found sitting on Austrian works councils. Consequently, not only are there no works councils representing employees at McDonalds, but there is no employee representation through a supervisory board.

France

The French system of employee representation is somewhat different from that in Germany and Austria. It is based not just on works councils but also on trade union sections, employee delegates, and union delegates. Individual trade unions can each establish a trade union section that brings its workplace members together. These union sections can be established regardless of the number of union members in the business, and they have specific rights under the law. In workplaces with over 50 employees, furthermore, unions have the right to appoint a trade union delegate to represent the union and the interests of employees. In addition, two separately elected bodies have specific rights and duties to represent the entire workforce. First, in businesses with more than 10 employees, the workforce is entitled to an employee delegate. Second, for all companies with more than 50 employees the workforce is entitled to a works council. Unlike the German system, the establishment of French works councils does not rely on the instigation of employees. In smaller companies with fewer than 200 employees, on the other hand, management can decide that there will not be a separate works council and that employee delegates will undertake both roles of representative and works council member. As with the German model, large companies with several plant locations, each with its own works council, are expected to establish a company-level works council. In companies with several plants and more than 2,000 employees, unions can also assign a central trade union delegate. Finally, businesses with several companies are expected to form a group-level works council (IDS, 1996).

As in Germany, French works councils are joint management–employee bodies. Representatives of management chair French works councils, whereas employee representatives serve as council secretaries. Councils are expected to meet once a month in companies with more than 150 employees but normally meet only once every two months in smaller companies. Works councils are entitled to use financial experts, who can be called in at the company's expense to examine annual accounts and large-scale redundancy proposals. In companies with more than 300 employees, councils can also call in technology experts and use financial experts to examine financial forecasts.

Although the rights of the French works councils are not as substantial as in Germany or Austria (there are no codetermination rights), they do provide the French unions with the advantage that only they (as "representative" trade unions) can nominate a list of candidates in a first-round election. If these candidates receive more than half of the votes, they are elected to the council, and seats are allocated on a proportional basis across unions. Only if union-selected candidates fail to obtain a majority vote in the election is a second round held, at which time nonunion employees can stand for election. As argued by Tchobanian (1995), the 1982 Auroux reforms have made works councils central to employee collective action, reaffirming the central role of unions in worker representation.

Despite some of the advantages granted unions within the French system, unions have found it very difficult, nonetheless, either to establish works councils or to appoint union delegates at McDonald's. In many cases, delegates have simply been dismissed, and, although unions have generally won their unfair dismissal cases in court, such victories have not improved union opportunities. McDonald's, that is, has simply compensated these employees but usually has not reinstated them. It has been extremely difficult, therefore, to retain union delegates in the company. Similarly, once unions have notified the company of their candidate lists for works council elections, these union-sponsored candidates have "disappeared." The unions allege that they were either dismissed or "bought out." An additional problem in establishing union delegates and works councils is the calculation of employee thresholds. Businesses must have more than 10 full-time employees for appointment of a union delegate and over 50 full-time employees for establishment of a works council. Many of McDonald's employees, of course, work part-time. These workers' hours can be included in the calculation of thresholds, but it takes two or three part-time employees to secure the equivalent of one full-time employee.

Moreover, it is often difficult to obtain accurate and up-to-date information on workers' hours.

Manipulation and interference with works council elections are also commonplace at McDonald's. For example, on the morning of July 6, 1994, 12 McDonald's managers were arrested at their place of work and put under judicial investigation. They were accused of impeding union rights and the election of a works council. This conflict involved 12 franchise restaurants in Lyon. The CFDT union argued that because all 12 franchises were operated by the same franchisee, they should be considered as a single business or "economic and social unit" (*unité économique et sociale*—UES). Having the restaurants defined as an UES would then have allowed the establishment of a *comité d'entreprise*. McDonald's argued against UES status, taking its case to the French high court. The court, nevertheless, decided in favor of the CFDT, and 10 of the 12 managers were found to have violated the exercise of union rights and interfered with the election of a works council. In the end, they were forbidden to return to their restaurants.

Another example of manipulation and interference is found in the election of the Lyon works council, the results of which were perplexing. In the first vote, when only union representatives could be elected, a mere 38 of 458 eligible employees voted. In the second vote (when any employee could stand for election), 260 employees voted, electing all nonunion representatives to the council. CFDT officials allege that management threatened anyone voting for the union with dismissal. Defeated, the CFDT has since focused its activities in Paris, where most of the restaurants are wholly owned and McDonald's has a higher public profile. In 1995, elections for union delegates and works councils were held. The CFDT claims that the same kind of voting manipulation that took place in Lyons likewise initially took place in Paris. However, with an increasing amount of bad publicity, it appeared that the company's overtly antiunion approach began to change. In particular, in 1995 a new senior human resource manager was appointed, and McDonald's declared itself to be a driving force in the field of social relations, wishing to integrate itself into the "social landscape" ("McDonald's Serves Up Improved Social Relatons," 1997: 20).

A CFDT official stated that, on one level, relations with the company have improved since the appointment of the human resource manager. Indeed, one of the first steps of the company's new approach was to agree to the establishment of a company-level works council in April 1996. In June 1996, the corporation also concluded a pay agreement with the CFDT for the company-owned restaurants. In October 1996, McDonald's then signed an agreement with the CFDT on the recognition of union rights, an agreement that covers all other trade unions representing employees in the company. Like the other agreements, however, this recognition agreement is restricted to its wholly owned restaurants, not the 90 percent of restaurants operated as franchises and joint ventures. The CFDT suggest that the pay element of the agreement was not especially significant, but the recognition agreement has had a small impact on the union's ability to establish both union delegates and works councils in the company-owned restaurants. In addition, when the company-level council was established in 1996, some of its seats were occupied by nonunion members. In the most recent election, however, all seats were captured by union representatives. The central or principal union delegate is a CDFT member who also serves as secretary of the *comité central d'entreprise* and the EWC employee representative.

By early 1999, McDonald's operated over 720 restaurants employing roughly 35,000 workers in France. Among these restaurants were five works councils and one central works council representing the company-owned restaurants. Since the problems at Lyon in 1994, McDonald's has bought back the franchise restaurants in Lyon and Nice. Four of the five *comité d'entreprise* are union-controlled, and in three of these, the CFDT has the majority of members. One of the four union-controlled works councils represents managers and some office workers, organized by the professional and managerial staff federation (*Conféderation générale des cadres*—CGC). The fifth is nonunion and represents about 10 restaurants all managed by one franchise operator. Consequently, of the total of the more than 720 McDonald's restaurants, the approximately 80 company-owned restaurants are represented by two *comité d'entreprise* and a number of *délegué syndical*. In addition, one works council represents workers in 20 restaurants operated by a joint venture (90 percent owned by McDonald's). Therefore, approximately 620 remaining franchise and joint-venture restaurants have no trade union representation whatsoever.

Since passage of the Auroux laws (introduced in 1982 and amended in 1986), workers have had a right of expression, or *group d'expression*, in which workers have the right to express their views about their working conditions. McDonald's has not created any such groups, claiming that workers can already express their views in the company's existing RAP sessions. As we have already suggested, however, RAP sessions appear to offer very little for employees in practice. French law, furthermore, provides for two or four representatives of a company's works council (depending on the number of managers employed) to attend board meetings (or supervisory board meetings where these exist). Although restricted to only consultative roles, no such representatives have been appointed at McDonald's.

In a more positive light, the recognition of the unions in the company-owned restaurants has had some impact on the functioning of works councils. In accordance with the works council legislation, the employer must provide exclusive use of an office and all equipment necessary for a works council to function effectively, as well as a budget amounting to 0.02 percent of the total wage bill. In addition, union representatives, works councillors, and employee delegates are entitled to paid time off for their activities depending on their range of responsibilities and the number of employees in the business (IDS, 1996; Goetschy, 1998). Since the recognition agreement, the principal union delegate has been able to obtain 50 percent paid time off to carry out his union duties, and the works council representatives/union delegates now have a budget and the use of an office with fax and telephone.

Nevertheless, in terms of representation of the vast majority of French workers and the exercise of any real influence by works councils over corporate decisions, the end results have been quite limited. Even in the smaller number of company-owned restaurants, many managers are still outspokenly antiunion and do not welcome employees' asking questions about the calculation of their pay entitlement or their rights to representation. If a restaurant does not have a union delegate, employees are often too inhibited to question managers about employee rights. Union delegates also report that a number of unfair dismissals relating to union activities are still occurring and that there are frequent instances in which restaurants do not adhere to national collective agreements.

The effectiveness of the existing works councils may also have been undermined by the continuing rivalry that often exists between the different union federations (Goetschy, 1998). In this case, there were some disagreements between union officials of different union federations and different regional offices in the same federation about who should be appointed as the principal trade union delegate and to the more influential positions on the company-level works council (e.g., secretary and treasurer). Making matters worse, representatives and union officials suggest that the corporation has attempted to exploit these inter- and intraunion differences. In one case, management allegedly spread rumors that one union confederation was reaching side agreements with McDonald's to exclude the other unions. Similar divisive tactics were used in Germany, where management allegedly attempted to divide individual works councils (Royle, 1998). In spite of inter- and intraunion differences, the company-level works council established in 1996 has allowed union representatives from different regions to meet face-to-face. It has been useful, moreover, in terms of obtaining a better picture of how McDonald's is organized and has allowed the works councils and unions to appoint additional union representatives at the appropriate level. If the unions were to fail to make these appointments, the company could simply refuse such appointments, arguing that they are invalid.

The company-level works council, however, can do nothing for the majority of workers employed in franchise operations. McDonald's stated in 1996 that it "hoped" that the franchisees would adopt similar practices and establish works councils. Indeed, it arranged a number of two-day seminars for franchisees at which the company explained the reasoning behind its change in direction ("McDonald's," 1997). In the three years since that time, nonetheless, there has been virtually no response from franchisees. In early 1999, there was only one works council representing franchise restaurants, a nonunion works council representing just 10 or so of the close to 650 franchise restaurants. Finally, according to a CFDT official, the new human resource manager appointed in 1995 may be genuinely trying to improve relations with the unions, but he is very much on his own at McDonald's. The changes introduced in 1996 have yet to achieve concrete improvements for the majority of workers, and with hindsight, these changes look increasingly more like a clever public relations exercise than a serious desire to be "integrated into the social landscape."

Spain
Spanish legislation provides for both employee delegates and works councils, the rights and duties of which are essentially identical. Workers are

entitled to delegates in firms with 10 or more employees or in firms with as few as 6 employees, provided a majority wants a delegate. Works councils comprise only employees and can be established in firms with 50 or more employees. Although having either works councils or employee delegates is not dependent on union involvement, where unions are well organized, they usually play central roles. In fact, Spanish unions dominate works council elections, nominating some 90 percent of elected representatives. As in France, unions are also entitled to establish trade union sections to bring together all the members of a particular union in the workplace. In companies with over 250 employees, members of each union with seats on the works council have a legal right to elect trade union delegates. Works councils are entitled to information and consultation with employers and have some protective functions regarding individual employees. Works councils, furthermore, have a duty to monitor employer compliance with the law, but barring employer violations, works councils cannot prevent management from acting as it wishes in the final instance (Escobar, 1995; Martinez Lucio, 1998).

National-level collective agreements are still relatively rare in Spain, but in recent years some have been negotiated to deal with key issues in the Spanish labor market. Such agreements have not dealt with pay since the mid-1980s, but Spain does have a statutory minimum wage, which is normally revised each January. Sectoral or company agreements often cover such issues as pay and working time. Indeed, there is a sectoral-level agreement for the broader hotel and restaurant industries, but it covers only job classifications, training, discipline, and sanctions for noncompliance. In the fast-food industry, therefore, improving basic rates of pay is highly dependent on achieving company-level agreements.

Despite the fact that the Spanish works council does not enjoy any codetermination rights, it is still a key institution in terms of employee representation. Unlike their counterparts in some other European countries, Spanish works councils can negotiate binding collective agreements covering pay and conditions in their company. In fact, at McDonald's, two company-level agreements have been negotiated with works councils, one covering a group of franchise restaurants in Madrid and one covering the 30 or so wholly owned company restaurants in the Madrid area. These negotiated agreements, however, do not appear beneficial to workers and certainly not to unions. According to trade union officials at FECOHT, both of these agreements are remarkably similar in that they offer very little to the employees. Neither the FECOHT nor any other union has been able to get involved in either of the agreements. FECOHT officials suggest that no real negotiations took place, and the works council representatives simply signed agreements that were merely presented to them by management.

McDonald's has approximately 160 restaurants in Spain employing about 8,000 workers. FECOHT officials report that there are currently some 33 separate works councils established in both franchise and company-owned restaurants. Only in two of these works councils has it been possible for the union to nominate candidates and elect any delegates. Currently, they have just two union delegates, one in a franchise restaurant and one in a company-owned restaurant. Elections are held every four years, and nominations for positions on the works councils are made on the basis of lists drawn up by either unions or groups of individual employees (provided that the number of voters supporting a list is three times greater than the number of places to be filled). Lists that receive less than 5 percent of the vote are eliminated, and any disputes that arise can be referred to the labor court.

Union officials suggest that the reason that there is such a minuscule number of union delegates at McDonald's is that the corporation has been very successful in promoting the election of nonunion candidates who will represent company interests. In many cases, works council representatives at McDonald's Spain are salaried managers. Union officials suggest that McDonald's groups a number of its restaurants together for the purpose of elections (typically five or so restaurants with a total of between 250 and 350 employees) in an effort to ensure that a large works council, not just a delegate, will be elected. Since most employees do not know the employees working in other restaurants, when the list of candidates is presented, workers often have no idea who to vote for. The problem for unions is not in attaining the 5 percent of votes required but in being able to nominate union candidates early enough. The result is that unions often have no candidates or that workers do not know their identity, and, thus, management usually acquires the majority of votes for the candidates whom it prefers. The FECOHT suggests that there is no contact or coordination between the existing works councils, and the union has yet to come across an incident where there has been a disagreement between works council representatives and the corporation.

As stated earlier, there is no technical difference between the rights of union delegates and those of the works council. The FECOHT contends that it would be much easier to get union delegates elected in individual restaurants with fewer than 50 workers and where no works council is required. In firms with more than 250 employees, on the other hand, the union has the right to appoint union delegates if they have a seat on the works council. Since McDonald's employs approximately 1,500 employees in its company-owned Spanish restaurants, FECOHT could nominate union delegates because they have a minimum level of representation, albeit a small number of union members. However, without representation on the works council, such delegates are not entitled to time off for union activities. Union officials argue that such nominations would be pointless, therefore, and would not allow any meaningful union influence. Finally, Spanish law also allows for company-level works councils to be established in firms with more than one site but only if so negotiated in collective agreements. As the unions in Spain have not played significant roles in reaching the two agreements at McDonald's, no such company-level works council has been established. We surmise that even if a company-level works council were established, it is unlikely to enhance employee interest representation given management's apparent success in blocking the appointment of union delegates and dominating the existing works councils.

Sweden

In Sweden, there are no separate channels providing a voice for employees outside the traditional union-employer bipartite system. Consequently, there is no elected works council structure as one finds in Germany and other European countries. Indeed, the current Swedish system was established to avoid institutions similar to works councils, of which Swedish unions have tended to be very skeptical.[4] The trade unions provide employee representation for Swedish workers both centrally and at the local level. In theory at least, there is no absence of monitoring and enforcement arrangements at the workplace. Codetermination councils, health and safety committees, and board representatives ensure that negotiated rules are observed. Trade union powers are largely derived from the 1977 Co-determination at Work Act, together with collective agreements that aim to increase union influence over company decisions. The most important of these agreements in the private sector is the 1982 Framework Agreement on Efficiency and Participation (Utvecklingsavtalet—UVA), which was concluded between SAF (the main employer's organization) and the LO (the primary labor organization). That agreement states that: "the forms of participation and co-determination shall be adapted to local circumstances at the workplace. The local parties have a joint responsibility for developing suitable participation and co-determination practices" (Brulin, 1995: 199).

The agreement also states that there are three possible forms of codetermination among which local agreements must clearly indicate which form of codetermination is chosen. Brulin (1995) suggests that, in practice, very few local agreements have been concluded, although the parties often act as if they have a local agreement. Joint consultative bodies are created for dealing with particular problems, or union representatives are included in the ordinary line of management. This appears to be the case at McDonald's Sweden, wherein McDonald's and the Swedish HRF union agreed some time ago to assign a union representative to work full-time on union matters in the head office of McDonald's in Stockholm. Workers are also supposed to be represented by union representatives, which could mean one or more union representatives servicing every restaurant. As suggested by Brulin (1995), arrangements of this kind are viewed by both parties as bipartite "participation and information bodies" or "line negotiations." These arrangements have no formal legitimization, however, and their juridical status remains unclear.

The Co-determination Act gives all unions and employers or employer organizations the right to negotiate but not necessarily any assurance that an agreement must be reached on any subject affecting the employment relationship. In particular, employers are obliged to consult local unions before implementing decisions that involve major changes affecting either employees in general or individual employees. For other less important matters, unions have the right to demand consultation. If agreement cannot be reached at a local level, the matter can be referred to the national level, and employers can be made to pay damages if they fail in their duty of consultation (IDS, 1996). Having been informed and consulted in the proper way, nonetheless, unions must in the end accept employer decisions. Brulin (1995) also points out that in cases where employee representation is weak, as may be the case at McDonald's, unions receive only minimum information strictly in line with the act and central agreements. Under such relationships, employers do not generally allow unions to take part in the planning and monitoring of change processes.

McDonald's has approximately 150 restaurants in Sweden employing about 7,500 workers. The main problem for union representation at McDonald's is that, although they have a full-time union representative at the head office, there are very few union representatives in the restaurants. One union representative estimated that there were no more than 10 union representatives across the roughly 150 restaurants. The potential shortcoming is that the senior union representative located at headquarters may often be out of touch with what occurs in the restaurants and may experience problems of role identification. Without representatives in every restaurant, the head office representative must rely on ordinary union members or other employees to bring problems to her attention. In addition, given the relatively low levels of union membership, there are likely to be few workers willing to take on the role of union representative in the restaurants. Although there would appear to be little need for the corporation to actively oppose union representatives, some union representatives report that restaurant managers have been openly hostile to them. Furthermore, union leaders themselves may feel that the struggle to appoint union representatives in the majority of McDonald's restaurants would be too costly and that more effective outcomes can be achieved by focusing on collective bargaining arrangements. Without sufficient union representation in the restaurants, however, frequent infringements of such agreements are more likely.

McDONALD'S AND THE EUROPEAN WORKS COUNCIL DIRECTIVE

The McDonald's EWC or European Communications Council, as McDonald's prefers to call it, was set up in November 1995 by voluntary agreement under Article 13 of the EWC Directive. There are currently 17 European countries represented on the McDonald's EWC, and, in theory at least, it is made up of both "employee" representatives and management representatives. It meets once per year, usually in September and usually in an expensive hotel and in a different country each year. For example, the first meeting took place in Vienna in 1996, the second took place in Barcelona, and the third in Athens. However, the manner in which the EWC was established and is "operated" suggests that the corporation has blatantly ignored the intent and the spirit of the directive (Royle, 1999b, 2000).

An examination of the McDonald's European Works Council reveals a number of problems. It appears that as far as the corporation is concerned, the EWC means "business as usual," with the EWC perceived as a mechanism to be captured primarily for management purposes. Of course, McDonald's is not the only American MNC that perhaps views EWCs as an unwelcome interference, the EWC at PepsiCo being a case in point ("Pepsi-Co," 1996; Overell, 1996). In addition, there have been a number of other EWCs where MNCs have attempted to marginalize trade union representation, including Marks and Spencer, BP, Unilever, and Honda (LRD, 1995; Barnett, 1996). Both Schulten (1996) and Marginson et al. (1998) are of a similar view that EWCs are likely to fall into two basic categories. First are those in which there is some form of independent cooperation on the employee side, and, hence, EWCs serve as *active institutions*. Second are those in which the EWCs are merely formal *symbols* or *procedures*, in that there is little or no influence over management decisions. McDonald's clearly falls into the second category.

There are several reasons for such an evaluation. First, since most EWC members are salaried managers, the majority of employee representatives are not truly *employees* in the sense that one might have assumed was intended by the directive. It is questionable, therefore, whether EWC members can honestly claim to represent the interests of the predominantly part-time and hourly paid employees who make up over 90 percent of the company's workforce. Second, premeetings for employees require the consent of management, meetings that McDonald's has ruled out presumably on the grounds of unjustified costs. Without such meetings, however, how are employee representatives expected to develop a meaningful employee-side strategy?

Third, despite the supposed joint agenda setting, in practice the structure and organization of meetings are largely determined by management. Fourth, there is the near exclusion of trade union-backed members serving as employee representatives, the result of dubious election processes. As discussed earlier, the combination of weak EU legislation and loopholes in national-level legislation has undermined election processes. One need look no further than the establishment and the election of the German EWC employee representative. In that case, McDonald's Germany successfully sidestepped the existing union-backed GBR chairman by an organized capture of the GBR election procedures. The company candidate who had already been selected by management consequently kept his seat on the EWC and in technical terms appeared to have legitimacy. A closer assessment of the election procedures revealed that this was far from the truth (Royle, 1999b, 2000).

Fifth, international sectoral trade union organizations have been kept out of the process, and outside "experts" can be brought in only with the permission of management. Sixth, there is no effective means by which the employee representatives can provide necessary feedback to the majority of employees about their concerns or their interpretation of the meetings. Finally, there is the question of franchise operations and holding companies. Some 65 percent of McDonald's 200,000 European workers employed in these companies are not covered by the directive and have no representation whatsoever. The franchise arrangement appears to be something that has not been adequately addressed in the directive's provisions. In theory, employees could challenge the agreement in the European labor courts, requesting that a special negotiating body be set up under Article 5. If McDonald's were to refuse, the case could then go to the courts. In view of the nature of the industry and workforce characteristics (Royle, 1999a), however, it seems unlikely that such a challenge will be mounted.

The EWC Directive was under review by the social partners until September 1999, during which the ETUC had set out a number of proposals, such as reducing the required employee thresholds. There is one brief mention of franchises under the question of joint ventures, where they are referred to as "contracts of domination." The ETUC argued that there is scope within the EWC Directive to address this issue. Whereas much of the emphasis on the interpretation of the directive has centered on the definition of "ownership," the ETUC has argued that this definition is too narrow and that the focus should be on the issue of the "controlling undertaking" (which is covered under Article 3.1 of the directive). The key determining issue would be to prove in each case that one organization had a "dominant" influence over another, by virtue, for example, of ownership, financial participation, or the rules that govern it. Part of the problem is that in order to determine whether or not an undertaking is a "controlling undertaking," the applicable law has to be the law of the member state that governs that undertaking.

Even if a legal solution to the issue of ownership and control were forthcoming, it may not be enough for unions to get past the various practical difficulties that remain. In addition to the many problems already outlined, there is the problem of an imbalance in education and negotiating and language skills between employee and management members on the EWC (Miller and Stirling, 1998). Furthermore, the individual capacity of EWC employee members to effectively counter a powerful management group and the ability of EWC members to develop a cohesive, employee-side strategy are considerable obstacles. Finally, enlisting individuals willing and able to effectively confront management at this level and over the long term is likely to be an added difficulty in this industry.

Lastly, the aim of the EWC Directive is to ensure that management consults and provides information to the workforce on a wide range of issues. While it is not directly intended to provide collective bargaining at a European level, management perhaps fears that it will interfere with its decision-making process or that there may be some added capacity for labor to reinforce collective bargaining through improved intelligence of company operations and international labor networking. The preceding analysis suggests, however, that there is very little that labor gains from the directive at present; the substantive requirements of the directive are not especially extensive, and it is clear that Article 13 arrangements are a particular weakness. There seems little doubt that this voluntarist approach to regulation allows an exit for employers (Streeck and Vitols, 1995). Paradoxically, therefore, even if the directive is ultimately enhanced from a labor perspective, in many cases the directive may remain a symbolic rather than a practical threat to managerial prerogative.

SUMMARY AND CONCLUSION

The results of our study show that McDonald's to a substantial extent has been able to impose its normal mode of operation across a number of disparate European IR systems. Despite the acknowledged difficulty of diffusing preferred HRM/LR practices across national borders (see Chapters 6 and 7), our case study of McDonald's in the EU illustrates the degree to which MNCs can diffuse policies and practices independently of regulatory systems. The ability of McDonald's to impose its will may be, in part, attributable to the organization's corporate culture, in which it successfully molds standardized management behavior throughout its operations. As Willmott (1993) argues, strong corporate cultures "exclude and eliminate" values inconsistent with a given culture. The McDonald's corporate culture appears to do just that, as it rejects union representation, encouraging managers to view union representation as an unwarranted and destructive interference.

Also contributing to McDonald's success in acting independently of EU regulatory systems is its heavy reliance on franchise operations. Rather than being hindered by the large proportion of restaurants operated as franchises, the company has reaped considerable benefits from the legal separation but economic dependency of franchises. Despite having effective control over virtually all facets of franchise operations, McDonald's can distance itself from the HRM/LR practices of individual franchise operators (e.g., when they fail to apply collective agreements or interfere with the establishment of works councils and assignment of union delegates). The high proportion of franchise operations also makes it extremely difficult to establish either site-level works councils in every restaurant or one company-wide works council in any country. Finally, franchise operations allow for an extremely paternalistic form of management that allows the close monitoring of individual employees and is often associated with a nonunion management style typical of small firms (Rainnie, 1989; Abbott, 1993).

A third contributing factor to McDonald's ability to circumvent IR system regulations is the nature of the labor markets on which the company depends. Although there are some variations across European countries, a similar pattern emerges that may be called "recruited acquiescence" (Royle, 1999a). In most European countries, fast-food service workforces are predominantly made up of young workers, who tend to be either poorly informed about, or disinterested in, their rights in the workplace. In some countries like Germany and Austria, furthermore, there are large number of foreign workers whose job opportunities are very limited, either because of language barriers or because their qualifications are not recognized. In addition, the fast-food industry tends to serve as a repository for low-skilled and poorly educated workers unable to find work elsewhere. Add to this the part-time and temporary nature of employment at McDonald's, and one can readily see how a company can manipulate a workforce and regulatory systems of worker representation and trade union organization.

It is not just U.S. MNCs that are often in conflict with the kind of legislatively underpinned systems of workers' interest representation found in

Europe. However, it may be that American companies find such systems particularly hard to accept in view of the frequently antagonistic union–management environment of their home operations (Kochan and Weinstein, 1994; Towers, 1999). The endemic short-termism of Anglo-Saxon approaches to management, fueled by economic liberalism and the need to return maximum short-term gains to shareholders, furthermore, sits uneasily with mainland European notions of social partnership supported by legally mandated rights at work. More specifically, in those countries where McDonald's has finally had to give into negotiating collective agreements, it appears to be the issue of worker representation through union delegates and/or works councils that the corporation finds most difficult to accept. By its very nature the McDonald's system does not allow for codetermination or cooperative decision making, because it functions on the basis that workplace decisions have already been made. The post-Fordist notion of a new era in which employers will promote meaningful participation in order to seek a mutual accommodation of interests at the point of production is rather questionable in the case of McDonald's and, probably more generally, for the fast-food industry as a whole.

Our analysis suggests that where national legislative systems provide MNCs with less room to maneuver (as in Sweden), management cannot so easily avoid statutory regulation of HRM/LR practices, but even here, the effectiveness of such regulation can be undermined. In addition, neither the sophisticated "legislative" nor "negotiated" tracks of the EU's Social Dialogue have been even moderately successful in terms of creating supranational framework agreements. Here, a better route toward regulation through collective bargaining may lie in sectoral rather than supranational dialogue (Keller and Sörries, 1999). Our findings also emphasize the fact that works councils, like any other statutory mechanism of labor–management relations, are dependent on the action of individuals and the attitudes of the parties involved (Kotthoff, 1994). The case of McDonald's in the EU highlights the weakness of even highly regulated national and regional IR systems when confronted with powerful and determined MNCs.

NOTES

1. A more detailed analysis of these avoidance strategies is available in Duve (1987) and Royle (1998).

2. McDonalds distributes a memorandum to all German restaurant managers detailing what action should be taken in the event that workers attempt to establish a works council. We have translated this memorandum from German to English.

3. The issue of works council rights, "das passive *Betriebsratswahlrecht*", is covered in paragraph 53 of the ArbVG. For non-EU citizens this may be a particularly controversial issue in Austria at the moment, especially in view of the recent election success of Jorg Haider and his far-right Freedom Party and its hard-line anti-immigrant stance (Frey and Hall, 1999).

4. In fact, Sweden did operate a system of works councils between 1946 and 1977, but they were never very strong and the unions withdrew from the agreement in the late 1970s (IDS, 1996).

REFERENCES

"Abgebraten bis die Kasse Stimmt." (1999). *Stern* 45, November 4, pp. 115–28.

Abbott, B., (1993). "Small Firms and Trade Unions in Services in 1990's." *Industrial Relations Journal* 24 (4), pp. 308–17.

Barnett, A. (1996). "British Firms Defying Social Chapter Opt-Out." *The Observer* 4, August p. 20.

Brulin, G. (1995). "Sweden: Joint Councils under Strong Unionism." In Rogers, J. and Streeck, W. (eds.), *Works Councils : Consultation, Representation, and Co-operation in Industrial Relations*. London: University of Chicago Press, pp. 189–216.

De Vos, T. (1981). *U.S. Multinationals and Worker Participation in Management*. London: Aldwych.

Duve F. (1987). *Unternehmermethoden gegen Betriebsratswahlen (Reportagen aus Grauzonen der Arbeitswelt)*. Hamburg: Rowohlt aschenbuchverlag.

Escobar, M. (1995). "Spain: Works Councils or Unions." In Rogers, J. and Streeck, W. (eds.), *Works Councils : Consultation, Representation, and Cooperation in Industrial Relations*. London: University of Chicago Press, pp. 153–88.

Frey, E. and Hall, W. (1999). "Big Gain for Right in Austrian Elections." *Financial Times*, October 4, p. 9.

Goetschy, J. (1998). "France: The Limits of Reform". In Ferner, A. and Hyman, R. (eds.), *Changing Industrial Relations in Europe*. Oxford: Basil Blackwell, pp. 357–94.

Hepple, B. (1999). "A Race to the Top? International Investment Guidelines and Corporate Codes of Conduct." Paper presented to the WG Hart Workshop: Legal Regulation of the Employment Relationship, Institute of Advanced Legal Studies, University of London, July.

Income Data Services (IDS). (1996). *European Management Guides : Industrial Relations and Collective Bargaining*. London: Institute of Personnel Development.

Jacobi, O., Keller, B., and Müller-Jentsch, W. (1998). "Germany Facing New Challenges". In Ferner, A. and Hyman, R. (eds.) *Changing Industrial Relations in Europe*. Oxford: Basil Blackwell, pp. 190–238.

Keller, B. and Sörries, B. (1999). "Sectoral Social Dialogues: New Opportunities or More Impasses?" *Industrial Relations Journal European Annual Review* 31 (5), pp. 330–43.

Kochan, T. A. and Weinstein, M. (1994). "Recent Developments in US Industrial Relations." *British Journal of Industrial Relations* 32 (4), pp. 483–504.

Kotthoff, H. (1994) *Betriebsräte und Bürgerstatus, Wandel und Kontinuität betrieblicher Mitbestimmung*. München-Mehring: Rainer Hampp Verlag.

Labor Research Development (LRD). (1995). *A Trade Unionist's Guide to European Works Councils*. London: TUC.

Langenhuisen, R. (1995). "McDonald's Kauft Sich von Betriebsräten frei." *Kölner Express*, December 7, p. 36.

Levinson, C. (1972). *International Trade Unionism*. London: George Allen and Unwin.

Love, J. F. (1995). *McDonald's Behind the Arches*. London: Bantam Press, London.

Maitland, A. (1999). "The Value of Virtue in a Transparent World." *Financial Times*, August 5, p. 14.

Marchington, M. (1995). "Involvement and Participation." In Storey, J. (ed.), *Human Resource Management: A Critical Text*. London: Routledge, pp. 280–305.

Marginson, P., Gilmar, M., Jacobi, O., and Krieger, H. (1998). *Negotiating European Works Councils: An Analysis of Agreements under Article 13*. Luxembourg: European Foundation for Working and Living Conditions, Commission of the EU.

Martinez Lucio, M. (1998). "Spain: Regulating Employment and Social Fragmentation." In Ferner, A. and Hyman, R. (eds.), *Changing Industrial Relations in Europe*. Oxford: Basil Blackwell, pp. 426–58.

Martinez, M. and Weston, S. (1994). "New Management Practices in a Multi-national Corporation : Restructuring of Worker Representation and Rights." *Industrial Relations Journal* 25 (2), June, pp. 110–21.

"McDonald's Serves up Improved Social Relations." (1997). *European Industrial Relations Review* 279, April, pp. 19–21.

Miller, D. and Stirling, J. (1998). "European Works Council Training: An Opportunity Missed?" *European Journal of Industrial Relations*, 4 (1), pp. 33–56.

Müller-Jentsch, W. (1995). "Germany: From Collective Voice to Co-Management." In Rogers, J. and Streeck, W. (eds.), *Works Councils: Consultation, Representation, and Cooperation in Industrial Relations*. London: University of Chicago Press, pp. 53–78.

Overell, S. (1996). "Row Follows PepsiCo Works Council Deal." *Personnel Management*, September 12, p. 6.

"Pepsi-Co Accused of Works Council Fraud." (1996). *Eurofood*, June 19, p. 3.

Rainnie, A. (1989). *Industrial Relations in the Small Firm: Small Isn't Beautiful*. London: Routledge.

Royle, T. (1998). "Avoidance Strategies and the German System of Co-Determination." *The International Journal of Human Resource Management* 9 (6), pp. 1026–47.

Royle, T. (1999a). "Recruiting the Acquiescent Workforce: A Comparative Analysis of McDonald's in Germany and the UK." *Employee Relations* 21 (6), October/November pp. 540–55.

Royle, T. (1999b). "Where's the Beef? McDonald's and the European Works Council." *European Journal of Industrial Relations* 5 (3), November, pp. 327–47.

Royle, T. (2000). *Working for McDonald's in Europe: The Unequal Struggle?* London: Routledge.

Schulten, T. (1996). "European Works Councils: Prospects for a New System of European Industrial Relations." *European Journal of Industrial Relations* 2 (3), pp. 303–24.

Shire, K. (1994). "Bargaining Regimes and the Social Reorganization of Production: The Case of General Motors in Austria and Germany." In Belanger, J., Edwards P., and Haiven, L., (eds.), *Worker Industrial Relations and the Industrial Challenge*. Ithaca, NY: ILR Press, pp. 137–56.

Streeck, W. (1991). "More Uncertainties: German Unions Facing 1992." *Industrial Relations* 30 (3), pp. 317–49.

Streeck, W. and Vitols, S. (1995). "Europe : Between Mandatory Consultation and Voluntary Information". In Rogers, J. and Streeck, W. (eds.), *Works Councils: Consultation, Representation and Co-operation in Industrial Relations*, London: University of Chicago Press, pp. 243–82.

Tchobanian, R. (1995). "France : From Conflict to Social Dialogue?" In Rogers, J. and Streeck, W. (eds.) *Works Councils: Consultation, Representation and Co-operation in Industrial Relations*. London: University of Chicago Press, pp. 115–52.

Towers, B. (1999). "Editorial: the UK's Third Statutory Recognition Procedure." *Industrial Relations Journal* 30 (2), pp. 82–95.

Traxler, F. (1998). "Austria: Still the Country of Corporatism." In Ferner, A. and Hyman, R. (eds.), *Changing Industrial Relations in Europe*. Oxford: Basil Blackwell, pp. 239–61.

Vidal, J. (1997). *McLibel: Burger Culture on Trial*. London: Macmillan.

Wever, K. S. (1995). "Human Resource Management and Organisational Strategies in German- and US-Owned Companies", *The International Journal of Human Resource Management* 6 (3), September, pp. 606–25.

Willmott, H. (1993). "Strength Is Ignorance; Slavery is Freedom: Managing Culture in Modern Organisations." *Journal of Management Studies* 30 (4), pp. 515–52.

18

NAFTA's Labor Side Agreement: Withering as an Effective Labor Law Enforcement and MNC Compliance Strategy?

Mario F. Bognanno and Jiangfeng Lu

The North American Agreement on Labor Cooperation (NAALC), also dubbed the "labor side agreement," was executed as a supplement to the North American Free Trade Agreement (NAFTA).[1] Both accords became effective on January 1, 1994, and with their adoption, Canada, Mexico, and the United States (for the first time) linked the region's trade to the operation and regulation of its labor markets (Herzstein, 1995). NAFTA calls for falling tariffs, increasing trade, and freer international capital flows among Canada, Mexico, and the United States. Organized labor in Canada and the United States opposed NAFTA, contending among other things, that it would cost jobs north of Mexico's border (Adams and Singh, 1997).[2] In coalition with human rights, environmental, and other nongovernmental organizations (NGOs), organized labor launched a whirlwind of political activity, calling attention to its concerns. Labor's voice was heard, but the resulting NAALC (ostensibly a quid pro quo to appease some members of the U.S. Congress who otherwise might not have supported NAFTA) fell far short of labor's goal.

In this chapter, we evaluate the NAALC's review and postreview dispute resolution procedures. Specifically, we examine the extent to which it has caused (1) the three signatory governments to adopt and enforce labor laws that are consistent with the side agreement's labor principles and (2) multinational companies (MNCs), as well as other organizations doing business in the NAFTA countries, to implement human resource management and labor relations (HRM/LR) policies that are consistent with prevailing labor laws. Given the NAALC's limited sanction and remedial authority, organized labor contends that the side agreement lacks the required means to prompt labor law enforcement and employer-compliant behavior. However, the so-called sunshine factor is often advanced to qualify this contention. That is, the public nature of the NAALC's submission process and the public's adverse reaction to substantiated claims of NAALC violations should be sufficient to pressure the

NAFTA governments to enforce their labor laws and employers to follow the rule of law. While the existing literature tends to support the sunshine hypothesis, we find limited support for it.

We first discuss organized labor's concerns with, and opposition to, NAFTA and the resulting compromise side agreement, the NAALC. We then describe the NAALC's submission and dispute resolution procedures and analyze the level of submissions or complaint activity reported during the NAALC's first six years, 1994–1999. We subsequently present and discuss specific submission scenarios within the context of the public nature of the formal complaint procedures. Here, we examine whether the transparency of the NAALC's dispute resolution process motivates NAALC-compliant behavior. Against the literature's general support of the sunshine factor hypothesis, we critically examine new evidence bearing on some of the early submissions. Furthermore, we assess this hypothesis using the data presented in the previous section. Finally, based on a survey of trade union and worker rights representatives who have filed submissions under the NAALC complaint procedures, we conclude our evaluation of whether the NAALC's sunshine potential promotes compliance. The last section presents our summary and conclusions.

BACKGROUND AND PROCEDURES

Opposition and Compromise

Before NAFTA's adoption, organized labor forcefully emphasized that in comparison to Canada and the United States, Mexico's wages were sharply lower, and enforcement of its labor laws was much more lax. In particular, labor's advocates pointed to Mexico's lax prosecution of labor law violators and to the discriminatory treatment that "independent" unions often received before Mexico's regulatory and judicial bodies.[3] Consequently, labor wanted NAFTA's scope expanded to include measures for improving the standard of living of Mexican workers and bringing Mexico's labor laws and their enforcement up to the level of its northern neighbors (Befort and Cornett, 1996).[4] Without these measures, organized labor argued, Mexico would attract increasingly large capital flows from Canadian and U.S. MNCs in their search for cheap labor, which, in turn, would undermine labor's bargaining power. It was argued further that since Canada and the United States are the region's "high wage" production and export venues, in the absence of a regional labor accord *with teeth,* Canadian and U.S. workers would be displaced and their wages and other employment conditions depressed (Anderson, 1993; Campbell, 1993; Cypher, 1993; Faux and Lee, 1993).

Labor and the other NGOs were not alone in arguing that the region's economic playing field was not level. The "giant sucking sound" (that would be heard as U.S. jobs moved from north to south of the Mexican border with NAFTA's adoption) was the refrain that Ross Perot used in opposing NAFTA during his 1991 presidential bid. In contrast, presidential candidate Bill Clinton endorsed NAFTA (much to labor's chagrin), while at the same time endorsing the idea of a labor side agreement (Clinton, 1992; Adams and Singh, 1997). Hence, after Clinton's election, organized labor in the United States had "hopes that the side agreements would guarantee the effective enforcement of Mexican labor and environmental laws, thus reducing the incentives for U.S. manufacturers to relocate plants to that country" (Shoch, 2000: 2). In the summer of 1993 the new Clinton administration proposed the establishment of an independent commission charged with the enforcement of labor and environmental laws, including reasonable allowances for trade sanctions if they were not enforced. In the face of opposition from Canada and Mexico, however, this proposal was dropped, and the resulting NAALC was much weaker than organized labor had hoped for (Shoch, 2000).

The version of the labor side agreement that was adopted pledges to improve, promote, and protect workers' rights in the three countries.[5] It further committed the NAFTA governments to cooperative and consultative activities, programs, studies, and reports.[6] Finally, it allowed the signatory countries and NGOs to file "submissions" alleging that any one of the three governments was failing to uphold its obligations under the NAALC (Compa, 1995).[7] This synthesis makes it clear that the partner countries pushed cooperative and consultative activities relevant to labor markets, worker rights, and labor law administrative issues to the trinational forefront.[8] In addition, through the submission or dispute resolution process, the partner countries allow for the review of alleged violations of worker rights under the NAALC. That is, while recognizing the sovereignty of each signature country, the NAALC establishes a National Administration Office (NAO) in each county empowered to review "labor law matters arising in the territory of another Party." [9] Consequently, the three governments and NGOs may seek NAO review of allegations that a signatory country is not NAALC-compliant.

The resulting side agreement was unacceptable, nevertheless, to organized labor in Canada and the United States. The rub, from labor's point of view, is that neither the reviewing NAO nor the NAALC's postreview dispute resolution mechanisms provide for meaningful sanctions. For example, with narrow exceptions, the side agreement does not allow for fines or punitive trade measures, such as might be made by increasing tariffs or imposing import barriers (Compa, 1995).[10] Prohibited labor practices by employers and MNCs, moreover, cannot be corrected through the equivalent of restraining orders or remedied through reinstatement or "make-whole" orders. In short, the NAOs do not sit as surrogate national labor relations boards, issuing complaints and conducting trials and handing down awards and remedies (Beckman, 1997; Levinson, 1997).[11]

Submission and Dispute Resolution Procedures

The NAALC does not establish regional labor standards, but it does list 11 principles that the three governments agreed to promote, to the maximum extent possible. The side agreement's Annex 1 itemizes the principles as follows:

1. freedom of association and protection of the right to organize;
2. the right to bargain collectively;
3. the right to strike;
4. prohibition of forced labor;
5. labor protections for children and young persons;
6. minimum employment standards, such as minimum wages and over-time pay, for wage earners, including those not covered by collective agreements;
7. elimination of employment discrimination on such grounds as race, religion, age, sex or other grounds;
8. equal pay for women and men;
9. prevention of occupational injuries and illnesses;
10. compensation in cases of occupational injuries and illnesses; and
11. protection of migrant workers.

The allegations of NAALC violations that are raised in NAO submissions generally correspond to one or more of the preceding principles. Among other things, the side agreement commits each government to effectively enforce its own labor laws, to promote high labor standards, and to promote compliance with its labor laws. These commitments do not similarly bind private parties, like MNCs. Nevertheless, since the side agreement invites submissions relative to "labor law matters arising in the territory of another Party,"[12] the name or names of the MNCs as well as the relevant country's government and the challenged conduct of both appear in submissions and become part of the public record. Upon receipt of a submission, the relevant NAO determines whether to accept it for review, and, if so, it proceeds to investigate the submission's claims.[13] The relevant NAO may consult with the charged private parties and request consultations with the charged NAFTA country's government.[14] Additionally, it will hold public fact-finding hearings and issue public reports.[15] The public reports include findings relevant to the issues raised in the submission and make recommendations such as commissioning studies, hosting conferences, and holding ministerial consultations.[16]

If worker rights are being violated, an NAO may recommend ministerial consultations. The Canadian minister of labor and the secretaries of labor from Mexico and the United States may consult about any matter within the scope of the side agreement and specifically about any matter related to the 11 principles.[17] If ministerial consultations fail, a minister (secretary) may direct most issues to an Evaluation Committee of Experts (ECE) upon petition.[18] However, specific conditions must first be met. The matter under investigation must be "trade-related," "covered by mutually recognized labor laws," not previously considered by an ECE in the absence of "new information," and involve a question of occupational safety and health or pertain to principles 4 through 11.[19]

The three ECE "expert" members are to conduct objective and nonadversarial investigations bearing on a NAFTA government's "pattern of practice" relevant to the enforcement of its labor laws, with the important exception of laws governing freedom of association, rights to bargain collectively, and rights to strike.[20] Finally, after consultations with the subject governments and consideration of statements submitted by private parties and/or the subject governments in response to its "draft" report,[21] the ECE will prepare a final and public report with recommendations, unless the council decides otherwise.[22]

If the ECE recommendations fail to resolve the matter in dispute, the submission may proceed to arbitration upon a two-thirds vote of the council.[23] For this to occur, however, the issue must pertain to a signatory government's "persistent pattern" of failure to enforce its occupational safety and health, child labor, or minimum wage laws; otherwise, the dispute process ends.[24] Of the 11 principles that the parties agreed to promote, therefore, only principles 5, 6, and 9 may be advanced to arbitration and possibly result in sanctions (Sack, 1997; McGrady, 1998; Massimino, 1997).[25]

Arbitration panels consist of 5 professionally qualified neutral members drawn from the council's roster of 45 such individuals. Panels will hold hearings and issue initial reports containing findings of facts, determinations of whether there has been a "persistent pattern" of failure to effectively enforce the subject laws, and recommendations, if any, in the form of "action plans" to correct the pattern of nonenforcement. Following a period for comments, each panel will issue a final public report. If the panel determines that there has been wrongdoing and that the charged government has not implemented the recommended "action plan" or any other mutually satisfactory remedy entered into among the parties, the panel may be reconvened. The panel, at that time, may impose a "monetary enforcement assessment" against the charged government of no more than .007 percent of the total trade in goods between the parties during the most recent year for which data are available.[26] If the charged government fails to pay the monetary enforcement assessment, the complaining governments may suspend year-after-year application of its NAFTA benefits in an amount sufficient to collect the monetary enforcement assessment.[27] Sanctions conclude when the arbitration panel determines that the assessment has been paid and the sanctioned government is fully implementing the action plan.[28]

ANALYSIS OF SIX YEARS OF SUBMISSION ACTIVITIES: NUMBERS AND ISSUES

The literature addressing the NAALC's propensity to motivate public and private HRM/LR policies and practices that are consistent with the side agreement's objectives and principles is anecdotal in nature and mainly involves the governments and businesses cited in NAO submissions. Table 18.1 succinctly presents historical information on NAO submissions filed between 1994 and 1999. In addition to the year, Table 18.1 identifies by country, the NAO and submission number, the charged party, and the status of the submission, as of December 31, 1999.

Table 18.1
NAO Submissions by Year: Country NAO, Submission Number, Charged Party, and Status

Year	U.S. NAO Submission Number and Charged Party	Status	Mexican NAO Submission Number and Charged Party	Status	Canadian NAO Submission Number and Charged Party	Status	Total
1994	No. 940001—Honeywell	4					4
	No. 940002—G.E. Corp.	4					
	No. 940003—Sony Corp.	6					
	No. 940004—G.E. Corp.	2					
1995			No. 9501—Sprint Corp.	6			1
1996	No. 9601—Mex. Government (Ministry of Environment)	6					2
	No. 9602—Silitek Corp. of Taiwan (Maxi-Switch)	2					
1997	No. 9701—Maquiladora companies	6					3
	No. 9702—Han Young	5					
	No. 9703—Echlin, Inc.	5					
1998	No. 9801—Mex. Government (Aeromexico)	1	No. 9801—Solec, Inc.	5	No. 98-1—Echlin, Inc.	5	10
	No. 9802—Vegetable farmers in Mexico	1	No. 9802—Washington State Apple Industry	5	No. 98-2—U.S. Government (DOL/INS)	1	
	No. 9803—St. Hubert McDonald's Restaurant	2	No. 9803—DeCoster Egg Farm	3			
	No. 9804—Canadian Government (Postal)	1	No. 9804—U.S. Government (DOL/INS)	3			
1999	No. 9901—Executive Air Transport, Inc.	3			No. 99-1—U.S. Government (NLRB)	1	2
Total	14		5		3		22

Notes: 1. NAO denied review; 2. submission withdrawn or settled before review process completed; 3. NAO accepted for review, public hearing/report issued, ministerial consultation denied; 4. NAO accepted for review, public hearing pending; 5. NAO accepted for review, public hearing/report issued, ministerial consultation pending; 6. NAO accepted for review, public hearing/report issued, ministerial consultation concluded.

During the NAALC's first six years, 22 submissions were filed, 6 alleging wrongdoings on the part of the NAFTA governments as regulators or employers and 16 alleging unchecked wrongdoings on the part of MNCs and other private organizations. On two occasions, separate submissions covering the same events were filed with two NAOs.[29] Therefore, after correcting for these dual filings, only 20 distinct case submissions were filed between 1994 and 1999, 5 challenging a signatory government and 15 challenging private parties. Critically, none of the submissions have evolved to the point of ECE evaluations, let alone arbitration.

Of the 22 submissions, 14 were filed with the U.S. NAO, 3 with the Canadian NAO, and 5 with the Mexican NAO. On an annual basis, about 2.4 submissions were filed, excluding 1998, when 10 submissions were filed. Other relevant facts in Table 18.1 are: [30]

1. Five submissions have been denied review, and 3 submissions were either withdrawn or settled before the review process was completed, leaving 14 candidate submissions for reviews, public hearings, requests for ministerial consultations, organizing and convening an ECE, and organizing and convening an arbitration panel. Countin Echlin, Inc. as 1 submission, the total of candidate submissions is 13, of which

   a. NAO hearings are pending for 3 submissions;
   b. NAO public hearings were held and reports were issued that did not recommend ministerial consultations in two instances, and these cases are closed;
   c. NAO public hearings were held and reports were issued recommending ministerial consultations in four cases with said consultations pending; and
   d. NAO public hearings were held and reports were issued that recommended ministerial consultations, which were held in four cases, and these cases are closed.

2. Although the U.S. NAO accepted 7 submissions for review during the NAALC's first four years, it accepted only 2 submissions for review in 1998 and 1999, and one of these was withdrawn (U.S. NAO Submission No. 9803, St. Hubert McDonald's Restaurant). The one viable submission accepted for review is U.S. NAO Submission No. 9901, involving the Association of Flight Attendants (AFA) and the Association of Flight Attendants of Mexico (ASSA) versus a privately owned Mexican airline company, Executive Air Transport, Inc. A public hearing is being scheduled.

3. Four of the 6 accepted submissions filed in 1998 and 1999 charge the U.S. government, as a regulator, and specific businesses with labor law violations. Brought to the Mexican NAO, the latter submissions include Mexican NAO Submissions No. 9801 (Solec, Inc.), 9802 (Washington State Apple Industry), 9803 (DeCoster Egg Farm) and 9904 (U.S. Government, DOL and INS).

4. The Canadian NAO has received three submissions, but only one has been accepted for review.

Effectiveness of the NAALC's Complaint Procedures: The "Sunshine Factor"

The NAALC first commits the signatory countries to labor-specific cooperative and consultative activities, programs, studies, and reports. Second, it allows each country to be challenged for failing to improve, promote, and protect workers' rights, as incorporated in the 11 principles. Driving this second purpose are organized labor and its allies, who argue that the doctrines of "free trade" and "fair trade" will converge only when the trading partners' commitments to the 11 principles are honored.

NAALC's Unique Contribution to Knowledge.

As to the labor side agreement's first purpose, over the past six years there have been several dozen NAALC-sponsored cooperative activities.[31] Other researchers have rightly concluded that through cooperative conferences, seminars, research, and other educational activities, the public's understanding of the differences and similarities of labor markets, labor laws, and employment practices in North America has increased markedly. Regional labor and industrial relations questions are being raised and addressed through research that would not have been conducted in the NAALC's absence. For example, it is doubtful (1) that studies of North America's labor market profiles, female employment, or plant closings would have been published, (2) that forthcoming publications comparing the three countries' labor laws and labor standards would have been launched or that industry studies and a comparative income security study would have been completed, and (3) that tricountry seminars on topics like income and productivity, labor market trends, or transnational labor–management relations would have been hosted.

These activities may help to shape future trade relations between the region's three governments, and they may influence corporate HRM/LR policies and practices as well. However, to many workers, the education and research activities of trade unions and labor activists' per se do not change labor laws, let alone plant-floor realities. More, the critics aver, needs to be done.

NAALC's Dispute Resolution Procedures.

As for the NAALC's second purpose of promoting the 11 principles through submissions, investigations, reviews, and dispute resolution via ministerial negotiations, our review leads us to conclude that the NAALC's record is mixed. Clearly, the NAALC provides unions and labor rights organizations access to forums that allows for critical reviews of the HRM/LR policies and practices of employers, including MNCs, and to "flag" for all to see alleged labor law enforcement failures on the part of the NAFTA governments. During the side agreement's first six years, approximately 80 organizations have used NAOs as platforms for airing alleged wrongdoings. These organizations are as diverse as the United Steelworkers of America, the Union of Telephone Workers of Mexico, the Canadian Automobile Workers, the Human Rights Watch and the Support Committee for Maquiladora Workers.

Further, the NAALC has been a valuable vehicle for unions and labor rights organizations to cooperate across national borders. In fact, about a dozen NAO submissions have been filed by cross-border petitioners; and in some cases, intraborder and cross-border unions and nonunion organizations have combined as copetitioners (Cook, 1996). This cooperative heterogeneity has created the potential for coalition building that has been valuable, furthermore, to organized labor's non-NAALC strategies. Examples include the labor alliances that (1) staged anti-World Trade Organizations (WTO) activities in Seattle in December 1999, (2) opposed the Clinton administration's year 2000 proposal granting Permanent Normal Trade Relations to China, and (3) built a foundation to support coordinated cross-border bargaining strategies among unions doing business with the same MNCs.

From labor's perspective, the preceding are positive NAALC-related developments, but there is also a negative side. As we have observed, organized labor generally holds that the side agreement's submission and review procedures lack meaningful remedies and as such are "all bark and no bite." Consequently, labor leaders continue to criticize the agreement, charging that it has not been effective in protecting workers and advancing labor rights. Others contend, nonetheless, that the "public nature" of the NAALC's submission, investigation, review, report, recommendation, and consultation activities has produced indirect benefits (Adams and Singh, 1997; Compa, 1995; Singh and Adams, 2000; and Cook et al., 1997). They argue, in particular, that the sunshine factor has had preventive and corrective effects via the pressure that it exerts on governments, MNCs, and other organizations to behave legally (Adams and Singh, 1997; Cook et al., 1997). The NAALC procedures, that is, bring public pressure to bear on the three governments, impelling them to maintain, improve, and enforce their labor laws. The publicity associated with NAO reviews and ministerial consultations also pressures MNCs to develop and implement private HRM/LR policies that are consistent with public labor policy (Compa, 2000).[32]

In essence, the sunshine hypothesis asserts that governments and businesses respond to the risk of reputation loss and related political and economic costs. With increasing communication efficiencies brought on by satellite broadcasting and television technologies, the internationalization of newsprint, and the Internet, bad news receives instantaneous and worldwide coverage. Consequently, it is hypothesized, government and business organizations not wishing to put their "political" and "physical" capital investments at risk are sensitive to adverse shifts in public opinion. To illustrate, the threat of sunshine has been offered as an explanation for the U.S. government's policy change in Canadian NAO Submission No. 98-2 (U.S. government, DOL/INS) (replicated in Mexican NAO Submission No. 9804). This submission was led by the Yale Law School Workers Rights Project, and it alleges that the U.S. government is not enforcing the minimum wage and overtime pay provisions of the Fair Labor Standards Act (FLSA), at least when it comes to employers who hire foreign nationals. Specifically, the submission challenges a U.S. policy that allows the Department of Labor to turn over evidence on undocumented workers to the U.S. Immigration and Naturalization Service. This policy, the submission asserts, has a "chilling effect" on immigrants who otherwise would report FLSA violators to the Department of Labor, and it encourages the employment of undocumented workers by businesses wishing to circumvent the law. On the day that the submission was accepted for review by the Mexican NAO, the United States announced that it had changed this policy. The Workers' Rights Project claims this as a "major victory," suggesting that it was the threat of Mexico's public review and public exposure that resulted in the policy change.[33]

U.S. NAO Submission No. 9803 is another example of a favorable outcome brought on by the threat of NAALC-related public exposure. This case involves the closing of a McDonald's franchise in St. Hubert, Quebec, during union representation proceedings. Within five months of being accepted for review, the U.S. NAO was asked to close its file. The government of Quebec and the submitters had agreed to study antiunion plant closing infractions and to make appropriate recommendations to the government, the alternative being to have one's "dirty laundry aired in public" (Singh and Adams, 2000).

These two examples have merit. Yet it is risky to generalize about the benefits of sunshine based on such scant foundation. Exhibit 18.1 contains short sketches of the facts, contentions, and present status of 10 additional NAO submissions, to which we now turn for a more comprehensive examination of the sunshine hypothesis. Approximately one-half of these submissions have been previously cited as support for the sunshine factor, but in light of more current information, it seems that this conclusion was premature in some instances. (The NAO case scenarios appearing in Exhibit 18.1, should be reviewed before proceeding.)

Joel Solomon, research director, Human Rights Watch/Americas, sees increased public awareness as a significant "indirect benefit" of the NAALC (Solomon, 1997). Specifically, he points to the government of Mexico, Ministry of Environment, Natural Resources and Fishing (scenario 4) and Maquiladoras (scenario 6) submissions as examples of how public awareness can help resolve labor rights problems. As with the two cases previously noted, the sunshine factor may have played important and positive roles in these cases. However, in the Government of Mexico case, one can identify other factors that may have been at work. As stated in scenario 4, the three pro-independent union decisions that the Mexican Supreme Court handed down in 1996 may indicate the beginning of a "truly" independent judiciary in Mexico, and, as such, these decisions may have little to do with the NAALC. As Torriente suggests, it is too early to tell (Torriente, 1997).

The sunshine potential of the *maquiladoras* case is more conclusive. The Mexican government and MNCs know that woman's rights' advocates are watching them closely, as are the international media. The Mexican secretary of labor and social welfare is undertaking to educate both female employees and businesses about their lawful rights and responsibilities, and it would seem that *postemployment,* gender-based discrimination aimed at screening out pregnant women is waning in the *maquiladora* sector. The same cannot be said about *preemployment* selection and screening practices, which are legal in Mexico.

However, the attributions of positive sunshine effects in the Silitek Corporation (Maxi-Switch) (scenario 5), Han Young (scenario 7), and Echlin, Inc. (scenario 8) submissions are more equivocal (Singh and Adams, 2000). The Silitek Corporation anecdote is actually a "threat" case. In April 1997, the Communications Workers of America (CWA) et al. withdrew its Maxi-Switch submission before the U.S. NAO's review commenced, largely because the

Exhibit 18.1 NAO Case Scenarios

1. Honeywell and General Electric (GE) (1994),[1] These submissions allege, inter alia, that the identified MNCs illegally threatened and dismissed workers for union activity. The Honeywell case alleges that 24 pro-union workers were fired, all supporters of the independent Union of Workers of the Steel, Metal, Iron, and Related Industries—an affiliate of the Authentic Labor Front (FAT). At GE, 11 workers were allegedly dismissed for organizing and for having pro-FAT sympathies. Both MNCs deny wrongdoing. Honeywell argues that all but one of the identified employees was laid off, all signed "resignation" forms, and all collected severance pay. Consequently, these employees have waived their right to protest their dismissals. GE states that 10 dismissals were disciplinary and one was a layoff. Six of the terminated workers were offered reinstatement or "additional severance pay," and they took the latter. Of the five terminated employees not offered reinstatements, three signed severance agreements, and two filed antiunion animus claims with the local CAB. The latter lost their CAB cases.[2] Neither the Honeywell nor GE facility was successfully organized, although these cases led to a number of CLC-led seminars and conferences on the freedom of association and the right to organize.

2. Sony (1994).[3] The Sony *maquiladora* allegedly interfered in an intraplant union rivalry, involving a nonaligned union slate opposite a Confederation of Mexican Workers (CTM) slate. It is alleged that approximately 13 non-CTM sympathizers were harassed and fired. It is further alleged that Sony aided the compliant CTM to ensure its success and that the local CAB denied attempts to register the nonaligned union. Sony denies all wrongdoing, pointing to unsuccessful employee actions before the local CAB and properly executed severance payments. However, the U.S. NAO report of review is harsh, observing in relevant part that, "it appears plausible that the workers' discharges occurred for the causes alleged, namely for participation in union organizing activities." As of 1997, the identified workers remain unemployed, and Sony remains CTM-represented.[4]

3. Sprint (1995).[5] Independent Union of Telephone Workers of Mexico alleges before the Mexican NAO that closure of the Sprint/La Conexion Familiar in San Francisco was motivated by antiunion animus. Sprint workers began to organize in February 1994, with a National Labor Relations Board (NLRB) election scheduled for July 1994. Between February and July Sprint allegedly mounted an illegal campaign to block a CWA organizing victory. Approximately 200 workers were released on July 14, 1994, and the facility was later closed.[6] The Mexican NAO report of review tends to support the allegations raised in the submission. In 1996 the NLRB found Sprint guilty of numerous

---

1. See *U.S. NAO Public Report of Review*, NAO Submission Nos. 940001and 940002, respectively.
2. Under Mexican labor law, dismissed workers may either elect to take severance pay and end the matter or seek reinstatement through CAB proceedings. In the Honeywell and GE cases, the U.S. NAO found that dismissed workers elect severance pay in such large proportions for several reasons. First, they lack sufficient personal resources to pursue reinstatement before the CAB; second, Mexico has no unemployment insurance system; and third, workers perceive the CAB procedures as being lengthy (and, as IBT and UE would argue, biased against independent union sympathizers).
3. See *U.S. NAO Public Report of Review*, NAO Submission No. 940003.
4. See Torriente. (1997: 21).
5. See *Report of Review of Public Submission 9501/NAO MEX*.
6. "Complaint against Sprint Filed by Mexican Telephone Workers Union," text of a release published by the Bureau of National Affairs, Inc., Washington, D.C. (February 9, 1995).

8(a)(1) violations, including the illegal threatening, interrogating, and surveillance of workers.[7] Appealed to the D.C. Circuit, the NLRB's decision was reversed in 1997.[8]

4. Government of Mexico, Ministry of the Environment, Natural Resources, and Fishing (SEMARNAP; 1996).[9] Submission arose out of the 1994 consolidation of the Mexican Fishing Ministry and parts of the Ministry of Agriculture and Water Resources. Pursuant to law governing federal labor relations, employees in the resulting new ministry were precluded from having more than one union. The submission alleges that the Mexican government is wrongly blocking workers' rights to organize and to free association by statutorily preventing more than one union per federal public sector workplace. Further, the impartiality of the Federal Conciliation and Arbitration Tribunal is challenged. The U.S. NAO recommended ministerial consultations, which have transpired. In 1996 the Mexican Supreme Court struck down the law precluding more than one federation of public sector employee unions. In that same year, it decided two additional cases eliminating the one-union-per-workplace restriction in both state and federal public sector employment.[10] Some see these decisions as an attack by an increasingly independent judiciary on Mexico's corporatist system of labor relations. They argue that the judges may be challenging PRI labor unions (e.g., CTM and CROC) that have long supported low-wage policies to attract foreign investments. It is also possible that these decisions were a response to pressure brought to bear by the ILO and the U.S. NAO submissions.[11]

5. Silitek Corporation (Maxi-Switch; 1996).[12] The independent Federation of Unions of Goods and Services Companies assisted in an organizing drive. Maxi-Switch, a computer keyboard manufacturer, allegedly opposed the organizing campaign, threatened a plant closure, participated in physical abuse intimidation and firings, and signed a so-called contract of protection with a CTM "phantom union" to avoid bargaining with the independent union in formation. The workers proceeded to form the independent local union and attempted to have it registered with the local CAB, chaired by a member of the CTM. The CAB denied the registration petition, asserting the "contract bar" principle. The submission alleges, inter alia, that the local CAB arbitrarily denied the registration request. Before the U.S. NAO completed its 1996 review, the submission was withdrawn because the Cananea, Mexico, CAB ultimately registered the independent union. The Mexican Supreme Court's 1996 decisions made it clear (to CABs) that more than one union per workplace was permissible in both the private and public sectors.[13] The plant's CTM union remains in place, and the workers who were allegedly dismissed for their pro-independent union sympathies were not reinstated.

6. Maquiladoras (1997).[14] Under Mexican law, employed women are entitled to six weeks' paid maternity leave before and after delivery, and individual companies are

---

7. *LCF, Inc. d/b/a La Conexion Familiar and Sprint Corporation and Communication Workers of America, District Nine and Local 9401, AFL-CIO*, 322 NLRB 774 (1996).

8. *LCF, Inc. d/b/a LaConexion Familiar and Sprint Corporation v. NLRB*, 327 U.S. App. D.C. 164 (1997).

9. *U.S. NAO Public Report of Review*, NAO Submission No. 9601.

10. See Torriente, pp. 155–56.

11. Ibid., pp. 176–77.

12. *The Case of Maxi-Switch, Inc. in Cananea, Mexico*, submitted by Communication Workers of America, et al., October 11, 1996 and submitted to the U.S. NAO.

13. See Torriente, pp. 23, 156.

14. *U.S. NAO Public Report of Review*, NAO Submission No. 9701. *Maquiladoras* are companies operating in Mexico that import components free of duty provided that they are reexported as assembled products. By 1997 the *maquiladora* sector had grown to include nearly 1 million workers

responsible for making said payments for short-term employees (i.e., those with fewer than 30 weeks of employment). Mexico's social security system makes these payments for long-term employees. Submission alleges gender discrimination through <u>preemployment</u> pregnancy screening (denying jobs to pregnant women) and <u>postemployment</u> dismissal or mistreatment due to pregnancy. According to the submitters, pregnancy-based gender discrimination is widespread among *maquiladora* employers, which include companies like Teledyne Corporation, Carlisle Plastics, W. R. Grace, American Zettler, Sanyo, General Motors, and Zenith. These and other companies deny the charges outright, and/or respondents maintain that their practices are legal.[15] Moreover, it is alleged that the CABs are inefficient in dealing with gender discrimination issues. The Mexican government holds that only "employed" women have CAB-related rights. Thus, preemployment, pregnancy-based discrimination is beyond the reach of the CABs and is not illegal per se. In 1997 the Office of the Secretary of Labor and Social Welfare inspected 437 *maquiladoras* and found that they were substantially in compliance with the law. Moreover, the secretary's office maintains an ongoing dialogue with the National Council of the Maquiladora Industry, which cooperates in securing the compliance of its member companies with labor laws and standards and in correcting deficiencies. Finally, since 1996 the secretary's office has conducted "consciousness awareness" programs with *maquiladora* employers on discrimination against women, including preemployment pregnancy testing. Formally, however, preemployment pregnancy screening is neither illegal nor widespread, according to the Mexican NAO. Presently, woman's rights organizations are monitoring gender-based employment policies of the *maquiladoras*.

7. Han Young (1997).[16] A subsidiary of Hyundai Corporation, Han Young assembles truck trailer chassis. To address safety and health and other issues, workers began organizing. They elected a union executive committee, but management allegedly directed it to meet with the "existing" local union with which it had an agreement. Said union was affiliated with the Revolutionary Confederation of Workers and Peasants (CROC)—a member of the Labor Congress (CT) that is aligned with the PRI. The workers' assert that the CROC union had never met with them, nor had they ever seen a copy of the labor agreement. The workers suspended organizing efforts, electing to affiliate with the Union of Workers in the Metal, Related Iron and Similar Industries (STIMAHCS), which was registered nationally. STIMAHCS filed for representation rights with the local CAB, challenging the CROC's exclusive rights to representation. The submission alleges that Han Young launched a vicious antiunion campaign that included dismissals and the hiring of CTM sympathizers to dilute STIMAHCS' support. In the face of alleged election irregularities, STIMAHCS defeated the CROC, but the company continued to fight the new union, fired 12 STIMAHCS supporters, and hired 50 anti-STIMAHCS replacements. The local CAB ultimately nullified the election results, in part because it held that STIMAHCS lacked the proper registration. The latter appealed, four workers began a hunger strike, and ultimately, the federal government intervened, mediating a settlement agreement between the parties. A second election was held. STIMAHCS won the election and was recognized by the CAB, and all but one discharged worker were reinstated. Moreover, the CAB granted registration to the "October 6," a local union formed to eventually supplant STIMAHCS. Nevertheless, by

---

in more than 2,700 establishments. Roughly 80 percent of these are production workers, and women constitute nearly 60 percent of this total.

15. "Mexico: No Guarantees—Sex Discrimination in Mexico's Maquiladora Sector," *Human Rights Watch Women's Rights Project*, August 1996, 8 (6(B)).

16. *U.S. NAO Public Report of Review*, NAO Submission No. 9702.

mid-1998, the October 6 union and Han Young had not executed a labor agreement, and a new representation election was pending. Even though this case received extensive press coverage, we understand that Han Young's newly relocated facility remains a so-called yellow factory (i.e., one without independent union representation).

8. Echlin, Inc. (1997 and 1998).[17] This submission raises freedom of association and health and safety issues at the ITAPSA export processing plant in the state of Mexico, Mexico. ITAPSA is a subsidiary of Echlin Inc. a U.S. corporation that produces and distributes automobile replacement parts. Workers concerned about workplace safety and health and other issues attempted to change their union. In response, the existing union and the company allegedly began a campaign of intimidation, physical violence, and job losses. STIMAHCS initiated a representation petition, challenging the plant's CTM union. The submission states that the federal CAB changed the scheduled election date without notifying STIMAHCS, and as its supporters showed up to vote, they were surreptitiously filmed. Altogether 50 pro-STIMAHCS workers were fired: 22 filed for reinstatement, and 28 took severance pay. Ultimately, an election was held, but it was allegedly replete with irregularities such as "voice voting" rather than voting by "secret ballot," 170 CTM "armed thugs" allegedly patrolled the polling area, nonworkers were allowed to vote, and so forth. STIMAHCS lost the election and, thereafter, challenged the election results. After going into Federal Court twice, in June 1998 the Court ultimately found in STIMAHCS' favor and ordered the CAB to conduct a *de novo* hearing on the allegations of election improprieties. Moreover, according to the submission, the CAB ordered 11 discharged workers to be reinstated, but they were barred from entering the plant by security guards. Elchin, Inc. denies all allegations of wrongdoing; further, it states that it reinstated the 11 workers found to be wrongfully terminated. However, its existing union exercised its agreement's "exclusion clause" (i.e., "closed shop" clause), demanding that the 11 workers be discharged since they had been expelled by the union. Among the U.S. NAO's numerous findings of impropriety is that to use the exclusion clause against workers who vote against an existing union amounts to a reprisal for exercising a constitutional right. The details of this case are difficult to pin down. However, we understand that Echlin, Inc., recently acquired by Dana Corp., has been relocating work from its ITAPSA plant to its other plants in Mexico and that STIMAHCS maintains only an informal presence at ITAPSA and that the workers who were allegedly dismissed without cause have not been reinstated

9. Solec, Inc. (1998).[18] Solec, Inc., located in Carson, California, is owned by two independent subsidiaries of two corporate giants, Sanyo and Sumitomo. Solec manufactures solar panels largely for export to Japan. A review of the submitters' freedom of association allegations follows. The company employs approximately 130 production workers whose interest in organizing was motivated by safety and health and economic issues. Next, the company's workforce, mainly Latinos, desired to organize, but this effort was repeatedly thwarted. Unit determination and election delay tactics were followed by harassment, threats of plant closing, and promises of rewards for speaking out against the union; further, the company filed a section 8(b)(1) complaint against the union. Balloting took place, but votes were not counted pending the 8(b)(1) determination, and the company continued to challenge the "employee" status of the

17. *U.S. NAO Public Report of Review*, NAO Submission No. 9703; *Review of Public Communication CAN 98-1*. The instant discussion abstracts from the safety and health aspect of this case.
18. "The Case of Solec, Inc. in Carson, California, USA," prepared by OCAWIU, Local I-675 and other NGOs on April 9, 1998, and accepted for review by the Mexican NAO as Submission No. 9801.

union leaders, even though the board had ruled that they were not "supervisory." Ultimately, the administrative law judge (ALJ) dismissed the 8(b)(1) complaint, and the company appealed to the NLRB. The board dismissed Solec's complaint, and the votes, taken four months earlier, were finally tallied. The company continued to resist the "employee" status of about 15 percent of its workers, causing the NLRB to reverse its earlier decisions in the matter and to yield to the company's demands. Nevertheless, the union won 62 to 37. On February 13, 1998, slightly more than five months after the election, the company petitioned the NLRB to have the election set aside. In addition to safety and health complaints culminating in a charge that the Occupational Safety and Health Administration (OSHA) has been pro-company, the submission alleges that the NLRB is company-complicit through its dilatory conduct. Moreover, the NLRB fails to enforce the labor laws that provide for the freedom of association and to correct ongoing violation of the labor law. On March 6, 2000, we interviewed Kelly J. Quinn, president of OCAW, Local I-675, by telephone. He advised us that shortly after the company petitioned the NLRB to set aside the election, the company withdrew its petition and voluntarily recognized the union. Indeed, the parties have entered into a three-year collective bargaining agreement, effective August 1, 1998. The union has also written to the Mexican NAO withdrawing its submission; however, it has not received formal indication whether or not the case has been closed.

Cananea, Mexico, Conciliation and Arbitration Board (CAB) agreed to register the independent Federation of Unions of Goods and Services Companies. This appeared to be a major worker–NAALC victory. The Mexican government's change of course in this case may have been prompted by the Mexican Supreme Court's 1996 pro-independent union decisions and/or the threat of a potentially embarrassing U.S. NAO public hearings. Attenuating these conclusions, however, are the views of Morton Bahr, president, CWA, who recently observed: "In fact, as of January 1998, fired Maxi-Switch workers have not been reinstated and a contract has not been negotiated, the [independent union] has gone to court to enforce the [registration] order; the outcome of the case is still pending" (Bahr, 1997: 9). In communications with CWA officials, we have learned that the Maxi-Switch plant is still represented by a CTM-affiliated "phantom union," and the workers who were allegedly dismissed for exercising their freedom of association rights have not yet been reinstated.

Han Young and Echlin, Inc. also appear to be Pyrrhic victories. Like Maxi-Switch, these two cases center on allegations that workers were improperly denied their freedom of association and collective bargaining rights (as well as alleged health and safety violations). They also involve challenges to in-house unions. At Han Young, the independent union involved (following CAB-supervised elections replete with irregularities that triggered considerable negative press and international attention and, ultimately, the intervention of the Mexican government) won its representation election, and the CAB extended representation rights to it. Nevertheless, even though the NAO report has been issued in this case and ministerial consultations are pending, Han Young remains in the hands of the CTM.

Indeed, it may be that there are no workers in Mexico's *maquiladora* sector that are represented by an independent union even after six years of

NAALC sunshine. This, however, is not to say that there are not independent-minded affiliates of the CTM, CROC, and other labor affiliates of the CT, particularly in automobile assembly and automobile parts manufacturing in Mexico (see Chapters 10 and 11 of this volume).

At Echlin, Inc., the Han Young story is repeated, as summarized in scenario 8. The CTM-affiliated local union remains in place, and, although the CAB directed the reinstatement of 11 workers found to be wrongfully discharged, they still remain out of work. This evidence suggests that the sunshine hypothesis has not worked for employees who were legally seeking representation by independent unions. In addition, in the Honeywell (scenario 1), General Electric (scenario 1), Sony (scenario 2), and Sprint (scenario 3) cases (all of which involved public hearings with public reports of reviews and media attention), the sunshine factor did not lead to the recognition of independent unions and to reinstatements. Arguably, recognition and reinstatements may not have been called for in any of these cases. It is possible that all four companies acted lawfully in response to the unions' organizing drives and that the Mexican and U.S. governments properly enforced their labor laws. By the same token, it seems reasonable to question whether the charges brought by the myriad of unions and worker rights' advocates in these four cases were totally without merit. In fact, the NAO reports of review certainly leave the reader with the impression that the governments and MNCs involved in these cases ought not to be totally exonerated.

Commenting on the Sony and Han Young cases, Jerome Levinson observed:

The Mexican government could not be sanctioned for depriving workers at MDM [aka Sony] of their constitutional right of free association. The CABs continue to exist with their current composition and acknowledged conflict of interest. The Han Young workers are as much victims of this system as are the MDM workers who lost their jobs for trying to organize an independent union. The commitment, which candidate Clinton made to American workers in his October 4, 1992 Raleigh, North Carolina speech that he would not place them in competition with Mexican workers unable to exercise core worker rights such as freedom of association, remains unfulfilled. (Levinson, 1997: 24)

Solec, Inc. (scenario 9) presents an interesting case that ended as workers would have hoped. However, according to Kelly J. Quinn, president, OCAW, Local I-675, the NAALC submission that he filed with the Mexican NAO had nothing to do with the union's ultimate organizing success. Quinn told us that while there was relatively little local media attention given to the Solec, Inc. organizing drive, some national stories did run, dealing with union organizing generally in the solar panel industry. Apparently these stories were strictly "news accounts" that did not criticize Solec, Inc. for its alleged union-avoidance tactics. Ultimately, Quinn observed, Solec, Inc. decided to recognize his local union because it knew that "we were not going away" and because its "union-resistance budget was at its limit." Quinn estimates that the company spent roughly U.S.$300,000 resisting unionization.

Our search for sunshine potential among the submissions in Exhibit 18.1 suggests that the benefits that unions and worker rights advocates derive from the public nature of the NAALC's complaint procedures may be overstated, even minuscule. Indeed, a look back at the data analyzed earlier offers added cause to discount the advantages presumably wrought by the public nature of the NAALC's proceedings. For instance, as a general matter, if the NAALC's dispute resolution procedures yielded practical, pro-labor rights payoffs, we would expect labor advocate groups to use them extensively and to use them increasingly with the passage of time.

However, as shown in Table 18.1, only 20 submissions (without double counting) were filed during the NAALC's first six years, and since Canadian NAO Submission No. 99-1 was filed on behalf of business interests, labor's interests are advanced in only 19 submissions. With a North American workforce of nearly 150 million and with thousands of MNCs and local unions in the region, the potential for actual or alleged compliance/enforcement challenges under the NAALC can reasonably be assumed to have been vastly in excess of 19 union-filed complaints over a six-year period. Indeed, this argument would hold even if we further assumed that the tricountry labor agencies' administrative procedures and judicial determinations were true to the labor principles enumerated in the side agreement. Labor's incidental utilization of the NAALC's dispute resolution procedures suggests to us that it views its payoffs as being borderline at best.

If the public reviews or the threat of public reviews were successful in pressuring government authorities to enforce their domestic labor laws and discouraging HRM/LR abuses by MNCs and other businesses, more NAO submissions surely would have been filed. Of course, it could be argued that, at the "margin," 19 union submissions in six years cast enough sunlight to influence the "average" behavior of errant businesses (and governments), causing them to correct (enforce) illegal HRM/LR practices (labor laws) and, thus, eliminating problems of noncompliance (enforcement). But such an argument is hardly compelling. If the sunshine created by these 19 union submissions, at the "margin," revealed that the labor laws were not being enforced and that prohibited business practices were going unpunished, then, on "average," adverse business and government behaviors would be reinforced, and labor's use of the NAALC's dispute resolution procedures would wane.

Unions and labor rights advocates seem to be using the NAALC's procedures very selectively, preferring instead to challenge alleged labor law violations through non-NAALC strategies. We surmise that labor has concluded that, in most cases, the costs of adverse publicity are not great enough to overcome the benefits that the NAFTA governments and businesses reap from not enforcing their labor laws, opposing union representation, paying substandard wages, or operating unsafe workplaces. Indeed, organized labor is quick to remind us that the NAFTA governments and businesses behave prohibitively in the first place because of the benefits derived from such behavior.

As reported in Table 18.1, except for 1998, when 10 NAO submissions were filed, the average annual number of filings totals slightly more than two per year. Aside from the fact that one-half of the 1998 submissions were either denied reviews or withdrawn and that the Echlin, Inc. submission was a duplicate, we note that in 1999 only 2 submissions were filed, a drop back to the non-1998 annual mean number of filings. Thus, it is hard to identify a discernible upward trend in the number of NAO submissions filed to date. However, what is more discernible is that as of December 31, 1999, the Canadian NAO had no public hearing on its docket; the Mexico NAO had two; and the U.S. NAO had one hearing pending. In addition to these three hearings, there were four cases awaiting ministerial consultations. It seems as though the NAFTA government's NAOs and the ministerial council's dispute resolution workloads are dwindling to embarrassingly low levels. The effectiveness of the NAALC's complaint procedure is withering, and, in our view, the sunshine factor is not the source for its reinvigoration.

Seven submissions (counting Echlin, Inc. only once) await either NAO review or ministerial consultations. Five raise safety and health issues. Thus, if need be, the Ministerial Council could initiate ECE proceedings and even arbitration in these cases. The safety and health allegations raised in the Han Young, Echlin, Inc., Washington State Apple Industry, and DeCoster Egg Farm submissions could attract more media attention if determined by ECE examiners or arbitrators rather than merely discussed in NAO reports of review or considered in ministerial consultations. The opinions and remedies proposed by neutral and expert ECE examiners or arbitrators, unencumbered by national political agendas, might be viewed as being more credible and deserving of media support.

The NAO reports of review present rich accounts of the labor and worker advocates' contentions and testimonies, but the positions of the business and government interests involved do not appear to be as complete. The reason for this is that business and government representatives, with few exceptions, have chosen not to testify at NAO hearings but rather to file posthearing written statements, which is within their rights.[34] However, because the accused generally does not participate in NAO hearings, NAO finding of facts and recommendations may be seen as less authoritative than otherwise would be the case.[35] In contrast, the charged parties may see fit to cooperate with ECE examiners and arbitration panels. If so, their findings and recommendations might be deemed as more authoritative, attracting more worldwide news coverage, and, if that were the case, public and political pressure could build to the point where the offending governments would be forced to enforce their safety and health laws. It will be interesting to see whether or not the NAFTA governments are willing to push legitimate occupational safety and health issues high enough on their policy agendas to risk "fourth"-party interventions, with more teeth.

On May 27, 1998, four Mexican trade unions filed a complaint against the United States. The Union of Workers in the Metal, Steel, Related Iron and Similar Industries (STIMAHCS), the Authentic Labor Front (FAT), the National Workers Union (UNT), and the Democratic Farm Workers Front (FDC) charged the United States with prohibited practices centered on Washington state's apple industry. This complaint cites the United States for failure to provide farmworkers with the right to organize and bargain; prevent discrimination against migrants; correct substandard safety and health standards, including worker exposure to highly toxic chemical products; abate discrimination (via threats, intimidation, coercion, interrogation, monitoring, and illegal layoffs) against apple warehouse and packing company workers' in the exercise of their organizing rights; improve and efficiently enforce workers' right to organize under the National Labor Relations Act; establish minimum wage and overtime pay for agriculture workers; provide for workers' compensation; and to protect migrant workers.[36]

The Mexican NAO accepted this submission for review and issued a public report on August 31, 1999, recommending ministerial consultations covering the whole litany of charges (Greenhouse, 1999, 2000).[37] The allegations of labor and human rights abuses brought against the Washington state apple industry may have merit, and they may also represent an illegal trade subsidy because Mexico is the Washington apple industry's largest single export market. Among the allegations, moreover, are safety and health and minimum wage violations, matters that are regulated by the laws of both countries. These aspects of the case and the publicity that it has received have led experts like Compa to suggest that this may be the submission that actually reaches the side agreement's arbitration procedures (Compa, 2000).

Given organized labor's interest in workplace unionization and representation, it is not surprising that 17 of the 20 (not counting double filings) submissions filed to date allege illegal resistance to workers' exercise of their freedom of association. Among this number, however, freedom of association is a focal issue in 10 cases.[38] Several of these 10 cases have led to cooperative programs and research activities. However, except in the Solec, Inc. case, not a single independent union is representing workers at any of the remaining locations.

Survey of Labor and Human Rights Advocates

To further test the viability of the sunshine hypothesis, we examine how well it holds up against the opinions of labor and human rights leaders from Canada and the United States, whose organizations have filed NAO submissions. We first compiled the names of every organization that filed or cofiled a NAO submission between 1994 and 1999, with the exception of the Labor Policy Association and EFCO Corporation (i.e., Canadian NAO Submission No. 99-1).[39] Approximately 80 different trade union and labor rights organizations have joined in 1 or more of the 21 (19 without double counting) union submissions filed with the three NAOs.[40] Among these, 44 were Canadian and U.S. organizations.[41] Mexican organizations were not surveyed simply because we lack fluency in written and spoken Spanish. We next compiled the names and addresses of the individuals representing the 44 Canadian and U.S. organizations. In some cases more than one person represented an organization when, for example, the latter was a party to more than one submission or when multiple individuals were named in the submission. Ultimately, our survey list included 53 individual names.

Between December 30, 1999, and January 29, 2000, we mailed questionnaires to the 53 representatives, soliciting opinions that have bearing on the side agreement. Specifically, we᾽ asked whether the charged NAFTA governments' and/or employers' law enforcement and HRM/LR policies and practices changed for the better, following the filing of their submissions. To encourage responses to our mailed questionnaire, we made follow-up mailings and telephone calls. Six individuals representing two organizations had left their respective organizations at the time of the survey. In these instances, only one replacement name was suggested (but both organizations remained in the survey). We dropped three other individuals from human rights organizations who were listed as copetitioners on relevant submissions but who reported that they knew little about the NAALC and its dispute resolution procedures. Thus, our adjusted population of surveyed individuals is 45, representing 41 Canadian and U.S. organizations. We received 23 completed questionnaires for a 51 percent response rate.[42] The response rate was higher for the subsample of unions, as 15 of the 23 unions surveyed responded, for a response rate of 65 percent.

About one-half of the questions asked in the survey are paraphrased in Tables 18.2 and 18.3. Questions 1 and 2 in Table 18.2 provide respondents' overall opinions about the NAFTA's countries' promotion of "core labor rights"[43] and the side agreements' labor principles. Not surprisingly, the respondents have different opinions about the promotion of "core labor rights" and the NAALC's labor principles across the three countries. Chi-square tests establish that these differences are statistically significant ($p = .001$ for question 1 and $p = .002$ for question 2).

With respect to question 1, the respondents' opine that Canada does a much better job of promoting labor's core rights than does the United States. Furthermore, while about 65 percent do not agree that the United States is a promoter of "core labor rights," the proportion jumps to nearly 83 percent in the case of Mexico. More critically, however, Mexico and the United States are largely viewed as countries that do not promote the NAALC's labor principles for economic reasons (see question 2). In this vein, when asked whether the NAALC has motivated labor law enforcement and whether the NAFTA countries are meeting their obligations under the labor side agreement, the dominant answer was no.

Turning to the questions bearing directly on the sunshine hypothesis, a majority of respondents agree that the NAALC complaint procedures can be useful in "highlighting" particular cases where the NAFTA governments have failed to enforce their labor laws and MNCs fail to comply with the labor laws. (Note the responses to questions 3 and 4 in Table 18.2). Moreover, as seen from the responses to question 3 in Table 18.3, approximately 48 percent of respondents believe that "adverse publicity" can "pressure signatory countries to enforce their labor laws" in the case of Mexico, but less so in the cases of

Table 18.2

Distribution of NAALC Survey Responses: Opinions of Union and Worker Rights Organizations with Experience Using NAALC's Complaint Procedures: Part I (1–5 Scale)

Variable/Question	Percentage of Responses (%)	Full Sample (n = 23)					Unions (n = 15)				
		1	2	3	4	5	1	2	3	4	5
1. As regulated by their domestic labor laws, the governments of the signatory countries promote core labor rights, particularly where "independent and democratic" unions are involved.[a]	Canada	4.3	43.4	34.7	17.4	0	6.7	46.7	20	26.7	0
	Mexico	0	4.3	13.0	17.4	65.2	0	6.7	6.7	26.7	60
	U.S.	4.3	21.7	4.3	52.2	13.0	0	13.3	6.7	53.3	20
2. As regulated by their domestic labor laws, the governments of the signatory countries promote the NAALC's labor principles, even if doing so may imply increasing employment costs and decreased foreign direct investments.[b]	Canada	0	26.1	34.8	21.7	17.4	0	26.7	20	33.3	20
	Mexico	0	4.3	4.3	26.1	65.2	0	6.7	0	20	73.3
	U.S.	4.3	8.7	17.4	34.8	34.8	0	13.3	13.3	33.3	40
3. The NAO submission procedure can be a useful way of highlighting particular cases and possibly embarrassing the governments that fail to enforce their labor laws.		8.7	60.9	26.1	4.3	0	0	60	33.3	6.7	0
4. The NAO submission procedure can be a useful way of highlighting particular cases and possibly embarrassing the multinational corporations that fail to enforce their labor laws.		8.7	56.5	21.7	13.0	0	0	60	26.7	13.3	0
5. The NAO submission procedure has led to more communications, cooperation, and solidarity among organized labor in the NAFTA countries.		8.7	52.2	30.4	4.3	0	6.7	53.3	26.7	6.7	0

Notes: 1. Responses are scaled 1 – 5: 1.Strongly agree; 2. Agree; 3. Uncertain; 4. Disagree; 5. Strongly disagree. One respondent failed to answer question 1, and another respondent failed to answer question 5. The actual N-sizes in the two questions are 22 and 14, respectively.
2. Chi-square tests on questions 1 and 2 reveal significant differences across signatory countries: a. $\chi^2(2)=21.02$, p=0.001; b. $\chi^2(2)=12.79$, p=0.002.

Table 18.3
Distribution of NAALC Survey Responses: Opinions of Union and Worker Rights Organizations with Experience Using the NAALC's Complaint Procedures: Part II (1–3 Scale)

Variable/Question — Percentage of Responses (%)		Full Sample (n = 23)			Unions (n = 15)		
		1	2	3	1	2	3
1. Has the NAALC treaty motivated a more effective enforcement of the labor laws in …?[a]	Canada	0	65.2	34.8	0	73.3	26.7
	Mexico	8.7	69.6	21.7	6.7	73.3	20
	U.S.	8.7	87.0	4.3	0	100	0
2. Are the signatory countries fulfilling their NAALC obligations … ?[b]	Canada	8.7	43.5	47.8	13.3	53.3	33.3
	Mexico	0	91.3	8.7	0	93.3	6.7
	U.S.	4.3	87.0	8.7	0	93.3	6.7
3. Does the possibility of adverse publicity arising out of the public nature of NAO communications pressure signatory countries to enforce their labor law … ?[c]	Canada	30.4	17.4	47.8	26.7	26.7	40
	Mexico	47.8	26.1	21.7	46.7	26.7	20
	U.S.	39.1	30.4	26.1	26.7	33.3	33.3
4. Is the public nature of NAO communications sufficient to motivate NAALC compliance by the governments of … ?[d]	Canada	4.3	73.9	21.7	6.7	80	13.3
	Mexico	0	87.0	13.0	0	93.3	6.7
	U.S.	4.3	91.3	4.3	6.7	93.3	0
5. Are the escalating ministerial consultations, expert evaluation committees (EECs), and arbitration panel enforcement procedures sufficient to motivate NAALC compliance by the governments of … ?[e]	Canada	4.3	78.3	17.4	6.7	86.7	6.7
	Mexico	0	87.0	13.0	0	93.3	6.7
	U.S.	0	91.3	8.7	0	93.3	6.7
6 Do you find it ironic that the US is being targeted for violating the objectives, principles and obligations of the NAALC?		8.7	91.3	0	0	100	0
7. Does the possibility of adverse publicity arising out of the public nature of NAO communications pressure MNCs to enforce the labor law?		52.2	34.8	13.0	46.7	40	13.3
8. If the charged parties identified in NAO submissions were required to appear at NAO hearings, would the governments' compliance with the NAALC's provisions improve?		52.2	17.4	30.4	40	26.7	33.3
9. If the charged parties identified in NAO submissions were required to appear at NAO hearings, would the employers' IR polices improve?		47.8	21.7	30.4	33.3	33.3	33.3
10. Do the NAO submission procedures create an unwarranted expectation that the NAO proceeding will remedy meritorious issues?		52.2	34.8	8.7	60	26.7	6.7

Notes: 1.Responses are scaled 1 - 3: 1. Yes; 2. No, 3. Don't know. One respondent failed to answer question 3, and another respondent failed to answer question 10. The N-size for these two questions is 22 and 14, respectively.
2. Chi-square tests of whether the responses to questions 1, 2, 3, 4, and 5 are the same across signatory countries follow: a. $\chi^2(2)=3.16$, p=0.21; b. $\chi^2(2)=16.70$, p=0.001; c. $\chi^2(2)=0.27$, p=0.872; d. $\chi^2(2)=2.79$, p=0.247; e. $\chi^2(2)=1.63$, p=0.444.

Canada (30.4 percent) and the United States (39.1 percent). Question 7 in Table 18.3 raises the same issue with respect to MNCs. Slightly more than one-half of the respondents answered yes. Hence, it appears that the opinions of a large proportion of NAALC-experienced trade union and worker rights advocates are consistent with holding that the sunshine factor matters particularly among MNCs, as suggested by the literature.

We do not doubt that negative publicity will create pressure for better labor law enforcement and HRM/LR change on the part of MNCs, if such pressure is widespread. Our point, however, is that the NAFTA governments' enforcement of their labor laws and MNC compliance with them will result only if the costs of widespread negative publicity are greater than the benefits from not enforcing and/or from flaunting labor laws in the first instance. At issue here is the matter of sufficiency, and question 4 in Table 18.3 goes more directly to this point. This question asks whether "the public nature of NAO communications is <u>sufficient</u> (emphasis added) to motivate NAALC compliance by the governments of...?" The dominant response is no and the intercountry differences are not statistically significant at the .05 level. Specifically, 74, 87, and 91 percent responded no in the case of Canada, Mexico and the United States, respectively. Question 5 raises a related point, namely, whether the NAALC's dispute resolution stages (i.e., ministerial consultations to ECEs to arbitration panels) are "<u>sufficient</u> (emphasis added) to motivate NAALC compliance by the governments...?" Again, the clearly dominant response is no and the intercountry differences are not statistically significant. Specifically, 78, 87, and 91 percent responded no in the case of Canada, Mexico, and the United States, respectively.

The responses to these questions strongly suggest that neither the sunshine factor *alone* nor the given threat of existing NAALC conflict resolution procedures and potential restricted sanctions *alone* are sufficient to bring about enforcement and compliance. The dilemma, we surmise, is that the existing NAALC conflict resolution procedures lack authority to impose meaningful sanctions that would "signal" to NAFTA countries that they are obligated to enforce their own labor laws and that MNCs are obligated to comply with those laws. Although the existing procedures allow for certain sanctions following arbitration, to date no cases have even gone to arbitration. If meaningful sanctions were exercised, on the other hand, then the *combination* of both the direct costs of sanctions arising from the dispute resolution procedures and indirect costs of bad publicity arising from the sunshine factor would hold promise of achieving compliance under the NAALC. Standing alone, however, the sunshine factor is not sufficient to bring about the labor law enforcement and MNC-compliant behavior that trade unions and labor rights activists seek.

SUMMARY AND CONCLUSIONS

As adopted in 1993, the NAALC fell far short of what the Canadian and U.S. labor and their allies had hoped for. For one thing, the NAALC does not offer remedies to workers whose legal rights are abridged; and for another, it is procedurally difficult to sanction NAFTA governments that fail to enforce their labor laws and violate the NAALC's 11 labor principles. Arbitration offers a tariff-based sanction. However, to traverse the procedural terrain from the point of filing a NAO submission to the point of arbitration is objectively cumbersome and, moreover, limited since only occupational safety and health, child labor, and minimum wage issues may be arbitrated. The core labor rights of freedom of association, to bargain collectively, and to strike are not arbitratable. Indeed, alleged violations of these fundamental and internationally recognized labor rights may not even be taken up by an ECE. To date, neither ECE examiners nor arbitration panels have been called into service.

The literature suggests, nonetheless, that all is not lost from labor's perspective, and to some extent, we agree. For instance, the NAALC is an important educational and research asset. It has given trade unions and labor advocates a stage on which to "flag" abuses for all to see, and it has brought on cross-border coalitions among unions and other NGOs that may not have otherwise formed. The literature further suggests that on the labor law enforcement and compliance fronts, the sunshine resulting from the public nature of the NAALC's complaint procedures has been effective to some degree, although nobody is making the case that the NAALC has succeeded in leveling the playing field with respect to North American trade competition. To evaluate whether the NAALC has motivated, through sunshine, law enforcement and compliance behaviors on behalf of the NAFTA governments and MNCs, we looked closely at the NAALC's record from 1994 to 1999.

After six full years, 19 NAO union submissions have been filed under the NAALC.[44] Widespread and negative publicity or the threat of negative publicity may have helped to bring four of these cases to equitable resolution. These are U.S. NAO Submission Nos. 9601 (Mexican Government, a federal employment case), 9701 (Maquiladora, a gender-based discrimination for pregnancy case), and 9803 (St. Hubert McDonald's Restaurant); and Canadian NAO Submission No. 98-2 (U.S. Government, a DOL/INS interagency federal case). Among these cases, only St. Hubert McDonald's touched (lightly) on the private sector's most contentious issue, the freedom of association. This was and is a critical issue among the balance of submissions that have not been denied NAO reviews.

The literature initially held that sunshine also played a positive role in the U.S. NAO Submission Nos. 9602 (Silitek Corp., Maxi-Switch), 9702 (Han Young), and 9701 (Echlin, Inc.) cases. Our examination of these submissions found, however, that many of the issues raised therein have not been satisfactorily addressed or remedied. The independent unions involved in these cases have failed to successfully unionize any of the targeted MNC facilities, and many workers who were allegedly discharged in the exercise of their freedom of association rights have never been reinstated. These outcomes are essentially repeated in U.S. NAO Submission Nos. 940001 (Honeywell), 940002 (General Electric Corp.), and 940003 (Sony Corp.) and in Mexican NAO No. 9501 (Sprint Corp.). This record of outcomes does not make a strong case in support of the sunshine factor, at least where MNCs and the freedom of association issue are involved. Moreover, the sunshine factor does not explain the resolution of Mexico NAO No. 9801 (Solec, Inc.).

A small number of submissions were filed during the NAALC's first six years, and only a handful of disputes are pending at the NAOs and before the Ministerial Council. These facts add to our misgivings about the so-called sunshine factor and the effectiveness of the NAALC's conflict resolution procedures. It is conjectured that without meaningful remedies and sanctions, the NAALC's public nature is not sufficient to motivate the NAFTA countries to enforce their laws and to compel businesses, including MNCs, to comply with them. In most cases, failure to enforce the labor laws and to comply with them may create benefits that exceed the costs associated with the negative media attention caused by the public nature of the NAALC dispute resolution procedures.

Implicit in our critique of the sunshine factor is the assumption that nonenforcement and noncompliance behaviors are manifest in North America, particularly in Mexico. Indeed, numerically speaking, such anti-NAALC occurrences dramatically exceed the mere 19 union submissions filed between 1994 and 1999. If the sunshine factor worked as hypothesized, organized labor would surely have been observed relying far more heavily on the NAALC's dispute resolution procedures. Not surprisingly, our sample of the opinions from 23 trade union and labor rights advocate organizations with experience under the NAALC procedures strongly reinforces our interpretation of the effects of sunshine on compliance. Based on their experiences, the representatives of these organizations make it quite clear that, in their opinions, the public nature of the NAALC's communications is not sufficient to motivate the NAALC countries to enforce their labor laws.

In conclusion, there is but a sliver of support for the argument that corrective influences have been brought on by the NAALC's sunshine factor, and, ultimately, we conclude that the labor side agreement is withering as an effective labor law enforcement and MNC compliance strategy. To sustain as an institution designed in part to motivate labor law enforcement and business compliance with labor policy, the remedy and penalty aspects of the NAALC will need to be revisited.

NOTES

1. *North American Agreement on Labor Cooperation*, September 14, 1993, United States-Canada-Mexico, 32 I.L.M. 1499, Article 51 (henceforth denoted as NAALC). The administrative structure of the NAALC includes, first, the Commission of Labor Cooperation (CLC), comprising of the Ministerial Council and a Secretariat. The Secretariat provides the administrative support required to implement the agreement; the Ministerial Council, made up of the top labor official in each country, is mandated to promote cooperative activities. Second, each country has a National Administrative Office (NAO) which compiles and disseminates labor-relevant information and receives and responds to complaints—"submissions" or "communications"—regarding labor law issues arising in NAFTA countries.

2. The Confederation of Mexican Workers (CTM) supported NAFTA but opposed the NAALC, "stating that it would reject any non-national organization seeking

to regulate labour rights and standards in Mexico." Other labor organizations in Mexico, like the independent Authentic Labour Front (FAT), took positions similar to those of labor in Canada and the United States (see Adams and Singh, 1997; 163).

3. An "independent" union is defined as a labor organization that is not affiliated with the Labor Congress (CT)—a collection of unions aligned with Mexico's largest political party, the Institutional Revolutionary Party (PRI), which has dominated Mexican politics for 70 years. About 85 percent of Mexico's organized labor is affiliated with the CT. The CTM, the Revolutionary Confederation of Workers and Peasants (CROC), and most of the other 35 confederations, federations, and national unions affiliated with the CT are closely associated with the PRI. See U.S. NAO, *Public Report of Review of NAO Submission No. 9702*, April 28, 1998.

4. The assertion that Mexico's labor and employment laws are inferior to, and more poorly enforced than, comparable U.S. laws may be exaggerated (see Befort and Cornett, 1996).

5. See NAALC, arts. 1–6.

6. See ibid., arts. 11–12.

7. See ibid., arts. 16.3 and 21–41. Article 15 directs each party to establish an NAO. Article 16.3 provides that among the NAOs' other responsibilities, each shall allow for the "submission and receipt" of "public communications on labor law matters arising in the territory of another Party," and each NAO shall establish its own "review" procedures. Compa discusses the labor–management tug-of-war over the development of the U.S. NAO's guidelines covering "review" procedures. He points out that filings by private parties to the U.S. NAO are referred to as "submissions" and not "complaints," per the guidelines. We use both terms in this chapter. (see Compa, 1995: 3).

8. Through broad-based cooperation and consultative activities, the NAALC seeks to achieve a number of objectives, specifically, to:

> (a) improve working conditions and living standards in each Party's territory; (b) promote, to the maximum extent possible, the labor principles set out in Annex 1; (c) encourage cooperation to promote innovation and rising levels of productivity and quality; (d) encourage publication and exchange of information, data development and coordination, and joint studies to enhance mutually beneficial understanding of the laws and institutions governing labor in each Party's territory; (e) pursue cooperative labor-related activities on the basis of mutual benefit; (f) promote compliance with, and effective enforcement by each Party of, its labor laws; and (g) foster transparency in the administration of labor law. (see NAALC, art. 1)

9. See ibid., art. 16.3.

10. Like the NAALC, multinational organizations such as the International Labor Organization, Organization for Economic Cooperation and Development, and the European Union have labor standards and complaint procedures, and like the NAALC, the labor standards are not enforced through "hard" sanctions but through tactics like negotiations, reports, behind-the-scenes political pressures, and moral suasion through embarrassing publicity. However, trade sanctions do exist under several labor rights systems established by several U.S. trade laws. For example, the Generalized System of Preferences as of 1984, the Overseas Private Investment Corporation as of 1985, the Caribbean Basin Initiative as of 1986, Section 301 of the Trade Act of 1988, and AID funding for economic development grants overseas all threaten, in one way or another, the loss or suspension of another country's beneficiary status for violating internationally recognized labor rights (see Compa, 1995: 1–2).

11. Steve Beckman, economist, United Automobile Workers (UAW), argues that:

> "the agreement's provisions for the assessment of penalties, if and when that ever occurs under the NAALC's excessively cumbersome procedures, should be changed to impose the burden on the companies that have violated the rights of workers rather than shifting the cost to the government, and the remedy for violations of the rights of workers should go to the workers hurt by the violation; otherwise, they receive no remedy at all from the process." (Beckman, 1997: 14).

Jerome I. Levinson, attorney for Mexican Workers of Magneticos de Mexico (MDM), observes that:

> "there is no legal bridge between the NAALC and the NAFTA," and he criticized the NAALC as being "a commitment, in principle, on the part of the Clinton Administration to worker rights, but an unwillingness to do anything concrete to implement that principle which might risk the displeasure of the Mexican authorities, or, of the MNCs." (Levinson, 1997: 24).

12. See NAALC, art. 16.3.

13. id. See also "Revised Notice of Establishment of U.S. National Administrative Office and Procedural Guidelines," *Federal Register* 59 (67), Thursday, April 7, 1994, pp. 16660–62; and *Canadian NAO Guidelines for Public Communications under Articles 16.3 and 21 of the North American Agreement on Labour Cooperation (NAALC)*, dated November 23, 1998. http://labour.hrdc-drhc.gc.ca/doc/ialc-cidt/eng/e/guidlins-e.html.

14. NAALC, art. 21.

15. The CLC's Secretariat office informed us that hearings and reports are public under the procedural rules adopted by all three NAOs.

16. NAALC, art. 22.

17. Ibid.

18. Ibid., art. 23.

19. Ibid.

20. Ibid.

21. Ibid., arts. 24, 25, 26.

22. Commenting on the dispute resolution system's complexities, Thea Lee (1997) observes that:

> "the consultation and dispute resolution procedures are so lengthy and tortuous as to discourage complaints and petitions: The period of time from when the ECE is established to final resolution could last as long as 1,225 days—more than three years." (Lee, 1997: 2).

23. See NAALC, art. 29.

24. Ibid.

25. From the Canadian perspective, the three-tier dispute resolution process relegates the most significant of worker rights "to the lowest level of scrutiny" (Greckol, et al., 1997: 3). McGrady, lists some NAALC flaws including "the ever-shrinking range of subjects over which complaints are admissible, reducing from 11 to 8, and then 3"; and only occupational health and safety, child labor, and minimum wage are subject to arbitration and enforcement through monetary sanctions (McGrady, 1998: 23–25). Massimino, director of the Washington office, Lawyer's Committee for Human Rights, points out, "Disputes surrounding industrial relations [freedom of association, collective bargaining and the right to strike] are restricted to the consultation processes" (Massimino, 1997: 11).

26. Annex 41A provides that if a panel hands down a monetary enforcement assessment against Canada, the CLC shall file the panel's assessment in a Canadian court of competent jurisdiction and the court shall issue the order to pay. This arrangement obviates the need to exercise the Suspension of Benefits provisions in Article 41 (see NAALC, Annex 41A).

27. Ibid.

28. Annex 39 provides that monetary enforcement assessments are put in a fund established to improve the enforcement of labor laws in the country against which the sanctions where leveled (Ibid., Annex 39).

29. Both U.S. NAO Submission No. 9703 and Canadian NAO Submission No. 98-1 allege that the Mexican government failed to remedy prohibited antiunion practices and substandard safety and health conditions at an Elchin, Inc. plant in Mexico. The trinational ministerial council has consolidated these two submissions, and ministerial consultations are pending. Similarly, both Canadian NAO Submission No. 98-2 and Mexico NAO Submission No. 9804 allege that the U.S. government is not enforcing its minimum wage and overtime pay standards in workplaces employing foreign nationals under a memorandum of understanding between the U.S. Department of Labor (DOL) and the Immigration and Naturalization Service (INS). In this instance, the Canadian NAO refused to review CAN 98-2, pointing out that the challenged memorandum of understanding changed after the submission was filed, while the Mexican NAO accepted Submission No. 9804 for review, and a hearing is pending.

30. Not shown in Table 18.1 is that many submissions allege violation of more than one labor principle. Counting the Echlin, Inc. submission once, 16 of the 21 submissions allege the denial of labor's basic right to freedom of association. Allegation of substandard occupational safety and health working conditions ranks as the second most often cited violation—8 submissions cite safety and health issues, again counting Echlin, Inc. once. Fair labor standards issues are cited seven times, ranking third.

31. In October 1999, the U.S. NAO Information Room maintained over 100 NAFTA-related program documents; proceedings; articles, papers, and books; and numerous CLC and NAO reports.

32. Compa cautions that, "one should not underestimate the power of public opinion informed by public exposure of labor rights violations, or the pressure for accountability generated by thorough oversight mechanisms like the NAO" (the submission and downstream processes) (Compa, 2000: 2–3).

33. See the "The Students of Yale Law School in the Public Service 1998–1999,"*Workers' Rights Project*, at http://www.yale.edu/lawweb/lawschool/pibroch.htn#n.

34. There have been two exceptions. In U.S. NAO submission 9702, the general manager of Han Young spoke on behalf of his company, as did the company council. In U.S. NAO submission 1996, the general coordinator of international affairs, secretary of labor and social welfare, testified on behalf of Mexico. See the U.S. NAO's Web site at www.dol.gov/dol/ilab/public/programs/nao/sumiss.htm.

35. Why business refuses to participate in NAO hearings is a matter of conjecture. However, nonparticipation may diminish the "sunshine factor."

36. Taken from the complaining parties' May 27, 1998, submission to C. Rafael Aranda, NAO secretary in Mexico.

37. Two recent and related developments bear on this point. Already covered by the FLSA and OSHA, illegal immigrant prospects for equal employment opportunities protections recently took a step forward when the Equal Employment Opportunity Commission announced its intent to extend the antidiscrimination laws to illegal immigrants (although its remedies may not include reinstatements) (see Greenhouse, 1999). Moreover, the American Federation of Labor and Congress of Industrial Organizations (AFL-CIO), changing its long-standing position, now is calling

for blanket amnesty for illegal immigrants in the United States and for secession of sanctions against U.S. employers who hire them, as opposed to employers who knowingly induce through advertisements illegal immigrants to enter the United States (see Greenhouse, 2000).

38. These 10 include Honeywell, G.E. Corp. (U.S. NAO Submission No. 940002), Sony Corp., Silitek Corp., Han Young, Echlin, Inc., Executive Air Transport, Inc., Sprint, Solec, Inc., and Washington State Apple Industry.

39. Filed on behalf of business interests, this submission alleges that the U.S. government's enforcement of section 8(a)(2) of the National Labor Relations Act violates the NAALC because the United States refuses to permit the unfettered participation of employees in HRM/LR decision-making processes in nonunion workplaces.

40. The total number of organizations filing submissions is unclear because we did not contact Mexico's "major" submitters, requesting the names and addresses of the "minor" cosubmitters.

41. We are fairly confident that we have the complete list of "minor" submitters who participated in Mexico NAO Submission No. 9804 (DOL/INS). The Yale Law School Workers' Rights Project kindly provided us with the information that it still had available. However, we could not locate the addresses of two of the "minor" organizations that joined in this submission. The two organizations not surveyed are the Korea Immigrant Workers' Advocates and Latino Workers Center (California). Therefore, we ultimately surveyed representatives from 44 organizations.

42. The responding organizations include outside counsel representing the International Brotherhood of Teamsters (United States) and International Brotherhood of Teamsters (Canada); Human Rights Watch/Americas; Maquiladora Health and Safety Support Committee; Worksafe! Southern California; United Steelworkers of America; United Automobile Worker—AFL-CIO; National Automobile Workers Union of Canada; Association of Flight Attendants; Florida Tomato Exchange; American Postal Workers Union; Communication, Energy, and Paper Worker Union of Canada; United Electrical, Radio and Machine Workers of America; Communications Workers of America; Paper, Allied-Industrial, Chemical and Energy Workers International Union; National Association of Letter Carriers; Washington, D.C., law firm; Yale Law School; Canadian Labour Congress; National Employment Law Project; Oil, Chemical, and Atomic Workers International Union, Local I-675; ACLU Immigrants' Rights Project; and Service Employees International Union.

43. The question reads as follows: "the signatory countries tend to promote (1) the freedom of association and the right to organize, (2) the right to bargain collectively, and (3) the right to strike."

44. Counting as one each the dual filings of U.S. Government (DOL/INS)) and Echlin, Inc. and not counting the employer-tendered Canadian Submission No. 99-1.

REFERENCES

Adams, R. J. and Singh, P. (1997). "Early Experience with NAFTA's Labour Side Accord." *Comparative Labor Law Journal* 18 (2), pp. 161–81.

Anderson, M. (1993). "North American Free Trade Agreement's Impact on Labor." In Bognanno, M. F. and Ready, K .J. (eds.), *The North American Free Trade Agreement: Labor, Industry, and Government Perspectives*. Westport, CT: Praeger, pp. 55–60.

Bahr, M. (1997). "Review of the North American Agreement on Labor Cooperation, Annex 5." Public comments, Commission of Labor Cooperation, Council of Ministers, Dallas, pp. 8–10.

Beckman, S. (1997). "Review of the North American Agreement on Labor Cooperation, Annex 5." Public comments, Commission of Labor Cooperation, Council of Ministers, Dallas, pp. 12–15.

Befort, S. F. and Cornett, V. E. (1996). "Beyond the Rhetoric of the NAFTA Treaty Debate: A Comparative Analysis of Labor and Employment Law in Mexico and the United States." *Comparative Labor Law Journal* 17 (2), pp. 269–313.

Campbell, B. (1993). "A Canadian Labor Perspective on a North American Free Trade Agreement on Industrial Labor." In Bognanno, M. F. and Ready, K. J. (eds.), *The North American Free Trade Agreement:Labor, Industry, and Government Perspectives*. Westport, CT: Praeger, pp. 61–68.

Clinton, W. J. (1992). "Expanding Trade and Creating American Jobs." October 4. Speech at North Carolina State University, Raleigh, NC.

Compa, L. A. (1995). "The First NAFTA Labor Cases: A New International Labor Rights Regime Takes Shape." *United States-Mexico Law Journal* 3 (Spring), pp. 159–81.

Compa, L. A. (2000). "Free Trade, Fair Trade, and the Battle for Labor Rights." Unpublished manuscript, School of Industrial and Labor Relations, Cornell University.

Cook, M. L. (1996). "Mexican Industrial Relations in Transition—What's New Since NAFTA?" Paper presented at the IRRA 48th Annual Meetings, San Francisco.

Cook, M. L., Gunderson, M., Thompson, M., and Verma, A. (1997). "Making Free Trade More Fair: Developments in Protecting Labor Rights." *Labor Law Journal* 48 (8), pp. 519–29.

Cypher, J..M. (1993). "Estimating the Impact of the U.S.–Mexican Free Trade Agreement on Industrial Labor." In Bognanno, M. F. and Ready, K. J. (eds.) *The North American Free Trade Agreement: Labor, Industry, and Government Perspectives*. Westport, CT: Praeger, pp. 85–97.

Faux, J. and Lee, T. (1993). "The Road to the North American Free Trade Agreement: Laissez-Faire or a Ladder Up?" In Bognanno, M. F. and Ready, K. J. (eds.), *The North American Free Trade Agreement: Labor, Industry, and Government Perspectives*. Westport, CT: Praeger, pp. 97–115.

Greckol, S., Sack, J., and Melancon, C. (1997). "Review of the North American Agreement on Labor Cooperation, Annex 5." Public comments, Commission of Labor Cooperation, Council of Ministers, Dallas, pp. 1–6.

Greenhouse, S. (1999). "US to Expand Anti-Discrimination Rights for Illegal Immigrants Working in this Country." *New York Times*, October 28, p. A28.

Greenhouse, S. (2000). "Labor Urges Amnesty for Illegal Immigrants." *New York Times*, February 17, p. A26.

Herzstein, R. E. (1995). "The Labor Cooperation Agreement Among Mexico, Canada, and the United States: Its Negotiation and Prospects." *United States-Mexico Law Journal* 3 Spring, pp. 121–31.

Lee, T. (1997). "Review of the North American Agreement on Labor Cooperation, Annex 5." Public comments, Commission of Labor Cooperation, Council of Ministers, Dallas, pp. 1–7.

Levinson, J. I. (1997). "Review of the North American Agreement on Labor Cooperation, Annex 5." Public comments, Commission of Labor Cooperation, Council of Ministers, Dallas, pp. 21–26.

Massimino, E. (1997). "Review of the North American Agreement on Labor Cooperation, Annex 5." Public comments, Commission of Labor Cooperation, Council of Ministers, Dallas, pp. 10–12.

McGrady, L. (1998). " NAFTA and Workers' Rights: A Canadian Perspective." Paper presented at the National Lawyers Guild Annual Convention, Detroit.

Shoch, J. (2000). "Rising from the Ashes of Defeat: Organized Labor and the 1997 and 1998 'Fast-Track' Fights." Unpublished manuscript, Department of Government, Dartmouth College.

Singh, P. and Adams, R. J. (2000). "Neither a Gem nor a Scam: The Progress of the North American Agreement of Labor Cooperation," Unpublished manuscript presented at the 52nd IRRA Annual Proceedings, Boston.

Solomon, J. (1997). "Review of the North American Agreement on Labor Cooperation, Annex 5." Public comments Commission of Labor Cooperation, Council of Ministers, Dallas, p. 10.

Torriente, A. L. (ed.). (1997). *Mexican and U.S. Labor Law and Practice*. Tucson, AZ: National Law Center for Inter-American Free Trade.

Part V

Summary and Conclusion

19

The Role of Power and Implications for Transnational Workplace Outcomes

William Cooke

In this final chapter, I frame transnational workplace outcomes as a product of power exercised by labor and management. Although not explicitly stated in each of the chapters of this volume, the theme of power as exercised by multinational companies (MNCs) and labor organizations implicitly runs throughout the various analyses. This central notion of organizational power underpinning human resource management and labor relations (HRM/LR) strategies pursued by MNCs and organized labor plays a dominant role in determining whether employment and workplace outcomes are more or less favorable for labor, management, or both. I first lay out a conceptual framework of the role of power in a labor–management context. I then synthesize and integrate the common themes of power underlying the analyses in this volume by highlighting salient factors acting as sources of power that influence the development and implementation of strategies and, consequently, workplace outcomes. Based on this synthesis and assessment of sources of power, I close by addressing the broader transnational implications and challenges ahead for labor–management relations.

THE ROLE OF POWER

A Conceptual Framework

As stated in Chapter 1, I begin with the highly simplified assumption that MNCs generally seek to act in ways *perceived* as optimizing profits and that unions generally seek to act in ways *perceived* as optimizing gains to workers. The ability of either party to act rationally, however, is bounded by limits of information and knowledge, by environmental uncertainty and unpredictability, and by the sheer complexity and politics of organizations, all of which can lead to organizational mistakes. Hence, both labor and management are susceptible to acting irrationally at times, failing to pursue or fully implement strategies that optimize organizational gains. Those parties that fail to correct such irrational, suboptimal behavior consequently reduce their opportunities and ability to achieve the gains that they seek and would otherwise optimize. The analyses presented in this volume provide a rich context in which to better understand such behavior and to address the factors that shape the workplace strategies of labor and management and, in turn, the transnational workplace outcomes of strategies pursued.

Toward synthesizing the analyses presented herein, I argue that optimization of workplace outcomes is dependent on (1) the total gain achievable through the employment relationship and (2) the sharing of that gain between labor and management. The extent to which either employers or unions optimize gains can be viewed as a product of both "relative power" and "total organizational power" (Cooke, 1990: Chapter 2).[1] Assuming that there are inherent conflicts of interests between labor and capital over the distribution of wealth and the means of generating such wealth, we can expect that there is always some degree of conflict or confrontation between labor and management. That party that can exercise greater relative power, in turn, has greater say over the means of creating and distributing wealth. Consequently, it behooves each party to find ways to maximize and sustain its relative power.

As the fate of labor and management is, however, inextricably linked to the success of the MNCs of which they are a part, the parties also share a common interest in maximizing wealth from which both parties would optimize their respective gains. Under those circumstances in which labor can exercise sufficient relative power to restrain management from dominating employment and workplace decisions regarding the means and distribution of wealth, labor and management have reason to cooperate with each other to maximize the wealth generated by the employment relationship. The ability of an organization to maximize wealth is dependent on its capacity to outperform competitors in the marketplace. That capacity is a function of what I call "total organizational power," which is the ability of an organization to extract from its environment the kind and magnitude of benefits sought. By increasing total organizational power vis-à-vis that of competitors, that is, greater total gain from the employment relationship can be created.

Toward optimizing gains, therefore, both labor and management must assess whether more can be gained from pursuing cooperative labor–management relations strategies fashioned to increase total organizational power or, alternatively, whether more can be gained by exercising relative power alone. If both parties perceive that greater gain can be achieved by increasing total organizational power than by exercising relative power alone, both parties have reason to pursue cooperative labor–management strategies, equitably sharing the added gain resulting from cooperation. If either party, however, perceives that greater gain can be achieved by exercising relative power alone, then cooperative strategies will not be pursued. Consequently, this exercise of relative and total organizational power, as constrained by the environment and limitations to rational organizational behavior, largely determines workplace outcomes.[2]

Toward understanding the role of power, Chamberlain's definition provides a useful basis on which to build: "[I]f the cost to B of disagreeing on A's terms is greater than the cost of agreeing on A's terms, while the cost to A of disagreeing on B's terms is less than the cost of agreeing on B's terms, then A's bargaining power is greater than B's" (Chamberlain, 1951: 221). Chamberlain's definition focuses on the costs of agreeing and disagreeing on the other party's terms in determining which party at any point in time can exercise greater relative power to optimize the outcomes that it seeks. Chamberlain's definition, nonetheless, also provides the basis for the parties to consider working cooperatively toward maximizing total organization power and, hence, total gain. That is, if each party offers terms to the other party that increase total organizational power and, consequently, entail lesser cost (or greater gain) to agreeing than disagreeing, then rational parties will work cooperatively to increase total organizational power. The notion of relative and total organizational power can be further extended in a slightly modified form to also apply to interunion, transnational cooperation. Where such cooperation can increase the total organizational power of cooperating unions to the point that the relative power of each participating union vis-à-vis the companies that they represent is enhanced, unions across borders have reason to forge transnational partnerships.

My objective here is to identify the sources of such power on which labor and management draw or leverage (1) to increase the costs to the second party of disagreeing with the first party's terms and (2) to reduce the cost (or increase the gain) to the second party of agreeing with the first party's terms. Stated differently, my objective is to identify the sources of power on which MNCs and unions can rely (or are constrained by) in forging and pursuing their respective HRM/LR strategies, strategies intended to influence both the distribution of wealth and the means of generating such wealth via the employment relationship and workplace practices. As conceptualized herein, greater or lesser relative and total organizational power is derived from (1) the broader economic and sociopolitical environments within which the parties find themselves and (2) the capacity and effectiveness by which labor and management draw upon and strategically utilize the sources of power available to them.[3] To illustrate the currency of this conceptual framework, I next draw on various analyses in the preceding chapters to identify salient sources of power and how labor and management have utilized these sources in pursuing their strategies for optimizing gain.

The Sources and Exercise of Power

Market Dynamics and Government Policies.
First, the dynamics of the marketplace make a difference. In particular, increasing international competition, advances in technologies, globalization of markets, and industry restructuring have had the effect of altering the relative and total organizational power of MNCs and unions. As described by Gennard and Ramsay (Chapter 13), for example, the changing economic environment of the printing and publishing sector, largely driven by continuing advances in

digital technology, continues to reshape the industry and modify the relative power of labor and management. Ongoing restructuring is marked by increasing industry concentration, with the emergence of large MNCs arising out of substantial merger and acquisition activity. Given the new forms of media, the graphical sector is increasingly shifting production to remote, low labor cost locations, becoming more segmented as a result of heightened outsourcing, and diversifying into various media outlets, including broadcasting. This ongoing industry restructuring has had a decidedly negative effect on union membership and union penetration and, hence, relative power among graphical sector unions.

Similarly, Bair and Ramsay's account (Chapter 3) of highly fluid, emerging global commodity chains has provided MNCs with increasing leverage over labor as core firms can more readily shift operations to links within chains where labor is cheaper and weaker. As discussed by Köhler (Chapter 2), furthermore, company executives have had to increasingly appease a volatile financial market by meeting shareholder earnings expectations, which have usually placed a strong emphasis on short-term horizons. Acting to meet these expectations, MNCs have too often hastily pursued mergers and acquisitions and sharply reduced employment. Although frequently having negative long-term consequences for companies, workers and their unions tend to have borne the brunt of restructuring and downsizing associated with these kinds of efforts to appease investors.

Influencing these broader market forces and, in turn, power relationships have been government restructuring and changes in market-related policies. For example, as discussed by Köhler (Chapter 2), some central governments have restructured themselves via privatization and outsourcing of traditional responsibilities. In some developing countries, decentralization of government activity has allowed local governments to play more important roles, especially with regard to offering foreign direct investment (FDI) incentives to MNCs, for example, by providing tax advantages, industrial parks, technology centers, and export processing zones (EPZs). Clamping the lid on wages to preserve its competitive advantage, Mexico has, likewise, attempted to attract FDI and improve its trade position (Babson, Chapter 10). By placing greater emphasis on achieving efficiency than on equity (Kleiner and Ham, Chapter 5), these kinds of government restructuring actions and shifts in business and market policies have generally changed the balance of power away from organized labor and toward MNCs.

As discussed by several authors, recently established multilateral regional policy agreements in Europe and North America have also had indirect effects on the balance of power between labor and management as a result of reducing barriers and costs to MNCs in choosing to move operations or shift production across borders. Given concerns that such movement and restructuring would have negative effects on some workers, the governments signatory to these agreements included provisions addressing the HRM/LR practices of MNCs with the purpose of minimizing such negative effects. Hence, the European Union (EU) European Works Council (EWC) Directive and the labor side agreement of NAFTA can be viewed as added sources of power for unions. The evidence, however, shows that these provisions have yielded minimal benefit to workers and their unions.

The early experience with EWCs strongly suggests that the promise and objectives of the EWC Directive have largely gone unfulfilled. Bain and Hester's evaluation (Chapter 15) of the potential costs and benefits of reaching voluntary versus mandatory agreements explains why MNCs overwhelmingly chose to create voluntary EWCs. In particular, based on the earlier voluntary agreements established, MNCs have minimized the extent to which they share information and engage in dialogue and consultation with employee representatives. This is certainly the case for the EWC established at McDonald's, as described and evaluated by Royle and Towers (Chapter 17) and for the several Belgian-U.K. EWCs examined by Beaupain, Jefferys and Annand (Chapter 16).

Unlike the EWC Directive, which requires MNCs to establish cross-national forums for information sharing and consultation with employee representatives, the NAALC agreement under the North American Free Trade Agreement (NAFTA) pledged Canada, Mexico, and the United States to improve, promote, and protect workers' rights in their respective countries. In their assessment of the labor side agreement, Bognanno and Lu (Chapter 18) conclude that the agreement has withered as an effective supranational mechanism for labor law enforcement and MNC compliance with host country employment and workplace laws. The authors' assessment of the labor side agreement is based on the fact that the law offers no remedies for violations, that the procedures for sanctioning NAFTA governments are exceptionally cumbersome and limited, and that no cases have been taken beyond ministerial consultations. Although there is some evidence that the three signatory governments and MNCs have corrected their illegal behavior in the face of negative public exposure and embarrassment (i.e., the "sunshine" factor), this appears to have occurred at most in a mere handful of cases. It follows, therefore, that as sources of power for labor, neither the NAFTA labor side agreement nor the European EWC Directive has proved to be an important source of relative power to labor.

IR Systems and MNC Strategies.

As addressed by a number of authors, differences in national industrial relations (IR) systems influence workplace outcomes, in particular, as a result of the relative power derived from employment and workplace regulations, collective bargaining contexts, and workplace cultures. Donn's analysis of the international shipping industry (Chapter 14) illustrates what can happen at the extreme when companies pursue their HRM/LR strategies in unregulated international labor markets. As he describes, "flag-of-convenience" (FOC) ships have escaped the reach of virtually any regulation of employment conditions on board ships that otherwise would be governed by traditional maritime nations. Additionally, given the nature of dispersed labor markets and the employment of "crew-of-convenience" workforces, FOC ships have virtually avoided all legitimate unionization, albeit the International Transport Workers Federation has had some modest success in forcing owners to reach minimal provision agreements with it. As a consequence, the relative power and HRM/LR strategies of most FOC shippers have gone unchallenged, resulting in deplorable living and employment conditions on board FOC ships, at least measured against minimal Western standards.

As I addressed in Chapter 4, MNCs are influenced in part by the restrictiveness of workplace regulations in deciding on their global operational configurations. For example, MNCs choose to invest less in countries with greater restrictions on employer freedom to lay off workers and in countries requiring the establishment of works councils. In essence, the greater the restrictions placed on employers (provided that at the same time such restrictions are viewed by unions as beneficial), the lesser the relative power of employers in setting the terms and conditions of employment. Furthermore, as I addressed in Chapter 4 and Kleiner and Ham addressed in Chapter 5, FDI decisions are influenced by collective bargaining contexts. It appears evident that MNCs invest less in countries in which the power of unions is generally greater. Hence, where unions have more successfully organized workers, and have extended contract coverage more widely and where negotiations are more highly centralized, MNCs have invested less than they would otherwise. This investment behavior can be viewed as an effort by MNCs to maximize their relative power via the global configuration of their operations.

Where they have invested, moreover, some MNCs have sought to avoid or minimize the restrictions of government workplace regulations and to avoid unionization. Royle and Towers' account of the HRM/LR strategy pursued by McDonald's across several European countries (Chapter 17) demonstrates how intensive such efforts can be. Evidence that union penetration among foreign-owned subsidiaries located in the United States dropped from nearly 30 percent in 1980 to below 15 percent by 1998 shows that it is not only U.S.-based MNCs that attempt to bolster their relative power by aggressively avoiding unionization, as well as by closing and downsizing foreign operations that have been unionized. Such efforts by MNCs to rid themselves of unions are well illustrated in Juravich and Bronfenbrenner's analysis of Bridgestone/Firestone's assault on the Rubber Workers and Steelworkers representing employees in the company's U.S. subsidiaries (Chapter 12).

Central to most analyses in this volume is the assessment of MNC success in diffusing preferred HRM/LR practices across their global operations. Underlying these efforts and explaining why some MNCs have been more or less successful is the exercise of power manifested by targeted local recipients resistant to such diffusion. The wide range of local responses appears to be a factor of differences in cultures and norms regarding workplace practices and the capacity of local constituents to resist. The capacity to resist, moreover, is clearly bolstered by the relative power of union organizations. As evaluated by Martin, Beaumont, and Pate in their analysis of AT&T and NCR (Chapter 6), it is critical that managers understand and be highly sensitive to the local context and culture of the subsidiaries in which new HRM/LR practices are being diffused. Change programs that do not take into account the incentive and ability of the local management and workforce to support or resist significant change are more likely to fail than those that do. Hence, both the message and the corporate messenger of change must have credibility at the foreign local level, and allowances must be made to amend strategies to take into account cross-cultural differences and basic organizational politics. Kenney and Tanaka's assessment of the diffusion of HRM/LR practices (Chapter 7) demonstrates, furthermore, how deep-rooted HRM/LR cultures and traditions (embraced by organized labor, as well as local management) made it virtually impossible for Japanese MNCs to diffuse their production systems intact to U.S. television assembly plants. Specifically, Japanese efforts to transplant their preferred "learning bureaucracies" failed in the face of Fordist workplace systems based on distinct divisions between labor and management and governed by hierarchical job-protection and seniority rights.

Similarly, as assessed by Huxley (Chapter 11), deep-rooted labor–management traditions led to differences in the deployment of GM's continental standardization of production and work in truck assembly. For instance, whereas the unionized workforce at the Canadian plant has long rejected management overtures to create a formalized system of work teams and rotation, the unionized workforce at GM's greenfield Mexican plant has accepted such a system. Such acceptance is consistent with Babson's account (Chapter 10) of Ford's Hermosillo operation in Mexico. The comparative ease with which GM and Ford were able to diffuse their preferred HRM/LR practices to their Mexican operations is, in part, attributable to the local union's affiliation with, and dominance by, the Confederation of Mexican Workers (CTM). The CTM, which long accommodated the former ruling political party (the Institutional Revolutionary Party), had endorsed that party's policy that workers fully accept new forms of work organization introduced by foreign-owned MNCs.

Brewster and Tregaskis (Chapter 8) examined the extent to which MNCs with operations in several European countries have diffused contingent employment and workplace practices. These practices are often viewed by MNCs as critical to achieving optimal workforce flexibility but are among the most contentious HRM/LR practices given their inherent threat to stable, long-term employment opportunities. The authors find that the use of contingent practices among MNCs parallels the usage common to host countries and sectors within countries. Brewster and Tregaskis conclude that differences in the extent to which contingent employment and workplace practices are deployed are primarily a matter of the extent to which such practices are generally accepted or rejected by workers in a given country. Hence, it appears that the institutional and cultural antecedents of host countries and sectors within countries have dominant effects on the extent to which MNCs can diffuse preferred HRM/LR practices. Stated differently, the power of MNCs to impose their preferred HRM/LR practices on the local workforces of their subsidiaries is generally quite limited, at least with regard to the diffusion of contingent employment and workplace practices in European countries.

The diffusion of preferred HRM/LR practices beyond foreign subsidiaries to indigenous firms also appears mixed. In their study of such diffusion in developing nations, Kuruvilla, Frenkel, and Peetz (Chapter 9) found only modest support for the argument that local firms in developing countries would adopt the so-called best practices deployed by lead MNCs in selected industries. The authors conclude that where diffusion does occur, it is more likely to occur within industries in which the market dominance of foreign subsidiaries is greater, the focus on serving international markets is greater than on serving domestic markets, and the labor market for qualified employees is tighter. The authors also find that government involvement can have the effect of shaping the balance of power between labor and management, as well as the total organizational power of firms within an industry. This was the case of the Indian government's insistence on the diffusion of selected practices in the banking industry and the case of the Penang Skills Development Center in the Malaysian electronics industry.

In contrast to most of the analyses presented in this volume but consistent with the Ford and GM success in diffusing practices to Mexico is the case of McDonald's in Europe. As detailed by Royle and Towers (Chapter 17), McDonald's has been able to impose to a substantial extent its "McParticipation" HRM/LR strategy throughout its European fast-food restaurants, largely through the exercise of relative power. That successful exercise of relative power over labor can be attributed to several sources of power.   First, McDonald's has a strong corporate culture that molds management behavior across all of its highly standardized operations and that views union representation as unwarranted and destructive.   Second, the company has taken full advantage of the nature of its workforce, which is predominantly made up of young, often poorly skilled and poorly educated workers who seek only temporary employment and/or are employed on a part-time basis.   Third, given the characteristics of its workforce and its corporate culture, the company has been diligent about "discouraging" any interest among workers for union representation and has successfully circumvented distinctly different legislated systems of employee interest representation at both the national and supranational levels. In particular, it has maneuvered to avoid or minimize union representation, the appointment of union delegates, and compliance with collective bargaining agreements; to evade creating local and national works councils or to dominate such councils where they have been established; and to capture the EWC primarily to serve management's agenda.   Fourth, McDonald's has relied heavily on operating franchises, which allow it to effectively control all facets of operations while remaining legally separated. As such, it has been able to distance itself from charges of noncompliance with various workplace regulations.

Although eventually destroyed by a change in top management strategy, Japanese-owned Bridgestone, likewise, successfully diffused its preferred HRM/LR strategy (based on extensive employee involvement and labor–management cooperation) to its U.S. Firestone tire manufacturing plants (Juravich and Bronfenbrenner, Chapter 12). Faced by the inevitable closure of Firestone plants, the Rubberworkers accepted Bridgestone's preferred HRM/LR strategy. This case illustrates how management approached the union to work cooperatively with the company toward increasing total organizational power. Gaining widespread support (if not enthusiasm) among workers to engage in nontraditional forms of work, the company indeed turned the Firestone plants into highly competitive operations.   However, with a change in company leadership that apparently believed more could be gained by exercising its relative power alone, Bridgestone/Firestone sought major concessions and a break from labor–management cooperation. Had the Steelworkers not come to the rescue, the company's aggressive assault on the union would have likely succeeded. In the end, however, the Steelworkers exercised sufficient relative power to deny the company its way.

Transnational Union Strategies.

In response to MNC global configuration and HRM/LR strategies (some of which include efforts to avoid, marginalize, or eliminate unions across locations), organized labor has sometimes developed successful countervailing strategies but often has not. The global campaign forged by the United Steel Workers of America against Bridgestone/Firestone provides a model of union coalition building and labor solidarity in the face of MNCs bent on destroying unions representing workers in foreign subsidiaries. Juravich and Bronfenbrenner make a strong case for the value of enlisting support from unions in both the home country and across the foreign subsidiaries of MNCs. By successfully coordinating cross-national public declarations and demonstrations of support in Japan, Europe, and Latin America, the Steelworkers gained sufficient relative power to force Bridgestone/Firestone back to the bargaining table to reach an acceptable agreement.

This case demonstrates the importance to unions of optimizing and maintaining relative power. Once the company perceived (1) that its relative power over the union was great enough to impose greater cost on the union to disagreeing than agreeing with the company and (2) that more could be gained by exercising relative power alone than could be gained by cooperative efforts at increasing total organizational power, the company chose to exercise its relative power alone. Had only the Rubberworkers been able to leverage sufficient relative power to offer Bridgestone/Firestone terms that would entail greater gain (or lesser costs) to agreeing than to disagreeing (whether such terms included continued cooperation or a return to more traditional relations), Bridgestone/Firestone would have backed away from its assault on the union. It is critical, therefore, that unions optimize and maintain their relative power, whether relationships with employers are more confrontational or more cooperative.

Toward enhancing union relative power, Bair and Ramsay (Chapter 3) emphasize the need for organized labor to dissect the commodity chains in which MNCs are embedded. Such a dissection can expose both the strengths and vulnerabilities of companies and, in turn, the optional sources of power (i.e., points of leverage) available to them. Toward optimizing relative power and developing the most effective organizing and countervailing strategies, unions must recognize key differences in commodity chains. MNCs embedded in some commodity chains have much greater flexibility to rely on remote supply and to disperse and relocate production (e.g., in apparel, electrical goods, and semiconductor chains) than others that require greater integration of supply, closer proximity to production or service, and more visibility in the marketplace (e.g., in hotel, banking, and newspaper chains). By tracing more fully the set of firms linked to given MNCs within a commodity chain, unions can identify the various unions representing employees of other companies within the commodity chain. The forging of interunion communication and cooperation among unions throughout a commodity chain, one based on mutual cause and understanding of each other, allows each to enhance its relative power.

By placing MNCs within the broader cross-national economic and sociopolitical environments in which they operate, moreover, organized labor can better design strategies for modifying public policy and enlisting the support of nongovernmental organizations (NGOs), consumer groups, and citizens concerned about the effects of globalization on workers and the environment. Indeed, unions have a potentially important source of relative power via NGOs that have used the "sunshine" factor to expose and embarrass MNCs that rely on remote, "sweatshop" production but whose brand marketing success depends on public image and approval (à la campaigns against the Gap, Liz Claiborne, Nike, and Guess).

Initiating communication, information exchange, and deeper understanding between unions representing workers of the same MNC across countries is a central theme for both Babson (Chapter 10) in his study of Ford's dual sourcing of production in the United States and Mexico and Huxley (Chapter 11) in his study of GM's program of continental standardization of truck production and work organization. To date, virtually no communication by the United Automobile Workers (UAW) in the United States or the Canadian Automobile Workers (CAW) in Canada with unions in Mexico has taken place. Following the Canadian workers' withdrawal from the UAW in 1984, moreover, the CAW and UAW have operated as separate entities without interunion coordination of strategies. However, as Huxley points out, both have supported each other over the last few years when either has struck GM plants.

Both Babson and Huxley argue that the American and Canadian unions would benefit by thinking differently about their southern counterparts in Mexico, not as strictly low-wage, low-skill competitors and docile organizations but as unions that share common interests, concerns, and struggles. Given that in the cases analyzed, auto industry unions across the continent are producing similar, if not identical, products primarily for the same U.S. market, their long-term well-being is inextricably linked to the transformation and reconfiguration of the auto sector. In addition, they have common concerns and struggles over health and safety issues, work organization, outsourcing, and possible whipsawing, all of which would appear to suggest that unions in all three countries have reason to communicate and exchange information, at least for locals across multisourced plants.

These cases, however, raise two basic challenges to cross-national cooperation. First, unions may view each other as competitors for product and work. Second, local unions from each country must be able to identify with the struggles of each other. As Huxley emphasizes, the emergence of worker solidarity depends on unions' having developed a capacity to pursue struggles that focus on achieving gains for workers at that locality. The extension of solidarity beyond the local level and the willingness of locals to even consider reordering their priorities require that local unions can identify with similar struggles elsewhere. Cross–border solidarity also presumes that gains to each workplace would be achieved from any coordinated strategies and that support for local unions elsewhere will be reciprocated. Within my conceptual framework, local unions must perceive that solidarity across borders enhances their own relative power vis-à-vis their local management, as well as the relative power of other local unions.

Based on the experiences of graphical worker unions, Gennard and Ramsay (Chapter 13) describe what is clearly one of the most ambitious transnational, interunion coordination strategies unfolding in any given industry. Central to such success in developing cross-national coordination are (1) the need for unions to collect, share, and analyze data across the locations of MNCs in a given industry or commodity chain and (2) the pursuit of longer-term common claims across locations, while recognizing institutional differences and priorities of different unions and their need for autonomy in how they pursue coordinated claims. Gennard and Ramsay conclude, nonetheless, that the ability of unions to develop transnational strategies is especially challenging given differences in union policies, languages, and laws across countries, the lack of resources, and outdated organizational structures. In addition, the authors believe that the most challenging obstacle to creating effective transnational coordination is the continued erosion of union membership and coverage, which allows MNCs to pit nonunion locations against unionized locations.

Lastly, Beaupain, Jefferys, and Annand (Chapter 16) raise a number of obstacles faced by unions in coordinating transnational strategies, namely, those of interunion differences. In spite of having a unique opportunity to coordinate strategies across unions representing employees from the subsidiaries of a given MNC via EWC arrangements, the authors found that elements of interunion rivalry and suspicion have undermined effective interunion cooperation and cohesion. A lack of trust between unions, it appears, stems from the lack of understanding of each other's respective organizational goals, structures, and priorities and the distinct, national IR systems in which they are embedded. Furthermore, natural concerns over competition between an MNC's subsidiaries for investment and product and over any reorganization of MNCs via mergers and acquisitions exacerbate rivalry and distrust. Divisiveness, in turn, can lead to outright disdain by one union for another, the withholding of valuable information between unions, and the unwillingness of unions to allocate resources necessary for travel and interunion planning meetings. The capacity of unions to maximize relative power by developing and coordinating effective interunion, transnational strategies, therefore, requires that they find ways to overcome distrust and divisiveness.

IMPLICATIONS FOR LABOR–MANAGEMENT RELATIONS AND TRANSNATIONAL WORKPLACE OUTCOMES

We began by tracing the emerging reach and restructuring of MNCs. As Köhler (Chapter 2) reports, there are more than 60,000 MNCs employing some 45 million workers across their foreign subsidiaries and another 50 million workers in their home operations. Although accounting for only about 1 percent of total world employment, today's MNCs account for two-thirds to three-fourths of total exports. Furthermore, FDI continues to rise steadily, and, based on the rate of expansion over the last five years, the number of foreign-owned subsidiaries will double from roughly 800,000 today to 1.8 million by 2010. Most of this increase is being driven by merger and acquisition investment, which generally does not lead to increases in employment but instead to changes and concentration in MNC ownership. The growing economic influence and restructuring of MNCs can have major implications, nonetheless, for the workplaces of the reorganized firms both abroad and at home (as demonstrated in the recent "merger" of Daimler Benz and Chrysler and subsequent controlling investment in Mitsubishi; "Riding Together," 2001).

The foregoing analysis and review have emphasized the underlying role of relative power in determining transnational workplace outcomes. Whether workplace outcomes are more favorable for labor or capital depends in large part on how successfully both parties have been able to capture various sources of power in their development and pursuit of HRM/LR strategies. Given the increasingly competitive and uncertain global market, the mobility and resources of MNCs would appear to give them greater leverage than organized labor to decide on the means and distribution of wealth derivable from the employment relationship. As shown by numerous accounts in this volume, however, the ability of MNCs to diffuse or impose their preferred HRM/LR practices across their operations across countries is limited. It is limited, that is, when the local workforce has sufficient relative power and interest in blocking the unilateral imposition of management strategies.

The subject of organized labor's generally diminished relative power in a rapidly changing global marketplace is taken up by authors of several chapters. Indeed, a central theme has been one of extending the degree of communication, information exchange, and, ultimately, strategy coordination of unions across borders. Presently, there is but a modest degree of such cooperation, and history has shown that nearly all earlier efforts at transnational strategy coordination have been short-lived. At a conceptual level, it would appear that unions have simply not seen sufficient benefit from sustained transnational interunion cooperation. That is, the potential, added relative power that might be derived by national or local unions from interunion cooperation across borders does not justify the potential sacrifice (costs) associated with developing or sustaining transnational partnerships.

At the heart of this issue is the perception that the potential gain to one is the potential loss to the other as MNCs pit one location against another via whipsawing and FDI decision making. Although public declarations and actions of support by one union for another union's struggle are valuable, they do not put much at risk in regard to the well-being or very livelihood of the unionized workforce providing such support. Within a context in which MNCs can and are willing to move production between unionized sites or to move work to nonunion locations, the development of cross-border, interunion strategies will require that each union see greater gain or lesser cost to such cooperation than any one union perceives it would incur without interunion cooperation. The challenge before unions, therefore, is to forge strategies that each union sees as maximizing its relative power vis-à-vis its own management. Such strategies will necessarily need to incorporate agreements that the potential loss of work or compensation to any given national or local union is less than it would be absent interunion cooperation. In short, interunion transnational strategies must demonstrate that by enhancing the total organizational power of unions involved, the relative power of each is, likewise, enhanced.

One can surmise that the reason that well-coordinated, interunion transnational strategies are not widespread is that unions have not been able to structure strategies that, indeed, truly increase the relative power of each union. Hence, to date, transnational strategies have been quite limited. They have almost exclusively been restricted to (1) sharing information, (2) consultation, (3) showing public support but incurring limited organizational sacrifice for given struggles, and (4) participating in international trade secretariats and associated world company councils as forums for facilitating greater understanding of the varied circumstances faced by unions across borders and, in turn, searching for common ground across locations. Even in the exceptional case of the EWC Directive, it appears that unions across borders have used these mandated councils for little more than the exchange of information and limited consultation about the subsidiaries of given MNCs. These kinds of interunion transnational efforts are not to be dismissed, but they cannot shift the balance of power between labor and MNCs very far.

The many practical obstacles (as identified by authors herein) to developing interunion, transnational strategies are, without question, substantial (if not daunting), an observation that helps explain why few unions have sought to forge them and why others have failed in the process. In addition to practical matters of insufficient financial resources and language barriers, unions in different countries have evolved differently with regard to strategic orientations and identities (Hyman, 1999). As a consequence, their organizational priorities, structures, forms of governance, policies, practices, and customs have evolved differently. There are also marked differences in the IR systems and welfare policies between countries, as addressed in part in Chapters 4 and 5. Given the generally deep-rooted desire for organizational autonomy and national identity, these kinds of differences have presented substantial organizational challenges to national unions in finding common ground and workable accommodations over setting priorities and developing practical mechanisms for pursuing coordinated collective bargaining strategies across countries.

Toward shifting the balance of power much further, however, unions across borders will need to create transnational partnerships in which their objectives and activities go well beyond those generally pursued to date.[4] Along these lines, it would appear that transnational partnerships would benefit from finding ways to bolster and leverage their existing relative power to enhance opportunities to negotiate over FDI and transnational movement-of-work decisions. Bearing in mind the logic of relative and total organizational power presented earlier, the challenge before unions is to offer terms to MNCs that (1) increase the total organizational power of organized employers and (2) entail less cost (or greater gain) to employers of agreeing to the union's terms than disagreeing to those terms. Here, the focus of transnational union partnerships would be to work cooperatively with MNCs to optimize total organizational power as a quid pro quo for (say) rights to joint decision making with MNCs over FDI and movement-of-work decisions.

Under such agreements (by way of example, only), when MNCs contemplate moving work across borders or making further investments abroad, the union partnership would be provided an opportunity to assess such investment decisions and make alternative recommendations. The logic underlying this proposal derives from existing outsourcing agreements between the UAW and the Big Three automakers in the United States. My suggested example merely extends such agreements to include any possible displacement of workers attributable to FDI and cross-border movement-of-work decisions. Under such an arrangement, members of the transnational union partnership would have opportunities for consultation and the making of recommendations to the relevant national union.

During this consultation among unions, the transnational union partnership would be seriously tested. As with the existing outsourcing arrangements in which UAW local unions can counterbid management's outsourcing options under consideration, the transnational partnership would need to devise alternative plans that would match any cost savings or increased profitability contained in management's plan. Whereas the location that would have received the added foreign investment or transfer of work under the management plan (say a Mexican operation at the expense of an American operation or vice versa), would have benefited at the expense of the location that would have forgone added investment or would have lost work, any alternative endorsed by the transnational partnership would also possibly benefit one operation at the expense of another. Herein lies the inherent "prisoner's dilemma," which unions across borders cannot escape. Nevertheless, caught in a prisoner's dilemma, it is better for the broader transnational partnership to find an optimal cooperative solution than to leave solutions to MNCs. Obviously, members of the transnational partnership would need to equitably share any sacrifices over time and reach consensus to any alternatives proposed to MNCs. Otherwise, national or local unions that would incur greater costs from transnational partnership recommendations than they would incur acting on their own would have reason to break from any such partnership.

One obstacle to forging transnational union partnerships that resonates, in particular, is one identified by Gennard and Ramsay as the most pressing, namely, nonunion competition within and across MNCs. Without having all sites of MNCs represented by unions and with the increasing opportunity for MNCs to establish or acquire nonunion sites through FDI decisions, the total organizational power underlying transnational union partnerships is especially limited. Consequently, it becomes imperative that unions incorporate into their transnational strategies concerted efforts at organizing, especially those locations that serve as essential links within given MNC value chains and/or within the broader commodity chains in which they are embedded. As part of this strategy, unions could (again, by way of example) demand union organizing neutrality agreements that would be applicable to all foreign locations of MNCs (much along the line of the UAW-DaimlerChrysler agreement recently reached).

Although this does not guarantee that foreign subsidiaries will become organized, it does neutralize companies from aggressively resisting efforts by members of the partnership that attempt to organize foreign subsidiaries.

With these neutrality agreements in hand, it follows that transnational union partnerships would assist and help coordinate organizing campaigns with the appropriate host country unions that have "jurisdiction" over given nonunion foreign operations. By achieving this kind of organizing neutrality agreement with MNCs and, in turn, increasing union penetration across MNCs, the relative power of the transnational partnership would increase over time. Hence, offsetting the potential losses that might be incurred by a given union as a result of MNC shifts in FDI and work across borders would be the added relative power gained by union partnerships via increased union penetration. Consequently, member unions that might consider breaking from union partnerships would have reason to pause, as they would sacrifice the value of the organizing neutrality clauses negotiated by union partnerships with MNCs.

Unless MNCs perceive that a net benefit to them will be gained by agreeing to these kinds of neutrality pledges and joint decision making over FDI and the movement of work, they would, of course, refuse to agree to any such terms. Hence, unions would need to agree to terms and conditions that increase the competitive position of MNCs in the sector (i.e., increase the total organizational power of employers). Because nonunion companies pose a serious competitive threat to unionized companies, where unions have organized MNCs and have sufficient relative power, unions have reason to cooperate with MNCs toward increasing total organizational power. Since MNCs are driven to optimize profits, that is, in highly competitive and uncertain markets (everything else the same), companies cannot endure incurring higher costs per unit of labor input than their nonunion competitors. Employees, on the other hand, have little to gain from selecting or retaining unions if unions do not increase compensation and/or improve workplace environments to levels better than those found in nonunion companies. It is imperative to unions and their companies, therefore, that they reach terms and conditions of employment (not ones, however, based on "smoke and mirrors") that generate value-added to that point that offsets any union cost differential in compensation and other terms and conditions of employment.

Lest the reader get the wrong impression, let me emphasize that labor–management "cooperation" does not imply that any given set of HRM/LR practices will be deployed, only that the parties find ways to continuously improve performance (i.e., increase total organizational power). What might be characterized as more "traditional" as opposed to "innovative" or "best practice" is not at issue; both approaches have been shown to succeed as well as fail. Cooperation requires only that labor and management find ways to jointly problem-solve around increasing a company's competitive position vis-à-vis its competitors and, importantly, to the benefit of both labor and management.

In addition to finding ways to jointly solving workplace inefficiencies unique to given locations, MNCs and transnational union partnerships will need to focus on the resolution of workplace inefficiencies in a global context. First, along these lines, members of a transnational union partnership could pledge to help management diffuse preferred HRM/LR practices between home and host locations. As reviewed earlier, unions have often resisted the diffusion of preferred HRM/LR practices to foreign subsidiaries and, thus, imposed substantial costs on MNCs. By helping tailor innovative practices to fit optimally within different IR systems and helping achieve local union leader and member endorsement of changes desired, the costs to diffusion of preferred HMR/LR practices can be minimized. Second, given the potentially high costs incurred by MNCs to disruptions in their global value chains (especially with just-in-time delivery systems in place), the transnational union partnership could also agree not to withhold its labor during the life of an agreement. Of course, what either MNCs or transnational union partnerships will be willing to agree to is a matter of the balance of relative power. In industries or sectors in which transnational partnerships can exercise greater relative power on a global basis, the more likely the kinds of options described herein would be agreed to by MNCs. The lesser the relative power that can be exercised by transnational partnerships, on the other hand, the less likely MNCs would agree to these kinds of options.

Critically, along these lines, unions must focus their organizing strategies on the subsidiaries and local suppliers of MNCs in developing countries. Greatly exacerbating this challenge to unions is the dependence of developing countries on FDI inflows from developed countries, in conjunction with the vast gulf between compensation, working conditions, and democratic union representation in developing and developed nations. Although there has been no pronounced shift in total FDI flowing toward low-wage, developing countries over the last two decades, FDI inflows into developing countries have continued to rise in magnitude and have become the dominant form of capital investment. Indeed, FDI accounted for 66 percent of total investment and financial assistance in developing countries by 1999, dramatically higher than the mere 5 percent that it accounted for in 1980 (Köhler, Chapter 2).

At the heart of the challenge are the contentious issues of perceived exploitation of workers in developing countries and perceived social dumping by MNCs of workers in developed nations. Indeed, ever sharper lines are being drawn between proponents and opponents of international regulation of labor standards. Proponents' arguments center around the setting of standards to protect workers (including children) from deplorable working conditions; eliminating unfair, low labor cost competitive advantages; and harmonizing standards upward. Opponents' arguments center around the priority of national development policies over international policies; undue infringement on national sovereignty and cultural identity; double standards and disguised protectionism by wealthy nations (given that the availability of low labor costs is usually the only competitive advantage available to developing nations); and the dependence of developing nations on FDI, which provides the most promising opportunity and avenue for developing countries to evolve as rapidly as possible out of poverty (see Tsogas, 1999 for detailed arguments).

Although there are deep disagreements about the international regulation of labor standards, there would appear to be no compelling reason to disagree about the desire to improve labor standards worldwide and as quickly as possible. That appears to be a premise shared by all in this heated debate. The means and timing by which that goal can be achieved, however, will continue to divide societies, to divide MNCs and organized labor, and, likewise, to divide organized labor in developed and developing countries for many years to come. As labor in both developed and developing nations arguably suffers the greater consequences of any exploitation and social dumping, organized labor and its allies have the most at stake in bridging this great divide. The development of much more extensive and well-coordinated, interunion transnational strategies will be required, therefore, to build that bridge.

Finally, in addition to forging transnational interunion partnerships for the purpose of *industrial* action, it would appear that international partnerships among unions must also find more effective ways of taking *political* action. Along these lines, unions will need to fashion coordinated strategies that change broader public opinion about labor standards and collective bargaining rights and, in turn, alter relevant government policies, especially across developing nations. Without government policies that protect the right of workers to organize and bargain collectively, unions will be thwarted in their efforts to represent employees of the foreign subsidiaries of MNCs and, in turn, bring nonunion locations within the transnational union partnership. Although much political activity has emerged in recent years under the auspices of the International Labor Organization (ILO), the International Confederation of Free Trade Unions, various international trade secretariats, national unions and federations acting independently, NGOs, and human rights organizations, it would appear that a much broader and more concerted effort among and across these various organizations is required of unions in seeking to optimize gains to workers.

In spite of the apparent differences between the priorities of organized labor, MNCs, and government policymakers, the fate of each is, nonetheless, inextricably linked to the success of each, at least in democratic societies. That is, the success of labor and management is dependent on favorable public policies; the success of government is dependent on favorable outcomes for both labor and management; the success of labor is dependent on the success of business; and where labor is organized and relatively strong, the success of business is dependent on labor. Under a scenario in which labor can exercise sufficient relative power, therefore, the interdependence of labor, MNCs, and government policymakers yields a setting in which leaders of all three entities have reason to work together toward increasing total gain from the employment relationship. At that point, government policymaking and labor–management negotiations can be directed at improving workplace conditions. The test of such policymaking and negotiations will necessarily hinge on finding ways to reduce *unit* labor costs by increasing labor productivity in order to offset the added costs associated with improving the standards of work.

CONCLUDING NOTE

In closing, in this volume we have sought to lay out, both in theory and in practice, the enormous complexity and challenges faced by MNCs, workers, and organized labor regarding a host of transnational workplace and labor–management issues. In so doing, we have presented a fairly comprehensive framework and a rich set of case examples and original analyses focusing on the HRM/LR strategies pursued by MNCs and organized labor. The workplace outcomes associated with these transnational strategies on workplaces are largely determined by the power that both labor and management can exercise and how that power is exercised. Since much of that power is ultimately derived directly and indirectly from the broader sociopolitical environment, concerned citizens and government policymakers can have a decidedly important effect on the balance of power between labor and management and, hence, workplace outcomes. As we aspire to improve the work lives and well-being of citizens worldwide in an ever-increasingly competitive, integrated, and uncertain global marketplace, we must embrace two fundamental and critical policy goals: (1) provide people with the greatest opportunities to have rewarding jobs that enhance the quality and value of their work lives and family lives and (2) provide the business community with the greatest opportunity to achieve sustainable competitive advantage, profitability, and growth. We cannot achieve the first goal without achieving the second, but the purpose of achieving the second goal surely must be to achieve the first.

NOTES

1. Readers familiar with Fox's (1974) and Lukes' (1974) seminal sociological analyses of power relations between labor and management will note similarities between their constructions of "power over" and "power for" and my use of relative and total organizational power.

2. My framing of this juxtaposing or balancing of the exercise of relative power while pursuing joint problem solving to increase total organizational power closely parallels Walton and McKersie's (1965) distinction between "distributive" and "integrative" bargaining, which have long been basic dimensions of labor–management negotiations.

3. The earlier conceptualizations of labor–management relations developed by Barbash (1984) and Kochan, Katz, and McKersie (1986) view the economic and sociopolitical environments and certain organizational factors as shaping the employment relationship and associated employment outcomes. The external environmental and internal organizational contexts of these two frameworks are basically extensions of Dunlop's (1958) systems framework of industrial relations. Although Barbash developed some fairly explicit behavioral assumptions about the interactions of labor and management, he was not explicit about how these behavioral assumptions might trigger the parties to cooperate. Although Kochan et al. addressed labor–management cooperation, they failed to develop any explicit underlying behavioral assumptions that would explain the conditions under which labor and management would forge cooperative relations.

4. The Union Network International (UNI) was formed in January 2000 with an expressed objective of promoting negotiations between MNCs and their unions across countries in a wide range of industries, including the telecommunications, graphical, and media industries. It is too early to assess UNI's success in engaging MNCs in transnational negotiations and how its approximately 1,000 affiliated unions have dealt with potential transnational tradeoffs. The creation of UNI, nonetheless, marks a recognition by unions across borders of their pressing need to pursue globally

coordinated strategies across MNCs. See "More Jobs are on the Line" (2000), and http://www.union-network.org.

REFERENCES

Chamberlain, N. W. (1951). *Collective Bargaining*, New York: McGraw-Hill.

Cooke W. N. (1990). *Labor-Management Cooperation: New Partnerships or Going in Circles?* Kalamazoo, MI: Upjohn Institute for Employment Research.

Barbash, J. (1984). *The Elements of Industrial Relations*. Madison : University of Wisconsin Press.

Dunlop, J. T. (1958). *Industrial Relations Systems*. New York: Holt, Rinehart, and Winston.

Fox, A. (1974). *Beyond Contract: Work, Power and Trust Relations*. London: Faber.

Hyman, R. (1999). "Five Alternative Scenarios for West European Unionism." In Munck, R. and Waterman, P. (eds.), *Labour Worldwide in the Era of Globalization*. New York: St. Martin's Press, pp. 121–30.

Kochan, T. A., Katz, H. C., and McKersie, R. B. (1986). *The Transformation of American Industrial Relations*. New York: Basic Books.

Lukes, S. (1974). *Power: A Radical View*. London: Macmillan.

"More Jobs are on the Line." (2001). *Financial Times*, September 19, p. 1X.

"Riding Together." (2001). *Business Week*, February 26, pp. 48–49.

Tsogas, G. (1999). "Labour Standards in International Trade Agreements: An Assessment of the Arguments." *International Journal of Human Resources* 10 (2), pp. 351–75.

Walton, R. E. and McKersie, R. B. (1965). *A Behavioral Theory of Labor Negotiations*. New York: McGraw-Hill.

Index

About the Editor and Contributors

William Cooke is the Director of the Douglas A. Fraser Center for Workplace Issues and Senior Research Professor in the College of Urban, Labor and Metropolitan Affairs, Wayne State University. His most recent research has focused on global business and workplace strategies (funded in part by the Russell Sage and Rockefeller Foundations) and on transnational interunion cooperation. Bill is also the Faculty Director of the *Strategic Collective Bargaining* executive education program at the University of Michigan and has been a consultant to a wide range of companies and unions regarding domestic and global labor relations strategies and contract negotiations.

Rachael Annand is a Senior Lecturer in the School of Business at Oxford Brookes University in Great Britain. Her main research focus has been on trade union organizations, both at the European and worldwide levels. She was an international officer in Britain's largest public sector union (UNISON) from 1989 to 2001.

Steve Babson is a Labor Program Specialist at the Labor Studies Center, Wayne State University in Detroit. His research focuses primarily on issues of work organization and labor relations in the North American auto industry. He is Codirector of the International Research Network on Autowork in the Americas, a trinational project linking union and university-based researchers in the United States, Mexico and Canada.

Trevor Bain is Professor Emeritus at the Manderson Graduate School of Business, University of Alabama. The primary focus of his research is on international industrial relations and human resources. He is the author of more than seventy five books, journal articles, chapters and monographs and is an active arbitrator and mediator.

Jennifer Bair is an Assistant Professor in the Department of Sociology at Yale University. Her current research explores how development outcomes are shaped in specific institutional contexts by transnational production networks between foreign and local firms. She is coeditor of *Globalization and Regionalism: NAFTA and the New Geography of the North American Apparel Industry* (Temple University, 2002).

Phillip Beaumont is a Professor of Employment Relations, Department of Business and Management, University of Glasgow. His current research interests include the impact of company lifelong learning programs, the diffusion of human resource management practices, and the outcomes of organizational downsizing. He has been an adviser and consultant to numerous companies, trade unions and government organizations.

Thérèse Beaupain is a Research Associate and at the Institute of Sociology, Free University of Brussels in Belgium. Her research has focused primarily on Belgian industrial relations and, more recently, on the European context of industrial relations. She has been a lecturer of industrial relations at the Free University of Brussels and taught comparative industrial relations at the Catholic University of Louvain.

Mario F. Bognanno is a Professor of Industrial Relations and former Director of the Industrial Relations Center, Carlson School of Management, at the University of Minnesota. His research has addressed topics in labor relations, labor economics, arbitration, and international industrial relations. He is an active arbitrator and recently served as chief-of-staff to the president of the University of Minnesota

Chris Brewster is a Professor of International Human Resource Management at South Bank University in London. His contribution, herein, was written while he was a Professor and Director of the Center for European Human Resource Management at the Cranfield School of Management in the United Kingdom. His research interests include comparative international human resource management, flexible working practices, and the management of trade unions, topics for which he has authored more than 10 books and 100 articles.

Kate Bronfenbrenner is the Director of Labor Education Research at Cornell University, School of Industrial and Labor Relations. Her primary research interests focus on union organizing and collective bargaining and on the impact of global trade and investment policy on workers, wages, and unions. She is the coauthor and editor of several books, including (with Tom Juravich) *Ravenswood: The Steelworkers' Victory and the Revival of American Labor* (Cornell University Press, 1999).

Clifford B. Donn is a Professor in the Department of Industrial Relations and Human Resource Managment at Le Moyne College in Syracuse, New York. His primary focus of research is on labor relations and employment conditions in the U.S.-flag and international ocean-going maritime industries. He is also an active mediator and arbitrator.

Stephen Frenkel is a Professor of Organization and Employment Relations at the Australian Graduate School of Management, University of New South Wales/University of Sydney. His research focuses on globalization and employment relations, and the social organization of innovation. He is on the editorial boards of the *Industrial and Labor Relations Review* and the *International Journal of Human Resource Management*.

John Gennard is a Professor in the Department of Human Resource Management, Business School, University of Strathclyde, Glasgow. His current research interests lie in the response of organized labor to the growth and strategies of multinational companies, with particular emphasis on the international graphical industry. He is also an industrial disputes arbitrator and is editor of the international journal *Employee Relations*.

Hwikwon Ham is a doctoral student in the Department of Economics at the University of Minnesota. His fields of specialization are labor economics, international economics and econometrics.

Kim Hester is an Associate Professor of Management in the Department of Management and Marketing, College of Business, at Arkansas State University. Her research interests mainly focus on union member attitudes and behaviors, union member commitment and participation, union support perceptions, organizational justice, and labor relations climates. She is the recipient of the 2001 College of Business Faculty Research Award.

Christopher Huxley is a Professor of Sociology and International Development Studies at Trent University, Canada. His current research focuses on the automobile assembly and supplier industries in Canada, the United States and Mexico. He has held visiting fellowships at the University of Warwick, the University of Windsor and Wayne State University (Visiting Fullbright Scholar, Fraser Center for Workplace Issues) and is coauthor of *Just Another Car Factory? Lean Production and Its Discontents* (Cornell University Press, 1997)

Steve Jefferys is a Professor of European Employment Studies at the Business School of the University of North London in the United Kingdom. His research interests focus largely on comparative European and Franco-British management and employment relations. He is the coauthor of *Management, Work and Welfare in Western Europe* (Edward Elgar, 2000), a study of the growing impact of American managerialism on Europe.

Tom Juravich is a Professor and Director of the Labor Center at the University of Massachusetts Amherst. His research has primarily focused on union organizing and collective bargaining, work and the labor process, and work and family issues. He is author of several books, including (with Kate Bronfenbrenner) *Ravenswood: The Steelworkers' Victory and the Revival of American Labor* (Cornell University Press, 1999).

Martin Kenney is a Professor at the University of California, Davis and Senior Project Director at the Berkeley Roundtable on the International Economy. His current research interests focus on the globalization of the electronics industry. He edited the book *Understanding Silicon Valley* (Stanford Press, 2000) and has consulted with various global organizations, including the United Nations and the World Bank

Morris Kleiner is a Professor of Public Affairs and Industrial Relations at the Humphrey Institute of Public Affairs and the Industrial Relations Center at the University of Minnesota. His research focuses on the role of labor market institutions in democratic societies and the performance of organizations. He is also a Research Associate at the National Bureau of Economic Research in Cambridge, Massachusetts.

Gabriele Köhler is a development economist with the United Nations Division on Investment, Technology and Enterprise Development, UN Conference on Trade and Development. Her research focuses on analytical and policy issues in international trade and investment, employment, and gender. She contributes regularly to the *World Investment Report* and has published on commodity issues, international development cooperation, and the history of the U.N.

Sarosh Kuruvilla is an Associate Professor of Industrial Relations and Asian Studies at Cornell University. His primary research interests concern the linkages between economic development strategies and industrial relations and human resource policies in developing countries. He serves as a consultant to the World Bank, the ILO, and to several Asian governments.

Jiangfeng Lu is a doctoral student in industrial relations at the Industrial Relations Center, Carlson School of Management, University of Minnesota. Her primary fields of study and research include labor-management relations, and organizational theory.

Graeme Martin is a Professor and Director of Research at the Dundee Business School, University of Abertay, Scotland. The focus of his research is primarily on international human resources and employee relations, management development, and organizational change. He is currently a visiting Professor of human resource management both at the University of Colorado in Denver and at Lulea Technological University in Sweden.

Judy Pate is a Lecturer in Human Resource Management at the Dundee Business School, University of Abertay, Scotland. Her research primarily focuses on psychological contracts, human resource development, and knowledge transfer.

David Peetz is an Associate Professor of Industrial Relations at Griffith University, Brisbane, Australia. His research has focused primarily on union membership and strategy, collective bargaining, working patterns, and public policy. He has previously worked as a senior executive in the Australian Public Service, and has been a consultant to the ILO in Malaysia, Thailand, and China.

Harvie Ramsay was a Professor of International Human Resource Management and Director of the Centre for European Employment Research at the University of Strathclyde, Scotland. His primary research interests focused on industrial democracy, gender issues in the workplace, and international labor-management relations. Prior to his death, he was leading a three-University research team studying the factors shaping the experience of work for software developers and call-center operatives.

Tony Royle is a Reader in International and Comparative Industrial Relations at Nottingham Trent University, United Kingdom. His primary research focus has been on industrial relations in multinational companies, especially across the food service sector in both Eastern and Western Europe. He is the author of *Working For McDonalds's in Europe: The Unequal Struggle?* (Routledge, 2000).

Shoko Tanaka is a consultant based in Davis, California. Her research has focused on the Japanese political economy, including industrial policies, small and medium size company policies, and venture capital in Japan. She has consulted widely with Japanese business and public officials in the United States and Japan.

Brian Towers is an Associate Fellow at the Industrial Relations Research Unit, University of Warwick, United Kingdom. His contribution, herein, was written while he was a Professor at Nottingham Trent University. His primary research focus has been on trade unions and industrial relations public policy. He is Consulting and Founding Editor of the *Industrial Relations Journal* and is author of *The Representation Gap: Change and Reform in British and American Industrial Relations* (Oxford University Press, 1997).

Olga Tregaskis is a Senior Research Fellow in the Department of Human Resource Management, Leicester Business School, DeMontfort University, United Kingdom. Her research centers on organizational and country context issues, in particular as they influence contingent employment patterns, employee learning, and development on an international basis. She has been a member of multiple international research teams and networks, and is member of the DeMontfort University International Management Research Group.